Philosophy of Communication

Philosophy of Communication

edited by Briankle G. Chang and Garnet C. Butchart

The MIT Press
Cambridge, Massachusetts
London, England

MIT Press books may be purchased at special quantity discounts for business or sales promotional use. For information, please email special_sales@mitpress.mit.edu or write to Special Sales Department, The MIT Press, 55 Hayward Street, Cambridge, MA 02142.

This book was set in Stone Sans and Stone Serif by Toppan Best-set Premedia Limited. Printed and bound in the United States of America.

Library of Congress Cataloging-in-Publication Data

Philosophy of communication / edited by Briankle G. Chang and Garnet C. Butchart.
    p. cm.
Includes bibliographical references and index.
ISBN 978-0-262-51697-6 (pbk. : alk. paper)
1. Communication. I. Chang, Briankle G. II. Butchart, Garnet C.
P90.P468 2012
302.2—dc23
2011040078

10 9 8 7 6 5 4 3 2 1

Contents

Acknowledgments

Considerable costs were incurred in the preparation of this book. We are therefore grateful to the many sources that provided funding to offset these costs. They include the following: The University of South Florida (College of Arts and Sciences Office of Research and Scholarship, the Humanities Institute, the USF Foundation, and the Department of Communication); the University of Massachusetts Amherst (the Office of Research Affairs and the Department of Communication). Deep gratitude goes to Philip Laughlin at the MIT Press for his advice and the confidence he placed in us from the beginning of this project. It was a pleasure working with him.

Publisher Credits

Introduction

Briankle G. Chang and Garnet C. Butchart

I

To philosophize is to communicate philosophically, and to communicate philosophically is to impart the wisdom of which philosophy speaks and which is spoken at the same time. Would philosophy—ever universalizing and universalized in its claims—be able to stand fast as what it claims to be if it did not impart anything, if it refused to communicate, if it simply remained silent? Even if philosophy managed somehow to keep silent, could this silence be anything other than philosophy's choice of expression, an expression wisely chosen by philosophy to keep its silence? And could this silence be anything other than an *expressive* silence? Could it keep itself from becoming a message, a silent message that is nonetheless heard, and heard as a refusal to communicate and, hence, as communicating this refusal? And continuing further in the direction indicated by these questions, one may ask whether the silence of philosophy—more exactly, the silence that philosophy succeeds in keeping—could ever not return finally to philosophy itself as a philosophical expression, as a message communicating, silently in this case, philosophy's own articulation as (the beginning of) a philosophy of silence, and, hence, a philosophy of silent *communication*?

From its inception, philosophy communicates forcefully. It begins by speaking against myths, incantatory poetry, oracular announcements, and received opinions (*doxa*), against, that is, storytellers, poets, seers, and, above all, the Sophists. Yet by speaking against its opponents, philosophy also speaks with and through them, voicing its own birth and worth through what others say, that is, articulating its identity as the purveyor of logos only in contrast to, or in the midst of, what is said by its others, its shadow congregation, its ineludible *supplement*. For instance, Socrates, Plato, and Aristotle talk a lot and talk ardently—in Socrates' case, nonstop and thus stopped only by the rendering of a death sentence; Plato and Aristotle write in and for the polis. And not to forget Descartes, the most solitary of all philosophers, who must also take a break from his meditations, looks out the window of his attic, and *judges*—in a flare of sophistry because he is not looking at the men on the busy street in *thought* but is seeing them, which, like past teachings or received opinions, is susceptible to methodic doubt—that the hats and coats down below are real men like himself.[1]

Born of the city, and flourishing nowhere but within the city walls, even if under the pretense of setting itself apart from the clamor of the streets, even if projecting itself as a solitary singing of rarefied wisdom for the purpose of "caring for the self" (*epimeleia heautou*) or for the elevation of cerebral solitude, philosophy is essentially of a place, a broad street (*platēa*), of commerce, both a product and a production of a *Kunstwollen* rooted in a space-time that is characteristically urban, public, and, palpably, market-oriented. (In point of fact, can one not see that the intensity with which philosophers, as "lovers of wisdom," inveigh against the Sophists, whom they impugn as "merchants or traders of words," is matched only by their covert desire to be heard, to win over as many souls as possible, that is, to triumph, under the claim of and to truth in its purity, in a communication campaign waged against chrematistics or any mercenary verbal *tekhnē*?) From the beginning, philosophy was nothing if not a discourse (*dis-cursus*) of circulation *in* circulation, a *communi*cative or *demo*cratic discourse, if that phrase is not redundant. Philosophy, always opposed to the occult or concealment and in favor of open exchange of bright ideas, is therefore always and already communicative in that it does not, and does not have to, enter into communication; it does not enter into communication because it is already in it. In principle and in fact, philosophy begins and ends as the communication of philosophy.

That philosophy and communication have belonged together from the beginning, that the former comes into its own and solidifies its stance through the latter, makes it logical—indeed philosophically proper—that we subject communication to philosophical investigation. Critical to this task—and also what provides the underlying frame of the present volume—is the move to establish communication as a proper topic of philosophy. Rather than *defining* communication, rather than *making* it *finite* in any way, we need to recall the idea of communication back into philosophy's own orbit, to seize it in such a way that it stands ready as an object of philosophical inquiry, as an instance of logos, so to speak, upon which logos can reflect and in which it can see itself working, critically. In so doing, a line of traffic may be reopened within philosophy's own border, a line through which communication may be brought to remark on philosophy and thus be brought back to itself, beyond the conventional relationship between philosophy and communication. To bring communication into philosophy's domain is to set up a line of communication *about* communication *and* philosophy in their constitutive intimacy, to break open a *platēa* from which we can see afresh not only how communication and philosophy necessarily complicate each other—how, that is, each appears as what may be called the other's "frontier" (not to say "boundary," which, unlike a frontier, can be clearly, even if contestably, drawn)—but also, more critically, how each works to draw the other, and thus itself as well, into a point of nondistinction where the telos of philosophy, ever distanced and distancing in its own voice and countervoice, finally and inevitably returns to meet its own *archē*, its *ancestral* beginning that, *tértium non datur*, turns out to lie at and as its end.

II

Communication takes place always under its own shadow, moving forward only insofar as it also speaks back to what it leaves behind. And thereby, in this speaking back, it keeps a degree of what is left behind. From this derives our sense of the reality of communication, our sense of its continuity, of our being in communication, even across silences, over noises, or through what are called mis-communications or communication breakdowns. It is through this continuity that we communicate, and it is through this continuity too that "communication" can be turned into a topic in our communication. After all, are we not now, as authors and readers, communicating about what is called, in this communication, philosophy of communication? With this fact as an interpretive key, let us consider an oft-heard statement that will help announce the theme underlying this volume: "One cannot not communicate."[2]

To the extent that this statement can be made, irrespective of the context in which it is said, it says that one—the speaker, first of all—cannot not do what he or she is doing at the moment of doing it. The two "nots" in the statement work in tandem to assert the unavoidability of communication, making absolute, in and through the message thus communicated, the impossibility of denying or refusing to communicate. Taken as such, with or without any empirical support (which has arguably never been stronger than now, when the smartest among us ebulliently declare that the whole universe can be reduced to "information" and "codes"), this statement is but one of self-evidence or self-evidencing.

For in saying "one cannot not communicate," one affirms and confirms that one is communicating, not only by stating that one cannot but do what one is doing, but also by admitting that one cannot not do what is being done while doing it. When a statement about communication is affirmed in this way, it communicates itself as its own affirmation, collapsing the saying and the said into one utterance whose enunciation attests to their identity all at once. Saying what it is doing and doing what it says it is doing, the statement no sooner saturates itself than is exhausted by its conformity with the fact that it is and that it establishes. In this event—and, by extension, in every communication event, to the extent that every communication *states*, makes public, something, itself above all, verbally or not—the dictum is the factum, and vice versa.[3]

Performative in this way, the statement "one cannot not communicate," for its offbeat sentence structure and stark propositional content, acts much like a deictic. And like a self-designating deictic, it signifies nothing but its own occasion, trapping and trapped by its own punctual *thisness*, thus appearing, given the verbal form it takes, as a mere self-report, a reflexive remark validated by its own performance *hic et nunc*, its own *taking place* as it is taking place. Read in this light, the statement does not so much communicate as *manifest* communication. It manifests the event of communication in and as the appearing of "this" self-report, which, as uttered, bears witness to the event that it is and that it hence cannot but make manifest. If the statement "one cannot not communicate" can still be said to communicate anything, it communicates the *taking place* of communication, a taking place that manifests itself by verbalizing itself. Manifesting the event from within what reflexively marks the event's very own manifestation, it communicates the unmistakable ability of communication to manifest itself, that is, to make manifest communication's own communicability, which gives itself to be seen, in this case, as a self-validating, self-referential announcement.

If one cannot not communicate, then "one cannot not communicate," too, cannot not be communicated. For, as just indicated, whenever "one cannot not communicate" is said, not only does the event of communication manifest itself, but this manifestation also chimes in in reflexive self-evidence and, as such, proceeds without breach in its own self-affirming and self-affirmed articulation. Simply put, when "one cannot not communicate" is affirmed absolutely, the statement communicates itself without condition, since it gives itself the canvas of expression that is none other than its very own communicability. That "one cannot not communicate" does not fail to be communicated as communication's inescapable self-expression, that the facture of communication is immediately born out by the dictum that the factum itself is, makes it clear that communication knows no negation. Communication cannot be negated because it cannot but take place, even if, and especially when, its denial or negation takes place, because, that is, to negate communication is to communicate the negation in question, thus affirming communication by reversal, by crossing out the negation that is being communicated. To put it in another way, communication cannot be (a)voided because a void, which avoidance or negation necessarily entails, is necessarily communicated whenever communication is (a)voided.[4]

Since a void in communication does not cease to communicate, which is to say, since the communication of a void does not and cannot (a)void communication, communication is at once contra- or counter-communication. It is, as just indicated, communication crossing itself out.[5] Seen in this light, communication does not so much begin and end in discrete events enchained by something other than those events; rather, it continues, or continues to survive, as punctuated moments in an ongoing process that has always and already begun and that, being (auto-)immune to negation, will never end either. Seen in this light too, contrary to popular belief, communication does not ever fail or break down.[6] Carrying its own contraries within itself, communication continues; more exactly, it survives and survives as itself. And it survives as itself because it turns and re-turns, because, when all is said and done, the return *of* communication is the return *to* communication, and vice versa. Communication, to repeat what was said earlier, takes place always under its own shadow, and this shadow of communication is also the communication of this shadow.

If communication takes place and does so continually, and if it manifests itself and therefore manifests itself across manifestations, then communication is neither identical with nor reducible to a particular taking place that manifests it.[7] Neither merely this nor merely that, always more and less than this or that, communication unfolds in what unfolds in it, demonstrating all that it cannot but continue to demonstrate. In this lies what can justifiably be called the *premise* (*pre-mittere*) of communication, a *fore-sending* that carries and is carried by all events of communication. A fore-sending, a sending *before* all that is sent, this premise presents itself as a first message, a message that sends and is sent before the sending begins. At the same time, however, presenting itself before the sending, it also transpires as the message that lasts in that it is the message that all messages re-present. Fore-sending itself in and through every sending that it brings in its wake, the premise of communication can no more *not not* communicate (itself) than it can *not not* be communicated by what it fore-sends, since, as just said, it outlasts all messages as the only message that lasts. It is in the lasting proposition of this premise that one also sees what can be called the *promise* (*pro-mittere*) of communication, a *sending forth* that opens the future for communication by keeping its promise, keeping it, in other words, as a fore-sending of expectation that, looking forward as much as forward looking, opens the future *of* communication. Projecting, as promises do, what is yet to come, the promise of communication projects the coming of communication and communicates the projection premised on this promise. For in saying in advance that what it says will be made good, the promise of communication keeps the premise of communication as a promise, indeed as a promised sending whose coming, to the extent it is coming, is yet to be. To the extent that communication is premised to take place, this taking place depends above all on the promise that the premise holds; conversely, to the extent that communication promises that it will be continued, this continuation results only from a sending that delivers itself as something yet to come. In the turning and returning of communication, the premise of communication turns out to be the promise of communication, and vice versa. This is the first and last gift of communication, a gift given to communication by itself, a communicative gift, if we might call it that, thanks to which communication is given a future, a certain future that will not not come.

III

The present volume brings together a selection of works under the title *Philosophy of Communication*. These works, written originally for purposes and audiences widely separated in space and time, are assembled here for the potential offered by them to articulate a unified project that places communication at the center of philosophical reflection. Although at times they might seem forced to converse with one another by the title under which they appear, they can nevertheless be heard in this new context to be speaking in one voice, a voice that not only affirms their continued relevance to their original topics but also confirms the opening of what henceforward may be known as philosophy of communication. If philosophy of communication, as a *nomen* as well as a *titel*, can begin to assert a topic of its own—to have its own "life and letters," so to speak—it is because the works collected here have already connected what they said to what they are now being called upon to say by their reappearance in this volume.

A title makes a sign. It predicts, or pre-says (*prae-dīcere*), that which it names and prepares one for what is coming under that name. But a title is more than a sign. A title also entitles: it lays claim to what it projects, to what is coming, and demands that a ground be given for this projection. It is with this sense of entitlement that we present this volume and, through it, what we think philosophy of communication should be like. In this volume, and in response to the demand implicit in the title, are the writings we consider to be foundational to what is being pursued here in the name of philosophy of communication. Brought together by a project that they help establish, these writings are truly *performative* in that they are brought together here to make happen what can happen only while, and only if, they are *making* it happen. Thus performative, these writings not only justify being collected in one place because they embody a vision of philosophy of communication, but also support this vision by giving it a shape and direction in thought. Just as what is here called philosophy of communication is to be envisioned through these selected writings, these writings themselves will also show themselves, after the fact, to have belonged properly to this anthology, under whose title our vision of philosophy of communication is projected.

If the title of a volume pre-says what is to come, and if what is pre-said to come is worthy of being introduced and, after the introduction, is to be pursued by others, then that volume must present something new, something productive. Rather than being a compilation of materials that reinforces some established program in philosophy, this project must be capable of standing on its own. *Philosophy of Communication* initiates a philosophical project that is in the end distinct from and independent of the various philosophies with which it will speak, and in this conversation, it speaks of something new. Our objective, then, even if only partially revealed by the fact of this volume, is not simply to ask that what is called "philosophy of communication" be granted a seat—next to, say, philosophy of language, philosophy of mind, and the like, each of which has its own topic and time-honored literature affirming that topic—in the forum of discourse devoted, according to its self-fashioning, to the love (*philia*) of wisdom (*sophia*). Our objective, more ambitiously, is to demonstrate that communication should itself be considered one of the central topics of philosophy, as the commonplace (*koinos topos*), in and toward which the love of wisdom, insofar as it is pursued through open exchange and does not exist just as an individual's private occupation, moves and re-moves itself according to its own origin and truth. If philosophy, understood in its classical sense, is distinguished as much by its way (*methodos*) of thinking as by the objects of thought it constructs, and, more important, if it does not forget its birth in a form of communication we call dialogue and does not forget its founding spirit, which is as argumentative as it is skeptical, then it is reasonable to recall communication back into philosophy's own circle of reflection and counter-reflection. It is reasonable, thus, to demand that communication, finally freed from its secondary or derivative status as "medium," be made a theme according to philosophy's own principle and vocation, that is, *philosophically*.

Nothing in discourse works by itself, and so too for this volume and the essays included in it. Just as in language each word articulates with every other word, and each sentence speaks with every other sentence, thus keeping afloat each one's meaning and identity either in isolation or in combination, each chapter in this volume, too, works off and against every other chapter to form a whole, through which the message indicated by the title of this collection may take shape and be delivered. A title, as just said, is a sign, a sign of promise: it predicates, or pre-shows (*prae-dicāre*), what is to come, communicating a message before the message it pre-says is communicated. In keeping with the promise made by the title of this volume, we now present the writings—some classical, some modern, others more recent or contemporary, but all significant—that bear directly on topics essential to philosophy of communication as we envision it.

This collection comprises thirty-two chapters. With the exception of the first essay, "Of 'This' Communication," an overture to themes that run throughout the volume, the chapters are organized into seven thematic parts. Each part consists of a selection of works that circumscribe a constellation of philosophical concerns, at the center of which the topic of communication may be situated. Rather than tracing the development of the idea of communication in the history of philosophy, we have arranged the parts in a way that we hope will allow philosophical thinking about communication to proceed cumulatively. Reflecting our views on what a philosophy of communication will involve, the themes we have identified for the seven parts not only help us frame the writings included in this volume, but, more important, they also make the framing itself part of the overall message; the framing, like each chapter in this book, makes its own incomparable contribution. It is our hope that the design of this volume will itself be viewed as a sign of what it makes possible, that, just as each piece in the volume speaks to one another, the volume as a whole will also be read as speaking to the topics that bring these pieces together.

Part I, "Openings," opens the volume with an extract from Plato's famed dialogue *Phaedrus*, which inspires much of the discussions on communication since then by setting up the portentous opposition between writing and speech and, by extension, between reason and nonreason, between truth and falsehood. This extract is followed by writings from four philosophers, Gottfried Wilhelm Leibniz, Georg Wilhelm Friedrich Hegel, Martin Heidegger, and Gilles Deleuze. When read in conjunction, these essays work agreeably to set a backdrop against which communication may be seen to emerge as a philosophical issue.

Part II, "Architecture of Intersubjectivity," addresses the question of intersubjectivity as central to any philosophy that has communication as its primary focus. Led by the "Fifth Meditation" in Edmund Husserl's *Cartesian Meditations*, which establishes the problematic of intersubjectivity in phenomenology and beyond, this section includes three additional works by Martin Heidegger, Alfred Schutz, and Michel Serres that carry Husserl's problematic beyond its transcendental horizon. Presented in this context, these writings can be read as founding statements about the basic condition that underpins the possibility of human communication.

Parts III to VII span five themes that translate communication into the domain of more or less established philosophical concerns. Part III, "Language before Communication," presents a selection of writings that constitute critical points of entry for a philosophical examination of the genesis of language, the function of linguistic code, the nature of symbolization as it relates to communicability, as well as the significance of power and human agency in the making of meaning. Part IV, "Writing, Meaning, Context," takes up longstanding issues surrounding language, meaning, context, and writing in their jointed hermeneutical contexts, into whose intersection communication can be situated as an essential but yet to be fully explored dimension.

Part V, "Difference, Subject, and Other," and Part VI, "Exchange, Gift, Communication," turn our attention to the notions of subjectivity and exchange as they relate to forms of mediation beyond their language-centered articulations. Individually and collectively, the authors presented in these two parts give us the task of thinking about "giving," "gift," and "exchange"—indeed, about their failure and success, their possibility and impossibility—not only as instances of intention and deliberation, out of which individuals, as subjects *of* communication, come to be and become communicative, but also, more crucially, exemplifying fundamental principles of Reason, on the basis of which presence in its manifold expressions appears to us as a gift and us to it as recipients in the light of our constituted subjectivity.

We should add at this point that if the authors represented in Parts IV, V, and VI appear to belong heavily to the Continental tradition in philosophy, perhaps even leaning toward the kind of thinking associated with what is called poststructuralism, it is because such writers confront, more directly and forcefully than others, the problems afflicting metaphysical thinking since the advent of phenomenology. In the wake of the critical reshaping of the challenge of metaphysical thinking, a challenge for which they are largely responsible, they give the problematic of communication a contemporary relevance otherwise impossible. In spite of, or precisely because of, the wide divergence among them, the writings in these parts can be read as cardinal points forming a grid for thinking about communication philosophically, mooring a system of lines according to which different outlines of philosophy of communication can be traced.

Part VII, "Community and Incommunicability," concludes the volume with four pieces of writing that offer contemporary perspectives on the topics addressed in the preceding Parts and Overture. By examining the logic of community and the problem of mediation, through which the reality of being human is constituted, these writings work together to end the volume as one argument that, in light of the arguments made therein, can only be read to communicate the possibility of its continuation.

To conclude, a few remarks must be made about the task of this selection. As we have suggested, a collection, like its title, is a promise. It is this promise that gives us the task of collection, and it is this task of collection that forces us to select. However, no selection is innocent, being determined, as it is, by the perspective adopted before any selection is made, and this collection dispenses with or rejects as much as it collects. For there is always more, much more, than one can collect. In preparing this volume, we, like all editors embarking on similar projects, faced the daunting task of deciding what to include and what not to include. If we erred in not including materials that perhaps ought to have been collected, we stand on the belief that these materials are better left where their original contributions shine most brilliantly. Now that this collection is completed, we, like all editors, are made even more aware of the possibility that readers may squint at the pages, finding problems or objecting to what we have done, or even rejecting what appears between the covers. In this case, we can only admit to the bias working behind us and behind the pages we collected. If nothing else, we have at least offered a vision of philosophy of communication that serves to prompt critical exchange.

Before ending, if that is ever possible, we wish to make one more observation. To communicate is, among other things, to perform the act of bringing the other closer while keeping the self intact. It is to invite the other for conversation, but only on the condition that the other is willing to converse. It is, in other words, premised on the conversants' promise to continue to communicate and to interrupt. Such is the case with editing and presenting this collection. If, as we said earlier, communication takes place as a promise, and if a promise is a promise only if it remains unfulfilled when it is made, then only future circumstances will tell us how the conversation initiated by this volume may fare.

Finally, recall what we said at the beginning. If philosophy must communicate, and if philosophy is distinguished by its capacity to reflect on itself, on what it has achieved and what it will continue to attempt to achieve, then philosophy is necessarily, not to say exclusively, a philosophy of communication. Just as one cannot not communicate, the need to communicate what philosophy of communication might look like cannot not be communicated continually. It is in light of this claim that this volume, and through it, we, dare to make its promises.

Notes

1. See Descartes, *Meditations on First Philosophy*, in *The Philosophical Writings of Descartes*, trans. John Cottinghann, Robert Stoothoff, and Dugald Murdoch, 2 vols. (Cambridge: Cambridge University Press, 1985), 2:21.

2. This statement is popularly known as one of the "axioms of communication" developed by the "Palo Alto Group," researchers at the Mental Research Institute in Palo Alto, California. Using a concept famously associated with this group, "the double-bind," we can say that individuals are not just bound to communicate or interact with one another; they are, often and unbeknownst to themselves, bound twice in a loop of paradoxical behaviors, which, according to this perspective, is potentially pathogenetic. For a summary of this theory, see Paul Watzlawick, Janet Helmick Beavin, and Don D. Jackson, *Pragmatics of Human Communication* (London: Faber and Faber, 1967), esp. chap. 2.

3. It is clear, *a la* Ludwig Wittgenstein and John. L. Austin, that one can identify *what* one does only through an *account* of what one does; words and deeds, speech and action, are interchangeable. But this does not mean that all speech acts—as types of doing, identifiable through the accounts that agents or observers can and will give of that doing—display the kind of self-referentiality observed in the present case.

4. For an insightful discussion of this idea, see Peter Fenves, *"Chatter": Language and History in Kierkegaard* (Stanford, CA: Stanford University Press, 1993), 145–190.

5. Concrete examples of this can be found throughout history. The practice of *damnatio memoriae* in the Roman tradition, for instance, by which the Senate would decree the destruction of all written and monumental traces of a citizen or tribune accused of treason or of bringing disgrace to the Republic, was itself an official, written, and duly recorded act. Similarly, attempts by those struggling for power and domination to erase or deface historical records or monuments have nonetheless been recorded if we can read and know about them. See also Fenves, *"Chatter,"* 145.

6. There is no failure or breaking down of communication because, never annulled because ever annulling itself, it has always and already failed, because what appears as a breakdown is what breaks open the possibility of communication, of its possible breakdowns. If one can speak of the failure or crisis of communication, it is because communication is always in crisis, always in trouble, always undecided. For a discussion of how what are normally regarded as "failures" of communication in fact open the possibility for communication to succeed or to proceed, see Briankle G. Chang, *Deconstructing Communication: Representation, Subject, and Economies of Exchange* (Minneapolis: University of Minnesota Press, 1996), 221–228.

7. The conflation of "idea" and "object," if not a total failure to observe the distinction between "token" and "type," is not uncommon when one speaks about communication. Without teasing out the various conceptual problems this conflation may cause for communication as a field of study, suffice it to point out that just as the "medium," to take a related idea for example, is not the same as the "message" contained in it, and a "channel" means more than a particular means of transmission (a power line, a telephone, or a transmission tower), the idea of communication is distinct and different from any object or manifestation so called.

Overture

1 Of "This" Communication

Briankle G. Chang

We speak suggesting that something not being said is speaking.
—Maurice Blanchot, *The Writing of the Disaster*

Communication happens on the side—or in some cases does not happen: then the sound of the voice fades away, or the text is left there.
—Hans-Jost Frey, *Interruptions*

I shall speak about communication.[1] With the statement "I shall speak about communication," I have just made known what I am about to do. However, in saying this, by saying, "I shall speak about communication," am I not communicating? In this instance, the act of my saying and what is thus said appear to stand in happy agreement, the latter being little more than a self-reflective report on the former, thereby saying nothing but affirming that this saying, this report, is taking place. Indeed, I begin by making a promise presaging what I shall speak about, and yet this making, this act by which the promise in question comes to pass, immediately dissolves the promise that is being made, since what is being promised by me is accomplished without delay by my *saying* so.

Nothing is more banal, more self-evident, than saying, "I am now speaking" as one speaks, yet there seems to be something troubling when one begins discussing communication by saying, "I shall speak about communication." This, I am quick to admit, is how I begin, which means that my quick beginning may be in trouble, or that I might begin without clarity, perhaps even blindly. Worse still, perhaps I should not even begin. But I did speak; I have already begun. In fact, it is in my having already spoken that my beginning becomes a problem, a problem made grave all the more by its having begun problematically. In any case, since I have already begun, I cannot but go on and go on beginning, if for no other reason than that I cannot unsay or undo what I have said or done so far. Having begun in this way, this beginning, this beginning of mine, turns out to be a nonbeginning. This nonbeginning will then be my beginning. For I do not begin; only this nonbeginning begins.

Curiously, a nonbeginning begins nonetheless. I cannot begin but with this nonbeginning. However, we recall that the nonbeginning I just spoke of is a beginning that has already begun and hence a beginning that should not be called a beginning. That being the case, when I say "Only this nonbeginning begins," I appear to be lying, for, in saying it, I contradict myself, saying that what I also say is not the case. Willingly or not, I seem to lie from the beginning because I say of what I claim to be a beginning that it begins and does not begin.

That a lie or contradiction arises when I begin to speak of communication suggests that any beginning of communication is not merely complicated or prohibitive, but essentially aporetic. Being aporetic (*a-poros*, not porous, not passable), a nonbeginning commences what it also enjoins from taking place, and conversely, it makes impossible what it nonetheless kicks off. Acknowledging the paradox implicit in my beginning and mindful of having said that one cannot really begin speaking, I can perhaps try to remain true to my initial promise by tracing the movements by which the *non-* in my nonbeginning is linked to the troubling and troubled way I begin, and is thereafter preserved in what I manage to say as I go on communicating. Inasmuch as my present condition, aporetic as it is, reflects the determination of contradicting voices articulated while I speak, the kind of tracing I propose should help us gain some access to my beginning's very inaccessibility, an inaccessibility that coordinates my starting point and prompts this tracing.

Tracking what I was led to say so far requires that I continue speaking about communication and do so by keeping in view the aporia within which I managed to begin and made the promise. Bearing this in mind, let me suggest, as a preamble to what follows, that the aporia in question not only marks an imperative underlying the condition of the possibility of communication, but, made manifest as an active response to the demand released by this imperative, it also works to overturn the condition of the possibility of communication into its condition of impossibility—an overturning that, as dictated by the imperative, demands in turn another demand in and of itself. This is the case because, as I will argue, it is in this aporetic nonbeginning, in this beginning that fails to—but nevertheless does—begin, that what might be called the force of communication is singularly concentrated, that communication, understood as sending and receiving of messages in general, including the message that begins by promising "I shall speak about communication," comes to take place and will continue to take place—always as instances of a self-announcement. Beginning only insofar as it exposes itself to the condition of nonbeginning, communication appears to begin by having begun already, for it begins only from and as a nonbeginning and ends, if at all, only as a response to a call that continues to re-call the message sent by a prior call, that is, by the imperative that does not fail to recall itself and thus to begin again. So, before I go further, let me pause and telegraph the point I shall develop later: To communicate is to communicate the imperative to communicate; to communicate is to demand communication, to demand, that is, the very demand that communicates it and that it in turn communicates.

Never too late to begin because it is always already too late (not) to begin. Since this is the condition in which I began and in which I promise to communicate, I can keep my promise only by communicating this promise endlessly. Acting in this way, not only do I communicate my promise and promise to communicate, but, most critically, I also find myself already and squarely in a space of communication, a space in which my promise is made and endlessly communicated. This space must be opened before I speak and must be kept open as long as I communicate. Presupposed and, at the same time, affirmed by my saying what I say now and will have said as I go on, this space marks off a welcome clearing as the very topos of communication, a discursive epoch (*epochē*) wherein the topic of communication can be established, and everything spoken thereof, questions regarding relevance aside, will be considered topical nevertheless. This opening—this epoch—will have been the first and last topic of communication, a topic from which all communications about communication come, and to which they ultimately return. In fact, it is within this epoch, within this opening that neither begins nor ends because it remains epochal, that communication begins to take place and continues to do so through the one, anyone, who communicates. This is what the epoch of communication makes possible, and it is in turn what keeps the epoch open, that is, keeping it as an epoch, our epoch. It is from within this epoch that one speaks and speaks about communication, failingly or not. And it is to this epoch that what I have to say ultimately speaks back.

I

No speech, no address to the other without the possibility of an elementary promise.
—Jacques Derrida, "Faith and Knowledge"

This world must be promised . . . and made possible before it can exist.
—Werner Hamacher, "Lingua Amissa"

I began this essay by saying "I shall speak about communication." Sincerely or not, I did say what I would do; I did appear to make a promise to speak about communication.[2] However, since I communicate my promise by promising to speak about communication, the promise I make returns in the same breath to, perhaps never departs from, my utterance, out of which it appears as such. This condition—a condition in which a promise in the making is compromised by the very act that is making it—seems to force itself on anyone who promises to speak about communication if only because the very force that anchors the speech act of promise-making seems to flood without remainder into one's *making* the promise as much as into the *promise* that is being made, and this by and through the non-distinction it effects, regardless of one's intention, between the fulfillment of what one does by saying it and the veracity of what one says as one is doing it. So, right from the beginning, from the very moment when I say "I shall speak about communication," not only do I, despite displaying a welcome instance of performative consistency, fall short of making a promise, but also, more momentously, my saying and what is therefore said by me also cross into each other to annihilate the so-called promise precisely by fully saturating, or what amounts to the same thing, by nullifying, the temporal distance upon which the speech act of promising depends for its felicity and intelligibility. Seen in this light, my promise—in fact, any promise—to speak about communication is hardly a promise at all, for no sooner do I begin to make the promise, indeed, before my sentence is even finished, than I am doing what, according to what my utterance suggests, is yet to be done. My promise, if one can still call it a promise, is at best a botched promise, a promise betrayed that, despite its appearance, promises nothing and hence cannot be kept. The promise to speak about communication, I repeat, cannot be and need not be kept because it is never properly made, and since it falls short of making itself as a promise, there is nothing for the speaker to unmake; still less is there a question of keeping, or failing to keep, it. Stated plainly, inasmuch as my saying that "I shall speak about communication" is an act of communication, this act communicates what it instantaneously enacts and it enacts what it decidedly communicates, for what is communicated by my act of communication, namely, my making a promise, returns in full force to attest to its own taking place, to the act itself as an event of communication.

I began by promising to speak about communication. However, since this promise is necessarily betrayed by its own making, I cannot be said to have spoken about anything effectively, except perhaps sending something that refuses to depart. Apparently, I have begun speaking, but in effect I have not said anything that is not already communicated by the *making* of the remarks I just made; or I appear to have made a promise to speak about communication, but this promise evaporates the moment it is communicated. In any case, I have begun and have not begun, have spoken but have not said anything, have promised and have not promised. From the beginning, my beginning fails to begin, suffering, regardless of my effort to the contrary, from having already undergone what it says it is about to start doing. Suffering in this way, I appear to begin, but not *at* the beginning, which is to say, I have begun, and can only begin, in the middle. This, then, means that instead of beginning, I continue. Simply put, I can succeed in beginning to speak about communication only on the condition that I continue speaking about it and keep doing so, irrespective of my failure to do so.

"To begin," "to begin to communicate," "the beginning of communication"—these are phrases with which one can only lie. For "what, having begun, cannot begin, cannot end," because ending is but a chance to begin and beginning is but a word that names no thing except a moment of what is of seamless succession.[3] Making all one (*continuāre*), communication continues: it transpires by crossing from *this* to *that*, from *this* this to *that* that, all the while taking place *here* and *now* precisely because it remains the same by becoming an other, by not being same, namely, by taking place nowhere else but *here* and *now*. Making a start on stopping, on what is being left behind, it moves on only to come back, unfolding ceaselessly in circles as the very circle that repeats, postpones, or resumes itself. Seen in this light, what is taken as the beginning lies as much ahead as behind, and what is taken as its ending lies behind as well as before. One thus finds oneself beginning to communicate only when one finds oneself interrupted in and by communication, since to begin to communicate is to resist what begins to end, and to end communication is to desist from what does not cease to begin anew. To the extent that to begin to communicate is to continue communicating, to continue communicating is to interrupt what unfolds continually. Communication affirms itself by interrupting itself, by being interrupted between *this* communication and the return of another *this* in no time. Whatever form it may take, whatever message it transmits, communication continues by way of interruption. It communicates interruption, which continues and communicates it.

Continually interrupting itself, communication continues; however, being interrupted continually, it also does not continue in that not only does it come to a stopping point, but it also does not remain unchanged as it separates itself from what has been transpiring all along. Inasmuch as I must speak to prove that I can go on speaking, I can be considered to continue speaking only if I say something more than, and other than, what I just said. Speaking and yet not allowing myself to speak unchanged, I continue speaking and do not continue speaking; thus establishing distance from communicating so as to continue communicating, I continue communicating and do not continue communicating. It is in this impossible connection between a yes and a no, between a coming and a going, between a repetition and its breaking, that I continue, and, continuing in this way, my continuation releases or survives itself: it outlasts itself by interrupting itself.[4] In fact, I cannot but interrupt my continuation, for I can succeed in continuing only if I also succeed in coming between what I continue to interrupt. Or, we can say, I succeed in communicating only if I fail to communicate, which is to say, I must fail to communicate so that communication can succeed and continue. Failing to succeed, or succeeding by failing, one no more succeeds than fails when one communicates. In this situation where the difference between failure and success is no longer distinct, it is also no longer certain whether one is the subject of one's own actions, except that one must continue and continue to interrupt. Continually interrupting and interrupted, "I"—the one who communicates—shall remain forever unfinished. Being unfinished, that is, when my being unfinished is definitive, I am finally open to that which never reaches me, but also to that which I never reach.

The logic of continuation underlying communication is thus one of incompletion, of (non)fulfillment in process predicated on self-deferral in principle. Breaking itself apart so as to go on, or, more exactly, converting its end into the means to renew itself, communication continually unfinishes as if autoimmune to its own success, surviving quiescently in its own nonfulfillment by producing the effect of nonfulfillment as its own cause. Always surviving as unfinished, it keeps itself open to itself, to its own continuation. It is, in a word, free: free from itself and free to become itself. Thanks to this freedom, it comes and goes, measured by nothing other than its ability to come and go freely. Between its coming and its going, each of which is no more a coming than a going, communication continues and, accordingly, remains in principle incomplete, because it is not free not to go on in this way.

(From a slightly different angle, we may say that in this free going and coming of communication, what is considered "past," "residual," or "emergent" is essentially a moment of the "ancestral," which, surpassing to yield and yielding to surpass, emerges constantly and thus remains always "contemporary."[5]) In this sense, and in this sense only, communication is *communicative*: it communicates its own possibility, coming off without fail as the very medium through which it comes to pass and, through the nondistinction between its success and its failure, makes common all that over which it crosses and interrupts continually. Or, we can say, communication is communicative because it does not cease to express or expose itself as such, ex-isting as a self-becoming owing to the profound ambiguity of the transcendence and immanence it embodies. The telos of communication, if there is any, is the perpetuation of its telos, the perpetual deferral of the telos by the telos itself, indeed, by a closure that is at once an opening.

The tautology, "*Communication* is *communicative*," expresses what I call the "fault of communication," a structural shortcoming inherent in transmission that, readily observed as the cause of incompletion described above, affects sending or receiving all the way so as to keep what is sent in a constant state of *being sent,* of being suspended in transmission. To the extent that the point of communication is *trans-mission*, is *sending across*, the fault of communication is that communication transmits its own disappointment, its incomplete crossing. It is in light of this fault that one can draw a parallel between the event of communication and that of promise-making. Just as communication necessarily falters in view of the teleology normally taken to characterize it, and for this reason, continues, making a promise likewise must keep saying what it only appears to say, since, when one says, "I promise," the word "promise" says that it does not yet say anything, and for this reason, speaks (un)failingly what it does not yet speak about. "To communicate" and "to promise" are therefore alike, one resembling the other in that when they take place, something other than a promise, something other than a transmission, also occurs, and when one speaks about them, something other than this speaking is also spoken of. The two acts parallel each other not only because they interact from the start and project comparable incomplete projections, as attested to by my troubled (non)beginning, but also because it is impossible for them not to be this way.

Lest I speak ahead of myself, let me recall that, as a common and deceptively simple mode of discourse, "to promise" is to say—to perform a speech act that says—"I *will* do X." It is to project X as possible, to project the possibility of X by *saying* "I will do X." However, since what corresponds to that which is being promised, X, is placed by the promise in a time yet to come—this speaking (of X) *ahead of* oneself in view of oneself being the necessary condition of "promise-making" as a performative—the promise thus made carries nothing but the very promise so performed. In principle and in fact, a promise promises, is capable of giving, only promise(s). When it is made, it says little more than the *saying* of the promise, giving, through the performative that it is, the said promise as the mere coming of a promise, as the mere promising of the coming of like promises, since, as just said, what is asserted to be effected by the promise at one moment can be secured only by the illocutionary act that depends for its reality entirely on a force that is exclusively possibility- or future-oriented.

Vouchsafed by a linguistically summoned future, a promise dispenses nothing but its own yet-to-come. Delivering nothing actual, only what lies ahead as spoken thereof, a promise guarantees that nothing is actually guaranteed. Or, we can say, promising by projecting, thus deferring the arrival of, what is being promised, a promise stretches itself across a fault-line that divides what it establishes, falling, in spite of itself, between "at least two 'times': a time of a future that can come and a time of a future that cannot come; a time that renders possible and one that renders impossible this very rendering."[6] Internally divided and dividing itself, a promise leaves open a possibility that defines it, but in leaving open this possibility, it also leaves open the possibility that none of what it promises will be preserved as a possibility. Faulty at the core, that is, temporally dislocating and dislocated with regard to itself, to promise is at once to keep the promise alive by keeping it at a distance, keeping it, that is, *away* and away *from* itself. Entirely and purely performative, a promise is from beginning to end a promise-in-the-making; it is never but a *performing* promise that plays out the necessity that it be open to future openings, future possibilities, including the possibility of their not being possible, of turning the promise into an unmistakable lie. Seen in this light, to promise is to continue to promise; it is to continue the promise-*making*, in short, to promise what is to be continued on the condition that it is continued.[7]

And the same holds for communication.[8] Just as a promise promises promise(s) and communicates the *making* of the promise(s), communication communicates, regardless of whatever else may happen with it, communication, and, that being always incomplete, communication promises its continuation. If a promise is always at the risk of being broken and is a promise only insofar as it is so at risk—otherwise it would not be a promise but a constative statement—communication is communicative only insofar as it remains promising, that is, incomplete, to be continued. Just as a promise is only *possible* and exceeds the speech that performs it because it says what it cannot actually speak about, communication likewise says that it has yet to speak, moving and re-moving only by removing itself, by doing away with what it imparts. Finally, to put it more economically, just as a promise must be prohibited, must be kept unfulfilled, by itself for the sake of promising, of there being this promise, communication necessarily faults itself so that it may continue. From the beginning, to communicate and to promise have never been apart from each other, not least because to promise is at once to communicate the promise being made, and to communicate is to promise that communication will have already begun and will have had no end. From the beginning, one necessarily begins *in* and *with* the other and, therefore, never begins by oneself. While we may say of communicating and promising that "they begin," what this statement really means is that they continue—each by itself as much as with the other.

From the above, one can easily ascertain why I was in trouble when I began this essay by saying "I shall speak about communication": from the moment I begin, from the moment I make the promise to speak about communication, both my promise as such and what I promise to discuss return, through the promise, from a future—from this promise's future—to render null my beginning as well as my promise. "To promise," "to speak," and "to communicate," individually or when tethered together, signify little that has not been taken as read when one begins to speak about them, as each term, being part of a chain, extends the syntagm by terminating in, without terminating, the others. This, as I just suggested, results necessarily from the fault of communication, a fault as continuous and long as it is horizonal. This fault marks the horizon, against which sending and receiving come to appear and continue to mistake each other, a faulty horizon, that is, from which arises the possibility of communication and to which this possibility falls only to rise again. In the end, I am permitted perhaps to say only this: Communication appears to begin and end, but it cannot, beginning, communicate its beginning or, ending, communicate its end.[9]

What, having begun, cannot begin, cannot end. That communication cannot begin or end does not merely mean that communication must be accepted as a fait accompli, or that it extends as long as one speaks about it. It means, principally, that communication first becomes a topic and can be posed as a problem only in communication, and this process is recursive. Indeed, as a notion whose "content" is easily turned into "form," and vice versa, and where discourses about it are easily objectivized to be discussed in turn—a situation reflected, for example, in such popular sayings as "the medium is the message"—"communication" floats fluently as its own going or ongoing concern, remaining topically relevant because of its self-reflective nature. More significant, to the extent that communication cannot begin or end, communication, beyond being incomplete, is also free from negation. It cannot be negated, annulled, or doubted, because to cross out or to doubt communication in any way is undeniably a communicative act, because the actuality of communication is necessarily implicated in the problematization that affirms *via negativum* this actuality and its continuation, and because, finally and from the start, the possibility of communication is already and irreducibly given in the presence of the concept as well as in the concept of a present fact.

Implicated when problematized, affirmed when negated, and its limits shown only when experienced in and made apparent by itself, communication performs the very fault that constitutes the opening for its performances which, being incomplete, can only continue. But it is an opening that also promises that the performances it so authors will be inadequate to—will be in excess and in want of—the performance as promised. It is an opening that does not fail to open the possibility of confusing the performance's own space and time, a faulty opening, indeed, where each moment of what it makes possible is both a "before" and an "after" and is therefore both an "already" and a "not yet." Thus confusing and being confused by its own occasioning, communication is *performa-communicative* in the strict sense that it is never—nor could it ever be—fully what it promises to be, since its performance, the taking place of *this* communication *here* and *now*, is always at the risk of being something and somewhere other than promised and, possibly, other than performed.[10] Just as a promise—insofar as it promises something—exceeds and hence exists not in the speech that performs it but, rather, in a horizon it projects, communication, insofar as it takes (its) place and does so continually, moves and re-moves itself only by removing itself. Moving in the (non)distinction between removing and re-moving, communication is at once ex-communication. To communicate is to exit communication at once. It is to come out of, while going beyond, what one is communicating, namely, to be ex-communicated by the communication one enacts continually. Like making a promise, like making a promise to speak about communication, in fact, like making a promise to promise any-thing, to communicate is to performa-communicate and is never not to ex-communicate, to leave itself behind, to render itself obsolete. Similarly, to be communicative is to be *ex*-communicative and is at once to be para-performa-communicative. Being ex-performa-communicative, communication keeps itself open to a future, to what makes it possible by rendering uncertain or doubtful what it thereby makes possible. In view of this promised future, of the coming of this future, which, since it is *coming*, does not and may not arrive, a past is retained, the present becomes active, and a future—always the future of a future—is kept open. Communication performa-ex-communicates in this way, and as a result and at once, everything, always to come even if having come, is brought back to it. In this way too, communication saves itself; it sets itself aside, reserving itself for the future, for the future of its own future. Herein lies what may be called the "confidence" of communi-cation, a presumed or projected assurance taken as certitude, to which one, anyone, who communicates submits and must submit. Thanks to this submission in confidence, one communicates continually, that is to say, (un)failingly. Without beginning and without ending, one simply communicates. A promise!

II

But if the imminence of what is thus owed to death suspends the moment it falls due . . . at the same time it signs its verdict. . . . It will have to die, it is assigned to residence and the date is set (*la mise en demeure est en marche*), the countdown has begun, there is simply a delay . . . but no one dreams of escaping death, and nothing will be saved.
—Jacques Derrida, *Counterpath*

A promise communicates nothing certain, except the certainty that, however promising, it is but a promise. Since a promise, as said earlier, is a promise only on the condition that it concedes its potential failure, it necessarily includes the possibility that it would no longer be promising, no longer be a promise. Entirely verbal in nature, a promise deliv-ers not more than do the words of which it is made. Not only that, but "in every promise," as Hamacher remarks, "there must be a non-promise, if it is to be and remain a promise."[11]

Promising—and thus communication and speech in general, to which promising owes its continuation—directs itself and is directed by this "non," a void or wound in the speaking of every language, and it is kept as a promise only so long as it is kept in this "non."[12] Signifying no logically based negation and unlike counterfactuals, this "non" opens a future worthy of its name—a future that only a promise can open and that it will performatively (dis)organize, a future that sees itself coming (*avoir venire*) and is decided, in this coming, as essentially undecidable, as something *possibly* other than a future.

In the same way that an act of promise is exposed to the uncertain possibilities of the future, an act of communication, too, fails to conform to the teleology that is supposed to guide it and, possibly going amiss in this way, does not fail to risk being *not* an act of communication. For, being promise-like, hence positing, like all promises do, a nascent fact the anticipation of which must have already been the very production of this fact, it also "must leave open at least one extreme possibility—and leaving open means risking and risking failure—the possibility of no longer falling under the regime of an intentional subject, and thereby no longer qualifying as an act."[13] Accordingly, the subject of communication is always a possible subject, a subject vulnerable to the possibility that it may not be the subject and may no longer be possible, since its actions, admitting, as they must, a horizon of possibilities not of their own, are but contingent performances, performances produced by the "possibilities not given *by* it but given *to* it, ceded, imparted, or left."[14] Always to come in that it is given the possibility to come or is made to come only *possibly*, the subject of communication, if it comes at all, is but a promised subject, a subject *made* to make possible the promise to communicate.

Only a subject acts, and only a subject can make promises that, as performatives, implicate the subject as the medium of their incomplete continuation. However, since a subject *of* an act becomes one only if it is first subject *to* what makes it possible, to what is not so gracefully termed "subjectivization," a subject of communication capable of promising to communicate also has to undergo what must have happened to it before it emerges as the medium of promising; it must suffer from what makes possible the promises it makes, and in so doing, it renders possible its failure to make good the promise made. The subject of communication is born in this way, arising from a formative trial that gives it the possibility of being possible. At the same time, however, since what arises must first fall, since what is possible must be made possible and thereafter be *kept* as possible, the birth of the subject implies that this subject comes to be only by being withdrawn in some way and by being withheld in this withdrawal; it must be made to disappear from the very scene on which it is also first made to appear and to act as a subject. Before becoming one, in other words, the subject must die, as it were, a performative death—a possible death (could death ever be more than a possibility?), a death before death as a certain withdrawal in its uncertainty. This withdrawal, this symbolic death, and above all, the life after made possible by this death, must have happened and will continue to happen. "The countdown has begun; there is simply the delay"—a delay that perhaps even death cannot delay. "No one," it is true, "dreams of escaping death, and nothing will be saved," but something, I suggest, is saved most certainly by this withdrawal and persists as the return of a disappearance that only death is able to promise.[15] It is out of this withdrawal, this performative death—the postal epoch, as I called it—that the possibility of communication comes and comes continually. To illustrate my point, let me retell a story.

The story is well-known. After running nonstop from Marathon to Athens, Philippides gasps out *Nenikkamen* (We have won) in the middle of the Agora and drops dead. Having completed his task, he perishes as did the Persian enemy to whose destruction he ran to bear witness. The death of our messenger in this case coincides with the successful delivery of a message—a death known to us as part of the story that this death itself helps make known.

Philippides is a courier. A courier ought to deliver, and Philippides delivers the news as he was ordered to do. Death is not usually a consequence of a courier fulfilling his job. However, Philippides dies upon finishing his job; he dies, quite literally, *on* and *for* the job. Seen in this way, Philippides is more than a reliable transporter; he is a mailman par excellence, the first postman, remembered in history because of his on-the-job performance. Indeed, not only does he deliver the message, but he also delivers himself into the very delivery, for which he works and, consequently, dies. From this vantage point, the tale of Philippides can be read as presenting a thesis about sending and receiving, about letters or the post, about mediation and communication in general, which would be hard to think without the figure of the postman.[16]

To deliver (*rederre*) means to make something arrive, to make something visible or known. Philippides, the postman, arrives in Athens and makes known the news to the waiting crowd. At the same time, "to deliver," as the German *zustellen* reminds us, also means to withdraw, to halt, to put oneself in suspension, and thus to set oneself free.[17] Once the delivery is made, the postman withdraws or undelivers himself from the given task. For once the delivery is made, the possibility of the message's being lost, which the postman carries no less than the message itself, can, happily, be eliminated. The postman now withdraws because he is no longer needed, and he is no longer needed because the message is no longer *with* him. In other words, insofar as Philippides succeeds in completing the delivery of a message to the people in Athens, and through this success, leaves the message behind him, he is perforce also left *behind* the message *by* the very message he delivered and left behind. As can easily been seen, just as the medium (a sheet of paper, for example) must recede and become invisible, so that the message (the words printed on the page) can be read, and just as the so-called ether, the empty space containing objects, as Aristotle insists against Democritus, cannot be a complete void but rather must be diaphanous (*to diaphones*) or appear transparent so that the objects in it can stand out and be seen as individual beings, what enables the message to appear must disappear or be kept invisible so as to make the delivered deliverable. The appearance of the message—we are speaking of "appearance" here in that the delivered message must come forth and be made visible to someone other than the one who carries it—is thus a determined appearance, a postal appearance, if I may so call it, into which the postman disappears. It is this moment of undelivery within the delivery that marks the event of delivery, ending the sending in a distant end, toward which it first began to move.

Philippides dies at the end of his run, extinguished, as it were, by the deed that distinguishes him as a reliable postman. As seen in his case, the end of a delivery spells the end of the postman that he is. The success of a delivery thus marks a break, a period, in transmission, an instance of sub- or ex-traction, whereby the messenger withdraws or is erased from the scene, upon which is then seen the possibilities of his performance—his failures as well as his successes. It is in this postal epoch (*epochē*) that Philippides, the postman, appears and reports to work, only to disappear from the message his work makes appear. In principle and in fact, then, Philippides' death is timed and timely, demanded, as it were, by the epochal principle of the post his life exemplifies.[18] According to this principle, and in view of how this principle plays itself out through the one who performs it, we can go so far as to say that Philippides, once chosen to deliver the news, is already dead, that he died before he left Marathon. Timely, more than timely, a messenger lost is the possibility of delivery regained, regained by being deleted at the end of the delivery so that the message can be delivered.

The post kills, and Philippides is put away accordingly. However, in being so erased, he lives on, delivered, as suggested earlier, from death by being delivered into history, reappearing, all the more vividly, in a tale as a figure exemplifying the principle for which he runs to his death, even before he started to run. Indeed, Philippides is saved by what kills him, remembered—well beyond the time of his physical expiration—precisely because of his physical disappearance. Or, we can say, Philippides, the running courier, must sacrifice himself, must be sacrificed, so as to open the postal epoch, to open the age of delivery, into which the postman is born and for which he can then serve, in life and in death alike. In this story about Philippides that we have all heard, in this figure that my reading has made of him, and, above all, in this postal epoch in which my reading of this story takes place is found the transcendence of the postal withdrawal as a self-effacing play (*Spielrung*), into which all of the above possibilities withdraw and, in turn, reappear.

Philippides's story is interesting in that, whatever morals one may find in it, the story tells essentially about itself: it communicates a message it embodies and does so by embodying as its message what grounds the communication of this message—a self-allegorizing tale, it seems. For, as can be easily seen by now, within this story about delivery is inscribed the very principle of delivery that motivates the story and that the story in turn motivates, and, in being so motivated and thus motivating its self-motivated readings, the story and its message revive each other in exchange—each commenting not only on the other like an echo, but through this resounding extension, also on all forms of delivery as long as they partake in the postal epoch that the principle of the post first opens and keeps open. The story asks to be read in this way because it is already (fore)closed by what it openly suggests, and because by opening the reading with an end in view, it ends in what begins it. Like the postman, like the post, and like the reading of a post, the story, thanks to a death it recounts, survives. It, its reading, delivers itself. Delivering itself to itself, it reads itself. What I read, I quickly learn, reads itself, it reads itself in me—its own reading. In this *reading*, in the survival of this reading, the end, says the postal principle, ends—and begins (itself) again. Like a promise.

Philippides dies, but, as a courier and because he is a courier, his death saves him. Philippides would not be known to us, certainly not in the way he is, if he did not die the way he did, if he did not fall for the sake of a "fault" that is called "delivery," by virtue of which this story is delivered to us and, through this delivery, is transmitted to a future that, seeing (itself) coming, promises the continuation of this delivery. "No one dreams of escaping death," because no one, I suppose, knows anyone who does not die.[19] But something is saved and arises when Philippides falls: not only is his story saved because it is read and reread, but, through the continuity of reading and rereading, one also finds oneself always and already in an opening of sending/receiving that only what remains beyond the death of delivery can make possible.

What withdraws remains, and it remains in withdrawal. If the postman can speak of withdrawal, it is because he speaks *in* and *through* the withdrawal he personifies. As such, consequently, he speaks only of the post he is. He does this, and does this necessarily, because, embodying the withdrawal that his death delivers and that, at the same time, also delivers him as an exemplary instance of delivery, he stands as *exceptional* with regard to the messages he carries as well as to the epoch that his withdrawal keeps open and in which he delivers his own demise as the message behind all the messages he delivers. Being excepted in this way, namely, being both inside and outside the topos in which he is always "absent from his own place," the postman, as a historical figure, as a figure of the figuration of delivery, exists in absence in the postal epoch, floating, as it were, across the open it looks over, and, in this free floating, he secures the unity of the open in one single catastrophe as it sends itself to wherever sending calls on him to perform. It is through this self-extraction that the postman can be said to *belong ecstatically* to the epoch that excludes or erases him and, in the same gesture, includes him as an exceptional one, as a floating void—an "empty square," to use a term of Gilles Deleuze's—that, *being outside* and yet *belonging*, "makes everything function."[20] This void, floating as an *extimate* remainder of the withdrawal, makes room for what comes to appear in the epoch, for what comes to be transmitted in it, including itself.[21] This is how the postal epoch establishes itself: it takes place by taking away its own place, in the very place in which it takes place.

It is in this place of loss, a lost place in which one can get lost only because one is already lost *in* and *to* it, that one sees the postman coming and going. Coming by going and going by coming, the postman arrives no sooner than he departs, and he departs only to return. It is in this turning and turning again that what may and may not come finds the rift in time whereby hours pass as so many moments of anticipation, of looking forward to that which is possible to come. And it is in this rift as a recurring element, in this emptiness in situ where what is lost returns through withdrawal, that the future unseen is given the possibility of being seen. Is it not true that Mary Magdalene finds the tomb empty? Is it also not true that the departed One is not recognized when she first sees him again? And even when she comes to recognize him somehow visible in his withdrawal, she is greeted with the injunction, *Noli me tangere* (Do not [even want to] to touch me).[22] He says it immediately, *Mē mou haptou*, as the phrase is given in the original Greek, wherein the verb *haptein* (to touch) can also mean "to hold back, to stop."[23] He does not want to be and could not be held back, because he, his resurrected body (*son corps ressuscité*) being visible notwithstanding, is departing and must depart. Departing, that is, in returning to where he was sent from, he reappears (to her) in disappearance. This reappearance—indeed a miracle that there is this *miracle*, something to wonder at and to be seen—means that he is now set free. For only those who are freed through withdrawal reappear in this way. And he is set free or taken away in this way so that those who choose to follow him can be free, freed to be set free. It is out of his spectral presence that a certain promise is dispatched, a promise that posts the future in its hallowed universality. There must be this coming of the promise through withdrawal if there is to be a future, a future that, in its coming, shall include all that takes place henceforward as promised possibilities, as possibilities that no sooner arise than they begin to fall, through the promise, into what will have been their future perfect. Herein is played out in archetypical form what can be called the freedom *of* the post(man), the postal performance of a free sending that communicates itself as the message of communication, a post forever and for all, a post that, surviving death, continues to post the message even if all is yet to receive it.

III

I have the impression that everything comes to resemble itself, and me first of all, in a post card, the post card that I am, am following (*qui je suis*). There is but that, this reproduction of a reproduction of which I am dying and which forbids me, which makes of you, my living one, an interdiction

they have *intercepted* us

. . . if the post card is a kind of open letter (like all letters), one can always . . . attempt to make it indecipherable without compromising its making its way. Indecipherable, my unique one, even for the addressee. And yet there are but post cards, it's terrifying.
—Jacques Derrida, *The Post Card*

If, as said earlier, the postman comes and does not stay, if he leaves only to return, it is because he is always in transit, always en route in the postal clearing, in an epoch of delivery, with which he, as the ideas of "return" and "en route" suggest, is in some way familiar, more or less feeling at home. This epoch, with which he is uncannily familiar but in which he is nevertheless susceptible to getting lost, defines the very regime of the post, and it accomplishes this *de-finition* precisely by *making finite* its own opening as a delimited topos, achieving this, that is, strictly by setting its own limits and hence making all movements within it unlimited, if only because the limit of the post in this case is none other than the post itself. Setting its own limits and hence unlimited with regard to all deliveries made within its spread, the postal topos is inclusively and appropriately (in)finite, since it permits, via its appropriative inclusion, infinite movements of sending and receiving in it as endless turning and returning.

In *The Post Card*, Derrida gives evidence to the general idea of the post's unlimited limits when he says, "To post is to send by 'counting' with a halt, a relay, or a suspensive delay, the place of a mailman, the possibility of going astray and of forgetting. . . . The *epokhé* and the *Ansichhalten* . . . is the place of the postal."[24] On this account, to post is to "send, *envoyer*, to 'expedite,' to cause to leave or to arrive, etc.," by way of a middleman who, always and already inside "the place of the postal," translates and transports.[25] Accordingly, to post is not only to send but also to receive; it is to give and to take, to go away and to come back, in a word, to exchange, even if the exchange is not equal, faithful, or symmetrical. It is thus against a certain "reason" of exchange, a certain economic ideal based on equivalence, correspondence, or assured arrival of goods, that Derrida reminds us of the possibilities of letters going astray, of their loss and destruction *in principle*. This warning stems, among other considerations, from the simple fact that once a letter is *sent*, once it is separate from and separated by the sender, it is no more and no less certain that it *was* sent (or even received) than that it *might* go anywhere or to anyone—even someone nonexistent—in the postal network. Efficiency of delivery aside, if it is possible for a letter to get lost, to be misdirected in any way, then this possibility of loss—seated factually in the distance or difference between sending and receiving, without which "delivery" would make no sense because there would be nothing to deliver (*dēlīberāre*), nothing to set free or to move across—belongs to delivery and belongs to it with no less certainty than the likelihood of the letter's expected arrival at its destination. Whatever form it may take, delivery implies a need for delivery, but this need turns around immediately to jeopardize the delivery so needed, not only because this need might not be fulfilled but also because it *must* remain potentially unfulfilled for the delivery to take place. In principle and in fact, delivery threatens and is threatened by delivery itself, by what calls for delivery in the first place. The condition of the possibility of delivery, as said earlier, spells at once the condition of the impossibility of delivery. Delivery does not and cannot deliver itself. It is *autoimmune*.

On the other hand, if it makes sense to speak of the possibility of the post's going astray, of its being forgotten, a possibility Derrida is known to emphasize, it makes equal sense to speak of the possibility of the letter's reaching its addressee as intended. If there is the possibility of forgetting, there must also be the possibility of remembering, of record keeping or archivization in general, without which there would nothing to forget and, as the logic goes, nothing to remember either. Just as the possibility of loss, of going astray, necessarily haunts the sending, the prospect of the message's fortunate arrival at its end blesses the delivery with equal tare when the letter leaves the addresser. From the beginning, sending and receiving are paired in their isotopic simplicity, each being the echo or mirror image of the other, thus affirming through each other the continuation of the promise of delivery made by the postman in withdrawal.

All deliveries take place in the wake of the postman's withdrawal, for all deliveries must trace and retrace the steps his withdrawal leaves behind and leaves open. Delivery—the setting free of what is to arrive—thus bears witness to the *epochē* and the *Ansichhalten* as "the place of the postal," the place of the mailman as one of relay or suspensive delay, into which the postman disappears and, consequently, survives as the promise that his delivery necessarily bears. Carried by and carrying on the sending, this promise becomes a promise of relay that also keeps relaying the promise as part of what it relays. Viewed in this light, every letter is a letter already sent and virtually received, if only because the letter would not be a letter, would not be written as a letter, without this relay that promises its writing as well as its being read, or being readable. Is it not true that the speaker hears his own speech first when speaking to another? Is it not true that one reads what one writes before others do? After all, if a message is to be transmitted across space and time, if it can be delivered after all, how can this transmission be accomplished without a system of relays already in place, that is, if the addresses of the sender and receiver are not identified or identifiable beforehand? Successful delivery requires the proper working of relays, but the relays serving the delivery depends for their proper working on the proper working of a delivery system that maps the delivery routes. There is no delivery unless there is a relay, but a relay works only via the paths made available by the delivery network, the paths that the deliverer must—but, again, may not—follow. Mutually dependent, delivery and relay define and undefine each other, each preceding and receding into the other. Each sends for the other via itself, and, in turn, receives itself in inverted form. In the end, we cannot but conclude that there is no delivery unless there is delivery, and that there is no relay unless there are relays. Only delivery delivers delivery; only relays relay relays.[26]

A letter leaves the writer's hand and sets out to reach the loved one. As the letter begins to leave, "everything ends up *passing through* . . . as dispensation, and even the gift of *es gibt Sein* or *es gibt Zein* . . . also says address, not the address of the addressee, but the skills of whoever's turn it is, in order to pull off this or that, chance too, somewhat. . . ."[27] Following the postman's withdrawal, in its sending and destining, a letter sets out on a path and goes *on leave*. Leaving so as to depart, the letter "becomes the way that gives all ways . . . and makes way for everything."[28] The opening of the letter by the addressee stops the sending, but this stop stops the stop itself, and stops to begin. Within the postal epoch, sending and receiving become but punctuations, moments of hesitation across a journey that in truth is one of self-transmission. For what is sent not only cannot be unsent but also demands that a reply be sent back. No doubt, a letter is sent to be received, yet receiving a letter forces the addressee to leave it to be sent and to be read again. Sending and receiving, despite the possibility of chance and regardless of "the skills of whoever's turn it is," are already included in each other. That is, before the letter is sent, it, like the one carrying it, must have already arrived at the other end. Similarly, what is received must have already arrived before its arrival. That arrival—ever ready "to come to the riverbank" (as the word "arrive" from *arrīpāre*, "to come to shore," picturesquely suggests)—is here but also not quite yet. In keeping with the principle that defines our postal epoch, we must conclude once more that only the post delivers a post, which, always arriv*ing*, makes its way in what proves to be a way of self-encounter. The post opens what it encloses, and it closes what it keeps open. "The post," as Derrida says, "is an epoch of the post."[29] It delivers itself to itself, thanks to the post, within the epoch of the post, into which all sending is drawn, if not drowned.

The withdrawal withdraws; it carries itself away. Since the withdrawal carries itself away, what happens with it would seem to add nothing to what was the case before, as what happens no sooner occurs than it is taken away by the *with*, the opposing force, with which the withdrawal moves and removes. *There is* withdrawal; it takes place. But since it goes away just as it comes, the withdrawal gives away nothing and hence appears not to take place. It cannot be said that with withdrawal nothing happens; it should be said that withdrawal leaves "nothing" behind. Leaving nothing behind, it happens, albeit quietly, taking place without making a scene. Against the *with* it carries, the withdrawal contracts, as it were, engulfing itself and engulfed (*abîme*) by itself in such a way that it gives nothing but its own concealment and self-erasure. Erasing itself by itself, the withdrawal re-places itself, performing, in keeping with its own nature, a self-cancellation that nonetheless gives: it gives into itself so as to give itself out as a "nothing," a "nothing that is not nothing," as Martin Heidegger says, since it *is* (a) *given*.[30] Without changing register, we could say that the withdrawal is strictly *apophatic*: it unsays and says itself away, existing by persisting groundlessly in the immanence of its silent effectivity. Withdrawal thus should be understood as a kind of "active annihilation" that releases the "nothing" it gives in a double movement: it holds back that which, in holding back, happens to give, and it gives, in this giving, by pulling itself back into a self-giving that it cannot hold back. Both passive and transitive, perhaps more passive than passive, and more transitive than transitive, the withdrawal withdraws. Withdrawing, it dispenses, and in dispensing, it also secedes to become, as silence is to speech, its own negative space, a shadow, a dim region in its original kinship with nothingness, within whose contour everything, as Heidegger would say, is illuminated. Thanks to the withdrawal, all sending and receiving are set on their way—given and given to be given again. Like a promise.

If the post is an epoch of the post, into which all sending, as I said, is drawn, it is because the epoch withdraws and must withdraw first. The epoch must withdraw so that the epoch of the post comes to be and sending can begin. At the same time, since what withdraws leaves nothing behind but the traces of its own erasure, the epoch of the post, like the postman, disappears into that which it opens and keeps open. It dispenses a lack, giving a shadow, as I called it, that nonetheless illuminates a region of illumination. It is in this sense, and in this sense only, that the epoch is strictly *absolute*—separate and separated because loosened and set loose—with regard to the topos it breaks open. And it is in this sense, too, that the topos of the post is also rigorously *topological*, or even *tropological*, in that it carries out all deliveries by a force of its own that is only and purely *form*ative. Finally, it is in this sense as well that the postal epoch, I suggest, is not only *religious* (*re-ligiōus*, *re-ligāre*) because, formatively effective with regard to the delivery it performs, it binds again or re-ties everything within its span, but also *catholic* in that, through this *religioun*, it establishes the epoch's absolute universality and universal validity. If the epoch of the post is given, if it is a gift *of* the withdrawal, it is a gift that one cannot refuse, for it is a gift one must have always and already accepted before anything can be given, before any exchange can take place.

Every epoch defines a "period," marking and making a round of time in which one makes one's way around by turning and returning. An epoch would be nothing, if not one of transition, of moving one thing to its next station and moving itself into another phase, all the while keeping everything that takes place within the limits it sets, within its distinct unity and coherence. If the post is an epoch of the post, the epoch is also the post of the epoch in question. Insofar as it makes sending possible, the epoch likewise gives itself away as a predestinal sending that occurrences of transition and transmission affirm and confirm. Within the epoch of the post, beginnings, ever epiphenomenal, have always and already begun, and endings, if at all, are but promises of beginning, since the epoch, causing the post to turn and to return, has always and already withdrawn into itself as the groundless *origin*, not to say beginning, of sending in general.

One can now see why Derrida says of the post that "there is only but . . . this reproduction of a reproduction," and that this forbids him, the sender, to say anything in confidence, and makes of the receiver, the living and loved one, an *inter*diction. Not only can a letter, once sent, go astray, be waylaid, or be misappropriated in every way, but the very transmission of the message, the successful delivery of the letter, also means scantly more than that it is *sent*; to the extent that it *is* sent, the letter is in a way already *lost*, lost to the sender, if not yet lost by the postman; and, therefore, that it needs to be *re*-sent time and again, doing so not only in anticipation of the cry, "They have intercepted us," but also to sidestep the risk that it might be misread, or even rejected, by the receiver. The same goes the other way around. What happens in sending happens also to the receiver, who will have known this in time, which is to say, the receiver, like the sender, will never know for sure what exactly is being sent and what is ever received. To send and to receive what the other intends to be shared is as desirable and as proper as it is impossible; it is to "have asked each other the impossible," laments Derrida, "as the impossible, both of us."[31] In the epoch of the post, every sending happens in this way in principle; in fact, it is *against* principle that it does not succeed in doing so, Popperian test and reliable postal service notwithstanding. For Derrida, this is terrifying. For this is the terrifying law of the post, a law, according to which Derrida and we, who write letters too, speak and speak lawfully of its terrifying effects.

Speaking of the post, I speak necessarily from within the epoch of the post, doing so, as I must, thanks to the withdrawal of the post. And speaking on this basis, I return naturally to what I said earlier: communication is communicative, and it continues. In saying this then and, again, now, I communicate according to the law of the post and attest to the effect and the force of its imperative. Moreover, since my saying follows the imperative in question, this imperative must have spoken first, must have made the demand to be spoken about prior to my saying it. Released by what has already withdrawn and, hence, appearing groundless, this imperative is (to be) its own activity, indistinguishable from the continuing project it projects continuously. In other words, having always and already abandoned itself, as do all imperatives, to what it commands and demands, the imperative of communication is at the same time a fact of communication, a factum, on the basis of which it establishes itself as reality, as a prior fact. Ever affirmative, ever performative, the imperative of communication is the communication of this very imperative. Communicating with each other, each obliges the other; obligingly, each communicates with the other. Between the two, the force of communication asserts itself across the topos cleared by the withdrawal of the post, wherein the imperative realizes the groundless decision that it is. In this topos, the post, having withdrawn, is forced to release in its wake the force given to it by the imperative and, through this force, it keeps afloat the promise delivered by the postman to all, including himself. As a result, as promised, communication continues, as does the imperative, to which its continuation submits.

"Communicate!" says the imperative of communication; it is both a saying and a demand that demands to be said and to be said as a demand. The saying of this demand, or the demand that is thereby said, cannot be contradicted, for in contradicting it, one says it and thus has already responded to the demand that it be said. "Communicate!" speaks before speaking, extending or prolonging itself forcefully while remaining in its place as the same, yet ever renewed, demand. However, since this saying, the saying of this demand, would make no sense and could not be announced unless to someone who already knows how to communicate and is free to continue doing so, the irreducible fact of communication necessarily, all but tautologically, implies the fact of both the sender and receiver as first recipients of the demand, as already freed into the fact of being addressed properly, not only so that the imperative can be announced, but also so that the pronouncement can be enacted with the force of communication. Seen in this light, the "first recipients" of the imperative are never *mere* recipients of messages but, rather, must actively give the imperative to themselves and do so by communicating from the power of the imperative, that is, by way of a free self-address.[32] It is by this self-delivery, which translates a groundless sending into a self-fulfilling prophesy, into a speaking before actual speech, that sender and receiver, never alone, and yet autonomous and relative, establish sending and receiving as an irreducible fact or objective reality, establishing it, that is, by freely and jointly making possible the communication of everything communicable, including saying that communication is impossible. To the extent that the imperative of communication must subject itself to the same imperative to take effect, sender and receiver answer to and thereby affirm the imperative only insofar as they have already responded to the call to partake in the announcement of this imperative.

To communicate, as suggested earlier, is to demand communication. However, since to demand communication, as just suggested too, is a self-directed, automatic, response to a prior call to communicate, to communicate amounts to demanding continuously that *there be* communication; it is, in short, to communicate continuously, to continue communicating. By demand, or more exactly, by a demand that demands itself, communication continues. This is the fundamental *proposition* of communication, an absolute proposition that communicates absolutely in that, demanding itself by responding to its own demand, it knows no opposition and has nothing to oppose. Knowing no opposition and having nothing to oppose, this proposition, we should have no trouble seeing, ultimately says nothing about communication, except that it is taking place and is continued, in a word, is re-promised (*respondēre*) or re-responded. Here, as I speak, I see before me what might be called "the primal scene of communication," the ever-environing and ever-environed topos, in and against which acts of communication, mine first of all, continue in response to their own calls. This topos, this scene, will have been the epoch of communication, an epoch, in which we, simultaneously senders and receivers, find our residence as permanent *skeptics* who, as the word "skeptic" (*skeptikōs, skopeîn,* "to consider, to look") suggests, look nonstop and diligently for the proper site of communication's continuing power without ever finding it, and who will keep looking and will keep failing to find any, all the while looking to a promise of communication that promises nothing but the possibility of its own coming.

Being "skeptical," sending and receiving can be read as an exercise of power for the sake of the separation of powers, as reflected in skepticism's most general procedure, the skeptical doubt, be it Pyrrhonian, Cartesian, or otherwise.[33] But, more than that, they are also fundamentally a matter of speaking in multiplicity, of sending multiple meanings in a single speech. To be skeptical is to give more than one, at least two, meaning(s) in the message. If communication is communicative, if it sends a message, this message, skeptical in nature, is accordingly multiple; it is, I argue, always triple, always and already three in one: not only does it say what is being said, namely, the message, its content, and not only does it say, ipso facto, that this *saying* is not just possible but actual and actually proven to be possible, because something is being said here and now, but it also says, more forcefully though obliquely, that *this* proof, the fact that *something has been said herewith* and the fact that *that* too is remarked (though obliquely) here and now and will be remarked again and again as long as anything is (to be) said—all these constitute a message affirming an original, authorless, sending that, sending itself as an imperative of sending, makes any message a message and makes it deliverable in principle, that is, infinitely quotable, repeatable, or sayable, as it speaks of the post that remains unsaid or withdrawn in actual speech. This last message within a message, within any message, is at once also the first message, the archi-message, as it were, of all communication, a message that the postman delivers to us even before he shows up in person, a message that must have been delivered before any message can then be delivered, a message, finally, that defines this epoch, in which "I," like everyone else, *am* the epoch's own unbroken promise, its indefatigable messenger.

As the postman withdraws, every sending and receiving is accomplished as promised, that is to say, becomes realizable, if not yet realized. What withdraws gives; however, since it, in giving, holds itself back, that which withdraws returns and releases itself only through a departing that traces the departure, of which, as a result, it is a trace. This trace, which traces and hence is a trace of traces, traces the story of the post, a story in which not only the sayable but also what is foreign to or remains withdrawn in the sayable can be traced, even if not directly constated or clearly heard. If this story can be told as one of Being, as, for example, in Heidegger, or as a fiction of (non)being, as in Derrida, I see no reason why it cannot be read as a story of communication, of how and why we communicate and do so (un)failingly.

Are we not, knowingly or not, telling and retelling this story of the post, of which we are part, whenever we speak or do not (want to) speak? Are we not, knowingly or not, communicating, communing, or coming together only to fall apart so as to start over again? What could the poet possibly have in mind when he says "Man is a sign," if not the understanding that communication makes a man and makes him by unmaking him into what makes him? Communication is communicative, and it continues. Nothing we do or say can stop it; not even silence, not even suicide, not even self-withdrawal, can deny that we are, knowingly or not, "a verbalism without end."[34] For, I said earlier and will say here one last time, communication cannot be avoided, if only because the avoidance of communication leaves a void that nonetheless communicates. The promise of communication always communicates what it promises, its promised coming . . . a promise.

What comes, always that which withdraws, must have been set out on its way, to come and also to go away. It is never certain that what is coming also arrives, but it is certain that what is coming, because it is *coming*, must not be here yet. Come what may, the possibility of whatever comes going away belongs to the condition of coming and to that of what comes.[35] "Without greeting, without a word, in a going even prior to coming and going," in a silent speech prior to the choice between saying "come" and saying "go," "it is there and gone away."[36] Communication comes and continues to come in this way because, given the way it promises to come, regardless of whether one admits seeing it coming or not, it has been coming and has already taken place in and as this coming. It is from within this coming—but also in its going away—that I now speak and have spoken. One always speaks and speaks without the power (not) to do so. So, without stopping, I say "look and see." Look and see the post turning and returning into itself, into the withdrawal at the post's center, into that of which communication, always plastic in form and in substance, is but a continuation of the post. In the end, there is no end. Like a promise—a promise of the post, in this epoch of the post.

Notes

1. Here I wish to point out that the word *this* in the title of this chapter should be taken as the cardinal deictic. Unlike "I," "here," and "now," which can refer to the agent of the speech, and the place and time in which what is said is said, "this" can only refer to itself as word or utterance or event. "'This,'" as Jeffrey Bennington remarks, "might mean just this, itself, its own self," this "this." Bennington, *Legislations: The Politics of Deconstruction* (London: Verso, 1994), 290. This essay is dedicated to Jacques Derrida in memory of his kindness, encouragement, and the future perfect of his thoughts.

2. I want to say at the outset that my ideas regarding promise and beyond, as I try to put them to work in this essay, are greatly influenced by the writings of Werner Hamacher. On this, see especially the essays collected in his *Premises* (Cambridge, MA: Harvard University Press, 1996), and his "Lingua Amissa," in *Futures of Jacques Derrida* (Stanford, CA: Stanford University Press, 2001). Having said that, I should add that the question of how the condition of sincerity relates to promising is complicated. For the purpose of making my point here, it suffices to say that I hold the more or less classic view, best represented by Paul Grice, that one cannot say insincerely what cannot be said sincerely. This is because, as David M. Rosenthal, explains, "When I speak insincerely, I intend you to take my speech act to be sincere. If it is impossible for tokens of a particular sentence type to be used to perform a sincere illocutionary act, I cannot hope to use such a token to produce in you the right response. Accordingly, I cannot intend to do so. So I cannot use it even to say something insincerely." Rosenthal, *Consciousness and Mind* (New York: Oxford University Press, 2005), 101.

3. Hans-Jost Frey, *Interruptions*, trans. Georgia Albert (Albany: State University of New York Press, 1996), 23.

4. On the idea of continuation as used here, see Werner Hamacher, "Ou, séance, touche de Nancy, ici," in *On Jean-Luc Nancy*, ed. Darren Sheppard, Simon Sparks, and Colin Thomas (New York: Routledge, 1997), 38–62.

5. I adopted the idea of "the ancestral" developed by Quentin Meillassoux. See his *After Finitude: An Essay on the Necessity of Contingency* (London: Continuum, 2009), esp. 1–27.

6. Hamacher, "Lingua Amissa," 174.

7. Promising must continue because, as just suggested, it is in principle incomplete, because, as Hamacher puts it, "missing is the truth of promising. If something promises—promises promising and thus promises language," which alone makes it possible, "it is missing. Missing releases the promise from promising, and it alone lets it go out freely." Hamacher, *Premises*, 142.

8. I must add here that the point I am making is already forcefully developed, though from a slightly different angle, by Hamacher in "Lingua Amissa," where he writes, "Communication—and therewith every being-with-another, every being—is a promise" (158), and later on, suggests that "the promise in question here must consequently be thought of first of all as the 'medium of all media.'" (160).

9. See Frey, *Interruptions*, 24.

10. For a nuanced discussion on the variations of performativity, see again, Hamacher, "Lingua Amissa," 163–165.

11. Hamacher, *Premises*, 128.

12. Ibid.

13. Hamacher, "Lingua Amissa," 175.

14. Ibid.

15. Catherine Malabou and Jacques Derrida, trans. David Wills, *Counterpath* (Stanford, CA: Stanford University Press, 2004), 108. A slightly different translation of the passage, from which the quoted sentence comes, can be found in Jacques Derrida, *Athens, Still Remains*, trans. Pascale-Anne Brault and Michael Naas (New York: Fordham University Press, 2010), 27–28.

16. For a detailed discussion on the idea of "post," see Bernhard Siegert, *Relays: Literature as an Epoch of the Postal System* (Stanford, CA: Stanford University Press), 1999.

17. Ibid., 10.

18. Epoch, *epochē*, refers to that which releases, to that which makes what is released possible, to a giving that makes what is given possible. This is the idea behind Heidegger's thinking of Being as epochal sending; he writes: "Epoch does not mean here the span of time in occurrence, but rather the fundamental characteristic of sending, the actual holding-back of itself in favor of the discernibility of the gift, that is, of Being with regard to the grounding of beings." Martin Heidegger, *On Time and Being*, trans. Joan Stambaugh (San Francisco: Harper & Row, 1972), 9.

19. Malabou and Derrida, *Counterpath*, 108.

20. Gilles Deleuze, *The Logic of Sense* (New York: Columbia University Press, 1990), 51.

21. Coined by Jacques Lacan from the term "intimacy" (*intimité*), the word *extimité* (extimacy) is meant to suggest that the most intimate in oneself, the Other, is at the same time the most hidden and unknown to oneself. I use it here to mean "externally intimate," "both inside and outside at the same time." For a brief discussion on this idea, see Jacques-Alain Miller, "Extimité," in *Lacanian Theory of Discourse: Subject, Structure, and Society*, ed. Mark Bracher, Marshall W. Alcorn Jr., Ronald J. Corthell, and Françoise Massardier-Kenny (New York: New York University Press, 1994), 74–87.

22. Jean-Luc Nancy, *Noli me tangere: On the Raising of the Body* (New York: Fordham University Press), 2008.

23. Ibid., 15.

24. Jacques Derrida, *The Post Card: From Socrates to Freud and Beyond* (Chicago: University of Chicago Press, 1987), 65.

25. Ibid., 63.

26. Niklas Luhmann is famously known for saying, "Only communication communicates." This claim, and variations of it, come from his systems theory-based idea of "operational closure," and means something different from what I try to suggest here. See, for example, his "What Is Communication?" in *Theories of Distinction: Redescribing the Descriptions of Modernity*, ed., William Rasch (Stanford, CA: Stanford University Press, 2002), 155–168.

27. Derrida, *The Post Card*, 65, emphasis added.

28. Martin Heidegger, *On the Way to Language,* trans. Peter D. Hertz (San Francisco: Harper & Row, 1982), 92.

29. Derrida, *The Post Card*, 63.

30. See Marlène Zarader, *The Unthought Debt: Heidegger and the Hebraic Heritage* (Stanford, CA: Stanford University Press, 2006), 130.

31. Derrida, *The Post Card*, 8.

32. See Peter Fenves, *"Chatter": Language and History in Kierkegaard* (Stanford, CA: Stanford University Press, 1993), 149.

33. See Odo Marquard, *In Defense of the Accidental* (New York: Oxford University Press, 1991), esp. chap. 1, 3–7.

34. Wiltold Gombrowicz, *A Guide to Philosophy* (New Haven, CT: Yale University Press, 2004), 84.

35. Hamacher, *Premises*, 386–387.

36. Ibid., 387.

I   Openings

2 Phaedrus

Plato

＊　＊　＊

Phaedrus.   By all means, let's talk.

Socrates.   Well, then, we ought to examine the topic we proposed just now: When is a speech well written and delivered, and when is it not?

Ph.   Plainly.

So.   Won't someone who is to speak well and nobly have to have in mind the truth about the subject he is going to discuss?

Ph.   What I have actually heard about this, Socrates, my friend, is that it is not necessary for the intending orator to learn what is really just, but only what will seem just to the crowd who will act as judges. Nor again what is really good or noble, but only what will seem so. For that is what persuasion proceeds from, not truth.

So.   Anything that wise men say, Phaedrus, "is not lightly to be cast aside";[1] we must consider whether it might be right. And what you just said, in particular, must not be dismissed.

Ph.   You're right.

So.   Let's look at it this way, then.

Ph.   How?

So.   Suppose I were trying to convince you that you should fight your enemies on horseback, and neither one of us knew what a horse is, but I happened to know this much about you, that Phaedrus believes a horse is the tame animal with the longest ears—

Ph.   But that would be ridiculous, Socrates.

So.   Not quite yet, actually. But if I were seriously trying to convince you, having composed a speech in praise of the donkey in which I called it a horse and claimed that having such an animal is of immense value both at home and in military service, that it is good for fighting and for carrying your baggage and that it is useful for much else besides—

Ph.   Well, that would be totally ridiculous.

So.   Well, which is better? To be ridiculous and a friend? Or clever and an enemy?

Ph.   The former.

So.   And so, when a rhetorician who does not know good from bad addresses a city which knows no better and attempts to sway it, not praising a miserable donkey as if it were a horse,[2] but bad as if it were good, and, having studied what the people believe, persuades them to do something bad instead of good—with that as its seed, what sort of crop do you think rhetoric can harvest?

Ph.   A crop of really poor quality.

So.   But could it be, my friend, that we have mocked the art of speaking more rudely than it deserves? For it might perhaps reply, "What bizarre nonsense! Look, I am not forcing anyone to learn how to make speeches without knowing the truth; on the contrary, my advice, for what it is worth, is to take me up only after mastering the truth. But I do make this boast: even someone who knows the truth couldn't produce conviction on the basis of a systematic art without me."

Ph.   Well, is that a fair reply?

So.   Yes, it is—if, that is, the arguments now advancing upon rhetoric testify that it is an art. For it seems to me as if I hear certain arguments approaching and protesting that that is a lie and that rhetoric is not an art but an artless practice.[3] As the Spartan said, there is no genuine art of speaking without a grasp of truth, and there never will be.[4]

Ph.   We need to hear these arguments, Socrates. Come, produce them, and examine them: What is their point? How do they make it?

So.   Come to us, then, noble creatures; convince Phaedrus, him of the beautiful offspring,[5] that unless he pursues philosophy properly he will never be able to make a proper speech on any subject either. And let Phaedrus be the one to answer.

Ph.   Let them put their questions.

So.   Well, then, isn't the rhetorical art, taken as a whole, a way of directing the soul by means of speech, not only in the lawcourts and on other public occasions but also in private?[6] Isn't it one and the same art whether its subject is great or small, and no more to be held in esteem—if it is followed correctly—when its questions are serious than when they are trivial? Or what have you heard about all this?

Ph.   Well, certainly not what *you* have! Artful speaking and writing is found mainly in the lawcourts; also perhaps in the Assembly.[7] That's all I've heard.

So.   Well, have you only heard of the rhetorical treatises of Nestor and Odysseus—those they wrote in their spare time in Troy? Haven't you also heard of the works of Palamedes?[8]

Ph.   No, by Zeus, I haven't even heard of Nestor's—unless by Nestor you mean Gorgias, and by Odysseus, Thrasymachus or Theodorus.[9]

So.   Perhaps. But let's leave these people aside. Answer this question yourself: What do adversaries do in the lawcourts? Don't they speak on opposite sides? What else can we call what they do?

Ph.   That's it, exactly.

So.   About what is just and what is unjust?

Ph.   Yes.

So.   And won't whoever does this artfully make the same thing appear to the same people sometimes just and sometimes, when he prefers, unjust?

Ph.   Of course.

So.   And when he addresses the Assembly, he will make the city approve a policy at one time as a good one, and reject it—the very same policy—as just the opposite at another.

Ph.   Right.

So.   Now, don't we know that the Eleatic Palamedes is such an artful speaker that his listeners will perceive the same things to be both similar and dissimilar, both one and many, both at rest and also in motion?[10]

Ph.   Most certainly.

So.   We can therefore find the practice of speaking on opposite sides not only in the law-courts and in the Assembly. Rather, it seems that one single art—if, of course, it is an art in the first place—governs all speaking. By means of it one can make out as similar anything that can be so assimilated, to everything to which it can be made similar, and expose anyone who tries to hide the fact that that is what he is doing.

Ph.   What do you mean by that?

So.   I think it will become clear if we look at it this way. Where is deception most likely to occur—regarding things that differ much or things that differ little from one another?

Ph.   Regarding those that differ little.

So.   At any rate, you are more likely to escape detection, as you shift from one thing to its opposite, if you proceed in small steps rather than in large ones.

Ph.   Without a doubt.

So.   Therefore, if you are to deceive someone else and to avoid deception yourself, you must know precisely the respects in which things are similar and dissimilar to one another.

Ph.   Yes, you must.

So.   And is it really possible for someone who doesn't know what each thing truly is to detect a similarity—whether large or small—between something he doesn't know and anything else?

Ph.   That is impossible.

So.   Clearly, therefore, the state of being deceived and holding beliefs contrary to what is the case comes upon people by reason of certain similarities.

Ph.   That is how it happens.

So.   Could someone, then, who doesn't know what each thing is ever have the art to lead others little by little through similarities away from what is the case on each occasion to its opposite? Or could he escape this being done to himself?

Ph.   Never.

So.   Therefore, my friend, the art of a speaker who doesn't know the truth and chases opinions instead is likely to be a ridiculous thing—not an art at all!

Ph.   So it seems.

So.   So, shall we look for instances of what we called the artful and the artless in the speech of Lysias you carried here and in our own speeches?

Ph.   That's the best thing to do—because, as it is, we are talking quite abstractly, without enough examples.

So.   In fact, by some chance the two speeches[11] do, as it seems, contain an example of the way in which someone who knows the truth can toy with his audience and mislead them. For my part, Phaedrus, I hold the local gods responsible for this—also, perhaps, the messengers of the Muses[12] who are singing over our heads may have inspired me with this gift: certainly *I* don't possess any art of speaking.

Ph.   Fine, fine. But explain what you mean.

So.   Come, then—read me the beginning of Lysias' speech.

Ph.   "You understand my situation: I've told you how good it would be for us, in my opinion, if we could work this out. In any case, I don't think I should lose the chance to get what I am asking for, merely because I don't happen to be in love with you. A man in love will wish he had not done you any favors—"[13]

So.   Stop. Our task is to say how he fails and writes artlessly. Right?

Ph.   Yes.

So.   Now isn't this much absolutely clear: We are in accord with one another about some of the things we discourse about and in discord about others?

Ph.   I think I understand what you are saying; but, please, can you make it a little clearer?

So.   When someone utters the word "iron" or "silver," don't we all think of the same thing?

Ph.   Certainly.

So.   But what happens when we say "just" or "good"? Doesn't each one of us go in a different direction? Don't we differ with one another and even with ourselves?

Ph.   We certainly do.

So.   Therefore, we agree about the former and disagree about the latter.

Ph.   Right.

So.   Now in which of these two cases are we more easily deceived? And when does rhetoric have greater power?

Ph.   Clearly, when we wander in different directions.

So.   It follows that whoever wants to acquire the art of rhetoric must first make a systematic division and grasp the particular character of each of these two kinds of thing, both the kind where most people wander in different directions and the kind where they do not.

Ph.   What a splendid thing, Socrates, he will have understood if he grasps *that!*

So.   Second, I think, he must not be mistaken about his subject; he must have a sharp eye for the class to which whatever he is about to discuss belongs.

Ph.   Of course.

So.   Well, now, what shall we say about love? Does it belong to the class where people differ or to that where they don't?

Ph.   Oh, surely the class where they differ. Otherwise, do you think you could have spoken of it as you did a few minutes ago, first saying that it is harmful both to lover and beloved and then immediately afterward that it is the greatest good?

So.   Very well put. But now tell me this—I can't remember at all because I was completely possessed by the gods: Did I define love at the beginning of my speech?

Ph.   Oh, absolutely, by Zeus, you most certainly did.

So.   Alas, how much more artful with speeches the Nymphs, daughters of Achelous, and Pan, son of Hermes, are, according to what you say, than Lysias, son of Cephalus! Or am I wrong? Did Lysias too, at the start of his love-speech, compel us to assume that love is the single thing that he himself wanted it to be? Did he then complete his speech by arranging everything in relation to that? Will you read its opening once again?

Ph.   If you like. But what you are looking for is not there.

So.   Read it, so that I can hear it in his own words.

Ph.   "You understand my situation: I've told you how good it would be for us, in my opinion, if we could work this out. In any case, I don't think I should lose the chance to get what I am asking for, merely because I don't happen to be in love with you. A man in love will wish he had not done you any favors, once his desire dies down—"

So.   He certainly seems a long way from doing what we wanted. He doesn't even start from the beginning but from the end, making his speech swim upstream on its back. His first words are what a lover would say to his boy as he was concluding his speech. Am I wrong, Phaedrus, dear heart?[14]

Ph.   Well, Socrates, that was the end for which he gave the speech!

So.   And what about the rest? Don't the parts of the speech appear to have been thrown together at random? Is it evident that the second point had to be made second for some compelling reason?[15] Is that so for any of the parts? I at least—of course I know nothing about such matters—thought the author said just whatever came to mind next, though not without a certain noble willfulness. But you, do you know any principle of speech-composition compelling him to place these things one after another in this order?

Ph.   It's very generous of you to think that I can understand his reasons so clearly.

So.   But surely you will admit at least this much: Every speech must be put together like a living creature, with a body of its own; it must be neither without head nor without legs; and it must have a middle and extremities that are fitting both to one another and to the whole work.

Ph.   How could it be otherwise?

So.   But look at your friend's speech: Is it like that or is it otherwise? Actually, you'll find that it's just like the epigram people say is inscribed on the tomb of Midas the Phrygian.[16]

Ph.   What epigram is that? And what's the matter with it?

So.   It goes like this:
A maid of bronze am I, on Midas' tomb I lie
As long as water flows, and trees grow tall.
Shielding the grave where many come to cry
That Midas rests here I say to one and all.

I'm sure you notice that it makes no difference at all which of its verses comes first, and which last.

Ph.   You are making fun of our speech, Socrates.

So.   Well, then, if that upsets you, let's leave that speech aside—even though I think it has plenty of very useful examples, provided one tries to emulate them as little as possible—and turn to the others. 1 think it is important for students of speechmaking to pay attention to one of their features.

Ph.   What do you mean?

So.   They were in a way opposite to one another. One claimed that one should give one's favors to the lover; the other, to the non-lover.

Ph.   Most manfully, too.

So.   I thought you were going to say "madly," which would have been the truth, and is also just what I was looking for: We did say, didn't we, that love is a kind of madness?

Ph.   Yes.

So.   And that there are two kinds of madness, one produced by human illness, the other by a divinely inspired release from normally accepted behavior?

Ph.   Certainly.

So.   We also distinguished four parts within the divine kind and connected them to four gods. Having attributed the inspiration of the prophet to Apollo, of the mystic to Dionysus, of the poet to the Muses, and the fourth part of madness to Aphrodite and to Love, we said that the madness of love is the best. We used a certain sort of image to describe love's passion; perhaps it had a measure of truth in it, though it may also have led us astray. And having whipped up a not altogether implausible speech, we sang playfully, but also appropriately and respectfully, a storylike hymn to my master and yours, Phaedrus—to Love, who watches over beautiful boys.

Ph.   And I listened to it with the greatest pleasure.

So.   Let's take up this point about it right away: How was the speech able to proceed from censure to praise?[17]

Ph.   What exactly do you mean by that?

So.   Well, everything else in it really does appear to me to have been spoken in play. But part of it was given with Fortune's guidance, and there were in it two kinds of things the nature of which it would be quite wonderful to grasp by means of a systematic art.

Ph.   Which things?

So.   The first consists in seeing together things that are scattered about everywhere and collecting them into one kind, so that by defining each thing we can make clear the subject of any instruction we wish to give.[18] Just so with our discussion of love: Whether its definition was or was not correct, at least it allowed the speech to proceed clearly and consistently with itself.

Ph.   And what is the other thing you are talking about, Socrates?

So.   This, in turn, is to be able to cut up each kind according to its species along its natural joints, and to try not to splinter any part, as a bad butcher might do. In just this way, our two speeches placed all mental derangements into one common kind. Then, just as each single body has parts that naturally come in pairs of the same name (one of them being called the right-hand and the other the left-hand one),[19] so the speeches, having considered unsoundness of mind to be by nature one single kind within us, proceeded to cut it up—the first speech cut its left-hand part, and continued to cut until it discovered among these parts a sort of love that can be called "left-handed," which it correctly denounced; the second speech, in turn, led us to the right-hand part of madness; discovered a love that shares its name with the other but is actually divine; set it out before us, and praised it as the cause of our greatest goods.

Ph.   You are absolutely right.

So.   Well, Phaedrus, I am myself a lover of these divisions and collections, so that I may be able to think and to speak; and if I believe that someone else is capable of discerning a single thing that is also by nature capable of encompassing many,[20] I follow "straight behind, in his tracks, as if he were a god."[21] God knows whether this is the right name for those who can do this correctly or not, but so far I have always called them "dialecticians." But tell me what I must call them now that we have learned all this from Lysias and you. Or is it just that art of speaking that Thrasymachus and the rest of them use, which has made them masters of speechmaking and capable of producing others like them—anyhow those who are willing to bring them gifts and to treat them as if they were kings?

Ph.   They may behave like kings, but they certainly lack the knowledge you're talking about. No, it seems to me that you are right in calling the sort of thing you mentioned dialectic; but, it seems to me, rhetoric still eludes us.

So.   What are you saying? Could there be anything valuable which is independent of the methods I mentioned and is still grasped by art? If there is, you and I must certainly honor it, and we must say what part of rhetoric it is that has been left out.

Ph.   Well, there's quite a lot, Socrates: everything, at any rate, written up in the books on the art of speaking.

So.   You were quite right to remind me. First, I believe, there is the Preamble with which a speech must begin. This is what you mean, isn't it—the fine points of the art?

Ph.   Yes.

So.   Second come the Statement of Facts and the Evidence of Witnesses concerning it;
third, Indirect Evidence; fourth, Claims to Plausibility. And I believe at least that excellent
Byzantine word-wizard adds Confirmation and Supplementary Confirmation.

Ph.   You mean the worthy Theodorus?[22]

So.   Quite. And he also adds Refutation and Supplementary Refutation, to be used both
in prosecution and in defense. Nor must we forget the most excellent Evenus of Paros,[23]
who was the first to discover Covert Implication and Indirect Praise and who—some
say—has even arranged Indirect Censures in verse as an aid to memory: a wise man indeed!
And Tisias[24] and Gorgias? How can we leave them out when it is they who realized that
what is likely must be held in higher honor than what is true; they who, by the power
of their language, make small things appear great and great things small; they who express
modern ideas in ancient garb, and ancient ones in modern dress; they who have discovered how to argue both concisely and at infinite length about any subject? Actually, when
I told Prodicus[25] this last, he laughed and said that only he had discovered the art of
proper speeches: What we need are speeches that are neither long nor short but of the
right length.

Ph.   Brilliantly done, Prodicus!

So.   And what about Hippias?[26] How can we omit him? I am sure our friend from Elis would
cast his vote with Prodicus.

Ph.   Certainly.

So.   And what shall we say of the whole gallery of terms Polus[27] set up—Speaking with
Reduplication, Speaking in Maxims, Speaking in Images—and of the terms Licymnius gave
him as a present to help him explain Good Diction?[28]

Ph.   But didn't Protagoras actually use similar terms?[29]

So.   Yes, Correct Diction, my boy, and other wonderful things. As to the art of making
speeches bewailing the evils of poverty and old age, the prize, in my judgment, goes to the
mighty Chalcedonian.[30] He it is also who knows best how to inflame a crowd and, once
they are inflamed, how to hush them again with his words' magic spell, as he says himself.
And let's not forget that he is as good at producing slander as he is at refuting it, whatever
its source may be.

As to the way of ending a speech, everyone seems to be in agreement, though some call
it Recapitulation and others by some other name.

Ph.   You mean, summarizing everything at the end and reminding the audience of what
they've heard?

So.   That's what I mean. And if you have anything else to add about the art of speaking—

Ph.   Only minor points, not worth making.

So.   Well, let's leave minor points aside. Let's hold what we do have closer to the light so
that we can see precisely the power of the art these things produce.

Ph.   A very great power, Socrates, especially in front of a crowd.

So.   Quite right. But now, my friend, look closely: Do you think, as I do, that its fabric is a little threadbare?

Ph.   Can you show me?

So.   All right, tell me this. Suppose someone came to your friend Eryximachus or his father Acumenus and said: "I know treatments to raise or lower (whichever I prefer) the temperature of people's bodies; if I decide to, I can make them vomit or make their bowels move, and all sorts of things. On the basis of this knowledge, I claim to be a physician; and I claim to be able to make others physicians as well by imparting it to them." What do you think they would say when they heard that?

Ph.   What could they say? They would ask him if he also knew to whom he should apply such treatments, when, and to what extent.

So.   What if he replied, "I have no idea. My claim is that whoever learns from me will manage to do what you ask on his own"?

Ph.   I think they'd say the man's mad if he thinks he's a doctor just because he read a book or happened to come across a few potions; he knows nothing of the art.

So.   And suppose someone approached Sophocles and Euripides and claimed to know how to compose the longest passages on trivial topics and the briefest ones on topics of great importance, that he could make them pitiful if he wanted, or again, by contrast, terrifying and menacing, and so on. Suppose further that he believed that by teaching this he was imparting the knowledge of composing tragedies—

Ph.   Oh, I am sure they too would laugh at anyone who thought a tragedy was anything other than the proper arrangement of these things: They have to fit with one another and with the whole work.

So.   But I am sure they wouldn't reproach him rudely. They would react more like a musician confronted by a man who thought he had mastered harmony because he was able to produce the highest and lowest notes on his strings. The musician would not say fiercely, "You stupid man, you are out of your mind!" As befits his calling, he would speak more gently: "My friend, though that too is necessary for understanding harmony, someone who has gotten as far as you have may still know absolutely nothing about the subject. What you know is what it's necessary to learn before you study harmony, but not harmony itself."

Ph.   That's certainly right.

So.   So Sophocles would also tell the man who was showing off to them that he knew the preliminaries of tragedy, but not the art of tragedy itself. And Acumenus would say his man knew the preliminaries of medicine, but not medicine itself.

Ph.   Absolutely.

So.   And what if the "honey-tongued Adrastus" (or perhaps Pericles)[31] were to hear of all the marvelous techniques we just discussed—Speaking Concisely and Speaking in Images and all the rest we listed and proposed to examine under the light? Would he be angry or rude, as you and I were, with those who write of those techniques and teach them as if they are rhetoric itself, and say something coarse to them? Wouldn't he—being wiser than we are—reproach us as well and say, "Phaedrus and Socrates, you should not be angry with these people—you should be sorry for them. The reason they cannot define rhetoric is that they are ignorant of dialectic. It is their ignorance that makes them think they have discovered what rhetoric is when they have mastered only what it is necessary to learn as preliminaries. So they teach these preliminaries and imagine their pupils have received a full course in rhetoric, thinking the task of using each of them persuasively and putting them together into a whole speech is a minor matter, to be worked out by the pupils from their own resources"?

Ph.   Really, Socrates, the art these men present as rhetoric in their courses and handbooks is no more than what you say. In my judgment, at least, your point is well taken. But how, from what source, could one acquire the art of the true rhetorician, the really persuasive speaker?

So.   Well, Phaedrus, becoming good enough to be an accomplished competitor is probably—perhaps necessarily—like everything else. If you have a natural ability for rhetoric, you will become a famous rhetorician, provided you supplement your ability with knowledge and practice. To the extent that you lack any one of them, to that extent you will be less than perfect. But, insofar as there is an art of rhetoric, I don't believe the right method for acquiring it is to be found in the direction Lysias and Thrasymachus have followed.

Ph.   Where can we find it then?

So.   My dear friend, maybe we can see now why Pericles was in all likelihood the greatest rhetorician of all.

Ph.   How is that?

So.   All the great arts require endless talk and ethereal speculation[32] about nature: This seems to be what gives them their lofty point of view and universal applicability. That's just what Pericles mastered—besides having natural ability. He came across Anaxagoras, who was just that sort of man, got his full dose of ethereal speculation, and understood the nature of mind and mindlessness[33]—just the subject on which Anaxagoras had the most to say. From this, I think, he drew for the art of rhetoric what was useful to it.

Ph.   What do you mean by that?

So.   Well, isn't the method of medicine in a way the same as the method of rhetoric?

Ph.   How so?

So.   In both cases we need to determine the nature of something—of the body in medicine, of the soul in rhetoric. Otherwise, all we'll have will be an empirical and artless practice. We won't be able to supply, on the basis of an art, a body with the medicines and diet that will make it healthy and strong, or a soul with the reasons and customary rules for conduct that will impart to it the convictions and virtues we want.

Ph.   That is most likely, Socrates.

So.   Do you think, then, that it is possible to reach a serious understanding of the nature of the soul without understanding the nature of the world as a whole?

Ph.   Well, if we're to listen to Hippocrates, Asclepius' descendant,[34] we won't even understand the body if we don't follow that method.

So.   He speaks well, my friend. Still, Hippocrates aside, we must consider whether argument supports that view.

Ph.   I agree.

So.   Consider, then, what both Hippocrates and true argument say about nature. Isn't this the way to think systematically about the nature of anything? First, we must consider whether the object regarding which we intend to become experts and capable of transmitting our expertise is simple or complex. Then, if it is simple, we must investigate its power: What things does it have what natural power of acting upon? By what things does it have what natural disposition to be acted upon? If, on the other hand, it takes many forms, we must enumerate them all and, as we did in the simple case, investigate how each is naturally able to act upon what and how it has a natural disposition to be acted upon by what.

Ph.   It seems so, Socrates.

So.   Proceeding by any other method would be like walking with the blind. Conversely, whoever studies anything on the basis of an art must never be compared to the blind or the deaf. On the contrary, it is clear that someone who teaches another to make speeches as an art will demonstrate precisely the essential nature of that to which speeches are to be applied. And that, surely, is the soul.

Ph.   Of course.

So.   This is therefore the object toward which the speaker's whole effort is directed, since it is in the soul that he attempts to produce conviction. Isn't that so?

Ph.   Yes.

So.   Clearly, therefore, Thrasymachus and anyone else who teaches the art of rhetoric seriously will, first, describe the soul with absolute precision and enable us to understand what it is: whether it is one and homogeneous by nature or takes many forms, like the shape of bodies, since, as we said, that's what it is to demonstrate the nature of something.

Ph.   Absolutely.

So.   Second, he will explain how, in virtue of its nature, it acts and is acted upon by certain things.

Ph.   Of course.

So.   Third, he will classify the kinds of speech and of soul there are, as well as the various ways in which they are affected, and explain what causes each. He will then coordinate each kind of soul with the kind of speech appropriate to it. And he will give instructions concerning the reasons why one kind of soul is necessarily convinced by one kind of speech while another necessarily remains unconvinced.

Ph.   This, I think, would certainly be the best way.

So.   In fact, my friend, no speech will ever be a product of art, whether it is a model[35] or one actually given, if it is delivered or written in any other way—on this or on any other subject. But those who now write *Arts of Rhetoric*—we were just discussing them[36]—are cunning people: they hide the fact that they know very well everything about the soul. Well, then, until they begin to speak and write in this way, we mustn't allow ourselves to be convinced that they write on the basis of the art.

Ph.   What way is that?

So.   It's very difficult to speak the actual words, but as to how one should write in order to be as artful as possible—that I am willing to tell you.

Ph.   Please do.

So.   Since the nature of speech is in fact to direct the soul, whoever intends to be a rhetorician must know how many kinds of soul there are. Their number is so-and-so many; each is of such-and-such a sort; hence some people have such-and-such a character and others have such-and-such. Those distinctions established, there are, in turn, so-and-so many kinds of speech, each of such-and-such a sort. People of such-and-such a character are easy to persuade by speeches of such-and-such a sort in connection with such-and-such an issue for this particular reason, while people of such-and-such another sort are difficult to persuade for those particular reasons.

The orator must learn all this well, then put his theory into practice and develop the ability to discern each kind clearly as it occurs in the actions of real life. Otherwise he won't be any better off than he was when he was still listening to those discussions in school. He will now not only be able to say what kind of person is convinced by what kind of speech; on meeting someone he will be able to discern what he is like and make clear to himself that the person actually standing in front of him is of just this particular sort of character he had learned about in school—to that he must now apply speeches of such-and-such a kind in this particular way in order to secure conviction about such-and-such an issue. When he has learned all this—when, in addition, he has grasped the right occasions[37] for speaking and for holding back; and when he has also understood when the time is right for Speaking Concisely or Appealing to Pity or Exaggeration or for any other of the kinds of speech he has learned and when it is not—then, and only then, will he have finally mastered the art well and completely. But if his speaking, his teaching, or his writing lacks any one of these elements and he still claims to be speaking with art, you'll be better off if you don't believe him.

"Well, Socrates and Phaedrus," the author of this discourse might say, "do you agree? Could we accept an art of speaking presented in any other terms?"

Ph.   That would be impossible, Socrates. Still, it's evidently rather a major undertaking.

So.   You're right. And that's why we must turn all our arguments every which way and try to find some easier and shorter route to the art: we don't want to follow a long rough path for no good reason when we can choose a short smooth one instead.

Now, try to remember if you've heard anything helpful from Lysias or anybody else. Speak up.

Ph.   It's not for lack of trying, but nothing comes to mind right now.

So.   Well, then, shall I tell you something I've heard people say who care about this topic?

Ph.   Of course.

So.   We do claim, after all, Phaedrus, that it is fair to give the wolf's side of the story as well.

Ph.   That's just what you should do.

So.   Well, these people say that there is no need to be so solemn about all this and stretch it out to such lengths. For the fact is, as we said ourselves at the beginning of this discussion,[38] that one who intends to be an able rhetorician has no need to know the truth about the things that are just or good or yet about the people who are such either by nature or upbringing. No one in a lawcourt, you see, cares at all about the truth of such matters. They only care about what is convincing. This is called "the likely" and that is what a man who intends to speak according to art should concentrate on. Sometimes, in fact, whether you are prosecuting or defending a case, you must not even say what actually happened, if it was not likely to have happened—you must say something that is likely instead. Whatever you say, you should pursue what is likely and leave the truth aside: the whole art consists in cleaving to that throughout your speech.[39]

Ph.   That's an excellent presentation of what people say who profess to be expert in speeches, Socrates. I recall that we raised this issue briefly earlier on, but it seems to be their single most important point.

So.   No doubt you've churned through Tisias' book quite carefully.[40] Then let Tisias tell us this also: By "the likely" does he mean anything but what is thought to be so by the crowd?

Ph.   What else?

So.   And it's likely it was when he discovered this clever and artful technique that Tisias wrote that if a weak but spunky man is taken to court because he beat up a strong but cowardly one and stole his cloak or something else, neither one should tell the truth.[41] The coward must say that the spunky man didn't beat him up all by himself, while the latter must rebut this by saying that only the two of them were there, and fall back on that well-worn plea, "How could a man like me attack a man like him?" The strong man, naturally, will not admit his cowardice, but will try to invent some other lie, and may thus give his opponent the chance to refute him. And in other cases, speaking as the art dictates will take similar forms. Isn't that so, Phaedrus?

Ph.   Of course.

So.   Phew! Tisias—or whoever else it was and whatever name he pleases to use for himself[42]—seems[43] to have discovered an art which he has disguised very well! But now, my friend, shall we or shall we not say to him—

Ph.   What?

So.   This: "Tisias, some time ago, before you came into the picture, we were saying that people get the idea of what is likely through its similarity to the truth. And we just explained that in every case the person who knows the truth knows best how to determine similarities. So, if you have something new to say about the art of speaking, we shall listen. But if you don't, we shall remain convinced by the explanations we gave just before: No one will ever possess the art of speaking, to the extent that any human being can, unless he acquires the ability to enumerate the sorts of characters to be found in any audience, to divide everything according to its kinds, and to grasp each single thing firmly by means of one form. And no one can acquire these abilities without great effort—a laborious effort a sensible man will make not in order to speak and act among human beings, but so as to be able to speak and act in a way that pleases the gods as much as possible. Wiser people than ourselves, Tisias, say that a reasonable man must put his mind to being pleasant not to his fellow slaves (though this may happen as a side effect) but to his masters, who are wholly good.[44] So, if the way round is long, don't be astonished: we must make this detour for the sake of things that are very important, not for what you have in mind. Still, as our argument asserts, if that is what you want, you'll get it best as a result of pursuing our own goal."

Ph.   What you've said is wonderful, Socrates—if only it could be done!

So.   Yet surely whatever one must go through on the way to an honorable goal is itself honorable.

Ph.   Certainly.

So.   Well, then, that's enough about artfulness and artlessness in connection with speaking.

Ph.   Quite.

So.   What's left, then, is aptness and ineptness in connection with writing: What feature makes writing good, and what inept? Right?

Ph.   Yes.

So.   Well, do you know how best to please god when you either use words or discuss them in general?

Ph.   Not at all. Do you?

So.   I can tell you what I've heard the ancients said, though they alone know the truth. However, if we could discover that ourselves, would we still care about the speculations of other people?[45]

Ph.   That's a silly question. Still, tell me what you say you've heard.

So.   Well, this is what I've heard. Among the ancient gods of Naucratis[46] in Egypt there was one to whom the bird called the ibis is sacred. The name of that divinity was Theuth,[47] and it was he who first discovered number and calculation, geometry and astronomy, as well as the games of draughts and dice, and, above all else, writing.

Now the king of all Egypt at that time was Thamus,[48] who lived in the great city in the upper region that the Greeks call Egyptian Thebes; Thamus they call Ammon.[49] Theuth came to exhibit his arts to him and urged him to disseminate them to all the Egyptians. Thamus asked him about the usefulness of each art, and while Theuth was explaining it, Thamus praised him for whatever he thought was right in his explanations and criticized him for whatever he thought was wrong.

The story goes that Thamus said much to Theuth, both for and against each art, which it would take too long to repeat. But when they came to writing, Theuth said: "O King, here is something that, once learned, will make the Egyptians wiser and will improve their memory; I have discovered a potion for memory and for wisdom."[50] Thamus, however, replied: "O most expert Theuth, one man can give birth to the elements of an art, but only another can judge how they can benefit or harm those who will use them. And now, since you are the father of writing, your affection for it has made you describe its effects as the opposite of what they really are. In fact, it will introduce forgetfulness into the soul of those who learn it: they will not practice using their memory because they will put their trust in writing, which is external and depends on signs that belong to others, instead of trying to remember from the inside, completely on their own. You have not discovered a potion for remembering, but for reminding; you provide your students with the appearance of wisdom, not with its reality. Your invention will enable them to hear many things without being properly taught, and they will imagine that they have come to know much while for the most part they will know nothing. And they will be difficult to get along with, since they will merely appear to be wise instead of really being so."

Ph.   Socrates, you're very good at making up stories from Egypt or wherever else you want!

So.   But, my friend, the priests of the temple of Zeus at Dodona say that the first prophecies were the words of an oak.[51] Everyone who lived at that time, not being as wise as you young ones are today, found it rewarding enough in their simplicity to listen to an oak or even a stone, so long as it was telling the truth, while it seems to make a difference to you, Phaedrus, who is speaking and where he comes from. Why, though, don't you just consider whether what he says is right or wrong?

Ph.   I deserved that, Socrates. And I agree that the Theban king was correct about writing.

So.   Well, then, those who think they can leave written instructions for an art, as well as those who accept them, thinking that writing can yield results that are clear or certain, must be quite naive and truly ignorant of Ammon's prophetic judgment: otherwise, how could they possibly think that words that have been written down can do more than remind those who already know what the writing is about?

Ph.   Quite right.

So.   You know, Phaedrus, writing shares a strange feature with painting. The offsprings of painting stand there as if they are alive, but if anyone asks them anything, they remain most solemnly silent. The same is true of written words. You'd think they were speaking as if they had some understanding, but if you question anything that has been said because you want to learn more, it continues to signify just that very same thing forever. When it has once been written down, every discourse roams about everywhere, reaching indiscriminately those with understanding no less than those who have no business with it, and it doesn't know to whom it should speak and to whom it should not. And when it is faulted and attacked unfairly, it always needs its father's support; alone, it can neither defend itself nor come to its own support.[52]

Ph.   You are absolutely right about that, too.

So.   Now tell me, can we discern another kind of discourse, a legitimate brother of this one? Can we say how it comes about, and how it is by nature better and more capable?

Ph.   Which one is that? How do you think it comes about?

So.   It is a discourse that is written down, with knowledge, in the soul of the listener; it can defend itself, and it knows for whom it should speak and for whom it should remain silent.

Ph.   You mean the living, breathing discourse of the man who knows, of which the written one can be fairly called an image.

So.   Absolutely right. And tell me this. Would a sensible farmer, who cared about his seeds and wanted them to yield fruit, plant them in all seriousness in the gardens of Adonis in the middle of the summer and enjoy watching them bear fruit within seven days? Or would he do this as an amusement and in honor of the holiday, if he did it at all?[53] Wouldn't he use his knowledge of farming to plant the seeds he cared for when it was appropriate and be content if they bore fruit seven months later?

Ph.   That's how he would handle those he was serious about, Socrates, quite differently from the others, as you say.

So.   Now what about the man who knows what is just, noble, and good? Shall we say that he is less sensible with his seeds than the farmer is with his?

Ph.   Certainly not.

So.   Therefore, he won't be serious about writing them in ink, sowing then, through a pen, with words that are as incapable of speaking in their own defense as they are of teaching the truth adequately.

Ph.   That wouldn't be likely.

So.   Certainly not. When he writes, it's likely he will sow gardens of letters for the sake of amusing himself, storing up reminders for himself "when he reaches forgetful old age"[54] and for everyone who wants to follow in his footsteps, and will enjoy seeing them sweetly blooming. And when others turn to different amusements, watering themselves with drinking parties and everything else that goes along with them, he will rather spend his time amusing himself with the things I have just described.

Ph.   Socrates, you are contrasting a vulgar amusement with the very noblest—with the amusement of a man who can while away his time telling stories of justice and the other matters you mentioned.[55]

So.   That's just how it is, Phaedrus. But it is much nobler to be serious about these matters, and use the art of dialectic. The dialectician chooses a proper soul and plants and sows within it discourse accompanied by knowledge—discourse capable of helping itself as well as the man who planted it, which is not barren but produces a seed from which more discourse grows in the character of others. Such discourse makes the seed forever immortal and renders the man who has it as happy as any human being can be.

Ph.   What you describe is really much nobler still.

So.   And now that we have agreed about this, Phaedrus, we are finally able to decide the issue.

Ph.   What issue is that?

So.   The issue which brought us to this point in the first place: We wanted to examine the attack made on Lysias on account of his writing speeches, and to ask which speeches are written artfully and which not. Now, I think that we have answered that question clearly enough.

Ph.   So it seemed; but remind me again how we did it.

So.   First, you must know the truth concerning everything you are speaking or writing about; you must learn how to define each thing in itself; and, having defined it, you must know how to divide it into kinds until you reach something indivisible. Second, you must understand the nature of the soul, along the same lines; you must determine which kind of speech is appropriate to each kind of soul, prepare and arrange your speech accordingly, and offer a complex and elaborate speech to a complex soul and a simple speech to a simple one. Then, and only then, will you be able to use speech artfully, to the extent that its nature allows it to be used that way, either in order to teach or in order to persuade. This is the whole point of the argument we have been making.

Ph.   Absolutely. That is exactly how it seemed to us.

Notes

1. "Is not lightly to be cast aside": *Iliad* 2.361.

2. "Miserable donkey": literally, "the shadow of a donkey," meaning a matter of no importance. An ancient commentator on Aristophanes' *Wasps*, 191, explains the origin of the story. A man rented a donkey to transport some things from Megara to Athens. As it was July, and noon, and the heat was terrible, the man stopped the donkey and sat in its shadow to cool off. The owner of the donkey, who was also there, claimed that the animal had been leased only for transporting baggage and not for providing shade. The two men had a terrible fight and ended up in court over it.

3. "Not an art but an artless practice": *atethnos tribē*. For a similar criticism of rhetoric as artless, see *Gorgias* 462b–c.

4. "As the Spartan said": Spartans were proverbially laconic, so this could mean simply, "to put it bluntly"; but the word used for "genuine" (*etumos*) is unusual in Plato and may come from the Dorian dialect of the Spartans.

5. "Beautiful offspring": Phaedrus' offspring are speeches or philosophical discussions. Cf. 242a–b and *Symposium* 209b–e.

6. Very similar to the definition of rhetoric Plato has Gorgias give at *Gorgias* 452e; except that Gorgias (1) does not mention private occasions, and (2) speaks simply of persuasion instead of "directing the soul" (*psychagōgia*). Cf. also Socrates' broad account of rhetoric as persuasion at *Gorgias* 453d–454a.

   Psychagōgia, literally "soul-leading," means something like "bewitchment." It evokes images of conjuring up souls from the underworld (see the play on words in Aristophanes, *Birds*, 1555—"unwashed

Socrates calls up [*psychagōgei*] souls from. the lake"). In the *Laws* the verb form of *psychagōgia* is used for the claims of those sophists who should be condemned to life imprisonment, their bodies to be cast across the borders of the state unburied (909h). Isocrates, however, uses it for the power of poetry that is denied to orators (*Evagoras* 10). In the *Timaeus* it is used for the irrational effect on the mind of images and phantasms (71a, cf. Xenophon, *Memorabilia* 3.10.6, and *Minos* 321a with Aristotle *Poetics* 1450a33–34).

7. Public speaking was at the center of all Greek political life (see Homer, *Iliad* 2.118–277), but it was especially prominent in Athens. Athenians prided themselves on their democratic Assembly, which could be influenced by any citizen who could speak well, regardless of his social rank. Effective speakers who did not hold office were known as demagogues. Athenian courts consisted of large juries of ordinary people—too many to bribe, but also too many to persuade without expert techniques of speaking. For an accused person, the ability to speak could make the difference between life and death, a point which paid teachers of rhetoric used to their advantage (*Gorgias* 485e–486b).

8. Nestor and Odysseus are Homeric heroes known for their speaking ability (*Iliad* 1.249, 3.223). Palarmedes, who does not figure in Homer, was proverbial for his cunning. He tricked Odysseus into joining the Greek expedition against Troy. According to a tradition different from that on which Plato relies below (274d–275b), Palarnedes was the inventor of the alphabet.

9. Gorgias of Leontini was the most famous teacher of rhetoric who visited Athens. Two model speeches have survived, one in praise of Helen, the other in defense of Palamedes (DK 11 and 11a). About Thrasymachus of Chalcedon (cf. 267c) we know little beyond what we can infer from his appearance in Book 1 of the *Republic*; a few paragraphs of his rhetoric survive (DK 1) and we may have a complete speech as well. The case can be made that a speech now attributed by most scholars to Critias should be assigned to Thrasymachus. From Theodorus of Byzantium (not to be confused with the mathematician who appears in the *Theaetetus*) we have no fragments (but see 266e and Aristotle *Rhetoric* 3.13.5).

10. The Eleatic Palaniedes is Zeno of Elea, the author of the famous paradoxes about motion (see *Parmenides* 127d–128a).

11. "The two speeches": Socrates' two speeches, since Socrates does not wish to imply that Lysias knows the truth about his subject, and since the messengers mentioned in the next sentence cannot have had an influence on Lysias in any case.

12. "Messengers of the Muses": *prophētai*, "interpreters." The messengers are the cicadas (259c).

13. In quoting the speech from 231e, here and at 263e Phaedrus changes the word order slightly, from *genomenōn toutōn to toutōn genomenōn*, from "if this could be *worked out*" to "if *this* could be worked out."

14. "End": *teieutē* (see 253c). "Dear heart": literally "dear head," an epic formula (*Iliad* 8.281).

15. "For some compelling reason?" The Greek is *anankē* (necessity). Socrates' first speech made conspicuously pedantic use of *anankē* at each stage in the argument, deriving conclusions by logical necessity from his definition of love.

16. The historical Midas was king of Phrygia in the eighth century BC.

17. Here Socrates treats his two speeches as one (see note 11).

18. On collecting many things into one kind, see 249c. Here, by introducing the idea of instruction, Socrates enlarges the context of rhetoric to include teaching (see Rowe's note).

19. The point is that each body has two hands, two feet, etc. The members of each pair are called the same (e.g., "hands") and are differentiated according to whether they are on the right or the left side.

20. "By nature capable of encompassing many": This is the version in the manuscripts, which read *pephukos*. Many editors, unable to make sense of the manuscript reading, wrongly prefer *pephukota*, which would give either of two meanings: (1) It may modify both "one" and "many"—"a natural unity and a natural plurality" (most versions; Hackforth cites *Philebus* 17a and 18 in support); (2) it may modify the agent—"anyone else who has the natural capacity to look to one and many."

21. "Straight behind, in his track, as if he were a god": Plato has adapted this line from Homer, *Odyssey* 2.406.

22. See note 9.

23. Evenus of Paros was active as a sophist toward the end of the fifth century BC. He is mentioned elsewhere in Plato (*Apology* 20b, *Phaedo* 60c–61c), but only a few tiny fragments of his work survive.

24. Tisias of Syracuse, with Corax, is credited with the founding of the Sicilian school of rhetoric, represented by Gorgias and Polus. For Gorgias, see note 9. Unlike sophists such as Hippias, Protagoras, and Prodicus, teachers of this school confined themselves to the art of speaking. For Corax's teaching on "what is likely" (*eikos*), see Aristotle *Rhetoric* 2.24.11.

25. Prodicus of Ceos, who lived from about 470 till after 400 BC, is frequently mentioned by Plato in connection with his ability to make fine verbal distinctions (*Protagoras* 339e–341d, *Meno* 75e, *Euthydemus* 277e*; cf. Aristotle, *Topics* 122b22). A parody of his style is to be found at *Protagoras* 337a–c, and a paraphrase of his speech on "The choice of Heracles" is in Xenophon, *Memorabilia* 2.1.21–33.

26. Hippias of Elis was born in the mid fifth century and traveled widely teaching a variety of subjects, including mathematics, astronomy, harmony, mnemonics, ethics, and history as well as public speaking. There is a parody of his style at *Protagoras* 337d–338b.

27. Polus was a pupil of Gorgias; Plato represents him in the *Gorgias*, esp. at 448c and 471a–c. He was said to have composed an *Art of Rhetoric* (*Gorgias*, 462b). "Gallery of terms": *mouseia logōn*. Hackforth interprets this as the title of another of his works (*The Muses' Treasury of Phrases*). This interpretation is rather unlikely: As Rowe remarks in his note on this passage, it destroys the syntax and gives an anachronistic meaning to *mouseiōn*.

28. Licymnius of Chios was a dithyrambic poet and teacher of rhetoric. See Aristotle, *Rhetoric* 3.13.5, 3.2.13.

29. Protagoras of Abdera, whose life spanned most of the fifth century BC, was the most famous of the early sophists. Only a handful of short fragments of his work survive, but we have a vivid portrayal of him in Plato's *Protagoras* and an intriguing reconstruction of his epistemology in the *Theaetetus*. With

his interest in Correct Diction (*orthoepeia*) compare *Cratylus* 391c (with 400d–401a) and *Protagoras* 338e–339d.

30. Literally, "the might of the Chalcedonian": a Homeric figure referring to Thrasymachus, who came from Chalcedon. See note 9.

31. "'The honey-tongued Adrastus' (or perhaps Pericles)": Socrates is pairing the Athenian statesman Pericles with the mythical Adrastus, just as he paired teachers of rhetoric with Homeric heroes at 261c.

   Pericles, who dominated Athens from the 450s until his death in 429 BC, was famous as the most successful orator-politician of his time. For an example of his oratory, see the funeral speech reconstructed by Thucydides at 2.35–46 with the historian's verdict at 2.65. Socrates takes a more critical view at *Gorgias* 503c and 515c–516d (but see *Meno* 94b).

   The quotation is from the early Spartan poet Tyrtaeus, fragment 9.8. Adrastus is a legendary warrior hero of Argos, one of the main characters in Euripides' *Suppliants*.

32. "Endless talk and ethereal speculation." These words (*adoleschia kai meteorologia*) represent the popular view of philosophy and the new learning (Aristophanes *Clouds* 1480 ff.). Since Plato took a dim view of Pericles' oratory (*Gorgias* 515), this paragraph is probably ironic. For Socrates' attitude toward Anaxagoras, see *Apology* 26d–e. For similar criticism of philosophy, see *Republic* 488e–489e and *Theaetetus* 175b ff.

33. "Mind and *mindlessness*": reading *anoias* with the manuscripts.

34. Hippocrates, who was contemporary with Socrates, was the famous doctor whose name is given to the Hippocratic Oath. None of the written works that have come down to us under his name express the view attributed to him in what follows. All doctors were said to be descendants of Asclepius, hero and god of healing.

35. In contrast to an actual speech given in an assembly or court of law, a model speech, or *epideixis*, was presented to display an orator's skill and to serve as an example for students. Gorgias has just given such a speech at *Gorgias* 447b–c. Lysias' speech above is also, of course, such a display.

36. See 266c ff.

37. "The right occasions": The concept of *kairos* or the right occasion to say this or that was at the center of ancient rhetorical theory. According to Dionysius of Halicarnassus, a critic of the first century BC, *kairos* was "the best measure of what gives pleasure or the opposite" in a speech. He goes on to say that Gorgias was the first to write about it, but that no expert general account could be given (*On Literary Composition*, 12).

38. See 259e ff.

39. Most of the surviving evidence of early oratory shows that speakers appealed to what is likely or plausible (*eikos*) only when evidence such as eyewitness testimony was not available. The defense of Antiphon, however, appealed to *eikos* when the evidence was fairly clear against him. Although highly praised by Thucydides, the defense was unsuccessful (Antiphon 1 in Gagarin & Woodruff; Thucydides 8.68).

40. "No doubt you've *churned through* Tisias' book quite carefully": For the colloquial verb in this sense, *patein* (literally, "thresh"), see Aristophanes, *Birds*, 471, and W. W. Merry's comment *ad loc*. For Tisias, see above 267a with note 24.

41. "Neither one should tell the truth": Antiphon uses a similar example as the hypothesis for his First Tetralogy, a set of four model speeches; in his example the man who is robbed is also killed, so there are no credible witnesses, and the only possible appeal is to *eikos*. Aristotle treats the use of likelihood in such a case in his *Rhetoric* 2.24.11; cf. 1.12.7.

42. Socrates may be referring to Corax, whose name happens also to be the Greek word for "crow."

43. "Seems": *eoiken*. Literally, "is likely to."

44. This may refer to Antisthenes, who is supposed to have said, "If you want to live with the gods, learn philosophy; if among men, rhetoric" (Fragment 125 Mullack). Antisthenes was a student of Socrates who held that happiness comes from virtue, which in turn comes from understanding.

45. The sense of the Greek is obscure. Socrates may be saying that only the ancients know whether the story he is about to relate is true. From here on, however, he focuses on the issue of truth in general and claims that if we could discover by ourselves what is true about aptness in writing, we would not need to rely on stories told by other people. The argument that follows the story of Theuth, which he tells partly under pressure from Phaedrus, is his effort to establish the truth independently.

46. Naucratis was a Greek trading colony in Egypt. The story that follows is probably an invention of Plato's (see 275b3) in which he reworks elements from Egyptian and Greek mythology. It is appropriately set in Egypt, since the Egyptians were known in Greece for their ancient records and their efforts to retain the memory of the past (Herodotus 2.77). The story picks up the theme of the conflict between Zeus and Prometheus; see Rowe's note on the passage.

47. Theuth (or Thoth) is the Egyptian god of writing, measuring, and calculation, who is represented on early monuments by an ibis. The Greeks identified Thoth with Hermes, perhaps because of his role in weighing the soul. Thoth figures in a related story about the alphabet at *Philebus* 18b.

48. Thamus is a Greek name for the god Ammon. As king of the Egyptian gods, Ammon was identified by Egyptians with the sun god Ra and by the Greeks with Zeus.

49. "Thamus they call Ammon": accepting Postgate's emendation of *Thamus* for *theon*. This implies that in Socrates' account Thamus is a god as well as the king.

50. "A *potion* for memory and for wisdom": *Pharmakon* ("potion") can refer to a medicinal drug, a poison, or a magical potion. Cf. its uses at 230d6 and 275a5.

51. "The first prophecies were the words of an oak": The oracle of Zeus was at Dodona in northwestern Greece. Homer reports the tradition that the message came from an oak (*Odyssey* 327–28). Herodotus tells a slightly different tale (2.55).

52. Cf. *Protagoras* 347c–348a, where Socrates argues that poetry cannot explain itself in the absence of its author, though he does not explicitly connect this with writing. For a related complaint against

writing see the *Seventh Letter* 344c. See also the essay "On Those Who Write Speeches" by Alcidamas, a pupil of Gorgias who was roughly contemporary with Plato.

53. Gardens of Adonis were pots or window boxes used for forcing plants during the festival of Adonis. It does seem difficult to believe, however, that seeds actually produced fruit within a week.

54. The diction here is poetic, but the source of this phrase, if one exists, is unknown.

55. Possibly a reference to the *Republic*, in which Socrates spends a great deal of time spinning a tale about justice.

3 New System of the Nature of the Communication of Substances

Gottfried Wilhelm Leibniz

1. On the system of occasional causes (March 1689–March 1690?)

The system of occasional causes must be partly accepted and partly rejected. Each substance is the true and real cause of its own immanent actions, and has the power of acting, and although it is sustained by the divine concourse nevertheless it cannot happen that it is merely passive, and this is true both in the case of corporeal substances and incorporeal ones. But on the other hand, each substance (excepting God alone) is nothing except the occasional cause of its transeunt actions towards another substance. Therefore the true reason of the union between soul and body, and the reason why one body adjusts itself to the state of another body, is nothing other than that the different substances of the same system of the world are created from the beginning in such a way that from the laws of their own nature they harmonize with one another.

2. New system of the nature of the communication of substances, as well as the union that exists between the soul and the body (27 June 1695)

It has been several years since I conceived this system and communicated some of it to learned men, and in particular one of the greatest theologians and philosophers of our time, who, having learned some of my opinions through a person of the highest rank, found them to be great paradoxes. But upon receiving my clarifications he retracted his objections in the most generous and edifying manner possible, and having approved some of my propositions he withdrew his censure of the others with which he did yet not agree. Since then I continued my meditations as and when I could, in order to give to the public only opinions that had been well examined, and I also endeavoured to answer the objections made against my essays on dynamics which have some connection with this. Finally, as some important people have desired to see my opinions further clarified, I ventured these opinions, although they are by no means popular or suitable to the taste of all sorts of mind. I am apt to do this principally to benefit from the judgement of those who are enlightened in these matters, because it would be too troublesome to seek out and ask separately all those who would be disposed to give me instruction, which I will always be delighted to receive, provided that the love of truth is evident in it rather than the passion for preconceived opinions.

Although I am one of those people who have worked much on mathematics, I have not ceased meditating on philosophy since my youth, because it seemed to me that there was a way of establishing something solid in it by clear demonstrations. I had gone far into the country of the Scholastics when mathematics and modern authors brought me out again while I was still quite young. Their beautiful ways of explaining nature mechanically charmed me, and I rightly scorned the method of those who only make use of forms or faculties, from which we learn nothing. But afterwards, having tried to go further into the very principles of mechanics, in order to explain the laws of nature that are known from experience, I realized that a consideration of an *extended mass* alone is not sufficient, and that we must also make use of the notion of *force*, which is perfectly intelligible, although it falls within the realm of metaphysics. It also seemed to me that the opinion of those who transform or degrade the beasts into pure machines, although it seems possible, is improbable, and even contrary to the order of things.

At first, when I freed myself from the yoke of Aristotle, I was seduced by the void and atoms, since they better satisfy the imagination. But returning to them after much medita-tion, I saw that it is impossible to find *the principles of a true unity* in matter alone, or in what is only passive, because it is only a collection or mass of parts to infinity. Now a mul-titude can only derive its reality from *true unities* which come from elsewhere and which are entirely different from mathematical points, which are only the extremities of extended things and modifications, and it is certain that *the continuum* could not be composed of such things. Therefore to find these *real unities*, I was compelled to have recourse to a real and animated point, so to speak, or to an atom of substance which must contain some form or activity in order to make a complete being. It was therefore necessary to recall and, as it were, rehabilitate the *substantial forms*, so disparaged today, but in a way that makes them intelligible and which separates the use that should be made of them from their previous misuse. I found, therefore, that their nature consists in force, and from that force follows something analogous to sensation and appetite, and thus it was necessary to conceive them as being rather like the notion we have of *souls*. But just as the soul ought not to be made use of to explain in detail the economy of an animal's body, I likewise judged that we must not use these forms to solve particular problems of nature, although they are necessary to establish its true general principles. Aristotle calls them *first entelechies*, I call them, perhaps more intelligibly, *primitive forces*, which do not contain only the *actuality* or the fulfilment of possibility, but also an original *activity*.

I saw that these forms and souls had to be indivisible, as well as our minds, as in effect I remembered that this was St. Thomas's opinion as regards the souls of beasts. But this truth revived the great difficulties of the origin and duration of souls and forms. For as every *simple substance* which has a true unity can begin or end only by a miracle, it follows that they could only begin by creation and only end by annihilation. Thus I was obliged to recognize that (except for the souls that God still wants to create specially) the constitutive forms of substances must have been created with the world and always subsist. Thus some Scholastics, such as Albert the Great and John Bacon, had glimpsed part of the truth of their origin. And the idea should not seem extraordinary, because we are only giving to forms the duration that Gassendists grant to their atoms.

Nevertheless I judged that we must not indiscriminately mix or confuse with other forms or souls the *mind* or rational soul, which is of a superior order, and has incomparably more perfection than these forms which are sunk in matter, which in my view can be found everywhere. In comparison with those, minds or rational souls are like little Gods made in the image of God, having within them some ray of the divine light. This is why God governs minds as a Prince governs his subjects, and even as a father cares for his children; whereas he arranges other substances as an engineer handles his machines. Thus minds have special laws, which place them above the revolutions of matter by the very order that God placed in them, and it can be said that everything else is made only for them, these very revolutions being adapted to the happiness of the good and the punishment of the wicked.

However, to return to ordinary forms, or *brute souls*, this duration that we must attribute to them, instead of the one that has been attributed to atoms, might give rise to the doubt whether they do not pass from body to body, which would be *metempsychosis*, and is more or less what some philosophers have believed with regard to the transmission of motion or of species. But this fancy is very far removed from the nature of things. There is no such passage of souls, and it is here that the transformations of Mr Swammerdam, Mr Malpighi and Mr Leeuwenhoek, who are some of the best observers of our times, came to my assistance, and have allowed me to accept more easily that the animal and every other organized substance does not begin when we believe it does, and that its apparent generation is only a development, and a kind of augmentation. I have also noticed that the author of the *Search after Truth*, Mr Régis, Mr Hartsoeker and other clever men, have not been far removed from this opinion.

But there still remained the most important question of what becomes of these souls or forms at the death of the animal, or at the destruction of the individual organized substance. And this question is all the more awkward inasmuch as it hardly seems reasonable that souls remain uselessly in a chaos of confused matter. Ultimately this made me think that there was only one reasonable view to take, and that is the one of the conservation not only of the soul, but also of the animal itself, and of its organic machine; although the destruction of its cruder parts has reduced it to such a small size that it escapes our senses in the same way that it did before birth. Thus there is no one who can tell the true time of death, which for a long time can pass for a simple suspension of observable actions. And death is ultimately nothing other than that in simple animals: witness the *resuscitations* of flies drowned and buried under pulverized chalk, and several similar examples which sufficiently show that there could be many other resuscitations, and in cases much further gone, if men were in a position to repair the machine. And apparently it was something approaching this idea of which the great Democritus spoke, complete atomist though he was, although Pliny made fun of it. It is therefore natural that the animal, having always been living and organized (as some insightful people are beginning to recognize), will also always remain so. And because there is thus no first birth or entirely new generation of the animal, it follows that there will never be any final extinction of it either, nor complete death taken in the metaphysical sense; and that consequently, rather than the transmigration of souls, there is only a transformation of the same animal, according to how its organs are differently folded, and more or less developed.

Rational souls, however, follow much higher laws, and are exempt from everything which could make them lose the position of citizens of the society of minds, God having provided for them so well that all the changes of matter could not make them lose the moral qualities of their personality. And it can be said that everything tends not only to the perfection of the universe in general, but also of these created beings in particular, which are destined for such a degree of happiness that the universe is concerned in it in virtue of the divine goodness which is communicated to each one insofar as the sovereign wisdom can permit.

As for the ordinary course of animals and other corporeal substances, whose complete extinction has until now been widely believed and whose changes depend on mechanical rules rather than moral laws, I have noted with pleasure that the ancient author of the book on *Diet*, which is attributed to Hippocrates, had caught a glimpse of the truth when he said in express terms that animals are not born and do not die, and that the things which are thought to begin and perish only appear and disappear. This was also the opinion of Parmenides, and also that of Melissus according to Aristotle. For these ancients were sounder than we think.

I am as well disposed as anyone to do justice to the moderns; nevertheless I find that they have carried reform too far, amongst other things by confusing natural things with artificial, through not having sufficiently grand ideas of the majesty of nature. They hold that the difference between nature's machine and ours is only that of great to small. This recently brought a very clever man to say that, by considering nature closely, we find it less admirable than we had thought, it being only like the workshop of a craftsman. I believe that this does not give a sufficiently just or worthy idea of nature, and there is only our system which ultimately shows the true and immense distance between the least productions and mechanisms of divine wisdom and the greatest masterpieces of art brought forth from a limited mind; this difference is not merely one of degree, but one of kind. We must therefore recognize that the machines of nature have a truly infinite number of organs, and are so well provided for and proofed against all accidents that it is not possible to destroy them. A natural machine still remains a machine in the least parts, and what is more, it always remains the same machine that it was, only being transformed by the different foldings that it receives, and it is sometimes extended, sometimes contracted and as it were concentrated, when we believe that it has disappeared.

Moreover, by means of the soul or form there is a true unity which answers to what is called "I" in us, which could not occur in the machines of art or in the simple mass of matters however organized it might be. This mass can only be regarded as like an army or a flock, or like a pond full of fish, or like a watch composed of springs and wheels. However if there were no true substantial unities, there would be nothing substantial or real in the collection. It was this that forced Mr Cordemoy to abandon Descartes by embracing the doctrine of Democritus's atoms, in order to find a true unity. But *atoms of matter* are contrary to reason; aside from the fact that they are also composed of parts, since the invincible attachment of one part to another (even if this could be conceived or reasonably supposed) would not destroy their diversity. There are only *atoms of substance*, that is to say, real unities absolutely devoid of parts, which are the sources of actions, and the absolute first principles of the composition of things, and as it were the ultimate elements of analysis of substantial things. They can be called *metaphysical points*: they have *something vital* in them, and a kind of *perception*, and *mathematical points* are their *points of view* for expressing the universe. But when corporeal substances are contracted, all their organs together make only one *physical* point as far as we are concerned. Thus physical points are only indivisible in appearance. Mathematical points are exact, but they are only modalities; it is only metaphysical points or substance (constituted by forms or souls) which are exact and real, and without them there would be nothing real, because without true unities there would be no multitude.

After establishing these things, I thought I had reached port, but when I set myself to meditate on the union of the soul with the body I was, as it were, thrown back onto the open sea. For I could not find any means of explaining how the body makes something pass into the soul, or vice versa, nor how one substance can communicate with another created substance. Mr Descartes left the game at that point, insofar as one can tell from his writings. But his disciples, seeing that the common opinion is inconceivable, thought that we sense the qualities of bodies because God arouses thoughts in the soul on the occasion of the motions of matter, and when our soul in its turn wants to move the body, they thought that it is God who moves the body for it. And as the communication of motions appeared to them to be inconceivable, they believed that God gives motion to a body on the occasion of the motion of another body. This is what they call the *system of occasional causes*, which has been very much in fashion because of the fine reflections of the author of the *Search after Truth*.

It must be acknowledged that this has gone a fair way into the difficulty, in explaining what cannot be the case; but their explanation of what really happens does not appear to have removed the difficulty. It is quite true that there is no real influence, in the strict metaphysical sense, of one created substance on another, and that all things, with all their realities, are continually produced by the power of God: but to resolve the problems, it is not enough to make use of the general cause and to bring in what is called *Deus ex machina*. For when this is done without there being any other explanation drawn from the order of secondary causes, it is in fact to have recourse to a miracle. In philosophy we must endeavour to explain by showing the way in which things are carried out by the divine wisdom, in accordance with the notion of the subject in question.

Being therefore obliged to grant that it is not possible that the soul or some other true substance could receive something from outside, except through divine omnipotence, I was led insensibly to a thought that surprised me, but which appears inevitable, and which in effect has some very great advantages and considerable beauty. Namely, that we should therefore say that God first created the soul, or any other real unity of such sort, so that everything must arise in it from its own nature, by a perfect *spontaneity* with regard to itself, and yet with a perfect *conformity* to things outside it. And thus our internal sensations (that is to say, those which are in the soul itself, and not in the brain or in the subtle parts of the body) being only phenomena following external beings, or rather true appearances and as it were well-ordered dreams, it must be the case that these internal perceptions in the soul itself come about through its own original constitution, that is to say through the representative nature (capable of expressing beings outside it in relation to its organs) which it was given at its creation and which constitutes its individual character. And this is what makes each of these substances represent accurately the whole universe in its way and according to a certain point of view, and makes the perceptions and expressions of external things occur in the soul at the right moment in virtue of its own laws, just as in a world apart, and just as if nothing existed beyond God and that soul (to make use of a manner of speaking used by a certain person who had an exalted mind, and whose holiness is famous), there will be a perfect agreement between all these substances, which gives rise to the same effect that would be noticed if they communicated with each other through a transmission of species or qualities, as ordinary philosophers believe. Moreover, the organized mass in which lies the soul's point of view, is expressed more immediately by it, and finds itself reciprocally ready to act of itself, following the laws of the corporeal machine, in the moment that the soul wills it, without one disturbing the laws of the other, the spirits and the blood having exactly at that time the motions that are needed to correspond to the passions and the perceptions of the soul. It is this mutual relationship, arranged in advance in each substance of the universe, which produces what we call their communication, and which alone constitutes *the union of the soul and the body*. And from that it can be understood how the soul has its seat in the body by an immediate presence, which could not be greater because the soul is in the body in the same way as unity is in the result of unities which is a multitude.

This hypothesis is perfectly possible. For why could God not initially give to a substance a nature or internal force which could produce in it in an orderly way (as in a *spiritual or formal automaton, but free* in the case of one which has received reason) everything that will happen to it, that is to say, all the appearances or expressions that it will have, and all that without the assistance of any created thing? It is all the more probable since the nature of substance necessarily requires and essentially contains a progress or a change, without which it would not have any force to act. And this nature of the soul is representative of the universe in a very exact way (although more or less distinct), the series of representations that the soul produces in itself will naturally correspond to the series of changes in the universe itself; just as, on the other hand, the body has been accommodated to the soul for the confluences in which it is conceived as acting outside itself. What is all the more reasonable is that bodies are made only for minds capable of entering into society with God, and of celebrating his glory. Thus as soon as we see the possibility of this *hypothesis of agreements*, we also see that it is the most reasonable, and that it gives a wonderful idea of the harmony of the universe and of the perfection of God's works.

It also has this great advantage, in that instead of saying that we are free only in appearance and in a way sufficient for practice, as some clever people have believed, we should rather say that we are determined only in appearance, and that in strict metaphysical terms we are perfectly independent of the influence of all other created things. This again puts the immortality of the soul in a wonderful light, as well as the forever uniform conservation of our individuality, perfectly well ordered by its own nature, sheltered from all external accidents, whatever the appearances to the contrary. Never has a system made our elevated position so evident. Every mind is like a world apart, sufficient unto itself, independent of every other created thing. It contains the infinite, expresses the universe; it is as durable, as subsistent, as the universe of created things itself. We should therefore hold that every mind should play its part in the manner most appropriate to contribute to the perfection of the society of all minds, which constitutes their moral union in the City of God. We also find here a new proof of the existence of God, which is extraordinarily clear. For this perfect agreement of so many substances, which have no communication with one another at all, could come only from a common cause.

Besides all these advantages, which make this hypothesis recommendable, it can be said that it is something more than a hypothesis, because it scarcely appears possible to explain things in any other intelligible way, and that several great difficulties which have exercised men's minds until now seem to disappear of themselves when it is properly understood. It also preserves our ordinary manners of speaking. For it can be said that the substance whose disposition explains change in an intelligible way, so that it can be thought that it is to this substance that others have been accommodated in this respect from the beginning, in accordance with the order of God's decrees, is the one that must be conceived in that respect as *acting* upon the others. Also the action of one substance on another is not an emission or transplantation of an entity as is commonly thought, and it could be reasonably taken only in the way that I have just said. It is true that we can very well conceive matter as emitting and receiving parts, by which we are right to explain mechanically all the phenomena of physics; but as a material mass is not a substance, it is evident that action in regard to substance itself could only be that which I have just said.

These considerations, however metaphysical they may seem, are still wonderfully useful in physics in order to establish the laws of motion, as our dynamics will be able to show. For it can be said that in the collision of bodies each suffers only from its own elasticity,

caused by the motion which is already in it. And as for absolute motion, nothing can determine it mathematically, since everything ends in relations. This ensures that there is always
a perfect equivalence of hypotheses, as in astronomy, so that whatever number of bodies
we take, it is arbitrary to assign rest or even such and such a degree of speed to whichever
one we choose without the phenomena of straight, circular or composite motion being able
to refute it. However it is reasonable to attribute true motion to bodies in accordance with
the supposition which explains phenomena in the most intelligible way, this denomination
being in accordance with the notion of action that we have just established.

4   Sense Certainty: Or the "This" and "Meaning"

Georg Wilhelm Friedrich Hegel

I.   Sense-Certainty: Or the "This" and "Meaning" [*Meinen*]

90. The knowledge or knowing which is at the start or is immediately our object cannot be anything else but immediate knowledge itself, a knowledge of the immediate or of what simply *is*. Our approach to the object must also be *immediate* or *receptive*; we must alter nothing in the object as it presents itself. In *ap*prehending it, we must refrain from trying to *com*prehend it.

91. Because of its concrete content, sense-certainty immediately appears as the *richest* kind of knowledge, indeed a knowledge of infinite wealth for which no bounds can be found, either when we *reach out* into space and time in which it is dispersed, or when we take a bit of this wealth, and by division *enter into* it. Moreover, sense-certainty appears to be the *truest* knowledge; for it has not as yet omitted anything from the object, but has the object before it in its perfect entirety. But, in the event, this very *certainty* proves itself to be the most abstract and poorest *truth*. All that it says about what it knows is just that it *is*; and its truth contains nothing but the sheer *being* of the thing [*Sache*]. Consciousness, for its part, is in this certainty only as a pure "I;" or I am in it only as a pure "This," and the object similarly only as a pure "This." I, *this* particular I, am certain of *this* particular thing, not because I, *qua* consciousness, in knowing it have developed myself or thought about it in various ways; and also not because *the thing* of which I am certain, in virtue of a host of distinct qualities, would be in its own self a rich complex of connections, or related in various ways to other things. Neither of these has anything to do with the truth of sense-certainty: here neither I nor the thing has the significance of a complex process of mediation; the "I" does not have the significance of a manifold imagining or thinking; nor does the "thing" signify something that has a host of qualities. On the contrary, the thing *is*, and it *is*, merely because it *is*. It *is*; this is the essential point for sense-knowledge, and this pure *being*, or this simple immediacy, constitutes its *truth*. Similarly, certainty as a *connection* is an *immediate* pure connection: consciousness is "I" nothing more, a pure "This"; the singular consciousness knows a pure "This," or the single item.

92. But when we look carefully at this *pure being* which constitutes the essence of this certainty, and which this certainty pronounces to be its truth, we see that much more is involved. An actual sense-certainty is not merely this pure immediacy, but an *instance* of it. Among the countless differences cropping up here we find in every case that the crucial one is that, in sense-certainty, pure being at once splits up into what we have called the two "Thises," one "This" as "I," and the other "This" as object. When *we* reflect on this difference, we find that neither one nor the other is only *immediately* present in sense-certainty, but each is at the same time *mediated*: I have this certainty *through* something else, viz. the thing; and it, similarly, is in sense-certainty *through* something else, viz. through the "I."

93. It is not just we who make this distinction between essence and instance, between immediacy and mediation; on the contrary, we find it within sense-certainty itself, and it is to be taken up in the form in which it is present there, not as we have just defined it. One of the terms is posited in sense-certainty in the form of a simple, immediate being, or as the essence, the *object;* the other, however, is posited as what is unessential and mediated, something which in sense-certainty is not *in itself* but through [the mediation of] an other, the "I," a *knowing* which knows the object only because the *object* is, while the knowing may either be or not be. But the object *is*: it is what is true, or it is the essence. It is, regardless of whether it is known or not; and it remains, even if it is not known, whereas there is no knowledge if the object is not there.

94. The question must therefore be considered whether in sense-certainty itself the object is in fact the kind of essence that sense-certainty proclaims it to be; whether this notion of it as the essence corresponds to the way it is present in sense-certainty. To this end, we have not to reflect on it and ponder what it might be in truth, but only to consider the way in which it is present in sense-certainty.

95. It is, then, sense-certainty itself that must be asked : "What is the *This*?" If we take the "This" in the twofold shape of its being, as "Now" and as "Here," the dialectic it has in it will receive a form as intelligible as the "This" itself is. To the question: "What is Now?", let us answer, e.g., "Now is Night." In order to test the truth of this sense-certainty a simple experiment will suffice. We write down this truth; a truth cannot lose anything by being written down, any more than it can lose anything through our preserving it. If *now*, *this noon*, we look again at the written truth we shall have to say that it has become stale.

96. The Now that is Night is *preserved*, i.e., it is treated as what it professes to be, as something that *is*; but it proves itself to be, on the contrary, something that is *not*. The Now does indeed preserve itself, but as something that is *not* Night; equally, it preserves itself in face of the Day that it now is, as something that also is not Day, in other words, as a *negative* in general. This self-preserving Now is, therefore, not immediate but mediated; for it is determined as a permanent and self-preserving Now *through* the fact that something else, viz. Day and Night, is *not*. As so determined, it is still just as simply Now as before, and in this simplicity is indifferent to what happens in it; just as little as Night and Day are its being, just as much also is it Day and Night; it is not in the least affected by this its other-being. A

simple thing of this kind which *is* through negation, which is neither This nor That, a *not-This*, and is with equal indifference This as well as That—such a thing we call a *universal*. So it is in fact the universal that is the true [content] of sense-certainty.

97. It is as a universal too that we *utter* what the sensuous [content] is. What we say is: "This," i.e. the *universal* This; or, "it is," i.e. *Being in general*. Of course, we do not *envisage* the universal This or Being in general, but we *utter* the universal; in other words, we do not strictly say what in this sense-certainty we *mean* to say. But language, as we see, is the more truthful; in it, we ourselves directly refute what we *mean* to say, and since the universal is the true [content] of sense-certainty and language expresses this true [content] alone, it is just not possible for us ever to say, or express in words, a sensuous being that we *mean*.

98. The same will be the case with the other form of the "This," with "Here." "Here" is, e.g., the tree. If I turn round, this truth has vanished and is converted into its opposite: "No tree is here, but a house instead." "Here" itself does not vanish; on the contrary, it abides constant in the vanishing of the house, the tree, etc., and is indifferently house or tree. Again, therefore, the "This" shows itself to be a *mediated simplicity*, or a *universality*.

99. *Pure being* remains, therefore, as the essence of this sense-certainty, since sense-certainty has demonstrated in its own self that the truth of its object is the universal. But this pure being is not an immediacy, but something to which negation and mediation are essential; consequently, it is not what we *mean* by "being," but is "being" defined as an abstraction, or as the pure universal; and our "meaning," for which the true [content] of sense-certainty is *not* the universal, is all that is left over in face of this empty or indifferent Now and Here.

100. When we compare the relation in which knowing and the object first came on the scene, with the relation in which they now stand in this result, we find that it is reversed. The object, which was supposed to be the essential element in sense-certainty, is now the unessential element; for the universal which the object has come to be is no longer what the object was supposed essentially to be for sense-certainty. On the contrary, the certainty is now to be found in the opposite element, viz, in knowing, which previously was the unessential element. Its truth is in the object as *my* object, or in its being *mine* [*Meinen*]; it is, because *I* know it. Sense-certainty, then, though indeed expelled from the object, is not yet thereby overcome, but only driven back into the "I." We have now to see what experience shows us about its reality in the "I."

101. The force of its truth thus lies now in the "I," in the immediacy of my *seeing, hearing*, and so on; the vanishing of the single Now and Here that we mean is prevented by the fact that *I* hold them fast. "Now" is day because I see it; "Here" is a tree for the same reason. But in this relationship sense-certainty experiences the same dialectic acting upon itself as in the previous one. I, *this* "I," see the tree and assert that "Here" is a tree; but another "I" sees the house and maintains that "Here" is not a tree but a house instead. Both truths have the same authentication, viz, the immediacy of seeing, and the certainty and assurance that both have about their knowing; but the one truth vanishes in the other.

102. What does not disappear in all this is the "I" as *universal*, whose seeing is neither a seeing of the tree nor of this house, but is a simple seeing which, though mediated by the negation of this house, etc., is all the same simple and indifferent to whatever happens in it, to the house, the tree, etc. The "I" is merely universal like "Now," "Here," or "This" in general; I do indeed *mean* a single "I," but I can no more say what I *mean* in the case of "I" than I can in the case of "Now" and "Here." When I say "this Here," "this Now," or a "single item," I am saying all Thises, Heres, Nows, all single items. Similarly, when I say "I", this singular "I", I say in general all "Is"; everyone is what I say, everyone is this singular "I." When Science is faced with the demand—as if it were an acid test it could not pass—that it should deduce, construct, find *a priori*, or however it is put, something called "this thing" or "this one man," it is reasonable that the demand should *say* which "this thing," or which "this particular man" is *meant*; but it is impossible to say this.

103. Sense-certainty thus comes to know by experience that its essence is neither in the object nor in the "I," and that its immediacy is neither an immediacy of the one nor of the other; for in both, what I *mean* is rather something unessential, and the object and the "I," are universals in which that "Now" and "Here" and "I" which I *mean* do not have a continuing being, or *are* not. Thus we reach the stage where we have to posit the *whole* of sense-certainty itself as its *essence*, and no longer only one of its moments, as happened in the two cases where first the object confronting the "I", and then the "I,", were supposed to be its reality. Thus it is only sense-certainty as a *whole* which stands firm within itself as *immediacy* and by so doing excludes from itself all the opposition which has hitherto obtained.

104. This pure immediacy, therefore, no longer has any concern with the otherness of the "Here," as a tree which passes over into a "Here" that is not a tree, or with the otherness of the "Now" as day which changes into a "Now" that is night, or with another "I" for which something else is object. Its truth preserves itself as a relation that remains self-identical, and which makes no distinction of what is essential and what is unessential, between the "I" and the object, a relation therefore into which also no distinction whatever can penetrate. I, *this* "I," assert then the "Here" as a tree, and do not turn round so that the Here would become for me *not* a tree; also, I take no notice of the fact that another "I" sees the Here as *not* a tree, or that I myself at another time take the Here as not-tree, the Now as not-day. On the contrary, I am a pure [act of] intuiting; I, for my part, stick to the fact that the Now is day, or that the Here is a tree; also I do not compare Here and Now themselves with one another, but stick firmly to *one* immediate relation: the Now is day.

105. Since, then, this certainty will no longer come forth to *us* when we direct its attention to a Now that is night, or to an "I" to whom it is night, we will approach *it* and let ourselves point to the Now that is asserted. We must let ourselves *point to it*; for the truth of this immediate relation is the truth of *this* "I" which confines itself to one "Now" or one "Here." Were we to examine this truth *afterwards*, or stand *at a distance* from it, it would lose its significance entirely; for that would do away with the immediacy which is essential to it. We must therefore enter the same point of time or space, point them out to ourselves,

i.e., make ourselves into the same singular "I" which is the one who knows with certainty. Let us, then, see how that immediate is constituted that is pointed out to us.

106. The Now is pointed to, *this* Now. "Now"; it has already ceased to be in the act of pointing to it. The Now that *is*, is another Now than the one pointed to, and we see that the Now is just this: to be no more just when it is. The Now, as it is pointed out to us, is Now that *has been*, and this is its truth; it has not the truth of *being*. Yet this much is true, that it has been. But what essentially *has been* [*gewesen ist*] is, in fact, not an essence that *is* [*kein Wesen*]; *it is not,* and it was with *being* that we were concerned.

107. In this pointing-out, then, we see merely a movement which takes the following course: (1) I point out the "Now," and it is asserted to be the truth, I point it out, however, as something that *has been*, or as something that has been superseded; I set aside the first truth. (2) 1 now assert as the second truth that it *has been*, that it is superseded. (3) But what has been, *is not*; I set aside the second truth, its *having been*, its supersession, and thereby negate the negation of the "Now," and thus return to the first assertion, that the "*Now*" *is*. The "Now," and pointing out the "Now," are thus so constituted that neither the one nor the other is something immediate and simple, but a movement which contains various moments. A *This* is posited; but it is rather an *other* that is posited, or the This is superseded: and this *otherness*, or the setting-aside of the first, is itself *in turn set aside*, and so has returned into the first. However, this first, thus reflected into itself, is not exactly the same as it was to begin with, viz. something *immediate*; on the contrary, it is *something that is reflected into itself,* or a *simple* entity which, in its otherness, remains what it is: a Now which is an absolute plurality of Nows. And this is the true, the genuine Now, the Now as a simple day which contains within it many Nows—hours. A Now of this sort, an hour, similarly is many minutes, and this Now is likewise many Nows, and so on. The pointing-out of the Now is thus itself the movement which expresses what the Now is in truth, viz. a result, or a plurality of Nows all taken together; and the pointing-out is the experience of learning that Now is a *universal*.

108. The *Here pointed out*, to which I hold fast, is similarly a *this* Here which, in fact, is *not* this Here, but a Before and Behind, an Above and Below, a Right and Left. The Above is itself similarly this manifold otherness of above, below, etc. The Here, which was supposed to have been pointed out, vanishes in other Heres, but these likewise vanish. What is pointed out, held fast, and abides, is a *negative* This, which *is* negative only when the Heres are taken as they should be, but, in being so taken, they supersede themselves; what abides is a simple complex of many Heres. The Here that is *meant* would be the point; but it *is* not: on the contrary, when it is pointed out as something that *is*, the pointing-out shows itself to be not an immediate knowing [of the point], but a movement from the Here that is *meant* through many Heres into the universal Here which is a simple plurality of Heres, just as the day is a simple plurality of Nows.

109. It is clear that the dialectic of sense-certainty is nothing else but the simple history of its movement or of its experience, and sense-certainty itself is nothing else but just this

history. That is why the natural consciousness, too, is always reaching this result, learning from experience what is true in it; but equally it is always forgetting it and starting the movement all over again. It is therefore astonishing when, in face of this experience, it is asserted as universal experience and put forward, too, as a philosophical proposition, even as the outcome of Scepticism, that the reality or being of external things taken as Thises or sense-objects has absolute truth for consciousness. To make such an assertion is not to know what one is saying, to be unaware that one is saying the opposite of what one wants to say. The truth for consciousness of a This of sense is supposed to be universal experience; but the very opposite is universal experience. Every consciousness itself supersedes such a truth, as, e.g., Here is a tree, or, Now is noon, and proclaims the opposite: Here is *not* a tree, but a house; and similarly, it immediately again supersedes the assertion which set aside the first so far as it is also just such an assertion of a sensuous This. And what consciousness will learn from experience in all sense-certainty is, in truth, only what we have seen viz. the This as a *universal*, the very opposite of what that assertion affirmed to be universal experience.

With this appeal to universal experience we may be permitted to anticipate how the case stands in the practical sphere. In this respect we can tell those who assert the truth and certainty of the reality of sense-objects that they should go back to the most elementary school of wisdom, viz. the ancient Eleusinian Mysteries of Ceres and Bacchus, and that they have still to learn the secret meaning of the eating of bread and the drinking of wine. For he who is initiated into these Mysteries not only comes to doubt the being of sensuous things, but to despair of it; in part he brings about the nothingness of such things himself in his dealings with them, and in part he sees them reduce themselves to nothingness. Even the animals are not shut out from this wisdom but, on the contrary, show themselves to be most profoundly initiated into it; for they do not just stand idly in front of sensuous things as if these possessed intrinsic being, but, despairing of their reality, and completely assured of their nothingness, they fall to without ceremony and eat them up. And all Nature, like the animals, celebrates these open Mysteries which teach the truth about sensuous things.

110. But, just as our previous remarks would suggest, those who put forward such an assertion also themselves say the direct opposite of what they mean: a phenomenon which is perhaps best calculated to induce them to reflect on the nature of sense-certainty. They speak of the existence of *external* objects, which can be more precisely defined as *actual*, absolutely *singular, wholly personal, individual* things, each of them absolutely unlike anything else; this existence, they say, has absolute certainty and truth. They *mean* "this" bit of paper on which I am writing—or rather have written—"this"; but what they mean is not what they say. If they actually wanted to *say* "this" bit of paper which they mean, if they wanted to *say* it, then this is impossible, because the sensuous This that is meant *cannot be reached* by language, which belongs to consciousness, i.e., to that which is inherently universal. In the actual attempt to say it, it would therefore crumble away; those who started

to describe it would not be able to complete the description, but would be compelled to leave it to others, who would themselves finally have to admit to speaking about something which *is not*. They certainly mean, then, *this* bit of paper here which is quite different from the bit mentioned above; but they say "actual *things*," "*external* or *sensuous objects*," "*absolutely singular entities*" [*Wesen*] and so on; i.e., they say of them only what is *universal*. Consequently, what is called the unutterable is nothing else than the untrue, the irrational, what is merely meant [but is not actually expressed].

If nothing more is said of something than that it is "an actual thing," an "external object," its description is only the most abstract of generalities and in fact expresses its sameness with everything rather than its distinctiveness. When I say: "a single thing," I am really saying what it is from a wholly universal point of view, for everything is a single thing; and likewise "this thing" is anything you like. If we describe it more exactly as "this bit of paper," then each and every bit of paper is "this bit of paper," and I have only uttered the universal all the time. But if I want to help out language—which has the divine nature of directly reversing the meaning of what is said, of making it into something else, and thus not letting what is meant *get into words* at all—by *pointing out* this bit of paper, experience teaches me what the truth of sense-certainty in fact is: I point it out as a "Here," which is a Here of other Heres, or is in its own self a "simple togetherness of many Heres"; i.e., it is a universal. I take it up then as it is in truth, and instead of knowing something immediate I take the truth of it, or *perceive* it.[1]

II. Perception: Or the Thing and Deception

111. Immediate certainty does not take over the truth, for its truth is the universal, whereas certainty wants to apprehend the This. Perception, on the other hand, takes what is present to it as a universal. Just as universality is its principle in general, the immediately self-differentiating moments within perception are universal: "I" is a universal and the object is a universal. That principle has arisen for us, and therefore the way we take in perception is no longer something that just happens to us like sense-certainty; on the contrary, it is logically necessitated. With the emergence of the principle, the two moments which in their appearing merely *occur*, also come into being: one being the movement of pointing-out or the *act of perceiving*, the other being the same movement as a simple event or the *object perceived*. In essence the object is the same as the movement: the movement is the unfolding and differentiation of the two moments, and the object is the apprehended togetherness of the moments. For us, or in itself, the universal as principle is the essence of perception, and, in contrast to this abstraction, both the moments distinguished—that which perceives and that which is perceived—are the unessential. But, in fact, because both are themselves the universal or the essence, both are essential. Yet since they are related to each other as opposites, only one can be the essential moment in the relation, and the distinction of essential and unessential moment must be shared between them. One of

them, the object, defined as the simple [entity], is the essence regardless of whether it is perceived or not; but the act of perceiving, as a movement, is the unessential moment, the unstable factor which can as well be as not be.

112. This object must now be defined more precisely, and the definition must be developed briefly from the result that has been reached; the more detailed development does not belong here. Since the principle of the object, the universal, is in its simplicity a *mediated* universal, the object must express this its nature in its own self. This it does by showing itself to be *the thing with many properties*. The wealth of sense-knowledge belongs to perception, not to immediate certainty, for which it was only the source of instances; for only perception contains negation, that is, difference or manifoldness, within its own essence.

113. The This is, therefore, established as *not* This, or as something superseded; and hence not as Nothing, but as a determinate Nothing, the Nothing of a content, viz. of the This. Consequently, the sense-element is still present, but not in the way it was supposed to be in [the position of] immediate certainty: not as the singular item that is "meant," but as a universal, or as that which will be defined as a *property*. *Supersession* exhibits its true twofold meaning which we have seen in the negative: it is at once a *negating* and a *preserving*. Our Nothing, as the Nothing of the This, preserves its immediacy and is itself sensuous, but it is a universal immediacy. Being, however, is a universal in virtue of its having mediation or the negative within it; when it *expresses* this in its immediacy it is a *differentiated, determinate* property. As a result *many* such properties are established simultaneously, one being the negative of another. Since they are expressed in the simplicity of the universal, these determinacies—which are properties strictly speaking only through the addition of a further determination—are related [only] to themselves; they are indifferent to one another, each is on its own and free from the others. But the simple, self-identical universality is itself in turn distinct and free from these determinate properties it has. It is pure relating of self to self, or the *medium* in which all these determinacies are, and in which as a *simple* unity they therefore interpenetrate, but without *coming into contact* with one another; for it is precisely through participating in this universality that they exist indifferently on their own account.

This abstract universal medium, which can be called simply "thinghood" or "pure essence," is nothing else than what Here and Now have proved themselves to be, viz. a *simple togetherness* of a plurality; but the many are, *in their determinateness*, simple universals themselves. This salt is a simple Here, and at the same time manifold; it is white and *also* tart, *also* cubical in shape, of a specific gravity, etc. All these many properties are in a single simple "Here," in which, therefore, they interpenetrate; none has a different Here from the others, but each is everywhere, in the same Here in which the others are. And, at the same time, without being separated by different Heres, they do not affect each other in this interpenetration. The whiteness does not affect the cubical shape, and neither affects the tart taste, etc.; on the contrary, since each is itself a simple relating of self to self it leaves the others alone, and is connected with them only by the indifferent Also. This Also is thus the pure universal itself, or the medium, the "thinghood," which holds them together in this way.

114. In the relationship which has thus emerged it is only the character of positive universality that is at first observed and developed; but a further side presents itself, which must also be taken into consideration. To wit, if the many determinate properties were strictly indifferent to one another, if they were simply and solely self-related, they would not be determinate; for they are only determinate in so far as they *differentiate* themselves from one another, and *relate* themselves *to others* as to their opposites. Yet, as thus opposed to one another they cannot be together in the simple unity of their medium, which is just as essential to them as negation; the differentiation of the properties, in so far as it is not an indifferent differentiation but is exclusive, each property negating the others, thus falls outside of this simple medium; and the medium, therefore, is not merely an Also, an indifferent unity, but a *One* as well, a unity which *excludes* an other. The One is the *moment of negation*; it is itself quite simply a relation of self to self and it excludes an other; and it is that by which "thinghood" is determined as a Thing. Negation is inherent in a property as a *determinateness* which is immediately one with the immediacy of being, an immediacy which, through this unity with negation, is universality. As a One, however, the determinateness is set free from this unity with its opposite, and exists in and for itself.

115. In these moments, taken together, the Thing as the truth of perception is completed, so far as it is necessary to develop it here. It is (a) an indifferent, passive universality, the *Also* of the many properties or rather "matters"; (b) negation, equally simply; or the *One*, which excludes opposite properties ; and (c) the many *properties* themselves, the relation of the first two moments, or negation as it relates to the indifferent element, and therein expands into a host of differences; the point of singular individuality in the medium of subsistence radiating forth into plurality. In so far as these differences belong to the indifferent medium they are themselves universal, they are related only to themselves and do not affect one another. But in so far as they belong to the negative unity they are at the same time exclusive [of other properties]; but they necessarily have this relationship of opposition to properties remote from *their* Also. The sensuous universality, or the *immediate* unity of being and the negative, is thus a *property* only when the One and the pure universality are developed from it and differentiated from each other, and when the sensuous universality unites them; it is this relation of the universality to the pure essential moments which at last completes the Thing.

116. This, then, is how the Thing of perception is constituted; and consciousness is determined as percipient in so far as this Thing is its object. It has only to *take* it, to confine itself to a pure apprehension of it, and what is thus yielded is the True. If consciousness itself did anything in taking what is given, it would by such adding or subtraction alter the truth. Since the object is the True and universal, the self-identical, while consciousness is alterable and unessential, it can happen that consciousness apprehends the object incorrectly and deceives itself. The percipient is aware of the possibility of deception; for in the universality which is the principle, *otherness* itself is immediately present for him, though

present as what is *null* and superseded. His criterion of truth is therefore *self-identity*, and his behaviour consists in apprehending the object as self-identical. Since at the same time diversity is explicitly there for him, it is a connection of the diverse moments of his apprehension to one another; but if a dissimilarity makes itself felt in the course of this comparison, then this is not an untruth of the object—for this is the self-identical—but an untruth in perceiving it.

117. Let us see now what consciousness experiences in its actual perceiving. *For us*, this experience is already contained in the development of the object, and of the attitude of consciousness towards it given just now. It is only a matter of developing the contradictions that are present therein. The object which I apprehend presents itself purely as a *One*; but I also perceive in it a property which is *universal*, and which thereby transcends the singularity [of the object]. The first being of the objective essence as a One was therefore not its true being. But since the *object* is what is true, the untruth falls in me; my apprehension was not correct. On account of the *universality* of the property, I must rather take the objective essence to be on the whole a *community*. I now further perceive the property to be *determinate, opposed* to another and excluding it. Thus I did not in fact apprehend the objective essence correctly when I defined it as a *community* with others, or as a continuity; on account of the *determinateness* of the property, I must break up the continuity and posit the objective essence as a One that excludes.

In the broken up One I find many such properties which do not affect one another but are mutually indifferent. Therefore, I did not perceive the object correctly when I apprehended it as exclusive; on the contrary, just as previously it was only continuity in general, so now it is a universal *common medium* in which many properties are present as sensuous *universalities*, each existing on its own account and, as *determinate*, excluding the others. But this being so, what I perceive as the simple and the True is also not a universal medium, but the *single property* by itself which, however, as such, is neither a property nor a determinate being; for now it is neither in a One nor connected with others. Only when it belongs to a One is it a property, and only in relation to others is it determinate. As this pure relating of itself to itself, it remains merely *sensuous being* in general, since it no longer possesses the character of negativity; and the consciousness which takes its object to be a sensuous being is only "my" *meaning* [*ein Meinen*], i.e., it has ceased altogether to perceive and has withdrawn into itself. But sensuous being and *my* meaning themselves pass over into perception: I am thrown back to the beginning and drawn once again into the same cycle which supersedes itself in each moment and as a whole.

118. Consciousness, therefore, necessarily runs through this cycle again, but this time not in the same way as it did the first time. For it has experienced in perception that the outcome and the truth of perception is its dissolution, or is reflection out of the True and into itself. Thus it becomes quite definite for consciousness how its perceiving is essentially constituted, viz. that it is not a simple pure apprehension, but *in its apprehension* is at the same time *reflected out of the True and into itself*. This return of consciousness into itself which

is directly *mingled* with the pure apprehension [of the object]—for this return into itself has shown itself to be essential to perception—alters the truth. Consciousness at once recognizes this aspect as its own and takes responsibility for it; by doing so it will obtain the true object in its purity. This being so, we have now in the case of perception the same as happened in the case of sense-certainty, the aspect of consciousness being driven back into itself; but not, in the first instance, in the sense in which this happened in sense-certainty, i.e., not as if the *truth* of perception fell in consciousness. On the contrary, consciousness recognizes that it is the *untruth* occurring in perception that falls within it. But by this very recognition it is able at once to supersede this untruth; it distinguishes its apprehension of the truth from the untruth of its perception, corrects this untruth, and since it undertakes to make this correction itself, the truth, *qua* truth of *perception, falls* of course *within consciousness*. The behaviour of consciousness which we have now to consider is thus so constituted that consciousness no longer merely perceives, but is also conscious of its reflection into itself, and separates this from simple apprehension proper.

119. At first, then, I become aware of the Thing as a *One*, and have to hold fast to it in this its true character; if, in the course of perceiving it, something turns up which contradicts it, this is to be recognized as a reflection of mine. Now, there also occur in the perception various properties which seem to be properties of the Thing; but the Thing is a One, and we are conscious that this diversity by which it would cease to be a One falls in us. So in point of fact, the Thing is white only to *our eyes, also* tart to *our* tongue, *also* cubical to *our* touch, and so on. We get the entire diversity of these aspects, not from the Thing, but from ourselves; and they fall asunder in this way for us, because the eye is quite distinct from the tongue, and so on. We are thus the *universal medium* in which such moments are kept apart and exist each on its own. Through the fact, then, that we regard the characteristic of being a universal medium as *our* reflection, we preserve the self-identity and truth of the Thing, its being a One.

120. But, regarded as existing each for itself in the universal medium, these *diverse aspects* for which consciousness accepts responsibility are *specifically determined*. White is white only in opposition to black, and so on, and the Thing is a One precisely by being opposed to others. But it is not as a One that it excludes others from itself, for to be a One is the universal relating of self to self, and the fact that it is a One rather makes it like all the others; it is through its *determinateness* that the thing excludes others. Things are therefore in and for themselves determinate; they have properties by which they distinguish themselves from others. Since the property [*Eigenschaft*] is the Thing's *own* [*eigene*] property or a determinateness in the Thing itself, the Thing has a number of properties. For, in the first place, the Thing is what is true, i.e., it *possesses intrinsic being*; and what is in it, is there as the Thing's essence, and not on account of other things. Secondly, therefore, the determinate properties do not only exist on account of other things and *for* other things, but in the Thing itself; yet they are determinate properties *in it* only because they are a plurality of reciprocally self-differentiating elements. And thirdly, since this is how they are in the "thinghood" [i.e.,

the essence of the *one* thing of which they are properties], they exist in and for themselves, indifferent to one another. It is in truth, then, the Thing itself that is white, and *also* cubical, *also* tart, and so on. In other words, the Thing is the *Also*, or the *universal medium* in which the many properties subsist apart from one another, without touching or cancelling one another; and when so taken, the Thing is perceived as what is true.

121. Now, in perceiving in this way, consciousness is at the same time aware that it is *also* reflected into itself, and that, in perceiving, the opposite moment to the Also turns up. But this moment is the *unity* of the Thing with itself, a unity which excludes difference from itself. Accordingly, it is this unity which consciousness has to take upon itself; for the Thing itself is the *subsistence of the many diverse and independent properties*. Thus we say of the Thing: *it is* white, *also* cubical, and *also* tart, and so on. But *in so far* as it is white, it is not cubical, and *in so far* as it is cubical and also white, it is not tart, and so on. Positing these properties as a oneness is the work of consciousness alone which, therefore, has to prevent them from collapsing into oneness in the Thing. To this end it brings in the "in so far," in this way preserving the properties as mutually external, and the Thing as the Also. Quite rightly, consciousness makes itself responsible for the oneness, at first in such a way that what was called a property is represented as "free matter." The Thing is in this way raised to the level of a genuine Also, since it becomes a collection of "matters" and, instead of being a One, becomes merely an enclosing surface.

122. If we look back on what consciousness previously took, and now takes, responsibility for, on what it previously ascribed, and now ascribes, to the Thing, we see that consciousness alternately makes itself, as well as the Thing, into both a pure, many-less *One*, and into an *Also* that resolves itself into independent "matters." Consciousness thus finds through this comparison that not only *its* truthful perceiving [*Nehmen des Wahren*], contains the *distinct moments of apprehension* and *withdrawal into itself*, but rather that the truth itself, the Thing, reveals itself in this twofold way. Our experience, then, is this, that the Thing exhibits itself *for the consciousness apprehending it*, in a specific manner, but is *at the same time* reflected out of the way in which it presents itself to consciousness and back into itself; in other words, it contains in its own self an opposite truth [to that which it has for the apprehending consciousness].

123. Thus consciousness has got beyond this second type of attitude in perceiving, too, i.e., the one in which it takes the Thing as truly self-identical, and itself for what is not self-identical but returns back into itself out of identity. The object is now for consciousness this whole movement which was previously shared between the object and consciousness. The Thing is a One, reflected into itself; it is *for itself*, but it is also *for an other*; and, moreover, it is an *other* on its own account, just *because* it is for an other. Accordingly, the Thing is for itself and *also* for an other, a being that is *doubly* differentiated but *also* a One; but the oneness contradicts this diversity. Hence consciousness would again have to assume responsibility for placing [the diversity] in the One and for keeping it away from the Thing. It would have to say that *in so far* as it is for itself, the Thing is *not* for an other. But the

oneness also belongs to the Thing itself as consciousness has found by experience: the Thing is essentially reflected into itself. The Also, or the indifferent difference, thus falls as much within the Thing as does the oneness; but since the two are different they do not fall within the same Thing, but in *different* Things. The contradiction which is present in the objective essence as a whole is distributed between two objects. In and for itself the Thing is self-identical, but this unity with itself is disturbed by other Things. Thus the unity of the Thing is preserved and at the same time the otherness is preserved outside of the Thing as well as outside of consciousness.

124. Now, although it is true that the contradiction in the objective essence is in this way distributed among different Things, yet the difference will, for that reason, attach to the singular separated Thing itself. The *different Things* are thus established as existing on their own account; and the conflict between them is so far reciprocal that each is different, not from itself, but only from the other. But each is thereby determined as being itself a *different* Thing, and it has its essential difference in its own self; but all the while not as if this difference were an opposition in the Thing itself. On the contrary, for itself it is a *simple determinateness* which constitutes the Thing's essential character, and differentiates it from others. As a matter of fact, since differentness is present in it, it is of course necessarily present as an *actual* difference manifoldly constituted. But because the determinateness constitutes the essence of the Thing, by which it distinguishes itself from other Things and is for itself, this further manifold constitution is the unessential aspect. Consequently, the Thing does indeed have the twofold "in so far" within its unity, but the aspects are unequal in value. As a result, this state of opposition does not develop into an actual opposition in the Thing itself, but in so far as the Thing through its *absolute difference* comes into a state of opposition, it is opposed to another Thing outside of it. Of course, the further manifoldness is necessarily present in the Thing too, so that it cannot be left out; but it is the unessential aspect of the Thing.

125. This determinateness, which constitutes the essential character of the Thing and distinguishes it from all others, is now defined in such a way that the Thing is thereby in opposition to other Things, but is supposed to preserve its independence in this opposition. But it is only a *Thing*, or a One that exists on its own account, in so far as it does not stand in this relation to others; for this relation establishes rather its continuity with others, and for it to be connected with others is to cease to exist on its own account. It is just through the *absolute character* of the Thing and its opposition that it *relates* itself to *others*, and is essentially only this relating. The relation, however, is the negation of its self-subsistence, and it is really the essential property of the Thing that is its undoing.

126. The conceptual necessity of the experience through which consciousness discovers that the Thing is demolished by the very determinateness that constitutes its essence and its being-for-self, can be summarized as follows. The Thing is posited as being *for itself*, or as the absolute negation of all otherness, therefore as purely *self*-related negation; but the

negation that is self-related is the suspension of *itself*; in other words, the Thing has its essential being in another Thing.

127. In fact, the definition of the object, as it has emerged, has shown itself to contain nothing else. The object is defined as having within it an essential property which constitutes its simple being-for-self; but along with this simple nature the object is also to contain diversity which, though *necessary*, is not to constitute its *essential* determinateness. This, however, is a distinction that is still only nominal; the unessential, which is none the less supposed to be necessary, cancels itself out. It is what has just been called the negation of itself.

128. With this, the last "in so far" that separated being-for-self from being-for-another falls away; on the contrary, the object is *in one and the same respect the opposite of itself: it is for itself, so far as it is for another*, and *it is for another, so far as it is for itself*. It is for itself, reflected into itself, a One; but this "for-itself," this reflection into itself, this being a One, is posited in a unity with its opposite, with its "being-for-another," and hence only as cancelled; in other words, this being-for-self is just as unessential as the only aspect that was supposed to be unessential, viz. the relationship to another.

129. Thus the object in its pure determinatenesses, or in,the determinatenesses which were supposed to constitute its essential being, is overcome just as surely as it was in its sensuous being. From a sensuous being it turned into a universal; but this universal, since it *originates in the sensuous,* is essentially *conditioned* by it, and hence is not truly a self-identical universality at all, but one *afflicted with an opposition*; for this reason the universality splits into the extremes of singular individuality and universality, into the One of the properties, and the Also of the "free matters." These pure determinatenesses seem to express the essential nature itself, but they are only a "being-for-self that is burdened with a "being-for-another." Since, however, both are essentially in a *single unity*, what we now have is *unconditioned absolute universality*, and consciousness here for the first time truly enters the realm of the Understanding.

130. Thus the singular being of sense does indeed vanish in the dialectical movement of immediate certainty and becomes universality, but it is only a *sensuous universality. My* "meaning" has vanished, and perception takes the object as it is *in itself*, or as a universal as such. Singular being therefore emerges in the object as true singleness, as the in-itself of the One, or as a reflectedness-into-self. But this is still a *conditioned* being-for-self *alongside which* appears another being-for-self, the universality which is opposed to, and conditioned by singular being. But these two contradictory extremes are not merely *alongside each other* but in a single unity, or in other words, the defining characteristic common to both, viz. "being-for-self," is burdened with opposition generally, i.e., it is at the same time *not* a "being-for-self." The sophistry of perception seeks to save these moments from their contradiction, and it seeks to lay hold on the truth, by distinguishing between the *aspects*, by sticking to the "Also" and to the "in so far," and finally, by distinguishing the "unessential" aspect from an "essence" which is opposed to it. But these expedients,

instead of warding off deception in the process of apprehension, prove themselves on the contrary to be quite empty; and the truth which is supposed to be won by this logic of the perceptual process proves to be in one and the same respect the opposite [of itself] and thus to have as its essence a universality which is devoid of distinctions and determinations.

131. These empty abstractions of a "singleness" and a "universality" opposed to it, and of an "essence" that is linked with something unessential—a "non-essential" aspect which is necessary all the same—these are powers whose interplay is the perceptual understanding, often called "sound common sense." This "sound common sense" which takes itself to be a solid, realistic consciousness is, in the perceptual process, only the play of these *abstractions*; generally, it is always at its poorest where it fancies itself to be the richest. Bandied about by these vacuous "essences," thrown into the arms first of one and then of the other, and striving by its sophistry to hold fast and affirm alternately first one of the "essences" and then the directly opposite one, it sets itself against the truth and holds the opinion that philosophy is concerned only with mental entities. As a matter of fact, philosophy does have to do with them too, recognizing them as the pure essences, the absolute elements and powers; but in doing so, recognizes them *in their specific determinateness* as well, and is therefore master over them, whereas perceptual understanding [or "sound common sense"] takes them for the truth and is led on by them from one error to another. It does not itself become conscious that it is simple essentialities of this kind that hold sway over it, but fancies that it has always to do with wholly substantial material and content; just as sense-certainty is unaware that the empty abstraction of pure being is its essence. But it is, in fact, these essentialities within which perceptual understanding runs to and fro through every kind of material and content; they are the cohesive power and mastery over that content and they alone are what the sensuous is *as essence* for consciousness, they are what determines the relations of the sensuous to it, and it is in them that the process of perception and of its truth runs its course. This course, a perpetual alternation of determining what is true, and then setting aside this determining, constitutes, strictly speaking, the steady every-day life and activity of perceptual consciousness, a consciousness which fancies itself to be moving in the realm of truth. It advances uninterruptedly to the outcome in which all these essential essentialities or determinations are equally set aside; but in each single moment it is conscious only of this *one determinateness* as the truth, and then in turn of the opposite one. It does indeed suspect their unessentiality, and to save them from the danger threatening them it resorts to the sophistry of asserting to be true what it has itself just declared to be untrue. What the nature of these untrue essences is really trying to get [perceptual] understanding to do is to *bring together*, and thereby supersede, the *thoughts* of those non-entities, the thoughts of that universality and singular being, of "Also" and "One," of the essentiality that is *necessarily* linked to the unessential moment, and of an unessential moment that yet is necessary. But the Understanding struggles to avoid doing this by resorting to "in so far as" and to the various "aspects," or by making itself responsible for one

thought in order to keep the other one isolated as the true one. But the very nature of these abstractions brings them together of their own accord. It is "sound common sense" that is the prey of these abstractions, which spin it round and round in their whirling circle. When common sense tries to make them true by at one time making itself responsible for their untruth, while at another time it calls their deceptiveness a semblance of the unreliability of Things, and separates what is essential from what is necessary to them yet supposedly unessential, holding the former to be their truth as against the latter—when it does this, it does not secure them *their* truth, but convicts *itself* of untruth.

III.   Force and the Understanding: Appearance and the Supersensible World

132. In the dialectic of sense-certainty, Seeing and Hearing have been lost to consciousness; and, as perception, consciousness has arrived at thoughts, which it brings together for the first time in the unconditioned universal. This, now, if it were taken as an inert simple essence, would itself in turn be nothing else than the one-sided extreme of *being-for-self*, for it would then be confronted by non-essence; but, if it were related to this, it would itself be unessential, and consciousness would not have escaped from the deceptions of the perceptual process. However, this universal has proved to be one which has returned into itself out of such a conditioned being-for-self. This unconditioned universal, which is now the true object of consciousness, is still just an *object* for it; consciousness has not yet grasped the Notion of the unconditioned as *Notion*. It is essential to distinguish the two: for consciousness, the object has returned into itself from its relation to an other and has thus become Notion *in principle*; but consciousness is not yet *for itself* the Notion, and consequently does not recognize itself in that reflected object. *For us*, this object has developed through the movement of consciousness in such a way that consciousness is involved in that development, and the reflection is the same on both sides, or, there is only one reflection. But since in this movement consciousness has for its content merely the objective essence and not consciousness as such, the result must have an objective significance for consciousness; consciousness still shrinks away from what has emerged, and takes it as the essence in the *objective* sense.

133. With this, the Understanding has indeed superseded its own untruth and the untruth of the object. What has emerged for it as a result is the Notion of the True—but only as the *implicit* being of the True, which is not yet Notion, or which lacks the *bring-for-self* of consciousness, and which the Understanding, without knowing itself therein, lets go its own way. This truth follows out its own essence, so that consciousness plays no part in its free realization, but merely looks on and simply apprehends it. To begin with, therefore, *we* must step into its place and be the Notion which develops and fills out what is contained in the result. It is through awareness of this completely developed object, which presents itself to consciousness as something that immediately *is*, that consciousness first becomes explicitly a consciousness that comprehends [its object].

134. The result was the unconditioned universal, initially, in the negative and abstract sense that consciousness negated its one-sided Notions and abstracted them: in other words, it gave them up. But the result has, implicitly, a positive significance: in it, the unity of "being-for-self" and "being-for-another" is posited; in other words, the absolute antithesis is posited as a self-identical essence. At first sight, this seems to concern only the form of the moments in reciprocal relation; but "being-for-self" and "being-for-another" are the *content* itself as well, since the antithesis in its truth can have no other nature than the one yielded in the result, viz. that the content taken in perception to be true, belongs in fact only to the form, in the unity of which it is dissolved. This content is likewise universal; there can be no other content which by its particular constitution would fail to fall within this unconditioned universality. A content of this kind would be some particular way or other of being for itself and of being in relation to an other. But, in general, to be for itself and to be in relation to an other constitutes the nature and essence of the content, whose truth consists in its being unconditionally universal; and the result is simply and solely universal.

135. But because this unconditioned universal is an object for consciousness, there emerges in it the distinction of form and content; and in the shape of content the moments look like they did when they first presented themselves: on one side, a universal medium of many subsistent "matters," and on the other side, a One reflected into itself, in which their independence is extinguished. The former is the dissolution of the Thing's independence, i.e., the passivity that is a being-for-another; the latter is being-for-self. We have to see how these moments exhibit themselves in the unconditioned universality which is their essence. It is clear at the outset that, since they exist only in this universality, they are no longer separated from one another at all but are in themselves essentially self-superseding aspects, and what is posited is only their transition into one another.

136. One moment, then, appears as the essence that has stepped to one side as a universal medium, or as the subsistence of independent "matters." But the independence of these "matters" is nothing else than this medium; in other words, the [unconditioned] universal is simply and solely the *plurality* of the diverse universals of this kind. That within itself the universal is in undivided unity with this plurality means, however, that these "matters" are each where the other is; they mutually interpenetrate, but without coming into contact with one another because, conversely, the many diverse "matters" are equally independent. This also means that they are absolutely porous, or are sublated. This sublation in its turn, this reduction of the diversity to a pure *being-for-self*, is nothing other than the medium itself, and this is the *independence* of the different "matters." In other words, the "matters" posited as independent directly pass over into their unity, and their unity directly unfolds its diversity, and this once again reduces itself to unity. But this movement is what is called *Force*. One of its moments, the dispersal of the independent "matters" in their [immediate] being, is the *expression* of Force; but Force, taken as that in which they have disappeared, is Force *proper*, Force which has been *driven back* into

itself from its expression. First, however, the Force which is driven back into itself *must* express itself; and, secondly, it is still Force remaining *within itself* in the expression, just as much as it is expression in this self-containedness.

When *we* thus preserve the two moments in their immediate unity, the Understanding, to which the Notion of Force belongs, is strictly speaking the *Notion* which sustains the different moments *qua* different; for, *in themselves*, they are not supposed to be different. Consequently, the difference exists only in thought. That is to say, what has been posited in the foregoing is in the first instance only the Notion of Force, not its reality. In point of fact, however, Force is the unconditioned universal which is equally in its own self what it *is for an other*; or which contains the difference in its own self—for difference is nothing else than being-*for-another*. In order, then, that Force may in truth *be*, it must be completely set free from thought, it must be posited as the substance of these differences, i.e., *first* the *substance*, as this whole Force, remaining essentially *in and for itself, and then* its *differences* as possessing *substantial being*, or as moments existing on their own account. Force as such, or as driven back into itself, thus exists on its own account as an *exclusive One*, for which the unfolding of the [different] "matters" is *another* subsisting essence; and thus two distinct independent aspects are set up. But Force is also the whole, i.e., it remains what it is according to its Notion; that is to say, these *differences* remain pure forms, superficial *vanishing* moments. At the same time there would be no difference at all between Force proper which has been driven back into itself, and Force unfolded into independent "matters," if they had no *enduring* being, or, there would be no Force if it did not *exist* in these opposite ways. But that it does exist in these opposite ways simply means that the two moments are at the same time themselves *independent*. It is therefore this movement of the two moments in which they perpetually give themselves independence and then supersede themselves again which we are now to consider.

In general, it is clear that this movement is nothing else than the movement of perceiving, in which the two sides, the percipient and what is perceived, are indistinguishably one in the *apprehension* of the True, and yet each side is at the same time equally *reflected into itself*, or has a being of its own. Here, these two sides are moments of Force; they are just as much in a unity, as this unity, which appears as the middle term over against the independent extremes, is a perpetual diremption of itself into just these extremes which exist only through this process. Thus the movement which previously displayed itself as the self-destruction of contradictory Notions here has *objective* form and is the movement of Force, the outcome of which is the unconditioned universal as something *not* objective, or as the *inner* being of Things.

137. Force, as thus determined, since it is conceived *as* Force or as *reflected into itself*, is one side of its Notion, but posited as a substantial extreme and, moreover, with the express character of a One. The subsistence of the unfolded "matters" outside of Force is thus precluded and is something other than Force. Since it is necessary that *Force itself* be this *subsistence*, or that it *express* itself, its expression presents itself in this wise, that the said "other"

approaches *it* and solicits it. But, as a matter of fact, since its expression is *necessary*, what is posited as another essence is in Force itself. We must retract the assertion that Force is posited as *a One*, and that its essence is to express itself as an "other" which approaches it externally. Force is rather itself this universal medium in which the moments subsist as "matters"; or, in other words, Force *has expressed itself*, and what was supposed to be something else soliciting it is really Force itself. It exists, therefore, now as the medium of the unfolded "matters." But equally essentially it has the form of the supersession of the subsisting "matters," or is essentially a *One*. Consequently, this *oneness*, since *Force* is posited as the medium of the "matters," is *now* something *other* than Force, which has this its essence outside of it. But, since Force must of necessity be this oneness which it is not as yet *posited* as being, this "other" *approaches it*, soliciting it to reflect itself into itself: in other words, Force supersedes its expression. But in fact Force is *itself* this reflectedness-into-self, or this supersession of the expression. The oneness, in the form in which it appeared, viz. as an "other," vanishes; Force is this "other" itself, is Force that is driven back into itself.

138. What appears as an "other" and solicits Force, both to expression and to a return into itself, directly proves to be *itself Force*; for the "other" shows itself to be as much a universal medium as a One, and in such a way that each of these forms at the same time appears only as a vanishing moment. Consequently, Force, in that there is an "other" for it, and it is for an "other," has not yet altogether emerged from its Notion. There are at the same time two Forces present; the Notion of both is no doubt the same, but it has gone forth from its unity into a duality. Instead of the antithesis remaining entirely and essentially only a moment, it seems, by its self-diremption into two wholly *independent* forces, to have withdrawn from the controlling unity. We have now to see more closely the implications of this independence.

In the first place, the second Force appears as the one that solicits and, moreover, in accordance with its content, as the universal medium in relation to the Force characterized as the one solicited. But since the second Force is essentially an alternation of these two moments and is itself Force, it is likewise the universal medium *only through its being solicited to be such*; and similarly, too, it is a negative unity, i.e., it solicits the retraction of Force [into itself], *only through its being solicited to do so*. Consequently, this distinction, too, which obtained between the two Forces, one of which was supposed to be the soliciting, the other the solicited, Force is transformed into the same reciprocal interchange of the determinatenesses.

139. The interplay of the two Forces thus consists in their being determined as mutually opposed, in their being for one another in this determination, and in the absolute, immediate alternation of the determinations—consists, i.e., in a transition through which alone these determinations *are* in which the Forces seem to make an *independent* appearance. The soliciting Force, e.g., is posited as a universal medium, and the one solicited, on the other hand, as Force driven back into itself; but the former is a universal medium only through the other being Force that is driven back into itself; or, it is really the latter

that is the soliciting Force for the other and is what makes it a medium. The first Force has its determinateness only through the other, and solicits only in so far as the other solicits it to be a soliciting Force; and, just as directly, it loses the determinateness given to it, for this passes over—or rather has already passed over—to the other. The external, soliciting Force appears as a universal medium, but only through its having been solicited by the other Force to do so; but this means that the latter *gives* it that character and is really *itself essentially* a universal medium; it gives the soliciting Force this character just because this other determination is essential to it, i.e., because *this is really its own self*.

140. To complete our insight into the Notion of this movement it may further be noticed that the differences themselves are exhibited in a twofold difference: once as a difference of *content*, one extreme being the Force reflected into itself, but the other the medium of the "matters"; and again as a difference of *form*, since one solicits and the other is solicited, the former being active and the other passive. According to the difference of content they are distinguished [merely] in principle, or *for us*; but according to the difference of form they are independent and in their relation keep themselves separate and opposed to one another. The fact that the extremes, from the standpoint of both these sides, are thus nothing *in themselves*, that these sides in which their different essences were supposed to consist are only vanishing moments, are an immediate transition of each into its opposite, this truth becomes apparent to consciousness in its perception of the movement of Force. But *for us*, as remarked above, something more was apparent, viz. that the differences, *qua differences of content and form*, vanished in themselves; and on the side of form, the essence of the *active, soliciting* or *independent* side, was the same as that which, on the side of content, presented itself as Force driven back into itself; the side which was passive, which was *solicited* or for an *other*, was, from the side of form, the same as that which, from the side of content, presented itself as the universal medium of the many "matters."

141. From this we see that the Notion of Force becomes *actual* through its duplication into two Forces, and how it comes to be so. These two Forces exist as independent essences; but their existence is a movement of each towards the other, such that their being is rather a pure *positedness* or a being that is *posited by an other*, i.e., their being has really the significance of a sheer *vanishing*. They do not exist as extremes which retain for themselves something fixed and substantial, transmitting to one another in their middle term and in their contact a merely external property; on the contrary, what they are, they are, only in this middle term and in this contact. In this, there is immediately present both the repression within itself of Force, or its *being-for-self*, as well as its expression: Force that solicits and Force that is solicited. Consequently, these moments are not divided into two independent extremes offering each other only an opposite extreme: their essence rather consists simply and solely in this, that each *is* solely through the other, and what each thus is it immediately no longer is, since it *is* the other. They have thus, in fact, no substances of their own which might support and maintain them. The *Notion* of Force rather preserves itself as the *essence* in its very *actuality*; Force, as *actual*, exists simply and solely in its *expression*, which at the

same time is nothing else than a supersession of itself. This *actual* Force, when thought of as free from its expression and as being for itself, is Force driven back into itself; but in fact this determinateness, as we have found, is itself only a moment of Force's expression. Thus the truth of Force remains only the *thought* of it; the moments of its actuality, their substances and their movement, collapse unresistingly into an undifferentiated unity, a unity which is not Force driven back into itself (for this is itself only such a moment), but is its *Notion qua Notion*. Thus the realization of Force is at the same time the loss of reality; in that realization it has really become something quite different, viz. this *universality*, which the Understanding knows at the outset, or immediately, to be its essence and which also proves itself to be such in the supposed reality of Force, in the actual substances.

142. In so far as we regard the *first* universal as the Understanding's Notion in which Force is not yet *for itself*, the second is now Force's *essence* as it exhibits itself in and for itself. Or, conversely, if we regard the first universal as the *Immediate*, which was supposed to be an *actual* object for consciousness, then this second is determined as the *negative* of Force that is objective to sense; it is Force in the form of its true essence in which it exists only as an *object for the Understanding*. The first universal would be Force driven back into itself, or Force as Substance; the second, however, is the *inner being* of things *qua* inner, which is the same as the Notion of Force *qua* Notion.

143. This true essence of Things has now the character of not being immediately for consciousness; on the contrary, consciousness has a mediated relation to the inner being and, as the Understanding, looks *through this mediating play of Forces into the true background of Things*. The middle term which unites the two extremes, the Understanding and the inner world, is the developed *being* of Force which, for the Understanding itself, is henceforth only a vanishing. This "being" is therefore called *appearance*; for we call *being* that is directly and in its own self a *non-being*, a surface show. But it is not merely a surface show; it is appearance, a *totality* of show. This *totality*, as totality or as a *universal*, is what constitutes the inner [of Things], the play of Forces as a reflection of the inner into itself. In it, the Things of perception are expressly present for consciousness as they are in themselves, viz. as moments which immediately and without rest or stay turn into their opposite, the One immediately into the universal, the essential immediately into the unessential, and vice versa. This play of Forces is consequently the developed negative; but its truth is the positive, viz. the *universal*, the object that, *in itself*, possesses being. The *being* of this object for consciousness is mediated by the movement of *appearance*, in which the *being of perception* and the sensuously objective in general has a merely negative significance. Consciousness, therefore, reflects itself out of this movement back into itself as the True; but, *qua* consciousness, converts this truth again into an objective *inner*, and distinguishes this reflection of Things from its own reflection into itself: just as the movement of mediation is likewise still objective for it. This inner is, therefore, for consciousness an extreme over against it; but it is for consciousness the True, since in the inner, as the in-itself, it possesses at the same time the certainty of itself, or the moment of its being-for-self. But it is not yet conscious of this

ground or basis, for the *being-for-self* which the inner was supposed to possess in its own self would be nothing else but the negative movement. This, however, is for consciousness still the *objective* vanishing appearance, not yet its *own* being-for-self. Consequently, the inner is for it certainly Notion, but it does not as yet know the nature of the Notion.

144. Within this *inner truth*, as the *absolute universal* which has been purged of the *antithesis* between the universal and the individual and has become the object of the *Understanding*, there now opens up above the *sensuous* world, which is the world of *appearance*, a *supersensible* world which henceforth is the *true* world, above the vanishing *present* world there opens up a permanent *beyond;* an in-itself which is the first, and therefore imperfect, appearance of Reason, or only the pure element in which the truth has its *essence*.

145. *Our object* is thus from now on the syllogism which has for its extremes the inner being of Things and the Understanding, and for its middle term, appearance; but the movement of this syllogism yields the further determination of what the Understanding descries in this inner world through the middle term, and the experience from which Understanding learns about the close-linked unity of these terms.

146. The inner world is, for consciousness, still a *pure beyond*, because consciousness does not as yet find itself in it. It is *empty*, for it is merely the nothingness of appearance, and positively the *simple* or *unitary* universal. This mode of the inner being [of Things] finds ready acceptance by those who say that the inner being of Things is unknowable; but another reason for this would have to be given. Certainly, we have no knowledge of this inner world as it is here in its immediacy; but not because Reason is too short-sighted or is limited, or however else one likes to call it—on this point, we know nothing as yet because we have not yet gone deep enough—but because of the simple nature of the matter in hand, that is to say, because in the *void* nothing is known, or, expressed from the other side, just because this inner world is determined as the *beyond* of consciousness. The result is, of course the same if a blind man is placed amid the wealth of the supersensible world (if it has such wealth, whether it be its own peculiar content, or whether consciousness itself be this content), and if one with sight is placed in pure darkness, or if you like, in pure light, just supposing the supersensible world to be this. The man with sight sees as little in that pure light as in pure darkness, and just as much as the blind man, in the abundant wealth which lies before him. If no further significance attached to the inner world and to our close link with it through the world of appearance, then nothing would be left to us but to stop at the world of appearance, i.e., to perceive something as true which we know is not true. Or, in order that there may yet be something in the void—which, though it first came about as devoid of *objective* Things must, however, as *empty in itself*, be taken as also void of all spiritual relationships and distinctions of consciousness *qua* consciousness—in order, then, that in this *complete void*, which is even called the *holy of holies*, there may yet be something, we must fill it up with reveries, *appearances*, produced by consciousness itself. It would have to be content with being treated so badly for it would not deserve anything better, since even reveries are better than its own emptiness.

147. The inner world, or supersensible beyond, has, however, *come into being*: it *comes from* the world of appearance which has mediated it; in other words, appearance is its essence and, in fact, its filling. The supersensible is the sensuous and the perceived posited as it is *in truth*; but the *truth* of the sensuous and the perceived is to be *appearance*. The supersensible is therefore *appearance qua appearance*. We completely misunderstand this if we think that the supersensible world is *therefore* the sensuous world, or the world as it exists for immediate sense-certainty and perception; for the world of appearance is, on the contrary, *not* the world of sense-knowledge and perception as a world that positively *is*, but this world posited as superseded, or as in truth an *inner world*. It is often said that the supersensible world is *not* appearance; but what is here understood by appearance is not appearance, but rather the *sensuous* world as itself the really actual.

148. The Understanding, which is our object, finds itself in just this position, that the inner world has come into being for it, to begin with, only as the universal, still unfilled, *in-itself*. The play of Forces has merely this negative significance of being *in itself* nothing, and its only positive significance that of being the *mediating agency*, but outside of the Understanding. The connection of the Understanding with the inner world through the mediation is, however, its own movement through which the inner world will fill itself out for the Understanding. What is *immediate* for the Understanding is the play of Forces; but what is the *True* for it, is the simple inner world. The movement of Force is therefore the True, likewise only as something altogether *simple*. We have seen, however, that this play of Forces is so constituted that the Force which is *solicited* by another Force is equally the *soliciting* Force for that other, which only thereby becomes itself a soliciting Force. What is present in this interplay is likewise merely the immediate alternation, or the absolute interchange, of the *determinateness* which constitutes the sole *content* of what appears: to be either a universal medium, or a negative unity. It ceases immediately on its appearance in determinate form to be what it was on appearing; by appearing in determinate form, it solicits the other side to *express* itself, i.e., the latter is now immediately what the first was supposed to be. Each of these two sides, the *relation* of soliciting and the *relation* of the opposed determinate content, is *on its own account* an absolute reversal and interchange [of the determinateness]. But these two relations themselves are again one and the same; and the difference of *form*, of being the solicited and the soliciting Force, is the same as the difference of *content*, of being the solicited Force as such, viz. the passive medium on the one hand, and the soliciting Force, the active, negative unity or the One, on the other. In this way there vanishes completely all distinction of *separate*, mutually contrasted *Forces* which were supposed to be present in this movement, for they rested solely on those distinctions; and the distinction between the Forces, along with both those distinctions, likewise collapses into only one. Thus there is neither Force, nor the act of soliciting or being solicited, nor the determinateness of being a stable medium and a unity reflected into itself, there is neither something existing singly by itself, nor are there diverse antitheses; on the contrary, what there is in this absolute flux is only *difference* as a *universal* difference, or as a difference

into which the many antitheses have been resolved. This difference, as a *universal* difference, is consequently the *simple element in the play of Force itself* and what is true in it. It is the *law of Force.*

149. The absolute flux of appearance becomes *a simple difference* through its relation to the simplicity of the inner world or of the Understanding. The inner being is, to begin with, only implicitly the universal; but this implicit, simple *universal* is essentially no less absolutely *universal difference*, for it is the outcome of the flux itself, or the flux is its essence; but it is a flux that is posited in the *inner* world as it is in truth, and consequently it is received in that inner world as equally an absolute universal difference that is absolutely at rest and remains selfsame. In other words, negation is an essential moment of the universal, and negation, or mediation in the universal, is therefore a *universal difference.* This difference is expressed in the *law*, which is the *stable* image of unstable appearance. Consequently, the *supersensible* world is an inert *realm of laws* which, though beyond the perceived world—for this exhibits law only through incessant change—is equally *present* in it and is its direct tranquil image.

150. This realm of laws is indeed the truth for the Understanding, and that truth has its *content* in the law. At the same time, however, this realm is only the *initial* truth for the Understanding and does not fill out the world of appearance. In this the law is present, but is not the entire presence of appearance; with every change of circumstance the law has a different actuality. Thus appearance retains *for itself* an aspect which is not in the inner world; i.e., appearance is not yet truly posited as *appearance,* as a *superseded* being-for-self. This defect in the law must equally be made manifest in the law itself. What seems to be defective in it is that while it does contain difference, the difference is universal, indeterminate. However, in so far as it is not law in general, but *a* law, it does contain determinateness; consequently, there are indefinitely *many* laws. But this plurality is itself rather a defect; for it contradicts the principle of the Understanding for which, as consciousness of the simple inner world, the True is the implicitly universal *unity.* It must therefore let the many laws collapse into *one* law, just as, e.g., the law by which a stone falls, and the law by which the heavenly bodies move, have been grasped as one law. But when the laws thus coincide, they lose their specific character. The law becomes more and more superficial, and as a result what is found is, in fact, not the unity of *these specific* laws, but a law which leaves out their specific character; just as the *one* law which combines in itself the laws of falling terrestrial bodies and of the motions of the heavenly bodies, in fact expresses neither law. The unification of all laws in *universal attraction* expresses no other content than just the *mere Notion of law itself*, which is posited in that law in the form of *being.* Universal attraction merely asserts that *everything has a constant difference in relation to other things.* The Understanding imagines that in this unification it has found a universal law which expresses universal reality *as such*; but in fact it has only found the *Notion* of *law itself*, although in such a way that what it is saying is that *all* reality is *in its own self,* conformable to law. The expression, *universal attraction,* is of great importance in so far as it is directed against the thoughtless

way in which everything is pictured as contingent, and for which determinateness has the form of sensuous independence.

151. Thus, in contrast to specific laws, we have universal attraction, or the pure Notion of law. In so far as this pure Notion is looked on as the essence, or the true inner being, the *determinateness* of the specific law itself still belongs to appearance, or rather to sensuous being. But the pure *Notion* of law transcends not merely the law which, being itself a specific law, stands contrasted with other specific laws, but also transcends law as such. The determinateness of which we spoke is itself really only a vanishing moment which can no longer occur here as something essential, for here it is only the law that is the True; but the *Notion* of law is turned against *law* itself. That is to say, in the law the difference itself is grasped *immediately* and taken up into the universal, thereby, however, giving the moments whose relation is expressed by the law a *subsistence* in the form of indifferent and [merely] implicit essentialities. But these parts of the difference present in the law are at the same time themselves determinate sides; the pure Notion of law as universal attraction must, to get its true meaning, be grasped in such a way that in it, as what is absolutely simple or unitary, the differences present in law as such themselves return again *into the inner world as a simple unity*. This unity is the inner *necessity* of the law.

152. The law is thereby present in a twofold manner: once, as law in which the differences are expressed as independent moments; and also in the form of a *simple* withdrawal into itself which again can be called *Force*, but in the sense not of a Force that is driven back into itself, but Force as such, or the Notion of Force, an abstraction which absorbs the differences themselves of what attracts and what is attracted. In this sense, *simple* electricity, e.g., is *Force*; but the expression of difference falls within the *law*; this difference is positive and negative electricity. In the case of the motion of falling, *Force* is the simple factor, *gravity*, whose *law* is that the magnitudes of the different moments of the motion, the time elapsed and the *space* traversed, are related to one another as root and square. Electricity itself is not difference *per se*, or is not in its essence the dual essence of positive and negative electricity; hence, it is usually said that it *has* the law of this mode of *being*, and, too, that it *has the property* of expressing itself in this way. It is true that this property is the essential and sole property of this Force, or that it belongs to it *necessarily*. But necessity here is an empty word; Force *must*, just *because* it *must,* duplicate itself in this way. Of course, given *positive* electricity, negative too is given *in principle*; for the positive *is*, only as related to a negative, or, the positive is *in its own self* the difference from itself; and similarly with the negative. But that electricity as such should divide itself in this way is not in itself a necessity. Electricity, as *simple Force*, is indifferent to its law—*to be* positive and negative; and if we call the former its Notion but the latter its being, then its Notion is indifferent to its being. It merely *has* this property, which just means that this property is not *in itself* necessary to it. This indifference is given another form when it is said that to be positive and negative belongs to the *definition* of electricity, and that this is simply *its Notion and essence*. In that case, its being would simply mean its actual existence. But that definition does not

contain the *necessity of its existence*; it exists, either because we *find* it, i.e., its existence is not necessary at all, or else it exists through, or by means of, other Forces, i.e., its necessity is an external necessity. But, in basing this necessity on the determinateness of *being through another*, we relapse again into the *plurality* of specific laws which we have just left behind in order to consider *law* as law. It is only with law as law that we are to compare its *Notion* as Notion, or its necessity. But in all these forms, necessity has shown itself to be only an empty word.

153. There is still another form than that just indicated in which the indifference of law and Force, or of Notion and being, is to be found. In the law of motion, e.g., it is necessary that motion be split up into time and space, or again, into distance and velocity. Thus, since motion is only the relation of these factors, it—the universal—is certainly divided *in its own self*. But now these parts, time and space, or distance and velocity, do not in themselves express this origin in a One; they are indifferent to one another, space is thought of as able to be without time, time without space, and distance at least without velocity—just as their magnitudes are indifferent to one another, since they are not related to one another *as positive* and *negative*, and thus are not related to one another through *their own essential nature*. The necessity of the *division* is thus certainly present here, but not the necessity of the *parts* as such for one another. But it is just for this reason that that first necessity, too, is itself only a sham, false necessity. For motion is not itself thought of as something *simple*, or as a pure essence, but as *already* divided; time and space are *in themselves* its *independent* parts or essences, or, distance and velocity are modes of being or ways of thinking, either of which can well be without the other; and motion is, therefore, only their superficial relation, not their essence. If it is thought of as a simple essence or as Force, motion is no doubt *gravity*, but this does not contain these differences at all.

154. The difference, then, in both cases is not a difference *in its own self*: either the universal, Force, is indifferent to the division which is the law, or the differences, the parts, of the law are indifferent to one another. The Understanding, however, *has* the Notion of this *implicit difference* just because the law is, on the one hand, the inner, *implicit* being, but is, at the same time, inwardly differentiated. That this difference is thus an *inner* difference follows from the fact that the law is a *simple* Force or is the *Notion* of the difference, and is therefore a difference belonging to the *Notion*. But this inner difference still falls, to begin with, only within the Understanding, and is not yet posited *in the thing itself*. It is, therefore, only its *own* necessity that is asserted by the Understanding; the difference, then, is posited by the Understanding in such a way that, at the same time, it is expressly stated that the difference is not *a difference belonging to the thing itself*. This necessity, which is merely verbal, is thus a recital of the moments constituting the cycle of the necessity. The moments are indeed distinguished, but, at the same time, their difference is expressly said to be *not* a difference of the thing itself, and consequently is itself immediately cancelled again. This process is called *"explanation."* A *law* is enunciated; from this, its implicitly universal element or ground is distinguished as *Force*; but it is said that this difference is no difference, rather

that the ground is constituted exactly the same as the law. The single occurrence of light-ning, e.g., is apprehended as a universal, and this universal is enunciated as the *law* of electricity; the "explanation" then condenses the *law* into *Force* as the essence of the law. This Force, then, is *so constituted* that when it is expressed, opposite electricities appear, which disappear again into one another; that is, *Force is constituted exactly the same as law*; there is said to be no difference whatever between them. The differences are the pure, universal expression of law, and pure Force; but both have the *same* content, the *same* constitution. Thus the difference *qua* difference of content, of the thing, is also again withdrawn.

155. In this tautological movement, the Understanding, as we have seen, sticks to the inert unity of its object, and the movement falls only within the Understanding itself, not within the object. It is an explanation that not only explains nothing, but is so plain that, while it pretends to say something different from what has already been said, really says nothing at all but only repeats the same thing. In the Thing itself this movement gives rise to nothing new; it comes into consideration [only] as a movement of the Understanding. In it, however, we detect the very thing that was missing in the law, viz. the absolute flux itself; for this *movement*, when we look at it more closely, is directly the opposite of itself. That is to say, it posits a difference which is not only *not* a difference for us, but one which the movement itself cancels as a difference. This is the same flux which presented itself as the play of Forces. This contained the distinction of soliciting and solicited Force, or Force expressing itself and Force repressed into itself; but these were distinctions which in reality were no distinctions, and therefore were also immediately cancelled again. What is present here is not merely bare unity in which *no difference* would be *posited*, but rather a *movement* in which *a distinction is certainly made but*, because it is no distinction, is *again cancelled*. In the process, then, of explaining, the to and fro of change which before was outside of the inner world and present only in the appearance, has penetrated into the supersensible world itself. Our consciousness, however, has passed over from the inner being as object to the other side, into the *Understanding*, and it experiences change there.

156. Thus this change is not yet a change of the thing itself, but rather presents itself as pure change by the very fact that the *content* of the moments of change remains the same. But since the *Notion*, *qua* Notion of the Understanding, is the same as the *inner being* of things, this change becomes for the Understanding the law of the inner world. The Under-standing thus *learns* that it is a law of *appearance itself*, that differences arise which are no differences, or that what is *selfsame repels* itself from itself; and similarly, that the differences are only such as are in reality no differences and which cancel themselves; in other words, what is *not selfsame* is *self-attractive*. And thus we have a second law whose content is the opposite of what was previously called law, viz. difference which remains constantly self-same; for this new law expresses rather that *like* becomes *unlike* and *unlike* becomes *like*. The Notion demands of the thoughtless thinker that he bring both laws together and become aware of their antithesis. The second is certainly also a law, an inner self-identical being,

but a selfsameness rather of the unlike, a permanence of impermanence. In the play of Forces this law showed itself to be precisely this absolute transition and pure change; the selfsame, viz. Force, *splits* into an antithesis which at first appears to be an independent difference, but which in fact proves *to be none*; for it is the *selfsame* which repels itself from itself, and therefore what is repelled is essentially self-attractive, for it is the *same*; the difference created, since it is no difference, therefore cancels itself again. Consequently, the difference exhibits itself as difference of the *thing itself* or as absolute difference, and this difference of the *thing* is thus nothing else but the selfsame that has repelled itself from itself, and therefore merely posits an antithesis which is none.

157. Through this principle, the first supersensible world, the tranquil kingdom of laws, the immediate copy of the perceived world, is changed into its opposite. The law was, in general, like its differences, that which remains selfsame; now, however, it is posited that each of the two worlds is really the opposite of itself. The *selfsame* really repels itself from itself, and what is not selfsame really posits itself as selfsame. In point of fact, it is only when thus determined that the difference is *inner* difference, or the difference *in its own self*, the like being unlike itself, and the unlike, like itself. *This second supersensible world* is in this way the *inverted* world and, moreover, since one aspect is already present in the first supersensible world, the inversion of the first. With this, the inner world is completed as appearance. For the first supersensible world was only the *immediate* raising of the perceived world into the universal element; it had its necessary counterpart in this perceived world which still retained *for itself the principle of change and alteration*. The first kingdom of laws lacked that principle, but obtains it as an inverted world.

158. According, then, to the law of this inverted world, what is *like* in the first world is *unlike* to itself, and what is *unlike* in the first world is equally *unlike to itself*, or it becomes *like* itself. Expressed in determinate moments, this means that what in the law of the first world is sweet, in this inverted in-itself is sour, what in the former is black is, in the other, white. What in the law of the first is the north pole of the magnet is, in its other, supersensible in-itself [viz. in the earth], the south pole; but what is there south pole is here north pole. Similarly, what in the first law is the oxygen pole of electricity becomes in its other, supersensible essence, hydrogen pole; and conversely, what is there the hydrogen pole becomes here the oxygen pole. In another sphere, revenge on an enemy is, according to the *immediate law*, the supreme satisfaction of the injured individuality. This law, however, which bids me confront him as himself a person who does not treat me as such, and in fact bids me destroy him as an individuality—this law is *turned round* by the principle of the other world into its opposite: the reinstatement of myself as a person through the destruction of the alien individuality is turned into self-destruction. If, now, this inversion, which finds expression in the punishment of crime, is made into a *law*, it, too, again is only the law of one world which is confronted by an *inverted* supersensible world where what is despised in the former is honoured, and what in the former is honoured, meets with contempt. The punishment which under the law of the *first* world disgraces and destroys a man,

is transformed in its *inverted* world into the pardon which preserves his essential being and brings him to honour.

159. Looked at superficially, this inverted world is the opposite of the first in the sense that it has the latter outside of it and repels that world from itself as an inverted *actual world*: that the one is appearance, but the other the in-itself; that the one is the world as it is for an other, whereas the other is the world as it is for itself. So that to use the previous examples, what tastes sweet is *really*, or *inwardly* in the thing, sour; or what is north pole in the actual magnet in the world of appearance, would be south pole in the *inner* or *essential being*; what presents itself as oxygen pole in the phenomenon of electricity would be hydrogen pole in unmanifested electricity. Or, an action which in the world of *appearance* is a crime would, in the *inner* world, be capable of being really good (a bad action may be well-intentioned); punishment is punishment *only in the world of appearance*; *in itself*, or in another world, it may be a benefit for the criminal. But such antitheses of inner and outer, of appearance and the supersensible, as of two different kinds of actuality, we no longer find here. The repelled differences are not shared afresh between two substances such as would support them and lend them a separate subsistence: this would result in the Understanding withdrawing from the inner world and relapsing into its previous position. The one side, or substance, would be the world of perception again in which one of the two laws would be operative, and confronting it would be an inner world, *just such a sense-world* as the first, but in the *imagination*; it could not be exhibited as a sense-world, could not be seen, heard, or tasted, and yet it would be thought of as such a sense-world. But, in fact, if the one *posited world* is a perceived world, and its *in-itself*, as its inversion, is equally *thought of as sensuous*, then sourness which would be the in-itself of the sweet thing is actually a thing just as much as the latter, viz. a *sour thing*; black, which would be the in-itself of white, is an actual black; the north pole which is the in-itself of the south pole is the north pole *actually present in the same magnet*; the oxygen pole which is the in-itself of the hydrogen pole is *actually present* in the same voltaic pile. The *actual* crime, however, has *its inversion* and *its in-itself* as *possibility*, in the *intention* as such, but not in a good intention; for the truth of intention is only the act itself. But the crime, as regards its content, has its reflection-into-self, or its inversion, in the *actual* punishment; this is the reconciliation of the law with the actuality opposed to it in the crime. Finally, the *actual* punishment has its *inverted* actuality present in it in such a way that the punishment is an actualization of the law, whereby the activity exercised by the law as punishment *suspends itself*, and, from being active, the law becomes again quiescent and is vindicated, and the conflict of individuality with it, and of it with individuality, is extinguished.

160. From the idea, then, of inversion, which constitutes the essential nature of one aspect of the supersensible world, we must eliminate the sensuous idea of fixing the differences in a different sustaining element; and this absolute Notion of the difference must be represented and understood purely as inner difference, a repulsion of the selfsame, as selfsame, from itself, and likeness of the unlike as unlike. We have to think pure change, or

think antithesis within the antithesis itself, or *contradiction*. For in the difference which is an inner difference, the opposite is not merely *one of two*—if it were, it would simply *be*, without being an opposite—but it is the opposite of an opposite, or the other is itself immediately present in it. Certainly, I put the "opposite" here, and the "other" of which it is the opposite, there; the "opposite," then, is on one side, is in and for itself without the "other." But just because I have the "opposite" here in and for itself, it is the opposite of itself, or it has, in fact, the "other" immediately present in it. Thus the supersensible world, which is the inverted world, has at the same time overarched the other world and has it within it; it is *for itself* the inverted world, i.e., the inversion of itself; it is itself and its opposite in one unity. Only thus is it difference as *inner* difference, or difference *in its own self*, or difference as an *infinity*.

161. We see that through infinity, law completes itself into an immanent necessity, and all the moments of [the world of] appearance are taken up into the inner world. That the simple character of law is infinity means, according to what we have found, (a) that it is self-*identical*, but is also in itself *different*; or it is the selfsame which repels itself from itself or sunders itself into two. What was called *simple Force duplicates* itself and through its infinity is law. (b) What is thus dirempted, which constitutes the parts thought of as in the *law*, exhibits itself as a stable existence; and if the parts are considered without the Notion of the inner difference, then space and time, or distance and velocity, which appear as moments of gravity, are just as indifferent and without a necessary relation to one another as to gravity itself, or, as this simple gravity is indifferent to them, or, again, as simple electricity is indifferent to positive and negative electricity. But (c) through the Notion of inner difference, these unlike and indifferent moments, space and time, etc. are a *difference* which is no *difference*, or only a difference of what is *selfsame*, and its essence is unity. As positive and negative they stimulate each other into activity, and their being is rather to posit themselves as not-being and to suspend themselves in the unity. The two distinguished moments both subsist; they are *implicit* and are *opposites in themselves*, i.e., each is the opposite of itself; each has its "other" within it and they are only one unity.

162. This simple infinity, or the absolute Notion, may be called the simple essence of life, the soul of the world, the universal blood, whose omnipresence is neither disturbed nor interrupted by any difference, but rather is itself every difference, as also their supersession; it pulsates within itself but does not move, inwardly vibrates, yet is at rest. It is self-*identical*, for the differences are tautological; they are differences that are none. This self-identical essence is therefore related only to itself; "to itself" implies relationship to an "other," and the *relation-to-self* is rather a *self-sundering*; or, in other words, that very self-identicalness is an inner difference. These *sundered moments* are thus *in and for themselves* each an opposite—*of an other*; thus in each moment the "other" is at the same time expressed; or each is not the opposite of an "other" but only a *pure opposite*; and so each is therefore in its own self the opposite of itself. In other words, it is not an opposite at all, but is purely for itself, a pure, self-identical essence that has no difference in it. Accordingly,

we do not need to ask the question, still less to think that fretting over such a question is philosophy, or even that it is a question philosophy cannot answer, the question, viz. "*How*, from this pure essence, how does difference or otherness *issue forth* from it?" For the division into two moments has already taken place, difference is excluded from the self-identical and set apart from it. What was supposed to be the *self-identical* is thus already one of these two moments instead of being the absolute essence. That the self-identical divides itself into two means, therefore, just as well that it supersedes itself as *already* divided, supersedes itself as an otherness. The *unity*, of which it is usual to say that difference cannot issue from it, is in fact itself one of the two moments; it is the abstraction of the simplicity or unitary nature over against the difference. But in saying that the unity is an abstraction, that is, is only one of the opposed moments, it is already implied that it is the dividing of itself; for if the unity is a *negative*, is *opposed* to something, then it is *eo ipso* posited as that which has an antithesis within it. The different moments of *self-sundering* and of *becoming self-identical* are therefore likewise only this movement of *self-supersession*; for since the self-identical, which is supposed first to sunder itself or become its opposite, is an abstraction or is *already itself* a sundered moment, its self-sundering is therefore a supersession of what it is, and therefore the supersession of its dividedness. Its *becoming self-identical* is equally a self-sundering; what becomes identical with itself thereby opposes itself to its self-sundering; i.e., it thereby puts itself on one side, or rather it *becomes* a *sundered moment*.

163. Infinity, or this absolute unrest of pure self-movement, in which whatever is determined in one way or another, e.g., as being, is rather the opposite of this determinateness, this no doubt has been from the start the soul of all that has gone before; but it is in the *inner* world that it has first freely and clearly shown itself. Appearance, or the play of Forces, already displays it, but it is as "*explanation*" that it first freely stands forth; and in being finally an object for consciousness, as *that which it is*, consciousness is thus *self-consciousness*. The Understanding's "explanation" is primarily only the description of what self-consciousness is. It supersedes the differences present in the law, differences which have already become pure differences but are still indifferent, and posits them in a single unity, in Force. But this unifying of them is equally and immediately a sundering, for it supersedes the differences and posits the oneness of Force only by creating a new difference, that of Law and Force, which, however, at the same time is no difference; and, moreover, from the fact that this difference is no difference, it goes on to supersede this difference again, since it lets Force be similarly constituted to Law. But this movement, or necessity, is thus still a necessity and a movement of the Understanding, or, the movement *as such* is not the Understanding's *object*; on the contrary, in this movement the Understanding has as objects positive and negative electricity, distance, force of attraction, and a thousand other things which constitute the content of the moments of the movement. The reason why "explaining" affords so much self-satisfaction is just because in it consciousness is, so to speak, communing directly with itself, enjoying only itself; although it seems to be busy with something else, it is in fact occupied only with itself.

164. In the contrary law, as the inversion of the first law, or in the inner difference, it is true that infinity itself becomes the *object* of the Understanding; but once again the Understanding falls short of infinity as such, since it again apportions to two worlds, or to two substantial elements, that which is a difference in itself—the self-repulsion of the selfsame and the self-attraction of the unlike. To the Understanding, the *movement*, as it is found in experience, is here a [mere] happening, and the selfsame and the unlike are *predicates*, whose essence is an inert substrate. What is, for the Understanding, an object in a sensuous covering, is *for us* in its essential form as a pure Notion. This apprehension of the difference as it is *in truth*, or the apprehension of *infinity* as such, is *for us*, or *in itself* [i.e. is merely implicit]. The exposition of its Notion belongs to Science; but consciousness, in the way that it *immediately* has this Notion, again comes on the scene as a form belonging to consciousness itself, or as a new shape of consciousness, which does not recognize in what has gone before its own essence, but looks on it as something quite different. Since this Notion of infinity is an object for consciousness, the latter is consciousness of a difference that is no less *immediately* cancelled; consciousness is for its own self, it is a distinguishing of that which contains no difference, or *self-consciousness*. I distinguish myself from myself, and in doing so I am directly aware that what is distinguished from myself is not different [from me]. I, the selfsame being, repel myself from myself; but what is posited as distinct from me, or as unlike me, is immediately, in being so distinguished, not a distinction for me. It is true that consciousness of an "other," of an object in general, is itself necessarily *self-consciousness*, a reflectedness-into-self, consciousness of itself in its otherness. The *necessary advance* from the previous shapes of consciousness for which their truth was a Thing, an "other" than themselves, expresses just this, that not only is consciousness of a thing possible only for a self-consciousness, but that self-consciousness alone is the truth of those shapes. But it is only *for us* that this truth exists, not yet for consciousness. But self-consciousness has at first become [simply] *for itself*, not yet *as a unity* with consciousness in general.

165. We see that in the *inner* world of appearance, the Understanding in truth comes to know nothing else but appearance, but not in the shape of a play of Forces, but rather that play of Forces in its absolutely universal moments and in their movement; in fact, the Understanding experiences only *itself*. Raised above perception, consciousness exhibits itself closed in a unity with the supersensible world through the mediating term of appearance, through which it gazes into this background [lying behind appearance]. The two extremes [of this syllogism], the one, of the pure inner world, the other, that of the inner being gazing into this pure inner world, have now coincided, and just as they, *qua* extremes, have vanished, so too the middle term, as something other than these extremes, has also vanished. This curtain [of appearance] hanging before the inner world is therefore drawn away, and we have the inner being [the "I"] gazing into the inner world—the vision of the undifferentiated selfsame being, which repels itself from itself, posits itself as an inner being containing different moments, but for which equally these moments are immediately *not*

different—*self-consciousness*. It is manifest that behind the so-called curtain which is supposed to conceal the inner world, there is nothing to be seen unless *we* go behind it ourselves, as much in order that we may see, as that there may be something behind there which can be seen. But at the same time it is evident that we cannot without more ado go straightway behind appearance. For this knowledge of what is the truth of appearance as ordinarily conceived, and of its inner being, is itself only a result of a complex movement whereby the modes of consciousness "meaning," perceiving, and the Understanding, vanish; and it will be equally evident that the cognition of *what consciousness knows in knowing itself,* requires a still more complex movement, the exposition of which is contained in what follows.

Note

1. The German for "to perceive" is *wahrnehmen*, which means literally "to take truly."

5 The End of Philosophy and the Task of Thinking

Martin Heidegger

The title designates the attempt at a reflection that persists in questioning. Questions are paths toward an answer. If the answer could be given it would consist in a transformation of thinking, not in a propositional statement about a matter at stake.

The following text belongs to a larger context. It is the attempt undertaken again and again ever since 1930 to shape the question of *Being and Time* in a more primordial fashion. This means to subject the point of departure of the question in *Being and Time* to an immanent criticism. Thus it must become clear to what extent the *critical* question as to what the matter of thinking is necessarily and continually belongs to thinking. Accordingly, the name of the task of *Being and Time* will change.

We are asking:

1. To what extent has philosophy in the present age entered into its end?
2. What task is reserved for thinking at the end of philosophy?

I To what extent has philosophy in the present age entered into its end?

Philosophy is metaphysics. Metaphysics thinks beings as a whole—the world, man, God—with respect to Being, with respect to the belonging together of beings in Being. Metaphysics thinks beings as beings in the manner of a representational thinking that gives grounds. For since the beginning of philosophy, and with that beginning, the Being of beings has shown itself as the ground (*archē*, *aition*, principle). The ground is that from which beings as such are what they are in their becoming, perishing, and persisting as something that can be known, handled, and worked upon. As the ground, Being brings beings in each case to presencing. The ground shows itself as presence. The present of presence consists in the fact that it brings what is present each in its own way to presence. In accordance with the given type of presence, the ground has the character of grounding as the ontic causation of the actual, the transcendental making possible of the objectivity of objects, the dialectical mediation of the movement of absolute spirit and of the historical process of production, and the will to power positing values.

What characterizes metaphysical thinking, which seeks out the ground for beings, is the fact that metaphysical thinking, starting from what is present, represents it in its presence and thus exhibits it as grounded by its ground.

What is meant by the talk about the end of philosophy? We understand the end of something all too easily in the negative sense as mere cessation, as the lack of continuation, perhaps even as decline and impotence. In contrast, what we say about the end of philosophy means the completion of metaphysics. However, completion does not mean perfection, as a consequence of which philosophy would have to have attained the highest perfection at its end. Not only do we lack any criterion that would permit us to evaluate the perfection of an epoch of metaphysics as compared with any other epoch; the right to this kind of evaluation does not exist. Plato's thinking is no more perfect than Parmenides'. Hegel's philosophy is no more perfect than Kant's. Each epoch of philosophy has its own necessity. We simply have to acknowledge the fact that a philosophy is the way it is. It is not for us to prefer one to the other, as can be the case with regard to various *Weltanschauungen*.

The old meaning of the word "end" means the same as place: "from one end to the other" means from one place to the other. The end of philosophy is the place, that place in which the whole of philosophy's history is gathered in its uttermost possibility. End as completion means this gathering.

Throughout the entire history of philosophy, Plato's thinking remains decisive in its sundry forms. Metaphysics is Platonism. Nietzsche characterizes his philosophy as reversed Platonism. With the reversal of metaphysics that was already accomplished by Karl Marx, the uttermost possibility of philosophy is attained. It has entered into its end. To the extent that philosophical thinking is still attempted, it manages only to attain an epigonal renaissance and variations of that renaissance. Is not then the end of philosophy after all a cessation of its way of thinking? To conclude this would be premature.

As a completion, an end is the gathering into the uttermost possibilities. We think in too limited a fashion as long as we expect only a development of new philosophies in the previous style. We forget that already in the age of Greek philosophy a decisive characteristic of philosophy appears: the development of the sciences within the field that philosophy opened up. The development of the sciences is at the same time their separation from philosophy and the establishment of their independence. This process belongs to the completion of philosophy. Its development is in full swing today in all regions of beings. This development looks like the mere dissolution of philosophy, yet in truth is precisely its completion.

It suffices to refer to the independence of psychology, sociology, anthropology as cultural anthropology, or to the role of logic as symbolic logic and semantics. Philosophy turns into the empirical science of man, of all that can become for man the experiential object of his technology, the technology by which he establishes himself in the world by working on it in the manifold modes of making and shaping. All of this happens everywhere on the basis of and according to the criterion of the scientific discovery of the individual areas of beings.

No prophecy is necessary to recognize that the sciences now establishing themselves will soon be determined and regulated by the new fundamental science that is called cybernetics.

This science corresponds to the determination of man as an acting social being. For it is the theory of the regulation of the possible planning and arrangement of human labor. Cybernetics transforms language into an exchange of news. The arts become regulated-regulating instruments of information.

The development of philosophy into the independent sciences that, however, interdependently communicate among themselves ever more markedly, is the legitimate completion of philosophy. Philosophy is ending in the present age. It has found its place in the scientific attitude of socially active humanity. But the fundamental characteristic of this scientific attitude is its cybernetic, that is, technological character. The need to ask about modern technology is presumably dying out to the same extent that technology more decisively characterizes and directs the appearance of the totality of the world and the position of man in it.

The sciences will interpret everything in their structure that is still reminiscent of their provenance from philosophy in accordance with the rules of science, that is, technologically. Every science understands the categories upon which it remains dependent for the articulation and delineation of its area of investigation as working hypotheses. Not only is their truth measured in terms of the effect that their application brings about within the progress of research, scientific truth is also equated with the efficiency of these effects.

The sciences are now taking over as their own task what philosophy in the course of its history tried to present in certain places, and even there only inadequately, that is, the ontologies of the various regions of beings (nature, history, law, art). The interest of the sciences is directed toward the theory of the necessary structural concepts of the coordinated areas of investigation. "Theory" means now supposition of the categories, which are allowed only a cybernetic function, but denied any ontological meaning. The operational and model-based character of representational-calculative thinking becomes dominant.

However, the sciences still speak about the Being of beings in the unavoidable supposition of their regional categories. They only do not say so. They can deny their provenance from philosophy, but never dispense with it. For in the scientific attitude of the sciences the certification of their birth from philosophy still speaks.

The end of philosophy proves to be the triumph of the manipulable arrangement of a scientific-technological world and of the social order proper to this world. The end of philosophy means the beginning of the world civilization that is based upon Western European thinking.

But is the end of philosophy in the sense of its evolving into the sciences also already the complete actualization of all the possibilities in which the thinking of philosophy was posited? Or is there a *first* possibility for thinking apart from the *last* possibility that we characterized (the dissolution of philosophy in the technologized sciences), a possibility from which the thinking of philosophy would have to start, but which as philosophy it could nevertheless not expressly experience and adopt?

If this were the case, then a task would still have to be reserved for thinking in a concealed way in the history of philosophy from its beginning to its end, a task accessible neither to philosophy as metaphysics nor, even less, to the sciences stemming from philosophy. Therefore we ask:

II   What task is reserved for thinking at the end of philosophy?

The mere thought of such a task of thinking must sound strange to us. A thinking that can be neither metaphysics nor science?

A task that has concealed itself from philosophy since its very beginning, even in virtue of that beginning, and thus has withdrawn itself continually and increasingly in the times that followed?

A task of thinking that—so it seems—includes the assertion that philosophy has not been up to the matter of thinking and has thus become a history or mere decline?

Is there not an arrogance in these assertions which desires to put itself above the greatness of the thinkers of philosophy?

This suspicion obtrudes. But it can easily be quelled. For every attempt to gain insight into the supposed task of thinking finds itself moved to review the whole history of philosophy. Not only that. It is even forced to think the historicity of that which grants a possible history to philosophy.

Because of this, the thinking in question here necessarily falls short of the greatness of the philosophers. It is less than philosophy. Less also because the direct or indirect effect of this thinking on the public in the industrial age, formed by technology and science, is decisively less possible for this thinking than it was for philosophy.

But above all, the thinking in question remains unassuming, because its task is only of a preparatory, not of a founding character. It is content with awakening a readiness in man for a possibility whose contour remains obscure, whose coming remains uncertain.

Thinking must first learn what remains reserved and in store for it, what it is to get involved in. It prepares its own transformation in this learning.

We are thinking of the possibility that the world civilization that is just now beginning might one day overcome its technological-scientific-industrial character as the sole criterion of man's world sojourn. This may happen, not of and through itself, but in virtue of the readiness of man for a determination which, whether heeded or not, always speaks in the destiny of man, which has not yet been decided. It is just as uncertain whether world civilization will soon be abruptly destroyed or whether it will be stabilized for a long time. Such stabilization, however, will not rest in something enduring, but establish itself in a sequence of changes, each presenting the latest novelty.

The preparatory thinking in question does not wish and is not able to predict the future. It only attempts to say something to the present that was already said a long time ago, precisely at the beginning of philosophy and for that beginning, but has not been explicitly thought. For the time being, it must be sufficient to refer to this with the brevity required. We shall take a directive that philosophy offers as an aid in our undertaking.

When we ask about the task of thinking, this means in the scope of philosophy to determine that which concerns thinking, is still controversial for thinking, and is the controversy. This is what the word *Sache* [matter] means in the German language. It designates that with which thinking has to do in the case at hand, in Plato's language, *to pragma auto* (see "The Seventh Letter," 341c 7).

In recent times, philosophy has of its own accord expressly called thinking "to the things themselves." Let us mention two cases that receive particular attention today. We hear this call "to the things themselves" in the Preface that Hegel placed at the front of the work he published in 1807, *System of Science*,[1] *First Part: The Phenomenology of Spirit*. This preface is not the preface to the *Phenomenology*, but to the *System of Science*, to the whole of philosophy. The call "to the things themselves" refers ultimately—and that means according to the matter, primarily—to *the Science of Logic*.

In the call "to the things themselves" the emphasis lies on the "themselves." Heard superficially, the call has the sense of a rejection. The inadequate relations to the matter of philosophy are rejected. Mere talk about the purpose of philosophy belongs to these relations, but so does mere reporting about the results of philosophical thinking. Neither is ever the actual whole of philosophy. The whole shows itself only in its becoming. This occurs in the developmental presentation of the matter. In the presentation, theme and method coincide. For Hegel, this identity is called the idea. With the idea, the matter of philosophy "itself" comes to appear. However, this matter is historically determined as subjectivity. With Descartes's *ego cogito*, says Hegel, philosophy steps on firm ground for the first time, where it can be at home. If the *fundamentum absolutum* is attained with the *ego cogito* as the distinctive *subiectum*, this means the subject is the *hypokeimenon* transferred to consciousness, is what truly presences; and this, vaguely enough, is called "substance" in traditional terminology.

When Hegel explains in the Preface (ed. Hoffmeister, p. 19), "The true (in philosophy) is to be understood and expressed, not as substance, but, just as much, as subject," then this means: the Being of beings, the presence of what is present, is manifest and thus complete presence only when it becomes present as such for itself in the absolute idea. But since Descartes, *idea* means *perceptio*. Being's coming to itself occurs in speculative dialectic. Only the movement of the idea, the method, is the matter itself. The call "to the thing itself" requires a philosophical method appropriate to its matter.

However, what the matter of philosophy should be is presumed to be decided from the outset. The matter of philosophy as metaphysics is the Being of beings, their presence in the form of substantiality and subjectivity.

A hundred years later, the call "to the thing itself" again is heard in Husserl's treatise *Philosophy as Rigorous Science*. It was published in the first volume of the journal *Logos* in 1910–11 (pp. 289ff.). Again, the call has at first the sense of a rejection. But here it aims in another direction than Hegel's. It concerns naturalistic psychology, which claims to be the genuine scientific method of investigating consciousness. For this method blocks access to the phenomena of intentional consciousness from the very beginning. But the call "to the thing itself" is at the same time directed against historicism, which gets lost in treatises about the standpoints of philosophy and in the ordering of types of philosophical *Weltanschauungen*. About this Husserl says in italics (ibid., p. 340): *"The stimulus for investigation must start, not with philosophies, but with issues* [Sachen] *and problems."*

And what is the matter at stake in philosophical investigation? In accordance with the same tradition, it is for Husserl as for Hegel the subjectivity of consciousness. For Husserl, the *Cartesian Meditations* were not only the topic of the Paris lectures in February of 1929. Rather, from the time following the *Logical Investigations*, their spirit accompanied the impassioned course of his philosophical investigations to the end. In its negative and also in its positive sense, the call "to the matter itself" determines the securing and elaborating of method. It also determines the procedure of philosophy, by means of which the matter itself can be demonstrated as a datum. For Husserl, "the principle of all principles" is first of all not a principle of content but one of method. In his work published in 1913, *Ideas toward a Pure Phenomenology and Phenomenological Philosophy*, Husserl devoted a special section (24) to the determination of "the principle of all principles." "No conceivable theory can upset this principle," says Husserl.

"The principle of all principles" reads:

. . . Every originarily giving intuition [is] *a source of legitimation for knowledge; everything* that presents itself to us *in the "Intuition" originarily* (in its bodily actuality, so to speak) [is] simply to be *accepted as it gives itself*, but also *only within the limits in which it gives itself there.* . . .

"The principle of all principles" contains the thesis of the precedence of method. This principle decides what matter alone can suffice for the method. "The principle of principles" requires absolute subjectivity as the matter of philosophy. The transcendental reduction to absolute subjectivity gives and secures the possibility of grounding the objectivity of all objects (the Being of these beings) in their valid structure and consistency, that is, in their constitution, in and through subjectivity. Thus transcendental subjectivity proves to be "the sole absolute being" (*Formal and Transcendental Logic*, 1929, p. 240). At the same time, transcendental reduction as the method of "universal science" of the constitution of the Being of beings has the same mode of Being as this absolute being, that is, the manner of the matter most native to philosophy. The method is not only directed toward the matter of philosophy. It does not merely belong to the matter as a key does to a lock. Rather, it belongs to the matter because it is "the matter itself." If one wished to ask: Where does "the principle of all principles" get its unshakable right? [T]he answer would have to be: from transcendental subjectivity, which is already presupposed as the matter of philosophy.

We have chosen a discussion of the call "to the matter itself" as our directive. It was to bring us to the path that leads us to a determination of the task of thinking at the end of philosophy. Where are we now? We have arrived, at the insight that for the call "to the matter itself" what concerns philosophy as its matter is established from the outset. From the perspective of Hegel and Husserl—and not only from their perspective—the matter of philosophy is subjectivity. It is not the matter as such that is controversial for the call, but rather the presentation by which the matter itself becomes present. Hegel's speculative dialectic is the movement in which the matter as such comes to itself, comes to its own presence [*Präsenz*]. Husserl's method is supposed to bring the matter of philosophy to its ultimate originary givenness, and that means to its own presence [*Präsenz*].

The two methods are as different as they could possibly be. But the matter that they are to present as such is the same, although it is experienced in different ways.

But of what help are these discoveries to us in our attempt to bring the task of thinking to view? They do not help us at all as long as we do not go beyond a mere discussion of the call. Rather, we must ask what remains unthought in the call "to the matter itself," Questioning in this way, we can become aware that something that it is no longer the matter of philosophy to think conceals itself precisely where philosophy has brought its matter to absolute knowledge and to ultimate evidence.

But what remains unthought in the matter of philosophy as well as in its method? Speculative dialectic is a mode in which the matter of philosophy comes to appear of itself and for itself, and thus becomes present [*Gegenwart*]. Such appearance necessarily occurs in luminosity. Only by virtue of some sort of brightness can what shines show itself, that is, radiate. But brightness in its turn rests upon something open, something free, which it might illuminate here and there, now and then. Brightness plays in the open and strives there with darkness. Wherever a present being encounters another present being or even only lingers near it—but also where, as with Hegel, one being mirrors itself in another speculatively—there openness already rules, the free region is in play. Only this openness grants to the movement of speculative thinking the passage through what it thinks.

We call this openness that grants a possible letting appear and show "clearing." In the history of language the German word *Lichtung* is a translation derived from the French *clairière*. It is formed in accordance with the older words *Waldung* [foresting] and *Feldung* [fielding].

The forest clearing [*Lichtung*] is experienced in contrast to dense forest, called *Dickung* in our older language. The substantive *Lichtung* goes back to the verb *líchten*. The adjective *licht* is the same word as "light." To lighten something means to make it light, free and open, e.g., to make the forest free of trees at one place. The free space thus originating is the clearing. What is light in the sense of being free and open has nothing in common with the adjective "light" which means "bright," neither linguistically nor materially. This is to be observed for the difference between clearing and light.[2] Still, it is possible that a material relation between the two exists. Light can stream into the clearing, into its openness, and let brightness play with darkness in it. But light never first creates the clearing. Rather, light presupposes it. However, the clearing, the open region, is not only free for brightness and darkness but also for resonance and echo, for sound and the diminishing of sound. The clearing is the open region for everything that becomes present and absent.

It is necessary for thinking to become explicitly aware of the matter here called clearing. We are not extracting mere notions from mere words, e.g., *Lichtung,* as it might easily appear on the surface. Rather, we must observe the unique matter that is named with the name "clearing" in accordance with the matter. What the word designates in the connection we are now thinking, free openness, is a "primal phenomenon." [*Urphänomen*], to use a word of Goethe's. We would have to say a "primal matter" [*Ursache*]. Goethe notes (*Maxims and Reflections,* no. 993): "Look for nothing behind phenomena: they themselves are what is to be learned." This means the phenomenon itself, in the present case the clearing, sets us the task of learning from it while questioning it, that is, of letting it say something to us.

Accordingly, we may suggest that the day will come when we will not shun the question whether the clearing, free openness, may not be that within which alone pure space and ecstatic time and everything present and absent in them have the place that gathers and protects everything.

In the same way as speculative dialectical thinking, originary intuition and its evidence remain dependent upon openness that already holds sway, the clearing. What is evident is what can be immediately intuited. *Evidentia* is the word that Cicero uses to translate the Greek *enargeia,* that is, to transform it into the Roman. *Enargeia,* which has the same root as *argentum* (silver), means that which in itself and of itself radiates and brings itself to light. In the Greek language, one is not speaking about the action of seeing, about *vidēre,* but about that which gleams and radiates. But it can radiate only if openness has already been granted. The beam of light does not first create the clearing, openness, it only traverses it. It is only such openness that grants to giving and receiving and to any evidence at all the free space in which they can remain and must move.

All philosophical thinking that explicitly or inexplicitly follows the call "to the matter itself" is in its movement and with its method already admitted to the free space of the clearing. But philosophy knows nothing of the clearing. Philosophy does speak about the light of reason, but does not heed the clearing of Being. The *lumen naturale,* the light of reason, throws light only on the open. It does concern the clearing, but so little does it form it that it needs it in order to be able to illuminate what is present in the clearing. This is true not only of philosophy's *method,* but also and primarily of its *matter,* that is, of the presence of what is present. To what extent the *subiectum,* the *hypokeimenon,* that which already lies present, thus what is present in its presence is constantly thought also in subjectivity, cannot be shown here in detail. (Refer to Heidegger, *Nietzsche,* vol. 2 [1961], pages 429ff.)[3]

We are concerned now with something else. Whether or not what is present is experienced, comprehended, or presented, presence as lingering in the open always remains dependent upon the prevalent clearing. What is absent, too, cannot be as such unless it presences in the *free space of the clearing.*

All metaphysics, including its opponent, positivism, speaks the language of Plato. The basic word of its thinking, that is, of its presentation of the Being of beings, is *eidos*, idea: the outward appearance in which beings as such show themselves. Outward appearance, however, is a manner of presence. No outward appearance without light—Plato already knew this. But there is no light and no brightness without the clearing. Even darkness needs it. How else could we happen into darkness and wander through it? Still, the clearing as such as it prevails through Being, through presence, remains unthought in philosophy, although it is spoken about in philosophy's beginning. Where does this occur and with which names? Answer:

In Parmenides' thoughtful poem which, as far as we know, was the first to reflect explicitly upon the Being of beings, which still today, although unheard, speaks in the sciences into which philosophy dissolves. Parmenides listens to the claim:

. . . χρεὼ δέ σε πάντα πυθέσθαι
ἠμὲν Ἀληθείης εὐκυκλέος ἀτρεμὲς ἦτορ
ἠδὲ βροτῶν δόξας, ταῖς οὐκ ἔνι πίστις ἀληθής.
Fragment I, 28ff.

. . . but you should learn all:
the untrembling heart of unconcealment, well-rounded,
and also the opinions of mortals
who lack the ability to trust what is unconcealed.

Alētheia, unconcealment, is named here. It is called well-rounded because it is turned in the pure sphere of the circle in which beginning and end are everywhere the same. In this turning there is no possibility of twisting, distortion, and closure. The meditative man is to experience the untrembling heart of unconcealment. What does the phrase about the untrembling heart of unconcealment mean? It means unconcealment itself in what is most its own, means the place of stillness that gathers in itself what first grants unconcealment. That is the clearing of what is open. We ask: openness for what? We have already reflected upon the fact that the path of thinking, speculative and intuitive, needs the traversable clearing. But in that clearing rests possible radiance, that is, the possible presencing of presence itself.

What prior to everything else first grants unconcealment is the path on which thinking pursues one thing and perceives it: *hopōs estin . . . einai*: that presencing presences. The clearing grants first of all the possibility of the path to presence, and grants the possible presencing of that presence itself. We must think *alētheia,* unconcealment, as the clearing that first grants Being and thinking and their presencing to and for each other. The quiet heart of the clearing is the place of stillness from which alone the possibility of the belonging together of Being and thinking, that is, presence and apprehending, can arise at all.

The possible claim to a binding character or commitment of thinking is grounded in this bond. Without the preceding experience of *alētheia* as the clearing, all talk about committed and non-committed thinking remains without foundation. Whence does Plato's determination of presence as *idea* have its binding character? With regard to what is Aristotle's interpretation of presencing as *energeia* binding?

Strangely enough, we cannot even ask these questions, always neglected in philosophy, as long as we have not experienced what Parmenides had to experience: *alētheia*, unconcealment. The path to it is distinguished from the lane along which the opinion of mortals wanders. *Alētheia* is nothing mortal, just as little as death itself.

It is not for the sake of etymology that I stubbornly translate the name *alētheia* as unconcealment, but for the sake of the matter that must be considered when we think adequately that which is called Being and thinking. Unconcealment is, so to speak, the element in which Being and thinking and their belonging together exist. *Alētheia* is named at the beginning of philosophy, but afterward it is not explicitly thought as such by philosophy. For since Aristotle it has become the task or philosophy as metaphysics to think beings as such ontotheologically.

If this is so, we have no right to sit in judgment over philosophy, as though it left something unheeded, neglected it and was thus marred by some essential deficiency. The reference to what is unthought in philosophy is not a criticism of philosophy. If a criticism is necessary now, then it rather concerns the attempt, which is becoming more and more urgent ever since *Being and Time*, to ask about a possible task of thinking at the end of philosophy. For the question now arises, late enough: Why is *alētheia* not translated with the usual name, with the word "truth"? The answer must be:

Insofar as truth is understood in the traditional "natural" sense as the correspondence of knowledge with beings, demonstrated in beings; but also insofar as truth is interpreted as the certainty of the knowledge of Being; *alētheia*, unconcealment in the sense of the clearing, may not be equated with truth. Rather, *alētheia*, unconcealment thought as clearing, first grants the possibility of truth. For truth itself, like Being and thinking, can be what it is only in the element of the clearing. Evidence, certainty in every degree, every kind of verification of *veritas*, already moves *with* that *veritas* in the realm of the clearing that holds sway.

Alētheia, unconcealment thought as the clearing of presence, is not yet truth. Is *alētheia* then less than truth? Or is it more, because it first grants truth as *adaequatio* and *certitudo*, because there can be no presence and presenting outside the realm of the clearing?

This question we leave to thinking as a task. Thinking must consider whether it can even raise this question at all as long as it thinks philosophically, that is, in the strict sense of metaphysics, which questions what is present only with regard to its presence.

In any case, one thing becomes clear: to raise the question of *alētheia*, of unconcealment as such, is not the same as raising the question of truth. For this reason, it was immaterial and therefore misleading to call *alētheia*, in the sense of clearing, "truth."[4] The talk about the "truth of Being" has a justified meaning in Hegel's *Science of Logic,* because here truth means the certainty of absolute knowledge. And yet Hegel, as little as Husserl, as little as all metaphysics, does not ask about Being as Being, that is, does not raise the question as to how there can be presence as such. There is presence only when clearing holds sway. Clearing is named with *alētheia*, unconcealment, but not thought as such.

The natural concept of truth does not mean unconcealment, not in the philosophy of the Greeks either. It is often and justifiably pointed out that the word *alēthes* is already used by Homer only in the *verba dicendi*, in statements, thus in the sense of correctness and reliability, not in the sense of unconcealment. But this reference means only that neither the poets nor everyday linguistic usage, nor even philosophy, see themselves confronted with the task of asking how truth, that is, the correctness of statements, is granted only in the element of the clearing of presence.

In the scope of this question, we must acknowledge the fact that *alētheia*, unconcealment in the sense of the clearing of presence, was originally experienced only as *orthotēs*, as the correctness of representations and statements. But then the assertion about the essential transformation of truth, that is, from unconcealment to correctness, is also untenable. Instead we must say: *alētheia*, as clearing of presence and presentation in thinking and saying, immediately comes under the perspective of *homoiōsis* and *adaequatio*, that is, the perspective of adequation in the sense of the correspondence of representing with what is present.

But this process inevitably provokes another question: How is it that *alētheia*, unconcealment, appears to man's natural experience and speech *only* as correctness and dependability? Is it because man's ecstatic sojourn in the openness of presencing is turned only toward what is present and the presentation of what is present? But what else does this mean than that presence as such, and together with it the clearing that grants it, remains unheeded? Only what *alētheia* as clearing grants is experienced and thought, not what it is as such.

This remains concealed. Does that happen by chance? Does it happen only as a consequence of the carelessness of human thinking? Or does it happen because self-concealing, concealment, *lēthē*, belongs to *a-lētheia*, not as a mere addition, not as shadow to light, but rather as the heart of *alētheia*? Moreover, does not a sheltering and preserving rule in this self-concealing of the clearing of presence, from which alone unconcealment can be granted, so that what is present can appear in its presence?

If this were so, then the clearing would not be the mere clearing of presence, but the clearing of presence concealing itself, the clearing of a self-concealing sheltering.

If this were so, then only with these questions would we reach the path to the task of thinking at the end of philosophy.

But is not all this unfounded mysticism or even bad mythology, in any case a ruinous irrationalism, the denial of *ratio*?

I ask in return: What does *ratio, nous, noein*, apprehending, mean? What do ground and principle and especially principle of all principles mean? Can this ever be sufficiently determined unless we experience *alētheia* in a Greek manner as unconcealment and then, above and beyond the Greek, think it as the clearing of self-concealing? As long as *ratio* and the rational still remain questionable in what is their own, talk about irrationalism is unfounded. The technological-scientific rationalization ruling the present age justifies itself every day more surprisingly by its immense results. But this says nothing about what first grants the possibility of the rational and the irrational. The effect proves the correctness of technological-scientific rationalization. But is the manifest character of what *is* exhausted by what is demonstrable? Does not the insistence on what is demonstrable block the way to what is?

Perhaps there is a thinking that is more sober-minded than the incessant frenzy of rationalization and the intoxicating quality of cybernetics. One might aver that it is precisely this intoxication that is extremely irrational.

Perhaps there is a thinking outside of the distinction of rational and irrational, more sober-minded still than scientific technology, more sober-minded and hence removed, without effect, yet having its own necessity. When we ask about the task of this thinking, then not only this thinking but also the question concerning it is first made questionable. In view of the whole philosophical tradition this means:

We all still need an education in thinking, and first of all, before that, knowledge of what being educated and uneducated in thinking means. In this respect Aristotle gives us a hint in Book IV of his *Metaphysics* (1006aff.): ἔστι γὰρ ἀπαιδευσία τὸ μὴ γιγνώσκειν τίνων δεῖ ζητεῖν ἀπόδειξιν καὶ τίνων οὐ δεῖ. "For it is uneducated not to have an eye for when it is necessary to look for a proof and when this is not necessary."

This sentence demands careful reflection. For it is not yet decided in what way that which needs no proof in order to become accessible to thinking is to be experienced. Is it dialectical mediation, or originarily giving intuition, or neither of the two? Only the peculiar quality of what demands of us above all else to be granted entry can decide about that. But how is this to make the decision possible for us when we have not yet granted it? In what circle are we moving here, indeed, inevitably?

Is it the *eukukleos Alētheiē,* well-rounded unconcealment itself, thought as the clearing?

Does the title for the task of thinking then read, instead of *Being and Time:* Clearing and Presence?

But where does the clearing come from and how is it given? What speaks in the "There is / It gives"?

The task of thinking would then be the surrender of previous thinking to the determination of the matter for thinking.

Notes

1. *Wissenschaft, scientia,* body of knowledge, not "science" in the present use of that word. For German Idealism, science is the name for philosophy.—Trans.

2. "Light" is also two adjectives in English, each having its own origin. "Light" in the sense of having little weight derives from the Sanskrit *laghu* and the Greek *elaphros, elachus* (slight, small); in the sense "bright, shining, luminous" it derives from the Indo-Germanic *leuk-* (white) and Sanskrit *ruc* (to shine). Yet already in Old English, though not yet in Old High German, the words take the same form; during the history of both languages they increasingly converge. The verb *lichten,* "to lighten," also has two senses: to illuminate and to alleviate. Heidegger emphasizes the less familiar second sense—to make less dense and heavy, for example, to lighten a ship by dispatching "lighters" to it to relieve it of cargo—see Whitman, "Crossing Brooklyn Ferry," lines 47–48 and 92.—Ed.

3. This material appears in English in Martin Heidegger, *The End of Philosophy,* trans. Joan Stambaugh (New York: Harper & Row, 1973), pp. 26ff.—Ed.

4. How the attempt to think a matter can for a time stray from what a decisive insight has already shown is demonstrated by a passage from *Being and Time,* 1927 (p. 219): "The translation [of the word *alētheia*] by means of the word 'truth,' and even the very theoretical-conceptual determinations of this expression [truth], cover up the meaning of what the Greeks established as basically 'self-evident' in the pre-philosophical understanding of their terminological employment of *alētheia.*"

6   The Conditions of the Question: What Is Philosophy?

Gilles Deleuze

Perhaps the question "What is philosophy?" can only be posed late in life, when old age has come, and with it the time to speak in concrete terms. It is a question one poses when one no longer has anything to ask for, but its consequences can be considerable. One was asking the question before, one never ceased asking it, but it was too artificial, too abstract; one expounded and dominated the question, more than being grabbed by it. There are cases in which old age bestows not an eternal youth, but on the contrary a sovereign freedom, a pure necessity where one enjoys a moment of grace between life and death, and where all the parts of the machine combine to dispatch into the future a trait that traverses the ages: Turner, Monet, Matisse. The elderly Turner acquired or conquered the right to lead painting down a deserted path from which there was no return, and that was no longer distinguishable from a final question. In the same way, in philosophy, Kant's *Critique of Judgment* is a work of old age, a wild work from which descendants will never cease to flow.

We cannot lay claim to such a status. The time has simply come for us to ask what philosophy is. And we have never ceased to do this in the past, and we already had the response, which has not varied: philosophy is the art of forming, inventing, and fabricating concepts. But it was not only necessary for the response to take note of the question; it also had to determine a time, an occasion, the circumstances, the landscapes and personae, the conditions and unknowns of the question. One had to be able to pose the question "between friends" as a confidence or a trust, or else, faced with an enemy, as a challenge, and at the same time one had to reach that moment, between dog and wolf, when one mistrusts even the friend.

This is because concepts need conceptual personae that contribute to their definition. "Friend" is one such persona, which is even said to attest to a Greek origin of philo-sophy: other civilizations had Wise Men, but the Greeks introduce these "friends," who are not simply more modest wise men. It was the Greeks who confirmed the death of the Wise Man and replaced him with the philosophers, the friends of wisdom, those who search for wisdom, but do not formally possess it. Yet few thinkers have asked themselves what "friend" means, even and especially the Greeks. Would "friend" designate a certain competent intimacy, a kind of material affinity [*goût matériel*] or potentiality, like that of the carpenter with the wood: the good carpenter knows the potential of the wood, he is the friend of the wood? The question is an important one, since the friend, as it appears in philosophy, no longer designates either an extrinsic person, an example, or an empirical circumstance, but rather a presence intrinsic to thought, a condition of possibility of thought itself—in short, a living category, a lived transcendental, a constitutive element of thought. And in fact, at the birth of philosophy, the Greeks made the friend submit to a power play [*coup de force*] that placed it in relation, no longer with another person, but with an Entity, an Objectivity, an Essence. This is what the oft-cited formula expresses, which must be translated, "I am the friend of Peter, of Paul, or even of the philosopher Plato, but even more so, I am the friend of the True, of Wisdom, or of the Concept." The philosopher knows a lot about concepts, and about the lack of concepts; he knows, in an instant, which are inviable, arbitrary, or inconsistent, and which, on the contrary, are well made and bear witness to a creation, even if it is a disturbing and dangerous one.

What does "friend" mean when it becomes a conceptual persona, or a condition for the exercise of thought? Or even "lover"; is it not rather the lover? And will not the friend reintroduce, within thought itself, a vital relation with the Other that one had believed excluded from pure thought? Or again, is it not a question of someone other than the friend or lover? For if the philosopher is the friend or lover of Wisdom, is it not because he lays a claim upon it, striving for it potentially rather than possessing it actually? Thus the friend would also be the claimant, and what he calls himself the friend of is the Thing on which the claim is made, but not the third party, who would become, on the contrary, a rival. Friendship would involve as much jealous distrust of the rival as it would amorous tension toward the object of desire. When friendship is turned toward essence, the two friends would be like the claimant and the rival (but who could distinguish them?). In this way, Greek philosophy would coincide with the formation of "cities": relations of rivalry were promoted between and within cities, opposing claimants in all domains, in love, in the games, the tribunals, the magistratures, politics—and even in thought, which would find its condition, not only in the friend, but in the claimant and the rival (the dialectic that Plato defined by *amphisbētēsis*).[1] A generalized athleticism. The friend, the lover, the claimant, and the rival are transcendental determinations which, for all that, do not lose their intense and animated existence, whether in a single persona or in several. And when, today, Maurice Blanchot, one of those rare thinkers to consider the meaning of the word "friend" in *philosophy*, takes up this question internal to the conditions of thought as such, does he not again introduce new conceptual personae into the heart of the most pure Thought, personae that are now hardly Greek, but come from elsewhere, bringing in their wake new living relations raised to the status of a priori figures: a certain fatigue, a certain distress between friends that converts friendship itself to the thought of the concept, as an infinite sharing and patience.[2] The list of conceptual personae is never closed, and for this reason plays an important role in the evolution or mutations of philosophy; their diversity must be understood without being reduced to the already complex unity of the philosopher.

The philosopher is the friend of the concept, he has the concept potentially. This means that philosophy is not a simple art of forming, inventing, or fabricating concepts, for concepts are not necessarily forms, discoveries, or products. Philosophy, more rigorously understood, is the discipline that consists of *creating concepts*. Would the friend then be the friend of his own creations? To create ever new concepts—this is the object of philosophy. It is because the concept must be created that it refers back to the philosopher as the one who has the concept potentially, or who has the potential and competence of the concept. One cannot object that creation is instead expressed through the sensible or through the arts, insofar as art brings spiritual entities into existence, and philosophical concepts are also "sensibilia." In fact, the sciences, arts, and philosophies are all equally creators, although it falls to philosophy alone to create concepts in the strict sense. Concepts do not wait for us ready-made, like celestial bodies. There is no heaven for concepts. They must be invented, fabricated, or rather created, and would be nothing without the signature of those who create them. Nietzsche specified the task of philosophy when he wrote, "Philosophers must no longer be content to accept the concepts that are given to them, so as merely to clean and polish them, *but must begin by fabricating and creating them, positing them and making them convincing to those who have recourse to them.* Hitherto they have generally trusted their concepts as if they were a miraculous gift from some sort of equally miraculous world,"[3] but this trust must be replaced by mistrust, and it is concepts that the philosopher must mistrust the most as long as he has not himself created them (Plato knew this well, though he taught the reverse . . .). What would be the worth of a philosopher of whom one could say: he did not create the concept? We at least see what philosophy is not: *it is neither contemplation, nor reflection, nor communication*, even if it can sometimes believe itself to be one or the other of these because of the capacity of every discipline to engender its own illusions, and to hide itself behind its own particular fog. It is not contemplation, for contemplations are things themselves, as viewed through the creation of their own concepts. It is not reflection, because no one needs philosophy in order to reflect on whatever one wants to reflect on: we believe that we are giving a great deal to philosophy by making it the art of reflection, but we take away everything from it, for mathematicians per se have never waited for philosophers in order to reflect on mathematics, nor artists, on painting or music; to say that they then become philosophers is a bad joke, as long as their reflection belongs to their respective creation. And philosophy finds no final refuge in communication, which works only with opinions, in order to create a "consensus" and not a concept.

Philosophy does not contemplate, it does not reflect, nor does it communicate, although it has to create the concepts of these actions or passions. Contemplation, reflection, and communication are not disciplines, but machines that constitute Universals in all disciplines. The Universals of contemplation, then of reflection, are like the two illusions that philosophy has already traversed in its dream of dominating the other disciplines (objective idealism and subjective idealism), and philosophy does not honor itself by now falling back upon the universals of communication that would give it an imaginary mastery of the marketplace and the media (intersubjective idealism). Every creation is singular, and the concept, as the properly philosophical creation, is always a singularity. The first principle of philosophy is that Universals explain nothing, but must themselves be explained. *Knowledge through pure concepts*—we can consider this definition of philosophy as decisive. But the Nietzschean verdict falls: you will know nothing by concepts if you have not first created them. . . . To philosophize is to create concepts, and great philosophers are thus very rare.

To know oneself—to learn to think—to act as if nothing were self-evident—to wonder, "to wonder why there is something . . . ," these determinations of philosophy and many others form interesting though, in the long run, tiresome attitudes, but they do not constitute a well-defined occupation, a true activity, even from a pedagogical point of view. To create concepts, at least, is to do something. The question concerning the use or utility of philosophy, or even its harmfulness, must be changed accordingly.

Many problems crowd in upon the hallucinating eyes of an old man who would see himself confronting all sorts of philosophical concepts and conceptual personae. First of all, these concepts are and remain signs: Aristotle's *substance*, Descartes's *cogito*, Leibniz's *monad*, Kant's *condition*, Schelling's *potency*, Bergson's *durée*. . . . But, also, certain concepts demand an extraordinary word, sometimes barbarous or shocking, that must designate them, while others are content with a very ordinary word in current usage, which is swelled with such distant harmonics that they risk being imperceptible to a nonphilosophical ear. Some concepts call forth archaisms, others neologisms, through almost mad etymological exercises: etymology as a properly philosophical athleticism. In each case, there must be a strange necessity for these words and their choice, like an element of style. The baptism of the concept solicits a properly philosophical taste that proceeds with violence or with insinuation, and that constitutes, within language, a language of philosophy—not only a vocabulary, but a syntax that rises to the sublime or a great beauty. Now, although they are dated, signed, and baptized, concepts have their own way of not dying, and yet are submitted to constraints of renewal, replacement, and mutation that give philosophy a history and also a restless geography, of which each moment and each place are conserved, but within time, and pass away, but outside of time. If concepts never cease changing, it will be asked what unity remains for the philosophies. Is it the same unity as that of the sciences or the arts, which do not proceed by concepts? Where do their respective histories lie? If philosophy is this continuous creation of concepts, we will obviously want to ask not only what a concept is as a philosophical Idea, but also what the other creative Ideas consist of, which are not concepts and which belong to the sciences and the arts, and that have their own history and their own becoming, and their own variable relations among themselves and philosophy. The exclusivity of the creation of concepts assures philosophy a function, but gives it no preeminence, no privilege, insofar as there are other ways of thinking and creating, other modes of ideation that do not have to pass through concepts—beginning, for example, with scientific thought. And we will always come back to the question of knowing of what use is this activity of creating concepts, given that it is differentiated from scientific or artistic activity. Why is it necessary to create concepts, and ever new concepts; under what necessity, for what use? Create them for what? To respond that the greatness of philosophy would lie precisely in having no use at all is a stupid coquetry. In any case, we have never had any problem concerning the death of metaphysics or the overcoming of philosophy: this is useless and tiresome drivel. People today speak of the bankruptcy of systems, whereas it is only the concept of system that has changed. If there is a place and a time to create concepts, the operation that is carried out there will always be called philosophy, or would not even be distinguished from it even if one gave it another name. Philosophy would willingly yield its place to any other discipline that could better fulfill the function of creating concepts, but as long as that function subsists, it will still be called philosophy, always philosophy.

We know, however, that the friend or the lover, as claimants, are not without rivals. If philosophy has a Greek origin as we have so often been told, it is because the city, unlike empires or states, invents the *Agon* as the rule of a society of "friends," the community of free men as rivals (citizens). This is the constant situation that Plato describes: if each citizen lays claim to something, he necessarily encounters rivals, so that it is necessary to be able to judge the well-foundedness of the claims. The carpenter claims the wood, but clashes with the forester, the lumberjack, and the joiner, who say, "*I* am the friend of the wood!" If it is a question of taking care of humans, there are many claimants who present themselves as the friend of humans—the peasant who nourishes them, the weaver who clothes them, the doctor who nurses them, the warrior who protects them. If in all these cases the selection is made, after all, from within a somewhat limited circle, it is no longer so in the case of politics, where, in the Athenian democracy as Plato sees it, anyone can claim anything. Hence the necessity for Plato to sort out these claims, to create instances according to which the well-foundedness of the claims can be judged: these are the Ideas as philosophical concepts. But even here, will we not encounter all sorts of claimants who say, "*I* am the true philosopher! I am the friend of Wisdom or of the Well-Founded"? The rivalry culminates with that of the philosopher and the sophist, who fight over the remains of the ancient sage. But how is one to distinguish the false friend from the true, and the concept from the simulacrum? The simulator and the friend: it is an entire Platonic theater that makes the conceptual personae proliferate by endowing them with the potential of the comic and the tragic.

Closer to us, philosophy has met with many new rivals. These were first of all the human sciences, and especially sociology, which wanted to replace it. But as philosophy had increasingly misunderstood its vocation of creating concepts, in order to take refuge in universals, it no longer knew very well what was at stake. Was it a matter of renouncing every creation of the concept in favor of a strict human science? Or, on the contrary, was it a matter of transforming the nature of concepts by making them either into collective representations, or into the conceptions of the world created by peoples, their vital, historical, and spiritual forces? Then it was the turn of epistemology, linguistics, or even psychoanalysis, and logical analysis. From test to test, philosophy confronted increasingly insolent and calamitous rivals, which Plato himself would not have imagined in his most comic moments. Finally, the deepest disgrace was reached when computer science, advertising, marketing, and design appropriated the word "concept" itself, and said, "This is our business, we are the *creative* ones, we are the '*conceptors*'! We are the friends of the concept, we put them into our computers." Information and creativity, concept and enterprise: already an abundant bibliography. . . . The general movement that replaced *Critique* by commercial promotion has not left philosophy unaffected. The simulacrum, the simulation of a package of noodles, has become the true concept, and the person who packages the product, merchandise, or work of art has become the philosopher, the conceptual persona, or the artist. But how could philosophy, an old person, line up with smart young executives in a race for the universals of communication in order to determine a marketable form of the concept, *Merz*? The more philosophy clashes with impudent and silly rivals, the more it encounters them in its own heart, the more it feels itself driven to fulfill its task of creating concepts, which are meteorites [*aérolithes*] rather than merchandise. It has mad smiles that wipe away its tears. The question of philosophy is thus the singular point where the concept and creation are linked together.

Philosophers are not sufficiently concerned with the nature of the concept as a philosophical reality. They have preferred to consider it as a given representation or piece of knowledge, which would be explained by the faculties capable of forming it (abstraction, or generalization) or using it (judgement). But the concept is not given, it is created, it is to be created; and it is not formed, it posits itself in itself, a self-positing. Each activity implies the other, since what is truly created, from the living being to the work of art, by that very fact enjoys a self-positing of itself, or a self-poetic character by which one recognizes it. The more the concept is created, the more it posits itself. What is dependent upon a free creative activity is also that which posits itself in itself, independently and necessarily: the most subjective will be the most objective. It is the post-Kantians, notably Schelling and Hegel, who paid the most attention, in this sense, to the concept as a philosophical reality. Hegel powerfully defined the concept by the Figures of its creation and the Moments of its self-positing: the Figures constitute the side under which the concept is created by and within consciousness, through the succession of minds, while the Moments make up the other side according to which the concept posits itself and brings together minds in the absolute of the Ego. Hegel thereby showed that the concept has nothing to do with a general or abstract idea that would not depend on philosophy itself. But he did so at the price of an indeterminate extension of philosophy that hardly allowed the independent movement of the sciences and arts to subsist, because it reconstituted universals with its own moments and no longer treated the personae of its own creation as anything but figuring phantoms. The post-Kantians circled around a universal *encyclopedia* of the concept that referred the creation of concepts to a pure subjectivity, instead of giving itself a more modest task, a *pedagogy* of the concept, that should analyze the conditions of creation as factors of moments that remain singular. If the three ages of the concept are the encyclopedia, pedagogy, and the professional commercial formation, only the second can prevent us from falling from the summits of the first into the absolute disaster of the third, an absolute disaster for thought, no matter what, of course, the social benefits from the point of view of universal capitalism.

Notes

1. Deleuze contrasts Plato's use of *amphisbētēsis* with Aristotle's use of *antiphasis* in *Différence et Répétition* (Paris, 1968), pp. 82–89.—Trans.

2. See Maurice Blanchot, *L'Amitié* (Paris, 1971).—Trans.

3. We have translated this quotation directly from the French. For an English translation from the German, see Friedrich Nietzsche, *The Will to Power*, trans. Walter Kaufmann and R. J. Hollingdale (New York, 1967), pp. 220–221.—Trans.

II   Architecture of Intersubjectivity

7 Fifth Meditation: Uncovering of the Sphere of Transcendental Being as Monadological Intersubjectivity

Edmund Husserl

§ 42. *Exposition of the problem of experiencing someone else, in rejoinder to the objection that phenomenology entails solipsism.*

As the point of departure for our new meditations, let us take what may seem to be a grave objection. The objection concerns nothing less than the claim of transcendental phenomenology to be itself transcendental *philosophy* and therefore its claim that, in the form of a constitutional problematic and theory moving within the limits of the transcendentally reduced ego, it can solve the transcendental problems pertaining to the *Objective world*. When I, the meditating I, reduce myself to my absolute transcendental ego by phenomenological epoché do I not become *solus ipse*; and do I not remain that, as long as I carry on a consistent self-explication under the name phenomenology? Should not a phenomenology that proposed to solve the problems of Objective being, and to present itself actually as philosophy, be branded therefore as transcendental solipsism?

Let us consider the matter more closely. Transcendental reduction restricts me to the stream of my pure conscious processes and the unities constituted by their actualities and potentialities. And indeed it seems[1] obvious that such unities are inseparable from my ego and therefore belong to his concreteness itself.

But what about other egos, who surely are not a mere intending and intended *in me*, merely synthetic unities of possible verification *in me*, but, according to their sense, precisely *others*? Have we not therefore done transcendental realism an injustice? The doctrine may lack a phenomenological foundation; but essentially it is right in the end, since it looks for a path from the immanency of the ego to the transcendency of the Other. Can we, as phenomenologists, do anything but agree with this and say: "The Nature and the whole world that are constituted 'immanently' in the ego are only my 'ideas' and have behind them the world that exists in itself. The way to this world must still be sought"? Accordingly can we avoid saying likewise: "The very question of the possibility of actually transcendent knowledge—above all, that of the possibility of my going outside my ego and reaching other egos (who, after all, as others, are not actually in me but only consciously intended in me)—this question cannot be asked purely phenomenologically"? Is it not *self-understood* from the very beginning that my field of transcendental knowledge does not reach beyond my sphere of transcendental experience and what is synthetically comprised therein? Is it not self-understood that all of that is included without residue in my own transcendental ego?

But perhaps there is some mistake in thoughts like these. Before one decides in favor of them and the "self-understood" propositions they exploit, and then perchance embarks on dialectical argumentations and self-styled "metaphysical" hypotheses (whose supposed possibility may turn out to be complete absurdity), it might indeed be more fitting to undertake the *task of phenomenological explication* indicated in this connexion by the "alter ego" and carry it through in concrete work. We must, after all, obtain for ourselves insight into the explicit and implicit intentionality wherein the alter ego becomes evinced and verified in the realm of our transcendental ego; we must discover in what intentionalities, syntheses, motivations, the sense "other ego" becomes fashioned in me[2] and, under the title, harmonious experience of someone else, becomes verified as existing and even as itself there in its own manner. These experiences and their works are facts belonging to my[3] phenomenological sphere. How else than by examining them can I explicate the sense, existing others, in all its aspects?

§ 43. The noematic-ontic mode of givenness of the Other, as transcendental clue for the constitutional theory of the experience of someone else.

First of all, my "transcendental clue" is the experienced Other, given to me in straightforward consciousness and as I immerse myself in examining the noematic-ontic content belonging to him (purely as correlate of my cogito, the particular structure of which is yet to be uncovered). By its remarkableness and multiplicity, that content already indicates the many-sidedness and difficulty of the phenomenological task. For example: In changeable harmonious multiplicities of experience I experience others as actually existing and, on the one hand, as world Objects—not as mere physical things belonging to Nature, though indeed as such things in respect of one side of them. They are in fact experienced also as *governing psychically* in their respective natural organisms.[4] Thus peculiarly involved with animate organisms, as "psychophysical" Objects, they are *"in" the world*. On the other hand, I experience them at the same time as *subjects for this world*, as experiencing it (this same world that I experience) and, in so doing, experiencing me too, even as I experience the world and others in it. Continuing along this line, I can explicate a variety of other moments noematically.

In any case then, within myself, within the limits of my transcendentally reduced pure conscious life, I *experience* the world, (including others)—and, according to its experiential sense, *not* as (so to speak) my *private* synthetic formation but as other than mine alone [*mir fremde*], as an *intersubjective* world, actually there for everyone, accessible in respect of its Objects to everyone. And yet each has his experiences, his appearances and appearance-unities, his world-phenomenon; whereas the experienced world exists in itself, over against all experiencing subjects and their world-phenomena.

What is the explanation of this? Imperturbably I must hold fast to the insight that every sense that any existent whatever has or can have for me—in respect of its "what" and its "it exists and actually is"—is a sense *in* and *arising from* my intentional life, becoming clarified and uncovered for me in consequence of my life's constitutive syntheses, in systems of harmonious verification. Therefore, in order to provide the basis for answering all imaginable questions that can have any sense <here>—nay, in order that, step by step, these questions themselves may be propounded and solved—it is necessary to begin with a systematic explication of the overt and implicit intentionality in which the being of others for me becomes "made" and explicated in respect of its rightful content—that is, its fulfilment-content.

Thus the problem is stated at first as a special one, namely that of the "thereness-for-me" of others, and accordingly as the theme of a *transcendental theory of experiencing someone else*, a transcendental theory of so-called "empathy." But it soon becomes evident that the range of such a theory is much greater than at first it seems, that it contributes to the founding of a *transcendental theory of the Objective world* and, indeed, to the founding of such a theory in every respect, notably as regards Objective Nature. The existence-sense [*Seinssinn*] of the world and of Nature in particular, as Objective Nature, includes after all, as we have already mentioned, thereness-for-everyone. This is always cointended wherever we speak of Objective actuality. In addition, Objects with "spiritual" predicates belong to the experienced world. These Objects, in respect of their origin and sense, refer us to subjects, usually other subjects, and their actively constituting intentionality. Thus it is in the case of all cultural Objects (books, tools, works of any kind, and so forth), which moreover carry with them at the same time the experiential sense of thereness-for-everyone (that is, everyone belonging to the corresponding cultural community, such as the European or perhaps, more narrowly, the French cultural community, and so forth).

§ 44. *Reduction of transcendental experience to the sphere of ownness.*

If the transcendental constitution of other subjects and accordingly the transcendental sense, "other subjects," are in question, and consequently a universal sense-stratum[5] that emanates from others[6] and is indispensible to the possibility of an Objective world for me is also in question, then the sense, "other subjects," that is in question here cannot as yet be the sense: "Objective subjects, subjects existing in the world." As regards method, a prime requirement for proceeding correctly here is that first of all we carry out, *inside the universal transcendental sphere, a peculiar kind of epoché* with respect to our theme. For the present we exclude from the thematic field everything now in question: we *disregard all constitutional effects of intentionality relating immediately or mediately to other subjectivity* and delimit first of all the total nexus of that actual and potential intentionality in which the ego constitutes *within himself a peculiar ownness.*[7]

This *reduction to my transcendental sphere of peculiar ownness* or to my transcendental concrete I-myself, by abstraction from everything that transcendental constitution gives me as Other, has an unusual sense. In the natural, the world-accepting attitude, I find differentiated and contrasted: myself and others. If I "abstract" (in the usual sense) from others, *I "alone"* remain. But such abstraction is not radical; such aloneness in no respect alters the natural world-sense, "experienceable by everyone," which attaches to the naturally understood Ego and would not be lost, even if a universal plague had left only me. Taken however in the transcendental attitude and at the same time with the constitutional abstraction that we have just characterized, my (the meditator's) ego in his transcendental ownness is not the usual I, this man, reduced to a mere correlate phenomenon and having his status within the total world-phenomenon. What concerns us is, on the contrary, *an essential structure, which is part of the all-embracing constitution* in which the transcendental ego, as constituting an Objective world, lives his life.[8]

What is specifically peculiar to me as ego, my concrete being as a monad, purely in myself and for myself *with an exclusive ownness*, includes <my> every intentionality and therefore, in particular, the intentionality directed to what is other[9]; but, for reasons of method, the synthetic effect of such intentionality (the actuality for me of what is other) shall at first remain excluded from the theme. In this pre-eminent intentionality there becomes constituted for me the new existence-sense that goes beyond my monadic very-ownness; there becomes constituted an ego, not as "I myself," but as mirrored in my own Ego, in my monad. The second ego, however, is not simply there and[10] strictly presented; rather is he constituted as "alter ego"—the ego indicated as one moment by this expression being I myself in my ownness. The "Other," according to his own constituted sense, points to me myself; the other is a "mirroring" of my own self and yet not a mirroring proper, an analogue of my own self and yet again not an analogue in the usual sense. Accordingly if, as a first step, the ego in his peculiar ownness has been delimited, has been surveyed and articulated in respect of his constituents—not only in the way of life-processes but also in the way of accepted unities concretely inseparable from him—, the question must then be asked: *How* can my ego, within his peculiar ownness, constitute under the name, "experience of something other," precisely something *other*—something, that is, with a sense that excludes the constituted from the concrete make-up of the sense-constituting I-myself, as somehow the latter's analogue? In the first place the question concerns no matter what alter egos; then however it concerns everything that acquires sense-determinations from them—in short, an Objective world in the proper and full signification of the phrase.

These problems will become more understandable if we proceed to characterize the ego's sphere of owness or, correlatively, to carry out explicitly the abstractive epoché that yields it. Thematic exclusion of the constitutional effects produced by experience of something other, together with the effects of all the further modes of consciousness relating to something other, does not signify merely phenomenological epoché with respect to naïve acceptance of the being of the other, as in the case of everything Objective existing for us in straightforward consciousness. After all, the transcendental attitude is and remains presupposed, the attitude according to which everything previously existing for us in straightforward consciousness is taken exclusively as "phenomenon," as a sense meant and undergoing verification, purely in the manner in which, as correlate of uncoverable constitutive systems, it has gained and is gaining existential sense. We are now preparing for just this uncovering and sense-clarification by the novel epoché, more particularly in the following manner.

As Ego in the transcendental attitude I attempt first of all to delimit, within my horizon of transcendental experience, *what is peculiarly my own*. First I say that it is *non-alien [Nicht-Fremdes]*. I begin by freeing that horizon abstractively from everything that is at all alien. A property of the transcendental phenomenon "world" is that of being given in harmonious straightforward experience; accordingly it is necessary to survey this world and pay attention to how something alien makes its appearance as jointly determining the sense of the world and, so far as it does so, to exclude it abstractively. Thus we abstract first of all from what gives men and brutes their specific sense as, so to speak, Ego-like living beings and consequently from all determinations of the phenomenal world that refer by their sense to "others" as Ego-subjects and, accordingly, presuppose these. For example, all cultural predicates. We can say also that we abstract from everything "*other-spiritual*," as that which makes possible, in the "alien" or "other" that is in question here, its specific sense. Furthermore the *characteristic of belonging to the surrounding world*, not merely for others who are also given at the particular time in actual experience, but also *for everyone*, the characteristic of being there for and accessible to everyone, of being capable of mattering or not mattering to each in his living and striving—a characteristic of all Objects belonging to the phenomenal world and the characteristic wherein their otherness consists—should not be overlooked, but rather excluded abstractively.

In this connexion we note something important. When we thus abstract, *we retain a unitarily coherent stratum of the phenomenon world*, a stratum of the phenomenon that is the correlate of continuously harmonious, continuing world-experience. *Despite* our abstraction, we can *go on continuously in our experiencing intuition*, while remaining exclusively in the aforesaid stratum. This unitary stratum, furthermore, is distinguished by being essentially the *founding* stratum—that is to say: I obviously cannot have the "alien" or "other" as experience, and therefore cannot have the sense "Objective world" as an experiential sense, without having this stratum in actual experience; whereas the reverse is not the case.

Let us observe more closely the result of our abstraction and, accordingly, what it leaves us. From the phenomenon world, from the world appearing with an Objective sense, a substratum becomes separated, as the "*Nature*" *included in my ownness*, a Nature that must always be carefully distinguished from Nature, pure and simple—that is to say: from the Nature that becomes the theme of the natural scientist. *This* Nature, to be sure, is likewise a result of abstraction, namely abstraction from everything psychic and from those predicates of the Objective world that have arisen from persons. But what is acquired by this abstraction on the part of the natural scientist is a stratum that belongs to the Objective world itself (viewed in the transcendental attitude, a stratum that belongs to the *objective sense*: "Objective world") and is therefore itself Objective—just as, on the other hand, what is abstracted *from* is Objective (the Objective psychic, Objective cultural predicates, and so forth). But in the case of *our* abstraction the sense "Objective," which belongs to everything worldly—as constituted intersubjectively, as experienceable by everyone, and so forth— *vanishes completely*. Thus there is included in my ownness, as purified from every sense pertaining to other subjectivity, *a sense*, "*mere Nature*," that has lost precisely that "by every- one" and therefore must not by any means be taken for an abstract stratum of the world or of the world's sense. Among the bodies belonging to this "Nature" and included in my peculiar ownness, I then find my *animate organism* as *uniquely* singled out—namely as the only one of them that is not just a body but precisely an animate organism: the sole Object within my abstract world-stratum to which, in accordance with experience, I ascribe *fields of sensation* (belonging to it, however, in different manners—a field of tactual sensations, a field of warmth and coldness, and so forth) the only Object "in" which I "*rule and govern*" *immediately*, governing particularly in each of its "organs." Touching kinesthetically, I per- ceive "with" my hands; seeing kinesthetically, I perceive also "with" my eyes; and so forth; moreover I can perceive thus at any time. Meanwhile the *kinesthesias* pertaining to the organs flow in the mode "I am doing," and are subject to my "I can"; furthermore, by calling these kinesthesias into play, I can push, thrust, and so forth, and can thereby "*act*" *somati- cally*—immediately, and then mediately. As *perceptively* active, *I experience* (or can experience) *all of Nature, including my own animate organism*, which therefore in the process is reflexively related to itself. That becomes possible because I "can" perceive one hand "by means of" the other, an eye by means of a hand, and so forth—a procedure in which *the functioning organ must become an Object and the Object a functioning organ*. And it is the same in the case of my generally possible original *dealing* with Nature and with my animate organism itself, by means of this organism—which therefore is reflexively related to itself *also in practice*.

Bringing to light my animate organism, reduced to what is included in my ownness, is itself part of bringing to light the *ownness-essence* of the Objective phenomenon: "*I, as this man.*" If I reduce *other* men to what is included in my ownness, I get *bodies* included therein; if I reduce *myself* as a man, I get "*my animate organism*" and "*my psyche*," or myself as a *psychophysical unity—in the latter, my personal Ego*, who operates in this animate organism and, "by means of" it, in the "*external world*," who is affected by this world, and who thus in all respects, by virtue of the continual experience of such unique modes of Ego- and life- relatedness, is constituted as psychophysically united with the animate corporeal organism. If *ownness-puriification of the external world, the animate organism, and the psychological whole*, has been effected, I have lost my natural sense as Ego, since every sense-relation to a pos- sible Us or We remains excluded, and have lost likewise all my worldliness, in the natural sense. But, in my spiritual ownness, I am nevertheless the identical Ego-pole of my manifold "pure" subjective processes, those of my passive and active intentionality, and the pole of all the habitualities instituted or to be instituted by those processes.

Accordingly this peculiar abstractive sense-exclusion of what is alien leaves us a *kind of* "*world*" still, a Nature reduced to what is included in our ownness and, as having its place in this Nature thanks to the bodily organism, the psychophysical Ego, with "body and soul" and personal Ego—utterly *unique* members of this reduced "world." Manifestly predicates that get significance from *this* Ego also occur in the reduced world—for example: "value" predicates and predicates of "works" as such. None of this is worldly in the natural sense (therefore all the quotation-marks); it is all exclusively what is mine in my world-experience, pervading my world-experience through and through and likewise cohering unitarily in my intuition. Accordingly the members we distinguish in this, my peculiarly own world-phenomenon, are *concretely* united, as is further shown by the fact that the *spatiotemporal form*—as reduced, however, to the form included in my ownness—also goes into this reduced world-phenomenon. Hence the reduced "Objects"—the "physical things," the "psychophysical Ego"—are likewise *outside one another*.

But here something remarkable strikes us: a sequence of evidences that yet, *in* their sequence, seem paradoxical. The psychic life of my Ego (this "psychophysical" Ego), including my whole world-experiencing life and therefore including my actual and possible experience *of* what is other, is wholly unaffected by screening off what is other. Consequently there belongs within my psychic being the whole constitution of the world existing for me and, in further consequence, the differentiation of that constitution into the systems that constitute what is included in my peculiar ownness and the systems that constitute what is other. I, the reduced "human Ego" ("psychophysical" Ego), am constituted, accordingly, as a member of the "world" with a multiplicity of "objects outside me." But I myself constitute all this in my "psyche" and bear it intentionally within me. If perchance it could be shown that everything constituted as part of my peculiar ownness, including then the reduced "world," belonged to the concrete essence of the constituting subject as an inseparable internal determination, then, in the Ego's self-explication, his peculiarly own world would be found as "inside" and, on the other hand, when running through that world straightforwardly, the Ego would find himself as a member among its "externalities" and would distinguish between himself and "the external world."

§ 45. *The transcendental ego, and self-apperception as a psychophysical man reduced to what is included in my ownness.*

These last meditations, like all the others, have been carried on by us in the attitude that effects transcendental reduction—carried on, that is to say, by me (the meditator) as transcendental ego. We now ask how I, the human Ego reduced to what is purely my own and, as thus reduced, included in the similarly reduced world-phenomenon and, on the other hand, I as transcendental ego are related to one another. The transcendental ego emerged by virtue of my "parenthesizing" of the entire Objective world and all other (including all ideal) Objectivities. In consequence of this parenthesizing, I have become aware of myself as the transcendental ego, who constitutes in his constitutive life every-thing that is ever Objective for me—the ego of all constitutions, who exists in his actual and potential life-processes and Ego-habitualities and who constitutes in them not only everything Objective but also himself as identical ego. We can say now: In that I, as this ego, have constituted and am continually further constituting as a phenomenon[11] (as a correlate) the world that exists for me, I have carried out a *mundanizing self-apperception*—under the title "Ego in the usual sense"—in corresponding constitutive syntheses and am maintaining a continuing acceptance and further development of it. By virtue of this mundanization everything included in the ownness belonging to me transcendentally (as this ultimate ego) enters, as something *psychic*, into "my psyche." I find the mundanizing apperception; and now, from the psyche as phenomenon and part of the phenomenon man, I can go back to the all-inclusive *absolute* ego, the *transcendental* ego. Therefore if I, as this ego, reduce my phenomenon, "the Objective world," to what is included in my peculiar ownness and take in addition whatever else I find as peculiarly my *own* (which can no longer contain anything "alien" or "other," after that reduction), then all this ownness of my ego is to be found again, in the reduced world-phenomenon, as the ownness of "*my psyche.*" Here, however, as a component pertaining to my world-apperception, it is something *transcendentally secondary*. Restricting ourselves to the ultimate transcendental ego and the universe of what is constituted in him, we can say that a division of his whole transcendental field of experience belongs to him immediately, namely the division into the sphere of his ownness—with the coherent stratum consisting in his experience of a world reduced to what is included in his ownness[12] (an experience in which everything "other" is "screened off")—and the sphere of what is "other." Yet every *consciousness of* what is other, every mode of appearance *of* it, belongs in the former sphere. Whatever the transcendental ego constitutes in that *first* stratum, whatever he constitutes as non-other, as his "peculiarly own"—that indeed belongs to him as *a component of his own concrete essence* (as we shall show); it is inseparable from his concrete being. Within and by means of this ownness the transcendental ego constitutes, however, the "Objective" world, as a universe of being that is other than himself—and constitutes, at the first level, the other in the mode: alter ego.

§ 46. *Ownness as the sphere of the actualities and potentialities of the stream of subjective processes.*

Up to now we have characterized the fundamental concept of "my own" only indirectly: as *non-alien* or *non-other*—a characterization that is based on, and thus presupposes, the concept of another ego. In order to clarify the sense of this "my own" it is important, however, to bring out its positive characteristic, or the positive characteristic of "the ego in his[13] ownness." This characteristic was merely indicated in the last sentences of the preceding section.

As our point of departure let us take something more general. If a concrete object stands out for us in experience as something particular, and our attentively grasping regard then becomes directed to it, it becomes appropriated in this simple grasping merely as "an undetermined object of empirical intuition." It becomes a determined object, and one undergoing further determination, in a continuation of the experience in the form of a determining experience, which at first unfolds only what is included in the object itself: a pure *explication*. In its articulated synthetic course, on the basis of the object given as self-identical in a continuous intuitive synthesis of identification, this pure explication unfolds, in a concatenation of particular intuitions the object's very own determinations, the "internal" determinations. These present themselves originaliter as determinations *in* which it, the Identical itself, is[14] what it is and, moreover, exists in itself, "in and of itself"— determinations wherein its identical being becomes explicated as the particulars making up its ownness: what it is, in particular. This own-essential content is only generally and horizonally anticipated beforehand; it then becomes constituted originaliter—with the sense: internal, own-essential feature (specifically, part or property)—by explication.

Let us apply this. When I am effecting transcendental reduction and reflecting on myself, the transcendental ego, I am given to myself *perceptually* as this ego—in a grasping perception. Furthermore I become aware that, although not grasped before this perception, I was "already given," already there for myself continually as an object of original intuition (as perceived in the broader sense). But I am given, in any case, with an open infinite horizon of still undiscovered *internal features of my own*. *My* own too is discovered by explication and gets its original sense by virtue thereof. It becomes uncovered originaliter when my experiencing-explicating regard is directed to myself, to my perceptually and even apodictically given "I am" and its abiding identity with itself[15] in the continuous unitary synthesis of original self-experience. Whatever is included in this identical being's own essence is characterized as its actual or possible explicatum, as a respect in which I merely unfold my own identical being as what it, as identical, is in particular: it in itself.

Now the following is to be noted here. Though I speak rightly of *self-perception*, and indeed as regards my concrete ego, that is not to say that, like explication of a perceptually given "visual thing," self-explication always goes on in particular *perceptions*, in the proper sense, and accordingly yields just perceptual explicata and no others. After all, when explicating the horizon of being that is included in my own essence, one of the first things I run into is my immanent temporality and, with it, my existence in the form of an open infiniteness, that of a stream of subjective processes, and in the form of all those "own-nesses" of mine that are somehow included in the stream—one of which is my explicating. Since it goes on in the living present, self-explication can find, strictly *perceptively*, only what is going on in the living present. In the most original manner conceivable it uncovers my own past by means of recollections. Therefore, though I am continually given to myself originaliter and can explicate progressively what is included in my own essence, this explication is *carried out largely in acts of consciousness that are not perceptions* of the own-essential moments it discovers. Thus alone can my stream of subjective processes, the stream in which I live as the identical Ego, become accessible to me: first of all, in respect of its actualities, and then in respect of the potentialities that manifestly are likewise moments of my own essence. All possibilities of the kind subsumed under the I "can" or "could have" set this or that series of subjective processes going (including in particular: I can look ahead or look back, I can penetrate and uncover the horizon of my temporal being)—all such possibilities manifestly belong to me as moments of my own essence.

In every case, however, explication is original if, precisely on the basis of original self-experience, it unfolds the experienced itself and confers upon the experienced that self-giveness which is, for it, the *most original conceivable*. The *apodictic evidence* of transcendental self-perception (the apodictic evidence of the "I am") extends into such explication, though with a previously stated *restriction*. In unqualifiedly apodictic evidence self-explication brings out only the all-embracing structural forms in which I exist as ego—that is to say: in which I exist with an essentially necessary all-inclusiveness and without which I could not exist. They include (among others) the mode of existence in the form of a certain all-embracing life of some sort or other, that of existence in the form of the continuous self-constitution of that life's own processes, as temporal within an all-embracing time, and so forth. In this *all-embracing apodictic Apriori*, with its undetermined universality and, on the other hand, its determinability, every explication of single egological data then participates—for example: as a certain, albeit imperfect, evidence contained in the recollection of my own past. The participation in apodicticity appears in the *formal law* (which is itself apodictic): So much illusion, so much being—which is only covered up and falsified thereby and which therefore can be asked about, sought, and (by following a predelineated way) found, even if only with approximation to its fully determined content. This fully determined content itself, with the sense of something firmly identifiable again and again, in respect of all its parts and moments, is an "idea," valid a priori.

§ 47. *The intentional object also belongs to the full monadic concretion of ownness. Immanent transcendence and primordial world.*

Manifestly (and this is of particular importance) the own-essentiality belonging to me as ego comprises more than merely the actualities and potentialities of the stream of subjective processes. Just as it comprises the constitutive systems, *it comprises the constituted unities*—but with a certain *restriction*. That is to say: Where, and *so far as, the constituted unity is inseparable from the original constitution itself*, with the inseparableness that characterizes an immediate[16] *concrete* oneness, not only the constitutive perceiving but also the perceived existent belongs to my concrete very-ownness.

That is not only the case with sensuous data, which, taken as mere data of sensation, become constituted as peculiarly my own: as "*immanent temporalities*" within the limits of my ego. It is also the case with all my *habitualities*, which are likewise peculiarly my own:

the habitualities that begin with institutive acts of my own and become constituted as abiding convictions in which *I myself* become abidingly convinced of such and such, and by virtue of which I, as polar Ego (Ego in the particular sense: mere Ego-pole), acquire determinations that are specifically Ego-determinations. But *"transcendent objects"* (for example: the objects of *"external"* sensuousness, unities belonging to multiplicites of sensuous modes of appearance) also belong here: if I, as ego, take into account just what is constituted *actually originaliter* as an appearing spatial object by my own sensuousness, my own apperceptions, *as itself concretely inseparable from them*. We see forthwith that the *entire reduced "world,"* which we previously obtained by excluding the sense-components pertaining to what is other or alien, belongs in this sphere and is rightly included in the positively defined concrete make-up of the ego: as something peculiarly his *own*. As soon as we exclude from consideration the intentional effects produced by "empathy," by our experience of others, we have a Nature (including an animate organism) that is constituted, to be sure, as a unity of spatial objects "transcending" the stream of subjective processes, yet constituted as merely a multiplicity of objects of possible experience—this experience being purely *my own* life, and what is experienced in this experience being nothing more than a synthetic unity inseparable from this life and its potentialities.

In this manner it becomes clear that *the ego, taken concretely*, has a *universe of what is peculiarly his own*, which can be uncovered by an original explication of his apodictic "ego sum"—an explication that is itself apodictic or at least predelineative of an apodictic form. *Within* this *"original sphere"* (the sphere of original self-explication) we find also a "transcendent world," which accrues on the basis of the intentional phenomenon, "Objective world," by reduction to what is peculiarly the ego's own (in the positive sense, which is now preferred). But, provided only that they are subjected to our reduction to what is included in the ego's ownness, all the corresponding illusions, phantasies, "pure" possibilities, and eidetic objectivities, which offer themselves as "transcendent," likewise belong in this domain—the domain of my peculiarly own essentiality, of what I am in myself, in my full concreteness or (as we may also say) what I am in myself as this monad.[17]

§ 48.   *The transcendency of the Objective world as belonging to a level higher than that of primordial transcendency.*

That my own essence can be at all contrasted for me with something else, or that I (who am I) can become aware of someone else (who is not I but someone other than I), presupposes that *not all my own modes of consciousness are modes of my self-consciousness*. Since actual being is constituted originally by harmoniousness of experience, my own self must contain, in contrast to self-experience and the system of its harmoniousness (the system, therefore, of self-explication into components of my ownness), yet other experiences united in harmonious systems. And now the *problem* is how we are to understand the fact that the ego has, and can always go on forming, in himself such intentionalities of a different kind, intentionalities with an existence-sense whereby *he wholly transcends his own being*. How can something actually existent for me—and, as that, not just somehow meant but undergoing harmonious verification in me—be anything else than, so to speak, a point of intersection belonging to my constitutive synthesis? As concretely inseparable from my synthesis, is it peculiarly my own? But even the possibility of a vaguest, emptiest intending of something alien is problematic, if it is true that, essentially, every such mode of consciousness involves its possibilities of an uncovering of what is intended, its possibilities of becoming converted into either fulfilling or disillusioning experiences of what is meant, and moreover (as regards the genesis of the consciousness), points back to such experiences of the same intended object or a similar one.

The fact of experience of something alien (something that is not I), is present as experience of an Objective world and others in it (non-Ego in the form: other Ego); and an important result of the ownness-reduction performed on these experiences was that it brought out a substratum belonging to them, an intentional substratum in which a reduced "world" shows itself, as an "immanent transcendency." In the order pertaining to constitution of a world *alien to my Ego*—a world "*external*" *to my own concrete Ego* (but not at all in the natural spatial sense)—that reduced world is the intrinsically first, the "*primordial*" *transcendency* (or "world"); and, regardless of its *ideality* as a synthetic unity belonging to an infinite system of my potentialities, it is *still a determining part of my own concrete being*, the being that belongs to me as concrete ego.

It must now be made understandable *how*, at the founded higher level, the sense-bestowal pertaining to transcendency proper, to constitutionally secondary *Objective transcendency*, comes about—and does so as an experience. Here it is not a matter of uncovering a genesis going on in time, but a matter of "*static analysis*." The Objective world is constantly there before me as already finished, a datum of my livingly continuous Objective experience and, even in respect of what is no longer experienced, something I go on accepting habitually. It is a matter of examining this experience itself and uncovering intentionally the manner in which it bestows sense, the manner in which it can occur as experience and become verified as evidence relating to an actual existent with an explicatable essence of *its* own, which is not *my* own essence and has no place as a constituent part thereof, though it nevertheless can acquire sense and verification only in my essence.

§ 49. *Predelineation of the course to be followed by intentional explication of experiencing what is other.*

Constitution of the existence-sense, "Objective world," on the basis of my primordial "world," involves a number of levels. As the *first* of these, there is to be distinguished the constitutional level pertaining to the "other ego" or to any "other egos" whatever—that is: to egos *excluded* from my own concrete being (from me as the "primordial ego"). In connexion with that and, indeed, motivated by it, there occurs a *universal super-addition of sense to my primordial world*, whereby the latter becomes the *appearance "of"* a determinate "Objective" world, as the identical world for everyone, myself included. Accordingly *the intrinsically first other* (the first "non-Ego") *is the other Ego*. And the other Ego makes constitutionally possible a new infinite domain of what is "other": an *Objective Nature* and a whole Objective world, to which all other Egos and I myself belong. This constitution, arising on the basis of the "*pure*" others (the other Egos who as yet have no worldly sense), is essentially such that the "others"-for-me do not remain isolated; on the contrary, an *Ego-community*, which includes me, becomes constituted (in my sphere of ownness, naturally) as a community of Egos existing with each other and for each other—*ultimately a community of monads*, which, moreover (in its communalized intentionality), constitutes the *one identical world. In this world* all Egos again present themselves, but *in an Objectivating apperception* with the sense "*men*" or "psychophysical men as worldly Objects."

By virtue of the mentioned communalization <of constitutive intentionality>, the transcendental intersubjectivity has an *intersubjective* sphere of ownness, in which it constitutes the Objective world; and thus, as the transcendencental "We," it is a subjectivity for this world and also for the world of men, which is the form in which it has made itself Objectively actual. If, however, intersubjective sphere of ownness and Objective world are to be distinguished here, nevertheless, when I as ego take my stand on the basis of the intersubjectivity constituted from sources within my own essence, I can recognize that the Objective world does not, in the proper sense, *transcend* that sphere or that sphere's own intersubjective essence, but rather inheres in it as an "immanent" transcendency. Stated more precisely: The Objective world as an *idea*—the ideal correlate of an intersubjective (intersubjectively communalized) experience, which ideally can be and is carried on as constantly harmonious—is essentially related to intersubjectivity (itself constituted as having the ideality of endless openness), whose component particular subjects are equipped with mutually corresponding and harmonious constitutive systems. Consequently *the constitution of the world essentially involves a "harmony" of the monads*: precisely this harmony among particular constitutions in the particular monads; and accordingly it involves also a harmonious generation that goes on in each particular monad. That is not meant, however, as a "metaphysical" hypothesizing of monadic harmony, any more than the monads themselves are metaphysical inventions or hypotheses. On the contrary, it is itself part of the explication of the intentional components implicit in the fact of the experiential world that exists for us. Here again it is to be noted that, as has been repeatedly emphasized, the ideas referred to are not phantasies or modes of the "as if," but arise constitutionally in integral connexion with all Objective experience and have their modes of legitimation and their development by scientific activity.

What we have just presented is a preliminary view of the course to be followed, level by level, in the intentional explication that we must carry out, if we are to solve the transcendental problem in the only conceivable way and actually execute the transcendental idealism of phenomenology.

§ 50.   *The mediate intentionality of experiencing someone else, as "appresentation"*
(analogical apperception).

After we have dealt with the prior stage, which is very important transcendentally—namely, definition and articulation of the primordial sphere—the genuine difficulties (and in fact they are not inconsiderable) are occasioned by the *first* of the above-indicated steps toward constitution of an Objective world: *the step taking us to the "other" ego.* They lie, accordingly, in the transcendental clarification of experiencing "someone else"—in the sense in which the other has not yet attained the sense "man."

Experience is original consciousness; and in fact we generally say, in the case of experiencing a man: the other is himself there before us "in person." On the other hand, this being there in person does not keeps us from admitting forthwith that, properly speaking, neither the other Ego himself, nor his subjective processes or his appearances themselves, nor anything else belonging to his own essence, becomes given in our experience originally. If it were, if what belongs to the other's own essence were directly accessible, it would be merely a moment of my own essence, and ultimately he himself and I myself would be the same. The situation would be similar as regards his animate organism, if the latter were nothing else but the "body" that is a unity constituted purely in my actual and possible experiences, a unity belonging—as a product of *my* "sensuousness" exclusively—in my primordial sphere. *A certain mediacy of intentionality* must be present here, going out from the substratum, "primordial world" (which in any case is the incessantly underlying basis), and making present to consciousness a "there too," which nevertheless is not itself there and can never become an "itself-there." We have here, accordingly, a kind of *making "co-present,"* a kind of *"appresentation."*

An appresentation occurs even in external experience, since the strictly seen front of a physical thing always and necessarily appresents a rear aspect and prescribes for it a more or less determinate content. On the other hand, experiencing someone else cannot be a matter of just this kind of appresentation, which already plays a role in the constitution of primordial Nature: Appresentation of this sort involves the possibility of verification by a corresponding fulfilling presentation (the back becomes the front); whereas, in the case of that appresentation which would lead over into the other original sphere, such verification must be excluded a priori. How can appresentation of another original sphere, and thereby the sense "someone else," be motivated in my original sphere and, in fact, motivated as experience—as the word "appresentation" (making intended as co-present) already indicates? Not every non-originary making-present can do that. A non-originary making-present can do it only in combination with an originary presentation, an itself-giving proper; and only as demanded by the originary presentation can it have the character of appresentation—somewhat as, in the case of experiencing a physical thing, what is there perceptually motivates <belief in> something else being there too.

The perception proper that functions as the underlying basis is offered us by our *perception of the primordially reduced world*, with its previously described articulation—a perception going on continually within the general bounds of the ego's *incessant self-perception*. The problem now is: In the perception of that reduced world, what in particular must be of account here? How does the motivation run? What becomes uncovered as involved in the very complicated intentional performance of the appresentation, which does in fact come about?

Initial guidance can be furnished by the verbal sense, *an Other*: an Other Ego. "Alter" signifies alter ego. And the ego involved here is I myself, constituted within my primordial ownness, and uniquely, as the psychophysical unity (the primordial man): as "personal" Ego, governing immediately in my animate organism (the only animate organism) and producing effects mediately[18] in the primordial surrounding world; the subject, moreover, of a concrete intentional life, <and (?)> of a psychic sphere relating to himself and the "world." All of that—with the grouping under types that arises in experiential life and the familiar forms of flow and combination—is at our disposal. As for the intentionalities by which it has become constituted (and they too are highly complicated)—admittedly we have not investigated them <in these meditations>. They belong to a distinct stratum and are the theme of vast investigations into which we did not and could not enter.

Let us assume that another man enters our perceptual sphere. Primordially reduced, that signifies: In the perceptual sphere pertaining to my primordial Nature, a body is presented, which, as primordial, is of course only a determining part of myself: an "immanent transcendency." Since, in this Nature and this world, my animate organism is the only body that is or can be constituted originally as an animate organism (a functioning organ), the body over there, which is nevertheless apprehended as an animate organism, must have derived this sense by an *apperceptive transfer from my animate organism*, and done so in a manner that excludes an actually direct, and hence primordial, showing of the predicates belonging to an animate organism specifically, a showing of them in perception proper. It is clear from the very beginning that only a similarity connecting, within my primordial sphere, that body over there with my body can serve as the motivational basis for the *"analogizing" apprehension* of that body as another animate organism.

There would be, accordingly, a certain assimilative apperception; but it by no means follows that there would be an inference from analogy. Apperception is not inference, not a thinking act. *Every* apperception in which we apprehend at a glance, and noticingly grasp, objects given beforehand—for example, the already-given everyday world—every apperception in which we understand their sense and its horizons forthwith, points back to a *"primal instituting,"* in which an object with a similar sense became constituted for the first time. Even the physical things of this world that are unknown to us are, to speak generally, known in respect of their type. We have already seen like things before, though not precisely this thing here. Thus *each everyday experience* involves an *analogizing transfer* of an originally instituted objective sense to a new case, with its anticipative apprehension of the object as having a similar sense. To the extent that there is givenness beforehand, there is such a transfer. At the same time, that sense-component in further experience which proves to be actually new may function in turn as institutive and found a pregivenness that has a richer sense. The child who already sees physical things understands, let us say, for the first time the final sense of scissors; and from now on he sees scissors at the first glance *as* scissors—but naturally not in an explicit reproducing, comparing, and inferring. Yet the manner in which apperceptions arise—and consequently in themselves, by their sense and sense-horizon, point back to their genesis—varies greatly. There are different levels of apperception, corresponding to different layers of objective sense. Ultimately we always get back to the *radical differentiation, of apperceptions* into those that, according to their genesis, belong purely to the *primordial sphere* and those that present themselves *with the sense "alter ego"* and, *upon* this sense, have built a new one—thanks to a genesis at a higher level.

§ 51.   *"Pairing" as an associatively constitutive component of my experience of someone else.*

If we attempt to indicate the peculiar nature of that analogizing apprehension whereby a body within my primordial sphere, being similar to my own animate body, becomes *apprehended as likewise an animate organism*, we encounter: first, the circumstance that here the *primally institutive original* is *always livingly present*, and the primal instituting itself is therefore always going on in a livingly effective manner; secondly, the peculiarity we already know to be necessary, namely that what is *appresented* by virtue of the aforesaid analogizing can never attain actual presence, never become an object of perception proper. Closely connected with the first peculiarity is the circumstance that *ego* and *alter ego* are always and necessarily given *in an original "pairing."*

Pairing, occurence in configuration as a pair and then as a group, a plurality, is a *universal* phenomenon of the transcendental sphere (and of the parallel sphere of intentional psychology); and, we may add forthwith, as far as a pairing is actually present, so far extends that remarkable kind of primal instituting of an analogizing apprehension—its continuous primal institution in living actuality—which we have already stressed as the first peculiarity of experiencing someone else. Hence it is not exclusively peculiar to this experience.

First of all, let us elucidate the essential nature of any "pairing" (or any forming of a plurality). Pairing is a *primal form of that passive synthesis* which we designate as *"association,"* in contrast to passive synthesis of "identification." In a *pairing association* the characteristic feature is that, in the most primitive case, two data are given intuitively, and with prominence, in the unity of a consciousness and that, on this basis—essentially, already in pure passivity (regardless therefore of whether they are noticed or unnoticed) —as data appearing with mutual distinctness, they *found phenomenologically a unity of similarity* and thus are always constituted precisely as a pair. If there are more than two such data, then a phenomenally unitary group, a plurality, becomes constituted. On more precise analysis we find essentially present here an intentional overreaching, coming about genetically (and by essential necessity) as soon as the data that undergo pairing have become prominent and simultaneously intended; we find, more particularly, a living mutual awakening and an overlaying of each with the objective sense of the other. This overlaying can bring a total or a partial coincidence, which in any particular instance has its degree, the limiting case being that of complete "likeness." As the result of this overlaying, there takes place in the paired data a mutual transfer of sense—that is to say: an apperception of each according to the sense of the other, so far as moments of sense actualized in what is experienced do not annul this transfer, with the consciousness of "different."

In that case of association and apperception which particularly interests us—namely apperception of the alter ego by the ego—pairing first comes about when the Other enters my field of perception. I, as the primordial psychophysical Ego, am always prominent in my primordial field of perception, regardless of whether I pay attention to myself and turn toward myself with some activity or other. In particular, my live body is always there and sensuously prominent; but, in addition to that and likewise with primordial originariness, it is equipped with the specific sense of an animate organism. Now in case there presents itself, as outstanding in my primordial sphere, a body "similar" to mine—that is to say, a body with determinations such that it must enter into a phenomenal *pairing* with mine—it *seems* clear without more ado that, with the transfer of sense, this body must forthwith appropriate from mine the sense: animate organism. But is the apperception actually so transparent? Is it a simple apperception by transfer, like any other? What makes this organism another's, rather than a second organism of my own? Obviously what we designated as the *second fundamental characteristic* of the apperception in question plays a part here: that none of the *appropriated* sense specific to an animate organism can become actualized originarily in my primordial sphere.

§ 52.   *Appresentation as a kind of experience with its own style of verification.*

But now there arises for us the difficult problem of making it understandable *that such an apperception is possible* and need not be annulled forthwith. How does it happen that, as the fact tells us, the transferred sense is appropriated with existence-status, as a set of "psychic" determinations existing in combination with that body over there, even though they can never show themselves *as* themselves in the domain of originality, belonging to the primordial sphere (which alone is available)?

Let us look at the intentional situation more closely. The appresentation which gives that component of the Other which is not accessible originaliter is combined with an original presentation (of "his" body as part of the Nature given as included in my ownness). In this combination, moreover, the Other's animate body and his governing Ego are given in the manner that characterizes *a unitary transcending experience*. Every experience points to further experiences that would fulfil and verify the appresented horizons, which include, in the form of non-intuitive anticipations, potentially verifiable syntheses of harmonious further experience. Regarding experience of someone else, it is clear that its fulfillingly verifying continuation can ensue *only by means of new appresentations that proceed in a synthetically harmonious fashion*, and only by virtue of the manner in which *these appresentations owe their existence-value to their motivational connexion with the* changing *presentations proper, within my ownness*, that continually appertain to them.

As a suggestive *clue* to the requisite clarification, this proposition may suffice: The experienced animate organism of another continues to prove itself as actually an animate organism, solely in its changing but incessantly *harmonious "behavior."* Such *harmonious* behavior (as having a physical side that indicates something psychic appresentatively) must present itself fulfillingly in original experience, and do so throughout the continuous change in behavior from phase to phase. The organism becomes experienced as a pseudo-organism, precisely if there is something discordant about its behavior.

The character of the existent "other" has its basis in this kind of verifiable accessibility of what is not originally accessible. Whatever can become presented, and evidently verified, *originally*—is something *I* am; or else it belongs to me as peculiarly my own. Whatever, by virtue thereof, is experienced in that founded manner which characterizes a primordially unfulfillable experience—an experience that does not give something itself originally but that consistently verifies something indicated—is "other." It is therefore conceivable only as an analogue of something included in my peculiar ownness. Because of its sense-constitution it occurs necessarily as an *"intentional modification"* of that Ego of mine which is the first to be Objectivated, or as an intentional modification of my primordial "world": the Other as phenomenologically a "modification" of myself (which, for its part, gets this character of being "my" self by virtue of the contrastive pairing that necessarily takes place). It is clear that, with the other Ego, there is appresented, in an analogizing modification, everything that belongs to his concretion: first, *his* primordial world, and then his fully concrete ego. In other words, *another monad* becomes constituted appresentatively in mine.

Similarly (to draw an instructive comparison), within my ownness and moreover within the sphere of its living present, my past is given only by memory and is characterized in memory *as* my past, a past present—that is: an intentional modification. The experiential verification of it, as a modification, then goes on necessarily in harmonious syntheses of recollection; only thus does a past as such become verified. Somewhat as my memorial past, as a modification of my living present, "transcends" my present, the appresented other being "transcends" my own being (in the pure and most fundamental sense: what is included in my primordial ownness). In both cases the modification is inherent as a sense-component in the sense itself; it is a correlate of the intentionality constituting it. Just as, in my living present, in the domain of "internal perception," my past becomes constituted by virtue of the harmonious memories occuring in this present, so in my primordial sphere, by means of appresentations occuring in it and motivated by its contents, an ego other than mine can become constituted—accordingly, in non-originary presentations [*in Vergegenwärtigungen*] of a new type, which have a modificatum of a new kind as their correlate. To be sure, as long as I consider non-originary presentations <of something lying> within the sphere of my ownness, the Ego in whom they center is the one identical I-myself. On the other hand, to everything alien (as long as it remains within the appresented horizon of concreteness that necessarily goes with it) centers in an appresented Ego who is not I myself but, relative to me, a modificatum: an *other* Ego.

An actually sufficient explication of the noematic complexes involved in experience of what is alien—such an explanation as is absolutely necessary to a complete clarification of what this experience does constitutively, by constitutive association—is not yet completed with what has been shown up to now. There is need of a supplement, in order to reach the point where, on the basis of cognitions already acquired, the possibility and scope of a transcendental constitution of the Objective world can become evident and transcendental-phenomenological idealism can thus become entirely manifest.

§ 53. *Potentialities of the primordial sphere and their constitutive function in the apperception of the Other.*

As reflexively related to itself, my animate bodily organism (in my primordial sphere)[19] has the central "Here" as its mode of givenness; every other body, and accordingly the "other's" body, has the mode "There." This orientation, "There," can be freely changed by virtue of my kinesthesias. Thus, in my primordial sphere, the *one spatial "Nature"* is constituted throughout the change in orientations, and constituted moreover with an intentional relatedness to my animate organism as functioning perceptually. Now the fact that my bodily organism can be (and is) apprehended as a *natural body existing and movable in space like any other* is manifestly connected with the possibility expressed in the words: By free modification of my kinesthesias, particularly those of locomotion, I can change my position in such a manner that I convert any There into a Here—that is to say, I could occupy any spatial locus with my organism. This implies that, perceiving from there, I should see the same physical things, only in correspondingly different modes of appearance, such as pertain to my being there. It implies, then, that not only the systems of appearance that pertain to my current perceiving "from here," but other quite determinate systems, corresponding to the change of position that puts me "there," belong constitutively to each physical thing. And the same in the case of every other "There."

Should not these interconnexions, or rather these instances of belonging together, which are involved in the primordial constitution of "my" Nature and are themselves characterized as associative—should not they be quite essential to clarification of the associative performance, experiencing someone else? After all, I do not apperceive the other ego simply as a duplicate of myself and accordingly as having my original sphere or one completely like mine. I do not apperceive him as having, more particularly, the spatial modes of appearance that are mine from here; rather, as we find on closer examination, I apperceive him as having spatial modes of appearance like those I should have if I should go over there and be where he is. Furthermore the Other is appresentatively apperceived as the "Ego" of a primordial world, and of a monad, wherein his animate organism is originally constituted and experienced in the mode of the absolute Here, precisely as the functional center for his governing. In this appresentation, therefore, the body in the mode *There*, which presents itself in *my* monadic sphere and is apperceived as another's live body (the animate organism of the alter ego)—that body indicates "the same" body in the mode *Here*, as the body experienced by the other ego in *his* monadic sphere. Moreover it indicates the "same" body concretely, with all the constitutive intentionality pertaining to this mode of givenness in the other's experience.

§ 54. *Explicating the sense of the appresentation wherein I experience someone else.*

Manifestly what has just now been brought to light points to the course of the association constituting the mode "Other." The body that is a member of my primordial world (the body subsequently of the other ego) is for me a body in the mode There. Its manner of appearance does not become paired in a direct association with the manner of appearance actually belonging at the time to my animate organism (in the mode Here); rather it awakens reproductively *another*, an immediately[20] similar appearance included in the system constitutive of my animate organism as a body in space. It brings to mind the way my body would look "if I were there." In this case too, although the awakening does not become a memory *intuition*, *pairing* takes place. The first-awakened manner of appearance of my body is not the only thing that enters into a pairing; my body itself does so likewise: as the synthetic unity pertaining to this mode, and the many other familiar modes, of its appearance. *Thus the assimilative apperception becomes possible* and established, by which the external body over there receives analogically from mine the sense, animate organism, and consequently the sense, organism belonging to another "world," analogous to my primordial world.

The *general style* of this and every other apperception that arises associatively is therefore to be described as follows: With the associative overlapping of the data founding the apperception, there takes place an association at a higher level. If the one datum is a particular mode of appearance of an intentional object, which is itself an index pointing to an associatively awakened system of manifold appearances wherein it would show itself, then the other datum is "supplemented" to become likewise an appearance *of* something, namely an analogous object. But it is not as though the unity and multiplicity "thrust upon" the latter datum merely supplemented it with modes of appearance taken from these others. On the contrary, the analogically apprehended object and its indicated system of appearances are indeed *analogically adapted* to the analogous appearance, which has awakened this whole system too. Every overlapping-at-a-distance, which occurs by virtue of associative pairing, is *at the same time a fusion* and[21] therein, so far as incompatibilities do not interfere, an assimilation, an accomodation of the sense of the one member to that of the other.

If we return to our case, that of apperception of the alter ego, it is now self-understood that what is appresented by the "body" over there, in my primordial "surrounding world," is not something psychic of mine, nor anything else in my sphere of ownness. I am *here* somatically, the center of a primordial "world" oriented around me. Consequently my entire primordial ownness, proper to me as a monad, has the content of the Here—not the content varying with some "I can and do," which might set in, and belonging to some There or other; accordingly, not the content belonging to that definite There.[22] Each of these contents excludes the other; they cannot both exist <in my sphere of ownness> at the same time. But, since the other body there enters into a pairing association with my body here and, being given perceptually, becomes the core of an appresentation, the core of my experience of a coexisting ego, that ego, according to the whole sense-giving course of the association, must be appresented *as an ego now coexisting in the mode There*, "such as I should be if I were there." My own ego, however, the ego given in constant self-perception, is actual now with the content belonging to his Here. Therefore an ego is *appresented*, as *other* than mine. That which is primordially incompatible, in simultaneous coexistence, becomes compatible: because my primordial ego constitutes the ego who is other for him by an appresentative apperception, which, according to its intrinsic nature, never demands and never is open to fulfillment by presentation.

Likewise easy to understand is the manner in which, as the effective association goes on continuously, such an appresentation of someone else continually furnishes new appresentational contents—that is to say, brings the changing contents of the other ego to definite notice; and, on the other hand, the manner in which, by virtue of the combination with a continual presentation and the associational demands expectantly addressed to this presentation, a *consistent confirmation* becomes possible. The *first determinate content* obviously must be formed by the understanding of the other's organism and specifically organismal conduct: the understanding of the members as hands groping or functioning in pushing, as feet functioning in walking, as eyes functioning in seeing, and so forth. With this the Ego at first is determined only as governing thus somatically [*so leiblich waltendes*] and, in a familiar manner, proves himself continually, so far as the whole stylistic form of the sensible processes manifest to me primordially must correspond to the form whose type is familiar from my own organismal governing [*leibliches Walten*]. It is quite comprehensible that, *as a further consequence*, an "empathizing" of definite contents belonging to the "*higher psychic sphere*" arises. Such contents too are indicated somatically and in the conduct of the organism toward the outside world—for example: as the outward conduct of someone who is angry or cheerful, which I easily understand from my own conduct under similar circumstances. Higher psychic occurrences, diverse as they are and familiar as they have become, have furthermore their style of synthetic interconnexions and take their course in forms of their own, which I can understand associatively on the basis of my empirical familiarity with the style of my own life, as examplifying roughly differentiated typical forms. In this sphere, moreover, every successful understanding of what occurs in others has the effect of opening up new associations and new possibilities of understanding; and conversely, since every pairing association is reciprocal, every such understanding uncovers my own psychic life in its similarity and difference and, by bringing new features into prominence, makes it fruitful for new associations.

§ 55. *Establishment of the community of monads. The first form of Objectivity: intersubjective Nature.*

But it is more important to clarify the *community*, developing at various levels, which is produced forthwith by virtue of experiencing someone else: the community between me, the primordial psychophysical Ego governing in and by means of my primordial organism, and the appresentatively experienced Other; then, considered more concretely and radically, between my monadic ego and his.

The first thing constituted in the form of community, and the *foundation for all other intersubjectively common things*, is the *commoness of Nature*, along with that of the *Other's organism* and *his psychophysical Ego*, as paired with *my own psychophysical Ego*.

Since other subjectivity, by appresentation within the exclusive own-essentialness of my subjectivity, arises with the sense and status of a subjectivity that is other in its own essence,[23] it might at first seem to be a mystery how community—even the first community, in the form of a common world—becomes established. The other organism, as appearing in my primordial sphere, is first of all a body in my primordial Nature, which is a synthetic unity belonging to me and therefore, as a determining part included in my own essence, inseparable from me myself. If that body functions appresentatively, then, in union with it, the other Ego becomes an object of my consciousness—and primarily the other Ego with his organism, as given to him in the manner of appearance pertaining to his "absolute Here." How can I speak at all of *the same* body, as appearing within my primordial sphere in the mode There and within his and to him in the mode Here? These two primordial spheres, mine which is for me as ego the original sphere, and his which is for me an appresented sphere—are they not *separated* by an abyss I cannot actually cross, since crossing it would mean, after all, that I acquired an original (rather than an appresenting) experience of someone else? If we stick to our de facto experience, our experience of someone else as it comes to pass at any time, we find that actually the *sensuously seen body* is experienced forthwith as *the body of someone else* and not as merely an indication of someone else. Is not this fact an enigma?

The body belonging to my original sphere and the body constituted, after all, quite separately in the other ego become identified and are called the identical body of someone else. How does this identification come about? How *can* it come about? But the enigma appears only if the two original spheres have already been distinguished—a distinction that already presupposes that experience of someone else has done its work. Since we are not dealing here with a temporal genesis of such experience, on the basis of a temporally antecedent self-experience, manifestly only a precise explication of the intentionality actually observable in our experience of someone else and discovery of the motivations essentially implicit in that intentionality can unlock the enigma.

As we said once before, appresentation as such presupposes a core of presentation. It is a making present combined by associations with presentation, with perception proper, but a making present that is fused with the latter in the particular function of "co-perception." In other words, the two are so fused that they stand within the *functional community of one perception*, which simultaneously presents and appresents, and yet furnishes for the total object a consciousness of its being itself there. Therefore, in the object of such a presentive-appresentive perception (an object making its appearance in the mode, itself-there), we must distinguish noematically between that part which is genuinely perceived and the rest, which is not strictly perceived and yet is indeed there too. Thus every perception of this type is transcending: it posits more as itself-there than it makes "actually" present at any time. Every external perception belongs here—for example, perception of a house (front—rear); but at bottom absolutely every perception, indeed every evidence, is thus described in respect of a most general feature, provided only that we understand "presenting" in a broader sense.

Let us apply this general cognition to the case of experiencing someone else. In this case too it should be noted that experience *can appresent only because it presents*, that here too appresentation can exist only in the aforesaid functional community with presentation. That implies, however, that, from the very beginning, *what this experience presents must belong to the unity of the very object appresented*. In other words: It is not, and cannot be, the case that the body belonging to my primordial sphere and indicating to me the other Ego (and, with him, the whole of the other primordial sphere or the other concrete ego) could appresent his factual existence and being-there-too, unless *this primordial body* acquired the sense, "a body belonging to the other ego," and, according to the whole associative-apperceptive performance, *the sense*: "*someone else's animate organism itself.*" Therefore it is not as though the body over there, in my primordial sphere, remained separate from the animate bodily organism of the other Ego, as if that body were something like a signal for its analogue (by virtue of an obviously inconceivable motivation); it is not as though consequently, with the spreading of the association and appresentation, my primordial Nature and the other's appresented primordial Nature—therefore my concrete ego and the other concrete ego—remained separate. On the contrary, this natural body belonging to my sphere appresents the other Ego, by virtue of the pairing association with my bodily organism, and with my Ego governing in my organism, within my primordially constituted Nature. In so doing, it appresents first of all the other Ego's governing in this body, the body over there, and mediately his governing in the Nature that appears to him perceptually—identically the Nature to which the body over there belongs, identically the Nature that is my primordial Nature. It is the same Nature, but in the mode of appearance: "as if I were standing over there, where the Other's body is." The body is the same, given to me as the body there, and to him as the body here, the central body. Furthermore, "my" whole Nature is the same as the Other's. In *my* primordial sphere it is constituted as an identical unity of my manifold modes of givenness—an identical unity in changing orientations around *my* animate organism (the zero body, the body in the absolute Here), an identical unity of even richer multiplicities that, as changing modes of appearance pertaining to different "senses," or else as changeable "perspectives," belong to each particular orientation as here or there and also, in a quite particular manner, belong to my animate organism, which is inseparable from the absolute Here. All of this has for me the originality of something included in my particular ownness, something directly accessible in original explication of my own self. *In the appresented other ego* the synthetic systems are *the same*, with all their modes of appearance, accordingly with all the possible perceptions and the noematic contents of these: except that the *actual* perceptions and the modes of givenness actualized therein, and also in part the objects actually perceived, are *not the same*; rather the objects perceived are precisely those perceivable *from there*, and *as* they are perceivable from there. Something similar is true of anything else of my own and the corresponding alien thing, even where original explication does not go on in perceptions. I do not have an appresented second original sphere with a second "Nature" and, in this Nature, a second animate bodily organism (the one belonging to the other ego himself), so that I must then ask how I can apprehend my Nature and this other as modes of appearance of the same Objective Nature. On the contrary, the *identity*-sense of "my" primordial Nature and the presentiated other primordial Nature is *necessarily* produced by the appresentation and the unity that it, *as* appresentation, necessarily has with the presentation co-functioning for it—this appresentation by virtue of which an Other and, consequently, his concrete ego are there for me in the first place. Quite rightly, therefore, we speak of *perceiving* someone else and then of perceiving the Objective world, perceiving that the other Ego and I are looking at the same world, and so forth—though this perceiving goes on exclusively within the sphere of my ownness. That does not at all contravene the fact that the intentionality of this sphere transcends my owness, or the fact that accordingly my ego constitutes in himself another ego—and constitutes this ego, moreover, as existent. What I actually see is not a sign and not a mere analogue, a depiction in any natural sense of the word; on the contrary, it is someone else. And what is grasped with actual originariness in this seeing—namely that corporeality over there, or rather only one aspect of its surface—is the Other's body itself, but seen just from my position and in respect of this aspect: According to the sense-constitution involved in perceiving someone else, what is grasped originaliter is the body of a psyche essentially inaccessible to me originaliter, and the two are comprised in the unity of one psychophysical reality.

On the other hand, it is implicit in the intentional essence of this perception of the Other—the Other who exists henceforth, as I do myself, within what is henceforth the Objective world—that I as perceiver can find the aforesaid distinction between my primordial sphere and the merely presentiated primordial sphere of the Other, and consequently can trace the peculiarities of the division into two noetic strata and explicate the complexes of associative intentionality. The experiential phenomenon, Objective Nature, has, besides the primordially constituted stratum, a superimposed second, merely appresented stratum originating from my experiencing of someone else; and this fact concerns, first of all, *the Other's animate bodily organism*, which is, so to speak, *the intrinsically first Object*, just as *the other man is constitutionally the intrinsically first <Objective> man*. In the case of this primal phenomenon of Objectivity, the situation is already clear to us: If I screen off my experience of someone else, I have the lowest constitution, the one-layered presentive constitution of the other body within my primordial sphere: if I add that experience, I have appresentationally, and as coinciding synthetically with the presentational stratum, the same animate organism as it is given to the other Ego himself, and I have the further possible modes of givenness available to him.

From that, as is easily understandable, *every* natural Object experienced or experienceable by me in the lower stratum receives an appresentational stratum (though by no means one that becomes explicitly intuited), a stratum united in an identifying synthesis with the stratum given to me in the mode of primordial originality: the same natural Object in its possible modes of givenness to the other Ego. This is repeated, *mutatis mutandis*, in the case of subsequently constituted mundanities of the concrete Objective world as it always exists for us: namely as a world of men and culture.

The following should be noted in this connexion. It is implicit in the sense of my successful apperception of others that their world, the world belonging to their appearance-systems, must be experienced forthwith as the same as the world belonging to my appearance-systems; and this involves an identity of our appearance-systems. Now we know very well that there are such things as *"abnormalities"* (for example: in the case of subjects who are blind or deaf); we know that therefore the appearance-systems are by no means always absolutely identical and that whole strata (though not all strata) can differ. But abnormality must first be *constituted* as such; and the constituting of abnormality is possible only on the basis of an intrinsically antecedent normality. This points to new tasks, which belong to a higher level of phenomenological analysis of the constitutional origin of the Objective world—as the Objective world existing for us and only by virtue of our own sense-producing sources, a world that can have neither sense nor existence for us otherwise. The Objective world has existence by virtue of a harmonious confirmation of the apperceptive constitution, once this has succeeded: a confirmation thereof by the continuance of experiencing life with a consistent harmoniousness, which always becomes re-established as extending through any "corrections" that may be required to that end. Now harmoniousness is preserved also by virtue of a recasting of apperceptions through distinguishing between normality and abnormalities (as modifications thereof), or by virtue of the constitution of new unities throughout the changes involved in abnormalities. Among the problems of abnormality the problem of non-human animality and that of the levels of "higher and lower" brutes are included. Relative to the brute, man is, constitutionally speaking, the normal case—just as I myself am the primal norm constitutionally for all other men. Brutes are essentially constituted for me as abnormal "variants" of my humanness, even though *among* them in turn normality and abnormality may be differentiated. Always it is a matter of intentional modifications in the sense-structure itself, as what becomes evinced. All of that, to be sure, needs a more thorough phenomenological explication. This general account, however, is enough for our present purposes.

After these clarifications it is no longer an enigma how I can constitute in myself another Ego or, more radically, how I can constitute in my monad another monad, and can experience what is constituted in me as nevertheless other than me. At the same time, this being indeed inseparable from such constitution, it is no longer an enigma how I can identify a Nature constituted in me with a Nature constituted by someone else (or, stated with the necessary precision, how I can identify a Nature constituted in me with one constituted in me *as* a Nature constituted by someone else). This identification is no greater [an] enigma than any other synthetic identification. It is therefore no more mysterious than any, by virtue of which, as an identification confined to my own original sphere, no matter what objective unity acquires sense and being for me through the medium of *presentiations*. Let us consider the following instructive example and use it to bring out a thought that takes us further: the notion of a *connexion* constituted through the medium of presentiation. How does one of my own subjective processes acquire for me the sense and status of an existent process, something existing with its identical temporal form and identical temporal content? The original is gone; but, in repeated presentiations, I go back to it and do so with the evidence: "I can always do so again." But these repeated presentiations are evidently themselves a temporal sequence; and each is separate from the others. In spite of that, however, an identifying synthesis connects them in the evident consciousness of "the Same"—which implies the same, never repeated temporal form, filled with the same content. Here, as everywhere else, "the Same" signifies therefore an *identical intentional object of separate conscious processes*, hence an object immanent in them only as something *non-really* inherent. Another case, very important in itself, is that of the constitution of objects that are ideal in the pregnant sense—for example: all logically ideal objects. In a living, many-membered thinking action I produce a structure: a theorem or a numerical structure. Subsequently I repeat the producing, while recollecting my earlier producing. At once, and by essential necessity, an identifying synthesis takes place; furthermore a new identifying synthesis occurs with each additional repetition (a repetition performed with a consciousness that the producing can be repeated again at will): It is identically the same proposition, identically the same numerical structure, *but repeatedly produced* or, this being equivalent, repeatedly made evident. Therefore in this case, through the medium of recollective presentiations, the synthesis extends—within my stream of subjective processes (which always is already constituted)—from my living present into my currently relevant separate pasts and thus makes a *connexion* between my present and these pasts. With that, moreover, the supremely significant *transcendental problem of ideal objectivities* ("ideal" in the specific sense) is solved. Their supertemporality turns out to be *omnitemporality*, as a correlate of free produceability and reproduceability at all times. After constitution of the Objective world with its Objective time and its Objective men as possible thinking subjects, that obviously carries over to ideal structures, as themselves Objectivated, and to their Objective omnitemporality. Thus the contrast between them and Objective *realities*, as spatiotemporally individuated structures, becomes understandable.

If we return now to our case, the experience of someone else, we find that, with its complicated structure, it effects a similar *connexion mediated by presentiation*: namely a connexion between, on the one hand, the uninterruptedly living self-experience (as purely passive original self-appearance) of the concrete ego—accordingly, his primordial sphere—and, on the other hand, the *alien sphere* presentiated therein. It effects this, first, by its identifying synthesis of the *primordially given* animate body of someone else and the same animate body, but *appresented* in other modes of appearance, and secondly, spreading out from there, by its identifying synthesis of the same Nature, given and verified primordially (with pure sensuous originality) and at the same time appresentationally. In that way the *coexistence of my <polar> Ego and the other Ego*, of my whole concrete ego and his, my intentional life and his, my "realities" and his—in short, a *common time-form*—is primally instituted; and thus every primordial temporality automatically acquires the significance of being merely an original mode of appearance of Objective temporality to a particular subject. In this connexion we see that the temporal community of the constitutively interrelated monads is indissoluble, because it is tied up essentially with the constitution of *a world and a world time*.

§ 56. *Constitution of higher levels of intermonadic community.*

With these considerations we have clarified the *first and lowest level of communalization* between me, the primordial monad for myself, and the monad constituted in me, yet as other and accordingly as existing for himself but only appresentationally demonstrable to me. The only conceivable manner in which others can have for me the sense and status of existent others, thus and so determined, consists in their being constituted *in me* as others. If they get that sense and status from sources that yield a continual confirmation, then they do indeed *exist* (as I am *compelled* to say), but exclusively as having the sense with which they are constituted: as monads, existing for themselves precisely as I exist for myself, yet existing also in communion, therefore (I emphasize the expression already used earlier) in *connexion with me* qua concrete ego, qua monad. To be sure, they are separate from my monad, so far as really inherent constituents are concerned, since no really inherent connexion leads from their subjective processes to my subjective processes or from anything included in their peculiar ownness to anything included in mine. To that separation there corresponds, after all, the "*real*," the mundane separation of my psychophysical existence from someone else's, a separation that shows itself as spatial, owing to the spatial character of our Objective animate organisms. On the other hand, this original communion is not just nothing. Whereas, really inherently, each monad is an absolutely separate unity, the "irreal" intentional reaching of the other into my primordiality is not irreal in the sense of being dreamt into it or being present to consciousness after the fashion of a mere phantasy. *Something that exists is in intentional communion with something else that exists.* It is an essentially *unique connectedness*, an actual community and precisely the one that makes transcendentally possible the being of a world, a world of men and things.

After the first level of communalization and (this being almost equivalent) the first constitution of an Objective world, starting from the primordial world, have been sufficiently clarified, the *higher levels* offer relatively minor difficulties. Though comprehensive investigations and a progressive differentiation of problems relating to these levels are necessary for purposes of an all-round explication, here we can be satisfied with rough general indications, easily understandable on the basis already laid. Starting from me, from the one who is constitutionally the primal monad, I acquire what are for the other monads and, correlatively, others as *psychophysical* subjects. This implies that I do *not* acquire the latter *merely as over against me* somatically and—by virtue of associative pairing—as *related back to my psychophysical existence* (which indeed is universally "central," and particularly the "central member" in the communalized world of the present level because of the necessarily oriented manner in which this world is given). On the contrary (and this carries over to the sociality of brute animals), in the sense of *a community of men* and in that of *man*—who, even as solitary, has the sense: member of a community—there is implicit a *mutual being for one another*, which entails an *Objectivating equalization* of my existence with that of all others— consequently: I or anyone else, as a man among other men. If, with my understanding of someone else, I penetrate more deeply into him, into his horizon of ownness, I shall soon run into the fact that, just as his animate bodily organism lies in my field of perception, so my animate organism lies in his field of perception and that, in general, he experiences me forthwith as an Other for him, just as I experience him as *my* Other. Likewise I shall find that, in the case of a plurality of Others, they are experienced also by one another as Others, and consequently that I can experience any given Other not only as himself an Other but also as related in turn to *his* Others and perhaps—with a mediatedness that may be conceived as reiterable—related at the same time to me. It is also clear that men become apperceivable only as finding Others and still more Others, not just in the realm of actuality but likewise in the realm of possibility, at their own pleasure. Openly endless Nature itself then becomes a Nature that includes an open plurality of men (conceived more generally: animalia), distributed one knows not how in infinite space, as subjects of possible intercommunion. To this community there naturally corresponds, in transcendental concreteness, a similarly[24] open *community of monads*, which we designate as *transcendental intersubjectivity*. We need hardly say that, as existing for me,[25] it is constituted purely within me, the meditating ego, purely by virtue of sources belonging to my intentionality; nevertheless it is constituted thus *as* a community constituted also in every other monad (who, in turn, is constituted with the modification: "other") as the same community—only with a different subjective mode of appearance—and as necessarily bearing within itself the same Objective world. Manifestly it is essentially necessary to the world constituted transcendentally in me (and similarly necessary to the world constituted in any community of monads that is imaginable by me) that it be a *world of men* and that, *in each particular man*, it be more or less perfectly constituted *intrapsychically*—in intentional processes and potential systems of intentionality, which, as "psychic life," are themselves already constituted as existing in the world. By "the psychic constitution of the Objective world" we mean, for example, my actual and possible experience of the world, as an experience belonging to me, the Ego who experiences himself as a man. Such experience of the world is more or less perfect; it always has its[26] open undetermined horizon. For each man, every other is implicit in this horizon—physically, psychophysically, in respect of what is internal to the other's psyche—and is thus in principle a realm of endless accessibilities, though in fact most other men remain horizonal.

§ 57. *Clarification of the parallel between explication of what is internal to the psyche and egological transcendental explication.*

On this basis it is not hard to clear up the *necessary parallel between explications of what is internal to the psyche and egological transcendental explications*, or the fact that, as was already said earlier, the pure psyche is a *self-Objectivation* of the monad, accomplished in the latter —a self-Objectivation the different levels of which are essential necessities, if Others are possibly to exist for the monad.

Connected with this is the fact that, a priori, every analysis or theory of transcendental phenomenology—including the theory whose main features have just been indicated, the theory of transcendental constitution of an Objective world—can be produced in the natural realm, when we give up the transcendental attitude. Thus transposed to the realm of transcendental naïveté, it becomes a theory pertaining to internal psychology. *Whether the two disciplines be eidetic or empirical*, a *"pure" psychology*—a psychology that merely explicates what belongs to a psyche, to a concrete human Ego, as its own intentional essence—corresponds to a *transcendental phenomenology*, and vice versa. That, however, is something to be made evident transcendentally.

§ 58. *Differentiation of problems in the intentional analysis of higher intersubjective communities. I and my surrounding world.*

The *constitution of humanity*, or of that community which belongs to the full essence of humanity, does not end with what has been considered up to now. On the basis, however, of community in the last sense acquired, it is easy to understand[27] the possibility of *acts of the Ego that reach into the other Ego through the medium of appresentative experience of someone else* and, indeed, the possibility of *specifically personal acts of the Ego* that have the character of acts of mine directed to you,[28] the character of *social acts*, by means of which all human personal communication is established. To study these acts carefully in their different forms and, starting from there, to make the essence of all *sociality* transcendentally understandable is an important task. With communalization proper, *social communalization*, there become constituted within the Objective world, as spiritual Objectivities of a peculiar kind, the various types of social communities with their possible hierarchical order, among them the pre-eminent types that have the character of *"personalities of a higher order."*

Consequently there would come into consideration, as inseparable from and (in a certain sense) correlative to the set of problems indicated, the problem of the constitution of the specifically human surrounding world, a surrounding world of culture for each man and each human community; likewise the problem of the genuine, though restricted, kind of Objectivity belonging to such a world. Its Objectivity is restricted, though concretely the world is given to me and to everyone only as a cultural world and as having the sense: accessible to everyone. But, as soon becomes apparent when its sense is explicated precisely, there are essential constitutional reasons why this accessibility is not unconditional. In this respect it is manifestly different from that absolutely unconditional accessibility to everyone which belongs essentially to the constitutional sense of Nature, of the animate organism, and therefore of the psychophysical man (understood with a certain generality). To be sure, the following is also included in the sphere of unconditional universality which is the correlate of the essential form of world constitution: Everyone, as a matter of a priori necessity, lives in the same Nature, a Nature moreover that, with the necessary communalization of his life and the lives of others, he has fashioned into a *cultural world* in his individual and communalized living and doing—a world having human significances, even if it belongs to an extremely low cultural level. But this, after all, does not exclude, either a priori or de facto, the truth that men belonging to one and the same world live in a loose cultural community—or even none at all—and accordingly constitute different surrounding worlds of culture, as concrete life-worlds in which the relatively or absolutely separate communities live their passive and active lives. Each man understands first of all, in respect of a core and as having its unrevealed horizon, *his* concrete surrounding world or *his* culture; and he does so precisely as a man who belongs to the community fashioning it historically. A deeper understanding, one that opens up the horizon of the past (which is co-determinant for an understanding of the present itself), is essentially possible to all members of that community, with a certain originality possible to them alone and barred to anyone from another community who enters into relation with theirs. At first such an individual necessarily understands men of the alien world as generically men, and men of a "certain" cultural world. Starting from there, he must first produce for himself, step by step, the possibilities of further understanding. Starting from what is most generally understandable, he must first open up ways of access to a sympathetic understanding of broader and broader strata of the present and then of the historical past, which in turn helps him to gain broader access to the present.

Constitution of "worlds" of any kind whatever, beginning with one's own stream of subjective processes, with its openly endless multiplicities, and continuing up through the Objective world with its various levels of Objectivation, is subject to the law of *"oriented" constitution*,[29] a constitution that presupposes at various levels, but within the extension of a sense conceived with maximal breadth, something "primordially" and something "secondarily" constituted. At each of the levels in question, the primordial enters, with a new stratum of sense, into the secondarily constituted world; and this occurs in such a fashion that the primordial becomes the central member, in accordance with orientational modes of givenness. The secondarily constituted, as a "world," is necessarily given as a horizon of being that is accessible from the primordial and is discoverable in a particular order. It is already thus in the case of the first, the "immanent" world, which we call the stream of subjective processes. As a system of mutual externalities, this stream is given in an orientation around the primordially constituted living present, from which everything else outside it (but belonging to immanent temporality) is accessible. Again, within the sphere that is primordial in our specific sense, my animate organism is the central member of "Nature," the "world" that becomes constituted by means of governance of my organism. In like manner, my psychophysical organism is primordial for the constitution of the Objective world of mutual externalities, and, in accordance with the oriented mode of givenness of this world, enters it as the central member. If the "world" that is primordial in our distinctive sense does not itself become the center of the Objective world, the reason is that this whole primordial "world" becomes Objectivated in such a fashion that it produces no new mutual externalities. On the other hand, the multiplicity of the Other's world is given as oriented peripherally to mine, and is thus a world, because it becomes constituted with a common Objective world immanent in it, and the spatiotemporal form of this Objective world functions at the same time as a form that gives access to it.

If we return to our case, that of the cultural world, we find that it too, as a world of cultures, is given orientedly on the underlying basis of the Nature common to all and on the basis of the spatiotemporal form that gives access to Nature and must function also in making the multiplicity of cultural formations and cultures accessible. We see that in this fashion the cultural world too is given "orientedly," in relation to a zero member or a <zero> "personality." Here I and my culture are primordial, over against every alien culture. To me and to those who share in my culture, an alien culture is accessible only by a kind of "experience of someone else," a kind of "empathy," by which we project ourselves into the alien cultural community and its culture. This empathy also calls for intentional investigations.[30]

We must forgo a more precise exploration of the sense-stratum that gives to the world of humanity and culture, as such, its specific sense, thus making it a world endowed with specifically "spiritual" predicates. Our constitutional explications have shown the intentional motivational complexes wherein accrued that coherent substratum of the full concrete world which is left us if we abstract from all predicates belonging to "Objective spirit." We retain the whole of Nature, already constituted as a concrete unity in itself. We retain, as included in Nature, the animate organisms of men and brutes; but we no longer retain psychic life as concretely complete, since human existence as such is always related consciously to an existent practical world as a surrounding world already endowed with humanly significant predicates, and this relationship presupposes a psychological constitution of such predicates.

That every such predicate of the world accrues from a *temporal* genesis and, indeed, one that is rooted in human undergoing and doing, needs no proof. A presupposition for the origin of such predicates in the particular subjects (and for the origin of their intersubjective acceptance as abiding predicates of the common life-world) is, consequently, that a community of men and each particular man are vitally immersed in a concrete surrounding world, are related to it in undergoing and doing—that all of this is already constituted. With this continual change in the human life-world, manifestly *the men themselves also change as persons*, since correlatively they must always be taking on new habitual properties. In this connexion far-reaching problems of static and genetic constitution make themselves keenly felt, those of genetic constitution as part of the problem of all-embracing genesis, which presents so many enigmas. For example: regarding personality, not only the problem of the static constitution of a unity of personal character, over against the multiplicity of instituted and subsequently annulled habitualities, but also the *genetic* problem, which leads back to enigmas concerning *"innate" character*.

For the present it must suffice that we have indicated these problems of a higher level as problems of constitution and thereby made it understandable that, with the systematic progress of transcendental-phenomenological explication of the apodictic ego, the transcendental sense of the world must also become disclosed to us ultimately in the *full concreteness* with which it is incessantly the *life-world* for us all. That applies likewise to all the particular formations of the surrounding world, wherein it presents itself to us according to our personal upbringing and development or according to our membership in this or that nation, this or that cultural community. All these matters are governed by essential necessities; they conform to an essential style, which derives its necessity from the transcendental ego and then from the transcendental intersubjectivity which discloses itself in that ego—accordingly, from the essential forms of transcendental motivation and transcendental constitution. If we succeed in uncovering these forms, the aforesaid a priori style acquires a rational clarification that has the highest dignity, the dignity of an ultimate, a transcendental intelligibility.

§ 59.   *Ontological explication and its place within constitutional transcendental phenomenology as a whole.*

By our coherent bits of actually executing analysis and, in part, by the accompanying pre-delineation of inevitable new problems and the form of order they demand, we have acquired philosophically fundamental insights. Starting from the experiential world given beforehand as existent and (with the shift to the eidetic attitude) from any experiential world whatever, conceived as given beforehand as existent, we exercised transcendental reduction—that is: we went back to the transcendental ego, who constitutes within himself givenness-beforehand and all modes of subsequent givenness; or (with eidetic self-variation) we went back to any transcendental ego whatever.

The transcendental ego was conceived accordingly as an ego who experiences within himself a world, who proves a world harmoniously. Tracing the essence of such constitution and its egological levels, we made visible an Apriori of a completely[31] novel kind, namely the Apriori of constitution. We learned to distinguish, on the one hand, the self-constitution of the ego for himself and in his primordial own-essentialness and, on the other hand, the constitution of all the aliennesses of various levels, by virtue of sources belonging to his own essentialness. There resulted the all-embracing unity of the essential form belonging to the total constitution accomplished in my own ego—the constitution as whose correlate the Objectively existing world, for me and for any ego whatever, is continually given beforehand, and goes on being shaped in its sense-strata, with a[32] correlative a priori form-style. And this constitution is itself an Apriori. With this most radical and consequential explication of what is intentionally included and what becomes intentionally motivated in "my" ego and in my essential variants, it becomes apparent that the universal de facto structure of the given Objective world—as mere Nature, as psychophysical being, as humanness, sociality of various levels, and culture—is, to a very great extent (and perhaps much further than we yet can see), an *essential necessity*. An understandable and necessary consequence is that the *task of an a priori ontology of the real* world—which is precisely discovery of the Apriori belonging to this world's universality—is inevitable but, on the other hand, one-sided and not philosophical in the final sense. Such an ontological Apriori (for example: of Nature, of the psychophysical, of sociality and culture) does indeed confer on the ontic fact, on the de facto world in respect of its "accidental" features, a relative intelligibility, that of an evident necessity of being thus and so by virtue of eidetic laws; but it does not confer *philosophical*—that is, *transcendental*, intelligibility. Philosophy, after all, demands an elucidation by virtue of the *ultimate* and *most concrete* essential necessities; and these are the necessities that satisfy the essential rootedness of any Objective world in transcendental subjectivity and thus make the world intelligible concretely: *as a constituted sense*. Only then, moreover, do the "supreme and final" questions become disclosed, those that are still to be addressed to the world even as understood in this manner.

One consequence of the beginning phase of phenomenology was that its method of pure but at the same time eidetic intuition led to attempts at a new ontology, fundamentally different in essence from the ontology of the eighteenth century, which operated logically with concepts remote from intuition; or, this being the same thing, attempts to draw *directly from concrete intuition*, in order to build particular a priori sciences (pure grammar, pure logic, pure jurisprudence, the eidetic theory of intuitively experienced Nature, and so forth) and, embracing them all, a universal ontology of the Objective world. As regards this, nothing prevents starting at first quite concretely with the human life-world around us, and with man himself as essentially related to this our surrounding world, and exploring, indeed purely intuitively, the extremely copious and never-discovered Apriori of any such surrounding world whatever, taking this Apriori as the point of departure for a systematic explication of human existence and of world strata that disclose themselves correlatively in the latter.

But what is acquired there straightforwardly, though it is a system of the Apriori, becomes philosophically intelligible and (according to what was said just now) an Apriori related back to the ultimate sources of understanding, only when problems of constitution, as problems of the specifically philosophical level, become disclosed and the natural realm of knowledge is at the same time exchanged for the transcendental. This implies that everything natural, everything given beforehand in straightforward intuition, must be built up again with a new originariness and not interpreted merely sequaciously as already definitive. That a procedure drawing insight from eidetic intuition is called phenomenological and claims philosophical significance is justified only by the circumstance that every genuine intuition has its place in the constitutional nexus. For this reason every intuitive ascertainment, in the attitude of positivity, concerning the sphere of eidetically necessary (axiomatic) fundamentals serves as *preliminary work* and is even indispensible a priori. It furnishes[33] the transcendental clue for discovery of the full constitutive concretion, as having both a noetic and a noematic aspect.

Regardless of the fact that it uncovers hidden horizons of sense on the ontic side (the overlooking of which seriously restricts the value of a priori ascertainments and makes their application uncertain), the significance and complete novelty of this going back into the constitutive is shown by the "monadological" results of our investigation.

§ 60. *Metaphysical results of our explication of experiencing someone else.*

Our monadological results are *metaphysical*, if it be true that ultimate cognitions of being should be called metaphysical. On the other hand, what we have here is *anything but metaphysics in the customary sense*: a historically degenerate metaphysics, which by no means conforms to the sense with which metaphysics, as "first philosophy," was instituted originally. Phenomenology's purely intuitive, concrete, and also apodictic mode of demonstration excludes all "metaphysical adventure," all speculative excesses.

Let us bring into relief some of *our* metaphysical results and at the same time draw further consequences.

A priori, my ego, given to me apodictically—the only thing I can posit in absolute apodicticity as existing—can be a world-experiencing ego only by being in communion with others like himself: a member of a community of monads, which is given orientedly, starting from himself. In that the Objective world of experience shows itself consistently, other monads show themselves consistently to be existent. Conversely, I cannot conceive a plurality of monads otherwise than as explicitly or implicitly in communion. This involves being a plurality of monads that constitutes in itself an Objective world and that spatializes, temporalizes, realizes itself—psychophysically and, in particular, as human beings—within that world. It is essentially necessary that the *togetherness* of monads, their mere *co*-existence, be a *temporal* co-existence and then also an existence temporalized in the form: "*real*" temporality.

But that entails further extremely important metaphysical results. Is it conceivable (to me, the subject who asks this, or, starting from me, any conceivable subject who might ask it)—is it, I ask, *conceivable* that two or more *separate pluralities of monads*, i.e., pluralities *not in communion*, co-exist, each of which accordingly constitutes *a world of its own*, so that together they constitute *two* worlds that are separate ad infinitum, *two* infinite *spaces and space-times*? Manifestly, instead of being a conceivability, that is a pure absurdity. A priori, as the *unity* of an intersubjectivity (an intersubjectivity, moreover, that possibly lacks every actual relation of community with the other intersubjectivity), each of two such groups of monads has, to be sure, its possibly quite different looking "world." But the two worlds are then necessarily *mere "surrounding worlds,"* belonging to these two intersubjectivities respectively, and mere aspects of a single Objective world, which is *common* to them. For indeed the two intersubjectivities are not absolutely isolated. As imagined by me, each of them is in necessary communion with me (or with me in respect of a possible variant of myself) as the constitutive primal monad relative to them. Accordingly they belong in truth to a single universal community, which includes me and comprises unitarily all the monads and groups of monads that can be conceived as co-existent. Actually, therefore, *there can exist only a single community of monads*, the community of *all* co-existing monads. Hence there can exist *only one Objective world*, only one Objective time, only one Objective space, only one Objective Nature. Moreover this one Nature *must* exist, if there are any structures in me that involve the co-existence of other monads. This alone is possible: that different groups of monads and different worlds are related to one another as those that may belong to stellar worlds we cannot see are related to us—that is, with animalia who lack all *actual* connexion with us. Their worlds, however, are surrounding worlds with open horizons that are only de facto, only accidentally, undiscoverable to them.

But the sense of this uniqueness of both the monadological world and the Objective world "innate" in it must be correctly understood. Naturally Leibniz is right when he says that infinitely many monads and groups of monads are conceivable but that it does not follow that all these possibilities are *compossible*; and, again, when he says that infinitely many worlds might have been "created," but not two or more at once, since they are imcompossible. It is to be noted in this connexion that, in a free variation, I can phantasy *first of all myself*, this apodictic de facto ego, as otherwise and can thus acquire the *system of possible variants of myself*, each of which, however, is annulled by each of the others and by the ego who I actually am. It is *a system of a priori incompossibility*. Furthermore the fact, "I am," prescribes *whether* other monads are others for me and *what* they are for me. I can only find them; I cannot create others that shall exist for me. If I phantasy myself as a pure possibility different from what I actually am, that possibility in turn prescribes what monads exist for him as others. And, proceeding in this fashion, I recognize that *each monad having the status of a concrete possibility predelineates a compossible universe*, a closed "world of monads," and that two worlds of monads are incompossible, just as two possible variants of my ego (or of any presupposedly phantasied ego whatever) are incompossible.

Such results and the course of the investigations leading to them enable us to understand how questions that, for traditional philosophy, had to lie beyond all the limits of science can acquire sense (regardless of how they may be decided)—for example, problems we touched on earlier.

§ 61. *The traditional problems of "psychological origins" and their phenomenological clarification.*

Within the world of men and brutes, we encounter the familiar natural-scientific problems of psychophysical, physiological, and psychological genesis. Among them is included the problem of psychic genesis. It is suggested to us by the development, in the course of which every child must build up his "idea of the world." The apperceptive system in which a world, as a realm of actual and possible experience, is there for him and always given beforehand must first of all become constituted in the course of the child's psychic development. The, child, considered Objectively, comes "into the world." How does he come to a "beginning" of his psychic life?

This psychophysical coming into the world leads back to the problem of live-bodily (purely "biological") individual development and phylogenesis, which, for its part, has its parallel in a psychological phylogenesis. But does that not point to corresponding interconnexions among the transcendental absolute monads, since indeed, so far as their psyches are concerned, men and brutes are self-Objectivations of monads? Should not this whole situation indicate most serious essential problems for a constitutional phenomenology, as "transcendental philosophy"?

To a great extent genetic problems, and naturally those of the first and most fundamental level, have indeed already been dealt with in the actual work of phenomenology. The fundamental level is, of course, the one pertaining to "my" ego in respect of his primordial own-essentialness. Constitution on the part of the consciousness of internal time and the whole phenomenological theory of association belong here; and what my primordial ego finds in original intuitive self-explication applies to every other ego forthwith, and for essential reasons. But with that, to be sure, the above-indicated *genetic problems of birth and death and the generative nexus of psychophysical being* have not yet been touched. Manifestly they belong to a higher dimension and presuppose such a tremendous labor of explication pertaining to the lower spheres that it will be a long time before they can become problems to work on.

Within the working sphere, however, let us indicate more precisely certain vast domains of problems (both static and genetic) that bring us into a closer relation to the philosophical tradition. Our connected intentional clarifications of the experience of someone else and the constitution of an Objective world took place on a basis given us beforehand in the transcendental attitude: a structural articulation of the primordial sphere, in which we already found a world, a primordial one. It had become accessible to us starting from the concrete world, taken qua "phenomenon," by means of that peculiar primordial reduction of the latter to what belongs to my ownness: a "world" of immanent transcendencies. It included the whole of Nature, reduced to the Nature appertaining to me myself by virtue of *my* pure sensuousness; but it included likewise the psychophysical man (with his psyche) as correspondingly reduced. As regards "Nature," not only "sight things," "touch things," and the like, but also to some extent complete physical things as substrates of causal properties were included, along with the all-embracing forms: space and time. Obviously the *first* problem for the constitutional clarification of the existential sense of the Objective world is to clarify the *origin of this primordial "Nature"* and that of the *primordial unity*[34] *of animate organism and psyche*—to clarify the constituting of them as immanent transcendencies. Actually to do so requires extraordinarily extensive investigations.

In this connexion we are again reminded of the problems concerning the "psychological origin" of the "idea of space," the "idea of time," the "idea of a physical thing"—problems dealt with so often in the last century by the most distinguished physiologists and psychologists. Much as the great projects bore the stamp of their distinguished authors, no actual clarification has as yet been attained.

When we turn from them to the set of problems that we have delimited and fitted into the phenomenological system of levels, it is evident that the whole of modern psychology and epistemology has failed to grasp the *proper sense* of the problems to be set here, both *psychologically and transcendentally*—their sense, namely, as problems of (static and genetic) *intentional explication*. To grasp it was, after all, impossible even for those who had accepted Brentano's doctrine of "psychic phenomena" as intentional processes. There was a lack of understanding for the peculiar character of an intentional "analysis" and all the tasks disclosed by consciousness as such, in respect of noesis and noema, a lack of understanding for the fundamentally novel methods these tasks require. About problems that concern the "psychological origins of the ideas of space, time, and the physical thing," no physics or physiology and no experimental or non-experimental psychology that moves similarly in the realm of inductive externalities has anything to say. Those are quite exclusively problems of intentional constitution that concern phenomena which are already given us beforehand as "clues" (or perhaps can become given beforehand, in particular, with the aid of an experiment), but which must now be interrogated for the first time according to the intentional method and *within the universal complexes of psychic constitution*. The kind of universality meant here is shown with sufficient distinctness in the case of the systematic unitary complex of those constitutions that are explicata of my ego, in respect of what is peculiar to my own self and what is other.

Phenomenology signifies indeed a fundamental refashioning of psychology too. Accordingly, by far the greater part of psychological research belongs in an *apriori and pure intentional psychology*. (Here the word "pure" means: kept free from everything psychophysical.) It is the same psychology, concerning which we have already indicated repeatedly that, by means of a change of the natural into the transcendental attitude, it is open to a "Copernican conversion," wherewith it assumes the new sense of a completely radical transcendental consideration of the world and impresses this sense on all phenomenological-psychological analyses. This sense alone makes such a psychology utilizable for transcendental philosophy and, indeed, gives it a place within a transcendental "metaphysics." Precisely in this lies the ultimate clarification and overcoming of the *transcendental psychologism* that has misled and paralysed the whole of modern philosophy.

As in the case of transcendental phenomenology, so also in the parallel case of intentional psychology (as a "positive" science) our exposition has manifestly predelineated a *fundamental structure*, a division of the corresponding investigations of eidetic psychology into those that explicate intentionally what is included in the *concrete own-essentiality of any psyche whatever* and those that explicate the intentionality pertaining to the otherness that becomes constituted therein. To the former sphere of research belongs the chief and fundamental part of the intentional explication of one's "idea of the world"—stated more precisely, explication of the "phenomenon," which makes its appearance within the human psyche: the existing world, as the world of universal experience. If this experiential world is reduced to the world constituted primordially in the single psyche, it is no longer everyone's world, the world that gets its sense from communalized human experience, but is exclusively this intentional correlate of the experiencing life that goes on in a single psyche, and first of all my experiencing life and its sense-fashionings in primordial originariness at various levels. Tracing these fashionings, intentional explication has to make constitutionally understandable this primordial core of the phenomenal world—this core, which every one of us men and, above all, every psychologist can acquire by the already-described exclusion of sense-moments pertaining to "otherness." If, within this primordial "world," we abstract from the reduced psychophysical being, "I, the man," primordial bare Nature remains, as the Nature pertaining to my own "bare sensuousness." As an initial problem concerning the psychological origin of the experiential world, there emerges here the problem concerning the origin of the "thing-phantom," or "thing pertaining to the senses," with its strata (sight thing, <touch thing,> and so forth) and their synthetic unity. The thing-phantom is given (always within the limits set by this primordial reduction) purely as a unity belonging to modes of sensuous appearance and their syntheses. The thing-phantom, in its variants as "near thing" and "far thing," all of which belong together synthetically, is not yet the "real thing" of the primordial psychic sphere. Even in this sphere the "real thing" becomes constituted at a higher level, as a causal thing, an identical substrate of causal properties (a "substance"). Obviously substance and causality indicate constitutional problems of a higher level. The constitutional problem of the thing pertaining to the senses, along with the problem of the spatiality and temporality that are fundamentally essential to it, is precisely the problem just now indicated. It is a problem of descriptive inquiry that concerns only the synthetic complexes of thing-appearances (apparencies, perspective aspects). Moreover, it is one-sided. The other side concerns the relation of the appearances back to the functioning animate organism, which in turn must be described in respect of its self-constitution and the signal peculiarity of its constitutive system of appearances.

When we proceed in this manner, new problems of descriptive explication continually arise, all of which must be solved systematically if even the constitution of the primordial "world," as a world of "realities"—along with the great problem of the constitution of spatiality and temporality, as essential to "realities" in that world—is to be dealt with seriously. As its execution shows, this task alone comprises a tremendous province of investigations; still it furnishes only the underlying level for a full phenomenology of Nature, as Objective and yet as pure Nature—which itself is far from being the concrete world.

Our discussion of psychology has given us occasion to translate the distinction between what is primordial and what is constituted as alien into terms of the purely psychic and to sketch as psychological problems (though only hastily) the problems relating to a primordial, and to an Objective, Nature.

If, however, we return to the transcendental attitude, our outlines of the problems relating to the psychological origin of the "idea of space," and the like, provide us conversely with outlines for the parallel problems of transcendental phenomenology—namely the problems involved in a concrete explication of primordial Nature and the primordial world as a whole. This fills a great gap in our earlier statement of the problems relating to constitution of the world as a transcendental phenomenon.

The extraordinarily vast complex of researches pertaining to the primordial world makes up a whole discipline, which we may designate as "transcendental aesthetics" in a very much broadened sense. We adopt the Kantian title here because the space and time arguments of the critique of reason obviously, though in an extraordinarily restricted and unclarified manner, have in view a noematic Apriori of sensuous intuition. Broadened to comprise the concrete Apriori of (primordial) Nature, as given in purely sensuous intuition, it then requires phenomenological transcendental supplementation by incorporation into a complex of constitutional problems. On the other hand, it would not be consistent with the sense of the correlative Kantian title, "transcendental analytics," if we used this as a name for the upper stories of the constitutional Apriori, which pertain to the *Objective* world itself and the multiplicities constituting it (at the highest level, the Apriori pertaining to the "idealizing" and theorizing acts that ultimately constitute scientific Nature and the scientific world). The theory of experiencing someone else, the theory of so-called "empathy," belongs in the first story above our "transcendental aesthetics." There is need only to indicate that what we said about the psychological problems of origin in the lower story applies here as well: For the first time, the problem of empathy has been given its true sense, and the true method for its solution has been furnished, by constitutional phenomenology. Precisely on that account all previous theories (including Max Scheler's) have failed to give an actual solution, and it has never been recognized that the otherness of "someone else" becomes extended to the whole world, as its "Objectivity," giving it this sense in the first place.

We would also state expressly that it would of course be pointless to treat the positive science of *intentional psychology* and *transcendental phenomenology separately*. Obviously the work of actual execution must devolve upon the latter, whereas psychology, unconcerned about the Copernican shift, will take over the results. Yet it is important to note that, just as the psyche and the whole Objective world do not lose their existence and existential sense when considered transcendentally (since they are merely rendered originarily understandable, by the uncovering of their concrete all-sidedness), so positive psychology does not lose its rightful content but rather, freed of naïve positivity, becomes a discipline within universal transcendental philosophy itself. From this point of view we may say that, among the sciences that have been raised above the level of naïve positivity, intentional psychology is intrinsically the first.

Indeed, it enjoys yet another advantage over all other positive sciences. If it is built up in the positive attitude according to the right method of intentional analysis, it can have no "problems of fundamentals," like those that infect the other positive sciences: problems that arise from the one-sidedness of naïvely constituted Objectivity, which finally demands that, in order to attain all-sidedness, we shift to a transcendental consideration of the world. But intentional psychology already has the transcendental hiddenly within itself; only a final clarification of its sense is needed in order to make the Copernican shift, which does not change the content of psychology's intentional results but only leads back to its "ultimate sense." Psychology has just one fundamental problem [*Fundamental-problem*], which (it may be objected) is ultimately a problem of fundamentals [*Grundlagenproblem*], albeit the only one: the concept of the psyche.

§ 62. *Survey of our intentional explication of experiencing someone else.*

Let us return now, at the conclusion of this chapter, to the objection by which at first we let ourselves be guided, the objection to our phenomenology, so far as, from the very beginning, it claimed to be transcendental philosophy and, as such, to have the ability to solve the problems that concern the possibility of Objective knowledge. The objection runs as follows. Starting from the transcendental ego of the phenomenological reduction and thenceforth restricted to him, phenomenology is incapable of solving those problems. Without admitting that it does so, it lapses into a transcendental solipsism; and the whole step leading to other subjectivity and to genuine Objectivity is possible only by virtue of an unacknowledged metaphysics, a concealed adoption of Leibnizian traditions.

Our actual explications have dissipated the objection as groundless. The following is to be noted above all. At no point was the transcendental attitude, the attitude of transcendental epoché abandoned; and our "theory" of experiencing someone else, our "theory" of experiencing others, did not aim at being and was not at liberty to be anything but explication of the sense, "others," as it arises from the constitutive productivity of that experiencing: the sense,[35] "truly existing others," as it arises from the corresponding harmonious syntheses. What I demonstrate to myself harmoniously as "someone else" and therefore have given to me, by necessity and not by choice, as an actuality to be acknowledged, is *eo ipso* the existing Other for me in the transcendental attitude: the alter ego demonstrated precisely within the experiencing intentionality of my ego. Within the bounds of positivity we say and find it obvious that, in my own experience, I experience not only myself but others—in the particular form: experiencing someone else. The indubitable[36] transcendental explication showed us not only that this positive statement is transcendentally legitimate but also that the concretely apprehended transcendental ego (who first becomes aware of himself, with his undetermined horizon, when he effects transcendental reduction) grasps himself in his own primordial being, and likewise (in the form of his transcendental experience of what is alien) grasps others: *other transcendental egos*, though they are given, not originaliter and in unqualifiedly apodictic evidence, but only in an evidence belonging to "external" experience. "In" myself I experience and know the Other; in me he becomes constituted—appresentatively mirrored, not constituted as the original. Hence it can very well be said, in a *broadened* sense, that the ego acquires—that I, as the one who meditatingly explicates, acquire by "self-explication" (explication of what I find in myself) every transcendency: as a transcendentally constituted transcendency and not as a transcendency accepted with naïve positivity. Thus the *illusion* vanishes: that *everything I*, qua transcendental ego, *know*[37] *as existing in consequence of myself*,[38] and explicate as *constituted in myself*, must *belong to me as part of my own essence*. This is true only of "immanent transcendencies." As a title for the systems of synthetic actuality and potentiality that confer sense and being on me as ego in my own essentialness, constitution signifies constitution of immanent objective actuality. *At the start of phenomenology*, when my attitude is that of someone who is *only starting*, who is instituting phenomenological reduction for the first time, as a universal condition under which to pursue constitutional research, *the transcendental ego who comes into view is, to be sure, grasped apodictically*—but as having *a quite undetermined horizon*, a horizon restricted only by the general requirement that the world and all I know about it shall become a mere "phenomenon." Consequently, when I am starting in this manner, all those distinctions are lacking which are made only subsequently by intentional explication but which nevertheless (as I now see) pertain to me essentially. There is lacking, above all, self-understanding with respect to my primordial essence, my sphere of ownness in the pregnant sense, and with respect to what, within that sphere itself, becomes constituted as an Other in experiencing someone else, as something appresented but essentially non-given (and never to become given) within my primordial sphere. I must first explicate *my own as such, in order to understand that, within my own, what is not my own likewise receives existential sense*—and does so as something appresented analogically. Therefore at the beginning I, the meditator, do not understand how I shall ever attain others and myself <as one among others>, since all other men are "parenthesized." At bottom moreover I do not yet understand, and I recognize only reluctantly, that, when I "parenthesize" myself qua man and qua human person, I myself am nevertheless to be retained qua ego. Thus I can as yet know nothing about a transcendental intersubjectivity; involuntarily I take myself, the ego, to be a *solus ipse* and still regard all constitutional components as merely contents of this one ego, even after I have acquired an initial understanding of constitutive performances. The further explications made in the present chapter were therefore necessary. Thanks to them, the *full and proper sense of phenomenological transcendental "idealism" becomes understandable* to us for the first time. The *illusion* of a solipsism is dissolved, *even though* the proposition that everything existing for me must derive its existential sense exclusively from me myself, from my sphere of consciousness retains its validity and fundamental importance. Phenomenological transcendental idealism has presented itself as a *monadology*, which, despite all our deliberate suggestions of Leibniz's metaphysics, draws its content purely from phenomenological explication of the transcendental experience laid open by transcendental reduction, accordingly from the most originary evidence, wherein all conceivable evidences must be grounded—or from the most originary legitimacy, which is the source of all legitimacies and, in particular, all legitimacies of knowledge. Actually, therefore, phenomenological explication is nothing like "metaphysical construction"; and it is neither overtly nor covertly a theorizing with adopted presuppositions or helpful thoughts drawn from the historical metaphysical tradition. It stands in sharpest contrast to all that, because it proceeds within the limits of pure "intuition," or rather of pure sense-explication based on a fulfilling givenness of the sense itself. Particularly in the case of the Objective world of realities (as well as in the case of each of the many ideal Objective worlds, which are the fields of purely a priori sciences)—and this cannot be emphasized often enough—phenomenological explication does nothing but *explicate the sense this world has for us all, prior to any philosophizing*, and obviously gets solely from our experience—*a sense which philosophy can uncover but never alter*, and which, because of an essential necessity, not because of our weakness, entails (in the case of any actual, experience) horizons that need fundamental clarification.

Notes

Editors' note: This chapter is extracted from *Cartesian Meditations*, translated by Dorion Cairns, which is based on the following texts: the first volume of *Husserliana*, published in 1950 by Martinus Nijhoff, Husserl's typescript cited as "Typescript C", and its French translation by Gabrielle Peiffer and Emmanuel Levinas in 1931.

1. Marginal note; Seems? Is.

2. The phrase rendered by "in me" crossed out.

3. The word rendered as "belonging to my" crossed out. Marginal comment: "The dangerous first person singular! This should be expanded terminologically."

4. This sentence crossed out. Three exclamation points in the margin.

5. Reading, with Typescript C, "*Sinnesschichte*" instead of "*Sinngeschichte*" (sense history).

6 Reading "*ihnen*" (them) instead of "*innen*" (within), as in both the published text and Typescript C.

7. Originally: constitutes himself in his peculiar ownness and synthetic unities inseparable from his peculiar ownness, which are therefore to be accounted as part of it.

The following comment was appended later:

§ 44. "inside the universal transcendental sphere"—"peculiar epoché." But it is misleading when the text goes on to say: "in that we exclude from the theoretical <*sic*> field everything now in question, in that we <disregard> all constitutional effects that relate immediately or mediately to other subjectivity," etc.

The question after all concerns, not other men, but the manner in which the ego (as the transcendental onlooker experiences him transcendentally) constitutes within himself the distinction between Ego and Other Ego—a difference, however, that presents itself first of all in the phenomenon, "world": as the difference between my human Ego (my Ego in the usual sense) and the other human Ego (the other Ego <likewise in the usual sense>).

8. Strasser attaches here the following note, which Husserl wrote on a separate sheet:

The total appearance of the world—the world always intended in the flux.

The total appearance of Nature.

The total intending of the world, the particular intending—the particular appearance of the particular wordly object. But the intending has strata; I can abstract. Physical-thing appearance, stratum of culture or stratum of human existence as <blank-space> in the flowing present. The stream of world-"appearances," of "perceptual appearances"; what is intended ontologically. Cogito-strata, such that each stratum has a stratum of the cogitatum. The ego directed to what is intended.

9. Marginal comment: ?! To men and to myself as a man.

10. Reading, with Typescript C, "und" instead of "uns" (to us).

11. The phrase "as a phenomenon" supplied in accordance with Typescript C and the French translation.

12. The phrase "reduced to what is included in his ownness" supplied in accordance with Typescript C and the French translation.

13. Reading "*seiner*" instead of "*meiner*" (my), as in both the published text and Typescript C.

14. Supplied in accordance with Typescript C and the French translation

15. According to Typescript C: "and my abiding identity with myself."

16. Reading "*unmittelbarer*" instead of "*unmittelbar*" (immediately), as in both the published text and Typescript C. Cf. the French: "*immédiate et concrète.*"

17. Reading with Typescript C and the French translation. According to the published text: "or (as we may also say) in my monad."

18. According to the published text, Typescript C and the French translation: "immediately."

19. Supplied in accordance with Typescript C and the French translation.

20. The words "another" and "immediately" supplied in accordance with Typescript C and the French translation.

21. Supplied in accordance with Typescript C and the French translation.

22. Reading with the original typescript, as given in the appendix to the published text.

23. Reading, with Typescript C, "*einer eigenwesentlich-anderen*" instead of "*einer eigenwesentlichen anderen*" (another subjectivity having its own essence). Cf. the French: "*ayant un être essentiellement propre.*"

24. Reading "*entsprechend*" instead of "*entsprechende*" (similar), as in both the published text and Typescript C.

25. Reading with Typescript C and the French version. According to the published text: "that for me."

26. Reading with Typescript C, "*sie hat stets ihren,*" instead of "*aber dock mindestens als.*" Cf. the French: "*elle a toujours ses.*"

27. Reading with Typescript C: "*Aber verständlick ist sehr leicht,*" instead of "*Aber selbstverständlick ist es sehr leicht*" (But of course it is very easy), which makes the sentence incomplete. Cf. the French: "*on comprend facilement.*"

28. The phrase, "the character of acts of mine directed to you," supplied in accordance with Typescript C, "*von Ich-Du-Akten,*" and the French, "*d'actes allant 'de moi a toi.'*"

29. In accordance with Typescript C and the French translation, the passage of the published text that follows here, p. 161, 11. 15–21, is assigned a later position. See the next note.

30. In accordance with Typescript C and the French translation, the passage beginning "We see . . ." has been transposed. See the preceding note.

31. Supplied in accordance with Typescript C and the French translation.

32. Reading "*einem*" instead of "*meinem*" (my), as in both the published text and Typescript C. Cf. the French translation: "*une forme.*"

33. Reading with Typescript C and the French translation. According to the published text: "Its result must become . . ."

34. Reading "*Einheit*" instead of "*Einheitern*" (unities) as in both the published text and Typescript C. In the French translation: "*unités.*"

35. Reading, with Typescript C, "*des Sinnes,*" instead of "*des Limes*" (the limit). Cf. the French: "*le sens.*"

36. Reading with Typescript C, "*zweifellose*" instead of "*zweifellos*" (indubitably).

37. Reading, with Typescript C, "*erkenne*" instead of "*erkennen.*"

38. Reading, with Typescript C, "*aus mir selbst*" instead of simply "*mir selbst.*"

8   Being-in-the-World as Being-With and Being-One's-Self. The "They"

Martin Heidegger

Our analysis of the worldhood of the world has constantly been bringing the whole phenomenon of Being-in-the-world into view, although its constitutive items have not all stood out with the same phenomenal distinctness as the phenomenon of the world itself. We have Interpreted the world ontologically by going through what is ready-to-hand within-the-world; and this Interpretation has been put first, because Dasein, in its everydayness (with regard to which Dasein remains a constant theme for study), not only is in a world but comports itself towards that world with one predominant kind of Being. Proximally and for the most part Dasein is fascinated with its world. Dasein is thus absorbed in the world; the kind of Being which it thus possesses, and in general the Being-in which underlies it, are essential in determining the character of a phenomenon which we are now about to study. We shall approach this phenomenon by asking *who* it is that Dasein is in its everydayness. All the structures of Being which belong to Dasein, together with the phenomenon which provides the answer to this question of the "who," are ways of its Being. To characterize these ontologically is to do so existentially. We must therefore pose the question correctly and outline the procedure for bringing into view a broader phenomenal domain of Dasein's everydayness. By directing our researches towards the phenomenon which is to provide us with an answer to the question of the "who," we shall be led to certain structures of Dasein which are equiprimordial with Being-in-the-world: *Being-with* and *Dasein-with* [*Mitsein* and *Mitdasein*]. In this kind of Being is grounded the mode of everyday Being-one's-Self [Selbstsein]; the explication of this mode will enable us to see what we may call the "subject" of everydayness—the "*they*."

Our chapter on the "who" of the average Dasein will thus be divided up as follows: 1. an approach to the existential question of the "who" of Dasein (Section 25); 2. the Dasein-with of Others, and everyday Being-with (Section 26); 3. everyday Being-one's-Self and the "they" (Section 27).[1]

§ 25.   An Approach to the Existential Question of the "Who" of Dasein

The answer to the question of who Dasein is, is one that was seemingly given in Section 9, where we indicated formally the basic characteristics of Dasein. Dasein is an entity which is in each case I myself; its Being is in each case mine. This definition *indicates* an *ontologically* constitutive state, but it does no more than indicate it. At the same time this tells us *ontically* (though in a rough and ready fashion) that in each case an "I"—not Others—is this entity. The question of the "who" answers itself in terms of the "I" itself, the "subject," the "Self."[2] The "who" is what maintains itself as something identical throughout changes in its Experiences and ways of behaviour, and which relates itself to this changing multiplicity in so doing. Ontologically we understand it as something which is in each case already constantly present-at-hand, both in and for a closed realm, and which lies at the basis, in a very special sense, as the *subjectum*. As something selfsame in manifold otherness,[3] it has the character of the *Self*. Even if one rejects the "soul substance" and the Thinghood of consciousness, or denies that a person is an object, ontologically one is still positing something whose Being retains the meaning of present-at-hand, whether it does so explicitly or not. Substantiality is the ontological clue for determining which entity is to provide the answer to the question of the "who." Dasein is tacitly conceived in advance as something present-at-hand. This meaning of Being is always implicated in any case where the Being of Dasein has been left indefinite. Yet presence-at-hand is the kind of Being which belongs to entities whose character is not that of Dasein.

The assertion that it is I who in each case Dasein is, is ontically obvious; but this must not mislead us into supposing that the route for an ontological Interpretation of what is "given" in this way has thus been unmistakably prescribed. Indeed it remains questionable whether even the mere ontical content of the above assertion does proper justice to the stock of phenomena belonging to everyday Dasein. It could be that the "who" of everyday. Dasein just is *not* the "I myself."

If, in arriving at ontico-ontological assertions, one is to exhibit the phenomena in terms of the kind of Being which the entities themselves possess, and if this way of exhibiting them is to retain its priority over even the most usual and obvious of answers and over whatever ways of formulating problems may have been derived from those answers, then the phenomenological Interpretation of Dasein must be defended against a perversion of our problematic when we come to the question we are about to formulate.

But is it not contrary to the rules of all sound method to approach a problematic without sticking to what is given as evident in the area of our theme? And what is more indubitable than the givenness of the "I"? And does not this givenness tell us that if we aim to work this out primordially, we must disregard everything else that is "given"—not only a "world" that is [einer seienden "Welt"], but even the Being of other "I"s? The kind of "giving" we have here is the mere, formal, reflective awareness of the "I"; and perhaps what it gives is indeed evident.[4] This insight even affords access to a phenomenological problematic in its own right, which has in principle the signification of providing a framework as a "formal phenomenology of consciousness."

In this context of an existential analytic of factical Dasein, the question arises whether giving the "I" in the way we have mentioned discloses Dasein in its everydayness, if it discloses Dasein at all. Is it then obvious *a priori* that access to Dasein must be gained only by mere reflective awareness of the "I" of actions? What if this kind of "giving-itself" on the part of Dasein should lead our existential analytic astray and do so, indeed, in a manner grounded in the Being of Dasein itself? Perhaps when Dasein addresses itself in the way which is closest to itself, it always says "I am this entity," and in the long run says this loudest when it is "not" this entity. Dasein is in each case mine, and this is its constitution; but what if this should be the very reason why, proximally and for the most part, Dasein *is not itself?* What if the aforementioned approach, starting with the givenness of the "I" to Dasein itself, and with a rather patent self-interpretation of Dasein, should lead the existential analytic, as it were, into a pitfall? If that which is accessible by mere "giving" can be determined, there is presumably an ontological horizon for determining it; but what if this horizon should remain in principle undetermined? It may well be that it is always ontically correct to say of this entity that "I" am it. Yet the ontological analytic which makes use of such assertions must make certain reservations about them in principle. The word "I" is to be understood only in the sense of a non-committal *formal indicator*, indicating something which may perhaps reveal itself as its "opposite" in some particular phenomenal context of Being. In that case, the "not-I" is by no means tantamount to an entity which essentially lacks "I-hood" ["Ichheit"], but is rather a definite kind of Being which the "I" itself possesses, such as having lost itself [Selbstverlorenheit].

Yet even the positive Interpretation of Dasein which we have so far given, already forbids us to start with the formal givenness of the "I," if our purpose is to answer the question of the "who" in a way which is phenomenally adequate. In clarifying Being-in-the-world we have shown that a bare subject without a world never "is" proximally, nor is it ever given. And so in the end an isolated "I" without Others is just as far from being proximally given. If, however, "the Others" already *are there with us* [*mit da sind*] in Being-in-the-world, and if this is ascertained phenomenally, even this should not mislead us into supposing that the *ontological* structure of what is thus "given" is obvious, requiring no investigation. Our task is to make visible phenomenally the species to which this Dasein-with in closest everydayness belongs, and to Interpret it in a way which is ontologically appropriate.

Just as the ontical obviousness of the Being-in-itself of entities within-the-world misleads us into the conviction that the meaning of this Being is obvious ontologically, and makes us overlook the phenomenon of the world, the ontical obviousness of the fact that Dasein is in each case mine, also hides the possibility that the ontological problematic which belongs to it has been led astray. *Proximally* the "who" of Dasein is not only a problem *ontologically*; even *ontically* it remains concealed.

But does this mean that there are no clues whatever for answering the question of the "who" by way of existential analysis? Certainly not. Of the ways in which we formally indicated the constitution of Dasein's Being in Sections 9 and 12 above, the one we have been discussing does not, of course, function so well as such a clue as does the one according to which Dasein's "Essence" is grounded in its existence.[5] *If the "I" is an Essential characteristic of Dasein, then it is one which must be Interpreted existentially.* In that case the "Who?" is to be answered only by exhibiting phenomenally a definite kind of Being which Dasein possesses. If in each case Dasein is its Self only in *existing*, then the constancy of the Self no less than the possibility of its "failure to stand by itself"[6] requires that we formulate the question existentially and ontologically as the sole appropriate way of access to its problematic.

But if the Self is conceived "only" as a way of Being of this entity, this seems tantamount to volatilizing the real "core" of Dasein. Any apprehensiveness however which one may have about this gets its nourishment from the perverse assumption that the entity in question has at bottom the kind of Being which belongs to something present-at-hand, even if one is far from attributing to it the solidity of an occurrent corporeal Thing. Yet man's "*substance*" is not spirit as a synthesis of soul and body; it is rather *existence*.

§ 26.   *The Dasein-with of Others and Everyday Being-with*

The answer to the question of the "who" of everyday Dasein is to be obtained by analysing that kind of Being in which Dasein maintains itself proximally and for the most part. Our investigation takes its orientation from Being-in-the-world—that basic state of Dasein by which every mode of its Being gets co-determined. If we are correct in saying that by the foregoing explication of the world, the remaining structural items of Being-in-the-world have become visible, then this must also have prepared us, in a way, for answering the question of the "who."

In our "description" of that environment which is closest to us—the work-world of the craftsman, for example—the outcome was that along with the equipment to be found when one is at work [in Arbeit], those Others for whom the "work" ["Werk"] is destined are "encountered too." If this is ready-to-hand, then there lies in the kind of Being which belongs to it (that is, in its involvement) an essential assignment or reference to possible wearers, for instance, for whom it should be "cut to the figure." Similarly, when material is put to use, we encounter its producer or "supplier" as one who "serves" well or badly. When, for example, we walk along the edge of a field but "outside it," the field shows itself as belonging to such-and-such a person, and decently kept up by him; the book we have used was bought at So-and-so's shop and given by such-and-such a person, and so forth. The boat anchored at the shore is assigned in its Being-in-itself to an acquaintance who undertakes voyages with it; but even if it is a "boat which is strange to us," it still is indicative of Others. The Others who are thus "encountered" in a ready-to-hand, environmental context of equipment, are not somehow added on in thought to some Thing which is proximally just present-at-hand; such "Things" are encountered from out of the world in which they are ready-to-hand for Others—a world which is always mine too in advance. In our previous analysis, the range of what is encountered within-the-world was, in the first instance, narrowed down to equipment ready-to-hand or Nature present-at-hand, and thus to entities with a character other than that of Dasein. This restriction was necessary not only for the purpose of simplifying our explication but above all because the kind of Being which belongs to the Dasein of Others, as we encounter it within-the-world, differs from readiness-to-hand and presence-at-hand. Thus Dasein's world frees entities which not only are quite distinct from equipment and Things, but which also—in accordance with their kind of Being *as Dasein* themselves—are "in" the world in which they are at the same time encountered within-the-world, and are "in" it by way of Being-in-the-world.[7] These entities are neither present-at-hand nor ready-to-hand; on the contrary, they are *like* the very Dasein which frees them, in that *they are there too, and there with it.* So if one should want to identify the world in general with entities within-the-world, one would have to say that Dasein too is "world."[8]

Thus in characterizing the encountering of *Others*, one is again still oriented by that Dasein which is in each case one's *own*. But even in this characterization does one not start by marking out and isolating the "I" so that one must then seek some way of getting over to the Others from this isolated subject? To avoid this misunderstanding we must notice in what sense we are talking about "the Others." By "Others" we do not mean everyone else but me—those over against whom the "I" stands out. They are rather those from whom, for the most part, one does *not* distinguish oneself—those among whom one is too. This Being-there-too [Auch-da-sein] with them does not have the ontological character of a Being-present-at-hand-along-"with" them within a world. This "with" is something of the character of Dasein; the "too" means a sameness of Being as circumspectively concernful Being-in-the-world. "With" and "too" are to be understood *existentially*, not categorially. By reason of this *with-like* [mithaften] Being-in-the-world, the world is always the one that I share with Others. The world of Dasein is a *with-world* [Mitwelt]. Being-in is *Being-with* Others. Their Being-in-themselves within-the-world is *Dasein-with* [Mitdasein].

When Others are encountered, it is not the case that one's own subject is *proximally* present-at-hand and that the rest of the subjects, which are likewise occurrents, get discriminated beforehand and then apprehended; nor are they encountered by a primary act of looking at oneself in such a way that the opposite pole of a distinction first gets ascertained. They are encountered from out of the *world*, in which concernfully circumspective Dasein essentially dwells. Theoretically concocted "explanations" of the Being-present-at-hand of Others urge themselves upon us all too easily; but over against such explanations we must hold fast to the phenomenal facts of the case which we have pointed out, namely, that Others are encountered *environmentally*. This elemental worldly kind of encountering, which belongs to Dasein and is closest to it, goes so far that even one's *own* Dasein becomes something that it can itself proximally "come across" only when it *looks away* from "Experiences" and the "centre of its actions," or does not as yet "see" them at all. Dasein finds "itself" proximally in *what* it does, uses, expects, avoids—in those things environmentally ready-to-hand with which it is proximally *concerned*.

And even when Dasein explicitly addresses itself as "I here," this locative personal designation must be understood in terms of Dasein's existential spatiality. In Interpreting this (see Section 23) we have already intimated that this "I-here" does not mean a certain privileged point—that of an I-Thing—but is to be understood as Being-in in terms of the "yonder" of the world that is ready-to-hand—the "yonder" which is the dwelling-place of Dasein as *concern*.[9]

W. von Humboldt has alluded to certain languages which express the "I" by "here," the "thou" by "there," the "he" by "yonder," thus rendering the personal pronouns by locative adverbs, to put it grammatically. It is controversial whether indeed the primordial signification of locative expressions is adverbial or pronominal. But this dispute loses its basis if one notes that locative adverbs have a relationship to the "I" *qua* Dasein. The "here" and the "there" and the "yonder" are primarily not mere ways of designating the location of entities present-at-hand within-the-world at positions in space; they are rather characteristics of Dasein's primordial spatiality. These supposedly locative adverbs are Dasein-designations; they have a signification which is primarily existential, not categorial. But they are not pronouns either; their signification is prior to the differentiation of locative adverbs and personal pronouns: these expressions have a Dasein-signification which is authentically spatial, and which serves as evidence that when we interpret Dasein without any theoretical distortions we can see it immediately as "Being-alongside" the world with which it concerns itself, and as Being-alongside it spatially—that is to say, as desevering and giving directionality. In the "here," the Dasein which is absorbed in its world speaks not towards itself but away from itself towards the "yonder" of something circumspectively ready-to-hand; yet it still has *itself* in view in its existential spatiality.

Dasein understands itself proximally and for the most part in terms of its world; and the Dasein-with of Others is often encountered in terms of what is ready-to-hand within-theworld. But even if Others become themes for study, as it were, in their own Dasein, they are not encountered as person-Things present-at-hand: we meet them "at work," that is, primarily in their Being-in-the-world. Even if we see the Other "just standing around," he is never apprehended as a human-Thing present-at-hand, but his "standing-around" is an existential mode of Being—an unconcerned, uncircumspective tarrying alongside everything and nothing [Verweilen bei Allem und Keinem]. The Other is encountered in his Dasein-with in the world.

The expression "Dasein," however, shows plainly that "in the first instance" this entity is unrelated to Others, and that of course it can still be "with" Others afterwards. Yet one must not fail to notice that we use the term "Dasein-with" to designate that Being for which the Others who are [die seienden Anderen] are freed within-the-world. This Dasein-with of the Others is disclosed within-the-world for a Dasein, and so too for those who are Daseins with us [die Mitdaseienden], only because Dasein in itself is essentially Being-with. The phenomenological assertion that "Dasein is essentially Being-with" has an existential-ontological meaning. It does not seek to establish ontically that factically I am not present-athand alone, and that Others of my kind occur. If this were what is meant by the proposition that Dasein's Being-in-the-world is essentially constituted by Being-with, then Being-with would not be an existential attribute which Dasein, of its own accord, has coming to it from its own kind of Being. It would rather be something which turns up in every case by reason of the occurrence of Others. Being-with is an existential characteristic of Dasein even when factically no Other is present-at-hand or perceived. Even Dasein's Being-alone is Being-with in the world. The Other can *be missing* only *in* and *for*[10] a Being-with. Being-alone is a deficient mode of Being-with; its very possibility is the proof of this. On the other hand, factical Being-alone is not obviated by the occurrence of a second example of a human being "beside" me, or by ten such examples. Even if these and more are present-at-hand, Dasein can still be alone. So Being-with and the facticity of Being with one another are not based on the occurrence together of several "subjects." Yet Being-alone "among" many does not mean that with regard to their Being they are merely present-at-hand there alongside us. Even in our Being "among them" they are *there with* us; their Dasein-with is encountered in a mode in which they are indifferent and alien. Being missing and "Being away" [Das Fehlen und "Fortsein"] are modes of Dasein-with, and are possible only because Dasein as Being-with lets the Dasein of Others be encountered in its world. Being-with is in every case a characteristic of one's own Dasein; Dasein-with characterizes the Dasein of Others to the extent that it is freed by its world for a Being-with. Only so far as one's own Dasein has the essential structure of Being-with, is it Dasein-with as encounterable for Others.[11]

If Dasein-with remains existentially constitutive for Being-in-the-world, then, like our circumspective dealings with the ready-to-hand within-the-world (which, by way of anticipation, we have called "concern"), it must be Interpreted in terms of the phenomenon of *care*; for as "care" the Being of Dasein in general is to be defined.[12] (Compare Chapter 6 of this Division.) Concern is a character-of-Being which Being-with cannot have as its own, even though Being-with, like concern, is a *Being towards* entities encountered within-the-world. But those entities towards which Dasein as Being-with comports itself do not have the kind of Being which belongs to equipment ready-to-hand; they are themselves Dasein. These entities are not objects of concern, but rather of *solicitude*.[13]

Even "concern" with food and clothing, and the nursing of the sick body, are forms of solicitude. But we understand the expression "solicitude" in a way which corresponds to our use of "concern" as a term for an *existentiale*. For example, "welfare work" ["Fürsorge"], as a factical social arrangement, is grounded in Dasein's state of Being as Being-with. Its factical urgency gets its motivation in that Dasein maintains itself proximally and for the most part in the deficient modes of solicitude. Being for, against, or without one another, passing one another by, not "mattering" to one another—these are possible ways of solicitude. And it is precisely these last-named deficient and Indifferent modes that characterize everyday, average Being-with-one-another. These modes of Being show again the characteristics of inconspicuousness and obviousness which belong just as much to the everyday Dasein-with of Others within-the-world as to the readiness-to-hand of the equipment with which one is daily concerned. These Indifferent modes of Being-with-one-another may easily mislead ontological Interpretation into interpreting this kind of Being, in the first instance, as the mere Being-present-at-hand of several subjects. It seems as if only negligible variations of the same kind of Being lie before us; yet ontologically there is an essential distinction between the "indifferent" way in which Things at random occur together and the way in which entities who are with one another do not "matter" to one another.

With regard to its positive modes, solicitude has two extreme possibilities. It can, as it were, take away "care" from the Other and put itself in his position in concern: it can *leap in* for him.[14] This kind of solicitude takes over for the Other that with which he is to concern himself. The Other is thus thrown out of his own position; he steps back so that afterwards, when the matter has been attended to, he can either take it over as something finished and at his disposal,[15] or disburden himself of it completely. In such solicitude the Other can become one who is dominated and dependent, even if this domination is a tacit one and remains hidden from him. This kind of solicitude, which leaps in and takes away "care," is to a large extent determinative for Being with one another, and pertains for the most part to our concern with the ready-to-hand.

In contrast to this, there is also the possibility of a kind of solicitude which does not so much leap in for the Other as *leap ahead* of him [*ihmvorausspringt*] in his existentiell potentiality-for-Being, not in order to take away his "care" but rather to give it back to him authentically as such for the first time. This kind of solicitude pertains essentially to authentic care—that is, to the existence of the Other, not to a "*what*" with which he is concerned; it helps the Other to become transparent to himself *in* his care and to become *free for* it.

Solicitude proves to be a state of Dasein's Being—one which, in accordance with its different possibilities, is bound up with its Being towards the world of its concern, and likewise with its authentic Being towards itself. Being with one another is based proximally and often exclusively upon what is a matter of common concern in such Being. A Being-with-one-another which arises [entspringt] from one's doing the same thing as someone else, not only keeps for the most part within the outer limits, but enters the mode of distance and reserve. The Being-with-one-another of those who are hired for the same affair often thrives only on mistrust. On the other hand, when they devote themselves to the same affair in common, their doing so is determined by the manner in which their Dasein, each in its own way, has been taken hold of.[16] They thus become *authentically* bound together, and this makes possible the right kind of objectivity [die rechte Sachlichkeit], which frees the Other in his freedom for himself.

Everyday Being-with-one-another maintains itself between the two extremes of positive solicitude—that which leaps in and dominates, and that which leaps forth and liberates [vorspringend-befreienden]. It brings numerous mixed forms to maturity;[17] to describe these and classify them would take us beyond the limits of this investigation.

Just as *circumspection* belongs to concern as a way of discovering what is ready-to-hand, solicitude is guided by *considerateness* and *forbearance*.[18] Like solicitude, these can range through their respective deficient and Indifferent modes up to the point of *inconsiderateness* or the perfunctoriness for which indifference leads the way.[19]

The world not only frees the ready-to-hand as entities encountered within-the-world; it also frees Dasein—the Others in their Dasein-with. But Dasein's ownmost meaning of Being is such that this entity (which has been freed environmentally) is Being-in in the same world in which, as encounterable for Others, it is there with them. We have interpreted worldhood as that referential totality which constitutes significance (Section 18). In Being-familiar with this significance and previously understanding it, Dasein lets what is ready-to-hand be encountered as discovered in its involvement. In Dasein's Being, the context of references or assignments which significance implies is tied up with Dasein's ownmost Being—a Being which essentially can have no involvement, but which is rather that Being *for the sake of which* Dasein itself is as it is.

According to the analysis which we have now completed, Being with Others belongs to the Being of Dasein, which is an issue for Dasein in its very Being.[20] Thus as Being-with, Dasein "is" essentially for the sake of Others. This must be understood as an existential statement as to its essence. Even if the particular factical Dasein does *not* turn to Others, and supposes that it has no reed of them or manages to get along without them, it *is* in the way of Being-with. In Being-with, as the existential "for the-sake-of" of Others, these have already been disclosed in their Dasein. With their Being-with, their disclosedness has been constituted beforehand; accordingly, this disclosedness also goes to make up significance– that is to say, worldhood. And, significance, as worldhood, is tied up with the existential "for-the-sake-of-which."[21] Since the worldhood of that world in which every Dasein essentially is already, is thus constituted, it accordingly lets us encounter what is environmentally ready-to-hand as something with which we are circumspectively concerned, and it does so in such a way that together with it we encounter the Dasein-with of Others. The structure of the world's worldhood is such that Others are not proximally present-at-hand as free-floating subjects along with other Things, but show themselves in the world in their special environmental Being, and do so in terms of what is ready-to-hand in that world.

Being-with is such that the disclosedness of the Dasein-with of Others belongs to it; this means that because Dasein's Being is Being-with, its understanding of Being already implies the understanding of Others. This understanding, like any understanding, is not an acquaintance derived from knowledge about them, but a primordially existential kind of Being, which, more than anything else, makes such knowledge and acquaintance possible.[22] Knowing oneself [Sichkennen] is grounded in Being-with, which understands primordially. It operates proximally in accordance with the kind of Being which is closest to us—Being-in-the-world as Being-with; and it does so by an acquaintance with that which Dasein, along with the Others, comes across in its environmental circumspection and concerns itself with—an acquaintance in which Dasein understands. Solicitous concern is understood in terms of what we are concerned with, and along with our understanding of it. Thus in concernful solicitude the Other is proximally disclosed.

But because solicitude dwells proximally and for the most part in the deficient or at least the Indifferent modes (in the indifference of passing one another by), the kind of knowing-oneself which is essential and closest, demands that one become acquainted with oneself.[23] And when, indeed, one's knowing-oneself gets lost in such ways as aloofness, hiding oneself away, or putting on a disguise, Being-with-one-another must follow special routes of its own in order to come close to Others, or even to "see through them" ["hinter sie" zu kommen].

But just as opening oneself up [Sichoffenbaren] or closing oneself off is grounded in one's having Being-with-one-another as one's kind of Being at the time, and indeed *is* nothing else but this, even the explicit disclosure of the Other in solicitude grows only out of one's primarily Being with him in each case. Such a disclosure of the Other (which is indeed thematic, but not in the manner of theoretical psychology) easily becomes the phenomenon which proximally comes to view when one considers the theoretical problematic of under-standing the "psychical life of Others" ["fremden Seelenlebens"]. In this phenomenally "proximal" manner it thus presents a way of Being with one another understandingly; but at the same time it gets taken as that which, primordially and "in the beginning," constitutes Being towards Others and makes it possible at all.

This phenomenon, which is none too happily designated as *"empathy"* [*"Einfühlung"*], is then supposed, as it were, to provide the first ontological bridge from one's own subject, which is given proximally as alone, to the other subject, which is proximally quite closed off.

Of course Being towards Others is ontologically different from Being towards Things which are present-at-hand. The entity which is "other" has itself the same kind of Being as Dasein. In Being with and towards Others, there is thus a relationship of Being [Seins-verhältnis] from Dasein to Dasein. But it might be said that this relationship is already constitutive for one's own Dasein, which, in its own right, has an understanding of Being, and which thus relates itself[24] towards Dasein. The relationship-of-Being which one has towards Others would then become a Projection[25] of one's own Being-towards-oneself "into something else." The Other would be a duplicate of the Self.

But while these deliberations seem obvious enough, it is easy to see that they have little ground to stand on. The presupposition which this argument demands—that Dasein's Being towards itself is Being towards an Other—fails to hold. As long as the legitimacy of this presupposition has not turned out to be evident, one may still be puzzled as to how Dasein's relationship to itself is thus to be disclosed to the Other as Other.

Not only is Being towards Others an autonomous, irreducible relationship of Being: this relationship, as Being-with, is one which, with Dasein's Being, already is.[26] Of course it is indisputable that a lively mutual acquaintanceship on the basis of Being-with, often depends upon how far one's own Dasein has understood itself at the time; but this means that it depends only upon how far one's essential Being with Others has made itself transparent and has not disguised itself.[27] And that is possible only if Dasein, as Being-in-the-world, already is with Others. "Empathy" does not first constitute Being-with; only on the basis of Being-with does "empathy" become possible: it gets its motivation from the unsociability of dominant modes of Being-with.[28]

But the fact that "empathy" is not a primordial existential phenomenon, any more than is knowing in general, does not mean that there is nothing problematical about it. The special hermeneutic of empathy will have to show how Being-with-one-another and Dasein's knowing of itself are led astray and obstructed by the various possibilities of Being which Dasein itself possesses, so that a genuine "understanding" gets suppressed, and Dasein takes refuge in substitutes; the possibility of understanding the stranger correctly presupposes such a hermeneutic as its positive existential condition.[29] Our analysis has shown that Being-with is an existential constituent of Being-in-the-world. Dasein-with has proved to be a kind of Being which entities encountered within-the-world have as their own. So far as Dasein *is* at all, it has Being-with-one-another as its kind of Being. This cannot be conceived as a summative result of the occurrence of several "subjects." Even to come across a number of "subjects" [einer Anzahl von "Subjekten"] becomes possible only if the Others who are concerned proximally in their Dasein-with are treated merely as "numerals" ["Nummer"]. Such a number of "subjects" gets discovered only by a definite Being-with-and-towards-one-another. This "inconsiderate" Being-with "reckons" ["rechnet"] with the Others without seriously "counting on them" ["auf sie zählt"], or without even wanting to "have anything to do" with them.

One's own Dasein, like the Dasein-with of Others, is encountered proximally and for the most part in terms of the with-world with which we are environmentally concerned. When Dasein is absorbed in the world of its concern—that is, at the same time, in its Being-with towards Others—it is not itself. *Who* is it, then, who has taken over Being as everyday Being-with-one-another?

§ 27. Everyday Being-one's-Self and the "They"

The *ontologically* relevant result of our analysis of Being-with is the insight that the "subject character" of one's own Dasein and that of Others is to be defined existentially—that is, in terms of certain ways in which one may be. In that with which we concern ourselves environmentally the Others are encountered as what they are; they *are* what they do [sie *sind* das, was sie betreiben].

In one's concern with what one has taken hold of, whether with, for, or against, the Others, there is constant care as to the way one differs from them, whether that difference is merely one that is to be evened out, whether one's own Dasein has lagged behind the Others and wants to catch up in relationship to them, or whether one's Dasein already has some priority over them and sets out to keep them suppressed. The care about this distance between them is disturbing to Being-with-one-another, though this disturbance is one that is hidden from it. If we may express this existentially, such Being-with-one-another has the character of *distantiality* [Abständigkeit]. The more inconspicuous this kind of Being is to everyday Dasein itself, all the more stubbornly and primordially does it work itself out.

But this distantiality which belongs to Being-with, is such that Dasein, as everyday Being-with-one-another, stands in *subjection* [*Botmässigkeit*] to Others. It itself *is* not;[30] its Being has been taken away by the Others. Dasein's everyday possibilities of Being are for the Others to dispose of as they please. These Others, moreover, are not *definite* Others. On the contrary, any Other can represent them. What is decisive is just that inconspicuous domination by Others which has already been taken over unawares from Dasein as Being-with. One belongs to the Others oneself and enhances their power. "The Others" whom one thus designates in order to cover up the fact of one's belonging to them essentially oneself, are those who proximally and for the most part *"are there"* in everyday Being-with-one-another. The "who" is not this one, not that one, not oneself [manselbst], not some people [einige], and not the sum of them all. The "who" is the neuter, the "*they*" [*das Man*].

We have shown earlier how in the environment which lies closest to us, the public "environment" already is ready-to-hand and is also a matter of concern [mitbesorgt]. In utilizing public means of transport and in making use of information services such as the newspaper, every Other is like the next. This Being-with-one-another dissolves one's own Dasein completely into the kind of being of "the Others," in such a way, indeed, that the Others, as distinguishable and explicit, vanish more and more. In this inconspicuousness and unascertainability, the real dictatorship of the "they" is unfolded. We take pleasure and enjoy ourselves as *they* [*man*] take pleasure; we read, see, and judge about literature and art as *they* see and judge; likewise we shrink back from the "great mass" as *they* shrink back; we find "shocking" what *they* find shocking. The "they," which is nothing definite, and which all are, though not as the sum, prescribes the kind of Being of everydayness.

The "they" has its own ways in which to be. That tendency of Being-with which we have called "distantiality" is grounded in the fact that Being-with-one-another concerns itself as such with *averageness*, which is an existential characteristic of the "they." The "they," in its Being, essentially makes an issue of this. Thus the "they" maintains itself factically in the averageness of that which belongs to it, of that which it regards as valid and that which it does not, and of that to which it grants success and that to which it denies it. In this averageness with which it prescribes what can and may be ventured, it keeps watch over everything exceptional that thrusts itself to the fore. Every kind of priority gets noiselessly suppressed. Overnight, everything that is primordial gets glossed over as something that has long been well known. Everything gained by a struggle becomes just something to be manipulated. Every secret loses its force. This care of averageness reveals in turn an essential tendency of Dasein which we call the "levelling down" [*Einebnung*] of all possibilities of Being.

Distantiality, averageness, and levelling down, as ways of Being for the "they," constitute what we know as "publicness"' ["die Offentlichkeit"]. Publicness proximally controls every way in which the world and Dasein get interpreted, and it is always right—not because there is some distinctive and primary relationship-of-Being in which it is related to "Things," or because it avails itself of some transparency on the part of Dasein which it has explicitly appropriated, but because it is insensitive to every difference of level and of genuineness and thus never gets to the "heart of the matter" ["auf die Sachen"]. By publicness everything gets obscured, and what has thus been covered up gets passed off as something familiar and accessible to everyone.

The "they" is there alongside everywhere [ist überall dabei], but in such a manner that it has always stolen away whenever Dasein presses for a decision. Yet because the "they" presents every judgment and decision as its own, it deprives the particular Dasein of its answerability. The "they" can, as it were, manage to have "them" constantly invoking it.[31] It can be answerable for everything most easily, because it is not someone who needs to vouch for anything. It "was" always the "they" who did it, and yet it can be said that it has been "no one." In Dasein's everydayness the agency through which most things come about is one of which we must say that "it was no one."

Thus the particular Dasein in its everydayness is *disburdened* by the "they." Not only that; by thus disburdening it of its Being, the "they" accommodates Dasein [kommt . . . dem Dasein entgegen] if Dasein has any tendency to take things easily and make them easy. And because the "they" constantly accommodates the particular Dasein by disburdening it of its Being, the "they" retains and enhances its stubborn dominion.

Everyone is the other, and no one is himself. The "*they*," which supplies the answer to the question of the "*who*" of everyday Dasein, is the "*nobody*" to whom every Dasein has already surrendered itself in Being-among-one-other [Untereinandersein].

In these characters of Being which we have exhibited—everyday Being-among-one-another, distantiality, averageness, levelling down, publicness, the disburdening of one's Being, and accommodation—lies that "constancy" of Dasein which is closest to us. This "constancy" pertains not to the enduring Being-present-at-hand of something, but rather to Dasein's kind of Being as Being-with. Neither the Self of one's own Dasein nor the Self of the Other has as yet found itself or lost itself as long as it is [seiend] in the modes we have mentioned. In these modes one's way of Being is that of inauthenticity and failure to stand by one's Self.[32] To be in this way signifies no lessening of Dasein's facticity, just as the "they," as the "nobody," is by no means nothing at all. On the contrary, in this kind of Being, Dasein is an *ens realissimum*, if by "Reality" we understand a Being that has the character of Dasein.

Of course, the "they" is as little present-at-hand as Dasein itself. The more openly the "they" behaves, the harder it is to grasp, and the slier it is, but the less is it nothing at all. If we "see" it ontico-ontologically with an unprejudiced eye, it reveals itself as the "Realest subject" of everydayness. And even if it is not accessible like a stone that is present-at-hand, this is not in the least decisive as to its kind of Being. One may neither decree prematurely that this "they" is "really" nothing, nor profess the opinion that one can Interpret this phenomenon ontologically by somehow "explaining" it as what results from taking the Being-present-at-hand-together of several subjects and then fitting them together. On the contrary, in working out concepts of Being one must direct one's course by these phenomena, which cannot be pushed aside.

Furthermore, the "they" is not something like a "universal subject" which a plurality of subjects have hovering above them. One can come to take it this way only if the Being of such "subjects" is understood as having a character other than that of Dasein, and if these are regarded as cases of a genus of occurrents—cases which are factually present-at-hand. With this approach, the only possibility ontologically is that everything which is not a case of this sort is to be understood in the sense of genus and species. The "they" is not the genus to which the individual Dasein belongs, nor can we come across it in such entities as an abiding characteristic. That even the traditional logic fails us when confronted with these phenomena, is not surprising if we bear in mind that it has its foundation in an ontology of the present-at-hand—an ontology which, moreover, is still a rough one. So no matter in how many ways this logic may be improved and expanded, it cannot in principle be made any more flexible. Such reforms of logic, oriented towards the "humane sciences," only increase the ontological confusion.

The *"they" is an existentiale; and as a primordial phenomenon, it belongs to Dasein's positive constitution*. It itself has, in turn, various possibilities of becoming concrete as something characteristic of Dasein [seiner daseinsmässigen Konkretion]. The extent to which its dominion becomes compelling and explicit may change in the course of history.

The Self of everyday Dasein is the *they-self*,[33] which we distinguish from the *authentic Self*—that is, from the Self which has been taken hold of in its own way [eigens ergriffenen]. As they-self, the particular Dasein has been *dispersed* into the "they," and must first find itself. This dispersal characterizes the "subject" of that kind of Being which we know as concernful absorption in the world we encounter as closest to us. If Dasein is familiar with itself as they-self, this means at the same time that the "they" itself prescribes that way of interpreting the world and Being-in-the-world which lies closest. Dasein is for the sake of the "they" in an everyday manner, and the "they" itself Articulates the referential context of significance.[34] When entities are encountered, Dasein's world frees them for a totality of involvements with which the "they" is familial, and within the limits which have been established with the "they's" averageness. *Proximally*, factical Dasein is in the with-world, which is discovered in an average way. *Proximally*, it is not "I," in the sense of my own Self, that "am," but rather the Others, whose way is that of the "they."[35] In terms of the "they," and as the "they," I am "given" proximally to "myself" [mir "selbst"]. Proximally Dasein is "they," and for the most part it remains so. If Dasein discovers the world in its own way [eigens] and brings it close, if it discloses to itself its own authentic Being, then this discovery of the "world" and this disclosure of Dasein are always accomplished as a clearing-away of concealments and obscurities, as a breaking up of the disguises with which Dasein bars its own way.

With this Interpretation of Being-with and Being-one's-Self in the "they," the question of the "who" of the everydayness of Being-with-one-another is answered. These considerations have at the same time brought us a concrete understanding of the basic constitution of Dasein: Being-in-the-world, in its everydayness and its averageness, has become visible.

From the kind of Being which belongs to the "they"—the kind which is closest—everyday Dasein draws its pre-ontological way of interpreting its Being. In the first instance ontological Interpretation follows the tendency to interpret it this way: it understands Dasein in terms of the world and comes across it as an entity within-the-world. But that is not all: even that meaning of Being on the basis of which these "subject" entities [diese seienden "Subjekte"] get understood, is one which that ontology of Dasein which is "closest" to us lets itself present in terms of the "world." But because the phenomenon of the world itself gets passed over in this absorption in the world, its place gets taken [tritt an seine Stelle] by what is present-at-hand within-the-world, namely, Things. The Being of those entities which *are there with us*, gets conceived as presence-at-hand. Thus by exhibiting the positive phenomenon of the closest everyday Being-in-the-world, we have made it possible to get an insight into the reason why an ontological Interpretation of this state of Being has been missing. *This very state of Being,*[36] *in its everyday kind of Being, is what proximally misses itself and covers itself up.*

If the Being of everyday Being-with-one-another is already different in principle from pure presence-at-hand—in spite of the fact that it is seemingly close to it ontologically—still less can the Being of the authentic Self be conceived as presence-at-hand. *Authentic Being-one's-Self* does not rest upon an exceptional condition of the subject, a condition that has been detached from the "they"; *it is rather an existentiell modification of the "they"—of the "they" as an essential existentiale.*

But in that case there is ontologically a gap separating the selfsameness of the authentically existing Self from the identity of that "I" which maintains itself throughout its manifold Experiences.

Notes

1. [*Editors' note*: The following passage is not identified in the original.] "Das Man." In German one may write "man glaubt" where in French one would write "*on croit*," or in English "they believe," "one believes," or "it is believed." But the German "man" and the French "*on*" are specialized for such constructions in a way in which the pronouns "they," "one," and "it" are not. There is accordingly no single idiomatic translation for the German "man" which will not sometimes lend itself to ambiguity, and in general we have chosen whichever construction seems the most appropriate in its context. But when Heidegger introduces this word with a definite article and writes "das Man," as he does very often in this chapter, we shall translate this expression as "the 'they,'" trusting that the reader will not take this too literally.

2. "dem 'Selbst.'" While we shall ordinarily translate the *intensive* "selbst" by the corresponding English intensives "itself," "oneself," "myself," etc., according to the context, we shall translate the *substantive* "Selbst" by the substantive "Self" with a capital.

3. ". . . als Selbiges in der vielfältigen Andersheit . . ." While the words "identisch" and "selbig" are virtually synonyms in ordinary German, Heidegger seems to be intimating a distinction between them. We shall accordingly translate the former by "identical" and the latter by "selfsame" to show its etymological connection with "selbst."

4. "Vielleicht ist in der Tat das, was diese Art von Gebung, das schlichte, formale, reflektive Ichvernehmen gibt, evident."

5. "as such a clue": here we read "als solcher," following the later editions. The earliest editions have "als solche," which has been corrected in the list of *errata*.

"Essence": while we ordinarily use "essence" and "essential" to translate "Wesen" and "wesenhaft," we shall use "Essence" and "Essential" (with initial capitals) to translate the presumably synonymous but far less frequent "Essenz" and "essentiell."

6. "... die Ständigkeit des Selbst ebensosehr wie seine mögliche 'Unselbständigkeit'. . ." The adjective "ständig," which we have usually translated as "constant" in the sense of "permanent" or "continuing," goes back to the root meaning of "standing," as do the adjectives "selbständig" ("independent") and "unselbständig" ("dependent"). These concepts will be discussed more fully in Section 64 below, especially H. 322, where "Unselbständigkeit" will be rewritten not as "Un-selbständkeit" ("failure to stand by one's Self") but as "Unselbst-ständigkeit" ("constancy to the Unself"). See also H. 128. (The connection with the concept of existence will perhaps be clearer if one recalls that the Latin verb "existere" may also be derived from a verb of *standing*, as Heidegger points out in his later writings.)

7. "... sondern gemäss seiner Seinsart *als Dasein* selbst in der Weise des In-der-Welt-seins "in" der Welt ist, in der es zugleich innerweltlich begegnet."

8. "Dieses Seiende ist weder vorhanden noch zuhanden, sondern ist *so, wie* das freigebende Dasein selbst—es *ist auch und mit da*. Wollte man denn schon Welt überhaupt mit dem innerweltlich Seienden identifizieren, dann müsste man sagen, 'Welt' ist auch Dasein."

9. "... dass dieses Ich-hier nicht einen ausgezeichneten Punkt des Ichdinges meint, sondern sich versteht als In-sein aus dem Dort der zuhandenen Welt, bei dem Dasein als *Besorgen* sich aufhält." The older editions have "In-Sein" for "In-sein," and "dabei" for "bei dem."

10. Italics [*in* and *for*] supplied in the later editions.

11. "... Mitdasein charakterisiert das Dasein anderer, sofern es für ein Mitsein durch dessen Welt freigegeben ist. Das eigene Dasein ist, sofern es die Wesensstruktur des Mitseins hat, als für Andere begegnend Mitdasein."

12. "... als welche das Sein des Daseins überhaupt bestimmt wird." The older editions omit "wird."

13. "Dieses Seiende wird nicht besorgt, sondern steht in der *Fürsorge*." There is no good English equivalent for "Fürsorge," which we shall usually translate by "solicitude." The more literal "caring-for" has the connotation of "being fond of," which we do not want here; "personal care" suggests personal hygiene; "personal concern" suggests one's personal business or affairs. "Fürsorge" is rather the kind of care which we find in "prenatal care" or "taking care of the children," or even the kind of care which is administered by welfare agencies. Indeed the word "Fürsorge" is regularly used in contexts where we would speak of "welfare work" or "social welfare"; this is the usage which Heidegger has in mind in his discussion of "Fürsorge" as "a factical social arrangement." (The etymological connection between "Sorge" ("care"), "Fürsorge" ("solicitude"), and "Besorgen" ("concern"), is entirely lost in our translation.)

14. "... sich an seine Stelle setzen, für ihn *einspringen*." Here, as on H. 100 (See our note 2, p. 133), it would be more idiomatic to translate "für ihn einspringen" as "intervene for him," "stand in for him" or "serve as deputy for him"; but since "einspringen" is to be contrasted with "vorspringen," "vorausspringen" and perhaps even "entspringen" in the following paragraphs, we have chosen a translation which suggests the etymological connection.

15. "... um nachträglich das Besorgte als fertig Verfügbares zu übernehmen ..."

16. "Umgekehrt ist das gemeinsame Sicheinsetzen für dieselbe Sache aus dem je eigens ergriffenen Dasein bestimmt."

17. Reading "... und zeitigt mannigfache Mischformen ..." with the older editions. The later editions have "zeigt" ("shows") instead of "zeitigt" ("brings to maturity").

18. "... Wie dem Besorgen als Weise des Entdeckens des Zuhandenen die *Umsicht* zugehört, so ist die Fürsorge geleitet durch die *Rücksicht* und *Nachsicht*." Heidegger is here calling attention to the etymological kinship of the three words which he italicizes, each of which stands for a special kind of *sight* or *seeing* ("Sicht").
   The italicization of "Umsicht" ("circumspection") is introduced in the newer editions.

19. "... bis zur *Rücksichtslosigkeit* und dem Nachsehen, das die Gleichgültigkeit leitet." This passage is ambiguous both syntactically and semantically. It is not clear, for instance, whether the subject of the relative clause is "die Gleichgültigkeit" or the pronoun "das," though we prefer the former interpretation. "Nachsehen," which is etymologically akin to "Nachsicht," means to "inspect" or "check" something; but it often means to do this in a very perfunctory manner, and this latter sense may well be the one which Heidegger has in mind.

20. "... zum Sein des Daseins, um das es ihm in seinem Sein selbst geht ..." The older editions have "darum" instead of "um das."

21. "Diese mit dem Mitsein vorgängig konstituierte Erschlossenheit der Anderen macht demnach auch die Bedeutsamkeit, d.h. die Weltlichkeit mit aus, als welche sie im existenzialen Worum-willen festgemacht ist." The word "sie" appears only in the later editions.

22. "Dieses Verstehen ist, wie Verstehen überhaupt, nicht eine aus Erkennen erwachsene Kenntnis, sondern eine ursprünglich existenziale Seinsart die Erkennen und Kenntnis allererst möglich macht." While we have here translated "Kenntnis" as "acquaintance" and "Erkennen" as "knowledge about," these terms must not be understood in the special senses exploited by Lord Russell and C. L. Lewis. The "acquaintance" here involved is of the kind which may be acquired whenever one is well informed about something, whether one has any direct contact with it or not.

23 "... bedarf das nächste und wesenhafte Sichkennen eines Sichkennenlernens." "Sichkennen" ("knowing oneself") is to be distinguished sharply from "Selbsterkenntnis" ("knowledge of the Self").

24. "... sich ... verhält ..." We have often translated this expression as "comports itself," compromising between two other possible meanings: "relates itself" and "behaves" or "conducts itself." In this passage, however, and in many others where this expression is tied up with "Verhältnis" ("relationship") rather than with "Verhalten" ("behaviour or conduct"), only "relates itself" seems appropriate.

25. "Projektion." Here we are dealing with "projection" in the familiar psychological sense, not in the sense which would be expressed by "Entwurf."

26. "Das Sein zu Anderen ist nicht nur ein eigenständiger, irreduktibler Seinsbezug, er ist als Mitsein mit dem Sein des Daseins schon seiend."

27. ". . . wie welt es das wesenhafte Mitsein mit anderen sich durchsichtig gemacht und nicht verstellt hat . . ." (The older editions have ". . . sich nicht undurchsichtig gemacht und verstellt hat . . .")

28. "Einfühlung" konstituiert nicht erst das Mitsein, sondern ist auf dessen Grunde erst möglich und durch die vorherrschenden defizienten Modi des Mitseins in ihrer Unumgänglichkeit motiviert."

29. ". . . welche positive existenziale Bedingung rechtes Fremdverstehen für seine Möglichkeit voraussetzt." We have construed "welche" as referring back to "Hermeneutik," though this is not entirely clear.

30. "Nicht es selbst *ist*; . . ."

31. "Das Man kann es sich gleichsam leisten, dass 'man' sich ständig auf es beruft."

32. "Man ist in der Weise der Unselbständigkeit und Uneigentlichkeit."

33. ". . . das Man-selbst . . ." This expression is also to be distinguished from "das Man selbst" ("the 'they' itself"], which appears elsewhere in this paragraph. In the first of these expressions "selbst" appears as a substantive, in the second as a mere intensive.

34. "Das Man selbst, worum-willen das Dasein alltäglich ist, attikuliert den Verweisungszusammenhang der Bedeutsamkeit." It is also possible to construe "alltäglich" as a predicate adjective after "ist"; in that case we should read: "Dasein is everyday for the sake of the 'they.'"

35. "*Zunächst* 'bin' niclit 'ich' im Sinne des eigenen Selbst, sondern die Anderen in der Weise des Man." In the earlier editions there are commas after "ich" and "Anderen," which would suggest a somewhat different interpretation.

36. We interpret Heidegger's pronoun "Sie" as referring to "Seinsverfassung" ("state of Being"); but there are other words in the previous sentence to which it might refer with just as much grammatical plausibility, particularly "Interpretation."

9 Foundations of a Theory of Intersubjective Understanding

Alfred Schutz

19. The General Thesis of the Alter Ego in Natural Perception

As we proceed to our study of the social world, we abandon the strictly phenomenological method. We shall start out by simply accepting the existence of the social world as it is always accepted in the attitude of the natural standpoint, whether in everyday life or in sociological observation. In so doing, we shall avoid any attempt to deal with the problem from the point of view of transcendental phenomenology. We shall, therefore, be bypassing a whole nest of problems whose significance and difficulty were pointed out by Husserl in his *Formal and Transcendental Logic*, although he did not there deal with these problems specifically.[1] The question of the "meaning" of the "Thou" can only be answered by carrying out the analysis which he posited in that work. Even now, however, it can be stated with certainty that the concept of the world in general must be based on the concept of "everyone" and therefore also of "the other."[2] The same idea was expressed by Max Scheler in his "Erkenntnis und Arbeit":

The reality of the world of contemporaries and community are taken for granted as *Thou-spheres* and *We-spheres*, first of all of the whole of nature both living and inorganic. . . . Furthermore, the reality of the "Thou" and of a community is taken for granted before the reality of the "I" in the sense of one's own Ego and its personal private experiences.[3]

We must, then, leave unsolved the notoriously difficult problems which surround the constitution of the Thou within the subjectivity of private experience. We are not going to be asking, therefore, how the Thou is constituted in an Ego, whether the concept "human being" presupposes a transcendental ego in which the transcendental alter ego is already constituted, or how universally valid intersubjective knowledge is possible. As important as these questions may be for epistemology and, therefore, for the social sciences, we may safely leave them aside in the present work.[4]

The object we shall be studying, therefore, is the human being who is looking at the world from within the natural attitude. Born into a social world, he comes upon his fellow men and takes their existence for granted without question, just as he takes for granted the existence of the natural objects he encounters. The essence of his assumption about his fellow men may be put in this short formula: The Thou (or other person) is conscious, and his stream of consciousness is temporal in character, exhibiting the same basic form as mine. But of course this has implications. It means that the Thou knows its experiences only through reflective Acts of attention. And it means that the Acts of attention themselves will vary in character from one moment to the next and will undergo change as time goes on. In short, it means that the other person also experiences his own aging.

So, then, all that we said in Chapter 2 about the consciousness of the solitary Ego will apply quite as much to the Thou. Since the Thou also performs intentional Acts, it also bestows meaning. *It* also selects certain items from its stream of consciousness and interprets these items by placing them within one or another context of meaning. *It* also pictures as whole units intentional Acts that took place step by step. *It* also lays down meaning-contexts in layers, building up its own world of experience, which, like my own, always bears upon it the mark of the particular moment from which it is viewed. Finally, since the Thou interprets its lived experiences, it gives meaning to them, and this meaning is intended meaning.

In Chapter 1 we already saw the difficulties standing in the way of comprehending the intended meaning of the other self. We found, in fact, that such comprehension could never be achieved and that the concept of the other person's intended meaning remains at best a limiting concept. Our temporal analysis has for the first time made clear the real reason why the postulate of comprehending the other person's intended meaning could never be carried out. For the postulate *means that I am to explicate the other person's lived experiences in the same way that he does*. Now we have seen that self-explication is carried out in a series of highly complex Acts of consciousness. These intentional Acts are structured in layers and are in turn the objects of additional Acts of attention on the part of the Ego. Naturally, the latter are dependent upon the particular Here and Now within which they occur. The postulate, therefore, that I can observe the subjective experience of another person precisely as he does is absurd. For it presupposes that I myself have lived through all the conscious states and intentional Acts wherein this experience has been constituted. But this could only happen within my own experience and in my own Acts of attention to my experience. And this experience of mine would then have to duplicate his experience down to the smallest details, including impressions, their surrounding areas of protention and retention, reflective Acts, phantasies, etc. But there is more to come: I should have to be able to remember all his experiences and therefore should have had to live through these experiences in the same order that he did; and finally I should have had to give them exactly the same degree of attention that he did. In short, my stream of consciousness would have to coincide with the other person's, which is the same as saying that I should have to *be* the other person. This point was made by Bergson in his *Time and Free Will*.[5] "Intended meaning" is therefore essentially subjective and is in principle confined to the self-interpretation of the person who lives through the experience to be interpreted. Constituted as it is within the unique stream of consciousness of each individual, *it is essentially inaccessible to every other individual*.

It might seem that these conclusions would lead to the denial of the possibility of an interpretive sociology and even more to the denial that one can ever understand another person's experience. But this is by no means the case. We are asserting neither that your lived experiences remain in principle inaccessible to me nor that they are meaningless to me. Rather, the point is that the meaning I give to your experiences cannot be precisely the same as the meaning you give to them when you proceed to interpret them.

To clarify the distinction between the two types of meaning involved, that is, between self-explication and interpretation of another person's experience, let us call in the aid of a well-known distinction of Husserl's:

Under *acts immanently directed*, or, to put it more generally, under *intentional experiences immanently related*, we include those acts which are *essentially* so constituted *that their intentional objects, when these exist at all, belong to the same stream of* experiences as themselves. . . . Intentional experiences for which this does not hold good are *transcendently directed*, as, for instance, all acts directed . . . towards the intentional experiences of other Egos with other experience-streams.[6]

It goes without saying that, not only are intentional Acts directed upon another person's stream of consciousness transcendent, but my experiences of another person's body, or of my own body, or of myself as a psychophysical unity fall into the same class. So we are immediately faced with the question of the specific characteristics of that subclass of transcendent Acts which are directed toward the lived experiences of another person. We could say that we "perceive" the other's experiences if we did not imply that we directly intuited them in the strict sense but meant rather that we grasped them with that same perceptual intention (*anschauliches Vermeinen*) with which we grasp a thing or event as present to us. It is in this sense that Husserl uses the word "perception" to mean "taking notice of": "The listener notices that the speaker is expressing certain subjective experiences of his and in that sense may be said to notice *them*; but he himself does not live through these experiences—his perception is 'external' rather than 'internal.'"[7] This kind of perception which is signitive[8] in character should not be confused with that in which an object directly appears to us. I apprehend the lived experiences of another only through signitive-symbolic representation, regarding either his body or some cultural artifact he has produced as a "field of expression" for those experiences.

Let us explain further this concept of signitive apprehension of another's subjective knowledge. The whole stock of my experience (*Erfahrungsvorrat*) of another from within the natural attitude consists of my own lived experiences (*Erlebnisse*) of his body, of his behavior, of the course of his actions, and of the artifacts he has produced. For the time being let us speak simply of the interpretation of the other person's *course of action* without further clarification. My lived experiences of another's acts consist in my perceptions of his body in motion. However, as I am always interpreting these perceptions as "body of another," I am always interpreting them as something having an implicit reference to "consciousness of another." Thus the bodily movements are perceived not only as physical events but also as a sign that the other person is having certain lived experiences which he is expressing through those movements. My intentional gaze is directed right through my perceptions of his bodily movements to his lived experiences lying behind them and signified by them. The signitive relation is essential to this mode of apprehending another's lived experiences. Of course he himself may be aware of these experiences, single them out, and give them his own intended meaning. His observed bodily movements become then for me not only a sign of his lived experiences as such, but of those to which he attaches an intended meaning. How interpretation of this kind is carried out is something which we shall study in detail later on. It is enough to say at this point that the signitive experience (*Erfahrung*) of the world, like all other experience in the Here and Now, is coherently organized and is thus "ready at hand."

Here it could be objected that the concept of lived experience excludes by definition everything but my own experience, since the very term "lived experience" is equivalent to "object of immanent awareness." A transcendent apprehension of someone else's lived experience would therefore be ruled out as absurd. For, the argument runs, it is only the indications of someone else's lived experience that I apprehend transcendently; having apprehended such indications, I infer from them the existence and character of the experiences of which they *are* indications. Against this point of view we should maintain emphatically that signitive apprehension of the other's body as an expressive field does not involve inference or judgment in the usual sense. Rather what is involved is a certain intentional Act which utilizes an already established code of interpretation directing us through the bodily movement to the underlying lived experience.[9]

In the everyday world in which both the I and the Thou turn up, not as transcendental but as psychophysical subjects, there corresponds to each stream of lived experience of the I a stream of subjective experience of the Thou. This, to be sure, refers back to my own stream of lived experience, just as does the body of the other person to my body. During this process, the peculiar reference of my own ego to the other's ego holds, in the sense that my stream of lived experience is for you that of another person, just as my body is another's body for you.[10]

20. The Other's Stream of Consciousness as Simultaneous with My Own

If I wish to observe one of my own lived experiences, I must perform a reflective Act of attention. But in this case, what I will behold is a past experience, not one presently occurring. Since this holds true for all my Acts of attention to my own experiences, I know it holds true for the other person as well. You are in the same position as I am: you can observe only your past, already-lived-through experiences. Now, whenever I have an experience of you, this is still my own experience.[11] However, this experience, while uniquely my own, still has, as its signitively grasped intentional object, a lived experience of yours which you are having at this very moment. In order to observe a lived experience of my own, I must attend to it reflectively. By no means, however, need I attend reflectively to *my* lived experience *of* you in order to observe *your* lived experience. On the contrary, by merely "looking" I can grasp even those of your lived experiences which you have not yet noticed and which are for you still prephenomenal and undifferentiated. This means that, whereas I can observe my own lived experiences only after they are over and done with, I can observe yours as they actually take place. This in turn implies that you and I are in a specific sense "simultaneous," that we "coexist," that our respective streams of consciousness intersect. To be sure, these are merely images and are inadequate since they are spatial. However, recourse to spatial imagery at this point is deeply rooted. We are concerned with the synchronism of two streams of consciousness here, my own and yours. In trying to understand this synchronism we can hardly ignore the fact that when you and I are in the natural attitude we perceive ourselves and each other as psychophysical unities.

This synchronism or "simultaneity" is understood here in Bergson's sense:

I call simultaneous two streams which from the standpoint of my consciousness are indifferently *one* or *two*. My consciousness perceives these streams as a single one whenever it pleases to give them an undivided act of attention; on the other hand it distinguishes them whenever it chooses to divide its attention between them. Again, it can make them both one and yet distinct from one another, if it decides to divide its attention while still not splitting them into two separate entities.[12]

I see, then, my own stream of consciousness and yours in a single intentional Act which embraces them both. The simultaneity involved here is not that of physical time, which is quantifiable, divisible, and spatial. For us the term "simultaneity" is rather an expression for the basic and necessary assumption which I make that your stream of consciousness has a structure analogous to mine. It endures in a sense that a physical thing does not: it subjectively experiences its own aging, and this experience is determinative of all its other experiences. While the duration of physical objects is no *durée* at all, but its exact opposite, persisting over a period of objective time,[13] you and I, on the other hand, have a genuine *durée* which experiences itself, which is continuous, which is manifold, and which is irreversible. Not only does each of us subjectively experience his own *durée* as an absolute reality in the Bergsonian sense, but the *durée* of each of us is given to the other as absolute reality. What we mean, then, by the simultaneity of two durations or streams of consciousness is simply this: the phenomenon of *growing older together*. Any other criterion of simultaneity presupposes the transformation of both durations into a spatiotemporal complex and the transformation of the real *durée* into a merely *constructed time*. This is what Bergson means by the time which is not experienced by you, nor by me, nor by anyone at all.[14] But in reality you and I can each subjectively experience and live through his own respective duration, each other's duration, and everyone's duration.[15]

I can therefore say without hesitation that the Thou is that consciousness whose intentional Acts I can see occurring as other than, yet simultaneous with, my own. Also I can say that I may become aware of experiences of the Thou which the latter never gets to notice: its prephenomenal subjective experiences. If, for instance, someone is talking to me, I am aware not only of his words but his voice. To be sure, I interpret these in the same way that I always interpret my own lived experiences. But my gaze goes right through these outward symptoms to the inner man of the person who is speaking to me. Whatever context of meaning I light upon when I am experiencing these outward indications draws its validity from a corresponding context of meaning in the mind of the other person. The latter context must be the very one within which his own present lived experience is being constructed step by step.[16]

What we have just described is the comprehension, at the very moment they occur, of the other person's intentional Acts, Acts which take place step by step and which result in syntheses of a higher order. Now, this is precisely what Weber means by observational as opposed to motivational understanding. But the essential thing about the simultaneity involved here is not bodily coexistence. It is not as if I could observationally understand only those whom I directly experience. Not at all. I can imaginatively place the minds of people of past ages in a quasisimultaneity with my own, observationally understanding them through their writings, their music, their art. We have yet to deal with the different forms taken on by this understanding in the different spheres of the social world.

The simultaneity of our two streams of consciousness, however, does not mean that the same experiences are given to each of us. My lived experience of you, as well as the environment I ascribe to you, bears the mark of my own subjective Here and Now and not the mark of yours. Also, I ascribe to you an environment which has already been interpreted from my subjective standpoint. I thus presuppose that at any given time we are both referring to the same objects, which transcend the subjective experience of either of us.[17] This is so at least in the world of the natural attitude, the world of everyday life in which one has direct experience of one's fellow men, the world in which I assume that you are seeing the same table I am seeing. We shall also see, at a later point, the modifications this assumption undergoes in the different regions of the social world, namely, the world of contemporaries, the world of predecessors, and the world of successors.

In what follows we shall be seeking confirmation for this general thesis of the other self in the concrete problems of understanding other people. However, even at this early point we can draw a few fundamental conclusions.

The self-explication of my own lived experiences takes place within the total pattern of my experience. This total pattern is made up of meaning-contexts developed out of my previous lived experiences. In these meaning-contexts all my past lived experiences are at least potentially present to me. They stand to a certain extent at my disposal, whether I see them once again in recognition or reproduction or whether, from the point of view of the already constituted meaning-context, I *can* potentially observe the lived experiences which they have built up. Furthermore, I can repeat my lived experiences in free reproduction (at least insofar as they have originated in spontaneous activities).[18] We say "in free reproduction" because I can leave unnoticed any phases whatsoever and turn my attention to any other phases previously unnoticed. In principle, however, the continuum which is my total stream of lived experience remains open in its abundance at all times to my self-explication.

Still, *your* whole stream of lived experience is *not* open to me. To be sure, your stream of lived experience is also a continuum, but I can catch sight of only disconnected segments of it. We have already made this point. If I could be aware of your whole experience, you and I would be the same person. But we must go beyond this. You and I differ from each other not merely with respect to how much of each other's lived experiences we can observe. We also differ in this: When I become aware of a segment of your lived experience, I arrange what I see within my own meaning-context. But meanwhile you have arranged it in yours. Thus I am always interpreting your lived experiences from my own standpoint. Even if I had ideal knowledge of all your meaning-contexts at a given moment and so were able to arrange your whole supply of experience, I should still not be able to determine whether the particular meaning-contexts of yours in which *I* arranged your lived experiences were the same as those which *you* were using. This is because your manner of attending to your experiences would be different from my manner of attending to them. However, if I look at my whole stock of knowledge of your lived experiences and ask about the structure of this knowledge, one thing becomes clear: *This is that everything I know about your conscious life is really based on my knowledge of my own lived experiences.* My lived experiences *of* you are constituted in simultaneity or quasisimultaneity with *your* lived experiences, to which they are intentionally related. It is only because of this that, when I look backward, I am able to synchronize *my* past experiences of you with *your* past experiences.

It might be objected that another person's stream of consciousness could still be constructed, without contradictions, as so synchronized with my own that they corresponded moment for moment. Furthermore, an ideal model might be constructed in which, at every moment, the Ego has lived experiences *of* the other self and is thereby simultaneously encountering the *other's* lived experiences. In other words, I might be able to keep track of your lived experiences *in their continuity* all through your lifetime. Yes, but only in their continuity, not in their completeness. For what I call the series of your lived experiences is merely one possible meaning-context which I have constructed out of a few of your lived experiences. I always fall far short of grasping the totality of your lived experience, which at this very moment is being transformed into a unique present moment for you. And, of course, what holds true of the series holds true of the single moment: comprehension falls short of fullness, even in simultaneity. In summary it can be said that my own stream of consciousness is given to me continuously and in all its fullness but that yours is given to me in discontinuous segments, never in its fullness, and only in "interpretive perspectives."

But this also means that our knowledge of the consciousness of other people is always in principle open to doubt, whereas our knowledge of our own consciousness, based as it is on immanent Acts, is always in principle indubitable.[19]

The above considerations will prove to be of great importance for the theory of the other self's action, which will be a predominant concern of ours in the pages to follow. It is in principle doubtful whether your experiences, as I comprehend them, are seized upon by your reflective glance at all, whether they spring from your spontaneous Acts and are therefore really "behavior" in the sense we have defined, and consequently whether they are really action, since the latter is behavior oriented to a goal. And so, in the concept of the other self's action, we come up against a profound theoretical problem. The very postulate of the comprehension of the intended meaning of the other person's lived experiences becomes unfulfillable. Not only this, but it becomes in principle doubtful whether the other person attends to and confers meaning upon those of his lived experiences which I comprehend.

21. The Ambiguities in the Ordinary Notion of Understanding the Other Person

Before we proceed further, it would be well to note that there are ambiguities in the ordinary notion of understanding another person. Sometimes what is meant is intentional Acts directed toward the other self; in other words, my lived experiences of you. At other times what is in question is *your* subjective experiences. Then, the arrangements of all such experiences into meaning-contexts (Weber's comprehension of intended meaning) is sometimes called "understanding of the other self," as is the classification of others' behavior into motivation contexts. The number of ambiguities associated with the notion of "understanding another person" becomes even greater when we bring in the question of understanding the signs he is using. On the one hand, what is understood is the sign itself, then again *what* the other person means by using this sign, and finally the significance of the fact *that* he is using the sign, here, now, and in this particular context.

In order to sort out these different levels in the meaning of the term, let us first give it a generic definition. Let us say that understanding (*Verstehen*) as such is correlative to meaning, for all understanding is directed toward that which has meaning (*auf ein Sinnhaftes*) and only something understood is meaningful (*sinnvoll*). In Chapter 2 we saw the implications for the sphere of the solitary Ego of this concept of that which has meaning (*des Sinnhaften*). In this sense, all intentional Acts which are interpretations of one's own subjective experiences would be called Acts of understanding (*verstehende Akte*). We should also designate as "understanding" all the lower strata of meaning-comprehension on which such self-explication is based.

The man in the natural attitude, then, understands the world by interpreting his own lived experiences of it, whether these experiences be of inanimate things, of animals, or of his fellow human beings. And so our initial concept of the understanding of the other self is simply the concept "our explication of our lived experiences *of* our fellow human beings as such." The fact that the Thou who confronts me is a fellow man and not a shadow on a movie screen—in other words, that he has duration and consciousness—is something I discover by explicating my own lived experiences of him.

Furthermore, the man in the natural attitude perceives changes in that external object which is known to him as the other's body. He interprets these changes just as he interprets changes in inanimate objects, namely, by interpretation of his own lived experiences of the events and processes in question. Even this second phase does not go beyond the bestowing of meaning within the sphere of the solitary consciousness.

The transcending of this sphere becomes possible only when the perceived processes come to be regarded as lived experiences belonging to another consciousness, which, in accordance with the general thesis of the other self, exhibits the same structure as my own. The perceived bodily movements of the other will then be grasped not merely as *my* lived experience of these movements within *my* stream of consciousness. Rather it will be understood that, simultaneous with *my* lived experience of you, there is *your* lived experience which belongs to you and is part of your stream of consciousness. Meanwhile, the specific nature of your experience is quite unknown to me, that is, I do not know the meaning-contexts you are using to classify those lived experiences of yours, provided, indeed, you are even aware of the movements of your body.

However, I can know the meaning-context into which I classify my own lived experiences of you. We have already seen that this is not your intended meaning in the true sense of the term. What can be comprehended is always only an "approximate value" of the limiting concept "the other's intended meaning."

However, talk about the meaning-context into which the Thou orders its lived experience is again very vague. The very question of whether a bodily movement is purposive or merely reactive is a question which can only be answered in terms of the other person's own context of meaning. And then if one considers the further questions that can be asked about the other person's schemes of experience, for instance about his motivational contexts, one can get a good idea of how complex is the theory of understanding the other self. It is of great importance to penetrate into the structure of this understanding far enough to show that we can only interpret lived experiences belonging to other people in terms of our own lived experiences of them.

In the above discussion we have limited our analysis exclusively to cases where other people are present bodily to us in the domain of directly experienced social reality. In so doing, we have proceeded as if the understanding of the other self were based on the interpretation of the movements of his body. A little reflection shows, however, that this kind of interpretation is good for only one of the many regions of the social world; for even in the natural standpoint, a man experiences his neighbors even when the latter are not at all present in the bodily sense. He has knowledge not only of his directly experienced consociates[20] but also about his more distant contemporaries. He has, in addition, empirical information about his historical predecessors. He finds himself surrounded by objects which tell him plainly that they were produced by other people; these are not only material objects but all kinds of linguistic and other sign systems, in short, artifacts in the broadest sense. He interprets these first of all by arranging them within his own contexts of experience.

However, he can at any time ask further questions about the lived experiences and meaning-contexts of their creators, that is, about why they were made.

We must now carefully analyze all these complex processes. We shall do so, however, only to the extent required by our theme, namely, "the understanding of the other person within the social world." For this purpose we must begin with the lowest level and clarify those Acts of self-explication which are present and available for use in interpreting the behavior of other people. For the sake of simplicity, let us assume that the other person is present bodily. We shall select our examples from various regions of human behavior by analyzing first an action without any communicative intent and then one whose meaning is declared through signs.

As an example of the "understanding of a human act" without any communicative intent, let us look at the activity of a woodcutter.

Understanding that wood is being cut can mean:

1. That we are noticing only the "external event," the ax slicing the tree and the wood splitting into bits, which ensues. If this is all we see, we are hardly dealing with what is going on in another person's mind. Indeed, we need hardly bring in the other person at all, for woodcutting is woodcutting, whether done by man, by machine, or even by some natural force. Of course, meaning *is* bestowed on the observed event by the observer, in the sense that he understands it as "woodcutting." In other words, he inserts it into his own context of experience. However, this "understanding" is merely the explication of his own lived experiences, which we discussed in Chapter 2. The observer perceives the event and orders his perceptions into polythetic syntheses, upon which he then looks back with a monothetic glance, and arranges these syntheses into the total context of his experience, giving them at the same time a name. However, the observer in our case does not as yet perceive the *woodcutter* but only *that the wood is being cut*, and he "understands" the perceived sequence of events as "woodcutting." It is essential to note that even this interpretation of the event is determined by the total context of knowledge available to the observer at the moment of observation. Whoever does not know how paper is manufactured will not be in a position to classify the component processes because he lacks the requisite interpretive scheme. Nor will he be in a position to formulate the judgment "This is a place where paper is manufactured." And this holds true, as we have established, for all arrangements of lived experiences into the context of knowledge.

But understanding that wood is being cut can also mean:

2. That changes in another person's body are perceived, which changes are interpreted as indications that he is alive and conscious. Meanwhile, no further assumption is made that an action is involved. But this, too, is merely an explication of the observer's own perceptual experiences. All he is doing is identifying the body as that of a living human being and then noting the fact and manner of its changes.

Understanding that someone is cutting wood can, however, mean:

3. That the center of attention is the woodcutter's own lived experiences as actor. The question is not one about external events but one about lived experiences: "Is this man acting spontaneously according to a project he had previously formulated? If so, what is this project? What is his in-order-to motive? In what meaning-context does this action stand for *him*?" And so forth. These questions are concerned with neither the facticity of the situation as such nor the bodily movements as such. Rather, the outward facts and bodily movements are understood as indications (*Anzeichen*) of the lived experiences of the person being observed. The attention of the observer is focused not on the indications but on what lies behind them. This is *genuine understanding of the other person*.

Now, let us turn our attention to a case where signs are being used and select as our example the case of a person talking German. The observer can direct his attention:

1. Upon the bodily movements of the speaker. In this case he interprets his own lived experience on the basis of the context of experience of the present moment. First the observer makes sure he is seeing a real person and not an image, as in a motion-picture film. He then determines whether the person's movements are actions. All this is, of course, self-interpretation.

2. Upon the perception of the sound alone. The observer may go on to discover whether he is hearing a real person or a tape recorder. This, too, is only an interpretation of his own experiences.

3. Upon the specific pattern of the sounds being produced. That is, he identifies the sounds first as words, not shrieks, and then as German words. They are thus ordered within a certain scheme, in which they are signs with definite meanings. This ordering within the scheme of a particular language can even take place without knowledge of the meanings of the words, provided the listener has some definite criterion in mind. If I am traveling in a foreign country, I know when two people are talking to each other, and I also know that they are talking the language of the country in question without having the slightest idea as to the subject of their conversation.

In making any of these inferences, I am merely interpreting my own experiences, and nothing is implied as to a single lived experience of any of the people being observed.

The observer "understands," in addition:

4. The word as the sign of its own word meaning. Even then he merely interprets his own experiences by coordinating the sign to a previously experienced sign system or interpretive scheme, say the German language. As the result of his knowledge of the German language, the observer connects with the word *Tisch* the idea of a definite piece of furniture, which he can picture with approximate accuracy. It matters not at all whether the word has been uttered by another person, a phonograph, or even a parrot. Nor does it matter whether the word is spoken or written, or, if the latter, whether it is traced out in letters of wood or iron.[21]

It does not matter when or where it is uttered or in what context. As long, therefore, as the observer leaves out of account all questions as to why and how the word is being used on the occasion of observation, his interpretation remains self-interpretation. He is concerned with the *meaning of the word,* not the *meaning of the user of the word.* When we identify these interpretations as self-interpretations, we should not overlook the fact that all previous knowledge of the other person belongs to the interpreter's total configuration of experience, which is the context from whose point of view the interpretation is being made.

The observer can, however, proceed to the genuine understanding of the other person if he:

5. Regards the meaning of the word as an indication (*Anzeichen*) of the speaker's subjective experiences—regards the meaning, in short, as *what the speaker meant.* For instance, he can try to discover what the speaker intended to say and what he meant by saying it on this occasion. These questions are obviously aimed at conscious experiences. The first question tries to establish the context of meaning within which the speaker understands the words he is uttering, while the second seeks to establish the motive for the utterance. It is obvious that the genuine understanding of the other person involved in answering such questions can only be attained if the objective meaning of the words is first established by the observer's explication of his own experiences.

All these, of course, are only examples. Later we shall have repeated opportunity to refer to the essential point which they illustrate. Let us now state in summary which of our interpretive acts referring to another self are interpretations of our own experience. There is first the interpretation that the observed person is really a human being and not an image of some kind. The observer establishes this solely by interpretation of his own perceptions of the other's body. Second, there is the interpretation of all the external phases of action, that is, of all bodily movements and their effects. Here, as well, the observer is engaging in interpretation of his own perceptions, just as when he is watching the flight of a bird or the stirring of a branch in the wind. In order to understand what is occurring, he is appealing solely to his own past experience, not to what is going on in the mind of the observed person.[22] Finally, the same thing may be said of the perception of all the other person's expressive movements and all the signs which he uses, provided that one is here referring to the general and objective meaning of such manifestations and not their occasional and subjective meaning.

But, of course, by "understanding the other person" much more is meant, as a rule. This additional something, which is really the only strict meaning of the term, involves grasping what is really going on in the other person's mind, grasping those things of which the external manifestations are mere indications. To be sure, interpretation of such external indications and signs in terms of interpretation of one's own experiences must come first. But the interpreter will not be satisfied with this. He knows perfectly well from the total context of his own experience that, corresponding to the outer objective and public meaning which he has just deciphered, there is this other, inner, subjective meaning. He asks, then, "What is that woodcutter really thinking about? What is he up to? What does all this chopping mean to him?" Or, in another case, "What does this person mean by speaking to me in this manner, at this particular moment? For the sake of what does he do this (what is his in-order-to motive)? What circumstance does he give as the reason for it (that is, what is his genuine because-motive)? What does the choice of these words indicate?" Questions like these point to the other person's *own* meaning-contexts, to the complex ways in which his own lived experiences have been constituted polythetically and also to the monothetic glance with which he attends to them.

22. The Nature of Genuine Intersubjective Understanding

Having established that all genuine understanding of the other person must start out from Acts of explication performed by the observer on his own lived experience, we must now proceed to a precise analysis of this genuine understanding itself. From the examples we have already given, it is clear that our inquiry must take two different directions. First we must study the genuine understanding of actions which are performed *without any communicative intent*. The action of the woodcutter would be a good example. Second we would examine cases where such communicative intent was present. The latter type of action involves a whole new dimension, the using[23] and interpreting of signs.

Let us first take actions performed without any communicative intent. We are watching a man in the act of cutting wood and wondering what is going on in his mind. Questioning him is ruled out, because that would require entering into a social relationship[24] with him, which in turn would involve the use of signs.

Let us further suppose that we know nothing about our woodcutter except what we see before our eyes. By subjecting our own perceptions to interpretation, we know that we are in the presence of a fellow human being and that his bodily movements indicate he is engaged in an action which we recognize as that of cutting wood.

Now how do we know what is going on in the woodcutter's mind? Taking this interpretation of our own perceptual data as a starting point, we can plot out in our mind's eye exactly how *we* would carry out the action in question. Then we can actually imagine ourselves doing so. In cases like this, then, we project the other person's goal as if it were our own and fancy ourselves carrying it out. Observe also that we here project the action in the future perfect tense as completed and that our imagined execution of the action is accompanied by the usual retentions and reproductions of the project, although, of course, only in fancy. Further, let us note that the imagined execution may fulfill or fail to fulfill the imagined project.

Or, instead of imagining for ourselves an action wherein we carry out the other person's goal, we may recall in concrete detail how we once carried out a similar action ourselves. Such a procedure would be merely a variation on the same principle.

In both these cases, we put ourselves in the place of the actor and identify our lived experiences with his. It might seem that we are here repeating the error of the well-known "projective" theory of empathy. For here we are reading our own lived experiences into the other person's mind and are therefore only discovering our own experiences. But, if we look more closely, we will see that our theory has nothing in common with the empathy theory except for one point. This is the general thesis of the Thou as the "other I," the one whose experiences are constituted in the same fashion as mine. But even this similarity is only apparent, for we start out from the general thesis of the other person's flow of duration, while the projective theory of empathy jumps from the mere fact of empathy to the belief in other minds by an act of blind faith. Our theory only brings out the implications of what is already present in the self-explicative judgment "I am experiencing a fellow human being." We know with certainty that the other person's subjective experience of his own action is in principle different from our own imagined picture of what we would do in the same situation. The reason, as we have already pointed out, is that the intended meaning of an action is always in principle subjective and accessible only to the actor. The error in the empathy theory is twofold. First, it naïvely tries to trace back the constitution of the other self within the ego's consciousness to empathy, so that the latter becomes the direct source of knowledge of the other.[25] Actually, such a task of discovering the constitution of the other self can only be carried out in a transcendentally phenomenological manner. Second, it pretends to a knowledge of the other person's mind that goes far beyond the establishment of a structural parallelism between that mind and my own. In fact, however, when we are dealing with actions having no communicative intent, all that we can assert about their meaning is already contained in the general thesis of the alter ego.

It is clear, then, that we imaginatively project the in-order-to motive of the other person as if it were our own and then use the fancied carrying-out of such an action as a scheme in which to interpret his lived experiences. However, to prevent misunderstanding, it should be added that what is involved here is only a reflective analysis of another person's completed act. It is an interpretation carried out after the fact. When an observer is directly watching someone else to whom he is attuned in simultaneity, the situation is different. Then the observer's living intentionality carries him along without having to make constant playbacks of his own past or imaginary experiences. The other person's action unfolds step by step before his eyes. In such a situation, the identification of the observer with the observed person is not carried out by starting with the goal of the act as already given and then proceeding to reconstruct the lived experiences which must have accompanied it. Instead, the observer keeps pace, as it were, with each step of the observed person's action, identifying himself with the latter's experiences within a common "we-relationship." We shall have much more to say about this later.

So far we have assumed the other person's bodily movement as the only datum given to the observer. It must be emphasized that, if the bodily movement is taken by itself in this way, it is necessarily isolated from its place within the stream of the observed person's living experience. And this context is important not only to the observed person but to the observer as well. He can, of course, if he lacks other data, take a mental snapshot of the observed bodily movement and then try to fit it into a phantasied filmstrip in accordance with the way he thinks he would act and feel in a similar situation. However, the observer can draw much more reliable conclusions about his subject if he knows something about his past and something about the over-all plan into which this action fits. To come back to Max Weber's example, it would be important for the observer to know whether the wood-cutter was at his regular job or just chopping wood for physical exercise. An adequate model of the observed person's subjective experiences calls for just this wider context. We have already seen, indeed, that the unity of the action is a function of the project's span. From the observed bodily movement, all the observer can infer is the single course of action which has directly led to it. If, however, I as the observer wish to avoid an inadequate interpretation of what I see another person doing, I must "make my own" all those meaning-contexts which make sense of this action on the basis of my past knowledge of this particular person. We shall come back later on to this concept of "inadequacy" and show its significance for the theory of the understanding of the other person.

23. Expressive Movement and Expressive Act

So far we have studied only cases where the actor seeks merely to bring about changes in the external world. He does not seek to "express" his subjective experiences. By an "expressive" action we mean one in which the actor seeks to project outward (*nach aussen zu projizieren*)[26] the contents of his consciousness, whether to retain the latter for his own use later on (as in the case of an entry in a diary) or to communicate them to others. In each of these two examples we have a genuinely planned or projected action (*Handeln nach Entwurf*) whose in-order-to motive is that someone takes cognizance of something. In the first case this someone is the other person in the social world. In the second it is oneself in the world of the solitary Ego. Both of these are expressive acts. We must clearly distinguish the "expressive act" (*Ausdruckshandlung*) from what psychologists call the "expressive movement" (*Ausdrucksbewegung*). The latter does not aim at any communication or at the expression of any thoughts for one's own use or that of others.[27] Here there is no genuine action in our sense, but only behavior: there is neither project nor in-order-to motive. Examples of such expressive movements are the gestures and facial expressions which, without any explicit intention, enter into every conversation.[28]

From my point of view as observer, your body is presented to me as a field of expression on which I can "watch" the flow of your lived experiences. I do this "watching" simply by treating *both* your expressive movements and your expressive acts as indications of your lived experiences. But we must look at this point in greater detail.

If I understand, as Weber says, certain facial expressions, verbal interjections, and irrational movements as an outbreak of anger, this understanding itself can be interpreted in several different ways. It can mean, for instance, nothing more than self-elucidation, namely my arrangement and classification of my own experiences of your body. It is only when I perform a further Act of attention involving myself intimately with *you*, regarding *your* subjective experiences as flowing simultaneously with *my* subjective experiences *of* you, that I really grasp or "get with" *your* anger. This turning to the genuine understanding of the other person is possible for me only because I have previously had experiences similar to yours even if only in phantasy, or if I have encountered it before in external manifestations. The expressive movement does, then, enter into a meaning-context, but only for the *observer*, for whom it is an indication of the lived experiences of the person he is observing. The latter is barred from giving meaning to his own expressive movements as they occur by the mere fact that he has not yet noticed them; they are, in our terminology, prephenomenal.

Expressive movements, then, have meaning only for the observer, not for the person observed. It is precisely this that distinguishes them from expressive acts. The latter always have meaning for the actor. Expressive acts are always genuine communicative acts (*Kundgabehandlungen*) which have as a goal their own interpretation.

The mere occurrence of a piece of external behavior, therefore, gives the interpreter no basis for knowing whether he is dealing with an expressive movement or an expressive act. He will be able to determine this only by appealing to a different context of experience. For instance, the play of a man's features and gestures in everyday life may be no different from those of an actor on the stage. Now we look upon the facial expressions and gestures of the latter as set signs that the stage actor is utilizing to express certain subjective experiences. In everyday life, on the other hand, we never quite know whether another person is "acting" in this sense or not unless we pay attention to factors other than his immediate movements. For instance, he may be imitating someone else for our benefit, or he may be playing a joke on us, or he may be hypocritically feigning certain feelings in order to take advantage of us.

It is quite immaterial to the understanding of expressive acts whether they consist of gestures, words, or artifacts. Every such act involves the use of signs. We must, then, turn next to the problem of the nature of signs.

24. Sign and Sign System

We must first distinguish the concept of "sign" or "symbol" from the general concept of "indication" or "symptom." In so doing we will be following Husserl's First *Logical Investigation*.[29] By an "indication" Husserl means an object or state of affairs whose existence indicates the existence of a certain other object or state of affairs, in the sense that belief in the existence of the former is a nonrational (or "opaque") motive for belief in the existence of the latter. For our purposes the important thing here is that the relation between the two exists solely in the mind of the interpreter.

Now, it is obvious that Husserl's "motive of belief" has nothing to do with our "motive of action." Husserl's so-called "motive" is, like ours, *a complex of meaning* or meaning-context. But it is a complex consisting of at least two interpretive schemes. However, when we interpret an indication, we do not attend to this causal relation, hence the motive is not "rational." The connection between the indication and what it indicates is therefore a purely formal and general one; there is nothing logical about it. There is no doubt that Husserl would agree with this point. Both animate and inanimate objects can serve as indications. For the geologist, a certain formation in the earth's surface is an indication of the presence of certain minerals. For the mathematician, the fact that an algebraic equation is of an odd degree is an indication that at least it has a real root. All these are relations—or correlations—within the mind of the interpreter and as such may be called contexts of meaning for him. In this sense, the perceived movements of the other person's body are indications for the observer of what is going on in the mind of the person he is observing.

"Signifying signs," "expressions," or "symbols" are to be contrasted with "indications."

First of all, let us see how a sign gets constituted in the mind of the interpreter. We say that there exists between the sign and that which it signifies the relation of representation.[30] When we look at a symbol, which is always in a broad sense an external object, we do not look upon it *as object* but *as representative* of something else. When we "understand" a sign, our attention is focused not on the sign itself but upon that for which it stands. Husserl repeatedly points out that it belongs to the essence of the signitive relation that "the sign and what it stands for have nothing to do with each other."[31] The signitive relation is, therefore, obviously a particular relation between the interpretive schemes which are applied to those external objects here called "signs." When we understand a sign, we do not interpret the latter through the scheme adequate to it as an external object but through the schemes adequate to whatever it signifies. We are saying that an interpretive scheme is *adequate* to an experienced object if the scheme has been constituted out of polythetically lived-through experiences of this same object as a self-existent thing. For example, the following three black lines, **A**, can be interpreted (1) *adequately*, as the diagram of a certain black and white visual Gestalt, or (2) *non-adequately*, as a sign for the corresponding vocal sound. The adequate interpretive scheme for the vocal sound is, of course, constituted not out of visual but out of auditory experiences.

However, confusion is likely to arise out of the fact that the interpretation of signs in terms of what they signify is based on previous experience and is therefore itself the function of a scheme.[32]

What we have said holds true of all interpretation of signs, whether the individual is interpreting his own signs or those of others. There is, however, an ambiguity in the common saying "a sign is always a sign for something." The sign is indeed the "sign for" what it means or signifies, the so-called "sign meaning" or "sign function." But the sign is also the "sign for" what it expresses, namely, the subjective experiences of the person using the sign. In the world of nature there are no signs (*Zeichen*) but only indications (*Anzeichen*).

A sign is by its very nature something used by a person to express a subjective experience. Since, therefore, the sign always refers back to an act of choice on the part of a rational being—a choice of this particular sign—the sign is also an indication of an event in the mind of the sign-user. Let us call this the "expressive function" of the sign.[33]

A sign is, therefore, always either an artifact or a constituted act-object.[34] The boundary between the two is absolutely fluid. Every act-object which functions as a sign-object (for instance, my finger pointing in a certain direction) is the end result of an action. But I might just as well have constructed a signpost, which would, of course, be classified as an artifact. In principle it makes no difference whether the action culminates in an act-object or in an artifact.[35]

It should be noted that in interpreting a sign it is not necessary to refer to the fact that someone made the sign or that someone used it. The interpreter need only "know the meaning" of the sign. In other words, it is necessary only that a connection be established in his mind between the interpretive scheme proper to the object which is the sign and the interpretive scheme proper to the object which it signifies. Thus when he sees a road sign, he will say to himself, "Intersection to the left!" and not "Look at the wooden sign!" or "Who put that sign there?"

We can, therefore, define signs as follows: Signs are artifacts or act-objects which are interpreted not according to those interpretive schemes which are adequate to them as objects of the external world but according to schemes not adequate to them and belonging rather to other objects. Furthermore, it should be said that the connection between the sign and its corresponding non-adequate scheme depends on the past experience of the interpreter. As we have already said, the applicability of the scheme of that which is signified to the sign is itself an interpretive scheme based on experience. Let us call this last-named scheme the "sign system." A sign system is a meaning-context which is a configuration formed by interpretive schemes; the sign-user or the sign-interpreter places the sign within this context of meaning.

Now there is something ambiguous in this idea of a sign context. Surely no one will maintain that the connection in question exists independently of the actual establishment, use, or interpretation of the signs. For the connection is itself an example of meaning and therefore a matter of either prescription or interpretation. In a strict sense, therefore, meaning-connections hold, not between signs as such, but between their meanings, which is just another way of saying between the experiences of the knowing self establishing, using, or interpreting the signs. However, since these "meanings" are understood only in and through the signs, there holds between the latter the connection we call the "sign system."

The sign system is present to him who understands it as a meaning-context of a higher order between previously experienced signs. To him the German language is the meaning-context of each of its component words; the sign system of a map is the meaning-context of every symbol on that map; the system of musical notation is the meaning-context of every written note; and so forth.

Knowing that a sign belongs to a certain sign system is not the same thing as knowing *what* that sign means and for what subjective experience of its user it is the expressive vehicle. Even though I do not know shorthand, still I know shorthand when I see it. Even though I may not know how to play a card game, still I can recognize the cards as *playing cards*, etc. The placing of a sign within its sign system is something I do by placing it within the total context of my experience. In doing this, all that is necessary is that I find within the store of my experience such a sign system together with the rules on the basis of which it is constituted. I do not have to understand the meaning of the individual signs or be fully conversant with the sign system. For instance, I can see that certain characters are Chinese without understanding their meaning.

As an *established* sign every sign is meaningful and therefore in principle intelligible. In general it is absurd to speak of a meaningless sign. A sign can properly be called meaningless only with respect to one or more established sign systems. However, to say that a sign is alien to one such system only means that it belongs to another. For instance, the meaninglessness per se of a definite auditory-visual symbol can never be determined but only its meaninglessness within a definite "language," in the broadest sense of that term. A letter combination which is quite unpronounceable can have a code meaning. It can be put together by one person according to the rules of the code and can then be interpreted by another person who knows those same rules. More than that, however, the audio-visual symbol "Bamalip" seems at first quite meaningless so far as the European languages are concerned. But the person who knows that "Bamalip" is the scholastic term for an entity of formal logic, namely, the first mood of the fourth figure of the syllogism, will be able to place it quite precisely within the structure of his own native language.

From this it follows that the sign meaning within a certain sign system must have been experienced previously. It is a question just what this phrase, "have been experienced," means. If we ask ourselves in what circumstances we have experienced the connection between the term "Bamalip" and the first mood of the fourth figure, we will find that we have learned it from a teacher or from a book. To have experienced the connection, however, means that we must on that occasion have established in our minds the term "Bamalip" as the sign of the first mood of the fourth figure. Therefore, the understanding of a sign (to be more precise, the possibility of its interpretation within a given system) points back to a previous decision on our part to accept and use this sign as an expression for a certain content of our consciousness.

Every sign system is therefore a scheme of our experience. This is true in two different senses. First, it is an *expressive scheme;* in other words, I have at least once used the sign for that which it designates, used it either in spontaneous activity or in imagination. Second, it is an *interpretive scheme;* in other words, I have already in the past interpreted the sign as the sign of that which it designates. This distinction is important, since, as already shown, I can recognize the sign system as an interpretive scheme, but only know that others do so. In the world of the solitary Ego the expressive scheme of a sign and its corresponding interpretive scheme necessarily coincide. If, for instance, I invent a private script, the characters of that code are established by me while I am inventing the script or using it to make notes. It is for me at such moments an expressive scheme. But the same scheme functions as an interpretive one for me when I later read what I have written or use it to make further notes.

To master fully a sign system such as a language, it is necessary to have a clear knowledge of the meaning of the individual signs within the system. This is possible only if the sign system and its component individual signs are known both as expressive schemes and as interpretive schemes for previous experiences of the knower. In both functions, as interpretive scheme and as expressive scheme, every sign points back to the experiences which preceded its constituting. As expressive scheme and as interpretive scheme a sign is only intelligible in terms of those lived experiences constituting it which it designates. Its meaning consists in its translatibility, that is, its ability to lead us back to something known in a different way. This may be either that scheme of experience in which the thing designated is understood, or another sign system. The philologist Meillet explains this point clearly as far as languages are concerned:

We cannot apprehend the sense of an unknown language intuitively. If we are to succeed in understanding the text of a language whose tradition has been lost, we must either have a faithful translation into a known language, that is, we must be closely related to one or more languages with which we are familiar. In other words, *we must already know it.*[36]

This property of "being already known" amounts to this: the meaning of the sign must be discoverable somewhere in the past experience of the person making use of the sign. To be fully conversant with a language, or in fact with any sign system, involves familiarity with given interpretive schemes on the basis of one's preceding experiences—even though this familiarity may be somewhat confused as to the implications of the schemes. It also involves the ability to transform these constituted objects into active experience of one's own, that is, in the ability to use expressively a sign system that one knows how to interpret.

We are now getting close to an answer to the question of what is meant by "connecting a meaning with a sign." Surely this involves something more than connecting words with behavior, which, as we pointed out in our Introduction, is a mere figure of speech. A meaning is connected with a sign, insofar as the latter's significance within a given sign system is understood both for the person using the sign and for the person interpreting it. Now we must be quite clear as to what we mean by speaking of the established membership of a sign in a given sign system. A sign has an "objective meaning" within its sign system when it can be intelligibly coordinated to what it designates within that system independently of whoever is using the sign or interpreting it. This is merely to say that he who "masters" the sign system will interpret the sign in its meaning-function to refer to that which it designates, regardless of who is using it or in what connection. The indispensable reference of the sign to previous experience makes it possible for the interpreter to repeat the syntheses that have constituted this interpretive or expressive scheme. Within the sign system, therefore, the sign has the ideality of the "I can do it again."[37]

However, this is not to say that the signs within the previously known sign system cannot be understood without an Act of attention to those lived experiences out of which the knowledge of the sign was constituted. On the contrary: as a genuine interpretive scheme for previous lived experiences, it is invariant with respect to the lived experiences of the I in which it was constituted.

What we have been considering is the objective meaning of the sign. The objective meaning is grasped by the sign-interpreter as a part of his interpretation of his own experience to himself. With this objective meaning of the sign we must contrast the sign's expressive function. The latter is its function as an indication of what actually went on in the mind of the communicator, the person who used the sign; in other words, of what was the communicator's own meaning-context.

If I want to understand the meaning of a word in a foreign language, I make use of a dictionary, which is simply an index in which I can see the signs arranged according to their objective meaning in two different sign systems or languages. However, the total of all the words in the dictionary is hardly the language. The dictionary is concerned only with the objective meanings of the words, that is, the meanings which do not depend on the users of the words or the circumstances in which they use them. In referring to subjective meanings, we do not here have in mind Husserl's "essentially subjective and occasional expressions," which we mentioned earlier. Such essentially subjective expressions as "left," "right," "here," "there," "this," and "I" can, of course, be found in the dictionary and are in principle translatable; however, they also have an objective meaning insofar as they designate a certain relation to the person who uses them. Once I have spatially located this person, then I can say that these subjective occasional expressions have objective meaning. However, *all* expressions, whether essentially subjective in Husserl's sense or not, have for both user and interpreter, over and above their objective meaning, a meaning which is both subjective and occasional. Let us first consider the *subjective* component. Everyone using or interpreting a sign associates with the sign a certain meaning having its origin in the unique quality of the experiences in which he once learned to use the sign. This added meaning is a kind of aura surrounding the nucleus of the objective meaning.[38] Exactly what Goethe means by "demonic"[39] can only be deduced from a study of his works as a whole. Only a careful study of the history of French culture aided by linguistic tools can permit us to understand the subjective meaning of the word "civilization" in the mouth of a Frenchman.[40] Vossler applies this thesis to the whole history of language in the following way: "We study the development of a word; and we find that the mental life of all who have used it has been precipitated and crystallized in it."[41] However, in order to be able to "study" the word, we must be able to bring to bear from our previous experience a knowledge of the mental structure of all those who have used it. The particular quality of the experiences of the user of the sign at the time he connected the sign and the *signatum* is something which the interpreter must take into account, over and above the objective meaning, if he wishes to achieve true understanding.

We have said that the added meaning is not only subjective but *occasional*. In other words, the added meaning always has in it something of the context in which it is used. In understanding someone who is speaking, I interpret not only his individual words but his total articulated sequence of syntactically connected words—in short, "what he is saying." In this sequence every word retains its own individual meaning in the midst of the surrounding words and throughout the total context of what is being said. Still, I cannot really say that I understand the word until I have grasped the meaning of the whole statement. In short, what I need at the moment of interpretation is the total context of my experience. As the statement proceeds, a synthesis is built up step by step, from the point of view of which one can see the individual acts of meaning-interpretation and meaning-establishment. Discourse is, therefore, itself a kind of meaning-context. For both the speaker and the interpreter, the structure of the discourse emerges gradually. The German language expresses the point we are making precisely in its distinction between *Wörter* ("unconnected words") and *Worte* ("discourse"). We can, in fact, say that when unconnected words receive occasional meaning, they constitute a meaningful whole and become discourse.

But what is that synthesis, what is that superimposed meaning-context which serves as an interpretive scheme for the understanding of a sign's occasional meaning? The answer is this: discourse is a sign-using act. The unity of a given speaker's discourse is, from his point of view, simply the unity that belongs essentially to every act. We have already seen in what this unity consists. It arises from the sign-user's own project or plan of action. It follows that the interpreter cannot grasp that unity until the act itself is completed. All he can do is arrive at an approximation based on his previous knowledge. This limitation, in fact, applies to the interpretation of objective as well as occasional meaning. One always has to wait until the last word has been said if one expects to make an effective interpretation. And it always remains a question of fact *what the unit is* whose end has to be awaited: whether it is a sentence, a book, the complete works of an author, or a whole literary movement.

The problem of the subjective and occasional meaning of signs is only one aspect of the larger problem of the distinction between objective and subjective meaning. It is to this dichotomy that we must now turn our attention.

25. Meaning-Establishment and Meaning-Interpretation

We have now seen that the sign has two different functions. First it has a *significative function*. By this we mean that it can be ordered by an interpreter within a previously learned sign system of his own. What he is doing here is interpreting the sign as an item of his own experience. His act is just another example of what we call self-interpretation. But there is a second kind of interpretation in which he can engage. He can inquire into the subjective and occasional meaning of the sign, in short, the *expressive* function which it acquires within the context of discourse. This subjective meaning can be his own, in which case he must go back in memory to the experiences he had at the moment of using the sign and establishing its meaning. Or it can be someone else's, in which case he must try to find out about the other person's subjective experiences when *he* used the sign. But in any case, when interpreting signs used by others, we will find two components involved, the objective and the subjective. Objective meaning is the meaning of the sign as such, the kernel, so to speak; whereas subjective meaning is the fringe or aura emanating from the subjective context in the mind of the sign-user.

Let us take a conversation between two people as an example. As one person speaks, thoughts are building up in his mind, and his listener is following him every step of the way just as the thoughts occur. In other words, none of the thoughts come out as prefabricated unities. They are constructed gradually, and they are interpreted gradually. Both speaker and listener live through the conversation in such a manner that on each side Acts of meaning-establishment or meaning-interpretation are filled in and shaded with memories of what has been said and anticipations of what is yet to be said. Each of these Acts can in turn be focused upon introspectively and analyzed as a unit in itself. The meaning of the speaker's discourse consists for him *and* for his listener in his individual sentences and these, in turn, in their component words as they come, one after another. The sentences for both of them serve as the meaning-contexts of the words, and the whole discourse as the meaning-context of the separate sentences.

Understanding the conscious Acts of another person who is communicating by means of signs does not differ in principle from understanding his other Acts (sec. 22). Like the latter, it occurs in the mode of simultaneity or quasi-simultaneity. The interpreter puts himself in the place of the other person and imagines that he himself is selecting and using the signs. He interprets the other person's subjective meaning as if it were his own. In the process he draws upon his whole personal knowledge of the speaker, especially the latter's ways and habits of expressing himself. Such personal knowledge continues to build itself up in the course of a conversation.

The same process goes on in the mind of the speaker. His words will be selected with a view to being understood by his listener. And the meaning he seeks to get across will not only be objective meaning, for he will seek to communicate his personal attitude as well. He will sketch out his communicative aim in the future perfect tense, just as he does the project of any other act. His choice of words will depend on the habits he has built up in interpreting the words of others, but it will, of course, also be influenced by his knowledge of his listener.

However, if the speaker is focused on what is going on in the mind of his listener, his knowledge of the latter is still quite uncertain. He can only estimate how much he is actually getting across. Any such estimate is necessarily vague, especially considering the fact that the listener's interpretation is always subsequent to the choice of words and fulfills or fails to fulfill the speaker's project in making that choice.

The listener is in a different position. For him the actual establishment of the meaning of the words has already occurred. He can start out with the objective meaning of the words he has heard and from there try to discover the subjective meaning of the speaker. In order to arrive at that subjective meaning, he imagines the project which the speaker must have had in mind. However, this picturing of the project starts out from the speaker's already spoken words. Contrary to the case of the speaker who is picturing something future on the basis of something present, the listener is picturing something pluperfect on the basis of something past. Another difference is that he is starting from words which have either succeeded or failed in fulfilling the speaker's project, and he is trying to uncover that project. The speaker, on the other hand, starts out with his own project as datum and tries to estimate whether it is going to be fulfilled by the listener's future interpretation.

Now since the words chosen by the speaker may or may not express his meaning, the listener can always doubt whether he is understanding the speaker adequately. The project of the speaker is always a matter of imaginative reconstruction for his interpreter and so is attended by a certain vagueness and uncertainty.

To illustrate what we mean, consider the fact that, in a conversation, thoughts like the following may run through the heads of the participants. The person about to speak will say to himself, "Assuming that this fellow speaks my kind of language, I must use such and such words." A moment later his listener will be saying to himself, "If this other fellow is using words the way I understand them, then he must be telling me such and such." The first statement shows how the speaker always chooses his words with the listener's interpretation in mind. The second statement shows how the listener always interprets with the speaker's subjective meaning in mind. In either case an intentional reference to the other person's scheme is involved, regardless of whether the scheme is interpretive or expressive.

As the speaker chooses his words, he uses, of course, his own interpretive scheme. This depends partly upon the way he himself usually interprets words and partly upon his knowledge of his listener's interpretive habits. When I read over a letter I have written to someone, I tend to interpret it just as if I were the receiver and not the sender. Now, my purpose in writing the letter was not merely to communicate an objective meaning to the reader but my subjective meaning as well. To put it in another way, I want him to rethink my thoughts. It may very well be, therefore, that when I read over my letter I shall decide that it falls short of this purpose. Knowing the person to whom I am writing and knowing his customary reactions to certain words and phrases, I may decide that this or that expression is open to misinterpretation or that he will not really be in a position to understand this or that thought of mine. Or I may fear that he will, as he reads, miss the point I am trying to make due to some subjective bias or some failure of attention on his part.

On the other hand, the recipient of the letter can carry out the opposite process. He can take a sentence and imagine that he himself wrote it. He can try to reconstruct the intention of the writer by guessing at some possible intentions and then comparing them with the actual propositional content of the sentence. He may conclude, "I see what he was trying to say, but he really missed his mark and said something else. If I had been he, I should have put it in such and such a way." Or the reader may say to himself instead, "My friend always uses that term in an odd way, but I see what he means, since I know the way he thinks. It's lucky that I am the one reading the letter. A third party would have been thrown off the track entirely at this point." In the last case, the reader really carries out a threefold interpretation. First, he interprets the sentence objectively on the basis of his ordinary habits of interpretation. Second, from his knowledge of the writer, he reconstructs what must be the latter's real meaning. Third, he imagines how the ordinary reader would understand the sentence in question.

These considerations hold true quite generally for all cases in which signs are either used or interpreted. This being the case, it ought to be clear that in interpreting the subjective meaning of the signs used by someone else, or in anticipating someone else's interpretation of the subjective meaning of our own signs, we must be guided by our knowledge of that person. Naturally, therefore, the degree of intimacy or anonymity in which the person stands to us will have a great deal to do with the matter. The examples we have just used were all cases where knowledge of the other person was derived from direct contact; they belong to what we call the domain of directly experienced social reality. However, the use and interpretation of signs are to be found in the other areas of social life as well, such as the worlds of contemporaries and of predecessors, where direct knowledge of the people with whom we are dealing is minimal or even absent. Our theory of the establishment and interpretation of the meaning of signs will naturally undergo various modifications as it is applied to these areas. We shall see what these modifications are when we come to Chapter 4. Even in the direct social relations we have used as examples, it was obviously impossible for the participants to "carry out the postulate of grasping each other's intended meaning," a point that we discussed in section 19. The subjective meaning that the interpreter *does* grasp is at best an approximation to the sign-user's intended meaning, but never that meaning itself, for one's knowledge of another person's perspective is always necessarily limited. For exactly the same reason, the person who expresses himself in signs is never quite sure of how he is being understood.

What we have been discussing is the content of communication. But we must remember that the actual *communicating* is itself a meaningful act and that we must interpret that act and the way it is done as things in their own right.

26. The Meaning-Context of Communication. Recapitulation

Once the interpreter has determined both the objective and subjective meanings of the content of any communication, he may proceed to ask why the communication was made in the first place. He is then seeking the in-order-to motive of the person communicating. For it is essential to every act of communication that it has an extrinsic goal. When I say something to you, I do so for a reason, whether to evoke a particular attitude on your part or simply to explain something to you. Every act of communication has, therefore, as its in-order-to motive the aim that the person being addressed takes cognizance of it in one way or another.

The person who is the object or recipient of the communication is frequently the one who makes this kind of interpretation. Having settled what are the objective and subjective meanings of the content of the communication by finding the corresponding interpretive or expressive schemes, he proceeds to inquire into the reason why the other person said this in the first place. In short, he seeks the "plan" behind the communication.

However, the seeker of the in-order-to motive need not be the person addressed at all. A nonparticipant observer may proceed to the same kind of interpretation. I can, indeed I must, seek the in-order-to motive of the communication if I am ever to know the goal toward which the communication is leading. Furthermore, it is self-evident that one can seek the in-order-to motives even of those acts of other people which have no communicative intent. We have already seen this in section 22. What an actor's subjective experience actually is we can only grasp if we find his in-order-to motive. We must first light upon his project and then engage in a play-by-play phantasy of the action which would fulfill it. In the case of action without communicative intent, the completed act itself is properly interpreted as the fulfillment of the in-order-to motive. However, if I happen to know that the completed act is only a link in a chain of means leading to a further end, then what I must do is interpret the subjective experiences the other person has of that further goal itself.

Now, we have already seen that we can go beyond the in-order-to motive and seek out the because-motive. Of course, knowledge of the latter presupposes in every case knowledge of the former. The subjective meaning-context which is the in-order-to motive must first be seen and taken for granted as an already constituted object in itself before any venture into deeper levels is undertaken. To speak of such deeper levels *as existing* by no means implies that the actor actually experiences them subjectively as meaning-contexts of his action. Nor does it mean that he can become aware even retrospectively of those polythetic Acts which, according to my interpretation, have constituted the in-order-to motive. On the contrary, there is every evidence against the view that the actor ever has any awareness of the because-motive of his action. This applies to one who is establishing a meaning as well as to any other actor. To be sure, he lives through the subjective experiences and intentional Acts which I have interpreted as his because-motive. However, he is not as a rule aware of them, and, when he is, it is no longer as actor. Such awareness, when it occurs, is a separate intentional Act independent of and detached from the action it is interpreting. It is then that a man can be said to understand himself. Such self-understanding is essentially the same as understanding others, with this difference—that usually, but not always, we have at our disposal a much richer array of information about ourselves and our past than others do.

Later on we shall describe the relation of the in-order-to motive to the because-motives in the various regions of the social world. At this point we shall merely try to recapitulate the complex structures involved in understanding another person insofar as these bear on communication and the use of signs. For to say, as we do, that for the user of the sign the sign stands in a meaning-context involves a number of separate facts which must be disentangled.

First of all, whenever I make use of a sign, those lived experiences signified by that sign stand for me in a meaning-context. For they have already been constituted into a synthesis, and I look upon them as a unit.

In the second place, for me the sign must already be part of a sign system. Otherwise I would not be able to use it. A sign must already have been interpreted before it can be used. But the understanding of a sign is a complicated synthesis of lived experiences resulting in a special kind of meaning-context. This meaning-context is a configuration involving two elements: the sign as object in itself and the *signatum*, each of which, of course, involves separate meaning-contexts in its own right. The total new meaning-context embracing them both we have called the "coordinating scheme" of the sign.

Third, the Act of selecting and using the sign is a special meaning-context for the sign-user to the extent that each use of a sign is an expressive action. Since every action comprises a meaning-context by virtue of the fact that the actor visualizes all the successive lived experiences of that action as one unified act, it follows that every expressive action is therefore a meaning-context. This does not mean that every case of sign-using is *ipso facto* a case of communication. A person may, talking to himself for instance, use a sign purely as an act of self-expression without any intention of communication.

Fourth, the meaning-context "sign-using as act" can serve as the basis for a superimposed meaning-context "sign-using as communicative act" without in any way taking into account the particular person addressed.

Fifth, however, this superimposed meaning-context can enter into a still higher and wider meaning-context in which the addressee *is* taken into account. In this case the communicating act has as its goal not merely that someone takes cognizance of it but that its message should motivate the person cognizing to a particular attitude or piece of behavior.

Sixth, the fact that this particular addressee is communicated with *here, now*, and *in this way* can be placed within a still broader context of meaning by finding the in-order-to motive of that communicative act.

All these meaning-contexts are in principle open to the interpreter and can be uncovered systematically by him. Just which ones he does seek to inquire into will depend upon the kind of interest he has in the sign.

However, the statement that all these meaning-contexts in principle lie open to interpretation requires some modification. As we have said repeatedly, the structure of the social world is by no means homogeneous. Our fellow men and the signs they use can be given to us in different ways. There are different approaches to the sign and to the subjective experience it expresses. Indeed, we do not even need a sign in order to gain access to another person's mind; a mere indication can offer us the opening. This is what happens, for instance, when we draw inferences from artifacts concerning the experiences of people who lived in the past.

27.   Subjective and Objective Meaning. Product and Evidence

We have now seen the different approaches to the genuine understanding of the other self. The interpreter starts with his own experience of the animate body of the other person or of the artifacts which the latter has produced. In either case he is interpreting Objectivations in which the other's subjective experiences manifest themselves. If it is the body of the other that is in question, he concerns himself with act-objectifications, i.e., movements, gestures, or the results of action. If it is artifacts that are in question, these may be either signs in the narrower sense or manufactured external objects such as tools, monuments, etc. All that these Objectivations have in common is that they exist only as the result of the action of rational beings. Because they are products of action, they are *ipso facto* evidence of what went on in the minds of the actors who made them. It should be noted that *not all evidences are signs*, but all signs are evidences. For an evidence to be a sign, it must be capable of becoming an element in a sign system with the status of coordinating scheme. This qualification is lacking in some evidence. A tool, for instance, although it is an evidence of what went on in the mind of its maker, is surely no sign. However, under "evidences" we mean to include not only equipment[42] that has been produced by a manufacturing process, but judgment that has been produced by thought, or the message content which has been produced by an act of communication.

The problematic of subjective and objective meaning includes evidences of all sorts. That is to say, anyone who encounters a given product can proceed to interpret it in two different ways. First, he can focus his attention on its status as an object, either real or ideal, but at any rate independent of its maker. Second, he can look upon it as evidence for what went on in the mind of its makers at the moment it was being made. In the former case the interpreter is subsuming his own experiences (*erfahrende Akte*) of the object under the interpretive schemes which he has at hand. In the latter case, however, his attention directs itself to the constituting Acts of consciousness of the producer (these might be his own as well as those of another person).

This relation between objective and subjective meaning will be examined in a more detailed way at a later point. *We speak, then, of the subjective meaning of the product if we have in view the meaning-context within which the product stands or stood in the mind of the producer. To know the subjective meaning of the product means that we are able to run over in our own minds in simultaneity or quasi-simultaneity the polythetic Acts which constituted the experience of the producer.*

We keep in view, then, the other person's lived experiences as they are occurring; we observe them being constituted step by step. For us, the other person's products are indications of those lived experiences. The lived experiences stand for him, in turn, within a meaning context. We know this by means of a particular evidence, and we can in an act of genuine understanding be aware of the constituting process in his mind.

Objective meaning, on the contrary, we can predicate only of the product as such, that is, of the already constituted meaning-context of the thing produced, whose actual production we meanwhile disregard. The product is, then, in the fullest sense the end result of the process of production, something that is finished and complete. It is no longer part of the process but merely points back to it as an event in the past. The product itself is, however, not an event but an entity (*ein Seiendes*) which is the sediment of past events within the mind of the producer. To be sure, even the interpretation of the objective meaning of the product occurs in step-by-step polythetic Acts. Nevertheless, it is exhausted in the ordering of the interpreter's experiences of the product within the total meaning-context of the interpretive act. And, as we have said, the interpreter leaves the original step-by-step creation of the product quite out of account. It is not that he is unaware that it has occurred; it is just that he pays no attention to it. Objective meaning therefore consists only in a meaning-context within the mind of the interpreter, whereas subjective meaning refers beyond it to a meaning-context in the mind of the producer.

A subjective meaning-context, then, is present if what is given in an objective meaning-context was created as a meaning-context by a Thou on its own part. Nothing, however, is thereby implied either about the particular kind of meaning-context into which the Thou orders its lived experiences or about the quality of those experiences themselves.

We have already noted that the interpreter grasps the other person's conscious experiences in the mode of simultaneity or quasi-simultaneity. Genuine simultaneity is the more frequent, even though it is a special case of the process. It is tied to the world of directly experienced social reality and presupposes that the interpreter witnesses the actual bringing-forth of the product. An example would be a conversation, where the listener is actually present as the speaker performs Acts that bring forth meaningful discourse and where the listener performs these Acts with and after the speaker. A case of quasi-simultaneous interpretation would be the reading of a book. Here the reader relives the author's choice of words as if the choice were made before his very eyes. The same would hold for a person inspecting some artifacts, such as tools, and imagining to himself how they were made. However, in saying that we can observe such subjective experiences on the part of the producer, we only meant that we can grasp the fact *that* they occur. We have said nothing about how we understand *what* experiences occur, nor how we understand *the way* in which they are formed. We shall deal with these problems when we analyze the world of contemporaries, the world of direct social experience, and the world of the genuine We-relationship. Still, it can be said even at this point that what is essential to this further knowledge is a knowledge of the person being interpreted. When we ask what the subjective meaning of a product is, and therefore what conscious experiences another person has, we are asking what particular polythetically constructed lived experiences are occurring or have occurred in a particular other person. This other person, this Thou, has his own unique experiences and meaning-contexts. No other person, not even he himself at another moment, can stand in his shoes at this moment.

The objective meaning of a product that we have before us is, on the other hand, by no means interpreted as evidence for the particular lived experience of a particular Thou. Rather, it is interpreted as already constituted and established, abstracted from every subjective flow of experience and every subjective meaning-context that could exist in such a flow. It is grasped as an objectification endowed with "universal meaning." Even though we implicitly refer to its author when we call it a "product," still we leave this author and everything personal about him out of account when we are interpreting objective meaning. He is hidden behind the impersonal "one" (someone, someone or other). This anonymous "one" is merely the linguistic term for the fact that a Thou exists, or has once existed, of whose particularity we take no account. I myself or you or some ideal type or Everyman could step into its shoes without in any way altering the subjective meaning of the product. We can say nothing about the subjective processes of this anonymous "one," for the latter has no duration, and the temporal dimension we ascribe to it, being a logical fiction, is in principle incapable of being experienced. But precisely for this reason the objective meaning remains, from the point of view of the interpreter, invariant for all possible creators of the meaningful object. Insofar as that object contains within its very meaning the ideality of the "and so forth" and of the "I can do it again," to that extent is that meaning independent of its maker and the circumstances of its origination. The product is abstracted from every individual consciousness and indeed from every consciousness as such. Objective meaning is merely the interpreter's ordering of his experiences of a product into the total context of his experience.

It follows from all we have said that every interpretation of subjective meaning involves a reference to a particular person. Furthermore, it must be a person of whom the interpreter has some kind of experience (*Erfahrung*) and whose subjective states he can run through in simultaneity or quasi-simultaneity, whereas objective meaning is abstracted from and independent of particular persons. Later we shall study this antithesis in greater detail, treating it as a case of polar opposition. Between the understanding of subjective meaning and the understanding of pure objective meaning there is a whole series of intermediate steps based on the fact that the social world has its own unique structure derived, as it is, from the worlds of direct social experience, of contemporaries, of predecessors, and of successors. We shall devote Chapter 4 to the study of these different worlds, meanwhile paying special attention to the process of anonymization in each. We shall explain the polar opposition between subjective and objective meaning as an ideal-typical formulation of heuristic principles of meaning-interpretation.

28. Excursus: A Few Applications of the Theory of Objective and Subjective Meaning in the Field of the Cultural Sciences

The theory of the two different types of meaning-interpretation of products which we have just developed is of great significance for the cultural sciences (*Geisteswissenschaften*) and not for these only. First of all, let us consider what are called "cultural objects," in other words, such ideal objectivities as "state," "art," "language," and so forth. These are all products according to our theory, for they bear upon them the mark of their production by our fellow men and are evidences of what went on in the minds of our fellow men. All cultural Objectivations can, therefore, be interpreted in a twofold manner. One interpretation treats them as completely constituted objectifications as they exist for us the interpreters, either now, as contemporaries in the present, or as coming later in history. These objectifications can be described quite simply or can be subjected to theoretical elaboration as objects of essential knowledge; that is, one can study the state as such, art as such, language as such.

All these products can, however, be treated as evidences for what went on in the minds of those who created them. Here highly complex cultural objects lend themselves to the most detailed investigation. The state can be interpreted as the totality of the acts of those who are oriented to the political order, that is, of its citizens; or it can be interpreted as the end result of certain historical acts and therefore itself as a historical object; or it can be treated as the concretization of a certain public-mindedness on the part of its rulers, and so forth. The art of a particular era can be interpreted as the expression of a particular artistic tendency of the time or as the expression of a particular interpretation of the world preceding and determining all artistic expression, in other words, as an expression of a particular way of "seeing." However, it can further be interpreted as a historical development which comes about in the form of a variation on the known style of an earlier epoch, whether due to the succession of schools or simply of generations. These are mere samples of the numerous possibilities of interpretation, and to each of them corresponds a special interpretive scheme and way of giving meaning to the object of interpretation.

We have already noted that the meaning-content of a product is more or less independent of what went on in the mind of the person creating it, according to whether the latter is understood by his interpreter in greater or lesser anonymity. In order to grasp a certain objectification in the ideality of the "I can do it again," one must conceive the author of that objectification simply as "one." Let us see how this works out in the field of economic theory. The so-called "principles of catallactics"[43] certainly have as their subject matter human acts considered as finished products, not actions in progress. The meaning-content of these principles is exhausted in the subsumption of such acts under the interpretive schemes of economic theory. To be sure, no economic act is conceivable without some reference to an economic actor, but the latter is absolutely anonymous; it is not you, nor I, nor an entrepreneur, nor even an "economic man" as such, but a pure universal "one."[44] This is the reason why the propositions of theoretical economics have just that "universal validity" which gives them the ideality of the "and so forth" and the "I can do it again." However, one can study the economic actor as such and try to find out what is going on in his mind; of course, one is not then engaged in theoretical economics but in economic history or economic sociology, of which Weber has furnished us an unparalleled example in the first book of his *Wirtschaft und Gesellschaft*. However, the statements of these sciences can claim no universal validity, for they deal either with the economic sentiments of particular historical individuals or with types of economic activity for which the economic acts in question are evidence.

To give examples from other fields of the significance of this question, we need only point out the importance of drawing a sharp distinction between subjective and objective meaning in those sciences which are interpretive in the narrow sense, namely, philology and jurisprudence. In philology it is always a basic question whether what is being studied is the objective meaning of a word at a definite time within a definite language area or, second, the subjective meaning which the word takes on in the usage of a particular author or of a particular circle of speakers or, third, the occasional meaning which it takes on in the context of discourse. Again, every student of law is familiar with the distinction between considering a point of law as a proposition within the legal system in accordance with philological and juridical canons of interpretation, on the one hand, and asking, on the other hand, what "the intention of the legislator" was. All these differences come down to the distinction between the objective and subjective meaning of the product, with which we have just been dealing.

One more point before we conclude this chapter. The tendency to look for a subjective meaning for everything in existence is so deeply rooted in the human mind, the search for the meaning of every object is so tied up with the idea that that object was once given meaning by some mind, that everything in the world can be interpreted as a product and therefore as evidence for what went on in the mind of God. Indeed, the whole universe can be regarded as the product of God, to whose creative act it bears witness. This is only to make passing reference, of course, to a whole area of problems that lie outside the strict sciences. In any case, the problem of subjective and objective meaning is the open door to every theology and metaphysics.

Notes

1. In the *Cartesian Meditations*, especially in Meditation V, Husserl has given us a profound analysis of the general significance of these questions and has also given us the essential starting point from which they must be solved.

2. This follows from Husserl's method of dealing with the problem. Cf. *Logik*, p. 212.

3. *Die Wissensformen und die Gesellschaft* (Leipzig, 1926), II, pp. 475 f.

4. [This paragraph is an adaptation.]

5. Cf. also Husserl's *Ideen*, p. 167 [E.T., p. 241]: "Closer inspection would further show that two *streams of experience* (spheres of consciousness for two pure Egos) *cannot be conceived as having an essential content that is identically the same;* moreover. . . . no *fully-determinate experience* of the one could ever belong to the other; only experiences of identically the same specification can be common to them both (although not common in the sense of being individually identical), but never two experiences which in addition have absolutely the same 'setting.'"

6. *Ideen*, p. 68 [E.T., p. 124].

7. *Logische Untersuchungen*, II., i, 34.

8. ["The term 'signification' is the same as 'meaning' for Husserl. Similarly, he often speaks of *significative* or *signitive acts* instead of acts of meaning-intention, of meaning, and the like. Signitive is also good as expressing opposition to intuitive. A synonym for *signitive* is *symbolic*" (Farber, *Foundation of Phenomenology*, p. 402, n.).]

9. Cf. Husserl's *Méditations cartésiennes*, p. 97: "The organism of another person keeps demonstrating that it *is* a living organism solely by its changing but always consistent behavior. And it does that in the following way: the physical side of the behavior is the index of the psychic side. It is upon this 'behavior' appearing in our experience and verifying and confirming itself in the ordered succession of its phases . . . it is in this indirect but genuine accessibility of that which is not in itself directly accessible that the existence of the other is, for us, founded." [The English rendering here is our own. Cf. Cairns' translation (from the German), *Cartesian Meditations*, p. 114.]

10. Cf. also, Husserl, *Logik*, p. 210.

11. [Or, literally, "all my experiences of the other self's experiences are still my own experiences" ("nun sind auch meine Erlebnisse von Fremden Erlebnissen noch immer je-meinige Erlebnisse.")

12. *Durée et simultanéité: A propos de la théorie d'Einstein*, 2d ed. (Paris, 1923) p. 66.

13. [". . . ein Beharren im Ablauf der objektiven Zeit." The words here are reminiscent of Kant. Cf. the *Critique of Pure Reason* B 183: "The schema of substance is the permanence of the real in time" ("die Beharrlichkeit des Realen in der Zeit").]

14. Bergson, *op. cit.*, p. 88 and *passim*.

15. Cf. Husserl, *Méditations cartésiennes*, p. 97: "From the phenomenological point of view, the other person is a modification of 'my' self."

16. Husserl comes to the same conclusion from an entirely different starting point: "It (the experience of the other person) establishes a connection between, on the one hand, the uninterrupted, unimpeded living experience which the concrete *ego* has of itself, *in other words, the ego's primordial sphere, and on the other hand* the alien sphere which appears within the latter by appresentation. It establishes this connection by means of a synthesis which identifies the primordially given animate body of the other person with his body as appresented under another mode of appearance. From there it reaches out to a synthesis of the same Nature, given and verified at once primordially (with pure sensuous originality) and in the mode of appresentation. Thus is definitely instituted for the first time *the coexistence of my 'I'* (as well as my concrete *ego* in general) and the *'I' of the other person*, the coexistence of my intentional life and his, of my 'realities' and his; in short what we have here is the creation of a *common time-form* (*Méditations cartésiennes*, § 55, p. 108. [See also E.T., Cairns, p. 128. Cf. the next footnote for an explanation of what Husserl means by "a synthesis of the same Nature."]

17. Husserl arrives at similar conclusions. He formulates the concept of the "intersubjective Nature" corresponding to the ordinary concept of environment, and he draws the profound distinction between

apperception in the mode of the *"hic"* and of the *"illic."* "It (the other's body as it appears to me) appresents, first of all, the activity of the other person as controlling his body (*illic*) as the latter appears to me. But also, and as a result of this, it appresents his action through that body on the *Nature* which he perceives. This Nature is the *same* Nature to which that body (*illic*) belongs, *my own* primordial Nature. It is the same Nature but it is given to me in the mode of 'If I were over there looking out through his eyes.' . . . Furthermore, *my whole* Nature is the same as his. It is constituted in my primordial sphere as an identical unity of my multiple modes of givenness, identical in all its changing orientations from the point of view of my body, which is the zero point, the absolute *here* (hic)" (*Méditations cartésiennes*, p. 104). [Cf. also E.T., Cairns, p. 123.]

18. For the sake of simplicity we are here leaving essentially actual lived experiences out of account.

19. Husserl, *Ideen*, p. 85 [E.T., p. 143].

20. [Schutz used the English term "consociates" (among others) to mean those whom we directly experience. We shall be using it in this technical sense to translate references to people in our *Umwelt* (domain of directly experienced social reality).]

21. Cf. Husserl, *Logische Untersuchungen* (3d ed.), II, ii, 89.

22. Of course, all such interpretations presume acceptance of the General Thesis of the Alter Ego, according to which the external object is understood to be animated, that is, to be the body of another self.

23. [*Setzung*; literally, "positing" or "establishing."]

24. The term "social relationship" is here being used in Weber's vague colloquial sense. Later, in sec. 31, we expect to subject it to detailed analysis.

25. For a critique of the empathy theory see Scheler, *Wesen und Formen der Sympathie*, pp. 277 ff. [E.T., Heath, p. 241].

26. [It is perhaps needless to caution the reader against any confusion of this concept with Schutz's "to project" (*entwerfen*), which means "to plan" or "design" an act.]

27. Husserl, *Logische Untersuchungen*, II, 31.

28. *Ibid.*

29. *Logische Untersuchungen*, II, i, 25–31.

30. Cf. Husserl's Sixth *Logical Investigation*.

31. *Ibid.*, II, ii, 55 [or II, 527 in the 1901 edition].

32. In effect, what we have here is a kind of metascheme connecting two others. This corresponds to Felix Kaufmann's so-called "coordinating scheme" (*Das Unendliche in der Mathematik und seine Ausschaltung* [Leipzig and Vienna, 1930], p. 42).

33. Our usage here diverges from the terminology of Husserl's *Logical Investigations*, I and VI.

34. [The words here translated "act-object" and "sign-object" are, respectively, *Handlungsgegenständlich-keit* and *Zeichengegenständlichkeit*. They refer to the act and sign considered as repeatable objects rather than as unique events.]

35. I cannot, therefore, admit as fundamental Hans Freyer's distinction between the physiognomic side of an action and its objectification in the material world. (See his *Theorie des objectiven Geistes* [Leipzig, 1923], pp. 29 ff.)

36. Quoted in Vossler, *Geist und Kultur in der Sprache* (Heidelberg, 1925), p. 115. [E.T., Oscar Oeser, *The Spirit of Language in Civilization* (London, 1932), p. 104. The reference is to A. Meillet, *Aperçu d'une histoire de la langue grecque* (Paris, 1913), p. 48.]

37. Cf. Husserl, *Logik*.

38. In fact, we can even say that the understanding of the objective meaning is an unrealizable ideal, which means merely that the subjective and occasional component in the sign's meaning should be explained with the utmost clarity by means of rational concepts. That language is "precise" in which all occasional subjective meanings are adequately explained according to their circumstances.

39. It was Jaspers who first called attention to the central importance of this concept in Goethe's image of the world. See his Psychologie der Weltanschauung 3d ed. (Berlin, 1925).

40. Curtius. *Frankreich* (Stuttgart, 1930), I, 2 ff.

41. Vossler, *Geist und Kultur in der Sprache*, p. 117 [E.T., p. 106].

42. *Zeug*. This is the term used by Heidegger for those objects of the external world which are "ready to hand." Cf. *Sein und Zeit*, p. 102 [E.T., *Being and Time*, Macquarrie and Robinson, p. 135].

43. [The theory of exchange. This term, originated by Whately, plays a major part in the economic thought of Ludwig von Mises, to which Schutz often refers. See Mises' *Human Action* (New Haven, 1966), esp. Part IV. Catallactics for Mises is part of a pure a priori theory of action considered as abstracted from its psychological and historical circumstances; Mises' concept is therefore especially useful as an example at this point. For a very recent major economic treatise based on the same concept see Murray N. Rothhard, *Man, Economy and the State* (Princeton, 1962).]

44. See the discussion of the anonymity of the world of contemporaries, sec. 39, below, for a further analysis of this concept of "one."

10 Platonic Dialogue

Michel Serres

The logicians' extended discussion of the notion of symbol is well known.[1] Without entering into the detail of the arguments that separate the Hilbertian realists, the nominalists following Quine, those who subscribe to the Polish school, and so on, I shall take up a fragment of the issue here, while giving it a new twist.

When I want to communicate with another person, I have at hand a number of old and new methods: languages, systems of writing, means of storing, of transmitting, or of multiplying the message—tapes, telephone, printing press, and so on.[2] It is not important for our present purposes to determine whether they are natural or synthetic. Writing is one of the simplest methods and, at the same time, one of the richest, since I can store, transmit, and multiply information with it. But before entering into these problems, as well as those of style, of the disposition of the narrative, of argumentation, and so on, there is first the physical appearance of the writing, its graphic form: writing is first and foremost a drawing, an ideogram, or a conventional graph. For the moment, let us agree that written communication is only possible between two persons used to the same graphic forms, trained to code and decode a meaning by using the same key.

Suppose, then, we take a written message at its source: it is understood only if the receptor possesses the key to the drawing. This is the condition of its reception, and it is essential. But there is another condition at the source of the message that, though it is only circumstantial, still merits analysis. The scribe must execute his drawing as well as possible. What does this mean? First, the graph comprises essential graphic signs, those charged with meaning; the form of the letters (standardized), properly formed clusters of letters and of words (regulated by the rules of morphology and of syntax), and so on. It also comprises inessential, accidental graphic signs, those without meaning whose presence depends on the ability, the clumsiness, the education, the passion, or the illness of he who writes: waverings in the graphic forms, failures in the drawing, spelling errors, and so on. The first condition presupposes an "orthogram" and a calligram. But this is never, or almost never, the case.[3] The calligram preserves form against accident, and if logicians are interested in form, it is also possible to be interested in pathology, in other words, in "cacography." Graphology is the misguided science (or the false science) dealing with the psychological motives of cacography: can we speak purely of the latter, that is to say, speak purely of an impurity?

Pathology of communication is not only a fact of writing. It also exists in spoken languages: stammerings, mispronunciations, regional accents, dysphonias, and cacophonies. Likewise in the technical means of communication: background noise, jamming, static, cut-offs, hyteresis, various interruptions. If static is accidental, background noise is *essential* to communication.

Following scientific tradition, let us call *noise* the set of these phenomena of interference that become obstacles to communication. Thus, cacography is the noise of graphic form or, rather, the latter comprises an essential form *and* a noise that is either essential or occasional. To write badly is to plunge the graphic message into this noise which interferes with reading, which transforms the reader into an epigraphist. In other words, simply to write is to risk jumbling a form. In the same way, to communicate orally is to risk losing meaning in noise. This set of phenomena has appeared so important to certain theoreticians of language[4] that they have not hesitated to transform our current conception of dialogue in reference to it: such communication is a sort of game played by two interlocutors considered as united against the phenomena of interference and confusion, or against individuals with some stake in interrupting communication.[5] These interlocutors are in no way opposed, as in the traditional conception of the dialectic game; on the contrary, they are on the same side, tied together by a mutual interest: they battle together against noise. The cacographer and the epigraphist, the cacophonous speaker and the auditor, exchange their reciprocal roles in dialogue, where the source becomes reception, and the reception source (according to a given rhythm). They exchange roles sufficiently often for us to view them as struggling together against a common enemy. *To hold a dialogue is to suppose a third man and to seek to exclude him*; a successful communication is the exclusion of the third man. The most profound dialectical problem is not the problem of the Other, who is only a variety—or a variation—of the Same, it is the problem of the third man. We might call this third man the *demon*, the prosopopeia of noise.[6]

The conception of the dialogue is immediately applicable to some famous philosophemes; it is capable of extracting from them some unexpected meanings. For example, the *Metaphysical Meditations* can be explained according to these principles: the *Meditations* seek out the other with whom one must join in order to expel the third man.[7] For the moment, let us go no further than the Platonic dialogues: the maieutic method, in fact, unites the questioner and the respondent in the task of giving birth. Dialectic makes the two interlocutors play on the same side; they do battle together to produce a truth on which they can agree, that is, to produce a successful communication. In a certain sense, they struggle together against interference, against the demon, against the third man. Obviously, this battle is not always successful. In the aporetic dialogues, victory rests with the powers of noise; in the other dialogues, the battle is fierce—attesting to the power of the third man. Serenity returns little by little when the exorcism is definitively(?) obtained.

It is not within the bounds of this study to develop at any great length the theme of the third man in the Platonic dialogue. That would take us too far afield, and we are, in fact, already very far from our premises—but not nearly as far as it would appear.

Let us return to logic and through it to writing. For the logician, a symbol is a drawing, a graph made on the blackboard with a piece of chalk.[8] A particular symbol can occur several times in a set of formulas. Mathematicians all agree to recognize a "same" symbol in two or more occurrences of this symbol. Yet by the graphic form itself every occurrence differs from another, whatever it may be: wavering of outline, errors of movement, and so forth. Consequently, the logician reasons not by using the concrete graph drawn on the black-board, here and now, but rather, as Tarski says, by using the class of objects having the same form.[9] The symbol is thus an abstract being that the graphs in question only evoke. This abstract being is recognized by the homeomorphism, if I dare say so, of the graphs. The recognition of this being presupposes that we distinguish the form of what I have already called cacography. The mathematician does not see any difficulty on this point, and more often than not the discussion appears idle to him.

But at the point where the scientist becomes impatient, the philosopher stops to wonder what would become of this question if mathematics did not exist. He sees all the mathematicians agreeing on this act of recognition of a same form, a form unvarying in the variation of graphic forms that evoke it. Now he knows, as does everyone, that no graph resembles any other and that if we wonder what are the respective portions of form and of cacography in writing, we must flatly admit that noise prevails—certain people will say that it prevails exhaustively. He will, consequently, come to the following conclusion if he takes into account what has been said above: it is one and the same act to recognize an abstract being through the occurrences of its concrete, standardized form and to come to an agreement about this recognition. In other words, the act of eliminating cacography, the attempt to eliminate noise, is at the same time the condition of the apprehension of the abstract form and the condition of the success of communication. If the mathematician becomes impatient, it is because he thinks inside a society that has triumphed over noise so well and for such a long time that he is amazed when the problem is raised anew. He thinks within the world of "we" and within the world of the abstract, two isomorphic and perhaps even identical worlds. The subject of abstract mathematics is the "we" of an ideal republic which is the city of communication maxi-mally purged of noise[10] (which, parenthetically, shows why Plato and Leibniz were not idealists). In general, to formalize is to carry out a process by which one passes from concrete modes of thinking to one or several abstract forms. It means to eliminate noise as well, in an optimal manner. It means to become aware of the fact that mathematics is the kingdom that admits only the absolutely unavoidable noise, the kingdom of quasi-perfect communication, the *manthánein*, the kingdom of the excluded third man, in which the demon is almost definitively exorcised. If there were no mathematics, it would be necessary to renew the exorcism.

The demonstration begins again. At the dawn of logic, that is to say, at both the historical and the logical beginning of logic, but also at the logical beginning of mathematics,
Hilbert and others repeated the Platonic reasoning concerning abstract idealities—which
was one of the conditions of the Greek miracle, at the historical dawn of mathematics. But
with us the discussion is truncated because it cannot bracket the inevitable fact of the historical existence of mathematics. With Plato, on the contrary, the discussion is full and
complete: it makes the recognition of the abstract form and the problem of the success of
the dialogue coexist. When I say "bed," I am not speaking of such and such a bed, mine,
yours, this one or that one; I am evoking the idea of the bed. When I draw a square and a
diagonal in the sand, I do not in any way want to speak of this wavering, irregular, and
inexact graph; I evoke by it the ideal form of the diagonal and of the square. I eliminate
the empirical, I dematerialize reasoning. By doing this, I make a science possible, both for
rigor and for truth, but also for the universal, for the *Universal in itself*. By doing this I
eliminate that which hides form—cacography, interference, and noise—and I create the
possibility of a science in the *Universal for us*. Mathematical form is both a Universal in itself
and a Universal for us: and therefore *the first effort to make communication in a dialogue successful is isomorphic to the effort to render a form independent of its empirical realizations*. These
realizations are the third man of the form, its interference and its noise, and it is precisely
because they intervene ceaselessly that the first dialogues are aporetic. The dialectical
method of the dialogue has its origins in the same regions as mathematical method, which,
moreover, is also said to be dialectical.

To exclude the empirical is to exclude differentiation, the plurality of others that mask
the same. It is the first movement of mathematization, of formalization. In this sense, the
reasoning of modern logicians concerning the symbol is analogous to the Platonic discussion of the geometric form drawn in the sand: one must eliminate cacography, the wavering
outline, the accident of the mark, the failure of a gesture, the set of conditions that ensure
that no graph is strictly of the same form as any other. In the same way, the object perceived
is indefinitely discernible: there would have to be a different word for every circle, for every
symbol, for every tree, and for every pigeon; and a different word for yesterday, today, and
tomorrow; and a different word according to whether he who perceives it is you or I, according to whether one of the two of us is angry, is jaundiced, and so on *ad infinitum*. At the
extreme limits of empiricism, meaning is totally plunged into noise, the space of communication is granular,[11] dialogue is condemned to cacophony: the transmission of communication is chronic transformation. Thus, the empirical is strictly essential and accidental *noise*.
The first "third man" to exclude is the empiricist, along with his empirical domain. And
this demon is the strongest demon, since one has only to open one's eyes and ears to see
that he is master of the world.[12] Consequently, in order for dialogue to be possible, one
must close one's eyes and cover one's ears to the song and the beauty of the sirens. In a
single blow, we eliminate hearing and noise, vision and failed drawing; in a single blow, we
conceive the form and we understand each other. And therefore, once again, the Greek

miracle, that of mathematics, must be born at the same time—historical time, logical time, and reflexive time—as a philosophy of dialogue and by dialogue.

In Platonism, the link between a dialectical method—in the sense of communication—and a progressive working diagram of abstract idealities in the manner of geometry is not an accident in the history of ideas, nor just an episode in the willful decisions of the philosopher: it is inscribed in the nature of things. To isolate an ideal form is to render it independent of the empirical domain and of noise. Noise is the empirical portion of the message just as the empirical domain is the noise of form. In this sense, the minor Socratic dialogues are pre-mathematical in the same way as is the measurement of a wheat field in the Nile valley.[13]

Notes

1. See Roger Martin, *Logique contemporaine et formalisation* (Paris: P. U. F., 1964), pp. 24–30.

2. It can be shown easily enough that no method of communication is universal: on the contrary, all methods are regional, in other words, isomorphic to one language. The space of linguistic communication (which, therefore, is the standard model of any space of communication) is not isotropic. An object that is the universal communicator or that is universally communicated does, however, exist: the technical object in general. That is why we find, at the dawn of history, that the first diffusion belongs to it: its space of communication is isotropic. Let there be no misunderstanding: at stake here is a definition of prehistory. History begins with regional language and the space of anisotropic communication. Whence this law of three states: technological isotropy, linguistic anisotropy, linguistic-technical isotropy. The third state should not be long in arriving.

3. It is hardly necessary to add that the first benefit of the printing press consists in permitting the reader not to be an epigraphist. A printed text is a calligram (but not always an orthogram). The possibility of an arbitrary multiplication is, of course, the second benefit.

4. For example. B. Mandelbrojt and Roman Jakobson. See Norbert Wiener, *The Human Use of Human Beings: Cybernetics and Society* (New York: Avon Books, 1967), chaps. 4 and 11.

5. Similarly, written communication is the battle of the scribe, and the reader, joined together by interest and by a project against any obstacles in the way of communication: the message in the bottle.

6. For an extended discussion of noise and the figures it assumes, see Michel Serres, *Le Parasite* (Paris: Grasset, 1980).

7. This interpretation has as a rough result the notion according to which the Cartesian text outlines the condition of possibility for a physics experiment and is therefore metaphysical in this sense. The Platonic texts had previously laid down the conditions of possibility for mathematical ideation.

8. See Martin, *Logique contemporaine*, pp. 26–27.

9. See Alfred Tarski, *Introduction to Logic and to the Methodology of Deductive Sciences* (New York: Oxford University Press, 1941), pp. 68 ff.—Ed.

10. Perhaps the only such city (along with that of music) as Leibniz liked to say.

11. Whence we see that if we admit the principle of undiscernibles, the monads neither listen to nor understand each other. They are without doors or windows, an implication that Leibniz made coherent. If Zeno is right, the Eleatics are condemned to silence.

12. And, as has often been seen in any discussion between an empiricist and a rationalist—Locke and Leibniz, for example—*empiricism would always be correct if mathematics did not exist*. Empiricism is the *true* philosophy as soon as mathematics is bracketed. Before the latter imposes itself and in order that it may do so, one must *want* not to listen to Protagoras and Callicles—because they are right. But the more they are right, the less we can hear them: they end up only making noise. The argument put forth against Locke by Leibniz, "You do not know mathematics," is not an *ad hominem* argument; it is the only logical defense possible.

13. One could object that the cacography of a circle and that of a letter cannot be made the same by reduction. Since the invention of topology, we know that, on the contrary, anexact idealities exist in the same way as exact ones as defined by measurement: so that here we have spoken purely only of the inverse of impurity. One would speak purely of impurity by attempting to pose the problem of cacography in an anexact form. That would already be more difficult, but it would take us out of the limits of this study. Besides, Leibniz assimilates the two forms, graph and graphic form, in a dialogue dating from 1677. See Leibniz, "Dialogue," in *Philosophical Papers and Letters*, ed. Leroy E. Loemker (Dordrecht, Holland: D. Reidel Publishing Company, 1970), pp. 182–85.

III   Language before Communication

11   On Language as Such and on the Language of Man

Walter Benjamin

Every expression of human mental life can be understood as a kind of language, and this understanding, in the manner of a true method, everywhere raises new questions. It is possible to talk about a language of music and of sculpture, about a language of justice that has nothing directly to do with those in which German or English legal judgments are couched, about a language of technology that is not the specialized language of technicians. Language in such contexts means the tendency inherent in the subjects concerned—technology, art, justice, or religion—toward the communication of mental meanings. To sum up: all communication of mental meanings is language, communication in words being only a particular case of human language and of the justice, poetry, or whatever underlying it or founded on it. The existence of language, however, is not only coextensive with all the areas of human mental expression in which language is always in one sense or another inherent, but with absolutely everything. There is no event or thing in either animate or inanimate nature that does not in some way partake of language, for it is in the nature of all to communicate their mental meanings. This use of the word "language" is in no way metaphorical. For to think that we cannot imagine anything that does not communicate its mental nature in its expression is entirely meaningful; the greater or lesser degree of consciousness that is apparently (or really) involved in such communication cannot alter the fact that we cannot imagine a total absence of language in anything. An existence entirely without relationship to language is an idea; but this idea can bear no fruit even within that realm of Ideas whose circumference defines the idea of God.

All that is asserted here is that all expression, insofar as it is a communication of mental meaning, is to be classed as language. And expression, by its whole innermost nature, is certainly to be understood only as *language*; on the other hand, to understand a linguistic entity it is always necessary to ask of which mental entity it is the direct expression. That is to say: the German language, for example, is by no means the expression of everything that we could—theoretically—express *through* it, but is the direct expression of that which communicates *itself* in it. This "itself" is a mental entity. It is therefore obvious at once that the mental entity that communicates itself in language is not language itself but something to be distinguished from it. The view that the mental essence of a thing consists precisely in its language—this view, taken as a hypothesis, is the great abyss into which all linguistic theory threatens to fall,[1] and to survive suspended precisely over this abyss is its task. The distinction between a mental entity and the linguistic entity in which it communicates is the first stage of any study of linguistic theory, and this distinction seems so unquestionable that it is, rather, the frequently asserted identity between mental and linguistic being that constitutes a deep and incomprehensible paradox, the expression of which is found in the ambiguity of the word logos. Nevertheless, this paradox has a place, as a solution, at the center of linguistic theory, but remains a paradox, and insoluble, if placed at the beginning.

What does language communicate? It communicates the mental being corresponding to it. It is fundamental that this mental being communicates itself *in* language and not *through* language. Languages therefore have no speaker, if this means someone who communicates *through* these languages. Mental being communicates itself in, not through, a language, which means: it is not outwardly identical with linguistic being. Mental is identical with linguistic being only insofar as it is capable of communication. What is communicable in a mental entity is its linguistic entity. Language therefore communicates the particular linguistic being of things, but their mental being only insofar as this is directly included in their linguistic being, insofar as it is capable of being communicated.

Language communicates the linguistic being of things. The clearest manifestation of this being, however, is language itself. The answer to the question "*What* does language communicate?" is therefore "All language communicates itself." The language of this lamp, for example, does not communicate the lamp (for the mental being of the lamp, insofar as it is *communicable*, is by no means the lamp itself), but: the language-lamp, the lamp in communication, the lamp in expression. For in language the situation is this: *the linguistic being of all things is their language.* The understanding of linguistic theory depends on giving this proposition a clarity that annihilates even the appearance of tautology. This proposition is untautological, for it means: that which in a mental entity is communicable *is* its language. On this "is" (equivalent to "is immediately") everything depends. Not that which *appears* most clearly in its language is communicable in a mental entity, as was just said by way of transition, but this *capacity* for communication is language itself. Or: the language of a mental entity is directly that which is communicable in it. What is communicable *of* a mental entity, *in* this it communicates itself. Which signifies: all language communicates itself. Or more precisely: all language communicates itself *in* itself; it is in the purest sense the "medium" of the communication. Mediation, which is the immediacy of all mental communication, is the fundamental problem of linguistic theory, and if one chooses to call this immediacy magic, then the primary problem of language is its magic. At the same time, the notion of the magic of language points to something else: its infiniteness. This is conditional on its immediacy. For just because nothing is communicated *through* language, what is communicated *in* language cannot be externally limited or measured, and therefore all language contains its own in commensurable, uniquely constituted infinity. Its linguistic being, not its verbal meanings, defines its frontier.

The linguistic being of things is their language; this proposition, applied to man, means: the linguistic being of man is his language. Which signifies: man communicates his own mental being *in* his language. However, the language of man speaks in words. Man therefore communicates his own mental being (insofar as it is communicable) by *naming* all other things. But do we know any other languages that name things? It should not be accepted that we know of no languages other than that of man, for this is untrue. We only know of no *naming* language other than that of man; to identify naming language with language as such is to rob linguistic theory of its deepest insights. *It is therefore the linguistic being of man to name things.*

Why name them? To whom does man communicate himself? But is this question, as applied to man, other than as applied to other communications (languages)? To whom does the lamp communicate itself? The mountain? The fox? But here the answer is: to man. This is not anthropomorphism. The truth of this answer is shown in knowledge and perhaps also in art. Furthermore, if the lamp and the mountain and the fox did not communicate themselves to man, how should he be able to name them? And he names them; *he* communicates himself by naming *them*. To whom does he communicate himself?

Before this question can be answered we must again inquire: how does man communicate himself? A profound distinction is to be made, a choice presented, in face of which an intrinsically false understanding of language is certain to give itself away. Does man communicate his mental being *by* the names that he gives things? Or *in* them? In the paradoxical nature of these questions lies their answer. Anyone who believes that man communicates his mental being *by* names cannot also assume that it is his mental being that he communicates, for this does not happen through the names of things, that is, through the words by which he denotes a thing. And, equally, the advocate of such a view can only assume that man is communicating factual subject matter to other men, for that does happen through the word by which he denotes a thing. This view is the bourgeois conception of language, the invalidity and emptiness of which will become increasingly clear in what follows. It holds that the means of communication is the word, its object factual, its addressee a human being. The other conception of language, in contrast, knows no means, no object, and no addressee of communication. It means: *in naming the mental being of man communicates itself to God.*

Naming, in the realm of language, has as its sole purpose and its incomparably high meaning that it is the innermost nature of language itself. Naming is that by which nothing beyond it is communicated, and *in* which language itself communicates itself absolutely. In naming the mental entity that communicates itself is *language*. Where mental being in its communication is language itself in its absolute wholeness, only there is the name, and only the name is there. Name as the heritage of human language therefore vouches for the fact *that language as such* is the mental being of man; and only for this reason is the mental being of man, alone among all mental entities, communicable without residue. On this is founded the difference between human language and the language of things. But because the mental being of man is language itself, he cannot communicate himself by it but only in it. The quintessence of this intensive totality of language as the mental being of man is naming. Man is the namer, by this we recognize that through him pure language speaks. All nature, insofar as it communicates itself, communicates itself in language, and so finally in man. Hence he is the lord of nature and can give names to things. Only through the linguistic being of things can he gain knowledge of them from within himself—in name. God's creation is completed when things receive their names from man, from whom in name language alone speaks. Man can call name the language of language (if the genitive refers to the relationship not of a means but of a medium) and in this sense certainly, because he speaks in name, man is the speaker of language, and for this very reason its only speaker. In terming man the speaker (which, however, according to the Bible, for example, clearly means the name giver: "As man should name all kinds of living creatures, so should they be *called*"), many languages imply this metaphysical truth.

Name, however, is not only the last utterance of language but also the true call of it. Thus in name appears the essential law of language, according to which to express oneself and to address everything else amounts to the same. Language—and in it a mental entity— only expresses itself purely where it speaks in name, that is, in its universal naming. So in name culminate both the intensive totality of language, as the absolutely communicable mental entity, and the extensive totality of language, as the universally communicating (naming) entity. By virtue of its communicating nature, its universality, language is incomplete where the mental entity that speaks from it is not in its whole structure linguistic, that is, communicable. *Man alone has a language that is complete both in its universality and in its intensiveness.*

In the light of this, a question may now be asked without the risk of confusion, a question that, though of the highest metaphysical importance, can be clearly posed first of all as one of terminology. It is whether mental being—not only of man (for that is necessary) but also of things, and thus mental being as such—can from the point of view of linguistic theory be described as of linguistic nature. If mental being is identical with linguistic, then a thing, by virtue of its mental being, is a medium of communication, and what is communicated in it is—in accordance with its mediating relationship—precisely this medium (language) itself. Language is thus the mental being of things. Mental being is therefore postulated at the outset as communicable, or, rather, is situated *within* the communicable, and the thesis that the linguistic being of things is identical with the mental, insofar as the latter is communicable, becomes in its "insofar" a tautology. *There is no such thing as a meaning of language; as communication, language communicates a mental entity, i.e., something communicable per se.* The differences between languages are those of media that are distinguished as it were by their density, that is, gradually; and this with regard to the density both of the communicating (naming) and of the communicable (name) aspects of communication. These two spheres, which are clearly distinguished yet united only in the name language of man, are naturally constantly interrelated.

For the metaphysics of language the equation of mental with linguistic being, which knows only gradual differences, produces a graduation of all mental being in degrees. This graduation, which takes place within mental being itself, can no longer be embraced by any higher category and so leads to the graduation of all being, both mental and linguistic, by degrees of existence or being, such as was already familiar to scholasticism with regard to mental being. However, the equation of mental and linguistic being is of great metaphysical moment to linguistic theory because it leads to the concept that has again and again, as if of its own accord, elevated itself to the center of linguistic philosophy and constituted its most intimate connection with the philosophy of religion. This is the concept of revelation. Within all linguistic formation a conflict is waged between what is expressed and expressible and what is inexpressible and unexpressed. On considering this conflict one sees, in the perspective of the inexpressible, at the same time the last mental entity. Now it is clear that in the equation of mental and linguistic being the notion of an inverse proportionality between the two is disputed. For this latter thesis runs: the deeper, i.e., the more existent and real the mind, the more it is inexpressible and unexpressed, whereas it is consistent with the equation proposed above to make the relation between mind and language thoroughly unambiguous, so that the expression that is linguistically most existent (i.e., most fixed) is linguistically the most rounded and definitive; in a word, the most expressed is at the same time the purely mental. Exactly this, however, is meant by the concept of revelation, if it takes the inviolability of the word as the only and sufficient condition and characteristic of the divinity of the mental being that is expressed in it. The highest mental region of religion is (in the concept of revelation) at the same time the only one that does not know the inexpressible. For it is addressed in name and expresses itself as revelation. In this, however, notice is given that only the highest mental being, as it appears in religion, rests solely on man and on the language in him, whereas all art, not excluding poetry, does not rest on the ultimate essence of language-mind, but on language-mind confined to things, even if in consummate beauty. "*Language, the mother* of reason and *revelation*, its alpha and omega," says Hamann.

Language itself is not perfectly expressed in things themselves. This proposition has a double meaning in its metaphorical and literal senses: the languages of things are imperfect, and they are dumb. Things are denied the pure formal principle of language—sound. They can only communicate to one another through a more or less material community. This community is immediate and infinite, like every linguistic communication; it is magical (for there is also a magic of matter). The incomparable feature of human language is that its magical community with things is immaterial and purely mental, and the symbol of this is sound. The Bible expresses this symbolic fact when it says that God breathes his breath into man: this is at once life and mind and language.

If in what follows the nature of language is considered on the basis of the first chapter of Genesis, the object is neither biblical interpretation, nor subjection of the Bible to objective consideration as revealed truth, but the discovery of what emerges of itself from the biblical text with regard to the nature of language; and the Bible is only *initially* indispensable for this purpose because the present argument broadly follows it in presupposing language as an ultimate reality, perceptible only in its manifestation, inexplicable and mystical. The Bible, in regarding itself as a revelation, must necessarily evolve the fundamental linguistic facts. The second version of the story of the Creation, which tells of the breathing of God's breath into man, also reports that man was made from earth. This is, in the whole story of the Creation, the only reference to the material in which the Creator expresses his will, which is doubtless otherwise thought of as creation without mediation. In this second story of the Creation the making of man did not take place through the word: God spoke—and there was—but this man, who is not created from the word, is now invested with the *gift* of language and is elevated above nature.

This curious revolution in the act of creation, where it concerns man, is no less clearly recorded, however, in the first story of the Creation, and in an entirely different context it vouches, with the same certainty, for a special relationship between man and language resulting from the act of creation. The manifold rhythm of the act of creation in the first chapter establishes a kind of basic form from which the act that creates man diverges significantly. Admittedly this passage nowhere expressly refers to a relationship either of man or of nature to the material from which they were created; and the question whether the words "He made" envisages a creation out of material must here be left open, but the rhythm by which the creation of nature (in Genesis 1) is accomplished is: Let there be—He made (created)—He named. In individual acts of creation (1:3; 1:11) only the words "Let there be" occur. In this "Let there be" and in the words "He named" at the beginning and end of the act, the deep and clear relation of the creative act to language appears each time. With the creative omnipotence of language it begins, and at the end language as it were assimilates the created, names it. Language is therefore both creative and the finished creation, it is word and name. In God name is creative because it is word, and God's word is cognizant because it is name. "And he saw that it was good"; that is: He had cognized it through name. The absolute relation of name to knowledge exists only in God, only there is name, because it is inwardly identical with the creative word, the pure medium of knowledge. That means: God made things knowable in their names. Man, however, names them according to knowledge.

In the creation of man the threefold rhythm of the creation of nature has given way to an entirely different order. In it, therefore, language has a different meaning: the trinity of the act is here preserved, but in this very parallelism the divergence is all the more striking: in the threefold "He created" of 1:27. God did not create man from the word, and he did not name him. He did not wish to subject him to language, but in man God set language, which had served *Him* as medium of creation, free. God rested when he had left his creative power to itself in man. This creativity, relieved of its divine actuality, became knowledge. Man is the knower in the same language in which God is creator. God created him in his image, he created the knower in the image of the creator. Therefore the proposition that the mental being of man is language needs explanation. His mental being is the language in which creation took place. In the word creation took place, and God's linguistic being is the word. All human language is only reflection of the word in name. Name is no closer to the word than knowledge to creation. The infinity of all human language always remains limited and analytical in nature in comparison to the absolutely unlimited and creative infinity of the divine word.

The deepest images of this divine word and the point where human language participates most intimately in the divine infinity of the pure word, the point at which it cannot become finite word and knowledge, are the human name. The theory of proper names is the theory of the frontier between finite and infinite language. Of all beings man is the only one who himself names his own kind, as he is the only one whom God did not name. It is perhaps bold, but scarcely impossible, to mention the second part of 2:20 in this context: that man named all beings, "*but* for man there was not found a helper fit for him." Accordingly, Adam names his wife as soon as he receives her (woman in the second chapter, Eve in the third). By giving names, parents dedicate their children to God; the names they give do not correspond—in a metaphysical, not etymological sense—to any knowledge, for they name newborn children. In a strict sense, no name ought (in its etymological meaning) to correspond to any person, for the proper name is the word of God in human sounds. By it each man is guaranteed his creation by God, and in this sense he is himself creative, as is expressed by mythological wisdom in the idea (which doubtless not infrequently comes true) that a man's name is his fate. The proper name is the communion of man with the *creative* word of God. (Not the only one, however; man knows a further linguistic communion with God's word.) Through the word man is bound to the language of things. The human word is the name of things. Hence it is no longer conceivable, as the bourgeois view of language maintains, that the word has an accidental relation to its object, that it is a sign for things (or knowledge of them) agreed by some convention. Language never gives *mere* signs. However, the rejection of bourgeois by mystical linguistic theory equally rests on a misunderstanding. For according to mystical theory the word is simply the essence of the thing. That is incorrect, because the thing in itself has no word, being created from God's word and known in its name by a human word. This knowledge of the thing, however, is not spontaneous creation, it does not emerge from language in the absolutely unlimited and infinite manner of creation; rather, the name that man gives to language depends on how language is communicated to him. In name the word of God has not remained creative; it has become in one part receptive, even if receptive to language. Thus fertilized, it aims to give birth to the language of things themselves, from which in turn, soundlessly, in the mute magic of nature, the word of God shines forth.

For conception and spontaneity together, which are found in this unique union only in the linguistic realm, language has its own word, and this word applies also to that conception which is enacted by the nameless in names. It is the translation of the language of things into that of man. It is necessary to found the concept of translation at the deepest level of linguistic theory, for it is much too far-reaching and powerful to be treated in any way as an afterthought, as has happened occasionally. Translation attains its full meaning in the realization that every evolved language (with the exception of the word of God) can be considered as a translation of all the others. By the relation, mentioned earlier, of languages as between media of varying densities, the translatability of languages into one another is established. Translation is removal from one language into another through a continuum of transformations. Translation passes through continua of transformation, not abstract areas of identity and similarity.

The translation of the language of things into that of man is not only a translation of the mute into the sonic; it is also the translation of the nameless into name. It is therefore the translation of an imperfect language into a more perfect one, and cannot but add something to it, namely knowledge. The objectivity of this translation is, however, guaranteed by God. For God created things; the creative word in them is the germ of the cognizing name, just as God, too, finally named each thing after it was created. But obviously this naming is only an expression of the identity of the creative word and the cognizing name in God, not the prior solution of the task that God expressly assigns to man himself: that of naming things. In receiving the unspoken nameless language of things and converting it by name into sounds, man performs this task. I would be insoluble were not the name-language of man and the nameless one of things related in God and released from the same creative word, which in things became the communication of matter in magic communion, and in man the language of knowledge and name in blissful mind. Hamann says: "Everything that man heard in the beginning, saw with his eyes, and felt with his hands was the living word; for God was the word. With this word in his mouth and in his heart, the origin of language was as natural, as close, and as easy as a child's game. . . ." Friedrich Müller, in his poem "Adam's Awakening and First Blissful Nights," has God summon man to name giving in these words: "Man of the earth step near, in gazing grow more perfect, more perfect through the word." By this combination of contemplation and naming is implied the communicating muteness of things (animals) toward the word language of man, which receives them in name. In the same chapter of the poem, the poet expresses the realization that only the word from which things are created permits man to name them, by communicating itself in the manifold languages of animals, even if mutely, in the image: God gives each beast in turn a sign, whereupon they step before man to be named. In an almost sublime way the linguistic community of mute creation with God is thus conveyed in the image of the sign.

As the unspoken word in the existence of things falls infinitely short of the naming word in the knowledge of man, and as the latter in turn must fall short of the creative word of God, there is reason for the multiplicity of human languages. The language of things can pass into the language of knowledge and name only through translation—as many translations, so many languages—once man has fallen from the paradisiac state that knew only one language. (According to the Bible, this consequence of the expulsion from paradise admittedly came about only later.) The paradisiac language of man must have been one of perfect knowledge; whereas later all knowledge is again infinitely differentiated in the multiplicity of language, was indeed forced to differentiate itself on a lower level as creation in name. For that the language of paradise was fully cognizant, even the existence of the tree of knowledge cannot conceal. Its apples were supposed to impart knowledge of good and evil. But on the seventh day, God had already cognized with the words of creation. And God saw that it was good. The knowledge to which the snake seduces, that of good and evil, is nameless. It is vain in the deepest sense, and this very knowledge is itself the only evil known to the paradisiac state. Knowledge of good and evil abandons name, it is a knowledge from outside, the uncreated imitation of the creative word. Name steps outside itself in this knowledge: the Fall marks the birth of the *human word*, in which name no longer lives intact, and which has stepped out of name language, the language of knowledge, from what we may call its own immanent magic, in order to become expressly, as it were externally, magic. The word must communicate *something* (other than itself). That is really the Fall of language-mind. The word as something externally communicating, as it were a parody by the expressly mediate word of the expressly immediate, the creative word of God, and the decay of the blissful, Adamite language-mind that stand between them. For in reality there exists a fundamental identity between the word that, after the promise of the snake, knows good and evil, and the externally communicating word. The knowledge of things resides in name, whereas that of good and evil is, in the profound sense in which Kierkegaard uses the word, "prattle," and knows only one purification and elevation, to which the prattling man, the sinner, was therefore submitted: judgment. Admittedly, the judging word has direct knowledge of good and evil. Its magic is different from that of name, but equally magical. This judging word expels the first human beings from paradise; they themselves have aroused it in accordance with the immutable law by which this judging word punishes—and expects—its own awakening as the only, the deepest guilt. In the Fall, since the eternal purity of names was violated, the sterner purity of the judging word arose. For the essential composition of language the Fall has a threefold significance (without mentioning its other meanings). In stepping outside the purer language of name, man makes language a means (that is, a knowledge inappropriate to him), and therefore also, in one part at any rate, a *mere* sign; and this later results in the plurality of languages. The second meaning is that from the Fall, in exchange for the immediacy of name damaged by it, a new immediacy arises, the magic of judgment, which no longer rests blissfully in itself. The third meaning that can perhaps be tentatively ventured is that the origin of abstraction, too, as a faculty of language-mind, is to be sought in the Fall. For good and evil, being unnamable, nameless, stand outside the language of names, which man leaves behind precisely in the abyss opened by this question. Name, however, with regard to existing language, offers only the ground in which its concrete elements are rooted. But the abstract elements of language—we may perhaps surmise—are rooted in the word of judgment. The immediacy (which, however, is the linguistic root) of the communicability of abstraction resides in judgment. This immediacy in the communication of abstraction came into being as judgment, when, in the Fall, man abandoned immediacy in the communication of the concrete, name, and fell into the abyss of the mediateness of all communication, of the word as means, of the empty word, into the abyss of prattle. For—it must be said again—the question as to good and evil in the world after creation was empty prattle. The tree of knowledge did not stand in the garden of God in order to dispense information on good and evil, but as an emblem of judgment over the questioner. This immense irony marks the mythical origin of law.

After the Fall, which, in making language mediate, laid the foundation for its multiplicity, it could be only a step to linguistic confusion. Since men had injured the purity of name, the turning away from that contemplation of things in which their language passes into man needed only to be completed in order to deprive men of the common foundation of an already shaken language-mind. *Signs* must become confused where things are entangled. The enslavement of language in prattle is joined by the enslavement of things in folly almost as its inevitable consequence. In this turning away from things, which was enslavement, the plan for the tower of Babel came into being, and linguistic confusion with it.

The life of man in pure language-mind was blissful. Nature, however, is mute. True, it can be clearly felt in the second chapter of Genesis how this muteness, named by man, itself became bliss, only of lower degree. Friedrich Müller has Adam say to the animals that leave him after he has named them, "And saw by the nobility with which they leaped away from me that the man had given them a name." After the Fall, however, when God's word curses the ground, the appearance of nature is deeply changed. Now begins its other muteness, which we mean by the deep sadness of nature. It is a metaphysical truth that all nature would begin to lament if it were endowed with language. (Though to "endow with language" is more than to "make able to speak.") This proposition has a double meaning. It means, first: she would lament language itself. Speechlessness: that is the great sorrow of nature (and for the sake of her redemption the life and language of *man*—not only, as is supposed, of the poet—are in nature). This proposition means, secondly: she would lament. Lament, however, is the most undifferentiated, impotent expression of language; it contains scarcely more than the sensuous breath; and even where there is only a rustling of plants, in it there is always a lament. Because she is mute, nature mourns. Yet the inversion of this proposition leads even further into the essence of nature; the sadness of nature makes her mute. In all mourning there is the deepest inclination to speechlessness, which is infinitely more than inability or disinclination to communicate. That which mourns feels itself thoroughly known by the unknowable. To be named—even when the namer is Godlike and blissful—perhaps always remains an intimation of mourning. But how much more melancholy to be named not from the one blessed, paradisiac language of names, but from the hundred languages of man, in which name has already withered, yet which, according to God's pronouncement, have knowledge of things. Things have no proper names except in God. For in his creative word, God called them into being, calling them by their proper names. In the language of men, however, they are over-named. There is, in the relation of human languages to that of things, something that can be approximately described as "over-naming": over-naming as the deepest linguistic reason for all melancholy and (from the point of view of the thing) of all deliberate muteness. Over-naming as the linguistic being of melancholy points to another curious relation of language: the overprecision that obtains in the tragic relationship between the languages of human speakers.

There is a language of sculpture, of painting, of poetry. Just as the language of poetry is partly, if not solely, founded on the name language of man, it is very conceivable that the language of sculpture or painting is founded on certain kinds of thing languages, that in them we find a translation of the language of things into an infinitely higher language, which may still be of the same sphere. We are concerned here with nameless, nonacoustic languages, languages issuing from matter; here we should recall the material community of things in their communication.

Moreover, the communication of things is certainly communal in a way that grasps the world as such as an undivided whole.

For an understanding of artistic forms it is of value to attempt to grasp them all as languages and to seek their connection with natural languages. An example that is appropriate because it is derived from the acoustic sphere is the kinship between song and the language of birds. On the other hand, it is certain that the language of art can be understood only in the deepest relationship to the doctrine of signs. Without the latter any linguistic philosophy remains entirely fragmentary, because the relationship between language and sign (of which that between human language and writing offers only a very particular example) is original and fundamental.

This provides an opportunity to describe another antithesis that permeates the whole sphere of language and has important relations to the antithesis already mentioned between language in a narrower sense and signs, with which, of course, language by no means necessarily coincides. For language is in every case not only communication of the communicable but also, at the same time, a symbol of the noncommunicable. This symbolic side of language is connected to its relation to signs, but extends more widely, for example, in certain respects, to name and judgment. These have not only a communicating function, but most probably also a closely connected symbolic function, to which, at least explicitly, no reference has here been made.

These considerations therefore leave us a purified concept of language, even though it may still be an imperfect one. The language of an entity is the medium in which its mental being is communicated. The uninterrupted flow of this communication runs through the whole of nature from the lowest forms of existence to man and from man to God. Man communicates himself to God through name, which he gives to nature and (in proper names) to his own kind, and to nature he gives names according to the communication that he receives from her, for the whole of nature, too, is imbued with a nameless, unspoken language, the residue of the creative word of God, which is preserved in man as the cognizing name and above man as the judgment suspended over him. The language of nature is comparable to a secret password that each sentry passes to the next in his own language, but the meaning of the password is the sentry's language itself. All higher language is a translation of those lower, until in ultimate clarity the word of God unfolds, which is the unity of this movement made up of language.

Note

1. Or is it, rather, the temptation to place at the outset a hypothesis that constitutes an abyss for all philosophizing?

12   Building Dwelling Thinking

Martin Heidegger

In what follows we shall try to think about dwelling and building. This thinking about building does not presume to discover architectural ideas, let alone to give rules for building. This venture in thought does not view building as an art or as a technique of construction; rather, it traces building back into that domain to which everything that *is* belongs. We ask:

1. What is it to dwell?
2. How does building belong to dwelling?

I

We attain to dwelling, so it seems, only by means of building. The latter, building, has the former, dwelling, as its goal. Still, not every building is a dwelling. Bridges and hangars, stadiums and power stations are buildings but not dwellings; railway stations and highways, dams and market halls are built, but they are not dwelling places. Even so, these buildings are in the domain of our dwelling. That domain extends over these buildings and so is not limited to the dwelling place. The truck driver is at home on the highway, but he does not have his lodgings there; the working woman is at home in the spinning mill, but does not have her dwelling place there; the chief engineer is at home in the power station, but he does not dwell there. These buildings house man. He inhabits them and yet does not dwell in them, if to dwell means solely to have our lodgings in them. In today's housing shortage even this much is reassuring and to the good; residential buildings do indeed provide lodgings; today's houses may even be well planned, easy to keep, attractively cheap, open to air, light, and sun, but—do the houses in themselves hold any guarantee that *dwelling* occurs in them? Yet those buildings that are not dwelling places remain in turn determined by dwelling insofar as they serve man's dwelling. Thus dwelling would in any case be the end that presides over all building. Dwelling and building are related as end and means. However, as long as this is all we have in mind, we take dwelling and building as two separate activities, an idea that has something correct in it. Yet at the same time by the means-end schema we block our view of the essential relations. For building is not merely a means and a way toward dwelling—to build is in itself already to dwell. Who tells us this? Who gives us a standard at all by which we can take the measure of the essence of dwelling and building?

It is language that tells us about the essence of a thing, provided that we respect language's own essence. In the meantime, to be sure, there rages round the earth an unbridled yet clever talking, writing, and broadcasting of spoken words. Man acts as though *he* were the shaper and master of language, while in fact *language* remains the master of man. Perhaps it is before all else man's subversion of *this* relation of dominance that drives his essential being into alienation. That we retain a concern for care in speaking is all to the good, but it is of no help to us as long as language still serves us even then only as a means of expression. Among all the appeals that we human beings, on our part, can help to be voiced, language is the highest and everywhere the first.

Now, what does *bauen*, to build, mean? The Old High German word for building, *buan*, means to dwell. This signifies to remain, to stay in a place. The proper meaning of the verb *bauen*, namely, to dwell, has been lost to us. But a covert trace of it has been preserved in the German word *Nachbar*, neighbor. The *Nachbar* is the *Nachgebur*, the *Nachgebauer*, the near-dweller, he who dwells nearby. The verbs *buri*, *büren*, *beuren*, *beuron*, all signify dwelling, the place of dwelling. Now, to be sure, the old word *buan* not only tells us that *bauen*, to build, is really to dwell; it also gives us a clue as to how we have to think about the dwelling it signifies. When we speak of dwelling we usually think of an activity that man performs alongside many other activities. We work here and dwell there. We do not merely dwell—that would be virtual inactivity—we practice a profession, we do business, we travel and find shelter on the way, now here, now there. *Bauen* originally means to dwell. Where the word *bauen* still speaks in its original sense it also says *how far* the essence of dwelling reaches. That is, *bauen*, *buan*, *bhu*, *beo* are our word *bin* in the versions: *ich bin*, I am, *du bist*, you are, the imperative form *bis*, be. What then does *ich bin* mean? The old word *bauen*, to which the *bin* belongs, answers: *ich bin*, *du bist* mean I dwell, you dwell. The way in which you are and I am, the manner in which we humans *are* on the earth, is *buan*, dwelling. To be a human being means to be on the earth as a mortal. It means to dwell. The old word *bauen*, which says that man *is* insofar as he *dwells*, this word *bauen*, however, *also* means at the same time to cherish and protect, to preserve and care for, specifically to till the soil, to cultivate the vine. Such building only takes care—it tends the growth that ripens into fruit of its own accord. Building in the sense of preserving and nurturing is not making anything. Ship-building and temple-building, on the other hand, do in a certain way make their own works. Here building, in contrast with cultivating, is a constructing. Both modes of building—building as cultivating, Latin *colere*, *cultura*, and building as the raising up of edifices, *aedificare*—are comprised within genuine building, that is, dwelling. Building as dwelling, that is, as being on the earth, however, remains for man's everyday experience that which is from the outset "habitual"—we inhabit it, as our language says so beautifully: it is the *Gewohnte*. For this reason, it recedes behind the manifold ways in which dwelling is accomplished, the activities of cultivation and construction. These activities later claim the name of *bauen*, building, and with it the matter of building, exclusively for themselves. The proper sense of *bauen*, namely dwelling, falls into oblivion.

At first sight this event looks as though it were no more than a change of meaning of mere terms. In truth, however, something decisive is concealed in it; namely, dwelling is not experienced as man's Being; dwelling is never thought of as the basic character of human being.

That language in a way retracts the proper meaning of the word *bauen*, which is dwelling, is evidence of the original one of these meanings; for with the essential words of language, what they genuinely say easily falls into oblivion in favor of foreground meanings. Man has hardly yet pondered the mystery of this process. Language withdraws from man its simple and high speech. But its primal call does not thereby become incapable of speech; it merely fails silent. Man, though, fails to heed this silence.

But if we listen to what language says in the word *bauen* we hear three things:

1. Building is really dwelling.
2. Dwelling is the manner in which mortals are on the earth.
3. Building as dwelling unfolds into the building that cultivates growing things and the building that erects buildings.

If we give thought to this threefold fact, we obtain a clue and note the following: as long as we do not bear in mind that all building is in itself a dwelling, we cannot even adequately *ask*, let alone properly decide, what the building of buildings might be in its essence. We do not dwell because we have built, but we build and have built because we dwell, that is, because we are *dwellers*. But in what does the essence of dwelling consist? Let us listen once more to what language says to us. The Old Saxon *wuon*, the Gothic *wunian*, like the old word *bauen*, mean to remain, to stay in a place. But the Gothic *wunian* says more distinctly how this remaining is experienced. *Wunian* means to be at peace, to be brought to peace, to remain in peace. The word for peace, *Friede*, means the free, das *Frye*; and *fry* means preserved from harm and danger, preserved *from* something, safeguarded. To free actually means to spare. The sparing itself consists not only in the fact that we do not harm the one whom we spare. Real sparing is something *positive* and takes place when we leave something before-hand in its own essence, when we return it specifically to its essential being, when we "free" it in the proper sense of the word into a preserve of peace. To dwell, to be set at peace, means to remain at peace within the free, the preserve, the free sphere that safeguards each thing in its essence. *The fundamental character of dwelling is this sparing.* It pervades dwelling in its whole range. That range reveals itself to us as soon as we recall that human being consists in dwelling and, indeed, dwelling in the sense of the stay of mortals on the earth.

But "on the earth" already means "under the sky." Both of these *also* mean "remaining before the divinities" and include a "belonging to men's being with one another." By a *primal* oneness the four—earth and sky, divinities and mortals—belong together in one.

Earth is the serving bearer, blossoming and fruiting, spreading out in rock and water, rising up into plant and animal. When we say earth, we are already thinking of the other three along with it, but we give no thought to the simple oneness of the four.

The sky is the vaulting path of the sun, the course of the changing moon, the wandering glitter of the stars, the year's seasons and their changes, the light and dusk of day, the gloom and glow of night, the clemency and inclemency of the weather, the drifting clouds and blue depth of the ether. When we say sky, we are already thinking of the other three along with it, but we give no thought to the simple oneness of the four.

The divinities are the beckoning messengers of the godhead. Out of the holy sway of the godhead, the god appears in his presence or withdraws into his concealment. When we speak of the divinities, we are already thinking of the other three along with them, but we give no thought to the simple oneness of the four.

The mortals are the human beings. They are called mortals because they can die. To die means to be capable of death *as* death. Only man dies, and indeed continually, as long as he remains on earth, under the sky, before the divinities. When we speak of mortals, we are already thinking of the other three along with them, but we give no thought to the simple oneness of the four.

This simple oneness of the four we call *the fourfold*. Mortals *are* in the fourfold by *dwelling*. But the basic character of dwelling is safeguarding. Mortals dwell in the way they safeguard the fourfold in its essential unfolding. Accordingly, the safeguarding that dwells is fourfold.

Mortals dwell in that they save the earth—taking the word in the old sense still known to Lessing. Saving does not only snatch something from a danger. To save properly means to set something free into its own essence. To save the earth is more than to exploit it or even wear it out. Saving the earth does not master the earth and does not subjugate it, which is merely one step from boundless spoliation.

Mortals dwell in that they receive the sky as sky. They leave to the sun and the moon their journey, to the stars their courses, to the seasons their blessing and their inclemency; they do not turn night into day nor day into a harassed unrest.

Mortals dwell in that they await the divinities as divinities. In hope they hold up to the divinities what is unhoped for. They wait for intimations of their coming and do not mistake the signs of their absence. They do not make their gods for themselves and do not worship idols. In the very depth of misfortune they wait for the weal that has been withdrawn.

Mortals dwell in that they initiate their own essential being—their being capable of death as death—into the use and practice of this capacity, so that there may be a good death. To initiate mortals into the essence of death in no way means to make death, as the empty nothing, the goal. Nor does it mean to darken dwelling by blindly staring toward the end.

In saving the earth, in receiving the sky, in awaiting the divinities, in initiating mortals, dwelling propriates as the fourfold preservation of the fourfold. To spare and preserve means to take under our care, to look after the fourfold in its essence. What we take under our care must be kept safe. But if dwelling preserves the fourfold, where does it keep the four-fold's essence? How do mortals make their dwelling such a preserving? Mortals would never be capable of it if dwelling were merely a staying on earth under the sky, before the divinities, among mortals. Rather, dwelling itself is always a staying with things. Dwelling, as preserving, keeps the fourfold in that with which mortals stay: in things.

Staying with things, however, is not merely something attached to this fourfold preservation as a fifth something. On the contrary: staying with things is the only way in which the fourfold stay within the fourfold is accomplished at any time in simple unity. Dwelling preserves the fourfold by bringing the essence of the fourfold into things. But things themselves secure the fourfold *only when* they themselves *as* things are let be in their essence. How does this happen? In this way, that mortals nurse and nurture the things that grow, and specially construct things that do not grow. Cultivating and construction are building in the narrower sense. *Dwelling*, inasmuch as it keeps the fourfold in things, is, as this keeping, a *building*. With this, we are on our way to the second question.

II

In what way does building belong to dwelling?

The answer to this question will clarify for us what building, understood by way of the essence of dwelling, really is. We limit ourselves to building in the sense of constructing things and inquire: what is a built thing? A bridge may serve as an example for our reflections.

The bridge swings over the stream "with ease and power." It does not just connect banks that are already there. The banks emerge as banks only as the bridge crosses the stream. The bridge expressly causes them to lie across from each other. One side is set off against the other by the bridge. Nor do the banks stretch along the stream as indifferent border strips of the dry land. With the banks, the bridge brings to the stream the one and the other expanse of the landscape lying behind them. It brings stream and bank and land into each other's neighborhood. The bridge *gathers* the earth as landscape around the stream. Thus it guides and attends the stream through the meadows. Resting upright in the stream's bed, the bridge-piers bear the swing of the arches that leave the stream's waters to run their course. The waters may wander on quiet and gay, the sky's floods from storm or thaw may shoot past the piers in torrential waves—the bridge is ready for the sky's weather and its fickle nature. Even where the bridge covers the stream, it holds its flow up to the sky by taking it for a moment under the vaulted gateway and then setting it free once more.

The bridge lets the stream run its course and at the same time grants mortals their way, so that they may come and go from shore to shore. Bridges initiate in many ways. The city bridge leads from the precincts of the castle to the cathedral square; the river bridge near the country town brings wagons and horse teams to the surrounding villages. The old stone bridge's humble brook crossing gives to the harvest wagon its passage from the fields into the village and carries the lumber cart from the field path to the road. The highway bridge is tied into the network of long-distance traffic, paced and calculated for maximum yield. Always and ever differently the bridge initiates the lingering and hastening ways of men to and fro, so that they may get to other banks and in the end, as mortals, to the other side. Now in a high arch, now in a low, the bridge vaults over glen and stream—whether mortals keep in mind this vaulting of the bridge's course or forget that they, always themselves on their way to the last bridge, are actually striving to surmount all that is common and unsound in them in order to bring themselves before the haleness of the divinities. The bridge *gathers*, as a passage that crosses, before the divinities—whether we explicitly think of, and visibly *give thanks for*, their presence, as in the figure of the saint of the bridge, or whether that divine presence is obstructed or even pushed wholly aside.

The bridge *gathers* to itself in *its own* way earth and sky, divinities and mortals.

Gathering [*Versammlung*], by an ancient word of our language, is called *thing*. The bridge is a thing—and, indeed, it is such *as* the gathering of the fourfold which we have described. To be sure, people think of the bridge as primarily and properly *merely* a bridge; after that, and occasionally, it might possibly express much else besides; and as such an expression it would then become a symbol, for instance a symbol of those things we mentioned before. But the bridge, if it is a true bridge, is never first of all a mere bridge and then afterward a symbol. And just as little is the bridge in the first place exclusively a symbol, in the sense that it expresses something that strictly speaking does not belong to it. If we take the bridge strictly as such, it never appears as an expression. The bridge is a thing and *only that*. Only? As this thing it gathers the fourfold.

Our thinking has of course long been accustomed to *understate* the essence of the thing. The consequence, in the course of Western thought, has been that the thing is represented as an unknown X to which perceptible properties are attached. From this point of view, everything *that already belongs to the gathering essence of this thing* does, of course, appear as something that is afterward read into it. Yet the bridge would never be a mere bridge if it were not a thing.

To be sure, the bridge is a thing of its *own* kind; for it gathers the fourfold in *such* a way that it allows a *site* for it. But only something *that is itself a locale* can make space for a site. The locale is not already there before the bridge is. Before the bridge stands, there are of course many spots along the stream that can be occupied by something. One of them proves to be a locale, and does so *because of the bridge*. Thus the bridge does not first come to a locale to stand in it; rather, a locale comes into existence only by virtue of the bridge. The bridge is a thing; it gathers the fourfold, but in such a way that it allows a site for the fourfold. By this site are determined the places and paths by which a space is provided for.

Only things that are locales in this manner allow for spaces. What the word for space, *Raum*, designates is said by its ancient meaning. *Raum, Rum*, means a place that is freed for settlement and lodging. A space is something that has been made room for, something that has been freed, namely, within a boundary, Greek *peras*. A boundary is not that at which something stops but, as the Greeks recognized, the boundary is that from which something *begins its essential unfolding*. That is why the concept is that of *horismos*, that is, the horizon, the boundary. Space is in essence that for which room has been made, that which is let into its bounds. That for which room is made is always granted and hence is joined, that is, gathered, by virtue of a locale, that is, by such a thing as the bridge. *Accordingly, spaces receive their essential being from locales and not from "space."*

Things which, as locales, allow a site we now in anticipation call buildings. They are so called because they are made by a process of building-construction. Of what sort this making—building—must be, however, we find out only after we have first given thought to the essence of those things that of themselves require building as the process by which they are made. These things are locales that allow a site for the fourfold, a site that in each case provides for a space. The relation between locale and space lies in the essence of these things as locales, but so does the relation of the locale to the man who lives there. Therefore we shall now try to clarify the essence of these things that we call buildings by the following brief consideration.

For one thing, what is the relation between locale and space? For another, what is the relation between man and space?

The bridge is a locale. As such a thing, it allows a space into which earth and sky, divinities and mortals are admitted. The space allowed by the bridge contains many places variously near or far from the bridge. These places, however, may be treated as mere positions between which there lies a measurable distance; a distance, in Greek *stadion*, always has room made for it, and indeed by bare positions. The space that is thus made by positions is space of a peculiar sort. As distance or "stadion" it is what the same word, *stadion*, means in Latin, a *spatium*, an intervening space or interval. Thus nearness and remoteness between men and things can become mere distance, mere intervals of intervening space. In a space that is represented purely as *spatium*, the bridge now appears as a mere something at some position, which can be occupied at any time by something else or replaced by a mere marker. What is more, the mere dimensions of height, breadth, and depth can be abstracted from space as intervals. What is so abstracted we represent as the pure manifold of the three dimensions. Yet the room made by this manifold is also no longer determined by distances; it is no longer a *spatium*, but now no more than *extensio*—extension. But from space as *extensio* a further abstraction can be made, to analytic-algebraic relations. What these relations make room for is the possibility of the purely mathematical construction of manifolds with an arbitrary number of dimensions. The space provided for in this mathematical manner may be called "space," the "one" space as such. But in this sense "the" space, "space," contains no spaces and no places. We never find in it any locales, that is, things of the kind the bridge is. As against that, however, in the spaces provided for by locales there is always space as interval, and in this interval in turn there is space as pure extension. *Spatium* and *extensio* afford at any time the possibility of measuring things and what they make room for, according to distances, spans, and directions, and of computing these magnitudes. But the fact that they are *universally* applicable to everything that has extension can in no case make numerical magnitudes the *ground* of the essence of spaces and locales that are measurable with the aid of mathematics. How even modern physics was compelled by the facts themselves to represent the spatial medium of cosmic space as a field-unity determined by body as dynamic center cannot be discussed here.

The spaces through which we go daily are provided for by locales; their essence is grounded in things of the type of buildings. If we pay heed to these relations between locales and spaces, between spaces and space, we get a clue to help us in thinking of the relation of man and space.

When we speak of man and space, it sounds as though man stood on one side, space on the other. Yet space is not something that faces man. It is neither an external object nor an inner experience. It is not that there are men, and over and above them *space*; for when I say "a man," and in saying this word think of a being who exists in a human manner—that is, who dwells—then by the name "man," I already name the stay within the fourfold among things. Even when we relate ourselves to those things that are not in our immediate reach, we are staying with the things themselves. We do not represent distant things merely in our mind—as the textbooks have it—so that only mental representations of distant things run through our minds and heads as substitutes for the things. If all of us now think, from where we are right here, of the old bridge in Heidelberg, this thinking toward that locale is not a mere experience inside the persons present here; rather, it belongs to the essence of our thinking *of* that bridge that *in itself* thinking *persists through* [durchsteht] the distance to that locale. From this spot right here, we are there at the bridge—we are by no means at some representational content in our consciousness. From right here we may even be much nearer to that bridge and to what it makes room for than someone, who uses it daily as an indifferent river crossing. Spaces, and with them space as such—"space"—are always provided for already within the stay of mortals. Spaces open up by the fact that they are let into the dwelling of man. To say that mortals *are* is to say that *in dwelling* they persist through spaces by virtue of their stay among things and locales. And only because mortals pervade, persist through, spaces by their very essence are they able to go through spaces. But in going through spaces we do not give up our standing in them. Rather, we always go through spaces in such a way that we already sustain them by staying constantly with near and remote locales and things. When I go toward the door of the lecture hall, I am already there, and I could not go to it at all if I were not such that I am there. I am never here only, as this encapsulated body; rather, I am there, that is, I already pervade the space of the room, and only thus can I go through it.

Even when mortals turn "inward," taking stock of themselves, they do not leave behind their belonging to the fourfold. When, as we say, we come to our senses and reflect on ourselves, we come back to ourselves from things *without ever abandoning* our stay among things. Indeed, the loss of rapport with things that occurs in states of depression would be wholly impossible if even such a state were not still what it is as a human state: that is, a staying *with* things. Only if this stay already characterizes human being can the things among which we are also *fail* to speak to us, *fail* to concern us any longer.

Man's relation to locales, and through locales to spaces, inheres in his dwelling. The relationship between man and space is none other than dwelling, thought essentially.

When we think, in the manner just attempted, about the relation between locale and space, but also about the relation of man and space, a light falls on the essence of the things that are locales and that we call buildings.

The bridge is a thing of this sort. The locale allows the simple onefold of earth and sky, of divinities and mortals, to enter into a site by arranging the site into spaces. The locale makes room for the fourfold in a double sense. The locale *admits* the fourfold and it *installs* the fourfold. The two—making room in the sense of admitting and in the sense of installing—belong together. As a double space-making, the locale is a shelter for the fourfold or, by the same token, a house. Things such as locales shelter or house men's lives. Things of this sort are housings, though not necessarily dwelling-houses in the narrower sense.

The making of such things is building. Its essence consists in this, that it corresponds to the character of these things. They are locales that allow spaces. This is why building, by virtue of constructing locales, is a founding and joining of spaces. Because building produces locales, the joining of the spaces of these locales necessarily brings with it space, as *spatium* and as *extensio*, into the thingly structure of buildings. But building never shapes pure "space." Neither directly nor indirectly. Nevertheless, because it produces things as locales, building is closer to the essence of spaces and to the essential origins of "space" than any geometry and mathematics. Building puts up locales that make space and a site for the fourfold. From the simple oneness in which earth and sky, divinities and mortals belong together, building *receives the directive* for its erecting of locales. Building *takes over* from the fourfold the standard for all the traversing and measuring of the spaces that in each case are provided for by the locales that have been founded. The edifices guard the fourfold. They are things that in their own way preserve the fourfold. To preserve the fourfold, to save the earth, to receive the sky, to await the divinities, to initiate mortals—this fourfold preserving is the simple essence of dwelling. In this way, then, do genuine buildings give form to dwelling in its essence, and house this essential unfolding.

Building thus characterized is a distinctive letting-dwell. Whenever it *is* such in fact, building already *has* responded to the summons of the fourfold. All planning remains grounded on this responding, and planning in turn opens up to the designer the precincts suitable for his designs.

As soon as we try to think of the essence of constructive building in terms of a letting-dwell, we come to know more clearly what that process of making consists in by which building is accomplished. Usually we take production to be an activity whose performance has a result, the finished structure, as its consequence. It is possible to conceive of making in that way; we thereby grasp something that is correct, and yet never touch its essence, which is a producing that brings something forth. For building brings the fourfold *hither* into a thing, the bridge, and brings *forth* the thing as a locale, out into what is already present, room for which is only now made *by* this locale.

The Greek for "to bring forth or to produce" is *tiktō*. The word *technē*, technique, belongs to the verb's root, *tec*. To the Greeks *technē* means neither art nor handicraft but, rather, to make something appear, within what is present, as this or that, in this way or that way. The Greeks conceive of *technē*, producing, in terms of letting appear. *Technē* thus conceived has been concealed in the tectonics of architecture since ancient times. Of late it still remains concealed, and more resolutely, in the technology of power machinery. But the essence of the erecting of buildings cannot be understood adequately in terms either of architecture or of engineering construction, nor in terms of a mere combination of the two. The erecting of buildings would not be suitably defined *even if* we were to think of it in the sense of the original Greek *technē* as *solely* a letting-appear, which brings something made, as something present, among the things that are already present.

The essence of building is letting dwell. Building accomplishes its essential process in the raising of locales by the joining of their spaces. *Only if we are capable of dwelling, only then can we build.* Let us think for a while of a farmhouse in the Black Forest, which was built some two hundred years ago by the dwelling of peasants. Here the self-sufficiency of the power to let earth and sky, divinities and mortals enter *in simple oneness* into things ordered the house. It placed the farm on the wind-sheltered mountain slope, looking south, among the meadows close to the spring. It gave it the wide overhanging shingle roof whose proper slope bears up under the burden of snow, and that, reaching deep down, shields the chambers against the storms of the long winter nights. It did not forget the altar corner behind the community table; it made room in its chamber for the hallowed places of childbed and the "tree of the dead"—for that is what they call a coffin there: the *Totenbaum*—and in this way it designed for the different generations under one roof the character of their journey through time. A craft that, itself sprung from dwelling, still uses its tools and its gear as things, built the farmhouse.

Only if we are capable of dwelling, only then can we build. Our reference to the Black Forest farm in no way means that we should or could go back to building such houses; rather, it illustrates by a dwelling that *has been* how it was able to build.

Dwelling, however, is *the basic character* of Being, in keeping with which mortals exist. Perhaps this attempt to think about dwelling and building will bring out somewhat more clearly that building belongs to dwelling and how it receives its essence from dwelling. Enough will have been gained if dwelling and building have become *worthy of questioning* and thus have remained *worthy of thought*.

But that thinking itself belongs to dwelling in the same sense as building, although in a different way, may perhaps be attested to by the course of thought here attempted.

Building and thinking are, each in its own way, inescapable for dwelling. The two, however, are also insufficient for dwelling so long as each busies itself with its own affairs in separation, instead of listening to the other. They are able to listen if both—building and thinking—belong to dwelling, if they remain within their limits and realize that the one as much as the other comes from the workshop of long experience and incessant practice.

We are attempting to trace in thought the essence of dwelling. The next step on this path would be the question: What is the state of dwelling in our precarious age? On all sides we hear talk about the housing shortage, and with good reason. Nor is there just talk; there is action too. We try to fill the need by providing houses, by promoting the building of houses, planning the whole architectural enterprise. However hard and bitter, however hampering and threatening the lack of houses remains, the *proper plight of dwelling* does not lie merely in a lack of houses. The proper plight of dwelling is indeed older than the world wars with their destruction, older also than the increase of the earth's population and the condition of the industrial workers. The proper dwelling plight lies in this, that mortals ever search anew for the essence of dwelling, that they *must ever learn to dwell*. What if man's homelessness consisted in this, that man still does not ever think of the *proper* plight of dwelling as *the* plight? Yet as soon as man *gives thought* to his homelessness, it is a misery no longer. Rightly considered and kept well in mind, it is the sole summons that *calls* mortals into their dwelling.

But how else can mortals answer this summons than by trying on *their* part, on their own, to bring dwelling to the fullness of its essence? This they accomplish when they build out of dwelling, and think for the sake of dwelling.

13   The A Priori Foundation of Communication and the Foundation of the Humanities

Karl-Otto Apel

(What sort of relation between science and the humanities should be postulated within the context of contemporary society?)

I.   Exposition

I do not believe that the question concerning the relation between science and the humanities is any more settled, or more clearly established, today than when it was brought to the fore in the days of Dilthey and Neo-Kantianism. It is true that, from time to time, speakers at congresses affirm that the old controversy between understanding and explanation has been overcome and rendered obsolete. And their audience may applaud their appeal not to split the unity of science, not to re-establish "two cultures," as Snow uses the term. But I think that appeasements and quasi-moral appeals of this kind should not intervene in, or worse, prevent, a serious meta-scientific analysis of the relations between science and the humanities. In my opinion, the chief question still is: whether it does or does not make a difference for the philosophy of science that in the human sciences, the *object* of science is also the *subject* of science, namely human society as a communication community. From this substantive question a methodological question arises: Should the humanities imitate the methods that have been so successful in the natural sciences in order thus to arrive at the status of genuine science, also? Or should they perhaps develop methods which are complementary to those used in the natural sciences, methods that flow from their own leading knowledge interests? In the latter case it could very well be that the knowledge interest guiding the humanities is equally complementary to that found in the natural sciences.

This question, or so it seems to me, is for us more significant than ever before, because we have learned—or must soon learn—to consider the methodological problems of science and the humanities in connection with their relations to social *praxis*. Dilthey's old question as to whether the goal of the humanities is or is not the same as that of natural science—namely, explanations according to laws as a basis for predictions—is today exemplified by the question as to whether, in the humanities, the relation to social *praxis* is or is not the same as in the case of natural science: that is, is it a social technology or not? This question is, in fact, answered in the affirmative by the prevailing philosophy of science, and the practical significance of this answer itself in the fact that, from this perspective, pedagogy, for example, is considered to be applied psychology, primarily in the sense of conditioning technology. Since, however, the human object in this conditioning technology is also a co-subject of the educator, the question arises as to whether there must not be a complementary method of critical-humanistic education to prevent splitting society into the manipulated and the manipulators. Such a split society would, of course, be the ideal presupposition of an objectifying social science and social technology. It could perform repeatable experiments without being disturbed by a feedback that turns controllable predictions into self-fulfilling or self-destroying prophecies. But the question remains as to whether the humanities, by their very method, should not presuppose a relation to social *praxis* that is complementary to the ideal objectification of human behavior, namely, unrestricted communication by way of intersubjective "understanding."

It is against this concrete and current background that I wish once again to raise the question of the relation between science and the humanities.[1] And I will do so by way of a critical examination of the neo-positivistic "logic of unified science."

I think that the clear-cut model of scientistic reductionism developed by this representative school of meta-science is even today a paradigm that dominates the tacit preconceptions even of those scientists and philosophers who would not wish to be understood to be neo-positivists. The most deeply rooted of these preconceptions, it seems, is the idea of knowledge as description and explanation of objectified data, conceived—a priori—as cases of instances of possible laws. Apparently even the understanding and the interpretation of symbolic meaning is to be subsumed under this conception of knowledge, if it is to be regarded as a topic of methodological relevance. In this context, my question is whether there are, perhaps, ultimate metaphysical presuppositions in the modern "logic of science" which imply conceptions of this kind, presuppositions that prevent the possibility of even imagining a "leading interest of knowledge" outside or beyond scientism. I would, indeed, reply to this question by way of a heuristic suspicion that a modern "logic of science" that does not reflect upon ultimate a priori presuppositions has just by this very fact inherited a tacit presupposition of traditional epistemology: namely, that one solitary subject of knowledge could objectify the whole world, including his fellowmen. To put it another way, it inherits the presupposition that the knowing subject can, in principle, win objective knowledge about the world without at the same time presupposing knowledge by sign-interpretation or intersubjective understanding, which cannot have the character of objectivity, and nevertheless may be improved upon in a methodical way. Let me explain—or better, explicate—this, by some remarks about the metaphysical background of the modern, analytical philosophy of science.

If one were to ask about the a priori presuppositions of modern neo-positivistic logic of science, several answers could be given. This first might be: the only a priori presupposition here implied is logic itself, which in science has to be combined in some way with the observation of facts. This might, perhaps, fit the original self-understanding of the logical positivists. But after some reflection, it becomes clear that, even in logical positivism, a few more a priori presuppositions are actually involved. Thus, it is not simply a matter of fact that there are facts; rather, is has to be presupposed, a priori, in the logic of science that there exist facts that are independent of human thinking about them, and that those facts can be recognized, intersubjectively, *as* facts. Now, what we have stated as presuppositions of logical positivism are, in fact, two of the metaphysical principles of Leibniz, namely, that there are "truths of reason" (*vérités de raison*) based on logic, and "truths of fact" (*vérités de fait*) based on experience.[2] And here, immediately, a further a priori presupposition comes to light which the logical positivists originally also shared with Leibniz: the presupposition of an ideal language of science which can bring together mathematical logic and experienced facts in an unequivocal manner (as Leibniz puts it: in a *lingua philosophica sive calculus ratiocinator*, which puts an end to misunderstandings in philosophical communication by providing recourse to a "calculemus"[3]). I might add that the logical positivists had at their disposal a theoretical basis for their semantical critique of metaphysics, only as long as the neo-Leibnizian metaphysics that they inherited from Russell and the young Wittgenstein remained hidden. Obviously, they lost this theoretical basis once they were forced to question these metaphysical presuppositions. And this happened once it became clear that the following ideal postulates simply could not be realized in the logic of science: first, the idea of one syntactico-semantical framework which could be presupposed as the universal language of science as a whole; second, the idea of observational sentences which could be considered as copies of facts (protocol sentences) independent of theoretical contexts already implied in the formulation of the observational sentences.

Since the language applicable in science always presupposes some reference to particular facts, while the observational statements always presuppose some orientation with respect to theoretical frameworks, a further a priori presupposition of the logic of science comes to light: "convention." Conventions are needed to construct "semantical frameworks" as possible languages of science and to interpret these frameworks as applicable to languages of science with the help of a metalanguage, which is, in practice, the non-formalized language of the science already being used. Conventions are also needed to establish observational statements which could function as basic propositions for confirmation and falsification of hypotheses or theories. But what are "conventions"? If one reads the literature of logical positivism one might think that a convention is some absolutely irrational factor that precedes all reasonable discourse, because it is already presupposed by the rules of a semantical framework. A convention seems to be the same thing as a solitary and arbitrary decision, such as, for instance, the decision of a sovereign ruler who, according to Hobbes, establishes and interprets the law by the authority of his will, or still earlier in the history of nominalism, the fiat of God's will which, according to the Franciscan theologians, precedes all reasoning.

While it is true that a convention precedes all rational operations which are conceivable according to the neo-positivistic idea of reason—for conventions cannot be deduced from first principles within a calculus—neither can they be derived from empirical observation or by induction from such observation. (In fact, the neo-positivists seriously tried to reduce the so-called pragmatic dimension of the language of science, which includes the ultimate conventions about the rules of semantical frameworks and their interpretations, to an object of empirical observation by way of another, behavioral science. But this enterprise was, of course, doomed to failure, for even if it were possible to describe conventions by means of a behavioral science, this would in turn presuppose conventions embedded in the observational sentences of this description, and so on, *ad infinitum*.)

Thus, for the neo-positivistic logic of science conventions are, indeed, ultimate presuppositions which have to be acknowledged as prior to all scientific rationality. But here the question arises as to whether scientific rationality, in the sense of the logic of science (i.e., logical inferences plus observation), in fact exhausts the whole of human rationality, so that beyond its limits only the irrationality of arbitrary decisions can exist. Such a limited view of rationality could, in my opinion, be justified only if one man, alone, could at least in principle practice science. For, in this case, the conventions which, so to speak, intervene in the rational operations of cognition would indeed have to be conceived of as completely irrational personal decisions. But the very word "con-vention" (in German *Überein-kunft*) speaks against this interpretation. Indeed, the later Wittgenstein even explained his conventionalism by pointing out that one person alone cannot be said to follow a rule. Thus he has shown that conventions presuppose language games. However, language games cannot be founded by conventions in the same way that artificial semantic frameworks can. Instead, they must on their own provide the foundations for rule conventions in a communication community. Now, is it possible to point out the pre-scientific rationality of meaning conventions in a communication community? Even tacit conventions about the use of words—not to mention explicit conventions about definitions, theoretical frameworks or statements of facts in empirical science—imply an intersubjective consensus about situational meanings and the aims of practical life which can only be achieved by a mutual understanding of intentions and motivations as the very sense of the conventions. While it is true that conventions cannot be deduced from their motives, and thus cannot be justified by the logic of an axiomatic system, they must nevertheless not be conceived of as arbitrary acts of a solitary will or—what amounts to the same thing in the context of justification—as events which can only be described and explained from the outside, as determined by extra-rational motives as causes. For it is by their *intelligibility* that meaning conventions must fulfill the condition of being presupposed by a communication community as a *common* basis of interaction and world interpretation, at the same time being improved in the course of improving such interaction and world interpretation. And it is by such improvements of meaning-conventions, implicit in public language games, that explicit conventions, for instance the definitions of concepts, come about.

Now the question arises whether there should not exist an intrinsic connection between the prescientific rationality of meaning conventions and the methodical *ratio* of the humanities. So far as I know, only the nearly forgotten American philosopher Josiah Royce realized this possibility of a nonscientistic and nonobjectivistic foundation of the humanities in his philosophy of "interpretation."[4] Royce made it clear indispensable conventions about the meanings of concepts needed in science presuppose that there are not only cognitive operations, such as perceptions and conceptions, which rest on an exchange between man and nature, but also cognitive operations, such as interpretation of signs, which rest on an exchange between men in a "community of interpretation."[5] This conception of Royce's which is, so to speak, a hermeneutical elaboration of the semiotical ideas of C.S. Peirce, in my opinion, provides the decisive suggestion as to the context in which conventions have their dimension of possible rationality. Conventions—so it seems to me—may be mediated by a rationality of a peculiar kind: it is not the scientific rationality of operations on objects which could be performed in a repeatable way by exchangeable human subjects, but rather the pre- and *meta-scientific rationality* of intersubjective discourse mediated by *explication of concepts* and interpretation of intentions. This dimension of reasonable discourse is inaccessible to those philosophies which proceed from methodical solipsism, that is, from the a priori presupposition that "one person alone could follow a rule," for example, that one person also could perform scientific research, etc. Therefore, I call the presupposition that makes the dimension of the rationality of conventions accessible the *A priori of Communication*, or rather, the *A priori of Language Communication*, because no other communication provides the possibility of rational conventions.

My first claim in this paper is that the *logic of science*, as it was developed by the logical positivists, has not, up to now, reflected upon the fact that, after the exposure of the hidden metaphysics of its early days moved to the new ground of the *A priori of Communication*. Instead of reflecting upon this new presupposition of its *conventionalist* phase, it has tacitly held on to its former presuppositions (inherited from *logical atomism* which implied methodical solipsism).[6] I will then illustrate my first thesis by displaying the consequences of methodical solipsism in the logic of science. My exposition of these consequences amounts to the assertion that methodical solipsism is one of the main reasons why the neo-positivistic logic of science has not, up to now, been able to cope with the peculiar interests and problems of the humanities, but has had to cling to the program of a scientistic reduction of the methods of the humanities to those of the natural sciences, or at least to those of the social sciences styled natural sciences. This assertion will make up the second thesis of my paper. Finally, the basis of this critique of reductive scientism as a consequence of methodological solipsism will be made explicit by my third thesis: that the *A priori of Language-Communication* provides an adequate presupposition for understanding the social function and the methodological approach of the humanities.

II. Methodical Solipsism as metaphysical presupposition of Logical Positivism

It might perhaps seem curious, at first sight, that modern analytical logic of science, based on semantical reconstruction of the language of science, should have *methodical solipsism* as its tacit presupposition. At first sight, the neo-Leibnizian postulate of a universal language of science lying at the ground of the Russell-Wittgenstein-Carnap program seems to be equivalent to an acknowledgement of the quasi-transcendental function of language communication as a condition of the possibility and validity of human knowledge. In particular, Carnap's transition from the language of private experience (in *Der logische Aufbau der Welt*, 1928) to the intersubjective "thing language" of "physicialism" (cf. "Die physikalische Sprache als Universalsprache der Wissenschaft," *Erkenntnis 3*, 1932) seems in principle to surmount the tradition of the *methodical solipsism* that is involved in the very foundations of traditional empiricism and positivism (and, by the way, also in that tradition of rationalistic philosophy which, from Descartes to Husserl, conceives of truths as evidence for consciousness). This view, however, is, it seems to me, unjustified. Indeed, I wish to maintain the thesis that a philosophy which postulates a physicalistic-behavioristic language for objectifying the phenomena of human intersubjectivity involves methodical solipsism to no less an extent than a philosophy that starts from the assumption that meaning and truth are matters of introspective evidence of private experiences of consciousness. The common bias of both philosophies lies in the tacit assumption that *objective* knowledge should be possible without *intersubjective* understanding by communication being presupposed. The traditional subjectivistic form of empiricism tries to realize this idea of knowledge without presupposing language as a condition of intersubjectivity at all. Modern logical (semantical) empiricism also leapfrogs the communicative function of language by postulating a language which would be a priori intersubjective by being simply objective and universal. It is, however, just this idea of intersubjectivity as warranted by objectivity that makes that neo-Leibnizian conception of a universal "thing-language" a new expression of the epistemological idea of methodical "solipsism."

In order to elucidate this point let me first make some remarks about the peculiarities of formalized languages as possible realizations of the neo-positivistic idea of a universal language of science.

At the outset let us note that the formalized languages of the logic of science, in principle, cannot be used for *intersubjective communication* in the full sense of that word. It is only *sentences* about *states of affairs* (not even *statements* about *facts!*) and *logical connections* between sentences that can be formulated in these languages, but not "utterances"[7] or "speech acts"[8] because these units of ordinary language do not get their meaning exclusively from the syntactical and semantical rules of a formal system, but only from the context of the pragmatical use of language in concrete situations of life. Now, among those parts of speech which cannot be expressed are, above all, personal identifiers such as "I," "you," "we," etc., which immediately express the situation of intersubjective communication, and the reflection upon this situation. Such utterances, which attest the human "competence of communication" by language can, in the logic of formalized "thing-languages," only be the object of descriptions of "verbal behavior" by an observer who does not himself participate in the communication. Now, strictly speaking, a description of verbal behavior in a formalized language cannot express an *understanding* of the intentions of the persons speaking, because this always implies that these persons and the "descriptor" participate in a common language game taking regard of the communicative competence of both sides.[9] The language of science as conceived by the neo-positivistic logic of science excludes—in principle—the existence of a language game common to the subjects and to the objects of science. It has to exclude this because the very point of constructing formalized languages for scientific use is to get rid of the *hermenteutic* problems of communication, that is, of interpreting one another's intentions, by establishing a framework of language which is *a priori* an *intersubjective* one and so provides the conditions of the possibility of objective knowledge. In short, the logically reconstructed language of science is destined for describing and explaining a world of pure objects; it is not suited to express communication which is the intersubjective dimension of language.

However, one could perhaps still ask what all this should have to do with methodical solipsism as an ultimate presupposition of thinking. I have to concede that the logic of science would not, in fact, imply methodical solipsism if it were to reflect upon two things: first, that even the constructor, let alone the user, of a formalized language of science already presupposes communication, in the full sense of understanding human intentions, for bringing about those conventions that are needed for introducing and testing the formalized languages; second, that human beings, so long as they are considered as possible partners of communication, and so of interaction, cannot be reduced to objects of description and/ or explanation of their behavior by means of formalized languages, but have to be dealt with in the context of a language game which is, in principle, common to the subjects and to the objects of science (i.e., the humanities).

The logical positivists would presumably not deny the first of these two points. Particularly in the school's recent stages, when the basic need for conventions could no longer be overlooked, it has begun to move in this direction. But still there are intrinsic reasons that prevent it from taking all the consequences of the *A priori of Communication* into account. The main such reason is the idea of a unified science, originally connected with the idea of the universal language. It is this reason that prevents logical positivism from methodically reflecting upon the intersubjective communication presupposed by constructive semantics in the manner of a transcendental pragmatics that does not reduce the intersubjective dimension of communication to "verbal behavior." And it is this same reason that prevents logical positivism from acknowledging as genuine the methods of understanding in the humanities, and so prevents it from acknowledging that human beings cannot be reduced to objects of description and/or explanation of their behavior by means of formalized languages.

If one really hopes to objectify the whole world, including the dimension of communication, by a language of a unified science, then one must, strictly speaking, cling to the a priori of methodical solipsism, for the totalization of the idea of scientific objectivity implies that the subject of the objectifying science could, in principle, practice science without being a member of a communication community. He should, on this view, be able to follow the rules of the universal "thing-language" as if they were rules of a "private language"—to speak as the later Wittgenstein does. It is well known that the later Wittgenstein denied this possibility; and, in my opinion, he has, indeed, refuted "methodical solipsism" with his notion of public "language games" as presuppositions of all intentionality of actions and cognitions. But the neo-positivistic "logic of unified science," as it is represented for instance by Hempel, Nagel, and Stegmüller, has not, up to now, drawn epistemological consequences from Wittgenstein's refutation of "methodical solipsism." Rather it clings to the idea of a universal "thing-language" as developed in the *Tractatus Logico-Philosophicus* of the younger Wittgenstein.

Let us, therefore, first pay some attention to the younger Wittgenstein, who explicitly confirms my thesis that *methodical solipsism* is the ultimate presupposition of a logic of a universal "thing language." In his early work, *Tractatus Logico-Philosophicus*, Wittgenstein traced the idea of a *universal language*, in which only the propositions of the natural sciences would be justified as meaningful, down to its last foundations, which he himself called "transcendental." Now, among these last foundations, were the following sentences of the *Tractatus*:

5.631: There is no such thing as the subject that thinks or entertains ideas. . . .

This sentence may be considered as the vantage point for a rigorous program of *behaviorism* within the neo-positivistic program of unified science. Nevertheless, Wittgenstein himself did not forget the *transcendental* presuppositions of behavioral science itself. These are condensed into the following sentence which seems to contradict the sentence I have already quoted:

5.641: Thus there really is a sense in which philosophy can talk about the self in a non-psychological way. What brings the self into philosophy is the fact that 'the world is my world.'. . .

The apparent contradiction between this sentence about a philosophical concept of "the self" and the previous denial of the existence of a thinking "subject" has to be resolved, according to Wittgenstein, by the transcendental consideration that the "self" expressed in the sentence, "the would is *my world*," is not *existing in* the world but is just the *limit* of that world which can be described in the language of natural sciences.

5.62: . . . The world is my world: this is manifest in the fact that the limits of language . . . mean the limits of my world.

So, according to Wittgenstein, the transcendental unity of the I as the unity of the language is the condition of the possibility of natural science just as, in Kant, the *transcendental unity* of the I is the *unity of consciousness*. But now there comes to light a point of Wittgenstein's critique of a pure language of science which goes, at any rate explicitly, beyond Kant's critique of pure reason: if the transcendental I does not exist in the world, but only as the limit of the world, so that all men in the world have to be conceived as objects of (description and explanation by) natural science, then there must be no need for intersubjective communication about the use of language. Every scientist, so to speak, must be completely self-sufficient as a transcendental subject of his language which is—by mystical guarantee—the language of all other scientists. In Wittgenstein's words:

5.64: Here it can be seen that solipsism, when its implications are followed out strictly, coincides with pure realism. The self of solipsism shrinks to a point without extension, and there remains the reality coordinated with it.

Precisely this presupposition is the point of methodical solipsism, which denies not just the existence of other minds, but the presupposition of other minds—for instance, by way of communication—for understanding oneself and the world. According to this position it should be possible for a scientist to reduce all other scientists—not to speak of laymen—to objects of his description and explanation of their behavior, including their verbal behavior if such a thing should exist in the world. It is my thesis that this very position has become the ultimate presupposition, one no longer reflected upon, of the neo-positivistic idea of a unified science, and it has remained so even after the shift from the metaphysics of logical atomism to the conventionalism of constructive semantics.

III.   Methodical Solipsism as presupposition of the neo-positivist idea of "understanding"

I will now go on to illustrate my first thesis by giving a critical sketch of the neo-positivist treatment of the humanities, especially of the old question about the relationship between nomological explanations and the understanding of meaning-intentions. Strictly speaking, it is not quite correct to speak of a neo-positivistic treatment of the humanities because the very heart of the humanities, *philology* in a broad sense, was not treated but simply ignored in the "logic of unified science." As has still to be shown, this exclusion is rather characteristic, and instructive with regard to the neo-positivists' strategy of argument. Nevertheless, there remains the fact that the "social sciences," and within their context also history, had to be dealt with by the logical positivists. In this context, they had also to discuss "understanding" which was claimed by Droysen, Dilthey, Croce, Collingwood and other philosophers to be the very method of the "Geisteswissenschaften."[10] Now, how did they proceed in dealing with "understanding"? Let us at this point take a closer look at their *strategy of argument*.

The first thing which strikes one upon reading the discussions by, say, O. Neurath, C. G. Hempel, P. Oppenheim, E. Nagel, Th. Abel, and W. Stegmüller,[11] is the fact that they do not at all discuss the *understanding of language-signs*, of statements, or whole texts of science, philosophy or literature. This is curious if one remembers the fact that the modern *logic of science* is, according to their own method, essentially an *analysis of language* which, for instance, transforms the older positivistic logic of explanation[12] into the *formal mode*, according to which it is no longer events that are explained by laws and causes, but sentences making up the *explanandum* that are deduced from sentences making up the explanans. Thus, the first thing analytic philosophers themselves do is always to *explicate* the concepts of traditional philosophy by reconstructing their semantical framework. But shouldn't this enterprise stand in close connection with the activity of those sciences that *interpret* texts, for instance, the history of science? That is what one might ask as an outsider; but one gets no answer to this question, for, as I have already mentioned, the neo-positivist logic of science does not deal with the philological, or, to use another term, with the hermeneutical, sciences. (I will return to this later on, with a conjecture as to the reasons why the neo-positivists' analyses of language overlook their most congenial relatives among the sciences, in a broad sense.)

But what about *understanding of actions* in history and sociology? As an outsider, again, one might think that this kind of understanding should itself stand in close connection with an *understanding of signs and texts* because ultimately the operation of understanding is directed to meaning as it is expressed by texts, works or actions, more or less according to the meaning-intentions of their authors.[13] One could here, perhaps, follow the later Wittgenstein and take it as a heuristic horizon that speech, actions and interpretations as meaning-intentions are always "interwoven" in *language-games* as "forms of life." One might thus be led to think that the historians and sociologists had to inquire into actions, institutions, etc., in a way similar to that in which philologists inquire into texts, in order to understand forms of life by interpreting the meaning of the goal-setting and the value-systems expressed by actions and institutions. Elaborated understanding of this kind is, indeed, needed not only for answering the question *why* certain actions of institutions came about but for answering the earlier question as to *what* is given: that is, as to what those actions (especially collective ones) and institutions are that are to be identified and described within a context of an historical situation and a socio-cultural form of life. Thus answering "what?" questions and answering teleological "why?" questions seems to be interwoven in historico-sociological descriptions with the so-called "hermeneutic circle" which also makes up the methodical rule of text interpretation. Sometimes the historian might even be interested in actions as supplements of texts; thus for instance, he could inquire into the political actions of Martin Luther as being elucidations or, perhaps also, contradictions of his theological writings. All these possibilities of methodical interpretation—which have nothing to do with *causal explanation*—have already been explored in a rich literature extending from Schleiermacher, Boeckh, Droysen to Dilthey, Weber, Croce, Collingwood, Rothacker, Gadamer, Betti and others.[14] And, as I have already mentioned, the later Wittgenstein has also given an important hint as to the possibility of a hermeneutic approach in sociology, as P. Winch, for instance has shown.[15] But if one hopes to find the neo-positivists dealing with this kind of understanding in history and sociology, one is once again disappointed. True, they do speak about the "so-called theoreticians of *understanding* or *Verstehen* in the *Geistes-wissenschaften*" and they try to come to terms with these people, but just at the beginning of the hoped-for discussion they introduce a rather cunning presupposition, namely: that the "theoreticians of the Geisteswissenschaften" conceive of understanding (*Verstehen*) as a method that competes with "covering law explanation" by appealing instead to higher, intuitive insights.[16] Thereby they assume that *understanding*, if it were a *method* of cognition, would answer the same kinds of questions as *explanation*, the only difference between the two operations being that "understanding" would have the additional ambition of reaching the same goal as explanation by a shortcut, so to speak. Having introduced these presuppositions—which, by the way, show that they are unable to conceive of any other leading interest of knowing[17] than that of the natural sciences—they start elaborating their own theory of "the operation called 'verstehen'."[18]

The neo-positivists are, then, generous enough to concede a place in science to the operation called "verstehen." But they do so by conceiving of "verstehen" as "empathy," and that means as "internalizing" special kinds of observable data, namely: human behavior as reaction to stimuli. By such internalizing empathy one is able—the neo-positivists say—to find *maxims* of behavior from one's own experience and to interpolate them into the observed behavior of others. By this interpolation of a behavior-maxim, the stimulus-data and the reaction-data become connected in such a way as to arouse in the observer the feeling of having understood with intuitive evidence *why* a human being reacted to a stimulus in the way that he actually did. For instance, one "understands" in this way, why one's neighbor stops working at his desk and lights a fire in his stove, by interpolating that he suddenly became cold. Presupposing this paradigm of "understanding," the neo-positivists, not surprisingly, come to the following estimate of its value as a scientific *method*: Understanding is only a psychologically interesting, *heuristic* device for hitting upon law-hypotheses in the context of explaining human behavior. But as such a heuristic device, it remains marginal to science because its results are only possible ingredients of the explanans. So what is relevant as a scientific method here, as in every case of neo-positivist explanation, becomes the deduction of the explanandum from the explanans in such a way that a prediction becomes possible which can be tested by observation. The first to formulate this argument against "understanding" as a method of science was, so far as I know, Otto Neurath, a member of the Vienna Circle, who wrote in his book *Empirishe Soziologie* (Wien, 1931, p. 56): "Empathy, understanding and the like may help the researcher, but it enters into a system of statements of science as little as does a good cup of coffee, which helped the researcher to do his work." (Translation by K.-O.A.) In this paper I will, therefore, call the neo-positivistic theory of understanding the *cup of coffee theory of understanding*.

C. G. Hempel, who, together with R. Oppenheim, gave the neo-positivistic theory of "explanation" its precise form in his so-called deductive-nomological model,[19] elaborated upon the cup of coffee theory of understanding as follows: ". . . understanding . . . in terms of one's own psychological function may prove a useful heuristic device in the search for general psychological principles which might provide a theoretical explanation: but the existence of empathy on the part of the scientist is neither a necessary, nor a sufficient, condition for explanation, or the scientific understanding [sic!] of any human action."[20] Let us examine this last, two-part thesis of Hempel and Oppenheim more closely. The first half of the thesis, namely, that understanding by empathy is not a *necessary* condition for the explanation of the scientific understanding, of any human action, is illustrated in the following way: "For the behavior of psychotics or of people belonging to a culture very different from that of the scientist may sometimes be explainable and predicable in terms of general principles even though the scientist who establishes or applies those principles may not be able to understand his subjects empathetically."[21] This is so characteristic and instructive an illustration that I will take it as a point of departure for my critical discussion of the whole neo-positivistic standpoint. First I will try to make clear under what tacit presuppositions the thesis of the illustration could be assumed to be true, and under what other presuppositions it is simply absurd; then I will try to show that it is, in fact, wrong, even under the tacit presuppositions of Hempel and Oppenheim.

The thesis that it is not necessary to "understand" human actions because one can sometimes explain them by general principles without understanding them by empathy can, in principle, be assumed to be true if, and only if, one is a priori *not interested* in understanding beliefs, reasons, or aims of human beings, but only in covering law explanations of what, in fact, is going on. But this means—properly speaking—that one is not interested in making a difference between human beings and their actions on the one hand, and any other natural events on the other, for only by *understanding* in the context of communication is one able to discover and to validate this difference. External explanation by general principles, even if they were confirmed by so-called observations of behavior, could never ascertain that the rules by which we "explain" behavior are followed, *as rules*, by the agents of the behavior, or, to put it in other words, that the concepts of our "explanation" could, in principle, be used by the agents themselves in order to conceptualize their own rule-following behavior. Now, to provide rules and concepts of just this kind makes up the leading interest of "understanding," as P. Winch has shown.[22] (Even Hempel and Oppenheim did, in fact, resort to "understanding" when they spoke of "psychotics" and "people belonging to very different cultures." For it is obvious that in their illustration they wish to introduce examples of human actions in a *deficient mode*, so to speak.)

Now it is clear that to exclude a priori an *interest* in understanding (and thus to exclude an *interest* in the distinctiveness of human actions) as a possible presupposition of cognition, prevents any reasonable discussion with so-called "theoreticians of understanding." It simply begs the question and reduces the assertion that understanding is not necessary to a blank tautology. This, again, may be illustrated by the kind of interpretations of the Hempel and Oppenheim examples that might be expected in a fair discussion. For, in the case of the behavior of psychotics, the theoreticians of understanding would of course say:

just this case illustrates that, in principle, understanding of human behavior is necessary, for only in cases of deficiency of humanity such as these may one, perhaps, have to give up understanding. In the case of foreign cultures, not even this argument would be plausible, for cultural anthropologists, ethnologists, historians, or linguists who are interested in recognizing these phenomena *as foreign cultures* simply would not give up "understanding." They eventually would—as, in fact, all cultural scientists, more or less, do—mediate or check their "empathy" *by other ways of understanding* and quasi-explanation which seem to be totally unknown to neo-positivists. I will return to this later. But cultural scientists would not by any means give up all claims to understanding in favor of covering law explanations. Not even social scientists who are not interested in understanding, but who wish rather to set up predictions for social engineering, can dispense with all presuppositions indebted to understanding; though in this case one can concede that they make only heuristic use of understanding in the service of explaining. But this case leads us back to our distinction between two kinds of possible answers to the thesis of Hempel and Oppenheim.

The most relevant answer, in my opinion, has already been put forward. It consists in the argument that a theory which a priori assesses *understanding* according to its value *for explaining*, simply begs the question by forgetting to ask for the proper aim of understanding as a way of cognition. For instance, it can never come to terms with what text interpretation is about. But even if one presupposes that covering law explanation, and thus prediction, is the only serious leading interest of science, as neo-positivists always tacitly do, one is not permitted to dispense completely with all *heuristic understanding*, as Hempel suggests, as long as one wishes to explain human behavior. And if historically relevant human behavior is to be explained, it is not even possible to treat understanding as only a heuristic device in the service of covering law explanation, for the simple reason that covering law explanations in history are not possible, as W. Dray has recently shown with striking arguments.[23] (The structure of so-called historical explanations which should better be called quasi-explanations cannot, in my opinion, be logically reduced to the Hempel-Oppenheim scheme of *deductive-nomological explanation*. They may well be answers to a question for causes, but even as such they cannot provide a basis for predictions but only for intelligibility in a sense of *ex post factum determinism*. As Dray has shown, the "because" sentences of historians, in contradistinction to those of an unhistorical social scientist, cannot, in principle, be replaced by an explanans in the sense of the Hempel-Oppenheim scheme. The main reason for this lies in the fact that historians cannot accept genuine empirical law-hypotheses as explications of the necessity meant by their "because" sentences. What they eventually should accept as an explication of that *ex post factum necessity* is either a pseudo-law with only one instance (stating formally the predictability of the explanandum in those cases where *all* individual circumstances of the singular event would return) or a progressive specification of the boundary-conditions of the searched-for law which must reconstruct the individual circumstances of the explanandum by the use of proper names and definite descriptions. In both cases only a pseudo-law can be proposed, and this is, indeed, intelligible, if one reflects upon the fact that historical explanations, even if not primarily interested in understanding intentions, must be mediated by an understanding of human actions against the background of singular situations. After all, in my opinion, we can here no longer presuppose, as we might in the case of nature, that the relevant data of experience are describable in terms of universal theories implying *universal*, that is, unchangeable *laws*. At least so much can be maintained: the elaboration of the very *understanding* of human motivations within the context of singular situations is an indispensable method of cognition even if one is interested only in historical (causal) explanations, whereas the idea that every historical event may be explained as a singular complexion of universally valid laws which, in principle, could be found without hermeneutic methods is, up to now, a metaphysical hypothesis of the neo-positivists. In natural science just the opposite is true; the renunciation of motivational understanding has been a methodological precondition of its progress since Galileo and Kepler.

From here I turn to the second half of the Hempel-Oppenheim thesis, namely, to the assertion that understanding is not a sufficient condition "for the explanation, or scientific understanding, of any human action." We have already learned how this thesis is taken by Th. Abel's analysis of "the operation called 'verstehen'" mentioned above. Abel's analysis, in fact, confirms Hempel's by stressing that "verstehen" provides only a *possible* hypothesis for explanation which has to be tested by observation, because our feeling of understanding a human action might be illusory. Now, the first thing to be said in reply to this is to once again call attention to the fact that Hempel and Oppenheim beg the question by tacitly equating "scientific understanding" with "explanation" according to laws, for it becomes immediately clear that testing the predictive value of the result of understanding by *observation* does not help you if what you are interested in is just *understanding*. If, for instance, one is interested in understanding, why, that is, *for what reasons*, a population of farmers left a certain stretch of land and settled in another region, no amount of testing nomological hypotheses in this and similar cases by observation can provide the decisive evidence. At most it can give hints, on the assumption that those hints can be integrated into the very attempt at *understanding*. For it is not just observation of data as in the case of a physicist's hypothesis, but communication by language with so-called objects as co-subjects, which would provide the best test of having understood someone's reasons for action.[24] Thus, in the case of the farmers, one would have to conduct interviews to provide a conclusive test for, say, the hypothesis that they left their old land because it had become barren, and not because they had heard about gold being discovered somewhere else. Incidentally, from this example one can see that the famous distinction between the "context of discovery" and the "context of justification"—stemming from Kant—cannot be used to show the methodological irrelevance of "understanding" as many "logicians of science" seem to suppose. For, as the analytical philosophers could have learned from Wittgenstein's theory of language games, the way by which knowledge has to be "justified" is not independent of the kind of question to which it is answering: *external explanations* may be justified by external observation; *intersubjective understanding* can only be justified by the *improvement of intersubjective understanding*. To neglect this internal connection between the context of discovery and the context of justification amounts to an abstractive fallacy which leads to a totalization of the leading interest of just one kind of knowledge and its corresponding kind of justification. It is important to remark here that the *relevant* hypotheses for understanding the characteristic actions of foreign peoples or cultures are not simply interpolations of our own experiences into their behavior, as Abel suggests; not are they hypotheses of a general nomological kind, to be confirmed by induction from observing as many cases of behavior as possible. If, for instance, we wish to know why in the ninth century B.C. the Mayans left their first area of settlement and in two migrations moved to the north of Yucatan, we presumably have to know, by some kind of indirect communication, something about their astrological religion. Similarly, in the case of Cleopatra's suicide we in fact know, from interpreting documents, that the queen took her life by means of a snake because this kind of death promised immortality to her, according to the Egyptian religious tradition.

These examples, in our present context, serve to indicate that the whole concept of *understanding* as *empathy* presupposed by the neo-positivists, is highly insufficient and misguiding, particularly if the only scientific alternative to evidence by empathy is sought in testing, by observation, the result of understanding as a hypothesis of covering law explanation. I do not, of course, wish to deny that empathy (*"Einfühlung"* as Herder said; or *"Nacherleben"* as Dilthey said) is an important ingredient of understanding, but, as even Dilthey maintained, it has to be integrated into, and checked by, the proper methods and contexts of understanding, which have been distinguished and diligently described in hermeneutics, particularly since Schleiermacher and Boeckh.[25] These canonical methods, as for instance, grammatical interpretation, interpretation in the light of literary genre or topic, interpretation of single utterances of a work by the whole of it, and vice versa, historical interpretation, psychological-biographical interpretation, in themselves already provide contexts in which the "divinations of understanding" (Hamann, Schleiermacher) are continually elaborated and corrected by way of a fruitful counterchecking of a priori and a posteriori, subjective and objective, universal and empirical, presuppositions of understanding. These traditional canons of interpretation may, today, be supplemented by sophisticated methods of, for instance, semiotical analysis, but this does not mean that understanding should be reduced to a heuristic device in the context of covering law explanation, in order to become controllable, and thus respectable, as a rational method of cognition. How misleading this claim of the logic of unified science is may be shown by two further arguments.

1. Hempel and Oppenheim take it for granted that, in the case of intentionally goal-directed actions, one has only two alternative ways of analyzing these phenomena.[26] Either one has to start a teleological analysis, presupposing the goal as a *cause finalis* which can determine people's actions from the future, *or* one must replace goals by *causal motives*, supposing for every single intended goal a corresponding wish or will to reach just this goal, thus providing antecedent conditions for a covering law explanation. Hempel and

Oppenheim, of course, decide in favor of the second alternative, but what is interesting in our context is the reason they give for this decision: if the motive were to be conceived as a goal lying in the future, they argue, we could not deal with cases where the goal was not attained at all.

Now, this argument, from my point of view, again shows that the neo-positivists are unable a priori to conceive of a *leading interest of cognition* other than *causal explanation*. For, the teleological alternative to their own approach, as they conceive of it, is only another type of causal explanation. If they could imagine a genuine interest in understanding goals as motives they would see that, even in the case where goals have not been reached, historians may, nevertheless, be concerned with understanding the goals as such, and not just the causes of what really happened. Human goals, for example social or political programs, even if not realized, may be the topic of detailed interpretation as possibilities of life to be discussed and eventually realized by later generations. From this one may realize that it is, indeed, possible and necessary for hermeneutical sciences to separate human motives *qua* goals from factual actions and to treat them like meaning intentions in texts. But even if, as in history and sociology, one is primarily interested in *explaining why* certain actions (or forbearances!) take place, it is far from being self-evident that hermeneutical methods could be dispensed with and understanding of reasons be reduced to *explanation by causal motives*. The problem here is whether those volitional cognitive complexes which may be formed out of wishes to reach some goals and beliefs such that, in a certain situation, certain actions become necessary and sufficient means for reaching those goals, may be considered as antecedent conditions in the sense of the Hempel-Oppenheim scheme. The difficulty here lies in the fact that the wishes and beliefs can only be defined with reference to their intentional objects. Thus they are internally (conceptually) connected with the "explanandum," whereas in genuine causal explanation an external (contingent) relation between the antecedent conditions and the explanandum is presupposed, and therefore an *empirical law*, instead of a *practical inference of understanding*, is required in order to bridge the gulf between the explanandum and the antecedent conditions. It may be objected that, within the context of an explanation, it is not the internal relation between wishes or beliefs and their intentional objects that is relevant, but the external relation between the occurrences of wishes and beliefs on the one hand and the explanandum on the other. But this objection overlooks the fact—in contradistinction to natural causes—the relevant occurrences of wishes and beliefs cannot be identified (or verified) without presupposing the internal relation to the explanandum as intentional object. And the explanandum, in turn, cannot be identified (verified) as a certain action without already presupposing the intentions by which the "antecedent conditions" are defined.[27] If one takes into consideration that, in any case, goal-directed action presupposes for its realization a genuine causal connection, one may wonder whether the search for such connections and thus for genuine natural laws is not obscured by claiming that all possible human intentions are possible causes within the context of covering law explanations. But even if this would be allowable, it would by no means prove that *hermeneutical* methods could be dispensed with, for in order to delineate the *volitional-cognitive complex* which is said to function as cause within the context of an explanation one has first to understand the corresponding human intentions, and for this one has to reconstruct the whole context of the corresponding forms of life, including value systems, world views, and so on. The unintended irony of Hempel's and Oppenheim's conception of causal motives lies in the fact that precisely as many different wishes and beliefs must be available as causes as were previously discovered by methodical efforts of understanding.

2. Our last hint, as to the reconstruction of whole forms of life including world views, may lead us to a further criticism of the whole conception of understanding as empathy, as it is presupposed in neo-positivism. The tacit presupposition of applying empathy as a paradigm for understanding is the idea of *empirical data* as results of a description which would precede all *understanding* as well as *explaining*. Among all the empirical data provided by description—so they would have us think—there are simply some kinds which may be internalized by empathy and thus connected by so-called understanding. This positivistic idea of experience, stemming from Hume, J.S. Mill, and Mach, completely overlooks the fact that understanding must be presupposed in order to describe the experienced data of the world *as something*, that is, for answering the question *what* a thing is. This primary understanding of the data of the world is internally connected with understanding human language and forms of life. This circumstance may be neglected in the case of natural science because here the fundamental world-interpretation which precedes all single explanations (as answers to the question of why this or that is the case) is generally not called into question except, perhaps, in a so-called fundamental crisis of normal science.[28] In the case of the humanities, however, such a fundamental crisis is, in a sense, the normal situation, for here one has always to understand human utterances, works, and actions in the light of their world-interpretation. On the other hand, one also has to interpret the data of the world as those of a historical "*Lebenswelt*" (E. Husserl) in the light of human language games and forms of life. It is just in this fruitful *circle of a transcendental hermeneutic* that, in my opinion, the point of convergence between Dilthey, Heidegger, and the latter Wittgenstein is to be sought. One thus sees that the concept of empathy does not throw much light upon the operation called "verstehen." Taken in psychologistic isolation, as is presupposed by the neo-positivists, it rather leads to overlooking the elementary faculty of *sign-understanding* or *communicative experience* which is at the center of all interpretation in the humanities. It is much more useful for hermeneutics to start from "pragmatical understanding" of signs, actions and circumstances of a situation within the context of a "common sphere" of life, as the later Dilthey did.[29] If one does so, one has however, to take into account that Dilthey's "pragmatical understanding," which comes near to Wittgenstein's idea of understanding within a language game, is not yet understanding in the sense of the humanities, as hermeneutic sciences. Only if the "pragmatical understanding" within the "common sphere" of life becomes doubtful, for example when a crisis in

understanding religious or legal traditions comes about, does *methodical understanding* in the sense of hermeneutics arise, according to Dilthey.[30] And now, when the problem is no longer understanding within the framework of an established language game or "common sphere," but rather finding the access to a foreign language game as a foreign form of life, empathy (*Einfühlung*), as a key to the phenomena of *sense-expression*, also fulfills its heuristic function within the context of hermeneutic methods, as already suggested.[31]

It is now time to close this criticism by asking the question: why, after all, are the neo-positivists prevented from coping with the humanities by those shortcomings which I have tried to reveal? This question may, as a function of my criticism, be divided into three parts.

1) Why do the neo-positivists ignore, in their "logic of science," *philology* in the broadest sense as the heart of the humanities considered as hermeneutic sciences? Why, in particular, do they overlook the fact that these empirico-hermeneutic sciences stand in a close connection to their own meta-scientific business of reconstructing the language of science?

2) Why do the neo-positivists, in the historical and in the social sciences, from the outset overlook the genuine *interest in understanding goals and reasons* as being different from the interest in causal explanation? In other words: why do they beg the question in their discussion with the "theoreticians of understanding" by presupposing that explanation is the aim of understanding, and thus bring about the cup-of-coffee theory of understanding.

3) Why, finally, do the Logical Positivists overlook the fact that the function of understanding lies not only in answering *why*-questions but, more fundamentally, in answering *what*-questions, and that answering these questions is "interwoven" with answering questions as to the meaning of language-signs?

I think that these three questions point to three fundamental shortcomings of neo-positivism that have this in common: they spring from a lack of reflection upon the fact that all cognition of objects presupposes understanding as a means of intersubjective communication. The most curious aspect of this lack of reflection lies in the fact that even the idea of constructing semantical frameworks (as a means of fixing, a priori, the ontological categories implied in a language of science), that even this method of language analysis has not prevented logical positivists from excluding all genuine interest of understanding from their methodology of possible sciences. They, so to speak, try to anticipate the results of intersubjective understanding once and for all in their semantic frameworks, leaving to science only the description and explanation of objective data within the framework they have established. But even this practice would be all right if they were to reflect upon the fact that constructing semantical frameworks has to be conceived as only an indirect way[32] of improving intersubjective communication—a way that always remains dependent upon, and indebted to, understanding and interpreting meaning within the context of communication in natural languages. If they did reflect upon this thoroughly, they would have to acknowledge that behind the construction of semantical frameworks there stand not just irrational *ad hoc* conventions, but long chains of rational discourse mediated by interpretation and criticism of the tradition of philosophy and science. And by reflecting upon this fact they would, furthermore, have to acknowledge that there are "sciences" in a broader sense of the word which make up a continuum with their own meta-scientific language analysis by understanding and interpreting the form and the context of traditional languages. They would thus not try to reduce understanding to an auxiliary function of scientific explanation, as they do in the cup-of-coffee theory, but would rather see the meta-scientific function of understanding already presupposed in all description and explanation of science.

By a consideration of these criticisms, in my opinion, an answer is suggested to our question regarding the shortcomings of the logic of unified science with respect to the humanities: the answer was already anticipated by our first thesis and is only to be illustrated in this paragraph. Methodical solipsism is, so far as I can see, the ultimate, tacit presupposition of the positivists' idea of cognition. It is for this reason that they can only deal with cognition by inference and observation; that is, with cognition as an exchange between man and the world of objects, but not with cognition as understanding and interpretation, that is, primarily with cognition as an exchange between men in a communication-community.

IV. The A priori of Communication and the Foundation of the Humanities

I think that by the preceding explication of my two initial theses concerning methodical solipsisms and its consequences in the philosophy of science, I have already sufficiently suggested my own position to the point where I can now be brief in the exposition of my third thesis: that *the A priori of Language-Communication is*, in fact, the adequate basis for understanding the social function and the methodology of the humanities. I will try to divide this thesis into two partial theses, or figures of argument, the first dealing with intersubjective communication as the ideal frame of the humanities, the second one introducing a methodological restriction on pure hermeneutics, and so perhaps on the humanities themselves, in favor of critical social science.

My first partial thesis starts from the fact that natural science itself, that is, describing and explaining objective spatio-temporal events, presupposes understanding and interpretation in a communication-community, because one man alone cannot follow a rule and thus cannot practice science. From this it follows that understanding and interpretation as means of communication fulfil a complementary function to description and explanation. This means, taking "complementarity" in the sense of N. Bohr, that cognition by objectifying and cognition as intersubjective understanding, supplement and exclude one another at the same time. You can test this phenomenon of *complementarity* in every discussion by trying to "reduce" your partner's utterances to mere verbal behavior (say, in the sense of Skinner). If you succeed in objectifying them in this way, you will lose your partner as a communication-partner and you will need other partners (not yet objectified) to whom to tell the results of your behavioral science. From this I conclude that philosophy of science in a broad sense, including the humanities, has to take into account two quite different, but complementary, leading interests of cognition. Only one of them is that of science in the narrow sense of the modern logic of science, that is, the leading interest of describing and explaining objectified data of the world. I would assume a close connection between this interest of cognition and instrumental labor, that is, operating upon nature as an environment to be adapted to by experimental behavior, learning by trial and error, and so on. In any event, the relation of scientific cognition in this sense to the practice of life is, nowadays, a *technological* one. Now, the other leading interest of cognition, complementary to the interest of an objectifying science, is, in my opinion, the *interest in improving communication in its own dimension of intersubjectivity.*

One has to stress this last remark in our age of science because most people may perhaps be disposed to think that the rational improvement of communication can also be brought about only by objectifying communication itself and by explaining its functions, as is done, partly by information theory and, in a sense, also by linguistics.[33] But I do not think that these narrowly scientific means are the only ways of improving intersubjective communication. In any case, these methods are not the way in which the humanities improve communication. They do so not by objectifying and explaining instruments and functions of communication but by elaborating the very understanding of meaning by methods of interpretation. That there is a decisive difference between this kind of hermeneutic rationalizing of communication and scientific objectifying becomes clear by reflection on the fact that all the objectifying sciences themselves, including linguistics, already presuppose the result of rationalized intersubjective conventions about the meanings of their language and about the aims of their practice. Thus, the hermeneutic preliminaries to meaning-conventions are conditions of the possibility and validity of scientific objectivity and, for this reason, cannot themselves be objective in the same sense that the results of science have to be. Explication of conceptual meanings, for instance, is a precondition for scientific objectivity and therefore cannot presuppose that exchangability and repeatability of subjective operations of cognition which it is predestined to make possible. Instead, it must engage in creative interpretation of ordinary language and of those contexts—mostly of philosophical character—in which the relevant conceptual meanings are already articulated. If one conceives of hermeneutics from this meta-scientific point of view, it becomes clear that the conjectures of understanding cannot be tested in the same way as explanatory hypotheses can. They cannot themselves presuppose fixed meaning-conventions and standards of significance, but in the long run the pragmatic criterion of their validity may be found in their contribution to the formation of meaning-conventions in the interpretation-community.

This leads us to the question of the practical significance of the humanities. If the relation between the objectifying science and the practice of life is a technological one, then the relation between the humanities and the practice of life must also, in my opinion, provide a complementary orientation with regard to technology. This may be performed by the humanities in a twofold manner: first, in a narrower sense, by way of hermeneutics, simply ensuring the understanding of meaning-intentions among people, and not least between scientists and technicians, and between these experts and society as a whole (here, if seems to me, the need for a comprehensive philosophy and history of science as a new, and even paradigmatic, branch of the humanities actually arises); second, in a broader sense, by suggesting world-views and ways of life, that is, ultimate values and possible aims of practice which could provide criteria for discussions and conventions about the requirements of a good life, including the very application of science and technology. And at this point, I would think, all our historical research, all our study of past ages and foreign cultures ought to contribute its results to the shaping and reshaping of an educated public opinion. I cannot imagine that this function of the humanities could be replaced at any time by reducing understanding and interpretation to the method of objectifying science, as is suggested by positivism. On the contrary, I am inclined to think that the need for *intersubjective understanding* in the narrow sense, as well as in the broad sense of goal-orientation, will grow in direct proportion to the growth of science and technology as primary productive forces of modern industrial society.

So much for the first part of my thesis about the *A priori of Communication* as the basis and frame for understanding the social function of the humanities. I will call this first part, for the sake of brevity, the *Thesis of Complementarity*, and I explicitly state my claim that this thesis refutes very kind of *scientistic reductionism*. Nevertheless, I have still to restrict this approach to the humanities by setting forth another thesis, or figure of argument.

It is not literally true that the humanities should never objectify human behavior, that they should, so to speak, deal with men only as co-subjects of communication. Perhaps the closest approximation to this idea which I have summarized in the complementarity thesis, is text-interpretation as the heart of the hermeneutic sciences.

Texts, as so-called "objects" of interpretation, are, in the last analysis, only objectified manifestations of the meaning-intentions of their authors and thus of a communication between human beings which surmounts, so to speak, space and time as the very realm of objectification. But this function of texts in the humanistic dialogue of the great spirits of all ages (to speak with Petrarch and P. Bembo) is already essentially modified if texts are only taken as *documents* ("source" or "remains") by which historians get information about spatio-temporal events. For history must objectify men and their actions in a spatio-temporal frame, and so must a fortiori the generalizing social sciences. It also has to be conceded that history and the social sciences ask not only for the meaning and the reasons of actions and institutions, but also ask for causes of what, in fact, happened or generally happens with men. Now the question arises as to how to deal with these phenomena from the point of view of a philosophy of the humanities.

To prepare for an appropriate answer to this question I will first exclude one type of social science which I would really not consider as an example for the concept of humanities. I mean those behavioral sciences which, in fact, are only interested in causal of statistical explanations and thus have become the basis for social engineering. I am not so much of a romantic as to think that these sciences could be dispensed with in a modern industrial society. Men have to calculate and even technically to manipulate their social behavior in order to survive as members of social systems. But this very concession has to be supplemented, in my opinion, by the urgent demand that all social technology has to be counterchecked by an improvement of intersubjective understanding, complementary of objectifying and manipulating men. Thus the narrowly scientific and technological type of social sciences has itself to be supplemented by another type of *humanistic social science* in order to prevent the very present danger of a technocracy.[34] I might add that, fortunately, in most cases, the human objects of science and social technology show that they are not mere natural objects in their relations to science. If they are able to understand the very theories by which their behavior is objectified and explained, they are able to join, at least in principle, the communication-community of the scientists and social engineers and thus they may emancipate themselves from the status of mere objects of science and technology. I shall come back to this later.

Nevertheless, even a critical and emancipatory type of social science,[35] including history, has to make use not only of understanding meaning-intentions but also of quasi-naturalistic causal explanation within the framework of a historical objectification of human life. The reason for this lies simply in the fact that men are still natural beings, and do not (yet!) really make or shape their own history as a result of their conscious and responsible decisions, but rather undergo history as a result of causally determined processes which evade the control of consciousness. So, in many aspects of their personal lives, and even more so of their social and historical lives, they themselves—or their behavior—lend themselves to being objectified and explained in a quasi-naturalistic way. What, however, does this mean? I now have to introduce the second half of my own conception of an adequate foundation of the humanities, that is, a figure of argument, or of thought, which may supplement and, in a sense, restrict, the thesis of the complementarity of explanation and understanding. (But it has to be noticed that the following restriction of the complementarity thesis presupposes the complementarity of understanding and explanation as an ideal model of what, in fact, must be anticipated in every genuine communication. Only a philosophy which starts out from that idealized distinction may win an adequate idea of what it means to treat human beings as quasi-natural objects of description and quasi-explanation, as is, in fact, possible and necessary; whereas a scientistic philosophy which derives from a naive totalization of our interest in causal explanation does not even *see* a problem in the transition from understanding to quasi-explanation, as may be concluded from Hempel's treatment of pathological behavior explaining as a paradigm for human science.)

We all know by experience that one sometimes can—and even must—unmask hidden motives of human beings, motives hidden to the agents themselves. This can take place in the middle of a conversation, and when that happens, we cannot help suspending the actual intersubjective communication to some extent or for some time, and reduce our partner to an object of description and of quasi-causal explanation. Nevertheless, this need not be the beginning of a natural science of human behavior in the service of social technology, although it, doubtless, may be (for instance in the case of a conditioning psychology which is apt to reduce education to mere drill). There exists, however, quite another possibility— the possibility, so to speak, of the application of quasi-*explanation* in the service of *emancipation*. In order to illustrate this I shall try to give a rough sketch of my conception of the methodology of psychoanalysis, the controversial details of the doctrine being of minor interest in this context.

S. Freud himself, as a physician, tried to understand his method of a new branch of natural science, later to be worked out completely in terms of physiology. And, in fact, there is a good deal of causal explanation according to presupposed drive-mechanisms in his theory, not to speak of the fact that the analyst always has to suspend, in a sense, the normal situation of intersubjective communication with respect to the patient, by objectifying his behavior, especially his neurotic symptoms. Nevertheless, there are, besides this, quite different features of the method which may be characterized as pre-eminently hermeneutic ones. Thus the analyst may never completely break off communication with the analysand, and, in a sense, he even tries to understand and interpret phenomena which a normal hermeneutician would never consider as understandable at all: for instance, the symbolic language of dreams and the purposeful strategy of evading conflicts by taking refuge in illness and, generally, the subconscious processing of experiences reaching back to the earliest days of childhood. So it is not surprising that many reflective psychoanalysts and philosophers, especially of the phenomenological stripe, claimed psychoanalysis to be a hermeneutical method, more precisely a method going beyond normal hermeneutics in the sense of a "depth hermeneutic" (*Tiefenhermeneutik*).

Now, I myself have come to the conclusion that psychoanalysis is neither a natural science nor a purely hermeneutical science. Rather, it incorporates a peculiar methodological model which constitutes the very heart of a branch of humanistic social science which I would call *critical-emancipatory* social science. The point of the model is, in my opinion, the *dialectical mediation* of *communicative understanding*—especially human self-understanding— by the quasi-naturalistic objectification and explanation of human behavior and human history.[36] It is true that the analyst has to objectify the behavior and the life story of the analysand as a quasi-determined section of nature, and he is, so to speak, entitled to this suspending of intersubjective communication by the fact that the patient is not able to communicate about his illness because he is undergoing a partial splitting off or estrangement of his true motives. He himself has, so to speak, objectified these contents of a "virtual communication" by repressing them into the reified pseudo-language of neurotical symptoms. Precisely to the extent that the patient undergoes, for instance, neurotic compulsion in his behavior, he presents himself as an object for causal explanation. But notwithstanding this quasi-naturalistic approach, the analyst, at the same time, tries to *understand* the reactions and the life-story of the patient as—in a way—meaningful, and even as resting on good reasons. He not only does so for himself, but he provokes self-reflection and, so to speak, reorganization of self-understanding in his patient. To that extent he is not concerned with objectifying a human being but, quite on the contrary, with rebuilding his autonomy as a subject of social interaction and intersubjective communication. The proper aim of psychoanalysis as a method—this is the crucial point, in my opinion—does not lie in the nomological deduction of predictions which could be tested by observation, but in the restitution of communication between the analyst and the analysand on a higher level. Thus the object of the analysis should himself confirm the hypotheses of the analyst and even supplement them by his self-understanding. Of course, the verification of the diagnosis would also lie in the elimination of the neurotic symptoms, but this means that the very object of causal explanation would be replaced by a new behavior, no longer compulsive, and therefore *understandable*.

I think that this methodological pattern of *dialectically mediating communicative understanding by methods of causal explanation* is, in fact, the model for a philosophical understanding of all those types of *critical social science* which have their relation to the practice of life, not in the realm of social engineering, but in provoking public self-reflection and in the emancipation of men as subjects. In the light of this idea, I would see, especially, the critique of ideology founded by Marx. By changing over from personal life to the life of the society, of course, a host of new problems arise;[37] nevertheless, the methodological analogies are striking. Within the frame of this paper I can mention only one point, which Habermas has stressed in his "Erkenntnis und Interesse."[38] *Psychoanalysis* as well as *critique* in the sense of Marx, presuppose as their theoretical basis not a universal deductive-nomological model, such as natural science since Newton has sought to realize as its ideal of knowledge. Rather, they presuppose the construction of a story of self-estrangement and possible emancipation, be it of personal life, be it of human history, and these stories must not be conceived as independent of one another, but rather as dialectically mediated by one another. Perhaps it is not unnecessary to point out that the postulated construction of a story as the basis of a *narrative explanation*[39] understanding. And thus it provides, I believe, the very foundation the character of an objectivist dogma in the sense of Popper's *Historicism*. It should rather be a hypothetical sketch which remains within the criticism frame of intersubjective communication and, so far as emancipatory practice is concerned, has the character of a proposal. From this one can conclude, I think, that the *A Priori of Language-Communication*—and of the indefinitive community of interpretation—is, in fact, the basis not only for the *thesis of complementarity* of understanding and explanation but also for the *thesis of dialectic mediation* of understanding of human self-estrangement and liberation, needs not have of the humanities.

Notes

1. Cf. the following of my papers: "Die Entfaltung der 'sprachanalytischen' Philosophie und das Problem der 'Geisteswissenschaft,'" in *Philos. Jahrbuch*, 72. Jg. (1965), pp. 239–89 (English trans.: "Analytic Philosophy of Language and the 'Geisteswissenschaften,'" in *Foundations of Language*, Suppl. series,

vol. 5, Dordrecht-Holland, 1967); "Wittgenstein und das Problem des hermeneutischen Verstehens," in *Zeitschrift für Theologie und Kirche*, 63. Jg. (1966) pp. 49–87; "Szientistik, Hermeneutik, Ideologiekritik: Entwurf einer Wissenschaftslehre in erkenntnisanthropologischer Sicht," in *Wiener Jahrbuch f. Philosophie*, Bd. I (1968), pp. 15–45 (shortened version in *Man and World*, 1968); "Die erkenntnisanthropologische Funktion der Kommunikationsgemeinschaft und die Grundlagen der Hermeneutik," in S. Moser (ed.), *Information und Kommunikation*, München/Wien (1968); "Szientismus oder transzendentale Hermeneutik? Zur Frage nach dem Subjekt der Zeicheninterpretation in der Semiotik des Pragmatismus," in *Hermeneutik und Dialektik*, Festschrift f. H. G. Gadamer, Tübingen (1970), Bd. I, pp. 105–44; "Die Kommunikationsgemeinschaft als transzendentale Voraussetzung der Sozialwissenschaften," in *Neue Hefte für Philosophie*, H. 2 (forthcoming). Cf. further G. Radnitzky, *Contemporary Schools of Metascience*, 2nd Vol.: "Continental Schools," 2nd Göteborg (1970).

2. The difference between Leibniz and the Neo-Leibnizianism of the founders of neo-positivism essentially lies in the fact that the latter do not take over Leibniz' idea that in the light of God's mind also the contingent truths may be demonstrated a priori. Nevertheless Carnap's Logicism and Syntacticism comes often close to the point of a model-Platonism which loses all empirical content.

3. Cf. L. Couturat, *La Logique de Leibniz*, Paris (1901); L. Couturat (ed.), *Opuscules et fragments inédits de Leibniz*, Paris (1903).

4. See L. Wittgenstein, *Philosophical Investigations*, I, par. 199.

5. See J. Royce, *The Problem of Christianity*, New York (1913), vol. 2, pp. 146 ff. Cf. K. O. Apel, "Szientismus oder transzendentale Hermeneutik?" *loc. cit.* (note 1).

6. For an interpretation of the internal connection of Methodical Solipsism with the thesis of extensionality within Logical Atomism, see K. O. Apel, *Analytic Philosophy of Language* (see note 1).

7. Cf. Y. Bar-Hillel, *Aspects of Language*, Jerusalem (1970), p. 364 ff.

8. Cf. J. R. Searie, *Speech Acts*, Cambridge, Mass. (1969).

9. I am here indebted to the ideas of P. Winch, *The Idea of a Social Science and Its Relation to Philosophy*, London (1958), and to unpublished papers of J. Habermas conerning the idea of Communication Competence. Cf. also my booklet, *Analytic Philosophy of Language and the "Geisteswissenschaften,"* *loc. cit.* (note 1).

10. Cf. K. O. Apel, "Das Verstehen. Eine Problemgeschichte als Begriffsgeschichte," in *Archiv f. Begriffsgeschichte*, Bd. I, Bonn (1995), pp. 142–199; cf. further my article, "Verstehen," in J. Ritter (ed.), *Historisches Wörterbuch der Philosophie* (forthcoming).

11. W. Stegmüller has summarized these discussions in his book *Resultate und Probleme der analytischen Philosophie und Wissenschaftstheorie*, Bd. 1: "Erklärung und Begründung," München-Wien-New York (1969).

12. See, for instance, the following definition of A. Comte: "L'explication des faits . . . n'est plus désormais que la liaison établie entre des divers phénomènes particuliers et quelques faits généraux, dont les progrès de la science tendent de plus à diminuer le nombre" (*Cours de Philosophie positive*, tom. I, rère lec.). J. S. Mill defines: "An individual fact is said to be explained, by pointing out its cause, that

is, by stating the law or laws of causation, of which its production is an instance" (*A System of Logic* (1943), Bk. III, Ch. 11, sect. 1).

13. The difference between the meaning-intentions of the author and the expressed meaning of texts, works, or actions constitutes one of the main problems of hermeneutics.

14. See note 10.

15. See note 9.

16. So does, for instance, W. Stegmüller (*l.c.*, p. 360 ff.) following Th. Abel and C. G. Hempel. The standard-presupposition of these authors is formulated by Stegmüller as follows (trans. by K. O. Apel): "The method in question, if it is not to be dismissed as something a priori completely unclear, therefore must be characterized as a procedure for acquiring appropriate explanations, i.e. for acquiring the hypotheses required by those explanations or non-hypothetical insights" (*l.c.*, p. 362).

17. This term ("Erkenntnisinteresse") was introduced by J. Habermas and myself in order to designate a transcendental condition of the possibility and validity of knowledge within the framework of "Wissenschaftstheorie in erkenntnisanthropologischer Sicht." So far the "leading interest of knowing" is not an *external* motivation which would be only psychologically interesting but an *internal* motivation which constitutes the meaning of different questions and so of different possible answers in explanatory and hermeneutic science respectively. See J. Habermas' "Erkenntnis und Interesse" in *Wissenschaft und Technik als Ideologie*, Frankfurt a/M. (1968), and his elaboration upon this in his book *Erkenntnis und Interesse*, Frankfurt a/M. 1968). Cf. K. O. Apek, *Analytic Philosophy of Language and the "Geistestoissenschaften,"* loc. cit., and "Szientistik, Hermeneutik, Ideologiekritik: Entwurf einer Wissenschaftslehre in erkenntnisanthropologischer Sicht," *loc. cit.* (note 1). Cf. also G. Radnitzky, *loc. cit.* (note 1).

18. Cf. Th. Abel, "The Operation called 'Verstehen,'" in H. Feigl and M. Brodbeck (eds.), *Readings in the Philosophy of Science*, New York (1953).

19. C. G. Hempel and P. Oppenheim, "Theory of Scientific Explanation," in *Philosophy of Science*, 15(1948), reprinted in H. Feigl and M. Brodeck (eds.), *loc. cit.*

20. C. G. Hempel and K. Oppenheim, *loc. cit.* p. 330.

21. *Ibid.*, p. 331.

22. See note 9.

23. See W. Dray, *Laws and Explanation in History*, Cambridge (1957).

24. This is true notwithstanding the fact that it is possible and even necessary to countercheck people's utterances—as possible deception or even quasi-delusions—by methods of quasi-explanation and quasi-observation. Cf. our interpretation of the structure of the critique of ideology below.

25. For a comprehensive historical account of hermeneutics, see J. Wach, *Das Verstehen*, 3 vols. Tübingen (1926–33). See further the classical account by W. Dilthey, "Die Entstehung der Hermeneutik" in *Gesammelte Schriften*, Bd. V. pp. 233 ff.

26. See Hempel and Oppenheim, *loc. cit.*, p. 327 f.; cf. Stengmüller, *loc. cit.*, pp. 329 ff. and 530 ff.

27. Cf. G. H. Von Wright, *Explanation and Understanding*, Ithaca, N. Y. (1971) Ch. III.

28. Cf. Th. Kuhn, *The Structure of Scientific Revolutions*, Chicago (1962). In the context of a confrontation of K. Popper's and his own view of science, Th. S. Kuhn sets the following provocative thesis: "In a sense, to turn Sir Karl's view on its head, it is precisely the abandonment of critical discourse that marks the transition to a science. Once a field has made that transition, critical discourse recurs only at moments of crisis when the bases of the field are again in jeopardy. Only when they must choose between competing theories do scientists behave like philosophers" (in I. Lakatos and A. Musgrave (eds.), *Criticism and the Growth of Knowledge*, Cambridge (1970), p. 6. f. It is precisely this transition to "normal science" that is, in my opinion, impossible for the humanities because innovative understanding of the world of human affairs in the light of critical discussion belongs to their very method of cognition.

29. See W. Dilthey, *Gesammelte Schriften*, Bd. VII ("Aufbau der geschichtlichen Welt in den Geisteswissenschaften"), 3rd ed. (1961), pp. 146 f.: "Every single human expression represents something that is common to many and therefore part of the realm of the objective mind. Every work, or sentence, every gesture or form of politeness, every work of art and every historical deed is only understandable, because the person expressing himself and the one understanding him are connected through something they have in common; the individual always thinks, experiences and acts as well as understands in this 'common sphere.'" (Translation by K. O. Apel.)

30. Cf. Dilethy, *loc. cit.*, p. 220 f. Something similar to a genuine crisis of "pragmatical understanding" may be intentionally provoked by an author by means of alienation (*Verfremdung* in the sense of B. Brecht). Thus, already in the level of grammar the ordinary understanding within the framework of a language game may be intentionally impeded by grammatically deviant (for instance, ironic) utterances which compel the reader to impose an *interpretation* on them by reflection on the very rules of the ordinary language games. These hints may suggest that hermeneutic understanding cannot be understood on the basis of Wittgenstein's closed (finite) language games but rather presupposes a reflective transcending of these games according to the regulative principles of the *transcendental* language game of the indefinite Community of Interpretation. Cf. my paper "Die Kommunikationsgemeinschaft als transzendentale Voraussezung der Sozialwissenschaften," *loc. cit.* (see note 1).

31. Cf. K. O. Apel, "Wiltlegenstein und das Problem des hermeneutischen Verstehens," *loc. cit.* (see note 1).

32. Cf. Yehoshua Bar-Hillel, "Argumentation in Pragmatic Languages," *Aspects of Language, loc. cit.*, pp. 206–21.

33. Cf. K. O. Apel, "Noam Chomsky's Sprachtheorie und die Philosophie der Gegenwart," in *Jahrbuch des Instituts für Deutsche Sprache*, Mannheim (1971), (forthcoming). Linguistics is here interpreted as a boundary case between natural science and hermeneutics.

34. Cf. K. O. Apel, "Wissenshaft als Emanzipation?" in *Zeitschrift f. allg. Wissenschafts-theoric*, Bd. I, Heft 2 (1970). All technocracy, of course, presupposes a split society, that is, labor division between the manipulators and the manipulated. This is overlooked by those naive totalizations of behavioral technology as B. F. Skinner's *Beyond Freedom and Dignity*, which cannot answer to the famous question of the young Marx: who educates the educators? (Cf. the second thesis on Feuerbach.)

35. I refer here in particular to what J. Habermas conceives of as "critique" in a neo-Marxist sense and what he associates with a third type of leading interest of knowing—besides technological objectifying and communicative understanding—which he calls "emancipatory." (Cf. note 11).

36. Cf. K. O. Apel, *Analytic Philosophy and the "Geistewissenschaften"*, *loc. cit.*, pp. 25 ff. and 55 ff.; K. O. Apel, "Szientistik, Hermeneutik, Ideologiekritik," *loc. cit.* Cf. also the works of Habermas (see note 11); Alfred Lorenzer, *Sprachzerstörung und Rekonstruktion*, Vorarbeiten zu einer Metatheorie der Psychoanalyse, Frankfurt (1970), and Paul Ricœur, *De l'Interprétation, Essay sur Freud*, Paris (1965).

37. For discussion of these problems cf. Apel/Bormann/Bubner/Gadamer/Giegel/Habermas, *Hermeneutik und Ideologiekritik*, Frankfurt (1971).

38. Cf. J. Habermas, *Erkenntnis und Interesse, loc. cit.*, pp. 315 ff.

39. Cf. also A. C. Danto, *Analytical Philosophy of History*, Cambridge (1955).

14 The Subject and Power

Michel Foucault

Why Study Power? The Question of the Subject

The ideas which I would like to discuss here represent neither a theory nor a methodology.

I would like to say, first of all, what has been the goal of my work during the last twenty years. It has not been to analyze the phenomena of power, nor to elaborate the foundations of such an analysis.

My objective, instead, has been to create a history of the different modes by which, in our culture, human beings are made subjects. My work has dealt with three modes of objectification, which transform human beings into subjects.

The first is the modes of inquiry which try to give themselves the status of sciences; for example, the objectivizing of the speaking subject in *grammaire générale*, philology, and linguistics. Or again, in this first mode, the objectivizing of the productive subject, the subject who labors, in the analysis of wealth and of economics. Or, a third example, the objectivizing of the sheer fact of being alive in natural history or biology.

In the second part of my work, I have studied the objectivizing of the subject in what I shall call "dividing practices." The subject is either divided inside himself or divided from others. This process objectivizes him. Examples are the mad and the sane, the sick and the healthy, the criminals and the "good boys."

Finally, I have sought to study—it is my current work—the way a human being turns himself into a subject. For example, I have chosen the domain of sexuality—how men have learned to recognize themselves as subjects of "sexuality."

Thus, it is not power but the subject which is the general theme of my research.

It is true that I became quite involved with the question of power. It soon appeared to me that, while the human subject is placed in relations of production and of signification, he is equally placed in power relations which are very complex. Now, it seemed to me that economic history and theory provided a good instrument for relations of production and that linguistics and semiotics offered instruments for studying relations of signification; but for power relations we had no tools of study. We had recourse only to ways of thinking about power based on legal models, that is: What legitimates power?

Or, we had recourse to ways of thinking about power based on institutional models, that is: What is the state?

It was therefore necessary to expand the dimensions of a definition of power if one wanted to use this definition in studying the objectivizing of the subject.

Do we need a theory of power? Since a theory assumes a prior objectification, it cannot be asserted as a basis for analytical work. But this analytical work cannot proceed without an ongoing conceptualization. And this conceptualization implies critical thought—a constant checking.

The first thing to check is what I shall call the "conceptual needs." I mean that the conceptualization should not be founded on a theory of the object—the conceptualized object is not the single criterion of a good conceptualization. We have to know the historical conditions which motivate our conceptualization. We need a historical awareness of our present circumstance.

The second thing to check is the type of reality with which we are dealing.

A writer in a well-known French newspaper once expressed his surprise: "Why is the notion of power raised by so many people today? Is it such an important subject? Is it so independent that it can be discussed without taking into account other problems?"

This writer's surprise amazes me. I feel skeptical about the assumption that this question has been raised for the first time in the twentieth century. Anyway, for us it is not only a theoretical question but a part of our experience. I'd like to mention only two "pathological forms"—those two "diseases of power"—fascism and Stalinism. One of the numerous reasons why they are, for us, so puzzling is that in spite of their historical uniqueness they are not quite original. They used and extended mechanisms already present in most other societies. More than that: in spite of their own internal madness, they used to a large extent the ideas and the devices of our political rationality.

What we need is a new economy of power relations—the word "economy" being used in its theoretical and practical sense. To put it in other words: since Kant, the role of philosophy is to prevent reason from going beyond the limits of what is given in experience; but from the same moment—that is, since the development of the modern state and the political management of society—the role of philosophy is also to keep watch over the excessive powers of political rationality, which is a rather high expectation.

Everybody is aware of such banal facts. But the fact that they're banal does not mean they don't exist. What we have to do with banal facts is to discover—or try to discover—which specific and perhaps original problem is connected with them.

The relationship between rationalization and excesses of political power is evident. And we should not need to wait for bureaucracy or concentration camps to recognize the existence of such relations. But the problem is: What to do with such an evident fact?

Shall we try reason? To my mind, nothing would be more sterile. First, because the field has nothing to do with guilt or innocence. Second, because it is senseless to refer to reason as the contrary entity to nonreason. Last, because such a trial would trap us into playing the arbitrary and boring part of either the rationalist or the irrationalist.

Shall we investigate this kind of rationalism which seems to be specific to our modern culture and which originates in *Aufklärung*? I think that was the approach of some of the members of the Frankfurt School. My purpose, however, is not to start a discussion of their works, although they are most important and valuable. Rather, I would suggest another way of investigating the links between rationalization and power.

It may be wise not to take as a whole the rationalization of society or of culture but to analyze such a process in several fields, each with reference to a fundamental experience: madness, illness, death, crime, sexuality, and so forth.

I think that the word "rationalization" is dangerous. What we have to do is analyze specific rationalities rather than always invoke the progress of rationalization in general.

Even if the *Aufklärung* has been a very important phase in our history and in the development of political technology, I think we have to refer to much more remote processes if we want to understand how we have been trapped in our own history.

I would like to suggest another way to go further toward a new economy of power relations, a way which is more empirical, more directly related to our present situation, and which implies more relations between theory and practice. It consists of taking the forms of resistance against different forms of power as a starting point. To use another metaphor, it consists of using this resistance as a chemical catalyst so as to bring to light power relations, locate their position, and find out their point of application and the methods used. Rather than analyzing power from the point of view of its internal rationality, it consists of analyzing power relations through the antagonism of strategies.

For example, to find out what our society means by sanity, perhaps we should investigate what is happening in the field of insanity.

And what we mean by legality in the field of illegality.

And, in order to understand what power relations are about, perhaps we should investigate the forms of resistance and attempts made to dissociate these relations.

As a starting point, let us take a series of oppositions which have developed over the last few years: opposition to the power of men over women, of parents over children, of psychiatry over the mentally ill, of medicine over the population, of administration over the ways people live.

It is not enough to say that these are anti-authority struggles; we must try to define more precisely what they have in common.

1. They are "transversal" struggles; that is, they are not limited to one country. Of course, they develop more easily and to a greater extent in certain countries, but they are not confined to a particular political or economic form of government.
2. The aim of these struggles is the power effects as such. For example, the medical profession is not criticized primarily because it is a profit-making concern but because it exercises an uncontrolled power over people's bodies, their health, and their life and death.

3. These are "immediate" struggles for two reasons. In such struggles people criticize instances of power which are the closest to them, those which exercise their action on individuals. They do not look for the "chief enemy" but for the immediate enemy. Nor do they expect to find a solution to their problem at a future date (that is, liberations, revolutions, end of class struggle). In comparison with a theoretical scale of explanations or a revolutionary order which polarizes the historian, they are anarchistic struggles.

But these are not their most original points. The following seem to me to be more specific.

4. They are struggles which question the status of the individual: on the one hand, they assert the right to be different, and they underline everything which makes individuals truly individual. On the other hand, they attack everything which separates the individual, breaks his links with others, splits up community life, forces the individual back on himself, and ties him to his own identity in a constraining way.

These struggles are not exactly for or against the "individual" but rather they are struggles against the "government of individualization."

5. They are an opposition to the effects of power which are linked with knowledge, competence, and qualification: struggles against the privileges of knowledge. But they are also an opposition against secrecy, deformation, and mystifying representations imposed on people.

There is nothing "scientistic" in this (that is, a dogmatic belief in the value of scientific knowledge), but neither is it a skeptical or relativistic refusal of all verified truth. What is questioned is the way in which knowledge circulates and functions, its relations to power. In short, the *régime du savoir*.

6. Finally, all these present struggles revolve around the question: Who are we? They are a refusal of these abstractions, of economic and ideological state violence, which ignore who we are individually, and also a refusal of a scientific or administrative inquisition which determines who one is.

To sum up, the main objective of these struggles is to attack not so much "such or such" an institution of power, or group, or elite, or class but rather a technique, a form of power.

This form of power applies itself to immediate everyday life which categorizes the individual, marks him by his own individuality, attaches him to his own identity, imposes a law of truth on him which he must recognize and which others have to recognize in him. It is a form of power which makes individuals subjects. There are two meanings of the word "subject": subject to someone else by control and dependence; and tied to his own identity by a conscience or self-knowledge. Both meanings suggest a form of power which subjugates and makes subject to.

Generally, it can be said that there are three types of struggles: either against forms of domination (ethnic, social, and religious); against forms of exploitation which separate individuals from what they produce; or against that which ties the individual to himself and submits him to others in this way (struggles against subjection, against forms of subjectivity and submission).

I think that in history you can find a lot of examples of these three kinds of social struggles, either isolated from each other or mixed together. But even when they are mixed, one of them, most of the time, prevails. For instance, in the feudal societies, the struggles against the forms of ethnic or social domination were prevalent, even though economic exploitation could have been very important among the revolt's causes.

In the nineteenth century, the struggle against exploitation came into the foreground.

And nowadays, the struggle against the forms of subjection—against the submission of subjectivity—is becoming more and more important, even though the struggles against forms of domination and exploitation have not disappeared. Quite the contrary.

I suspect that it is not the first time that our society has been confronted with this kind of struggle. All those movements which took place in the fifteenth and sixteenth centuries and which had the Reformation as their main expression and result should be analyzed as a great crisis of the Western experience of subjectivity and a revolt against the kind of religious and moral power which gave form, during the Middle Ages, to this subjectivity. The need to take a direct part in spiritual life, in the work of salvation, in the truth which lies in the Book—all that was a struggle for a new subjectivity.

I know what objections can be made. We can say that all types of subjection are derived phenomena, that they are merely the consequences of other economic and social processes: forces of production, class struggle, and ideological structures which determine the form of subjectivity.

It is certain that the mechanisms of subjection cannot be studied outside their relation to the mechanisms of exploitation and domination. But they do not merely constitute the "terminal" of more fundamental mechanisms. They entertain complex and circular relations with other forms.

The reason this kind of struggle tends to prevail in our society is due to the fact that, since the sixteenth century, a new political form of power has been continuously developing. This new political structure, as everybody knows, is the state. But most of the time, the state is envisioned as a kind of political power which ignores individuals, looking only at the interests of the totality or, I should say, of a class or a group among the citizens.

That's quite true. But I'd like to underline the fact that the state's power (and that's one of the reasons for its strength) is both an individualizing and a totalizing form of power. Never, I think, in the history of human societies—even in the old Chinese society—has there been such a tricky combination in the same political structures of individualization techniques and of totalization procedures.

This is due to the fact that the modern Western state has integrated in a new political shape an old power technique which originated in Christian institutions. We can call this power technique the pastoral power.

First of all, a few words about this pastoral power.

It has often been said that Christianity brought into being a code of ethics fundamentally different from that of the ancient world. Less emphasis is usually placed on the fact that it proposed and spread new power relations throughout the ancient world.

Christianity is the only religion which has organized itself as a church. And as such, it postulates in principle that certain individuals can, by their religious quality, serve others not as princes, magistrates, prophets, fortune-tellers, benefactors, educationalists, and so on but as pastors. However, this word designates a very special form of power.

1. It is a form of power whose ultimate aim is to assure individual salvation in the next world.

2. Pastoral power is not merely a form of power which commands; it must also be prepared to sacrifice itself for the life and salvation of the flock. Therefore, it is different from royal power, which demands a sacrifice from its subjects to save the throne.

3. It is a form of power which does not look after just the whole community but each individual in particular, during his entire life.

4. Finally, this form of power cannot be exercised without knowing the inside of people's minds, without exploring their souls, without making them reveal their innermost secrets. It implies a knowledge of the conscience and an ability to direct it.

This form of power is salvation oriented (as opposed to political power). It is oblative (as opposed to the principle of sovereignty); it is individualizing (as opposed to legal power); it is coextensive and continuous with life; it is linked with a production of truth—the truth of the individual himself.

But all this is part of history, you will say; the pastorate has, if not disappeared, at least lost the main part of its efficiency.

This is true, but I think we should distinguish between two aspects of pastoral power—between the ecclesiastical institutionalization, which has ceased or at least lost its vitality since the eighteenth century, and its function, which has spread and multiplied outside the ecclesiastical institution.

An important phenomenon took place around the eighteenth century—it was a new distribution, a new organization of this kind of individualizing power.

I don't think that we should consider the "modern state" as an entity which was developed above individuals, ignoring what they are and even their very existence, but, on the contrary, as a very sophisticated structure, in which individuals can be integrated, under one condition: that this individuality would be shaped in a new form and submitted to a set of very specific patterns.

In a way, we can see the state as a modern matrix of individualization or a new form of pastoral power.

A few more words about this new pastoral power.

1. We may observe a change in its objective. It was no longer a question of leading people to their salvation in the next world but rather ensuring it in this world. And in this context, the word "salvation" takes on different meanings: health, well-being (that is, sufficient wealth, standard of living), security, protection against accidents. A series of "worldly" aims took the place of the religious aims of the traditional pastorate, all the more easily because the latter, for various reasons, had followed in an accessory way a certain number of these aims; we only have to think of the role of medicine and its welfare function assured for a long time by the Catholic and Protestant churches.

2. Concurrently the officials of pastoral power increased. Sometimes this form of power was exerted by state apparatus or, in any case, by a public institution such as the police. (We should not forget that in the eighteenth century the police force was not invented only for maintaining law and order, nor for assisting governments in their struggle against their enemies, but for assuring urban supplies, hygiene, health, and standards considered necessary for handicrafts and commerce.) Sometimes the power was exercised by private ventures, welfare societies, benefactors, and generally by philanthropists. But ancient institutions, for example the family, were also mobilized at this time to take on pastoral functions. It was also exercised by complex structures such as medicine, which included private initiatives with the sale of services on market economy principles, but which also included public institutions such as hospitals.

3. Finally, the multiplication of the aims and agents of pastoral power focused the development of knowledge of man around two roles: one, globalizing and quantitative, concerning the population; the other, analytical, concerning the individual.

And this implies that power of a pastoral type, which over centuries—for more than a millennium—had been linked to a defined religious institution, suddenly spread out into the whole social body; it found support in a multitude of institutions. And, instead of a pastoral power and a political power, more or less linked to each other, more or less rival, there was an individualizing "tactic" which characterized a series of powers: those of the family, medicine, psychiatry, education, and employers.

At the end of the eighteenth century, Kant wrote, in a German newspaper—the *Berliner Monatschrift*—a short text. The title was "Was heisst Autklärung?" It was for a long time, and it is still, considered a work of relatively small importance.

But I can't help finding it very interesting and puzzling because it was the first time a philosopher proposed as a philosophical task to investigate not only the metaphysical system or the foundations of scientific knowledge but a historical event—a recent, even a contemporary event.

When in 1784 Kant asked, Was heisst Aufklärung?, he meant, What's going on just now? What's happening to us? What is this world, this period, this precise moment in which we are living?

Or in other words: What are we? as *Aufklärer*, as part of the Enlightenment? Compare this with the Cartesian question: Who am I? I, as a unique but universal and unhistorical subject? I, for Descartes, is everyone, anywhere at any moment?

But Kant asks something else: What are we? in a very precise moment of history. Kant's question appears as an analysis of both us and our present.

I think that this aspect of philosophy took on more and more importance. Hegel, Nietzsche . . .

The other aspect of "universal philosophy" didn't disappear. But the task of philosophy as a critical analysis of our world is something which is more and more important. Maybe the most certain of all philosophical problems is the problem of the present time and of what we are in this very moment.

Maybe the target nowadays is not to discover what we are but to refuse what we are. We have to imagine and to build up what we could be to get rid of this kind of political "double bind," which is the simultaneous individualization and totalization of modern power structures.

The conclusion would be that the political, ethical, social, philosophical problem of our days is not to try to liberate the individual from the state and from the state's institutions but to liberate us both from the state and from the type of individualization which is linked to the state. We have to promote new forms of subjectivity through the refusal of this kind of individuality which has been imposed on us for several centuries.

How Is Power Exercised?

For some people, asking questions about the "how" of power would limit them to describing its effects without ever relating those effects either to causes or to a basic nature. It would make this power a mysterious substance which they might hesitate to interrogate in itself, no doubt because they would prefer *not* to call it into question. By proceeding this way, which is never explicitly justified, they seem to suspect the presence of a kind of fatalism. But does not their very distrust indicate a presupposition that power is something which exists with three distinct qualities: its origin, its basic nature, and its manifestations?

If, for the time being, I grant a certain privileged position to the question of "how," it is not because I would wish to eliminate the questions of "what" and "why," Rather, it is that I wish to present these questions in a different way: better still, to know if it is legitimate to imagine a power which unites in itself a what, a why, and a how. To put it bluntly, I would say that to begin the analysis with a "how" is to suggest that power as such does not exist. At the very least it is to ask oneself what contents one has in mind when using this all-embracing and reifying term; it is to suspect that an extremely complex configuration of realities is allowed to escape when one treads endlessly in the double question: What is power? and Where does power come from? The little question, What happens? although flat and empirical, once scrutinized is seen to avoid accusing a metaphysics or an ontology of power of being fraudulent; rather, it attempts a critical investigation into the thematics of power.

"How," not in the sense of "How does it manifest itself?" but "By what means is it exercised?" and "What happens when individuals exert (as they say) power over others?" As far as this power is concerned, it is first necessary to distinguish that which is exerted over things and gives the ability to modify, use, consume, or destroy them—a power which stems from aptitudes directly inherent in the body or relayed by external instruments. Let us say that here it is a question of "capacity." On the other hand, what characterizes the power we are analyzing is that it brings into play relations between individuals (or between groups). For let us not deceive ourselves; if we speak of the structures or the mechanisms of power, it is only insofar as we suppose that certain persons exercise power over others. The term "power" designates relationships between partners (and by that I am not thinking of a zero-sum game but simply, and for the moment staying in the most general terms, of an ensemble of actions which induce others and follow from one another).

It is necessary also to distinguish power relations from relationships of communication which transmit information by means of a language, a system of signs, or any other symbolic medium. No doubt communicating is always a certain way of acting upon another person or persons. But the production and circulation of elements of meaning can have as their objective or as their consequence certain results in the realm of power; the latter are not simply an aspect of the former. Whether or not they pass through systems of communication, power relations have a specific nature. Power relations, relationships of communication, and objective capacities should not therefore be confused. This is not to say that there is a question of three separate domains. Nor that there is on one hand the field of things, of perfected technique, work, and the transformation of the real; on the other that of signs, communication, reciprocity, and the production of meaning; and finally, that of the domination of the means of constraint, of inequality, and the action of men upon other men.[1] It is a question of three types of relationships which in fact always overlap one another, support one another reciprocally, and use each other mutually as means to an end. The application of objective capacities in their most elementary forms implies relationships of communication (whether in the form of previously acquired information or of shared work); it is tied also to power relations (whether they consist of obligatory tasks, of gestures imposed by tradition or apprenticeship, of subdivisions and the more or less obligatory distribution of labor). Relationships of communication imply finalized activities (even if only the correct putting into operation of elements of meaning) and, by virtue of modifying the field of information between partners, produce effects of power. They can scarcely be dissociated from activities brought to their final term, be they those which permit the exercise of this power (such as training techniques, processes of domination, the means by which obedience is obtained) or those, which in order to develop their potential, call upon relations of power (the division of labor and the hierarchy of tasks).

Of course, the coordination between these three types of relationships is neither uniform nor constant. In a given society there is no general type of equilibrium between finalized activities, systems of communication, and power relations. Rather, there are diverse forms, diverse places, diverse circumstances or occasions in which these interrelationships establish themselves according to a specific model. But there are also "blocks" in which the adjustment of abilities, the resources of communication, and power relations constitute regulated and concerted systems. Take, for example, an educational institution: the disposal of its space, the meticulous regulations which govern its internal life, the different activities which are organized there, the diverse persons who live there or meet one another, each with his own function, his well-defined character—all these things constitute a block of capacity-communication-power. The activity which ensures apprenticeship and the acquisition of aptitudes or types of behavior is developed there by means of a whole ensemble of regulated communications (lessons, questions and answers, orders, exhortations, coded signs of obedience, differentiation marks of the "value" of each person and of the levels of knowledge) and by the means of a whole series of power processes (enclosure, surveillance, reward and punishment, the pyramidal hierarchy).

These blocks, in which the putting into operation of technical capacities, the game of communications, and the relationships of power are adjusted to one another according to considered formulae, constitute what one might call, enlarging a little the sense of the word, "disciplines." The empirical analysis of certain disciplines as they have been historically constituted presents for this very reason a certain interest. This is so because the disciplines show, first, according to artificially clear and decanted systems, the manner in which systems of objective finality and systems of communication and power can be welded together. They also display different models of articulation, sometimes giving preeminence to power relations and obedience (as in those disciplines of a monastic or penitential type), sometimes to finalize activities (as in the disciplines of workshops or hospitals), sometimes to relationships of communication (as in the disciplines of apprenticeship), sometimes also to a saturation of the three types of relationship (as perhaps in military discipline, where a plethora of signs indicates, to the point of redundancy, tightly knit power relations calculated with care to produce a certain number of technical effects).

What is to be understood by the disciplining of societies in Europe since the eighteenth century is not, of course, that the individuals who are part of them become more and more obedient, nor that they set about assembling in barracks, schools, or prisons; rather, that an increasingly better invigilated process of adjustment has been sought after—more and more rational and economic—between productive activities, resources of communication, and the play of power relations.

To approach the theme of power by an analysis of "how" is therefore to introduce several critical shifts in relation to the supposition of a fundamental power. It is to give oneself as the object of analysis power relations and not power itself—power relations which are distinct from objective abilities as well as from relations of communication. This is as much as saying that power relations can be grasped in the diversity of their logical sequence, their abilities, and their interrelationships.

What constitutes the specific nature of power?

The exercise of power is not simply a relationship between partners, individual or collective; it is a way in which certain actions modify others. Which is to say, of course, that something called Power, with or without a capital letter, which is assumed to exist universally in a concentrated or diffused form, does not exist. Power exists only when it is put into action, even if, of course, it is integrated into a disparate field of possibilities brought to bear upon permanent structures. This also means that power is not a function of consent. In itself it is not a renunciation of freedom, a transference of rights, the power of each and all delegated to a few (which does not prevent the possibility that consent may be a condition for the existence or the maintenance of power); the relationship of power can be the result of a prior or permanent consent, but it is not by nature the manifestation of a consensus.

Is this to say that one must seek the character proper to power relations in the violence which must have been its primitive form, its permanent secret, and its last resource, that which in the final analysis appears as its real nature when it is forced to throw aside its mask and to show itself as it really is? In effect, what defines a relationship of power is that it is a mode of action which does not act directly and immediately on others. Instead, it acts upon their actions: an action upon an action, on existing actions or on those which may arise in the present or the future. A relationship of violence acts upon a body or upon things; it forces, it bends, it breaks on the wheel, it destroys, or it closes the door on all possibilities. Its opposite pole can only be passivity, and if it comes up against any resistance, it has no other option but to try to minimize it. On the other hand, a power relationship can only be articulated on the basis of two elements which are each indispensable if it is really to be a power relationship: that "the other" (the one over whom power is exercised) be thoroughly recognized and maintained to the very end as a person who acts; and that, faced with a relationship of power, a whole field of responses, reactions, results, and possible inventions may open up.

Obviously the bringing into play of power relations does not exclude the use of violence any more than it does the obtaining of consent; no doubt the exercise of power can never do without one or the other, often both at the same time. But even though consensus and violence are the instruments or the results, they do not constitute the principle or the basic nature of power. The exercise of power can produce as much acceptance as may be wished for: it can pile up the dead and shelter itself behind whatever threats it can imagine. In itself the exercise of power is not violence; nor is it a consent which, implicitly, is renewable. It is a total structure of actions brought to bear upon possible actions; it incites, it induces, it seduces, it makes easier or more difficult; in the extreme it constrains or forbids absolutely; it is nevertheless always a way of acting upon an acting subject or acting subjects by virtue of their acting or being capable of action. A set of actions upon other actions.

Perhaps the equivocal nature of the term "conduct" is one of the best aids for coming to terms with the specificity of power relations. For to "conduct" is at the same time to "lead" others (according to mechanisms of coercion which are, to varying degrees, strict) and a way of behaving within a more or less open field of possibilities.[2] The exercise of power consists in guiding the possibility of conduct and putting in order the possible outcome. Basically power is less a confrontation between two adversaries or the linking of one to the other than a question of government. This word must be allowed the very broad meaning which it had in the sixteenth century. "Government" did not refer only to political structures or to the management of states; rather, it designated the way in which the conduct of individuals or of groups might be directed: the government of children, of souls, of communities, of families, of the sick. It did not only cover the legitimately constituted forms of political or economic subjection but also modes of action, more or less considered or calculated, which were destined to act upon the possibilities of action of other people. To govern, in this sense, is to structure the possible field of action of others. The relationship proper to power would not, therefore, be sought on the side of violence or of struggle, nor on that of voluntary linking (all of which can, at best, only be the instruments of power), but rather in the area of the singular mode of action, neither warlike nor juridical, which is government.

When one defines the exercise of power as a mode of action upon the actions of others, when one characterizes these actions by the government of men by other men—in the broadest sense of the term—one includes an important element: freedom. Power is exercised only over free subjects, and only insofar as they are free. By this we mean individual or collective subjects who are faced with a field of possibilities in which several ways of behaving, several reactions and diverse comportments, may be realized. Where the determining factors saturate the whole, there is no relationship of power; slavery is not a power relationship when man is in chains. (In this case it is a question of a physical relationship of constraint.) Consequently, there is no face-to-face confrontation of power and freedom, which are mutually exclusive (freedom disappears everywhere power is exercised), but a much more complicated interplay. In this game freedom may well appear as the condition for the exercise of power (at the same time its precondition, since freedom must exist for power to be exerted, and also its permanent support, since without the possibility of recalcitrance, power would be equivalent to a physical determination).

The relationship between power and freedom's refusal to submit cannot, therefore, be separated. The crucial problem of power is not that of voluntary servitude (how could we seek to be slaves?). At the very heart of the power relationship, and constantly provoking it, are the recalcitrance of the will and the intransigence of freedom. Rather than speaking of an essential freedom, it would be better to speak of an "agonism"[3]—of a relationship which is at the same time reciprocal incitation and struggle, less of a face-to-lace confrontation which paralyzes both sides than a permanent provocation.

How is one to analyze the power relationship?

One can analyze such relationships, or rather I should say that it is perfectly legitimate to do so, by focusing on carefully defined institutions. The latter constitute a privileged point of observation, diversified, concentrated, put in order, and carried through to the highest point of their efficacity. It is here that, as a first approximation, one might expect to see the appearance of the form and logic of their elementary mechanisms. However, the analysis of power relations as one finds them in certain circumscribed institutions presents a certain number of problems. First, the fact that an important part of the mechanisms put into operation by an institution are designed to ensure its own preservation brings with it the risk of deciphering functions which are essentially reproductive, especially in power relations between institutions. Second, in analyzing power relations from the standpoint of institutions, one lays oneself open to seeking the explanation and the origin of the former in the latter, that is to say, finally, to explain power to power. Finally, insofar as institutions act essentially by bringing into play two elements, explicit or tacit regulations and an apparatus, one risks giving to one or the other an exaggerated privilege in the relations of power and hence to see in the latter only modulations of the law and of coercion.

This does not deny the importance of institutions on the establishment of power relations. Instead, I wish to suggest that one must analyze institutions from the standpoint of power relations, rather than vice versa, and that the fundamental point of anchorage of the relationships, even if they are embodied and crystallized in an institution, is to be found outside the institution.

Let us come back to the definition of the exercise of power as a way in which certain actions may structure the field of other possible actions. What, therefore, would be proper to a relationship of power is that it be a mode of action upon actions. That is to say, power relations are rooted deep in the social nexus, not reconstituted "above" society as a supplementary structure whose radical effacement one could perhaps dream of. In any case, to live in society is to live in such a way that action upon other actions is possible—and in fact ongoing. A society without power relations can only be an abstraction. Which, be it said in passing, makes all the more politically necessary the analysis of power relations in a given society, their historical formation, the source of their strength or fragility, the conditions which are necessary to transform some or to abolish others. For to say that there cannot be a society without power relations is not to say either that those which are established are necessary or, in any case, that power constitutes a fatality at the heart of societies, such that it cannot be undermined. Instead, I would say that the analysis, elaboration, and bringing into question of power relations and the "agonism" between power relations and the intransitivity of freedom is a permanent political task inherent in all social existence.

The analysis of power relations demands that a certain number of points be established concretely:

1. *The system of differentiations* which permits one to act upon the actions of others: differentiations determined by the law or by traditions of status and privilege; economic

differences in the appropriation of riches and goods, shifts in the processes of production, linguistic or cultural differences, differences in know-how and competence, and so forth. Every relationship of power puts into operation differentiations which are at the same time its conditions and its results.

2. *The types of objectives* pursued by those who act upon the actions of others: the maintenance of privileges, the accumulation of profits, the bringing into operation of statutary authority, the exercise of a function or of a trade.

3. *The means of bringing power relations into being*: according to whether power is exercised by the threat of arms, by the effects of the word, by means of economic disparities, by more or less complex means of control, by systems of surveillance, with or without archives, according to rules which are or are not explicit, fixed or modifiable, with or without the technological means to put all these things into action.

4. *Forms of institutionalization*: these may mix traditional predispositions, legal structures, phenomena relating to custom or to fashion (such as one sees in the institution of the family); they can also take the form of an apparatus closed in upon itself, with its specific *loci*, its own regulations, its hierarchical structures which are carefully defined, a relative autonomy in its functioning (such as scholastic or military institutions); they can also form very complex systems endowed with multiple apparatuses, as in the case of the state, whose function is the taking of everything under its wing, the bringing into being of general surveillance, the principle of regulation, and, to a certain extent also, the distribution of all power relations in a given social ensemble.

5. *The degrees of rationalization*: the bringing into play of power relations as action in a field of possibilities may be more or less elaborate in relation to the effectiveness of the instruments and the certainty of the results (greater or lesser technological refinements employed in the exercise of power) or again in proportion to the possible cost (be it the economic cost of the means brought into operation or the cost in terms of reaction constituted by the resistance which is encountered). The exercise of power is not a naked fact, an institutional right, nor is it a structure which holds out or is smashed: it is elaborated, transformed, organized; it endows itself with processes which are more or less adjusted to the situation.

One sees why the analysis of power relations within a society cannot be reduced to the study of a series of institutions, not even to the study of all those institutions which would merit the name "political." Power relations are rooted in the system of social networks. This is not to say, however, that there is a primary and fundamental principle of power which dominates society down to the smallest detail; but, taking as point of departure the possibility of action upon the action of others (which is coextensive with every social relationship), multiple forms of individual disparity, of objectives, of the given application of power over ourselves or others, of, in varying degrees, partial or universal institutionalization, of more or less deliberate organization, one can define different forms of power. The forms and the specific situations of the government of men by one another in a given society are multiple;

they are superimposed, they cross, impose their own limits, sometimes cancel one another out, sometimes reinforce one another. It is certain that in contemporary societies the state is not simply one of the forms or specific situations of the exercise of power—even if it is the most important—but that in a certain way all other forms of power relation must refer to it. But this is not because they are derived from it; it is rather because power relations have come more and more under state control (although this state control has not taken the same form in pedagogical, judicial, economic, or family systems). In referring here to the restricted sense of the word "government," one could say that power relations have been progressively governmentalized, that is to say, elaborated, rationalized, and centralized in the form of, or under the auspices of, state institutions.

Relations of power and relations of strategy.
The word "strategy" is currently employed in three ways. First, to designate the means employed to attain a certain end; it is a question of rationality functioning to arrive at an objective. Second, to designate the manner in which a partner in a certain game acts with regard to what he thinks should be the action of the others and what he considers the others think to be his own; it is the way in which one seeks to have the advantage over others. Third, to designate the procedures used in a situation of confrontation to deprive the opponent of his means of combat and to reduce him to giving up the struggle; it is a question, therefore, of the means destined to obtain victory. These three meanings come together in situations of confrontation—war or games—where the objective is to act upon an adversary in such a manner as to render the struggle impossible for him. So strategy is defined by the choice of winning solutions. But it must be borne in mind that this is a very special type of situation and that there are others in which the distinctions between the different senses of the word "strategy" must be maintained.

Referring to the first sense I have indicated, one may call power strategy the totality of the means put into operation to implement power effectively or to maintain it. One may also speak of a strategy proper to power relations insofar as they constitute modes of action upon possible action, the action of others. One can therefore interpret the mechanisms brought into play in power relations in terms of strategies. But most important is obviously the relationship between power relations and confrontation strategies. For, if it is true that at the heart of power relations and as a permanent condition of their existence there is an insubordination and a certain essential obstinacy on the part of the principles of freedom, then there is no relationship of power without the means of escape or possible flight. Every power relationship implies, at least *in potentia*, a strategy of struggle, in which the two forces are not superimposed, do not lose their specific nature, or do not finally become confused. Each constitutes for the other a kind of permanent limit, a point of possible reversal. A relationship of confrontation reaches its term, its final moment (and the victory of one of the two adversaries), when stable mechanisms replace the free play of antagonistic reactions. Through such mechanisms one can direct, in a fairly constant manner and with reasonable certainty, the conduct of others. For a relationship of confrontation, from the moment it is not a struggle to the death, the fixing of a power relationship becomes a target—at one and the same time its fulfillment and its suspension. And in return, the strategy of struggle also constitutes a frontier for the relationship of power, the line at which, instead of manipulating and inducing actions in a calculated manner, one must be content with reacting to them after the event. It would not be possible for power relations to exist without points of insubordination which, by definition, are means of escape. Accordingly, every intensification, every extension of power relations to make the insubordinate submit can only result in the limits of power. The latter reaches its final term either in a type of action which reduces the other to total impotence (in which case victory over the adversary replaces the exercise of power) or by a confrontation with those whom one governs and their transformation into adversaries. Which is to say that every strategy of confrontation dreams of becoming a relationship of power, and every relationship of power leans toward the idea that, if it follows its own line of development and comes up against direct confrontation, it may become the winning strategy.

In effect, between a relationship of power and a strategy of struggle there is a reciprocal appeal, a perpetual linking and a perpetual reversal. At every moment the relationship of power may become a confrontation between two adversaries. Equally, the relationship between adversaries in society may, at every moment, give place to the putting into operation of mechanisms of power. The consequence of this instability is the ability to decipher the same events and the same transformations either from inside the history of struggle or from the standpoint of the power relationships. The interpretations which result will not consist of the same elements of meaning or the same links or the same types of intelligibility, although they refer to the same historical fabric, and each of the two analyses must have reference to the other. In fact, it is precisely the disparities between the two readings which make visible those fundamental phenomena of "domination" which are present in a large number of human societies.

Domination is in fact a general structure of power whose ramifications and consequences can sometimes be found descending to the most recalcitrant fibers of society. But at the same time it is a strategic situation more or less taken for granted and consolidated by means of a long-term confrontation between adversaries. It can certainly happen that the fact of domination may only be the transcription of a mechanism of power resulting from confrontation and its consequences (a political structure stemming from invasion); it may also be that a relationship of struggle between two adversaries is the result of power relations with the conflicts and cleavages which ensue. But what makes the domination of a group, a caste, or a class, together with the resistance and revolts which that domination comes up against, a central phenomenon in the history of societies is that they manifest in a massive and universalizing form, at the level of the whole social body, the locking together of power relations with relations of strategy and the results proceeding from their interaction.

Notes

1. When Jürgen Habermas distinguishes between domination, communication, and finalized activity, I do not think that he sees in them three separate domains but rather three "transcendentals."

2. Foucault is playing on the double meaning in French of the verb *conduire*, "to lead" or "to drive," and *se conduire*, "to behave" or "to conduct oneself"; whence *la conduite*, "conduct" or "behavior."—Translator's note.

3. Foucault's neologism is based on the Greek ἀγώνισμα meaning "a combat." The term would hence imply a physical contest in which the opponents develop a strategy of reaction and of mutual taunting, as in a wrestling match.—Translator's note.

15 An Eye at the Edge of Discourse

Catherine Malabou

> If one looks at the etymology, one finds that to denote directed vision French resorts to the word *regard* [gaze], whose root originally referred not to the act of seeing but to expectation, concern, watchfulness, consideration, and safeguard, made emphatic by the addition of a prefix expressing a redoubling or return. *Regarder* [to look at, to gaze upon] is a movement that aims to recapture, *reprendre sous garde* [to place in safekeeping once again]. Starobinski (1961/1989, p. 2)

I'd like to talk about a strange state of vision: *the vision of thought.* What is it to *see* a thought? To see a thought coming? To be present at its emergence, at the moment when it is still no more than a promise, plan, or sketch, but is already strong enough to live? What is it to see before writing, when a brand-new thought can already be apprehended sensibly, sensually, like a body? How should we approach that strange state of half-carnal, half-intelligible vision that oversees the torments of the text even as it establishes the suspended spatial presence of the text?

I am interested in the *schema* of discourse, where *schema* is understood in terms of the famous meaning Kant gave it as "a general procedure of the imagination for procuring an image for a concept" (1781/1965, p. 183). What I want to explore first of all are the processes by which a thought, an idea, or an intellectual motive allows itself to be figured before adhering to a definitive form. The second objective of this analysis is to explore these processes in the light of a philosophical fracture prevalent throughout the 20th century among thinkers who questioned a particular conception of the connection between the idea and the sensible, between idealization and writing, or between concept and text.

French philosophers such as Lyotard, Deleuze, Derrida, and Levinas, as well as writers such as Blanchot, to cite only a few, consider the question of the space and time of thought, as well as the sensibility of the idea, as central to their work, even as they redefine the notion of intellectual visibility. In the philosophical tradition, to see thought designates the actual act of contemplation. This is the Platonic meaning of *theoria*: The idea, by definition, is that which allows itself to be seen as an image (*eidos*) and the soul is the eye that apprehends it, in other words, receives it without ever inventing, creating, or forming it. In the traditional conception of thought, the visibility of thought is defined in terms of transcendence: The Idea is visible because it comes from elsewhere to impose itself on the mind as a phenomenon that the mind must welcome, interiorize, and make its own.

What happens to the possibility of seeing thought when this conception of transcendence, which implies that the ideal object is given as an absolute referent outside the intellect, is faced with a radical challenge? What happens when the visibility of thought is no longer ontologically guaranteed by the transcendence of the object? What happens when vision is enclosed by the limits of discourse and writing, with no real outside? How does thought figure itself when the figurable and thinkable, to draw a distinction between them, are nonetheless *coalescent*?[1]

We must assume that there is "an eye at the edge of discourse," to borrow an expression from Jean-François Lyotard's book, *Discours, figure* (1985/2006, p. 38). This eye is not mine, nor is it yours; it is not the eye of a subject or of a subject able to see herself[2] think. Instead, the eye is the eye of discourse itself, an optical arrangement that language brings up to its edge through its structure, so that talking gives birth to the visibility of its subject matter. The eye that borders discourse does see something other than discourse, but this "other thing" can only be envisaged as a function of discourse. This is another way of saying that language actually opens and founds that from which all too often it is thought to derive: namely, referentiality. The word that destines saying and seeing to each another is inscribed originally in their regard for each other. Thus, as Lyotard claims, "Language is not a homogenous milieu; it is divisive because it exteriorizes the sensible opposite itself" (1985, p. 83, my translation). The distance that both separates and brings together language and subject matter is, therefore, not a distance prior to language; it is not the prelinguistic gap regulating the relation of word to thing outside of language and without it. The distance is in fact given with language, from the outset. "The world is a function of language (. . .) all speech constitutes that which it designates in the world, as a thick object to synthesize, as an object to decode" (1985, p. 129, my translation).

However, this is not to say that language has the power to make things exist. Its demiurgical powers are not of this order. In fact, language begins by making things disappear since to speak is to reveal the possibility of naming things in their absence, while also naming the absence. To speak is to lose. But in this instance, to be able to lose is also to be able to see, to be able to see what one loses, and to be able to say that one sees it. The "world-function" of discourse, which ensures the constancy and possible evanescence of the world itself, is thus precisely what Lyotard means by the "distance where the eye settles at the edge of discourse" (1985, p. 129, my translation).

Before returning to our topic, other elements of the analysis are required: What is it to see a thought? How does a thought announce itself sensibly? To start with, it is worth noting that if the eye that settles at the edge of discourse comes from discourse, then to see another thought must designate one of the ways in which language both sees and schematizes itself. The question is then that of knowing how—and here we grasp the full meaning of Lyotard's title *Discours, figure*—language renders itself both discourse *and* figure, and how it unfolds in both linguistic *and* figural space.

Lyotard insists that it is a matter of unfolding. From the opening lines of his book, he shows that to recognize the presence of an eye in discourse in no way implies that "the given [is] a text" (1985, p. 9, my translation) or that the world is a book that can be reduced to linguistic units simply awaiting decoding. Far from it. The claim that language renders visible that to which it refers implies—and this is the function of this strange, foreign external eye—that what is irreducibly given is the heterogeneity (call it different nature, if you like) of discourse and figure, saying and form. Language involves a necessary spatial manifestation, but Lyotard says that this "cannot incorporate without being shaken" (1985/2006, p. 37). If the figure is not outside discourse, in the transcendent sense referred to above, it nevertheless constitutes the other of discourse within discourse, "an exteriority that cannot be interiorized as *signification*" (Lyotard, 1985/2006, p. 37). This exteriority, which is the thickness of the figural, is the sensible, opaque expanse in which thought is formed. The figural never offers itself as a simple signifier, the sensible reflection of ideality. Its very dependence makes it autonomous in relation to discourse, inasmuch as it is never more than *another* mode of being of the idea.

There is, therefore, an originary violence at work in language, causing an irremissible schism between discourse and figure, sense and sensible, and idea and flesh. Given this, when we ask what it means "to see a thought," we must examine the distortion between the sayable as a gaping tear, rent at the edge of language, and sound out the power of the eye, which is both language and look, without being one more than the other. To see a thought rise, to stand at the edge of its creation, to watch the figure of a new idea necessarily amounts to an intensification of the originary spectacle of language, to an opening of the eye twice by attempting to localize the eye of discourse, to give it form—the form of style, writing, and volume. Thus, Lyotard says that art generally goes "from the interior of discourse [. . .] into the figure" (1985/2006, p. 37). "The [artistic] figure is a deformation that imposes another form on the arrangement of linguistic units" (1985, p. 61, my translation). Lyotard shows that this other form is expressed in an infinite variety of forms in painting, fiction, poetry, and pure energy, "which folds, which crumples and creases the text and makes a work from it" (1985/2006, p. 39).

If one sticks to the presence of the idea in writing, one might then wonder how, by envisaging itself, thought can figure its own gaze. In *Difference and Repetition*, Deleuze (1968/1984) presents this figuring as a *mise-en-scène*, a *dramatization*. Essentially, he says that the schema is a "dramatization of the Idea" whose goal is to "specify" and "incarnate" it (1968/1984, p. 218).[3]

To see a thought is thus to specify it in the figural. But just as there is an irreducible distortion in language between discourse and figure, as I explained above, there is also an irreducible distortion between thought and form. In other words, there is neither speculation nor reflection between the two. Instead, the mirroring is breached, there is a breach of reflexivity, to the point that when thought allows itself to be seen, it is always revealed as unrecognizable, unknowable, taking the form of an outsider whose face is not an immediately identifiable reflection, even though it is visible, hence the invariable angst of writing.

Nevertheless, to see a thought is really to face a mirror game in which the relation between seeing and seen moves very quickly. In *The Space of Literature*, Blanchot (1955/1982) describes this movement as the opening of the realm of *fascination*. It is true that when thought allows itself to be seen, the eye of discourse catches sight of itself between word and figure, thus reflecting itself. As Blanchot says, it is precisely "the mirror image" grasping "one's own look" (1955/1982, p. 32), and thus "a vision that never comes to an end," "what one sees seizes sight and renders it interminable, [. . .] the gaze coagulates into light, [and] light is the absolute gleam of an eye one doesn't see but which one doesn't cease to see" precisely because it is "the mirror image of one's own look" (1955/1982, p. 32). The space between our eye and what it sees, in other words, once again, between our eye and itself, is the milieu of fascination. "Of whoever is fascinated it can be said that he doesn't perceive any real object, any real figure, for what he sees does not belong to the world of reality, but to the indeterminate milieu of fascination" (1955/1982, pp. 32–33).

In some respects, to see a thought amounts to seeing, to figuring, absence, because a thought, as Blanchot puts it, "points us constantly back to the presence of absence [. . .] to absence as its own affirmation" (1955/1982, p. 23). Perhaps then the idea, the very process of thought, consists in nothing more than this fascinating materialization of absence, which gives the impression that when one is thinking, *someone* is there; that the eye, at the edge of discourse, sees someone's face:

When I am alone, I am not alone, but, in this present, I am already returning to myself in the form of Someone. Someone is there, where I am alone. The fact of being alone is my belonging to this dead time which is not my time, or yours, or the time we share in common, but Someone's time. Someone is what is still present when there is no one. (Blanchot, 1955/1982, p. 24)

Idealization appears as presence, in solitude, of solitude. What the eye sees at the edge of discourse is the essence of solitude, namely a gaze fascinated by the fact of being captured by itself alone. At the same time, this presence, this someone, is a paradoxical figure of anonymity and impersonality. To see thought as someone is to see absence in person; that is, as much as it is to see no one, it is also to touch the limits of the figurable.

Consequently, this speculative dissymmetry, where the eye is not pointed back to something, but instead is pointed to its own mirage, i.e., to the impossibility of the face—caricature, Levinas (1995, pp. 129–137) would say—inverts the seeing and the seen. In the end, how do we know that it is not the idea that gazes upon us at the very moment we think we see it? Could we write without feeling gazed upon? The staring function of thought could be called the *superego*. How can we have ideas without satisfying the demands of the ideal self? A psychic function could be assigned to this searching power of the idea through which the eye of discourse in some senses turns back against its subject. But it is not clear that this spying scenario translates so easily, as it deconstitutes the subject instead of constituting it, thereby introducing into the narcissistic loop the sharp edge of a blade that threatens to take out the subject's eyes.

Thus, the staring *idée fixe* deconstitutes the subject. What does this mean? One might think that the original question, "what is it to see a thought?" implies analyzing a process of becoming, describing a thought's movement of maturation, indissociable from figurability. But in fact it all looks as if even as the thought is born, it was always more mature than us, which is why it stares at us. Furthermore, even when we think that we are modeling it, it has the power to deform or deface us. Scrutinized by the idea, we unfurl ourselves before it, returning to a liminal, embryonic, presubjective state through the very activity of thinking or creating. In *Difference and Repetition*, Deleuze claims

It is true that every Idea turns us into larvae, having put aside the identity of the I along with the resemblance of the self. This is badly described as a matter of regression, fixation, or arrestation of development, for we are never fixed at a moment or in a given state but always fixed by an Idea as though in the glimmer of a look, always fixed in a movement that is under way. (1968/1984, p. 219)

The stare of the idea is, therefore, not only a gaze but is truly a process of fixing, a sight taken of the becoming of one who thinks, a sight that momentarily fixes the thinker in an identity without simultaneously sending it back a self-image, that is, without giving it the possibility of saying *I* or *me*; it is even less a superego.

There is so much to say about this moment before the subject, the moment of these identity limbos to which the idea binds us with its stare. Inevitably, it evokes childhood. Doesn't one always feel infantilized on seeing a thought? Doesn't one always feel unmasked as the child one always was? And doesn't the idea always have our mother's eyes? Blanchot writes:

Perhaps the force of the maternal figure receives its intensity from the very force of fascination, and one might say then, that if the mother exerts this fascinating attraction it is because, appearing when the child lives altogether in fascination's gaze, she concentrates in herself all the powers of enchantment. It is because the child is fascinated that the mother is fascinating, and that is also why all the impressions of early childhood have a kind of fixity which comes from fascination. (1955/1982, pp. 26–27)

Blanchot describes the bond connecting the fascination of childhood with the fascination of writing; even if it is maternal, the face of the idea is no less impersonal: "Whoever is fascinated doesn't see, properly speaking, what he sees. Rather, it touches him in an immediate proximity; it seizes and ceaselessly draws him close, even though it leaves him absolutely at a distance. Fascination is fundamentally linked to neutral, impersonal presence, to the indeterminate They, the immense, faceless Someone" (1955/1982, p. 27).

The figure of the mother in the idea is always the photograph of an absence. Like my mother, the idea gazes at me, starting from the possibility of her disappearance, for we are always as afraid of losing an idea as we are of losing our mother.

Perhaps also, like a mother, the idea always threatens us with its disappointment. When we feel her harsh stare and regress before it, falling back into childhood, isn't that because we are as afraid of disappointing our idea as we were and will always be of disappointing our mother? A passage from *In Search of Lost Time* (Proust, 1919/2002) comes to mind. The hero is in Venice with his mother. She is waiting for him at the hotel, and from the balcony she sees him returning from a walk. Her anxious face appears behind the "multicolored" marble balusters, as if framed by a window, or rather, an arch. When the hero sees his mother looking at him like this, he is taken back to his childhood, which is also to return to the impossibility of writing. His mother's eyes harbor tenderness and disappointment at once. Tenderness: "[A]s soon as I called to her from the gondola, she sent out to me, from the bottom of her heart, a love which stopped only where there was no longer any corporeal matter to sustain it, on the surface of her impassioned gaze which she brought as close to me as possible" (Proust, 1954/1993, p. 847). Disappointment: "Of this sort was the window in our hotel behind the balusters of which my mother sat waiting for me, gazing at the canal with a patience which she would not have displayed in the old days at Combray, at a time when, cherishing hopes for my future which had never been realised, she was unwilling to let me see how much she loved me. Nowadays she was well aware that an apparent coldness on her part would alter nothing, and the affection she lavished upon me was like those forbidden foods which are no longer withheld from invalids when it is certain that they are past recovery" (Proust, 1954/1993, pp. 845–846).

The idea stares hard at us, with the cruelty of disappointed love, but without this cruelty it is impossible to write. For it is impossible to think without feeling helpless, that is, stripped naked by a gaze. This ravishing, this capturing of the I, which skins it, also results from the fact that even as she feels herself gazed at by that which she tries to see and figure, the child subject does not really see that which looks at her. Thus, the principle behind all writing, in its ideality as well as in its figurability, is the *confession*, whose form and paradox was expressed so powerfully by St. Augustine: Why should I confess to God if he already knows everything? St. Augustine's question shows that although God is watching me, I do not see him looking at me, which is why I confess to him, and why, in the end, I am and remain a child. All imaginative writing processes must therefore take the form of *blind* figuration, that of a blind person who cannot see what is staring at her even as she feels stripped naked by a gaze. All confessions assume that the Other, someone, already knows what I am going to say and that I am egged on to say it, so to speak, without being able to turn round. The idea watches me from behind, at my back, because as we know since Hegel, all conscience is constituted and deconstituted precisely by this *a tergo* perspective. This explains why Blanchot describes the writer as Orpheus, as the one who cannot turn back. In the night of hell, the impossibility of turning round renders "distance sensible." Yet, Orpheus is also the one who cannot not turn back. Essentially fallible, he gives in exactly to the temptation of the desire to see that which fascinates him, the desire to figure the eye that sees him, and the desire to stand face-to-face with him, and it is this specular weakness that kills him.

The attempt to see thought can also be seen as leading to the figuration of a secret. One can only write once that which is our most personal possession—our ideas, our plans—actually become secret, hidden from ourselves. It is worth recalling that, etymologically, secret means "separated," "withdrawn," "hidden from sight." The secret of the eye at the edge of discourse, the secret that the eye jealously guards by giving it form, is therefore that which is both closest and farthest from the one who tries to see the thought or to see herself think. Derrida devoted some essential analyses to the problem of the secret, in which he suggests that the writer or thinker is carried—put into gear, into action—by the secret of her own work, which is both unknown and unknowable to her.

To write always amounts, therefore, to simultaneously revealing and keeping the secret. It reveals the secret because one can only write under its dictation; yet, writing also keeps the secret, as the revelation does not exhaust and cannot dry up the mystery of the eye that looks, but that one cannot see. The more the secret is revealed, made manifest, the more it is kept—in the same way that a criminal or suspect feels protected in the public space of a crowd.

The inherent, well-known paradox of the secret, that one is never better hidden than by the visible, inevitably raises the ethical question of *responsibility*. Let us start again from the impossible face-to-face encounter between the eye on the edge of discourse that looks and one that tries to look to see the thought. There is no speculation, no reflection between them. I see nothing. Yet, from this nonvision or lack of foresight, one might say, responsibility is born, in the strict sense of the possibility of responding. To keep and to reveal a secret is always to respond: to answer *it* by revealing it, to answer *for it* by keeping it. To try to see the thought, thus, always results in seeing the structure of responsibility, in its very invisibility. Analyzing the structure of compassion, Derrida writes,

[An eye] looks at me and I don't see him and it is on the basis of this gaze that singles me out [*ce regard qui me regarde*] that my responsibility comes into being. Thus is instituted or revealed the "it concerns me" or "it's my lookout [*ça me regarde*] that leads me to say, 'it is my business, my affair [. . .] that will nevertheless be mine and which I alone will have to answer for.'" (1992/1995, p. 91)

So, "it's my concern." This gaze that gazes at me without my knowing what it sees, at the very moment when I am trying to see it, this gaze that is the gaze of the idea, with the double meaning of the genitive: the idea watched and the idea watching. This gaze of the idea makes me responsible for the idea at the very moment that the gaze frees me of responsibility as this eye is not mine, it is always that of another, of the Other. Derrida asks:

How can another see into me, into my most secret self, without my being able to see in there myself and without my being able to see him in me? And if my secret self, that which can be revealed only to the other, to the wholly other, to God if you wish, is a secret that I will never reflect on, that I will never know or experience or possess as my own, then what sense is there in saying that it is "my" secret? (1992/1995, p. 92)

Indeed, if the eye stares at me although I am unable to envisage it, then my thought is not mine, it is not my own. At the same time, because it is not mine, because it belongs to the Other, I must keep it as my own, as a treasure in transit, as if I had to hand it in, give it back before leaving, return it to the Other, in other words, make it public. This then is my responsibility.

I'll conclude by asking again: What is it to see a thought? What should I call this embryo of form, which exists without existing, which starts to live, and which scrutinizes everything even as it hides itself? As we know, Levinas (1965/1969) calls this strange presence of absence, or presence of the Other, the *face*. The meaning he gives this concept enables the joining of the two axes I have shown in relation to the vision of thought. On the one hand, it is the speaking being, as a thinker, who sees what he thinks starting from an eye at the edge of discourse. For Levinas in *Totality and Infinity*, as for Lyotard, discourse shows and thereby shows *itself*: "Better than comprehension, *discourse* relates with what remains essentially transcendent" (Levinas, 1965/1969, p. 195). Discourse puts thought outside itself, thus allowing thought to see itself. At the same time, by throwing thought out, discourse separates itself from thought in an absolute manner, digging an irreducible distance between thought and that which it figures in the distance: "Absolute difference, inconceivable in terms of formal logic, is established only by language. Language accomplishes a relation between terms that breaks up the unity of a genus" (Levinas, 1965/1969, p. 195). Thought, therefore, sees itself as another. On this basis, it succeeds in putting itself at a distance, as if it were objectivizing itself. But in separating itself in this manner, it also loses itself. Its own epiphany or revelation is a face. *Its own* face, but also thereby necessarily *a* face staring at it, which is no longer its own, but that of an other, that of the Other. The face appears; yet, one cannot grasp it. It reveals itself but prohibits the face-to-face encounter or symmetry. It is a phenomenon, yet exceeds any image. It refuses to be possessed. It escapes my vision, yet looks at me and calls me to the highest responsibility: "The other absolutely other—the Other—[calls for] responsibility" (Levinas, 1965/1969, p. 197). Levinas concludes that this structure of visibility–invisibility is *the very structure of ethics*.

To formulate my question, I began by unfolding discourse and figure. This led me to understand their proximity and distance within the face. The answer to my opening question is now clear: What the eye of discourse sees, what it sees of thought, is a particular figure, namely a face. It is a complex figure, which imagines and stares; which is someone, yet is no one; which is both me and other; which is secret and public; which withdraws (to hell, for example), yet which is in the world. It calls me to answer. The figure is the face of alterity. Before concluding, however, I ask myself, do *figure* and *face*[4] designate the *same* thing? I have shifted between one and the other—discourse-figure, discourse-face—as if they were one and the same. But even in the introduction to his book, Lyotard (1985) differentiates the concept of *figure* from the concept of *face*. Levinas too is careful to draw a rigorous distinction between figure and face. What is at stake is the meaning of *form*. For Lyotard, the face as defined by Levinas lacks form, it appears as a pure event without a contour and hence in the end without materiality. In *Totality and Infinity*, Levinas says, "[T]he face [. . .] breaks through the form that nevertheless delimits it" (1965/1969, p. 198). The face "explodes form," that is, the contours of figure and face that we usually take as synonymous with it. If indeed the face sees the eye of discourse when it tries to look at thought, then it is possible that it sees nothing and that in the end all thought dissipates. As Lyotard says in the opening section of *Discourse, figure*: "To want to make oneself a partisan of the event, an official of the event, is again an ethical illusion. Donation has the character of disempowering us; we cannot appoint ourselves to this disempowering" (1985, p. 23). In other words, not to want to figure or not to want to take the Other in form amounts to missing the Other.

Does the eye that sees thought see a figure or a face? The development of this single question has led me to posit the apparently irreconcilable difference between the two concepts, if they are indeed two concepts. Does the eye of thought see a form, or does it just see something that starts from the explosion of all form?

I have not spoken about what I might name, pretentiously, my own thought. Nor shall I talk about it; I only mention it in conclusion. I am working on the concept of plasticity, which refers to both the formation of the figure and the explosion of all form. Should we not turn to this concept to attempt to think through figure and face together, to try to see thought in the process of grasping itself? This is an open-ended question, to which I shall not respond, as it is no doubt too early to do so, for I have only just begun to be able to see myself think.

Notes

1. Coalescence: from the Latin *coalescere*, "to grow with." The knitting of two tissue surfaces that are in contact (for instance, two lips of a wound); a state of liquid particles in suspension joined in larger droplets; contraction of two or more phonic elements in a single element (*Le Robert Dictionary*, 1994, p. 395).

2. Note from the translator: An intentional choice was made to use *herself* rather than the gender-neutral *himself* or *herself*. This is a political move, intended to inscribe both author and translator as women in the text; furthermore, given the personal voice of the article, this choice also made stylistic sense.

3. Deleuze explains further that it is "a pure staging without author, without actors and without subjects" (1968/1984, p. 219).

4. In French, *figure* and *visage* have the same general meaning, but *face* is less "plastic" than *figure*, which means something more designed, more shaped (as in painting), than does *face*. This is why Levinas always uses *face* and never *figure*.

References

Blanchot, M. (1982). *The space of literature* (A. Smock, Trans.). Lincoln: University of Nebraska Press. (Original work published 1955)

Deleuze, G. (1984). *Difference and repetition* (P. Patton, Ttrans.). New York: Columbia University Press. (Original work published 1968)

Derrida, J. (1995). *The gift of death* (D. Wills, Trans.). Chicago: University of Chicago Press. (Original work published 1992)

Kant, I. (1965). *Critique of pure reason* (unabridged edition, N. K. Smith, Trans.). New York: Bedford/ St. Martin's Press. (Original work published in 1781)

Le Robert Dictionary. (1994). Paris: Le Dictionnaire Robert SNL.

Levinas, E. (1969). *Totality and infinity* (A. Lingis, Trans.). Pittsburgh, PA: Duquesne University Press.

Levinas, E. (1995). Interdit de la représentation et "Droits de 1'homme." In P. Hayat (Ed.), *Altérité et transcendence*. Montpellier, France: Fata Morgana.

Lyotard, J.-F. (1985). *Discours, figure*. Paris: Klincksieck.

Lyotard, J.-F. (2006). Taking the side of the figural (M. Sinclair, Trans.). In K. Crome and J. Williams (Eds.), *The Lyotard reader and guide*. New York: Columbia University Press.

Proust, M. (1993). *The fugitive* (C. K. Scott Moncrieff and T. Kilmartin, Trans.). New York: The Modern Library. (Original work published 1954)

Proust, M. (2002). *In search of lost time* (C. Prendergast, Ed.). London: Allen Lane. (Original work published 1919)

Starobinski, J. (1989). *The living eye* (A. Goldhammer, Trans.). Cambridge, MA: Harvard University Press. (Original work published 1961)

IV Writing, Meaning, Context

Ludwig Wittgenstein

1. "Cum ipsi (majores homines) appellabant rem aliquam, et cum secundum eam vocem corpus ad aliquid movebant, videbam, et tenebam hoc ab eis vocari rem illam, quod son- abant, cum eam vellent ostendere. Hoc autem eos velle ex motu corporis aperiebatur: tamquam verbis naturalibus omnium gentium, quae fiunt vultu et nutu oculorum, cetero- rumque membrorum actu, et sonitu vocis indicante affectionem animi in petendis, haben- dis, rejiciendis, fugiendisve rebus. Ita verba in variis sententiis locis suis posita, et crebro audita, quarum rerum signa essent, paulatim colligebam, measque jam voluntates, edomito in eis signis ore, per haec enuntiabam." (Augustine, *Confessions*, I. 8.)[1]

These words, it seems to me, give us a particular picture of the essence of human lan- guage. It is this: the individual words in language name objects—sentences are combinations of such names.——In this picture of language we find the roots of the following idea: Every word has a meaning. This meaning is correlated with the word. It is the object for which the word stands.

Augustine does not speak of there being any difference between kinds of word. If you describe the learning of language in this way you are, I believe, thinking primarily of nouns like "table," "chair," "loaf," and of people's names, and only secondarily of the names of certain actions and properties; and of the remaining kinds of word as something that will take care of itself.

Now think of the following use of language: I send someone shopping. I give him a slip marked "five red apples." He takes the slip to the shopkeeper, who opens the drawer marked "apples"; then he looks up the word "red" in a table and finds a colour sample opposite it; then he says the series of cardinal numbers—I assume that he knows them by heart—up to the word "five" and for each number he takes an apple of the same colour as the sample out of the drawer.——It is in this and similar ways that one operates with words.——"But how does he know where and how he is to look up the word 'red' and what he is to do with the word 'five'?"——Well, I assume that he *acts* as I have described. Explanations come to an end somewhere.—But what is the meaning of the word "five"?—No such thing was in question here, only how the word "five" is used.

2. That philosophical concept of meaning has its place in a primitive idea of the way language functions. But one may also say that it is the idea of a language more primitive than ours.

Let us imagine a language for which the description given by Augustine is right. The language is meant to serve for communication between a builder A and an assistant B. A is building with building-stones: there are blocks, pillars, slabs and beams. B has to pass the stones, and that in the order in which A needs them. For this purpose they use a language consisting of the words "block," "pillar," "slab," "beam." A calls them out;—B brings the stone which he has learnt to bring at such-and-such a call.——Conceive this as a complete primitive language.

3. Augustine, we might say, does describe a system of communication; only not everything that we call language is this system. And one has to say this in many cases where the question arises "Is this an appropriate description or not?" The answer is: "Yes, it is appropriate, but only for this narrowly circumscribed region, not for the whole of what you were claiming to describe."

It is as if someone were to say: "A game consists in moving objects about on a surface according to certain rules . . ."—and we replied: You seem to be thinking of board games, but there are others. You can make your definition correct by expressly restricting it to those games.

4. Imagine a script in which the letters were used to stand for sounds, and also as signs of emphasis and punctuation. (A script may be conceived as a language for describing sound-patterns.) Now imagine someone interpreting that script as if there were simply a correspondence of letters to sounds and as if the letters had not also completely different functions. Augustine's conception of language is like such an over-simple conception of the script.

5. If we look at the example in §1, we may perhaps get an inkling how much this general notion of the meaning of a word surrounds the working of language with a haze which makes clear vision impossible. It disperses the fog to study the phenomena of language in primitive kinds of application in which one can command a clear view of the aim and functioning of the words.

A child uses such primitive forms of language when it learns to talk. Here the teaching of language is not explanation, but training.

6. We could imagine that the language of §2 was the *whole* language of A and B; even the whole language of a tribe. The children are brought up to perform *these* actions, to use *these* words as they do so, and to react in *this* way to the words of others.

An important part of the training will consist in the teacher's pointing to the objects, directing the child's attention to them, and at the same time uttering a word; for instance, the word "slab" as he points to that shape. (I do not want to call this "ostensive defini-tion," because the child cannot as yet *ask* what the name is. I will call it "ostensive teaching of words."——I say that it will form an important part of the training, because it is so with human beings; not because it could not be imagined otherwise.) This ostensive teaching of words can be said to establish an association between the word and the thing. But what does this mean? Well, it may mean various things; but one very likely thinks first of all that a picture of the object comes before the child's mind when it hears the word. But now, if this does happen—is it the purpose of the word?—Yes, it *may* be the purpose.—I can imagine such a use of words (of series of sounds). (Uttering a word is like striking a note on the keyboard of the imagination.) But in the language of §2 it is *not* the purpose of the words to evoke images. (It may, of course, be discovered that that helps to attain the actual purpose.)

But if the ostensive teaching has this effect,—am I to say that it effects an understanding of the word? Don't you understand the call "Slab!" if you act upon it in such-and-such a way?—Doubtless the ostensive teaching helped to bring this about; but only together with a particular training. With different training the same ostensive teaching of these words would have effected a quite different understanding.

"I set the brake up by connecting up rod and lever."—Yes, given the whole of the rest of the mechanism. Only in conjunction with that is it a brake-lever, and separated from its support it is not even a lever; it may be anything, or nothing.

7. In the practice of the use of language (2) one party calls out the words, the other acts on them. But in instruction in the language the following process will occur: the learner names the objects; that is, he utters the word when the teacher points to the stone.—And there will be this still simpler exercise: the pupil repeats the words after the teacher——both of these being processes resembling language.

We can also think of the whole process of using words in (2) as one of those games by means of which children learn their native language. I will call these games "language-games" and will sometimes speak of a primitive language as a language-game.

And the processes of naming the stones and of repeating words after someone might also be called language-games. Think of much of the use of words in games like ring-a-ring-a-roses.

I shall also call the whole, consisting of language and the actions into which it is woven, a "language-game."

8. Let us now look at an expansion of language (2). Besides the four words "block," "pillar," etc., let it contain a series of words used as the shopkeeper in (1) used the numer-als (it may be the series of letters of the alphabet); further, let there be two words, which may as well be "there" and "this" (because this roughly indicates their purpose), that are used in connexion with a pointing gesture; and finally a number of colour samples. A

gives an order like: "d—slab—there." At the same time he shows the assistant a colour sample, and when he says "there" he points to a place on the building site. From the stock of slabs B takes one for each letter of the alphabet up to "d," of the same colour as the sample, and brings them to the place indicated by A.—On other occasions A gives the order "this—there." At "this" he points to a building-stone. And so on.

9. When a child learns this language, it has to learn the series of "numerals" a, b, c, . . . by heart. And it has to learn their use.—Will this training include ostensive teaching of the words?—Well, people will, for example, point to slabs and count: "a, b, c slabs."—Something more like the ostensive teaching of the words "block," "pillar," etc. would be the ostensive teaching of numerals that serve not to count but to refer to groups of objects that can be taken in at a glance. Children do learn the use of the first five or six cardinal numerals in this way.

Are "there" and "this" also taught ostensively?—Imagine how one might perhaps teach their use. One will point to places and things—but in this case the pointing occurs in the *use* of the words too and not merely in learning the use.—

10. Now what do the words of this language *signify*?—What is supposed to shew what they signify, if not the kind of use they have? And we have already described that. So we are asking for the expression "This word signifies *this*" to be made a part of the description. In other words the description ought to take the form: "The word . . . signifies . . . "

Of course, one may for short describe the use of the word "slab" by saying that this word signifies this object. This will be done when, for example, it is merely a matter of removing the mistaken idea that the word "slab" refers to the shape of building-stone that we in fact call a "block"—but apart from this point it is already known what sort of "*referring*" this is—that is, how these words are used.

Equally one may say that the signs "a," "b," etc. signify numbers; when for example this removes the mistaken idea that "a," "b," "c," play the part actually played in language by "block," "slab," "pillar." And one may also say that "c" means this number and not that one; when for example this serves to explain that the letters are to be used in the order a, b, c, d, etc. and not in the order a, b, d, c.

But assimilating the descriptions of the uses of words in this way cannot make the uses themselves any more like one another. For, as we see, they are absolutely unlike.

11. Think of the tools in a tool-box: there is a hammer, pliers, a saw, a screw-driver, a rule, a glue-pot, glue, nails and screws.—The functions of words are as diverse as the functions of these objects. (And in both cases there are similarities.)

Of course, what confuses us is the uniform appearance of words when we hear them spoken or meet them in script and print. For their *application* is not presented to us so clearly. Especially when we are doing philosophy!

12. It is like looking into the cabin of a locomotive. We see handles all looking more or less alike. (Naturally, since they are all supposed to be handled.) But one is the handle of a crank which can be moved continuously (it regulates the opening of a valve); another is the handle of a switch, which has only two effective positions, it is either off or on; a third is the handle of a brake-lever, the harder one pulls on it, the harder it brakes; a fourth, the handle of a pump: it has an effect only so long as it is moved to and fro.

13. When we say: "Every word in language signifies something" we have so far said *nothing whatever*; unless we have explained exactly *what* distinction we wish to make. (It might be, of course, that we wanted to distinguish the words of language (8) from words "without meaning" such as occur in Lewis Carroll's poems, or words like "Lilliburlero" in songs.)

14. Imagine someone's saying: "*All* tools serve to modify something. Thus a hammer modifies the position of a nail, a saw the shape of a board, and so on."—And what is modified by a rule, a glue-pot, and nails?—"Our knowledge of a thing's length, the temperature of the glue, and the solidity of a box."—Would anything be gained by this assimilation of expressions?—

15. The word "to signify" is perhaps used in the most straightforward way when the object signified is marked with the sign. Suppose that the tools A uses in building bear certain marks. When A shows his assistant such a mark, he brings the tool that has that mark on it.

It is in this and more or less similar ways that a name means and is given to a thing.—It will often prove useful in philosophy to say to ourselves: naming something is like attaching a label to a thing.

16. What about the colour samples that A shows to B: are they part of the *language*? Well, it is as you please. They do not belong among the words; yet when I say to someone: "Pronounce the word 'the,'" you will count the second "the" as part of the sentence. Yet it has a role just like that of a colour-sample in the language-game (8); that is, it is a sample of what the other is meant to say.

It is most natural, and causes least confusion, to reckon the samples among the instruments of the language.

((Remark on the reflexive pronoun "*this* sentence."))

17. It will be possible to say: In language (8) we have different *kinds of word*. For the functions of the word "slab" and the word "block" are more alike than those of "slab" and "d." But how we group words into kinds will depend on the aim of the classification,—and on our own inclination.

Think of the different points of view from which one can classify tools or chess-men.

18. Do not be troubled by the fact that languages (2) and (8) consist only of orders. If you want to say that this shows them to be incomplete, ask yourself whether our language is complete;—whether it was so before the symbolism of chemistry and the notation of the infinitesimal calculus were incorporated in it; for these are, so to speak, suburbs of our language. (And how many houses or streets does it take before a town begins to be a town?) Our language may be seen as an ancient city: a maze of little streets and squares, of old and new houses, and of houses with additions from various periods; and this surrounded by a multitude of new boroughs with straight regular streets and uniform houses.

19. It is easy to imagine a language consisting only of orders and reports in battle.—Or a language consisting only of questions and expressions for answering yes and no. And innumerable others.——And to imagine a language means to imagine a life-form.

But what about this: is the call "Slab!" in example (2) a sentence or a word?—If a word, surely it has not the same meaning as the like-sounding word of our ordinary language, for in §2 it is a call. But if a sentence, it is surely not the elliptical sentence: "Slab!" of our language.——As far as the first question goes you can call "Slab!" a word and also a sentence; perhaps it could be appropriately called a "degenerate sentence" (as one speaks of a degenerate hyperbola); in fact it *is* our "elliptical" sentence.—But that is surely only a shortened form of the sentence "Bring me a slab," and there is no such sentence in example (2).—But why should I not on the contrary have called the sentence "Bring me a slab" a *lengthening* of the sentence "Slab!"?—Because if you shout "Slab!" you really mean: "Bring me a slab."—But how do you do this: how do you *mean that* while you *say* "Slab!"? Do you say the unshortened sentence to yourself? And why should I translate the call "Slab!" into a different expression in order to say what someone means by it? And if they mean the same thing—why should I not say: "When he says 'Slab!' he means 'Slab!'"? Again, if you can mean "Bring me the slab," why should you not be able to mean "Slab!"?——But when I call "Slab!," then what I want is, *that he should bring me a slab*!——Certainly, but does "wanting this" consist in thinking in some form or other a different sentence from the one you utter?—

20. But now it looks as if when someone says "Bring me a slab" he could mean this expression as *one* long word corresponding to the single word "Slab!"——Then can one mean it sometimes as one word and sometimes as four? And how does one usually mean it?——I think we shall be inclined to say: we mean the sentence as *four* words when we use it in contrast with other sentences such as "*Hand* me a slab," "Bring *him* a slab," "Bring *two* slabs," etc.; that is, in contrast with sentences containing the separate words of our command in other combinations.——But what does using one sentence in contrast with others consist in? Do the others, perhaps, hover before one's mind? *All* of them? And *while* one is saying the one sentence, or before, or afterwards?—No. Even if such an explanation rather tempts us, we need only think for a moment of what actually happens in order to see that we are going astray here. We say that we use the command in contrast with other sentences because

our language contains the possibility of those other sentences. Someone who did not understand our language, a foreigner, who had fairly often heard someone giving the order: "Bring me a slab!," might believe that this whole series of sounds was one word corresponding perhaps to the word for "building-stone" in his language. If he himself had then given this order perhaps he would have pronounced it differently, and we should say: he pronounces it so oddly because he takes it for a *single* word.——But then, is there not also something different going on in him when he pronounces it,—something corresponding to the fact that he conceives the sentence as a *single* word?——Either the same thing may go on in him, or something different. For what goes on in you when you give such an order? Are you conscious of its consisting of four words *while* you are uttering it? Of course you have a *mastery* of this language—which contains those other sentences as well—but is this having a mastery something that *happens* while you are uttering the sentence?—And I have admitted that the foreigner will probably pronounce a sentence differently if he conceives it differently; but what we call his wrong conception *need* not lie in anything that accompanies the utterance of the command.

The sentence is "elliptical," not because it leaves out something that we think when we utter it, but because it is shortened—in comparison with a particular paradigm of our grammar.—Of course one might object here: "You grant that the shortened and the unshortened sentence have the same sense.—What is this sense, then? Isn't there a verbal expression for this sense?"——But doesn't the fact that sentences have the same sense consist in their having the same *use*?—(In Russian one says "stone red" instead of "the stone is red"; will the copula be missing in the sense, or as they attach it in *thought*?)

21. Imagine a language-game in which A asks and B reports the number of slabs or blocks in a pile, or the colours and shapes of the building-stones that are stacked in such-and-such a place.—Such a report might run: "Five slabs." Now what is the difference between the report or statement "Five slabs" and the order "Five slabs!"?—Well, it is the part which uttering these words plays in the language-game. No doubt the tone of voice and the look with which they are uttered, and much else besides, will also be different. But we could also imagine the tone's being the same—for an order and a report can be spoken in a *variety* of tones of voice and with various expressions of face—the difference being only in the application. (Of course, we might use the words "statement" and "command" to stand for grammatical forms of sentence and intonations; we do in fact call "Isn't the weather glorious to-day?" a question, although it is used as a statement.) We could imagine a language in which *all* statements had the form and tone of rhetorical questions; or every command the form of the question "Would you like to . . . ? " Perhaps it will then be said: "What he says has the form of a question but is really a command,"—that is, has the function of a command in the technique of using the language. (Similarly one says "You will do this" not as a prophecy but as a command. What makes it the one or the other?)

22. Frege's idea that every assertion contains an assumption,* which is the thing that is asserted, really rests on the possibility found in our language of writing every statement in the form: "It is asserted that such-and-such is the case."—But "that such-and-such is the case" is *not* a sentence in our language—so far it is not a *move* in the language-game. And if I write, not "It is asserted that . . . ," but "It is asserted; such-and-such is the case," the words "It is asserted" simply become superfluous.

We might very well also write every statement in the form of a question followed by a "Yes"; for instance: "Is it raining? Yes!" Would this show that every statement contained a question?

Of course we have the right to use an assertion sign in contrast with a question-mark, for example, or if we want to distinguish an assertion from a fiction or a supposition. It is only a mistake if one thinks that the assertion consists of two actions, entertaining and asserting (assigning the truth-value, or something of the kind), and that in performing these actions we follow the propositional sign roughly as we sing from the musical score. Reading the written sentence aloud or to oneself is indeed comparable with singing from a musical score, but "*meaning*" (thinking) the sentence that is read is not.

Frege's assertion sign marks the *beginning of the sentence*. Thus its function is like that of the full-stop. It distinguishes the whole period from a clause *within* the period. If I hear someone say "it's raining" but do not know whether I have heard the beginning and end of the period, so far this sentence does not serve to tell me anything.

23. But how many kinds of sentence are there? Say assertion, question, and command?— There are *countless* kinds: countless different kinds of use of what we call "symbols," "words," "sentences." And this multiplicity is not something fixed, given once for all; but new types of language, new language-games, as we may say, come into existence, and others become obsolete and get forgotten. (We can get a *rough picture* of this from the changes in mathematics.)

Here the term "*language-game*" is meant to bring into prominence the fact that the *speaking* of language is part of an activity, or of a life-form.

Review the multiplicity of language-games in the following examples, and in others:
Giving orders, and obeying them—
Describing the appearance of an object, or giving its measurements—
Constructing an object from a description (a drawing)—
Reporting an event—
Speculating about the event—
Forming and testing a hypothesis—

---

* Imagine a picture representing a boxer in a particular stance. Now, this picture may be used to tell someone how he should stand, should hold himself; or how he should not hold himself; or how a particular man did stand in such-and-such a place; and so on. One might (using the language of chemistry) call this picture a proposition-radical. This will be how Frege thought of the "assumption."

Presenting the results of an experiment in tables and diagrams—
Making up a story; and reading it—
Play-acting—
Singing catches—
Guessing riddles—
Making a joke; telling it—
Solving a problem in practical arithmetic—
Translating from one language into another—
Requesting, thanking, cursing, greeting, praying.
—It is interesting to compare the multiplicity of the tools in language and of the ways they are used, the multiplicity of kinds of word and sentence, with what logicians have said about the structure of language. (Including the author of the *Tractatus Logico-Philosophicus*.)

24. If you do not keep the multiplicity of language-games in view you will perhaps be inclined to ask questions like: "What is a question?"—Is it the statement that I do not know such-and-such, or the statement that I wish the other person would tell me . . . ? Or is it the description of my mental state of uncertainty?—And is the cry "Help!" such a description?

Think how many different kinds of thing are called "description": description of a body's position by means of its co-ordinates; description of a facial expression; description of a sensation of touch; of a mood.

Of course it is possible to substitute the form of statement or description for the usual form of question: "I want to know whether . . ." or "I am in doubt whether . . ."—but this does not bring the different language-games any closer together.

The significance of such possibilities of transformation, for example of turning all statements into sentences beginning "I think" or "I believe" (and thus, as it were, into descriptions of *my* inner life) will become clearer in another place. (Solipsism.)

※　※　※

37. What is the relation between name and thing named?—Well, what *is* it? Look at language-game (2) or at another one: there you can see the sort of thing this relation consists in. This relation may also consist, among many other things, in the fact that hearing a name calls before our mind the picture of what is named; and it also consists, among other things, in the name's being written on the thing named or being pronounced when that thing is pointed at.

38. But what, for example, is the word "this" the name of in language-game (8) or the word "that" in the ostensive definition "that is called . . ."?—If you do not want to produce confusion you will do best not to call these words names at all.—Yet, strange to say, the word "this" has been called the only *genuine* name; so that anything else we call a name was one only in an inexact, approximate sense.

This queer conception springs from a tendency to sublime the logic of our language—as one might put it. The proper answer to it is: we call very different things "names"; the word "name" is used to characterize many different kinds of use of a word, related to one another in many different ways;—but the kind of use that "this" has is not among them.

It is quite true that, in giving an ostensive definition for instance, we often point to the object named and say the name. And similarly, in giving an ostensive definition for instance, we say the word "this" while pointing to a thing. And also the word "this" and a name often occupy the same position in a sentence. But it is precisely characteristic of a name that it is defined by means of the demonstrative expression "That is N" (or "That is called 'N'"). But do we also give the definitions: "That is called 'this,'" or "This is called 'this'"?**

This is connected with the conception of naming as, so to speak, an occult process. Naming appears as a *queer* connexion of a word with an object.—And you really get such a queer connexion when a philosopher tries to bring out *the* relation between name and thing by staring at an object in front of him and repeating a name or even the word "this" innumerable times. For philosophical problems arise when language *goes on holiday*. And *here* we may indeed fancy naming to be some remarkable act of mind, as it were a baptism of an object. And we can also say word "this" *to* the object, as it were *address* the object as "this"—a queer use of this word, which doubtless only occurs in doing philosophy.

39. But why does it occur to one to want to make precisely this word into a name, when it evidently is *not* a name?—That is just the reason. For one is tempted to make an objection against what is ordinarily called a name. It may be put like this: *a name ought really to signify a simple*. And for this one might perhaps give the following reasons: The word "Excalibur," say, is a proper name in the ordinary sense. The sword Excalibur consists of parts combined in a particular way. If they are combined differently Excalibur does not exist. But it is clear that the sentence "Excalibur has a sharp blade" makes *sense* whether Excalibur is still whole or is broken up. But if "Excalibur" is the name of an object, this object no longer exists when Excalibur is broken in pieces; and as no object would then correspond to the name it would have no meaning. But then the sentence "Excalibur has a sharp blade" would contain a word that had no meaning, and hence the sentence would be nonsense. But it does make sense;

** What is it to *mean* the words "*That* is blue" at one time as a statement about the object one is pointing to—at another as an explanation of the word "blue"? Well, in the second case one really means "That is called 'blue.'"—Then can one at one time mean the word "is" as "is called" and the word "blue" as "blue," and another time mean "is" really as "is"?

It is also possible for someone to get an explanation of the words out of what was intended as a piece of information. [Marginal note: Here lurks a crucial superstition.]

Can I say "bububu" and mean "If it doesn't rain I shall go for a walk"?—It is only in a language that I can mean something by something. This shows clearly that the grammar of "to mean" is not like that of the expression "to imagine" and the like.

so there must always be something corresponding to the words of which it consists. So the word "Excalibur" must disappear when the sense is analysed and its place be taken by words which name simples. It will be reasonable to call these words the real names.

40. Let us first discuss *this* point of the argument: that a word has no meaning if nothing corresponds to it.—It is important to note that the word "meaning" is being used illicitly if it is used to signify the thing that "corresponds" to the word. That is to confound the meaning of a name with the *bearer* of the name. When Mr. N.N. dies one says that the bearer of the name dies, not that the meaning dies. And it would be nonsensical to say that, for if the name ceased to have meaning it would make no sense to say "Mr. N.N. is dead."

41. In §15 we introduced proper names into language (8). Now suppose that the tool with the name "N" is broken. Not knowing this, A gives B the sign "N." Has this sign meaning now or not?—What is B to do when he is given it?—We have not settled anything about this. One might ask: what *will* he do? Well, perhaps he will stand there at a loss, or show A the pieces. Here one might say: "N" has become meaningless; and this expression would mean that the sign "N" no longer had a use in our language-game (unless we gave it a new one). "N" might also become meaningless because, for whatever reason, the tool was given another name and the sign "N" no longer used in the language-game.—But we could also imagine a convention whereby B has to shake his head in reply if A gives him the sign belonging to a tool that is broken.—In this way the command "N" might be said to be given a place in the language-game even when the tool no longer exists, and the sign "N" to have meaning even when its bearer ceases to exist.

✳ ✳ ✳

111. The problems arising through a misinterpretation of our forms of language have the character of *depth*. They are deep disquietudes; their roots are as deep in us as the forms of our language and their significance is as great as the importance of our language.—Let us ask ourselves: why do we feel a grammatical joke to be *deep*? (And that is what the depth of philosophy is.)

112. A simile that has been absorbed into the forms of our language produces a false appearance, and this disquiets us. "But *this* isn't how it is!"—we say. "Yet *this* is how it has to *be!*"

113. "But *this* is how it is—" I say to myself over and over again. I feel as though, if only I could fix my gaze absolutely sharply on this fact, get it in focus, I must grasp the essence of the matter.

114. (*Tractatus Logico-Philosophicus*, 4.5): "The general form of propositions is: This is how things are."—That is the kind of proposition that one repeats to oneself countless times. One thinks that one is tracing the outline of the thing's nature over and over again, and one is merely tracing round the frame through which we look at it.

115. A *picture* held us captive. And we could not get outside it, for it lay in our language and language seemed to repeat it to us inexorably.

116. When philosophers use a word—"knowledge," "being," "object," "I," "proposition," "name"—and try to grasp the *essence* of the thing, one must always ask oneself: is the word ever actually used in this way in the language which is its original home?—
What *we* do is to bring words back from their metaphysical to their everyday use.

117. You say to me: "You understand this expression, don't you? Well then—I am using it in the sense you are familiar with."—As if the sense were an atmosphere accompanying the word, which it carried with it into every kind of application.
If, for example, someone says that the sentence "This is here" (saying which he points to an object in front of him) makes sense to him, then he should ask himself in what special circumstances this sentence is actually used. There it does make sense.

118. Where does our investigation get its importance from, since it seems only to destroy everything interesting, that is, all that is great and important? (As it were all the buildings, leaving behind only bits of stone and rubble.) What we are destroying is nothing but houses of cards and we are clearing up the ground of language on which they stood.

119. The results of philosophy are the uncovering of one or another piece of plain non-sense and bumps that the understanding has got by running its head up against the limits of language. These bumps make us see the value of the discovery.

120. When I talk about language (words, sentences, etc.) I must speak the language of every day. Is this language somehow too coarse and material for what we want to say? *Then how is another one to be constructed?*—And how strange that we should be able to do anything at all with the one we have!
In giving explanations I already have to use language full-blown (not some sort of pre-paratory, provisional one); this by itself shows that I can adduce only exterior facts about language.
Yes, but then how can these explanations satisfy us?—Well, your very questions were framed in this language; they had to be expressed in this language, if there was anything to ask!

And your scruples are misunderstandings.

Your questions refer to words; so I have to talk about words.

You say: the point isn't the word, but its meaning, and you think of the meaning as a thing of the same kind as the word, though also different from the word. Here the word, there the meaning. The money, and the cow that you can buy with it. (But contrast: money, and its use.)

121. One might think: if philosophy speaks of the use of the word "philosophy" there must be a second-order philosophy. But it is not so: it is, rather, like the case of orthography, which deals with the word "orthography" among others without then being second-order.

122. A main source of our failure to understand is that we do not *command a clear view* of the use of our words.—Our grammar is lacking in this sort of perspicuity. A perspicuous representation produces just that understanding which consists in "seeing connexions." Hence the importance of finding and inventing *intermediate cases*.

The concept of a perspicuous representation is of fundamental significance for us. It earmarks the form of account we give, the way we look at things. (Is this a "Weltanschauung"?)

123. A philosophical problem has the form: "I don't know my way about."

124. Philosophy may in no way interfere with the actual use of language; it can in the end only describe it.

For it cannot give it any foundation either.

It leaves everything as it is.

It also leaves mathematics as it is, and no mathematical discovery can advance it. A "leading problem of mathematical logic" is for us a problem of mathematics like any other.

125. It is the business of philosophy, not to resolve a contradiction by means of a mathematical or logico-mathematical discovery, but to make it possible for us to get a clear view of the state of mathematics that troubles us: the state of affairs *before* the contradiction is resolved. (And this does not mean that one is sidestepping a difficulty.)

The fundamental fact here is that we lay down rules, a technique, for a game, and that then when we follow the rules, things do not turn out as we had assumed. That we are therefore as it were entangled in our own rules.

This entanglement in our rules is what we want to understand (i.e. get a clear view of).

It throws light on our concept of *meaning* something. For in those cases things turn out otherwise than we had meant, foreseen. That is just what we say when, for example, a contradiction appears: "I didn't mean it like that."

The civil status of a contradiction, or its status in civil life: there is the philosophical problem.

126. Philosophy simply puts everything before us, and neither explains nor deduces anything.—Since everything lies open to view there is nothing to explain. For what is hidden, for example, is of no interest to us.

One might also give the name "philosophy" to what is possible *before* all new discoveries and inventions.

127. The work of the philosopher consists in assembling reminders for a particular purpose.

128. If one tried to advance *theses* in philosophy, it would never be possible to debate them, because everyone would agree to them.

129. The aspects of things that are most important for us are hidden because of their simplicity and familiarity. (One is unable to notice something—because it is always before one's eyes.) The real foundations of his enquiry do not strike a man at all. Unless *that* fact has at some time struck him.—And this means: we fail to be struck by what, once seen, is most striking and most powerful.

130. Our clear and simple language-games are not preparatory studies for a future regimentation of language—as it were first approximations, ignoring friction and air-resistance. The language-games are rather set up as *objects of comparison* which are meant to throw light on the facts of our language by way not only of similarities, but also of dissimilarities.

131. For we can avoid ineptness or emptiness in our assertions only by presenting the model as what it is, as an object of comparison—as, so to speak, a measuring-rod; not as a preconceived idea to which reality *must* correspond. (The dogmatism into which we fall so easily in doing philosophy.)

132. We want to establish an order in our knowledge of the use of language: an order with a particular end in view; one out of many possible orders; not *the* order. To this end we shall constantly be giving prominence to distinctions which our ordinary forms of language easily make us overlook. This may make it look as if we saw it as our task to reform language.

Such a reform for particular practical purposes, an improvement in our terminology designed to prevent misunderstandings in practice, is perfectly possible. But these are not the cases we have to do with. The confusions which occupy us arise when language is like an engine idling, not when it is doing work.

133. It is not our aim to refine or complete the system of rules for the use of our words in unheard-of ways.

For the clarity that we are aiming at is indeed *complete* clarity. But this simply means that the philosophical problems should *completely* disappear.

The real discovery is the one that makes me capable of stopping doing philosophy when I want to.—The one that gives philosophy peace, so that it is no longer tormented by questions which bring *itself* in question.—Instead, we now demonstrate a method, by examples; and the series of examples can be broken off.—Problems are solved (difficulties eliminated), not a *single* problem.

There is not *a* philosophical method, though there are indeed methods, like different therapies.

✳ ✳ ✳

153. We are trying to get hold of the mental process of understanding which seems to be hidden behind those coarser and therefore more readily visible accompaniments. But we do not succeed; or, rather, it does not get as far as a real attempt. For even supposing I had found something that happened in all those cases of understanding,—why should *it* be the understanding? And how can the process of understanding have been hidden, when I said "Now I understand" *because* I understood?! And if I say it is hidden—then how do I know what I have to look for? I am in a muddle.

154. But wait—if "Now I understand the principle" does not mean the same as "The formula . . . occurs to me" (or "I say the formula," "I write it down," etc.)—does it follow from this that I employ the sentence "Now I understand. . . ." or "Now I can go on" as a description of a process occurring behind or side by side with that of saying the formula?

If there has to be anything "behind the utterance of the formula" it is *particular circumstances*, which justify me in saying I can go on—when the formula occurs to me.

Try not to think of understanding as a "mental process" at all.—For *that* is the expression which confuses you. But ask yourself: in what sort of case, in what kind of circumstances, do we say, "Now I know how to go on," when, that is, the formula *has* occurred to me?—

In the sense in which there are processes (including mental processes) which are characteristic of understanding, understanding is not a mental process.

(A pain's growing more and less; the hearing of a tune or a sentence: these are mental processes.)

155. Thus what I wanted to say was: when he suddenly knew how to go on, when he understood the principle, then possibly he had a special experience—and if he is asked: "What was it? What took place when you suddenly grasped the principle?" perhaps he will describe it much as we described it above—but for us it is *the circumstances* under which he

had such an experience that justify him in saying in such a case that he understands, that he knows how to go on.

156. This will become clearer if we interpolate the consideration of another word, namely "reading." First I need to remark that I am not counting the understanding of what is read as part of "reading" for purposes of this investigation: reading is here the activity of rendering out loud what is written or printed; and also of writing from dictation, writing out something printed, playing from a score, and so on.

The use of this word in the ordinary circumstances of our life is of course extremely familiar to us. But the part the word plays in our life, and therewith the language-game in which we employ it, would be difficult to describe even in rough outline. A person, let us say an Englishman, has received at school or at home one of the kinds of education usual among us, and in the course of it has learned to read his native language. Later he reads books, letters, newspapers, and other things.

Now what takes place when, say, he reads a newspaper?——His eye passes—as we say—along the printed words, he says them out loud—or only to himself; in particular he reads certain words by taking in their printed shapes as wholes; others when his eye has taken in the first syllables; others again he reads syllable by syllable, and an occasional one perhaps letter by letter.—We should also say that he had read a sentence if he spoke neither aloud nor to himself during the reading but was afterwards able to repeat the sentence word for word or nearly so.—He may attend to what he reads, or again—as we might put it—function as a mere reading-machine: I mean, read aloud and correctly without attending to what he is reading; perhaps with his attention on something quite different (so that he is unable to say what he has been reading if he is asked about it immediately afterwards).

Now compare a beginner with this reader. The beginner reads the words by laboriously spelling them out.—Some however he guesses from the context, or perhaps he already partly knows the passage by heart. Then his teacher says that he is not really *reading* the words (and in certain cases that he is only pretending to read them).

If we think of *this* sort of reading, the reading of a beginner, and ask ourselves what *reading* consists in, we shall be inclined to say: it is a special conscious activity of mind.

We also say of the pupil: "Of course he alone knows if he is really reading or merely saying the words off by heart." (We have yet to discuss these propositions: "He alone knows. . . .")

But I want to say: we have to admit that—as far as concerns uttering any *one* of the printed words—the same thing may take place in the consciousness of the pupil who is "pretending" to read, as in that of the practised reader who is "reading" it. The word "to read" is applied *differently* when we are speaking of the beginner and of the practised reader.——Now we should of course like to say: What goes on in that practised reader and in the beginner when they utter the word *can't* be the same. And if there is no difference in what they happen to be conscious of there must be one in the unconscious workings of their minds, or, again, in the brain.—So we should like to say: There are at all events two different mechanisms at work here. And what goes on in them must distinguish reading from not reading.—But these mechanisms are only hypotheses, models designed to explain, to sum up, what you observe.

* * *

196. In our failure to understand the use of a word we take it as the expression of a queer *process*. (As we think of time as a queer medium, of the mind as a queer kind of being.)

197. "It's as if we could grasp the whole use of a word in a flash."—And that is just what we say we do. That is to say: we sometimes describe what we do in these words. But there is nothing astonishing, nothing queer, about what happens. It becomes queer when we are led to think that the future development must in some way already be present in the act of grasping the use and yet isn't present.—For we say that there isn't any doubt that we understand the word, and on the other hand its meaning lies in its use. There is no doubt that I now want to play chess, but chess is the game it is in virtue of all its rules (and so on). Don't I know, then, which game I want to play until I *have* played it? or are all the rules contained in my act of intending? Is it experience that tells me that this sort of game is the usual consequence of such an act of intending? so is it impossible for me to be certain what I was intending to do? And if that is nonsense—what kind of super-strong connexion exists between the act of intending and the thing intended?——Where is the connexion effected between the sense of the expression "Let's play a game of chess" and all the rules of the game?—Well, in the list of rules of the game, in the teaching of it, in the day-to-day practice of playing.

198. "But how can a rule show me what I have to do at *this* point? Whatever I do is, on some interpretation, in accord with the rule."—That is not what we ought to say, but rather: any interpretation still hangs in the air along with what it interprets, and cannot give it any support. Interpretations by themselves do not determine meaning.

"Then can whatever I do be brought into accord with the rule?"—Let me ask this: what has the expression of a rule—say a sign-post—got to do with my actions? What sort of connexion is there here?—Well, perhaps this one: I have been trained to react to this sign in a particular way, and now I do so react to it.

But that is only to give a causal connexion; to tell how it has come about that we now go by the sign-post; not what this going-by-the-sign really consists in. On the contrary; I have further indicated that a person goes by a sign-post only in so far as there exists a regular use of sign-posts, a custom.

199. Is what we call "obeying a rule" something that it would be possible for only *one* man to do, and to do only *once* in his life?—This is of course a note on the grammar of the expression "to obey a rule."

It is not possible that there should have been only one occasion on which only one person obeyed a rule. It is not possible that there should have been only one occasion on which a report was made, an order given or understood; and so on.—To obey a rule, to make a report, to give an order, to play a game of chess, are *customs* (uses, institutions).

To understand a sentence means to understand a language. To understand a language means to be master of a technique.

200. It is, of course, imaginable that two people belonging to a tribe unacquainted with games should sit at a chess-board and go through the moves of a game of chess; and even with all the appropriate mental accompaniments. And if *we* were to see it we should say they were playing chess. But now imagine a game of chess translated according to certain rules into a series of actions which we do not ordinarily associate with a *game*—say into yells and stamping of feet. And now suppose those two people to yell and stamp instead of playing the form of chess that we are used to; and this in such a way that their procedure is translatable by suitable rules into a game of chess. Should we still be inclined to say they were playing a game? What right would one have to say so?

201. This was our paradox: no course of action could be determined by a rule, because any course of action can be made out to accord with the rule. The answer was: if *any* action can be made out to accord with the rule, then it can also be made out to conflict with it. And so there would be neither accord nor conflict here.

It can be seen that there is a misunderstanding here from the mere fact that in the course of our argument we give one interpretation after another; as if each one contented us at least for a moment, until we thought of yet another standing behind it. What this shows is that there is a way of grasping a rule which is *not* an *interpretation*, but which is exhibited in what we call "obeying the rule" and "going against it" in actual cases.

Hence there is an inclination to say: any action according to the rule is an interpretation. But we ought to restrict the term "interpretation" to the substitution of one expression of the rule for another.

202. And hence also "obeying a rule" is a practice. And to *think* one is obeying a rule is not to obey a rule. Hence it is not possible to obey a rule "privately": otherwise thinking one was obeying a rule would be the same thing as obeying it.

203. Language is a labyrinth of paths. You approach from *one* side and know your way about; you approach the same place from another side and no longer know your way about.

✳   ✳   ✳

217. "How am I able to obey a rule?"—if this is not a question about causes, then it is about the justification for my following the rule in the way I do.

If I have exhausted the justifications I have reached bedrock, and my spade is turned. Then I am inclined to say: "This is simply what I do."

(Remember that we sometimes demand definitions for the sake not of their content, but of their form. Our requirement is an architectural one; the definition a kind of ornamental coping that supports nothing.)

218. Whence comes the idea that the beginning of a series is a visible section of rails invisibly laid to infinity? Well, we might imagine rails instead of a rule. And infinitely long rails correspond to the unlimited application of a rule.

219. "All the steps are really already taken" means: I no longer have any choice. The rule, once stamped with a particular meaning, traces the lines along which it is to be followed through the whole of space.——But if something of this sort really were the case, how would it help?

No; my description only made sense if it was to be understood symbolically.—I should have said: *This is how it strikes me.*

When I obey a rule, I do not choose.

I obey the rule *blindly*.

220. But what is the purpose of that symbolical proposition? It was supposed to bring into prominence a difference between being causally determined and being logically determined.

221. My symbolical expression was really a mythological description of the use of a rule.

222. "The line intimates to me the way I am to go."—But that is of course only a picture. And if I judged that it intimated this or that as it were irresponsibly, I should not say that I was obeying it like a rule.

223. One does not feel that one has always got to wait upon the nod (the whisper) of the rule. On the contrary, we are not on tenterhooks about what it will tell us next, but it always tells us the same, and we do what it tells us.

One might say to the person one was training: "Look, I always do the same thing: I . . ."

224. The word "agreement" and the word "rule" are *related* to one another, they are cousins. If I teach anyone the use of the one word, he learns the use of the other with it.

225. The use of the word "rule" and the use of the word "same" are interwoven. (As are the use of "proposition" and the use of "true.")

∗ ∗ ∗

"What is *internal* is hidden from us."—The future is hidden from us. But does the astronomer think like this when he calculates an eclipse of the sun?

If I see someone writhing in pain with evident cause I do not think: all the same, his feelings are hidden from me.

We also say of some people that they are transparent to us. It is, however, important as regards this observation that one human being can be a complete enigma to another. We learn this when we come into a strange country with entirely strange traditions; and, what is more, even given a mastery of the country's language. We do not *understand* the people. (And not because of not knowing what they are saying to themselves.) We cannot find our feet with them.

"I cannot know what is going on in him" is above all a *picture*. It is the convincing expression of a conviction. It does not give the reasons for the conviction. *They* are not readily accessible.

If a lion could talk, we could not understand him.

Note

1. "When they (my elders) named some object, and accordingly moved towards something, I saw this and I grasped that the thing was called by the sound they uttered when they meant to point it out. Their intention was shown by their bodily movements, as it were the natural language of all peoples: the expression of the face, the play of the eyes, the movement of other parts of the body, and the tone of voice which expresses our state of mind in seeking, having, rejecting, or avoiding something. Thus, as I heard words repeatedly used in their proper places in various sentences, I gradually learnt to understand what objects they signified; and after I had trained my mouth to form these signs, I used them to express my own desires."

17 Premises

Werner Hamacher

Understanding is in want of understanding.

The thoughts pursued here cannot be summarized in this proposition concerning understanding without encountering resistance—not in this proposition nor in the three or four sentences into which it can be analyzed and expanded.

That understanding is in want of understanding—a proposition to be read as the principle of understanding, as an announcement or summation, as a demand or complaint—will not have said anything about understanding unless it itself is understood, and unless it is understood that this proposition speaks also of the impossibility of understanding and thus the impossibility of this very proposition.

"Understanding is in want of understanding" means first of all that understanding is not only concerned with understanding things but must itself be understood whenever anything is to be understood. In understanding, something is doubtless made accessible, but it becomes accessible only in the very act of understanding—under its conditions or presuppositions. The object to which understanding refers may exist in the absence of any understanding of this object; but as the subject-matter of understanding, it is already a subject-matter affected by understanding, and as such it remains uncomprehended as long as its understanding is not understood as well. If the determining moments of understanding remain in the dark, if it is not even understood that there are such moments—both historical and structural—then the subject-matter to be understood also remains obscure. Among the structural conditions without which understanding can never take place is therefore this: in understanding not only something but also the understanding of this thing must be understood.

That understanding is not only a matter of understanding things and that it, too, wants to be understood means, furthermore, that understanding produces effects and remains incomplete without the understanding of these effects. Whether one defines understanding as an occurrence, a process, or an act, it is never a relation between two already given, immobile entities that somehow remain untouched by this relation; rather, it is a relation in which each term constitutes itself in the first place—the reader turns into the reader of this sentence, the sentence into the sentence of this reader. Understanding is thus a procedure of reciprocal affection and alteration. Unless it is understood that understanding is this constitutive alteration and indeed the alteration of all sedimented constitutions of the elements involved in its process, then not only does understanding itself remain uncomprehended but also everything that is all too easily called its subject and its object. If, by contrast, it is understood that understanding is change and alteration, then one must also concede that it cannot be arrested in a stable pattern of transformation. Even when understanding exercises control over itself through reflection, it does not stop transforming its transformative turns and ineluctably becoming another one. "Understanding is in want of understanding" thus also means that however much it may make itself into a theme, it still cannot be stabilized into an essence, a paradigm, or an Idea that would not then be exposed to another understanding, an understanding incommensurable with the first. Understanding wants to be understood by another understanding and wants to be understood otherwise: paradoxically, it is itself only as an understanding exposed to another one and, at the limit, exposed to something other than understanding.

To understand means "to be able," "to have the capacity," "to take something upon oneself," "to be in charge of it." The proposition concerning understanding thus means, in its third version, that understanding requires the ability to be performed. The dominant philosophical tradition since antiquity has interpreted this ability as *technē*, *ars*, art, and has furthermore taken it for a methodologically controllable procedure. This tradition proceeds in principle from an historically invariant analogy between the objects and subjects of understanding. The security of knowledge was based on the correspondence between the structure of the sentence and that of the subject-matter; the "art of understanding" could never go wrong as long as its rules corresponded to those of the "art of speaking." The structural analogy between the possibilities of understanding and the actuality of its objects underwent its first convulsion when it became doubtful whether knowledge had command over its own ground. The dissociation of the possible and the actual unleashed by this doubt—the dissociation between what can be thought and made, on the one hand, and what is given, on the other—did not weaken the faith in techniques and technology, in abilities and powers; rather, it culminated in a philosophy and a praxis of the will-to-power and of the will-to-will that was determined to convert the given into something made and thereby restore the broken unity of the experience of the self. Possibility and ability were defined ontotechnologically as self-enabling and self-empowerment, while understanding was interpreted as self-understanding, the understanding of the already understood, and thus the understanding of understanding itself. An echo of this formula of self-formation—a formula of the will-to-will and the will to self-understanding—may still be heard in the proposition "understanding is in want of understanding."

But the dissociation that was supposed to be healed in the pure self-relation of understanding once again erupts in this very relation. As a self-generating and self-realizing "faculty," understanding was supposed to have been its own unconditioned premise, its absolute autoprotasis, and it was supposed to have drawn from this premise a conclusion about itself. But the proposition "understanding is in want of understanding"—a proposition in which this self-relation is reclaimed—remains valid only as long as understanding is not yet understood, the will to understanding has not yet been fulfilled, no ability has yet secured itself, and no capacity has been saturated in a conclusive experience of understanding. The proposition is valid only under the premise that understanding cannot be fulfilled. As long as understanding still only *wants* to be understood, it *cannot* yet be understood: it cannot yet be enabled and is not yet even possible. The proposition of understanding—a proposition postulating that understanding provides its own possibility— thus touches upon something else, something that does not correspond, to understanding and cannot be assimilated to it. The proposition points toward something uncomprehended and incomprehensible, toward an incapacity and an impossibility. Not only is the privilege of technique and technology shaken by this other—by the impossible—but so too is the possibility of regulating and methodologically controlling understanding. And so too is the very possibility of understanding in general, its capacity to find its premises in itself, to understand its own understanding, to stand *before* and thus take charge of this understanding: its ability, in sum, *to be understanding* at all.

The proposition of understanding sidesteps understanding. Precisely what understanding means is supposed to be grasped and comprehended in this proposition; but since this understanding is tied to the unfulfilled and unfulfillable demand to grasp itself and to include itself in its comprehension, this proposition says that understanding must understand itself from its impossibility. That understanding is in want of understanding is, in short, an aporia: the proposition says that understanding—precisely because it is necessary— does not understand. And since the proposition must participate in this non-understanding of understanding, it says that it, the proposition, does not yet say anything. But with this aporetic result at least this much is said, however implicitly: understanding is not a formal-logical relation that must accommodate itself to the principle of non-contradiction; non-understanding is not opposed to understanding but is its inconceivable ground and ungraspable background; and understanding, like non-understanding, moves in an open arena that wants to be understood in terms *other* than those defined by the categories of the understanding and wants perhaps to be other than *understood*.

For it is always another who understands and whose difference from what is understood remains irreducible. Something else is always understood—even when one understands "oneself"—and indeed understood in such a way that a relation to this other, however familiar or well-known it may be, is each time created for the first time or for the first time anew. Hence understanding is indeed a relation, but a relation to something new, however old it may be; it is a relation to another, even when this other would be the nearest and closest to hand; and it is a relation to something that can offer itself only as something uncomprehended, even when it is already considered familiar. It is thus each time another, a new and non-anticipated relation to something uncomprehended and until now incomprehensible. But if it is indeed a relation to something incomprehensible *until now*, then it must also be a relation to something *still* incomprehensible in understanding, for otherwise precisely *this*—the thing uncomprehended until now—would not be understood. If understanding relates itself each time to something strange, then it must be an estranged relation. If it comports itself to another, then it must be a comportment altered by this other and opened to further alterations. Understanding is not therefore a simple relation but an insolubly aporetic one. At the limit, it is a relation to the non-relational, hence a relationless relation: a reference to retreat, hence a self-retreating reference.

Understanding stands off from itself—not just occasionally, because of the constitution of something called its object, or because of the individual incapacities of those who seek to understand. Understanding stands at a distance from itself only because it refers to something uncomprehended. Otherwise it would not be understanding at all: it would be knowledge. Something is understood only in its incomprehensibility. And this incomprehensibility does not simply accompany understanding as an unavoidable evil or a regrettable remnant of finitude that could be cast off under ideal conditions of communication; rather, incomprehensibility is what first grants understanding, discloses its possibility, and preserves it as a possibility. If something is understood, it is only because it stands back from understanding.

It is one of the remarkable features of the movement of understanding that the incomprehensible, the foreign, and the irreducibly other—each of which sets understanding into motion in the first place—can be brought to rest at the end of this movement (but it is precisely this end that is at issue here), can be stabilized into an object of representation, thematized by a subject, and thus made into a cognized, controlled, reduced other of this subject. Understanding does not start by referring to objects; rather, objects constitute themselves in the act of understanding. Once they are constituted (and this final constitution is, once again, in question) the movement of understanding comes to a halt and turns into a certification of the object and a self-securing of cognitive reason. Perhaps the best place to observe the leap from an understanding that is exposed to the incomprehensible into a self-consciousness that posits its objects is in Hegel's description of Greek "mantics." In his *Lectures on the Philosophy of History* Hegel explains that the mantic, like the philosopher, proceeds from *thaumazein*, from wonder or astonishment—indeed, from what Aristotle (in the same section of the *Metaphysics* to which Hegel refers) describes as an *aporon*: a place without any outlet, an impasse, something incomprehensible.[1] "For the Greeks only *eavesdrop* [*lauschen*] on natural objects," Hegel writes, "and *intimate* these objects with an inward-directed question concerning their meaning. Just as, according to Aristotle, philosophy proceeds from wonder, so does the Greek intuition of nature proceed from this wonder."[2] Not only does an aporia precede philosophy and set it into motion; in every one of its steps philosophy remains bound to it. The relation of spirit (*Geist*) to this aporia consists in a pause, a breakdown of knowledge, a mere "eavesdropping" on something that communicates itself, and as Hegel then indicates, this relation expresses itself in a question about an unfamiliar meaning:

None of this means that spirit encounters something extraordinary when compared with the usual. . . . On the contrary, Greek spirit, once excited, wonders about the *natural* of nature. It does not relate to it in a dull manner as something given: Greek spirit relates to it as something that is at first foreign to spirit but something to which it nevertheless has the intimating confidence and the faith that the natural bears something within itself that would be friendly to spirit, something to which spirit could relate in a positive manner. (Hegel, 12: 288; Lectures, 234)

According to Hegel, then, the "natural" of nature, its essence and its meaning, cannot be conceived in wonder as some sort of "given" but must be perceived, as a non-given, something that holds itself back, something "foreign" to which spirit entertains no "positive" relation, and that means an absence of any determinate relation of positing: no positing relation at all. The relation to the "natural" is thus at first the aporetic relation to the relationless. By relating itself to the "natural," spirit refers to something that is not given to it, something that it does not posit, and something that it therefore cannot make into an object of representation. "Nevertheless," Hegel writes—and this "nevertheless" marks the turning point from the aporia to representation and spirit—spirit has "the intimating confidence and faith that the natural bears something within itself, something that would be friendly to spirit, something to which it could relate in a positive manner." The foreign, the non-given, is not recognized as friendly but is, instead, "intimated," not known but believed. Whatever the natural is supposed to "bear in itself" must therefore already be *presupposed* in order for spirit to be able to enter into a "positive" relation to it. It is this *supposition* of faith that turns the foreign into something friendly, the non-given into a given, and makes that which withdraws from every determinate position into something positive.

Hegel does not dissolve the aporia of understanding. On the contrary, for him, the aporia constitutes the resistance from which experience must rebound and turn back on itself. By supposing that the incomprehensible has a meaning, spirit understands it as its object and understands itself as its positing. Hegel describes the leap from aporia to representation—or the contraction of difference into position—in the following terms: "Yet the Hellenes did not remain immobile before these feelings [wonder and intimation]; rather they brought out [*herausstellten*] the inwardness about which their intimation asked, making it into a determinate representation [*Vorstellung*], an object [*Gegenstand*] of consciousness" (Hegel, 12: 288; Lectures, 234). To suppose that the foreign would be something friendly is essentially to suppose that an interiority inhabits that absolute exteriority which hitherto could be experienced, only as an aporia, something impossible to experience. It is to presuppose an interiority that can be "brought out" and placed in the hands of knowledge as a "determinate representation" and thus as an "object of consciousness." The positing of spirit brings itself out in this bringing forth of representation, and from the aporia something is brought to light that ought no longer be aporetic at all: positionality itself. The "natural" of nature, its essence and meaning, is only the positing and self-positing of spirit. And this positing consists in the movement from wonder to mantic supposition and semantic explication, a movement leading understanding to representation, concept, and philosophy.

Positing, setting into place, position—these are always, for Hegel, placing together, co-positing, inaugurating a synthesis of spirit with itself in its other. Even in wonder, where spirit does not understand and does not understand itself, it can still consolidate its powers of cognition by presupposing an inwardness, a meaning, or a significance, and thereby achieve knowledge and self-knowledge. The path of spirit is in every case circular: it leads spirit from its presupposition of an absolute other to this other as the other *of itself*, and in this way it returns spirit to itself. Hegel thinks the course of autoposition not only as the path of thinking but also as the way of song, poetry, and literature:

> Similarly, the Greeks listened to the murmurings of the springs and asked what was the meaning of this. . . . The Naiads, or springs, are the external inception of the muses. Yet the muses' immortal songs are not what one hears when one listens to the murmurings of springs; they are the productions of spirit in its capacity for sensible hearing, which produces [them] in its eavesdropping on itself. (Hegel, 12: 289; Lectures, 235)

Spirit does not simply listen in astonishment, thus caught in an aporia; it hears "sensibly," *sinnig*, in a reasonable manner. Spirit thus listens for the sense and meaning of a murmuring that, as "something foreign at first," must have lacked sense. In this way, it can produce "in its eavesdropping" the song of meaning "in itself." The work of spirit is the appropriation of the foreign, the semanticization of the asemic, the positivizing of the aporetic. The song of the muses is not the mere murmuring of the springs but only the "sensibly" heard murmuring, the murmuring heard with a sense for its sense. Spirit hears itself singing in the spring as its muse. Song—and thus art in general—is not incomprehensible nature but a representation of spirit that perceives and understands itself in nature. Every muse is already the muse of the mantic and thus the muse of speculative auto-semanticization:

> The interpretation and explanation of nature . . . the demonstration of sense and significance in nature—this is the activity of subjective spirit to which the Greeks gave the name *manteia*. . . . Both the material and the explicator who brings out what is significant belong to *manteia*. . . . Nature answered the questions of the Greek: this is the sense in which the statement that man obtained answers to the questions of nature from his spirit is true. (Hegel, 12: 289–90; Lectures, 235)[3]

Wherever this speculative inversion of question and answer takes place there must be a circular path between spirit and nature. Its logical form is the self-presupposition of spirit in its other—and "spirit" is nothing but this self-presupposition. Interpretation, as the "bringing out" or understanding "of sense and significance," is for Hegelian spirit—whether in its subjective, objective, or absolute state—always only a "bringing forth" of something previously put into place, a laying out of something earlier laid down, an understanding of a previous positing. The hermeneutics of the *mantis* is autohermeneutics. It is self-understanding and, more exactly, the understanding of understanding itself as position.

But the aporia remains uncomprehended. In the aporia—and in the astonishment that responds to it—the Greeks, according to Hegel, do not simply stand still. On the contrary, "Greek spirit, once excited," spirit that has "the natural only as incitement" (Hegel, 12:

288–89; Lectures, 234), takes the only path that the blockage of the aporia leaves open: a path back to itself. Something is then understood, to be sure, but it is understood only by turning away from that which, as incomprehensible, first demands comprehension, whether it "excites" or "incites." It is thus understood at the cost of not understanding the very excitation to which the further course of understanding owes its impetus. The significance is grasped but not the *mania*: the *Sinn* (meaning) is understood but not the *Wahnsinn* (dementia)[4] that undoes the production of meaning. For de-mentia is not supposed by spirit nor posited in its representations and concepts but is, rather, whatever lies in advance of all positings and presuppositions and thus precedes every possible understanding. It is an other that is not the other *of* spirit and not the other *of* understanding but is other than any other still susceptible to semanticization and ontologization—an other that offers no point of support for the hermeneutic reduction to sense and enters into the horizon of self-positing only as its disruption.

The aporia incites understanding, but it remains incomprehensible—and with this abyss of understanding, so too does understanding itself. Understanding cannot, therefore, as Hegel proposes, obey the matrix of a thoroughgoing dialectization; rather, it obeys a double law—one could call it the law of dia-lecture,[5] double reading: the law of hermeneutic reduction whereby a stable semantic position is attained, on the one hand, and on the other, the dismaying law of de-posing under which no position, no understanding, and no mantic, semantic, or hermeneutic reduction are possible. If understanding understands itself, it has already forgotten the devastation, the astonishment, the wonder, and the eavesdropping from which it took its point of departure. Since, however, it does not understand its provenance, it does not understand. If, by contrast, it remains in astonishment, it does not understand yet again. Something is "understood" in every case only because it is not "understood." Understanding is possible only between these two impossibilities of understanding—the hermeneutic parousia of spirit in its autoposition and de-posing *sans phrase*—only *between* them, hence only insofar as the movement of self-positing must always be exposed and once again discharged by another understanding, and thus only insofar as its standing suspends itself in this unposited, groundless "between." There is understanding, including self-understanding, only from the aporia—and the aporia is what asemantically, alogically, and adialectically grants understanding, including dialectical understanding, by refusing it. When understanding fails, so too do philosophy and art.

With his interpretation of understanding as dialectical self-presupposition, Hegel does not simply react to the Platonic-Aristotelian aporia; he also links up with Kant's thesis on Being as absolute position. Kant first set down this formula for the fundamental thought of modern metaphysics in his treatise of 1763, *The One Possible Basis of Proof for a Demonstration of the Existence of God*: "Existence [*Dasein*] is the absolute position of a thing."[6] He then comments: "The concept of position or positing [*Position oder Setzung*] is completely simple and is the same as the concept of Being. . . . If a thing is considered posited in and for itself, then Being [*Sein*] is as much as existence [*Dasein*]." This position is absolute in the

Kantian sense because it refers purely to the existence of "a thing in and for itself" regardless of all relations to possible predicates. Just as the positing of Being cannot be the copula in the predicative judgment, this positing cannot be a predicate, since every predication must already presuppose the existence of its logical subject.[7] And this absolute, pre-predicative presupposition, as the unconditioned fiat of Being, does not become any less absolute because it must still entertain one relation: that of the subject to this positing. In the *Critique of Pure Reason* Kant explicitly defines the modalities of Being—being actual, being possible, being necessary—in such a way that they are said to "express the relation to the faculty of knowledge" (A 219; B 266).[8] Being thus consists in a positing with respect to the subject of knowledge, and this positing—whether it be a pure synthesis of transcendental apperception or, as in Fichte, a primordial "enactment"—is the original act of the cognitive subject. In this act the Being of the thing is posited along with the Being of its knowledge in the subject. The absolute positing of Being is a positing of knowledge. Because this positing, as a transcendental act, is absolutely foundational and because it conditions both conceptuality and intuition, the "supreme principle" of experiential synthesis resides in it: "The conditions of the possibility of experience in general are at the same time conditions of the possibility of the objects of experience" (A 158; B 198). The essence of knowledge, like the essence of the object known, is conceived as an original act of positing, as a dictate of subjective consciousness in which it dictates itself and affects itself.[9] Kant's ontology and that of his speculative followers can thus be characterized as autotheseology and ontotheseology.

Existence must be based on the transcendental positing of the self if knowledge is to have "objective reality," that is, if knowledge is supposed to refer to existence in such a way that, according to the *Critique of Pure Reason*, it can find in existence "meaning and sense" (A 155; B 194). If the criterion of existence—of its objectivity and reality—is "meaning and sense," if positing always posits an existing entity by simultaneously positing meaning, then ontotheseology is possible only within a logic of Being as meaning: only as semontology. But ontotheseology is at the same time only possible if the agent that posits Being and meaning posits itself in what it has posited, if it posits and knows itself as meaning. The fact that the existential position of the subject posits itself *as* positing immediately makes this position into a reflection. After Fichte's *Wissenschaftslehre*, this is most clearly expressed in Hegel's *Science of Logic*: "Existence [*Dasein*] is only being-posited [*Gesetztsein*]; this proposition expresses the essence of existence."[10] Since, however, being-posited originates from the "absolute presupposition" in which positing bends back on itself and reflects itself, Hegel can conclude: "Being-posited is thus a determination of reflection." And furthermore: "Being-posited is a relation to other, but to reflectedness-in-itself" (Hegel, 6: 33; Science, 407). As being-posited, Being is, for Hegel, other; but the absolute premise of this other—precisely the premise that it is posited unconditionally and thus posited as something unconditioned—refers the other back to its positing and turns its existence into reflectedness. Reflection takes being-other back into itself and is the very unity of itself and the other; more exactly, it is the other as self. The circle of position is thereby closed: the experience of the other has shown itself as an experience of the same, reflection as expanded position—or reposition—and the premises of theseology are once again secured, this time under the sign of speculative dialectics. In every relation to the other the original positing returns to itself, understands itself in this other as a form of its understanding, and is in this process of self-comprehension the unity of subject and substance, knowledge and meaning, thesis and semiosis. It is ontotautology—but therefore aporetic.

And yet the fundamental aporia—the aporia of positing, of founding itself—remains uncomprehended once again. A positing that is supposed to be unconditioned must be a positing without presupposition and thus a subjectless positing. It must purely posit itself; but by positing itself, *it* already posits *itself*, and so the positing that it is first supposed to perform must already *allow* itself to be presupposed. But such an allowance, admission, or concession of a presupposition can no longer be thought according to the logic of positing. It must be other than a presup-position and other than a positing of a prior support; on the contrary, in the very act of positing it must be precisely the opening that remains independent of the positing, an opening onto another that itself withdraws from the power, the faculty, and the possibility of positing. But if a positing can be a positing only by allowing something other than itself—other than its thetic Being—then an original positing cannot be performed. It is in need of a difference with respect to itself that can under no condition be reduced to a thetic act. Only by allowing something other than itself can it then grant admission to itself—and grant admission *to* itself, in turn, merely as that which it is not yet and never will have been, as the mere promise of a position, never as this position itself. But this is to say that any position is essentially defined from a distance from itself, and since this distance remains, for it, unmeasurable, it means that positing is an ineluctably aporetic act, the act of a non-action, an act of omission. And it means that positing, affected by something other than Being understood as position, never *is*—never "is" according to its own sense of "is," according to the sense of thetic Being. Philosophical negligence cannot then be held accountable for the fact that the aporia of positing is not understood, never analyzed, and has not been made into a theme. The aporia, as a displacement of every positing, *is* not—and therefore cannot be a theme for understanding. Making possible every theme and making every one impossible, it must be an *anathema* to understanding in every possible sense.

If positing must give leave to a non-positing; if positing, exposed, must break down in order for it to be a positing in the first place, then the structure of positing must be determined by a twofold leaving: by a leaving out (an ellipsis) and a letting in (the disclosure of a possibility). It must not be able to be what it must be able to become. It can claim to be only in the form of a demand for Being, not as a thetic Being but only as an imperative "Be!" And yet, since it is an aporetic claim, it must place this dictate of its fiat under this reservation: it cannot be pronounced and cannot be performed. Finite reason cannot ground itself; it can posit itself only by letting this positing be given out as an apodictic but unfulfillable imperative. And this not only applies to the transcendental act of theoretical reason—an act that posits the thing in itself in pure self-affection as an appearance of an appearance[11]—it also applies, *a fortiori*, to the law of practical reason, a law that can demand self-consistent, autonomous action and Being only because it, under the conditions of finitude, never offers this action and this Being as actual. It was Schelling who, in his *Philosophical Letters on Dogmaticism and Criticism*, gave the structure of the Kantian aporia of positing its most pregnant formula: "Be! That is the supreme demand of criticism."[12] The ontological imperative that Schelling deciphers in Kant's work transforms the principle of Being as position into the unfounded demand for a Being—unfounded because it first demands a foundation for any position. Demanded in this way, Being cannot persist as a result, a fact, or even only as a being. The imperative testifies to this: from its inception positing is exposed to something else, something that is neither realized nor even conceivable in this positing. Indeed, the imperative indicates that positing is exposed positing; abandoned by itself, it is thus ex-position. Since ontotheseology understands Being and language in such a manner that it can find an autonomous foundation only in the command that there be a foundation and only in the promise of a grounding, it itself must be constituted in an ex-thetic manner. It cannot be concerned with Being and the meaning of this Being as givens but only as tasks given out, as assignments demanded and omitted. And for its part, it can only be an ontotheseology that gives up. The principle of ontotheseology is a leap; its form—if it can still be called a form—is the aporia.

To the ontological imperative Schelling discovers in Kant's theory of position there corresponds the "hermeneutic imperative," whose existence Friedrich Schlegel asserts in one of his fragments: "There is a hermeneutic imperative."[13] The imperative "Understand!" does not simply mean "You must understand" but also "You do not yet understand—and you do not yet understand that you must understand." The hermeneutic imperative explicitly states that understanding is necessary, and it implies that understanding cannot be actual as long as it still must be demanded; indeed, it states that understanding is impossible as long as its possibility must be first disclosed in the imperative demand. Only in the not-yet and never-once of understanding can something be understood. Like Kant's and Schelling's ontological imperative, Schlegel's hermeneutic imperative thus expresses the aporia of position. There must be communication and understanding, but there can be communication and understanding only in view of them as *another* communication and *another* understanding—as a communication and understanding that are not and never will be given, as a communication and understanding of something other than the subject. In the imperative, whether ontological or hermeneutic, it thus becomes clear that there can be a position—and thus Being, subject, language, and understanding—only from the ex-position of this position: only, therefore, from what is precisely not an understanding of Being as position, not a subject, not a language, and not an understanding—and is, moreover, not a negation of any of these but the opening of every one. Only as an ex-posed, abandoned subject is there a subject in the first place, and only as exposed, disrupted language and understanding is there anything like language or understanding at all.

Schlegel captured this insight with the formula of philological self-affection: "Reading," he notes, "means to affect oneself philologically, limit, determine oneself philologically" (KA, 16.1: 68; no. 80). His plan for a "deduction of philology," which is perhaps not without irony, makes an effort to conceive of philology "as a logical affect and a subjectively necessary condition for the fulfillment of the logical imperative" (KA, 16.1: 72; no. 121).[14] The term "logical imperative" is here to be understood as an imperative of logic, but also as an imperative that demands a logic and a logos in the first place. Accordingly, the hermeneutic imperative is the one that will have commanded understanding from the position of an always only futurial hermeneutics. Like hermeneutics, philology is a "logical affect"—*philia* of the *logos*—as sheer self-affection of the logos, a logos that consists in nothing other than pure self-affection. The imperative that philology gives itself must therefore be understood as the self-affection of the logos—but for this reason as *affectio in distans*, for otherwise it would not be an imperative. The riddle of the logical and hermeneutic imperative leads back to the structure of logical and hermeneutic self-affection, which is to say, the aporia that the self can affect itself only as another. Understanding is self-affection, but affection only of a self that is unable to be affected in its otherness. Its homogeneity must be in itself heterogeneous; its temporality the torn temporality of asynchronicity and achronicity; its topic atopia. But this means that there is no understanding *itself*, and there is no language *itself* in which understanding could develop itself. There is, Schlegel insists, a hermeneutical imperative; but there can be such an imperative only when it refuses the very understanding and language that it makes possible—and even refuses itself in granting itself. The hermeneutic imperative is as little a part of actuality as any understanding that stands under this imperative, but it is hardly a projection of actuality either, since a teleological project can open itself up from this imperative alone. Neither substance nor presence nor even a project, the imperative—whether hermeneutic or ontological—is a mere admission of understanding and of Being without any of the conditions for their actualization. And this admission, this opening up, this unarrestable gift of understanding must be thought as the disclosure of the possibility of understanding and thus as itself incomprehensible.

Or, as Schlegel says in his essay "On Incomprehensibility," it must be thought as irony. Irony is, for him, neither the rhetorical figure that allows self-sufficient subjects to take flight to other meanings of their discourse, nor an occurrence within a tropologically well-defined and already constituted language. Rather, it is the structure by virtue of which language is possible but its complete constitution—as something like a *characteristica universalis* or a closed system of tropes—is impossible. Instead of being an inner-linguistic figure, for which it is often mistaken, irony is, for Schlegel, the limit figure of affiguration: the interminable opening of the domain of figures, always at their margin, noticeable in every particular figure as the quivering of its contours, and at the same time their defiguration. At once making language possible and making it impossible, irony—like the apodictic imperatives "be" and "understand"—is the aporia of its acconstitution: constitution and non-constitution of language in one. Schlegel can thus write the following fragment about Socratic irony, a fragment he first published in the *Lyceum* and later cites in "On Incomprehensibility": "It contains and incites a feeling of indissoluble antagonism . . . between the impossibility and the necessity of a complete communication," and as a version of the categorical, logical, and hermeneutic imperative, irony is in turn the law of freedom, for, as Schlegel writes in the same fragment, it "is the freest of all licenses, for by means of it one posits oneself way beyond oneself, and yet it is also the most lawful, for it is unconditionally necessary" (KA, 2: 68; Incomprehensibility, 265). The self does not posit itself in irony; rather, it posits itself *away*—way beyond itself. Irony is not a position but an excess beyond the form of subjectivity, and it thus cannot be reduced to a comprehensible thing: it is the incomprehensible, the "impossibility . . . of a complete communication." But it is just as much the necessity of this impossibility, for only in this excess—only by acceding to another—does the subject have the chance to constitute itself. Irony, incomprehensibility, is thus "the form of paradox" that must precede every form and every communication in order for them to be able to become form and communication. It is the necessary impossibility that inscribes itself in every possibility of language, and since it is also the form—without form—of unconditioned admission, "the freest of all licenses," it allows communication without limits and thus eclipses, leaves out, and leaves in the dark this giving-leave. It is the limitless admission of communication: "Indeed, the most precious thing human beings possess . . . depends in the final analysis, as anybody can easily know, on some such point of strength that *must be left* in the dark, but that nevertheless carries and supports the whole, and this force would give out at precisely the moment when one wanted to dissolve it through comprehension" (KA, 2: 370; Incomprehensibility, 268, italics added). This force left in the dark, Schlegel implies, is a non-force; it is the impossibility of complete communication, the impotence, incapacity, and inability to understand and to make comprehensible—"as anybody can easily know" from, for example, a passage in Aristotle's *Metaphysics* where he speaks of a force that is essentially a non-force in relation to the same thing for which it is a force: *dunamis adunamiai*, force non-force, possibility impossibility (1046a31). As the medium of the possibility and impossibility of communication, language—and that is in every case the language of irony—is always a broken, fragmented language, a language distanced from itself. It must offer itself in always other meanings, in an uncontrollable flight of allosemies and allegories, as always other than meaning, always other than language, and only thereby as language "itself": as exposed, disrupted, abandoned language, language without language.

Reason is not autonomous, only the demand that it should be so. The given—and thus retained—ground has given way to the movement of grounding ever since Kant's *Critiques*; but since this grounding in an injunction that language should lay down its own ground is infinite, it remains exposed to an irreparable abyss. If the imperative that there should be a self-grounding language, a language of reason, and therefore language as such is the absolute, unique, and unconditioned premise of language, then it will never have grounded itself: there will never have been *a* language and never a *language*. The apodictic imperative, language as the claim that there should be a language, always means this as well: there is not even one language, there has never been one, and none could ever be given. And so it, almost, has no meaning. In this imperative, the movement of semiosis remains exposed to an uncontrollable anasemiosis. By indicating a direction, it goes astray and becomes aberrant: every imperative is also an im*perrative*, its operation an ope*rration*, its reference refer*rence*. If the imperative of a rational, autonomous language is the premise of understanding—for only a thoroughly rational language can be understood, strictly speaking—then understanding will never have secured a ground and will never have come about. It remains in falling apart. "Premise" no longer means ground and presupposition but *Aussetzung*: ex-position, exposure, interruption, abandonment. In its premises language misses itself and thus misses its understanding. Only what goes astray and foregoes itself is promised in language.

The non-understanding—or incomplete understanding—that was decried or simply denied by rationalists who did not investigate the *ratio* of their own rationality is in truth what makes understanding possible. Non-understanding does not belong to the pathology of linguistic Being; it belongs to its logic. A rearticulation of this logic, which became necessary after the Kantian discovery of an apodictic aporia of action, demanded that the dominant lexicon of "understanding," which had suggested such a pathology, a deficiency, or even a degeneration of understanding, be subjected to a displacement and transformation. And this affected the entire vocabulary by which the concept of understanding had been defined: not only the vocabulary of thesis, position, positing, *Setzung, Gegenständlichkeit, Stellung, Vorstellung,* and *Darstellung* but also that of substance, constancy, and consistency.[15] All these concepts have their place in the topology of a metaphysics that essentially conceives itself as ontotheseology. Wherever the possibility of a non-understanding is no longer perceived as a contingent but as a structural devastation of the system of positings and emplacements, the axioms of these concepts are forfeited. This happens in Friedrich Schlegel's essay "On Incomprehensibility," in his theory of irony and fragmentary discourse, in the thought that whoever stands—or understands—can also fall, in his citation of Goethe's line, "Let everyone see where he stands / And let him that stands not fall."[16] This happens in Hölderlin's remark "Daß sich krümmt der Verstand daß nimmer das Forschen / Aufgeht."[17] It happens in Kleist's "Earthquake in Chile," where knowledge collapses under the weight of accidents. It happens in a note Kierkegaard wrote for *Fear and Trembling*: "Write for the dead, for those in earlier times whom you loved.—Will they read me?—No."[18] It is for this reason that Kafka's Odradek, another Hermes, roams in hallways, staircases, corridors, and lofts, between life and death, where he is not at home, cannot be placed, and cannot be arrested by understanding. It is for this reason that *Finnegans Wake* writes itself as "a fadograph of a yestern scene"[19]—as a writing not of saturated phenomenality but of aphanisis. And it is for this reason that Celan speaks of the "unreadability of this / world."[20] Something is readable only in its unreadability, comprehensible only in its resistance to comprehension—at the place where understanding writhes or falls, where its object slips away from it, and where its addressee is missing. The literature of recent centuries has indicated this with greater passion and honesty than its institutionally bound theory. Literature pursues the movements of language in which every stance starts to oscillate, quiver, or collapse. It is only from distance and difference, from the unattainable "before" (*Vor*) of understanding that understanding (*Verstehen*) is henceforth to be "understood."

It is from here—from the distance of understanding to standing, placing, and stating, from the distancing of a language that is infinitely addressed and claimed but never given and never fixed—that the following becomes clear: understanding can never be a passive absorption into a vessel of concepts or expectations; understanding must, instead, be a process in which the self and other are altered—and altered in ways impossible to anticipate. Understanding must be a standing-before-itself-toward-another-language, hence an exposure and ex-position of language. Understanding stands toward language—not simply toward a specific language, but in every language toward what is not yet said in it. It remains true to language, and in every language true to what is already thematically fixed in no language. In every one of its places it can be dispossessed by the theme of another language and indeed dispossessed by this other language. Understanding stands up to language: it allows speech and fosters further speaking. For this reason, its turning—and understanding is once again essentially a turning toward another—must be a turning toward what is unsaid, toward silence, speechlessness, and muteness. Before it can be the transition from one language to another, it must already be the transition to what no longer speaks or does not yet speak or will never be able to speak. Understanding is thus never without tension and pain; hence its strange pathos and apathy. What never stirs is touched upon in understanding: the apathetic itself. And it is for this reason that death and the dead obtain an outstanding place, a boundary position, in all attempts to think understanding: facing that which no longer understands and no longer lets itself be understood but which still defines all understanding as its limit. Thus Euripides writes in *Heracles*, after the hero of culture has murdered his children: "There inside is the horror. / You need no other interpreter."[21] Death itself gives the unsurpassable interpretation; in every surpassable one it must already be at work. It is what the journeyman in Johann Peter Hebel's story understands when "Kannitverstan," the supposed owner of limitless capital, presents himself as a corpse. And Kierkegaard tells himself in a note for *Fear and Trembling* to write for the dead, for those who will not read. Speaking is always also imparting to the dead and parting with them. Whoever speaks, whoever understands, dies—and, prosaically enough, does not stop dying. To use a word that was important to Nietzsche, Kafka, and Benjamin, one could say: whoever speaks, whoever understands, "outlives" and is "outlived."

Not even so-called "life philosophy," which has been reputed—not without justification—to promote the ideology of immediacy like no other, could deny the part played by the mute, the departed, and the incomprehensible in understanding. The bourgeois mentality expressed in the relevant reflections of Dilthey may have led to the tenacity with which the hermeneutics of empathy and reliving took hold of the question of understanding, and it may have contributed to the long-held view of hermeneutics as a technique of methodical identification with the author, the contexts of his life, and his intentions. The ideal of this comfortable identity of I and Thou that continues to flourish in consensualist theories of language and society even today was defined by Dilthey as a grounding form of understanding, and in a programmatic gesture he accorded it the status of an axiom to which the methodology of the "human sciences" had to conform. In his "Drafts for the Critique of Historical Reason" he writes: "Understanding is a rediscovery of the I in the Thou. Spirit finds itself again at ever higher levels of connectedness. This identity of spirit in the I, in the Thou, in every subject of a community, in every system of culture, finally, in the totality of spirit and universal history makes possible the successful cooperation of different processes in the human sciences. Here, the knowing subject is one with its object, and at all levels of its objectivation this is the same."[22] Using these words to announce its right to "universal history," the hermeneutics of the "human sciences" (*Geisteswissenschaften*) understands itself as the rediscovery of the I in the Thou, the subject in the object, spirit in its objectivations—and thus the same in the same. But if it is the same spirit that everywhere rediscovers itself and, like the hedgehog in the fairy tale, is already there whenever it, as a hare, reaches its goal; if spirit is always already understood and can never be understood as anything other than the same, then understanding is not only an exclusively reproductive process and not only a process that is superfluous in principle: it is also an impossible process. For it can no longer be understood; it can only have been understood. And the same goes for language: if it must already exist as an objectivation of "spirit" at the spot where the very same spirit should rediscover it, then all language is a mere reproduction of language; everything has already been said, and further speaking is superfluous, indeed impossible; there is no further speaking that does not for its part already belong to the stable stock of language. *Wir erleben Bestand*: "We experience stability" (Dilthey, 3: 195). In these words the hermeneut of "life philosophy" makes a statement that must be restated by anyone for whom understanding is the rediscovery of the I in the Thou, hence an understanding of what is already understood or is comprehensible in principle. But the ideal of language would then consist in the loss of language, and the ideal of understanding would be its renunciation.

"We experience stability"—this also means for Dilthey that we never experience life itself. "Lived experience," *Erlebnis*, is never the experience of life itself but always only an experience of its fixed stock of forms: "And if one wanted to try to experience the flux of life by means of any particular kind of effort . . . then one falls prey to the law of life itself yet again, a law according to which every moment of life that is observed . . . is a remembered moment, no longer flux. . . . And so we cannot grasp the essence of this life itself. What the young man of Saïs unveils is a statue, not life" (Dilthey, 7: 194–95). Life does not let itself be grasped as "lived experience." By saying this, Dilthey also acknowledges that only those things that are not alive and have thus departed from the "structural connectiveness" of life can be grasped as "lived experience." Since, however, to understand is to experience life, it is impossible to avoid the conclusion that only the fixed and dead forms of life, not life itself, can be understood. Understanding would not be the rediscovery of the self in the other; it would not be empathy and reanimation but sobriety before the image of Saïs. The continuum of life would not be universalized in understanding: it would be interrupted—and only something incomprehensible would ever be understood. But Dilthey avoids this obviously aporetic conclusion, for it means that the "sameness of spirit in the I, in the Thou, in every subject of a community" is only to be found in its otherness; spirit, subject, and society only in their collapse; identity only in difference. If Dilthey had yielded to his insight into what he called the "law of life," he would have had to admit that understanding cannot be the narcissistic "rediscovery of the I in the Thou" but only a "rediscovery" of what has never been before.

"The present never *is*" (Dilthey, 7: 194)—from this, his most pregnant formula, Dilthey avoids drawing the conclusion that there is never any past-present and no future-present either. He thus misses an opportunity to conceive of time as something other than a continuum and to think of understanding as something other than a process of homogenization. Instead of holding onto the experience of selfhood, he would have had to concede that this selfhood only constitutes itself in the medium of alteration—and that it cannot as a result ever stop deconstituting itself. The law of which he would have had to speak is not that of life but, instead, the law of life's law: a law of missed selfhood, of non-return, of ever-otherness. It is the law of delegation under which only another can ever be understood: a law under which the law must give leave to another and cede its rights to this other; a law—of the de-legation even of the law—under which the law itself must break down. It would be the law of a priori manifolding: a law commanding that there always be more than *one* law and always something other than the *law*, each one isolated and standing together with others only in its isolation. It is thus the law of a whole that converges in—and does not emerge out of—separation and division. Only where understanding stands under this law of delegation is it *itself* and yet open to *another*. It is understanding only when it touches, in itself, upon something incomprehensible.

"Rediscovery," repetition, returning to oneself and to the self are not simply obsessively cited and recited topoi of the philosophical tradition. Under the title "hermeneutic circle" the theorem of return holds an axiomatic status in all hermeneutic theories, regardless of whether they make universal claims or limit themselves to regional investigations into scholarly domains of historical philology. The "circle" in understanding is an expression of a difficulty that can be characterized as the paradox of presupposition, for this circle is at once demanded and prohibited. There is a demand that all understanding of a part be grounded in the understanding of a supposed whole, but it is forbidden that the whole be anticipated and set down as a formal structure in advance of the understanding of the part. The model of an organic connection among all individual phenomena lies at the basis of the demand, whereas the prohibition arises from the belief in demonstrative certainty; in order to achieve such certainty, no one is allowed to turn a proposition to be demonstrated into a premise of the demonstration. In his "Second Academic Discourse," Schleiermacher paraphrases the "founding proposition of hermeneutics" as the principle "that all parts can be understood by means of the whole and therefore every explanation of the particular already presupposes the understanding of the whole."[23] But this presupposition of the whole—and on this point Schleiermacher leaves no doubts—is a presupposition of something that is never given as a consistent phenomenon but always only as an ideal of understanding. The presupposition, the circle, and thus the "principle of hermeneutics" have the structure of a project, a prolepsis toward that which is not yet and never will be given: they are ground, principle, and premise only when they forever forestall every factual stance and every form of phenomenal consistency. The premise is a promise. This promise, it should be emphasized, is not founded on secure knowledge of particular states of affairs that it intends to complete in the future; rather, it is the only possible grounding of such knowledge, and thus a promise that not only precedes all acts of cognition and understanding but also, for this reason, precedes every predicative use of language, every predicative promise. If the ground (and thus the whole) is structured as a promise, then everything that was grounded in this whole, hence every part, must have functioned as its fulfillment. But in the same academic discourse Schleiermacher concedes that "non-understanding will never entirely disappear" (HK, 328). He thus admits that the whole of understanding, its ground, and its presupposition remain out of reach, and so the part, far from redeeming the promise of totality, must participate in the structure of promising, in the impossibility of its fulfillment.

Understanding remains an unfulfillable promise, always behind and ahead of itself at the same time. The objection lodged by formal logic against the "circle"—it takes for its premise what could only be its result—is in this way untenable: from the perspective of formal logic, the whole, which is precisely the result, is a conclusion whose certainty is in principle compelling; for understanding, by contrast, the whole remains a necessary but unredeemable project. Yet the notion of a "circle"—not a logical one, of course, but a hermeneutic one—is still justifiable. For understanding cannot do without an understanding of the whole and is understanding in an emphatic sense only when it can no longer be refuted by a single uncomprehended detail. The anticipation of its totality, the anticipation of *itself*, is thus constitutive of understanding; it consists essentially in *being* its own premise and thus being—being toward—that which it is not yet. No longer, then, is a "presupposition" the *proposition major* from which subsequent propositions can be derived for the understanding according to consistent logical rules; rather, understanding, structured as ahead-of-itself, is nothing other than "presupposing." Understanding cannot therefore succumb to the objection of a *petitio principii*; as an aporetic prolepsis, it is itself *principium petitsanis principii*.

In *Being and Time* Heidegger tried to defend the hermeneutic circle along similar lines. He took his point of departure from a concept of understanding that is not limited to the understanding of texts, discourses, or actions and does not allow the conventions of any particular science to proscribe its horizon: "In ontic discourse we use the expression 'to understand something' to mean 'to be in a stance of control over something,' 'to be capable of coping with it,' 'to be able to do something.' That which can be done as an existential in understanding is not a 'what' but rather Being as existing. The mode of Being of *Dasein* as being-able [*Sein-können*] lies in an existential manner in understanding."[24] Understanding thus means to be able, and as an existential it is, according to Heidegger, "the most primordial and the final positive ontological determination of *Dasein*" (SZ, 143–44). As a primordial and indeed as "the most primordial" mode of being-ahead-of-oneself and standing-in-advance-of-oneself, understanding is, once again, the "final positive determination of *Dasein*." It is for this reason that, as Heidegger always underlines, *Dasein* is "free for *its* possibilities" (SZ, 144). "What it is *not yet* in its ability-to-be, it *is* existentially" (SZ, 145). And by understanding in this way, *Dasein* is always already its own "not-yet": it stands ahead of itself where it does not yet stand, and it thus understands in its "not" each time itself, each time understands in another *its* other, and each time understands possibilities as *its* possibilities. There is no "there" of being-there that would not be a "before," and there is no "before" that could not be its own "before." *Dasein* does not therefore make any presuppositions; rather, as understanding, it *is* "the most primordial 'presupposing'" in which it "relates itself solely to itself" (SZ, 228).[25] Without any presuppositions, it is itself the performance of "presupposing" in which it understands itself as understanding—as premise and project. And this movement of Being called "understanding" is, according to Heidegger, related solely to itself, grasped as a circular self-relation.

The terminology of throwing, projection, and thrownness that Heidegger mobilizes in this context still moves within the horizon of a standing and a "positive" determination, even if it is a "final" one. However much *Being and Time* may reclaim a pre-positional and pre-propositional structure for the Being of *Dasein*, it nevertheless conceives of *Dasein* in its "before"—to the extent that it is *its* "before"—as a position and thus grasps *Dasein* within the horizon of ontotheseology. Heidegger is never more consistent than when he redefines the autonomy of *Dasein* as standing-on-its-own (*Selbst-ständigkeit*), which is to say: "the standing of the self in the sense of having achieved a stance" and "in the double sense of consistent standing-firm" (SZ, 322).[26] And Heidegger is equally consistent when he attempts to secure the status of the self-relation of understanding as a "circular Being of *Dasein*" (*SZ*, 315). The circle is the basic figure of the horizon of positionality: there is no position that would not stand in the horizon of self-movement, no horizon that would not be circular, no circle in which the position would not relate to itself by being out ahead of itself and would not therefore close in on itself. Thus Heidegger can write: "The ecstatic character of the primordial future lies precisely in the fact that this future concludes one's ability-to-be; that is, it is closed [*geschlossen*] and as such it makes possible the resolute [*entschlossene*: disclosed] existentiell understanding of nothingness" (SZ, 330). Understanding is conclusive; it is the closing and coming to an end of understanding. Thus the original finitude of understanding. The circle designates the figure of all possible figures, the primordial figure of the authentic, existentiell pre-position in which *Dasein* as understanding encounters itself as the end of understanding. The "presupposition" in which *Dasein* discloses itself is at the same time the conclusion in which it closes in on itself.

The "circular Being of *Dasein*," the "ontological circle-structure" (SZ, 330) of an entity that is concerned with its own being and with Being as its own, is not, for Heidegger, a deducible and further reducible phenomenon; on the contrary, it is the phenomenon that precedes all phenomenality and inscribes itself in every other phenomenon, including the "phenomenon" of phenomenality itself. For the very possibility that something will show itself *as* something—whether in the apophantic or hermeneutic mode of the "as"—is already "circular," since something can show itself only to a *Dasein* that therein understands one of its own possibilities and thus understands itself in anticipation of itself. In this way Heidegger draws all talk of a "circle" away from its restrictive use in regional hermeneutic investigations and reclaims it for a fundamental hermeneutics, and he likewise dismisses the charge lodged by formal logic against the circle—the charge that it is a *circulus vitiosus* and should therefore be banned from all further proceedings: "But to see a *vitiosum* in this circle and to be on the look-out for ways to avoid it, even if one only 'senses' it as an unavoidable imperfection—this is to misunderstand understanding from the ground up" (SZ, 153).[27] The circle of understanding cannot be avoided because it is an "expression of the existential fore-structure of *Dasein* itself" (SZ, 153). Avoiding this circle would then be nothing less than suicidal. Yet at the same time Heidegger insists that precisely this "circle" must be avoided if *Dasein* is to be characterized, in an ontological manner. At the very end of § 32 ("Understanding and Interpretation"), having formulated the "ontological circle-structure" of *Dasein*, Heidegger offers without further commentary the following sentence: "Nevertheless, if one notices that a 'circle' belongs ontologically to a kind of Being that is present-to-hand (subsistence [*Bestand*]), we must altogether avoid using the phenomenon to characterize in an ontological manner anything like *Dasein*" (SZ, 153). The "circle" thus *cannot* be avoided, and yet it *must* be avoided; it is not a vicious one, and yet it is one after all. This flagrant contradiction between the unavoidable and what is to be avoided "nevertheless"—the contradiction between understanding as event and advent of Being and understanding as a securing of something subsistent—gives rise to the suspicion that even authentic understanding is resistance to understanding. Indeed, it gives rise to the suspicion that the project of a fundamental-hermeneutic analysis is afflicted in its entirety by a deficient understanding, and at the same time it indicates the possibility of an opening up of the hermeneutic horizon toward an understanding that is not simply an understanding of itself and thus not simply an understanding of the Being of *Dasein*: it is the possibility of an opening of understanding to something other than a phenomenon, to another "before"—or something other than a "before"—and thus to another existential premise or something other than a premise.

Heidegger's analysis of the problem and metaproblem of understanding, being-ahead-of-oneself, projection, and *Dasein* becomes explosive at the very moment it reaches the *locus classicus* of hermeneutics and its question concerning the premises of understanding:

the moment, that is, it sets out to analyze the whole. According to Schleiermacher's formulation, an understanding of the whole must be "presupposed" for the explanation of the part. In accordance with the fundamental-hermeneutic deregionalization of this question carried out in *Being and Time*, such an understanding must refer to the "possible being-whole of *Dasein*" and this being-whole can only have the structure of a Being *toward* the whole, which is to say, the structure—*a limine*—of a being-toward-the-end, a being-toward-death. "This end," Heidegger writes, "which *belongs* to being-able, i.e., to existence, limits and determines the possible wholeness of *Dasein*" (SZ, 234).[28] Heidegger poses the question concerning the possibility of being-whole as a question concerning the possibility of death, hence as a question concerning an understood death, a death *Dasein* is in a position to die. Thus it is the question whether death "belongs" to being-able. Heidegger seems to answer this unequivocally in the affirmative whenever he speaks of the anticipation of death and the unbroken circularity of understanding—for example, in the following sentence, where the word "belonging" is underlined: "*Dasein* always already exists in just such a manner that its 'not-yet' *belongs* to it" (SZ, 243). Or, to take another example, when he asserts: "Just as *Dasein* already *is* as long as it is constantly its 'not yet,' likewise it *is* always already its end" (SZ, 245). This being-already of the "not-yet," this being-beforehand of *Dasein* forbids the interpretation of death as "outstanding" (*Ausstand*) and thus as a mode of "subsistence" (*Bestand*).[29] For death is never an actuality in the sense of the objectivity of something present-to-hand; it is always a futurial possibility of *Dasein*. And this possibility is from two points of view "distinguished" from all others: it is the most extreme possibility and thus the only one from which the ontological analysis of being-able can attain its completeness; but as this, the most extreme possibility, it is at the same time the one in which being-possible runs up against the end of all possibilities. In view of this "distinction," which represents an existential premise of Heidegger's entire existential analytic, the question concerning the possibility of being-whole, the horizon of *Dasein*, the structure of understanding and its "before," and finally the question whether the end "belongs" to *Dasein* must all open themselves to something other than a merely affirmative response.

Heidegger presents the aporia that death, as the possibility of the end, is at the same time the end of the possibility of *Dasein* in one of the most decisive and subsequently most famous passages of *Being and Time*:

The closest proximity of Being to death as possibility is as far removed from anything actual as possible. The more this possibility is understood without any veiling, the more purely does understanding penetrate into possibility as the possibility of the impossibility of existence as such. Death as possibility gives *Dasein* nothing that could be "actualized" and nothing that *Dasein* could ever actually *be*. It is the possibility of the impossibility of every way of comporting oneself toward . . . , of every mode of existing. In the anticipation of this possibility, it becomes "greater and greater"; that is to say, the possibility unveils itself to be such that it knows no measure at all, no more or less, but signifies the possibility of the measureless impossibility of existence. (SZ, 262)[30]

That understanding, as Heidegger writes, "penetrates into possibility as the possibility of the impossibility of existence as such" means that it "penetrates" into and anticipates this possibility, that it understands, is able and capable of this possibility as the dis-abling of precisely its ability. Hence understanding must always be an understanding of non-understanding if it is ever understanding at all. Insofar as it is understanding, it always already understands this understanding as an understanding of non-understanding; understanding still understands this non-understanding, the impossibility that is—never actual—death. This is to say that *Dasein* still grasps "the absolute impossibility of existence" (SZ, 265) as a possibility and indeed, as Heidegger emphasizes, makes it possible in the first place. But it also means that there is thus absolutely no limit and no measure for the possibilities and understanding of *Dasein*: it is always dying, and by dying in this way it is infinitely finite. *Dasein* still understands its end, and by still understanding, it is the infinite finitude of understanding. It still—and precisely here—understands itself in its Being toward death and is thus itself essentially the understanding of the absolutely incomprehensible. *Dasein* is understood, enabled death.[31]

The possible being-whole of *Dasein* as understanding would indeed be reached, the completeness of the hermeneutic situation would be attained, and the fundamental-hermeneutical circle would be closed with this "most extreme and ownmost" possibility. If the possibility of impossibility still "belongs" to the circuit of possibilities—which is the circuit of understanding as being-able—then there is nothing more that could withdraw from understanding, oppose itself to understanding as something exterior, or determine it from the outside. If the "absolute impossibility of existence" constitutively "belongs" to the possibilities of *Dasein*, if *Dasein* has from the beginning cut out the circle of its ability and understanding, if it has always already enabled its own not-being-able, then it not only never stops understanding itself and understanding itself as understanding, but, in making possible its own impossibility, it comes to the summa of its existence, to itself as ability. Death, the end of understanding, is understood; the end of being-able is enabled; the end of enabling is still enabled. And so death as a possibility and a capacity of *Dasein* is the absolute of its self-appropriation.

But Heidegger's formula—"the possibility of the impossibility of existence"—has another side. Death, Heidegger writes, "is the possibility of the impossibility of every way of comporting oneself toward . . . , of every mode of existing" (SZ, 262).[32] And death is, accordingly, the possibility of the impossibility of this very possibility. If finite Being is comportment toward the end of Being, then it is comportment toward the impossibility of this very comportment. Understanding—since it means being-able—must be structured as an understanding of the non-understanding of this understanding itself. It can understand itself only as possible non-understanding, and since this possibility does not remain exterior to it but rather determines it from the outset, it can understand itself likewise only by not understanding itself—and by not understanding itself as understanding. Making-impossible must then "belong" to the structure of making-possible; non-understanding must still "belong" to the most authentic and "the most primordial" understanding. And this affects every possibility of *Dasein*, including the possibility of ontology, phenomenology, and hermeneutics. The postulate that "death is, as long as it 'is,' essentially always my own" (SZ, 240), becomes untenable: the "ever mineness" (*Jemeinigkeit*) of death withdraws into ever otherness (*Jeandersheit*). Death, the end, the most extreme and "ownmost" limit of *Dasein* and its possibilities, insofar as it is non-comprehended death, cannot be one's *own* death without at the same time being *another* death, a death impossible to appropriate. Wherever understanding is supposed to be "the most primordial," it must turn into an incomprehensible, other understanding. The project of a fundamental hermeneutics of understanding thus collapses at its limit, at the very place where it was supposed to have secured the completeness of understanding and therefore its own wholeness. The "not-yet" of the end, as a "never-once," does not always "also belong" to *Dasein*; in the absence of every phenomenologically graspable marking, it marks the non-appurtenance, the non-belonging to *Dasein*. Whenever the horizon of understanding is affected by incomprehensibility, there is no longer simply a "hermeneutic situation"[33] that would allow an adequate ontological analysis. Whenever it is no longer possible to have, see, or grasp anything, the three forms in which interpretation unfolds—fore-having, fore-seeing, and fore-grasping (*Vorhabe, Vorsicht, Vorgriff*)[34]—are bound to fail; whenever understanding no longer grasps its "before" as its *own*, no longer grasps it as *its* possibility, and is no longer able to rediscover itself in this "before" and thence return to itself, the hermeneutic circle remains open.

Every "anticipation" of understanding, every understanding as being-in-anticipation-of-itself, must be an anticipation of its incomprehensibility. There is no "before" that would not also be its making-impossible and thereby de-structure the fore-structure of *Dasein*. The premise of understanding must also be a premise of its impossibility and thus dismissed: the making-impossible of every premise. "Before" is the prefix of the disappropriation and de-authentication of understanding. Every phenomenon is crossed out by this "before" and its movement of aphanisis.

Heidegger does not pursue this other side of the formula of the possibility of impossibility; nowhere does he analyze it and never does he draw out its consequences. The impossibility of understanding—of *Dasein*—continues for him to "belong" to the domain of understanding; it remains an understood, enabled impossibility and thus an existential of appropriation. He no longer understands, one could say, what he himself had indicated in his description of the "phenomenon" of being-toward-the-end, because he understands this mode of being only within the parameters of understanding *itself*. But his phrase concerning the "possibility of measureless impossibility" also indicates the impossibility of appropriation, thus the collapse of being-whole, the fall of every stance that understanding is supposed to be able to attain in its most extreme possibility, and the opening onto an other—and this other can no longer be understood according to the measure of the self, no longer according to the measure of the understanding, and no longer according to the measure of ability. The measureless understanding toward which Heidegger's phrase points—an understanding without stance and without standard—would have to be understood in the absence of every measure and thus in the absence even of understanding *itself*. Something, including understanding, would have to be understood always in such a way as if there were no understanding at all. For if understanding is supposed to understand *another*—and only then can it be called understanding at all—then for the sake of this other it must give up even its most minimal premise, namely, the premise that it is understanding. This hyperbolic demand, request, or hope defines—and undefines—every moment of understanding. Without it, understanding would be an imposition. What Heidegger's phrase thus discloses—and Heidegger's interpretation of this phrase immediately forecloses—is the possibility of thinking about understanding no longer as an archi-eschatological self-appropriation, no longer as a making-present, as a presentation or appresentation, but as an always singular alteration and thus an alteration of the very concept of understanding, even the most "radical" one. Only an understanding that was free of understanding would be a *free* understanding.

The "before" does not therefore "belong" to understanding: it absolves itself of understanding in the movement of its "presupposing." No longer—always already no longer—a "pre-" of positing, the self cannot understand or grasp itself in this "before," recognize itself as its other, and thence return to itself. Exposed to this "before," understanding breaks the circle that it itself draws. It always "belongs" to another that does not belong to it, to others to which nothing can belong.

Heidegger never denied the movement of understanding in the direction of the other, but he placed this movement under the sign of being-oneself and the possible wholeness of the self. One of the most remarkable statements devoted to this motif in *Being and Time* reads: "As non-relational possibility, death individualizes—but only in such a manner that, as the possibility not to be surpassed, it makes *Dasein* as being-with have an understanding of the being-able of others" (SZ, 264). Accordingly, being-with only becomes comprehensible within the horizon of the "ownmost" possibility of *Dasein* itself; "others" become comprehensible only in *Dasein*'s own "being-able" and thus on analogy with its "final positive" characteristic—without Heidegger even noting, much less discussing, this homogenization of the self and the other.[35] If, by contrast, the possibility of not-being-able already had to be admitted as one of the determinants of *Dasein*, then it cannot be considered any less constitutive—and deconstitutive—of being-with and must even be thought of as the opening of every access to another. But the fact that it is not only *my* death that I die, not only *my* other that I understand, means that the other, death, can be experienced neither according to my measure nor on analogy with a self. The fact that I am not simply *with* my death, that it does not simply "belong" to my being-there, my *Dasein*—this devastates the with-structure of my relation to another. Being with another, I am already without the "with" that secures my commensurability with it. Only in this with-without-with, only in an understanding-without-understanding, is another "understood" in such a manner that it is not subjected to the measure of *my* possibilities, and I in turn do not fall prey to its tyranny but, instead, experience the "measureless" possibility of the impossibility of our relation. Horizons can be fused only if they are analogical specimens of one and the same geometrical structure. As an analogue to the self, the other is always understood only as another self, never in its otherness, never from the perspective of its difference—and so precisely misunderstood. Not the "fusing of horizons" recommended by a diplomatic hermeneutics of mediation,[36] but only the draft of aporetic distancing and the disappropriation of the horizon allow for something called understanding, admit understanding from its withdrawal, and free up access—the aporia—to the other.

The fact that understanding must be free in order to be understanding at all means that it must open up and keep open a space that just as little "belongs" to it as to anything else that could arise therein as a possible object. Something is understand*able* only when it is set free from understanding. Heidegger does not describe this movement of laying bare, setting free, and opening up in *Being and Time*, and when years later he does so in the essay "On the Essence of Truth," he does not use the terminology of understanding and anticipation but that of leaving, and ex-posing: "As this letting-be, it exposes itself to beings as such and transposes all comportment into the open. Letting-be, that is, freedom, is in itself ex-posing [*aus-setzend*], ek-sistent. Seen from the perspective of the essence of truth, the essence of freedom shows itself as exposure [*Aussetzung*] to the unconcealment of beings."[37] With this ex-posure to an open arena where another can first appear, understanding abandons its ontotheseological horizon: no longer is it subordinated to a praxis and a theory of "position or positing," and no longer does it go in search of a certain stance, the constancy of objects, or the consistency of representation. As the ex-posure of positing—the *Aussetzung der Setzung*, the interruption of every positional act, the exposition of every possible position—it draws on an opening, an unposited space, and a place impossible to posit. Whatever still appears in this opening as an object of representation and comprehension must be tinged by its openness and cannot therefore, as Heidegger insists, simply appear *as* such an object. Just as ex-posure—this immemorial "premise" of understanding, a premise in which every act of communication and understanding is disclosed—can no longer be thought in accordance with the logic of positing and that of Being conceived as position, it is no longer possible to think of the "pre" of this "premise" simply as something that still "belongs" to positing and could be referred back to understanding; the "pre" of this "premise" can be thought only as something that no longer "belongs." Along with the exposure of understanding comes the a-position, abandonment, and loss of its "before."

Even the most defiant positivists cannot deny that this insight into the paradoxical structure—this de-structure—of understanding does not thrive on the soil of fundamental ontology alone. The peculiar crossing of understanding's possibility and impossibility is also found in the work of the most vehement critic of this ontology, namely Adorno. And in Adorno's writings this crossing of possibility and impossibility is formulated in less hidden, more categorical, and much more aggressive terms than in Heidegger's intricate phenomenological aporias. In his essay "Trying to Understand Endgame," Adorno says of Beckett's play: "Understanding it can only mean understanding its incomprehensibility, concretely reconstructing what it means that it has no meaning."[38] Concerning Rudolf Borchardt's "Position of the Poet," he writes: "He was 'cornered,' to use English, the language he loved: his work was an impasse, aporetic. That it gave shape to its own impossibility is the true seal of its modernity" (Notes, 553; 2: 208). In his "Speech on Lyric Poetry and Society," Adorno speaks of something that "suddenly flashes out, something in which the possible surpasses its own impossibility" (Notes, 64; 1: 50), and a little later he says: "the chimeric longing of language for the impossible becomes an expression of the insatiable erotic longing of the subject who discharges himself of himself in another" (Notes, 67; 1: 53).[39] Longing for another must mean longing for something "impossible," since this longing strives to break through the categorial forms of subjectivity that dominate every experience of the other and distort every other into a replica of the self: the other must be the impossible, the one beyond all possibilities of the subject— the other other—if the I is going to be able to discharge itself of itself in this other and come free. The language that turns itself toward this other can no longer conform to the communicative codes in which an egologically structured society comprehends itself. Indeed, this language must be impossible, incomprehensible—and in its incomprehensibility it must allow, as Adorno writes, that "sudden flash" that in language itself, under the conditions of its impossibility, is other.

In an essay entitled "Presuppositions" Adorno comments, referring to texts of modernity, that "The harsh light of the incomprehensible such artworks turn toward the reader renders customary comprehensibility suspect of being stale, shallow, thingly—preartistic" (Notes, 431; 2: 95).[40] In the same essay Adorno denounces any attempt to limit the principle of incomprehensibility to modernity and to the domain of art, or to a merely "aesthetic" concept of understanding, and this denunciation is undertaken with enough energy to make it clear that he does not conceive of the collapse of comprehensibility only as a regional and historically circumscribed phenomenon. Thus he writes: "In art—and, so I would like to think, not in art alone—history has retroactive force. The crisis of comprehensibility . . . drags even older works into itself" (Notes, 432; 2: 96). It is the incomprehensible—and incomprehensible in principle—that is torn open by the "crisis of comprehensibility" in modernity. And thus it is an aporia, a self-denial of both rationality and the course of history, that breaks through all the borders between epochs, institutions, and genres, between theories and practices, between conscious and unconscious acts. By "surpassing its own impossibility," the possible testifies to a language that no longer obeys the distinctions of subjectivity, and it testifies to an understanding that would have leaped clear of the categories of rational construction and leaped into another understanding—not an understanding that is somehow "irrational" but one that consists in the freeing of the *ratio*, the emancipation of an altered *ratio*. It is this event of the impossible that matters in the end—and matters not simply because it discloses an understanding that no longer conforms to conceptual and social forms of understanding but, most of all, because only in the arena of this other under-standing is it possible to experience *what* understanding, language, and society could be—and *that* they could be at all. More exactly: what and that they could *perhaps* be.

In a speech entitled "The Meridian," Paul Celan spoke of the paths of poetry and lan-guage: they are "paths of a voice to a perceiving You, creaturely paths, perhaps projects of existence [*Daseinsentwürfe vielleicht*], a sending oneself out toward oneself, in search of oneself . . ." (GW, 3: 201). One can understand Celan's progression of phrases in this way: the paths are not only toward a You; they are also toward oneself, toward another and toward an I, hence toward the other as an I or toward the I as another; they are paths, finally, in search of themselves. Indeed, there is no guarantee that they are paths; they move in the mode of "perhaps," more exactly, in the mode of suspending all modalities: "projects of existence *perhaps*," Celan says. There is, for these paths, no certainty, not even that they could have taken their point of departure from "art as something given in advance and something that is supposed to be unconditionally presupposed" (GW, 3: 193). This alone is certain: "The poem is in want of another, it needs this other, it needs an against to work. It seeks it out, it gives itself over to it in speaking" (GW 3: 198). But neither this other nor the path—which is to say, the art or the language able to lead to it—are presupposed or given in advance of the poem. A poem without presuppositions, even without the presup-position that it is a poem, is something that "sends itself out toward itself"—but toward a "self" impossible to secure, a merely virtual "self." It is a prolepsis into an other. "Perhaps," Celan writes, "here, with the I—with the *here* and estranged I set free *in this way*—perhaps here an other becomes free?—Perhaps the poem is from that point itself . . ." (GW, 3: 196). It is not from its own point of view but only from that of this other, the non-given and non-presupposed—an other who is without methodological guarantees of understanding and has thus "perhaps" become free—that the poem is then—but once again "perhaps"—"itself." Its language speaks from the place of a "perhaps," a possible other; but this possibil-ity is impossible to secure, and so the language of the poem can speak only "perhaps."

By describing the path of language and poetry in this way, Paul Celan describes the path of understanding as well. Understanding does not so much set out in search of the other as set out *from* it. Celan does not deny the "darkness" with which poetry is reproached, and one can doubtless understand this "darkness" as incomprehensibility; rather, he offers this by way of clarification: "the darkness assigned to poetry from a—perhaps self-projected—distance and foreignness for the sake of an encounter" (GW, 3: 195). If the poem is an apostrophe to an other, then it must speak in such a way that it is comprehensible to this other according to the measure of its otherness; but since this measure is uncertain, the poem can hope for comprehensibility only in its estrangement from comprehension. The poem is incomprehensible for the sake of *another* understanding. In its darkness the other-ness of its addressee already speaks too: the one addressed is the one who addresses. And this otherness speaks in a language other than that of commodious communication, in a language that is never already common language, never already language at all, and can therefore never be certain of its comprehensibility. The poem can be written only from something other than the poem; understanding—"perhaps," if it comes to the poem—can only come from something incomprehensible.

Celan called the path that he himself forged in his speech "this impossible path, this path of the impossible" (GW, 3: 195). The path was impossible, and so too are the paths of language, one can surmise, because "what is claimed and what is turned into a You, so to speak [*gleichsam*], by the act of naming brings its otherness along" on this path (GW 3: 198). The path of what is called a You "so to speak" and what must no less be called an I "so to speak" leads out into the open—and is thus an impossible path and a path of the impossible. "We are," Celan says, "if we speak with things in this way, always in the space of a question about their whence and whither: in an 'open-ended' question, a question 'coming to no conclusion,' a question pointing toward the open and empty and free—we are far outside" (GW 3: 199).[41] Far out-side, in a question pointing toward the open, not at a site definable by temporal and spatial parameters, not in a given or presupposed rhetorical topos, but at a site to be projected, a non-site: "u-topia" (GW, 3: 199). The path of language goes toward the otherness of one "turned into a You, so to speak," and it thus goes out into an opening that cannot be occupied or invested by methods and topics: the impossible. It goes to the otherness of language and is therefore, "perhaps," already the path of another language. It is the path of understanding toward the siteless, the unsecurable, toward the "otherness" of understanding—toward an understanding of Being other than as position— and is therefore, once again "perhaps," already other than understanding.

On March 26, 1969, Celan wrote this about poetry: "La poésie ne s'impose plus, elle s'expose" (GW, 3: 181).

And so, too, does understanding. It ex-poses itself.

Notes

1. See Aristotle, *Metaphysica*, ed. W. Jaeger (Oxford: Clarendon, 1957), 982b12; *Metaphysics*, trans. W. D. Ross, in *The Works of Aristotle*, ed. R. McKeon (New York: Random House, 1941), 692.

2. G. W. F. Hegel, *Vorlesungen über die Philosophic der Geschichte* in *Werke in zwanzig Bänden*, ed. E. Moldenhauer and K. M. Michel (Frankfurt am Main: Suhrkamp, 1970), 12: 288. Cf. *Lectures on the Philosophy of History*, trans. J. Sibree (New York: Dover, 1956), 234; hereafter, Lectures.

All translations in this chapter are new. Whenever possible, I have included references to readily available English translations; but in no case are these translations themselves quoted.—Trans.

3. Other passages from the same context point in a similar direction: "Thus the Delphic priestesses, without consciousness and without reflection, in the rapture of enthusiasm (*mania*) uttered unintelligible sounds from themselves, and only then did the *mantis* lay down a specific meaning for these noises" (12: 290; Lectures, 236). And: "*manteia* in general is poetry—not arbitrary fantasizing but a fantasy that puts spirit into the natural and is meaningful knowledge" (12: 291; Lectures, 236–37). Interpretation (*Auslegen*) is, one could say, a putting inside (*Hineinlegen*). It obeys the mechanism of

projection that Goethe ironically recommended in the "Tame Xenien II": "Im Auslegen seid frisch und munter,/ Legt ihr's nicht aus, so legt was unter" (In interpretation be fresh and cheerful; if you don't lay it out, lay something down) (Goethe, *Werke*, Hamburger Ausgabe, ed. Erich Trunz [Hamburg: Wegner, 1964], 1: 329). How little the Hegelian presentation grasps the peculiarity of Greek mantics becomes clear in Jean-Luc Nancy's commentary on its first philosophical discussion in Plato's *Ion*; see J.-L. Nancy, *Le partage des voix* (Paris: Galilée, 1982); cf. "Sharing Voices," trans. Gayle L. Ormiston, in *Transforming the Hermeneutic Context*, ed. G. L. Ormiston and A. D. Schrift (Albany, N.Y.: SUNY Press, 1990), 211–59.

4. See Hegel, 12: 290; *Lectures*, 236.

5. See my study, *pleroma—zu Genesis und Struktur einer dialektischen Hermeneutik bei Hegel*, in G. W. F. Hegel, *Der Geist des Christentums: Schriften 1796–1800*, ed. W. Hamacher (Berlin: Ullstein, 1978), 7–333. My work does not discuss premises but rather the structure of the dialectical "pre" and the speculative mass. I also make the suggestion that one should speak of diaporia rather than aporia—of an impasse in the passage itself.

6. Immanuel Kant, *Gesammelte Schriften*, ed. Königliche Preussische [later, Deutsche] Akademie der Wissenschaften (Berlin and Leipzig: Georg Reimer [later, Walter de Gruyter], 1900–) 2: 73. There is a reprint of the Akademie edition of this treatise alongside an English translation entitled *The One Possible Basis for a Demonstration, of the Existence of God*, trans. Gordon Treash (New York: Abaris, 1979). All subsequent citations of Kant refer to the Akademie edition, hereafter "Ak," except citations of the *Critique of Pure Reason*. In accordance with scholarly tradition, all citations of this work refer to its original editions (A, B).

7. Kant explicitly writes: "The relations of all predicates to their subject never indicate something existing, for the subject must have already have been *presupposed* as existing." And "if the subject is not already *presupposed* as existing, it remains in every predicate undecided whether it belongs to something existing or merely to a possible subject. Therefore, existence cannot itself be a predicate" (Ak, 2: 74; emphasis added).

8. Kant's thesis on Being should be compared to an essay of Martin Heidegger from *Wegmarken* (Frankfurt am Main: Klostermann, 1967), 273–307; cf. "Kant's Thesis on Being," trans. Ted Klein, Jr., and William Pohl, *The Southwestern Journal of Philosophy*, 4 (1973): 7–33. For Kant's later theory of positing, see Eckart Förster, "Kant's *Selbstsetzungslehre*" in *Kant's Transcendental Deductions*, ed. E. Förster (Stanford: Stanford University Press, 1989), 217–38.

9. These positio-ontological premises are universally valid and are thus even valid for things in themselves, hence for things with no relation to our modes of thinking and sensing—albeit with an important distinction. These premises have, for Kant, transcategorial validity. In a very important section of the *Critique of Judgment*, § 76, Kant says: "But our entire distinction between the merely possible and the actual rests on this: the merely possible means the position of representation of a thing with respect to our concept and the ability to think in general, whereas the actual means the positing of a thing in itself (apart from that concept)" (Ak, 5: 402).

10. Hegel, 6: 32; cf. *The Science of Logic*, trans. A. V. Miller (New York: Humanities Press, 1969), 406; hereafter, "Logic." (Miller translates *Dasein* as "determinate being.")

11. In one of his last notes Kant wrote about the thing in itself as *ens per se*: "It is an *ens rationis* = x of the position of itself according to the principle of identity wherein the subject, as self-affecting, hence according to the form, is thought only as appearance" (*Opus postumum*, AK, 22: 27).

12. F. W. J. Schelling, *Sämmtliche Werke* (Stuttgart: Cotta, 1856), 1.1: 335; cf. *Philosophical Letters on Dogmaticism and Criticism*, in *The Unconditional in Human Knowledge*, trans. Fritz Marti (Lewisburg, Pa.: Bucknell University Press, 1980), 192.

13. Friedrich Schlegel, *Fragmente zur Poesie und Literatur*, in *Kritische Friedrich-Schlegel Ausgabe*, ed. Ernst Behler, Jean-Jacques Anstett, and Hans Eichner (Paderborn: Schöningh, 1958–), 16.1: 69; section 4, "Zur Philologie," II no. 95. Hereafter, KA.

14. See KA, 16.1: 36; no. 14: "Not a deduction but TOWARD the deduction." In "On Incomprehensibility," he brings up the Idea of "constructing for the reader . . . as it were, before his eyes another new reader to my liking, indeed . . . even to deduce him" (KA, 2: 363). A translation of the last quotation can be found in "On Incomprehensibility" in *"Lucinde" and the Fragments*, trans. Peter Firchow (Minneapolis: University of Minnesota Press, 1971), 260. All citations of Schlegel have been newly translated for this volume.

15. Positing (*Setzung*), objectivity (*Gegenständlichkeit*), placing (*Stellung*), representation (*Vorstellung*), presentation (*Darstellung*) all refer in German to a certain stance or to the act of taking a stand.—Already in his earlier work Heidegger referred the tradition of these concepts, which he later collected under the title *Ge-stell*, back to Greek philosophy and its language. In his *Introduction to Metaphysics* he thus writes: "But this erect standing-there, coming to a stance [*zum Stande kommen*] and enduring in a stance [*im Stand Bleiben*], is what the Greeks understood by Being" (Martin Heidegger, *Ein-führung in die Metaphysik* (Tübingen: Niemeyer, 1966), 46; cf. *Introduction to Metaphysics*, trans. Ralph Manheim [Garden City, N.Y.: Anchor, 1961], 49). "'Being' meant for the Greeks *constancy* in a double sense: 1. standing-in-itself as emergence [*Ent-stehung*] (*phusis*) 2. 'standing' as such, that is, enduring, lingering (*ousia*)" (*Einführung in die Metaphysik*, 48; *Introduction to Metaphysics*, 52). Heidegger's terminology of "decline" (*Verfallen*) indicates that he does not simply have a critical relationship to this tradition and indeed lets it persist in its "destruction" through "fundamental" ontology.

16. Friedrich Schlegel, *Charakteristiken und Kritiken I* in KA, 2: 372: "Sehe jeder wo er bleibe, / Und wer steht daß er nicht falle."

17. Friedrich Hölderlin, *Sämtliche Werke*, ed. F. Beißner (Stuttgart: Kohlhammer, 1943–1985), 2.2: 606 (late variant to "Bread and Wine"): "that the understanding writhes that research never / arises."

18. Søren Kierkegaard, *Papirer*, ed. P. A. Heiberg, V. Kuhr, and E. Torsting, rev. ed. N. Thulstrup (Copenhagen: Gyldendal, 1968–1970), 4: 244 (B 96 1b); cf. *Fear and Trembling—Repetition*, trans. and ed. Howard V. Hong and Edna H. Hong (Princeton: Princeton University Press, 1983), 244.

19. James Joyce, *Finnegans Wake* (Landon: Faber and Faber, 1975), 7.

20. Paul Celan, *Gesammelte Werke*, ed. Beda Allemann and Stefan Reichert in association with Rolf Bücher (Frankfurt am Main: Suhrkamp, 1983), 2: 338: "Unlesbarkeit dieser / Welt." Hereafter, GW.

21. Euripides, *Heracles*, ed. G. W. Bond (Oxford: Clarendon, 1981), ll. 911–12; cf. *Heracles*, trans. William Arrowsmith, in *Euripides* (Chicago: University of Chicago Press, 1956), 2: 93–94.

22. Wilhelm Dilthey; "The Construction of the Historical World in the Human Sciences" in *Gesammelte Schriften* (Leipzig: Teubner, 1927), 7: 191; cf. Dilthey, *Selected Writings*, ed. H. P. Rickman (Cambridge, England: Cambridge University Press, 1976), 208. All citations of Dilthey refer to the collected works.

23. Friedrich Schleiermacher, *Hermeneutik und Kritik*, ed. and intro. Manfred Frank (Suhrkamp: Frankfurt am Main, 1977), 328. Hereafter, HK.

24. Martin Heidegger, *Sein und Zeit* (Tübingen: Niemeyer, 1967), 143; cf. *Being and Time*, trans. John Macquarrie and Edward Robinson (New York: Harper & Row, 1962), 183. Since the English translation includes the pagination of the German text in its margins, all citations refer to the German edition; hereafter "SZ." All translations of Heidegger are new.

25. This formulation from § 44 (on the "Presupposition of Truth") reads in context: "What does it mean to 'presuppose'? To understand something as the ground for the Being of some other entity. . . . Thus to presuppose 'truth' means to understand it as something for the sake of which *Dasein* is. But *Dasein* is already—this lies in its being constituted as care—ahead of itself in each case. . . . The most primordial 'presupposing' lies in *Dasein* being constituted as care, in its being ahead of itself. This 'presupposing' that lies in the being of *Dasein* relates itself . . . solely to itself."

26. The connection between "running ahead" or "anticipating" (*Vorlaufen*) and "standingness" (*Ständigkeit*) and is made explicit in the following sentence: "Standing-on-one's-own means existentially nothing but resoluteness running ahead" (322).

27. In the same vein, the section devoted to the "hermeneutic situation" and the "methodical character of existential analysis in general" (§ 63) speaks of the unavoidability of the "circa": "A 'circle' in proof can never be 'avoided' in the existential analytic, because such an analytic does not do any proving at all according to rules of the 'logic of consistency,' What common sense wishes to eliminate in avoiding the 'circle,' on the supposition that it is satisfying the loftiest rigor of scientific investigation, is nothing less than the basic structure of care. Because it is primordially constituted by care, *Dasein* is always already ahead of itself" (315). At the point where the "idea of existence" begins, "pre-supposing" has "the character of interpretive projecting" (314)—and so, one could add, runs for precisely this reason in a circle. Heidegger adds that the "project" does not somehow prejudice that which is to be understood; rather, it discloses it by "indicating [it] in a formal manner" and "allowing" it "to come into speech for the first time" (315). The circle thus discloses, but it discloses as a formal indication that already has a determinate structure and by means, of this structure determines the "word" of that which is disclosed for understanding. This "word" is spoken only as a word predisposed by the "circle"—of care, of understanding, of being-able, and being-able-to-be-oneself.

28. This comes from the opening of the "Second Section" of *Being and Time* ("*Dasein* and Temporality"), which integrates the "Results of the Preparatory Fundamental Analysis of *Dasein*."

29. See Heidegger's analysis in § 48, "Outstanding, End, Wholeness" (SZ, esp. 242–246).

30. In a more elliptical fashion than here, I commented upon this decisive thought of Heidegger in an earlier work. See my "Peut-être la question" in *Les fins de l'homme—A partir du travail de Jacques Derrida*,

ed. Philippe Lacoue-Labarthe and Jean-Luc Nancy (Paris: Galilée, 1981), 245–363. In this essay I pursue the structure of the apophantic and hermeneutic "as," the possibility of self-understanding in Being-toward-death, the possibility (the "perhaps" and "peut-être") of the impossibility of one's "own" death and one's "own" understanding, namely, being-able, and finally the possibility—of the impossibility—of the question of Being. A few sentences from this fragmentary commentary: "This possibility that bears the name death cannot be grasped or conceived under the schema of the 'as.' It is just as little possible to speak of death *as* death, to speak of death *as such* as it is to say that it *is*" (356). "Nothing can assure me that I die my own death, that I properly die, that I do not die the death of another" (362). "By virtue of its not-yet structure, its apo- and para-structure, authentic understanding compels its own inauthenticity" (363). The motifs of possibility and the possibility of the impossibility of existence as such are further pursued and questioned in Giorgio Agamben's essay "La passion de la facticité," in *Heidegger—Questions ouvertes* (Paris: Osiris, 1988), 63–84, and in Jacques Derrida's *Aporias*, trans. Thomas Dutoit (Stanford: Stanford University Press, 1993).

31. "Der verstandene Tod" (Understood Death) is the title of Dolf Sternberger's "Untersuchung zu Martin Heideggers Existential-Ontologie" of 1932–33; it has been reprinted in D. Sternberger, *Über den Tod* (Frankfurt am Main: Insel, 1977).

32. Heidegger's formulation reaches its peak in the paragraphs concerned with the "ability-to-be-whole of *Dasein* in an existentially authentic way as anticipating resoluteness" (§ 62): "We conceived of death in an existential manner as the characteristic possibility of the *im*possibility of existence, that is, as the absolute nothingness of *Dasein*" (306). It should be noted that Heidegger does not write that death is conceived "as a *possibility* of the absolute nothingness of existence" but "as the absolute nothingness of existence"—and that he thus conceals the double sense of this possibility: on the one hand, this possibility is itself already a nothingness and, on the other, nothingness is always still a possibility of existence. These distinctions stop sounding "sophistic" when one is clear about the degree to which the meaning of "possibility" and "*im*possibility," "nothingness," "being-guilty," "conscience," "self," and *Dasein* in Heidegger's work depends upon them.

33. The first paragraph of the chapter that concerns "The possible being-whole of *Dasein* and Being toward death" (§ 4.6) begins by calling attention to "The insufficiency of the hermeneutic situation from which the preceding analysis of *Dasein* has arisen" (235). But this situation remains "insufficient" and thus never turns into a "situation" at all.

34. See Heidegger's analysis in § 32, "Understanding and Interpretation" (SZ, esp. 150).

35. Being-there (*Dasein*), for Heidegger, is doubtless "equiprimordially" being-with (*Mit-sein*), but this being-with—if it is "primordial," which is to say, "authentic"—is always a being-with with another *Dasein* in its "ownmost" being-able and is thus *Dasein* understanding itself in its being-toward-death. The analogy between *Dasein* and *Dasein*-with in *Being and Time* is, so far as I can see, never relinquished. It is this analogy that allows Heidegger to conceive of *Dasein* constituted as being-with but not as co-constituted by *another*—and that means constituted as other than *Dasein*-with as well. It becomes free *for* another by becoming free *from* it (Michael Theunissen points this out in his analysis of "authentic being-with-another" in *Being and Time*; see M. Theunissen, *Der Andere—Studien zur Sozialontologie der Gegenwart* [Berlin: de Gruyter, 1965], 181; cf. *The Other: Studies in the Social Ontology of Husserl, Heidegger, Sartre, and Buber*, trans. Christopher Macann [Cambridge, Mass.: MIT Press, 1984], 192.) And *Dasein*

becomes free *for* another by submitting this other to the model of its "own" *Dasein*. For the Heidegger of *Sein und Zeit*, each one gains freedom out of what is most proper to it, not out of what is impossibly its own, not out of that which neither "belongs" to *Dasein* nor to *Dasein*-with. But doesn't *Dasein*, by relating itself to *Dasein*-with, relate to the possibility of its *im*-possibility and thus to an immensely other relatum and to this other in another manner than mere relation? If this relation—this irrelation— is constitutive for every being-with, then must it not also be constituted as being-without-with and thus irreducibly de-constituted? The point is to think through the relation to the other not only as constitutive but as deconstitutive as well.

36. In *Truth and Method* Hans-Georg Gadamer makes the fusion of horizons of understanding into the very form of hermeneutic acts in general. Despite his constant appeal to Heidegger, despite the claim that he continues the fundamental-ontological project, he thus falls back upon a position that can best be characterized as a doctrine of diplomatic moderation. "Historical consciousness," Gadamer writes, brings "together once again that from which it has kept itself apart in order to mediate itself with itself in the unity of the historical horizon that it thus acquires for itself" (*Wahrheit und Methode* [Tübingen: Mohr, 1965], 290; cf. *Truth and Method*, 2nd rev. ed., trans. J. Weinsheimer and D. Marshall [New York: Crossroads, 1989], 306). Unity and completion are the results of a diplomatic—not dialectical—mediation at the end of which it becomes clear that it has been the mediation of the self with itself. The other comes into consideration, for Gadamer, only insofar as it has already entered into the horizon of a common sense and thus shed its otherness in favor of commonality.

37. Martin Heidegger, *Wegmarken* (Frankfurt am Main: Klosterman 1967), 84; cf. "On the Essence of Truth," trans. John Sallis, in *Basic Writings*, ed. D. F. Krell (New York: Harper & Row, 1977), 128.

38. Theodor W. Adorno, *Noten zur Literatur*, ed. R. Tiedemann (Frankfurt am Main: Suhrkamp, 1981), 283; cf. *Notes on Literature*, trans. Shierry Weber Nicholsen (New York: Columbia University Press), 1: 243. Hereafter, "Notes."

39. Any time the disclosure of possibility and the impossible are discussed in connection with and understanding, a discussion of affect is sure to follow. In every case it is a privileged or even grounding affect, never a fleeting feeling. In Kant (and among his successors in Schlegel) it is a pure self-affection, more exactly, pain. In Nietzsche it is the pathos of distance, as in the aphorism from *The Gay Science* that bears the title "Toward the Question of Comprehensibility" and begins with the sentence: "One does not only wish to be understood when one writes; one wishes just as surely *not* to be understood" (*Fröhliche Wissenschaft*, in *Werke*, ed. K. Schlechta [Munich: Hanser, 1954], 2: 256; cf. *The Gay Science*, trans. Walter Kaufmann [New York: Vintage, 1974], 343; § 381). In Kierkegaard it is despair; in Heidegger anxiety or boredom; in Adorno erotic longing; in Bataille hate. In the foreword to the second edition of his book *L'impossible* (perhaps named in honor of "L'impossible" from Rimbaud's *Une saison en enfer*) Bataille explains in the first sentences why the first chapter bears the title "The Hatred of Poetry": "It seemed to me that only hate leads to real poetry. Poetry has power and sense only in the violence of revolt. But poetry achieves this violence only by evoking the *impossible*" (Georges Bataille, *L'impossible* in *Oeuvres complètes* [Paris: Gallimard, 1971], 3: 101; italics added).

40. Adorno's discussion then takes issue with an "aesthetic concept of understanding" (Notes, 433; 2: 96).

41. Just as Celan lets the movement of the poem proceed from a question, Emmanuel Lévinas lets the movement of understanding proceed from a "primordial" question that is always also a request and a prayer, and he characterizes this question as "a relation to the other that refuses thematization and therefore always also an assimilation to knowledge because of its irreducible difference. A relation that therefore does not make itself into a correlation. Hence a relation that strictly speaking cannot express itself as a relation, since under its terms there is an absence even of that commonality of synchrony that no relation is allowed to refuse for its terms. And yet to the other—relation. Relation and non-relation" (Emmanuel Lévinas, *De Dieu qui vient à l'idée* [Paris: Vrin, 1986], 168–69).

18 Signature Event Context

Jacques Derrida

Still confining ourselves, for simplicity, to *spoken* utterance.
—Austin, *How to Do Things with Words*, p. 113, n. 2

Is it certain that there corresponds to the word *communication* a unique, univocal concept, a concept that can be rigorously grasped and transmitted: a communicable concept? Following a strange figure of discourse, one first must ask whether the word or signifier "communication" communicates a determined content, an identifiable meaning, a describable value. But in order to articulate and to propose this question, I already had to anticipate the meaning of the word *communication*: I have had to predetermine communication as the vehicle, transport, or site of passage of a *meaning*, and of a meaning that is *one*. If *communication* had several meanings, and if this plurality could not be reduced, then from the outset it would not be justified to define communication *itself* as the transmission of a meaning, assuming that we are capable of understanding one another as concerns each of these words (transmission, meaning, etc.). Now, the word *communication*, which nothing initially authorizes us to overlook as a word, and to impoverish as a polysemic word, opens a semantic field which precisely is not limited to semantics, semiotics, and even less to linguistics. To the semantic field of the word *communication* belongs the fact that it also designates nonsemantic movements. Here at least provisional recourse to ordinary language and to the equivocalities of natural language teaches us that one may, for example, *communicate a movement*, or that a tremor, a shock, a displacement of *force* can be communicated—that is, propagated, transmitted. It is also said that different or distant places can communicate between each other by means of a given passageway or opening. What happens in this case, what is transmitted or communicated, are not phenomena of meaning or signification. In these cases we are dealing neither with a semantic or conceptual content, nor with a semiotic operation, and even less with a linguistic exchange.

Nevertheless, we will not say that this nonsemiotic sense of the word *communication*, such as it is at work in ordinary language, in one or several of the so-called natural languages, constitutes the *proper* or *primitive* meaning, and that consequently the semantic, semiotic, or linguistic meaning corresponds to a derivation, an extension or a reduction, a metaphoric displacement. We will not say, as one might be tempted to do, that semiolinguistic communication is *more metaphorico* entitled "communication," because by analogy with "physical" or "real" communication it gives passage, transports, transmits something, gives access to something. We will not say so:

1. because the value of literal, *proper meaning* appears more problematical than ever,
2. because the value of displacement, of transport, etc., is constitutive of the very concept of metaphor by means of which one allegedly understands the semantic displacement which is operated from communication as a nonsemiolinguistic phenomenon to communication as a semiolinguistic phenomenon.

(I note here between parentheses that in this communication the issue will be, already is, the problem of polysemia and communication, of dissemination—which I will oppose to polysemia—and communication. In a moment, a certain concept of writing is bound to intervene, in order to transform itself, and perhaps in order to transform the problematic.)

It seems to go without saying that the field of equivocality covered by the word *communication* permits itself to be reduced massively by the limits of what is called a *context* (and I announce, again between parentheses, that the issue will be, in this communication, the problem of context, and of finding out about writing as concerns context in general). For example, in a *colloquium* of *philosophy* in the *French language*, a conventional context, produced by a kind of implicit but structurally vague consensus, seems to prescribe that one propose "communications" on communication, communications in discursive form, colloquial, oral communications destined to be understood and to open or pursue dialogues within the horizon of an intelligibility and truth of meaning, such that in principle a general agreement may finally be established. These communications are to remain within the element of a determined "natural" language, which is called French, and which commands certain very particular uses of the word *communication*. Above all, the object of these communications should be organized, by priority or by privilege, around communication as *discourse*, or in any event as signification. Without exhausting all the implications and the entire structure of an "event" like this one, which would merit a very long preliminary analysis, the prerequisite I have just recalled appears evident; and for anyone who doubts this, it would suffice to consult our schedule in order to be certain of it.

But are the prerequisites of a context ever absolutely determinable? Fundamentally, this is the most general question I would like to attempt to elaborate. Is there a rigorous and scientific concept of the *context*? Does not the notion of context harbor, behind a certain confusion, very determined philosophical presuppositions? To state it now in the most summary fashion, I would like to demonstrate why a context is never absolutely determinable, or rather in what way its determination is never certain or saturated. This structural nonsaturation would have as its double effect:

1. a marking of the theoretical insufficiency of the *usual concept of* (the linguistic or non-linguistic) *context* such as it is accepted in numerous fields of investigation, along with all the other concepts with which it is systematically associated;

2. a rendering necessary of a certain generalization and a certain displacement of the concept of writing. The latter could no longer, henceforth, be included in the category of communication, at least if communication is understood in the restricted sense of the transmission of meaning. Conversely, it is within the general field of writing thus defined that the effects of semantic communication will be able to be determined as particular, secondary, inscribed, supplementary effects.

Writing and Telecommunication

If one takes the notion of writing in its usually accepted sense—which above all does not mean an innocent, primitive, or natural sense—one indeed must see it as a *means of communication*. One must even acknowledge it as a powerful means of communication which *extends* very far, if not infinitely, the field of oral or gestural communication. This is banally self-evident, and agreement on the matter seems easy. I will not describe all the *modes* of this extension in time and in space. On the other hand I will pause over the value of *extension* to which I have just had recourse. When we say that writing *extends* the field and powers of a locutionary or gestural communication, are we not presupposing a kind of *homogenous* space of communication? The range of the voice or of gesture certainly appears to encounter a factual limit here, an empirical boundary in the form of space and time; and writing, within the same time, within the same space, manages to loosen the limits, to open the *same field* to a much greater range. Meaning, the content of the semantic message, is thus transmitted, *communicated*, by different *means*, by technically more powerful mediations, over a much greater distance, but within a milieu that is fundamentally continuous and equal to itself, within a homogenous element across which the unity and integrity of meaning is not affected in an essential way. Here, all affection is accidental.

The system of this interpretation (which is also in a way *the* system of interpretation, or in any event of an entire interpretation of hermeneutics), although it is the usual one, or to the extent that it is as usual as common sense, has been *represented* in the entire history of philosophy. I will say that it is even, fundamentally, the properly philosophical interpretation of writing. I will take a single example, but I do not believe one could find, in the entire history of philosophy as such, a single counterexample, a single analysis that essentially contradicts the one proposed by Condillac, inspired, strictly speaking, by Warburton, in the *Essay on the Origin of Human Knowledge* (*Essai sur l'origine des connaissances humaines*).[1] I have chosen this example because an *explicit* reflection on the origin and function of the written (this explicitness is not encountered in all philosophy, and one should examine the conditions of its emergence or occultation) is organized within a philosophical discourse which like all philosophy presupposes the simplicity of the origin and the continuity of every derivation, every production, every analysis, the homogeneity of all orders. Analogy is a major concept in Condillac's thought. I choose this example also because the analysis which "retraces" the origin and function of writing is placed, in a kind of noncritical way, *under the authority of the category of communication.*[2] If men write, it is (1) because they have something to communicate; (2) because what they have to communicate is their "thought," their "ideas," their representations. Representative thought precedes and governs communication which transports the "idea," the signified content; (3) because men are *already* capable of communicating and of communicating their thought to each other when, in continuous fashion, they invent the means of communication that is writing. Here is a passage from chapter 13 of part 2 ("On Language and On Method"), section 1 ("On the Origin and Progress of Language"), (writing is thus a modality of language and marks a continuous progress in a communication of linguistic essence), section 13, "On Writing": "Men capable of communicating their thoughts to each other by sounds felt the necessity of imagining new signs apt to perpetuate them and to make them *known* to *absent* persons" (I italicize this value of *absence*, which, if newly reexamined, will risk introducing a certain break in the homogeneity of the system). As soon as men are capable of "communicating their thoughts," and of doing so by sounds (which is, according to Condillac, a secondary stage, articulated language coming to "supplement" the language of action, the unique and radical principle of all language), the birth and progress of writing will follow a direct, simple, and continuous line. The history of writing will conform to a law of mechanical economy: to gain the most space and time by means of the most convenient abbreviation; it will never have the least effect on the structure and content of the meaning (of ideas) that it will have to vehiculate. The same content, previously communicated by gestures and sounds, henceforth will be transmitted by writing, and successively by different modes of notation, from pictographic writing up to alphabetic writing, passing through the hieroglyphic writing of the Egyptians and the ideographic writing of the Chinese. Condillac continues: "Imagination then will represent but the *same* images that they had already expressed by actions and words, and which had, from the beginnings, made language figurative and metaphoric. *The most natural means* was therefore to draw the pictures of things. To *express the idea* of a man or a horse the form of one or the other will be represented, and the first attempt at writing was but a simple painting" (p. 252; my italics).

The representative character of written communication—writing as picture, reproduction, imitation of its content—will be the invariable trait of all the progress to come. The concept of *representation* is indissociable here from the concepts of *communication* and *expression* that I have underlined in Condillac's text. Representation, certainly, will be complicated, will be given supplementary way-stations and stages, will become the representation of representation in hieroglyphic and ideographic writing, and then in phonetic-alphabetic writing, but the representative structure which marks the first stage of expressive communication, the idea/sign relationship, will never be suppressed or transformed. Describing the history of the kinds of writing, their continuous derivation on the basis of a common radical which is never displaced and which procures a kind of community of analogical participation between all the forms of writing, Condillac concludes (and this is practically a citation of Warburton, as is almost the entire chapter): "This is the general history of writing conveyed by a *simple gradation* from the state of painting through that of the letter; for letters are *the last steps* which remain to be taken after the Chinese marks, which partake of letters precisely as hieroglyphs partake equally of Mexican paintings and of Chinese characters. These characters are so close to our writing that an alphabet *simply diminishes* the confusion of their number, and is their *succinct abbreviation*" (pp. 254–53).

Having placed in evidence the motif of the economic, *homogenous, and mechanical* reduction, let us now come back to the notion of *absence* that I noted in passing in Condillac's text. How is it determined?

1. First, it is the absence of the addressee. One writes in order to communicate something to those who are absent. The absence of the sender, the addressor, from the marks that he abandons, which are cut off from him and continue to produce effects beyond his presence and beyond the present actuality of his meaning, that is, beyond his life itself, this absence, which however belongs to the structure of all writing—and I will add, further on, of all language in general—this absence is never examined by Condillac.
2. The absence of which Condillac speaks is determined in the most classical fashion as a continuous modification, a progressive extenuation of presence. Representation regularly *supplements* presence. But this operation of supplementation ("To supplement" is one of the most decisive and frequently employed operative concepts on Condillac's *Essai*)[3] is not exhibited as a break in presence, but rather as a reparation and a continuous, homogenous modification of presence in representation.

Here, I cannot analyze everything that this concept of absence as a modification of presence presupposes, in Condillac's philosophy and elsewhere. Let us note merely that it governs another equally decisive operative concept (here I am classically, and for convenience, opposing *operative* to *thematic*) of the *Essai: to trace* and *to retrace*. Like the concept of supplementing, the concept of trace could be determined otherwise than in the way Condillac determines it. According to him, to trace means "to express," "to represent," "to recall," "to make present" ("in all likelihood painting owes its origin to the necessity of thus tracing our thoughts, and this necessity has doubtless contributed to conserving the language of action, as that which could paint the most easily," p. 253). The sign is born at the same time as imagination and memory, at the moment when it is demanded by the absence of the object for present perception ("Memory, as we have seen, consists only in the power of reminding ourselves of the signs of our ideas, or the circumstances which accompanied them; and this capacity occurs only by virtue of the *analogy* of *signs* (my italics; this concept of analogy, which organizes Condillac's entire system, in general makes certain all the continuities, particularly the continuity of presence to absence) that we have chosen, and by virtue of the order that we have put between our ideas, the objects that we wish to retrace have to do with several of our present needs" (p. 129). This is true of all the orders of signs distinguished by Condillac (arbitrary, accidental, and even natural signs, a distinction which Condillac nuances, and on certain points, puts back into question in his Letters to Cramer). The philosophical operation that Condillac also calls "to retrace" consists in traveling back, by way of analysis and continuous decomposition, along the movement of genetic derivation which leads from simple sensation and present perception to the complex edifice of representation: from original presence to the most formal language of calculation.

It would be simple to show that, essentially, this kind of analysis of written signification neither begins nor ends with Condillac. If we say now that this analysis is "ideological," it is not primarily in order to contrast its notions to "scientific" concepts, or in order to refer to the often dogmatic—one could also say "ideological"—use made of the word ideology, which today is so rarely examined for its possibility and history. If I define notions of Condillac's kind as ideological, it is that against the background of a vast, powerful, and systematic philosophical tradition dominated by the self-evidence of the *idea* (*eidos, idea*), they delineate the field of reflection of the French "ideologues" who, in Condillac's wake, elaborated a theory of the sign as a representation of the idea, which itself represents the perceived thing. Communication, hence, vehiculates a representation as an ideal content (which will be called meaning); and writing is a species of this general communication. A species: a communication having a relative specificity within a genus.

If we ask ourselves now what, in this analysis, is the essential predicate of this *specific difference*, we once again find *absence*.

Here I advance the following two propositions or hypotheses:

1. Since every sign, as much in the "language of action" as in articulated language (even before the intervention of writing in the classical sense), supposes a certain absence (to be determined), it must be because absence in the field of writing is of an original kind if any specificity whatsoever of the written sign is to be acknowledged.
2. If, perchance, the predicate thus assumed to characterize the absence proper to writing were itself found to suit every species of sign and communication, there would follow a general displacement: writing no longer would be a species of communication, and all the concepts to whose generality writing was subordinated (the concept itself as meaning, idea, or grasp of meaning and idea, the concept of communication, of sign, etc.) would appear as noncritical, ill-formed concepts, or rather as concepts destined to ensure the authority and force of a certain historic discourse.

Let us attempt then, while continuing to take our point of departure from this classical discourse, to characterize the absence which seems to intervene in a fashion specific to the functioning of writing.

A written sign is proffered in the absence of the addressee. How is this absence to be qualified? One might say that at the moment when I write, the addressee may be absent from my field of present perception. But is not this absence only a presence that is distant, delayed, or, in one form or another, idealized in its representation? It does not seem so, or at very least this distance, division, delay, *différance* must be capable of being brought to a certain absolute degree of absence for the structure of writing, supposing that writing exists, to be constituted. It is here that *différance* as writing could no longer (be) an (ontological) modification of presence. My "written communication" must, if you will, remain legible despite the absolute disappearance of every determined addressee in general for it to function as writing, that is, for it to be legible. It must be repeatable—iterable—in the absolute absence of the addressee or of the empirically determinable set of addressees. This iterability (*iter*, once again, comes from *itara*, *other* in Sanskrit, and everything that follows may be read as the exploitation of the logic which links repetition to alterity), structures the mark of writing itself, and does so moreover for no matter what type of writing (pictographic, hieroglyphic, ideographic, phonetic, alphabetic, to use the old categories). A writing that was not structurally legible—iterable—beyond the death of the addressee would not be writing. Although all this appears self-evident, I do not want it to be assumed as such, and will examine the ultimate objection that might be made to this proposition. Let us imagine a writing with a code idiomatic enough to have been founded and known, as a secret cipher, only by two "subjects." Can it still be said that upon the death of the addressee, that is, of the two partners, the mark left by one of them is still a writing? Yes, to the extent to which, governed by a code, even if unknown and nonlinguistic, it is constituted, in its identity as a mark, by its iterability in the absence of whoever, and therefore ultimately in the absence of every empirically determinable "subject." This implies that there is no code—an organon of iterability—that is structurally secret. The possibility of repeating, and therefore of identifying, marks is implied in every code, making of it a communicable, transmittable, decipherable grid that is iterable for a third party, and thus for any possible user in general. All writing, therefore, in order to be what it is, must be able to function in the radical absence of every empirically determined addressee in general. And this absence is not a continuous modification of presence; it is a break in presence, "death," or the possibility of the "death" of the addressee, inscribed in the structure of the mark (and it is at this point, I note in passing, that the value or effect of transcendentality is linked necessarily to the possibility of writing and of "death" analyzed in this way). A perhaps paradoxical consequence of the recourse I am taking to iteration and to the code: the disruption, in the last analysis, of the authority of the code as a finite system of rules; the radical destruction, by the same token, of every context as a protocol of a code. We will come to this in a moment.

What holds for the addressee holds also, for the same reasons, for the sender or the producer. To write is to produce a mark that will constitute a kind of machine that is in turn productive, that my future disappearance in principle will not prevent from functioning and from yielding, and yielding itself to, reading and rewriting. When I say "my future disappearance," I do so to make this proposition more immediately acceptable. I must be able simply to say my disappearance, my nonpresence in general, for example the nonpresence of my meaning, of my intention-to-signify, of my wanting-to-communicate-this, from the emission or production of the mark. For the written to be the written, it must continue to "act" and to be legible even if what is called the author of the writing no longer answers for what he has written, for what he seems to have signed, whether he is provisionally absent, or if he is dead, or if in general he does not support, with his absolutely current and present intention or attention, the plenitude of his meaning, of that very thing which seems to be written "in his name." Here, we could reelaborate the analysis sketched out above for the addressee. The situation of the scribe and of the subscriber, as concerns the written, is fundamentally the same as that of the reader. This essential drifting, due to writing as an iterative structure cut off from all absolute responsibility, from *consciousness* as the authority of the last analysis, writing orphaned, and separated at birth from the assistance of its father, is indeed what Plato condemned in the *Phaedrus*. If Plato's gesture is, as I believe, the philosophical movement par excellence, one realizes what is at stake here.

Before specifying the inevitable consequences of these nuclear traits of all writing—to wit: (1) the break with the horizon of communication as the communication of conscious-nesses or presences, and as the linguistic or semantic transport of meaning; (2) the subtraction of all writing from the semantic horizon or the hermeneutic horizon which, at least as a horizon of meaning, lets itself be punctured by writing; (3) the necessity of, in a way, *separating* the concept of polysemia from the concept I have elsewhere named *dissemination*, which is also the concept of writing; (4) the disqualification or the limit of the concept of the "real" or "linguistic" context, whose theoretical determination or empirical saturation are, strictly speaking, rendered impossible or insufficient by writing—I would like to demonstrate that the recognizable traits of the classical and narrowly defined concept of writing are generalizable. They would be valid not only for all the orders of "signs" and for all languages in general, but even, beyond semiolinguistic communication, for the entire field of what philosophy would call experience, that is, the experience of Being: so-called "presence."

In effect, what are the essential predicates in a minimal determination of the classical concept of writing?

1. A written sign, in the usual sense of the word, is therefore a mark which remains, which is not exhausted in the present of its inscription, and which can give rise to an iteration both in the absence of and beyond the presence of the empirically determined subject who, in a given context, has emitted or produced it. This is how, traditionally at least, "written communication" is distinguished from "spoken communication."

2. By the same token, a written sign carries with it a force of breaking with its context, that is, the set of presences which organize the moment of its inscription. This force of breaking is not an accidental predicate, but the very structure of the written. If the issue is one of the so-called "real" context, what I have just proposed is too obvious. Are part of this alleged real context a certain "present" of inscription, the presence of the scriptor in what he has written, the entire environment and horizon of his experience, and above all the intention, the meaning which at a given moment would animate his inscription. By all rights, it

belongs to the sign to be legible, even if the moment of its production is irremediably lost, and even if I do not know what its alleged author-scriptor meant consciously and intentionally at the moment he wrote it, that is abandoned it to its essential drifting. Turning now to the semiotic and internal context, there is no less a force of breaking by virtue of its essential iterability; one can always lift a written syntagma from the interlocking chain in which it is caught or given without making it lose every possibility of functioning, if not every possibility of "communicating," precisely. Eventually, one may recognize other such possibilities in it by inscribing or *grafting* it into other chains. No context can enclose it. Nor can any code, the code being here both the possibility and impossibility of writing, of its essential iterability (repetition/alterity).

3. This force of rupture is due to the spacing which constitutes the written sign: the spacing which separates it from other elements of the internal contextual chain (the always open possibility of its extraction and grafting), but also from all the forms of a present referent (past or to come in the modified form of the present past or to come) that is objective or subjective. This spacing is not the simple negativity of a lack, but the emergence of the mark. However, it is not the work of the negative in the service of meaning, or of the living concept, the *telos*, which remains *relevable* and reducible in the *Aufhebung* of a dialectics.

Are these three predicates, along with the entire system joined to them, reserved, as is so often believed, for "written" communication, in the narrow sense of the word? Are they not also to be found in all language, for example in spoken language, and ultimately in the totality of "experience," to the extent that it is not separated from the field of the mark, that is, the grid of erasure and of difference, of unities of iterability, of unities separable from their internal or external context, and separable from themselves, to the extent that the very iterability which constitutes their identity never permits them to be a unity of self-identity?

Let us consider any element of spoken language, a large or small unity. First condition for it to function: its situation as concerns a certain code; but I prefer not to get too involved here with the concept of code, which does not appear certain to me; let us say that a certain self-identity of this element (mark, sign, etc.) must permit its recognition and repetition. Across empirical variations of tone, of voice, etc., eventually of a certain accent, for example, one must be able to recognize the identity, shall we say, of a signifying form. Why is this identity paradoxically the division or dissociation from itself which will make of this phonic sign a grapheme? It is because this unity of the signifying form is constituted only by its iterability, by the possibility of being repeated in the absence not only of its referent, which goes without saying, but of a determined signified or current intention of signification, as of every present intention of communication. This structural possibility of being severed from its referent or signified (and therefore from communication and its context) seems to me to make of every mark, even if oral, a grapheme in general, that is, as we have seen, the nonpresent *remaining* of a differential mark cut off from its alleged "production" or origin. And I will extend this law even to all "experience" in general, if it is granted that there is no experience of *pure* presence, but only chains of differential marks.

Let us remain at this point for a while, and come back to the absence of the referent and even of the signified sense, and therefore of the correlative intention of signification. The absence of the referent is a possibility rather easily admitted today. This possibility is not only an empirical eventuality. It constructs the mark; and the eventual presence of the referent at the moment when it is designated changes nothing about the structure of a mark which implies that it can do without the referent. Husserl, in the *Logical Investigations*, had very rigorously analyzed this possibility. It is double:

1. A statement whose object is not impossible but only possible might very well be proffered and understood without its real object (its referent) being present, whether for the person who produces the statement, or for the one who receives it. If I say, while looking out the window, "The sky is blue," the statement will be intelligible (let us provisionally say, if you will, communicable), even if the interlocutor does not see the sky; even if I do not see it myself, if I see it poorly, if I am mistaken, or if I wish to trick my interlocutor. Not that it is always thus; but the structure of possibility of this statement includes the capability of being formed and of functioning either as an empty reference, or cut off from its referent. Without this possibility, which is also the general, generalizable, and generalizing iteration of every mark, there would be no statements.

2. The absence of the signified. Husserl analyzes this too. He considers it always possible, even if, according to the axiology and teleology which govern his analysis, he deems this possibility inferior, dangerous, or "critical": it opens the phenomenon of the *crisis* of meaning. This absence of meaning can be layered according to three forms:

a. I can manipulate symbols without in active and current fashion animating them with my attention and intention to signify (the crisis of mathematical symbolism, according to Husserl). Husserl indeed stresses the fact that this does not prevent the sign from functioning: the crisis or vacuity of mathematical meaning does not limit technical progress. (The intervention of writing is decisive here, as Husserl himself notes in *The Origin of Geometry*.)

b. Certain statements can have a meaning, although they are without *objective* signification. "The circle is square" is a proposition invested with meaning. It has enough meaning for me to be able to judge it false or contradictory (*widersinnig* and not *sinnlos*, says Husserl). I am placing this example under the category of the absence of the signified, although the tripartition signifier/signified/referent does not pertinently account for Husserl's analysis. "Square circle" marks the absence of a referent, certainly, and also the absence of a certain signified, but not the absence of meaning. In these two cases, the crisis of meaning (nonpresence in general, absence as the absence of the referent—of perception—or of meaning—of the actual intention to signify) is always linked to the essential possibility of writing; and this crisis is not an accident, a factual and empirical anomaly of spoken language, but also the positive possibility and "internal" structure of spoken language, from a certain outside.

c. Finally there is what Husserl calls *Sinnlosigkeit* or agrammaticality. For example, "green is or" or "abracadabra." In the latter cases, as far as Husserl is concerned, there is no more language, or at least no more "logical" language, no more language of knowledge as Husserl understands it in teleological fashion, no more language attuned to the possibility of the intuition of objects given in person and signified in *truth*. Here, we are confronted with a decisive difficulty. Before pausing over it, I note, as a point which touches upon our debate on communication, that the primary interest of the Husserlian analysis to which I am referring here (precisely by extracting it, up to a certain point, from its teleological and metaphysical context and horizon, an operation about which we must ask how and why it is always possible) is that it alleges, and it seems to me arrives at, a rigorous dissociation of the analysis of the sign or expression (*Ausdruck*) as a signifying sign, a sign meaning something (*bedeutsame Zeichen*), from all phenomena of communication.[4]

Let us take once more the case of agrammatical *Sinnlosigkeit*. What interests Husserl in the *Logical Investigations* is the system of rules of a universal grammar, not from a linguistic point of view, but from a logical and epistemological point of view. In an important note from the second edition,[5] he specifies that from his point of view the issue is indeed one of a purely *logical* grammar, that is the universal conditions of possibility for a morphology of significations in the relation of knowledge to a possible object, and not of a pure grammar in *general*, considered from a psychological or linguistic point of view. Therefore, it is only in a context determined by a will to know, by an epistemic intention, by a conscious relation to the object as an object of knowledge within a horizon of truth—it is in this oriented contextual field that "green is or" is unacceptable. But, since "green is or" or "abracadabra" do not constitute their context in themselves, nothing prevents their functioning in another context as signifying marks (or indices, as Husserl would say). Not only in the contingent case in which, by means of the translation of German into French "le vert est ou" might be endowed with grammaticality, *ou* (*oder*, or) becoming when heard *où* (where, the mark of place): "Where has the green (of the grass) gone (*le vert est où*)?," "Where has the glass in which I wished to give you something to drink gone (*le verre est où*)." But even "green is or" still signifies an *example of agrammaticality*. This is the possibility on which I wish to insist: the possibility of extraction and of citational grafting which belongs to the structure of every mark, spoken or written, and which constitutes every mark as writing even before and outside every horizon of semiolinguistic communication; as writing, that is, as a possibility of functioning cut off, at a certain point, from its "original" meaning and from its belonging to a saturable and constraining context. Every sign, linguistic or nonlinguistic, spoken or written (in the usual sense of this opposition), as a small or large unity, can be *cited*, put between quotation marks; thereby it can break with every given context, and engender infinitely new contexts in an absolutely nonsaturable fashion. This does not suppose that the mark is valid outside its context, but on the contrary that there are only contexts without any center of absolute anchoring. This citationality duplication, or duplicity, this iterability of the mark is not an accident or an anomaly, but is that (normal/abnormal) without which a mark could no longer even have a so-called "normal" functioning. What would a mark be that one could not cite? And whose origin could not be lost on the way?

The Parasites. Iter, of Writing: That Perhaps It Does Not Exist

I now propose to elaborate this question a little further with help from—but in order to go beyond it too—the problematic of the *performative*. It has several claims to our interest here.

1. Austin,[6] by his emphasis on the analysis of perlocution and especially illocution, indeed seems to consider acts of discourse only as acts of communication. This is what his French translator notes, citing Austin himself: "It is by comparing the *constative* utterance (that is, the classical 'assertion,' most often conceived as a true or false 'description' of the facts) with the *performative* utterance (from the English *performative*, that is, the utterance which allows us to do something by means of speech itself) that Austin has been led to consider *every* utterance worthy of the name (that is, destined to *communicate*, which would exclude, for example, reflex-exclamations) as being first and foremost a *speech act* produced in the *total* situation in which the interlocutors find themselves (*How to Do Things With Words*, p. 147)."[7]

2. This category of communication is relatively original. Austin's notions of illocution and perlocution do not designate the transport or passage of a content of meaning, but in a way the communication of an original movement (to be defined in a *general theory of action*), an operation, and the production of an effect. To communicate, in the case of the performative, if in all rigor and purity some such thing exists (for the moment I am placing myself within this hypothesis and at this stage of the analysis), would be to communicate a force by the impetus of a mark.

3. Differing from the classical assertion, from the constative utterance, the performative's referent (although the word is inappropriate here, no doubt, such is the interest of Austin's finding) is not outside it, or in any case preceding it or before it. It does not describe something which exists outside and before language. It produces or transforms a situation, it operates; and if it can be said that a constative utterance also effectuates something and always transforms a situation, it cannot be said that this constitutes its internal structure, its manifest function or destination, as in the case of the performative.

4. Austin had to free the analysis of the performative from the authority of the *value of truth*, from the opposition true/false,[8] at least in its classical form, occasionally substituting for it the value of force, of difference of force (*illocutionary* or *perlocutionary force*). (It is this, in a thought which is nothing less than Nietzschean, which seems to me to beckon toward Nietzsche; who often recognized in himself a certain affinity with a vein of English thought.)

For these four reasons, at least, it could appear that Austin has exploded the concept of communication as a purely semiotic, linguistic, or symbolic concept. The performative is a "communication" which does not essentially limit itself to transporting an already constituted semantic content guarded by its own aiming at truth (truth as an *unveiling* of that which is in its Being, or as an *adequation* between a judicative statement and the thing itself).

And yet—at least this is what I would like to attempt to indicate now—all the difficulties encountered by Austin in an analysis that is patient, open, aporetic, in constant transformation, often more fruitful in the recognition of its impasses than in its positions, seem to me to have a common root. It is this: Austin has not taken into account that which in the structure of *locution* (and therefore before any illocutory or perlocutory determination) already bears within itself the system of predicates that I call *graphematic in general*, which therefore confuses all the ulterior oppositions whose pertinence, purity, and rigor Austin sought to establish in vain.

In order to show this, I must take as known and granted that Austin's analyses permanently demand a value of *context*, and even of an exhaustively determinable context, whether de jure or teleologically; and the long list of "infelicities" of variable type which might affect the event of the performative always returns to an element of what Austin calls the total context.[9] One of these essential elements—and not one among others—classically remains consciousness, the conscious presence of the intention of the speaking subject for the totality of his locutory act. Thereby, performative communication once more becomes the communication of an intentional meaning,[10] even if this meaning has no referent in the form of a prior or exterior thing or state of things. This conscious presence of the speakers or receivers who participate in the effecting of a performative, their conscious and intentional presence in the totality of the operation, implies teleologically that no *remainder* escapes the present totalization. No remainder, whether in the definition of the requisite conventions, or the internal and linguistic context, or the grammatical form or semantic determination of the words used; no irreducible polysemia, that is no "dissemination" escaping the horizon of the unity of meaning. I cite the first two lectures of *How to Do Things with Words:* "Speaking generally, it is always necessary that the *circumstances* in which the words are uttered should be in some way, or ways, *appropriate*, and it is very commonly necessary that either the speaker himself or other persons should *also* perform certain *other* actions, whether 'physical' or 'mental' actions or even acts of uttering further words. Thus, for naming the ship, it is essential that I should be the person appointed to name her, for (Christian) marrying, it is essential that I should not be already married with a wife living, sane and undivorced, and so on; for a bet to have been made, it is generally necessary for the offer of the bet to have been accepted by a taker (who must have done something, such as to say 'Done'), and it is hardly a gift if I *say* 'I give it you' but never hand it over. So far, well and good" (pp. 8–9).

In the Second Lecture, after having in his habitual fashion set aside the grammatical criterion, Austin examines the possibility and origin of the failures or "infelicities" of the performative utterance. He then defines the six indispensable, if not sufficient, conditions for success. Through the values of "conventionality," "correctness," and "completeness" that intervene in the definition, we necessarily again find those of an exhaustively definable context, of a free consciousness present for the totality of the operation, of an absolutely full meaning that is master of itself: the teleological jurisdiction of a total field whose *intention* remains the organizing center (pp. 12–16). Austin's procedure is rather remarkable, and typical of the philosophical tradition that he prefers to have little to do with. It consists in recognizing that the possibility of the negative (here, the *infelicities*) is certainly a structural possibility, that failure is an essential risk in the operations under consideration; and then, with an almost *immediately simultaneous* gesture made in the name of a kind of ideal regulation, an exclusion of this risk as an accidental, exterior one that teaches us nothing about the language phenomenon under consideration. This is all the more curious, and actually rigorously untenable, in that Austin denounces with irony the "fetish" of opposition *value/fact*.

Thus, for example, concerning the conventionality without which there is no performative, Austin recognizes that *all* conventional acts are *exposed* to failure: "It seems clear in the first place that, although it has excited us (or failed to excite us) in connexion with certain acts which are or are in part acts of *uttering words*, infelicity is an ill to which *all* acts are heir which have the general character of ritual or ceremonial, all *conventional* acts: not indeed that *every* ritual is liable to every form of infelicity (but then nor is every performative utterance)" (pp. 18–19; Austin's italics).

Aside from all the questions posed by the very historically sedimented notion of "convention," we must notice here: (1) That in this specific place Austin seems to consider only the conventionality that forms the *circumstance* of the statement, its contextual surroundings, and not a certain intrinsic conventionality of that which constitutes locution itself, that is, everything that might quickly be summarized under the problematic heading of the "arbitrariness of the sign"; which extends, aggravates, and radicalizes the difficulty. Ritual is not an eventuality, but, as iterability, is a structural characteristic of every mark. (2) That the value of risk or of being open to failure, although it might, as Austin recognizes, affect the totality of conventional acts, is not examined as an essential predicate or *law*. Austin does not ask himself what consequences derive from the fact that something possible—a possible risk—is *always* possible, is somehow a necessary possibility. And if, such a necessary possibility of failure being granted, it still constitutes an accident. What is a success when the possibility of failure continues to constitute its structure?

Therefore the opposition of the success/failure of illocution or perlocution here seems quite insufficient or derivative. It presupposes a general and systematic elaboration of the structure of locution which avoids the endless alternation of essence and accident. Now, it is very significant that Austin rejects this "general theory," defers it on two occasions, notably in the Second Lecture. I leave aside the first exclusion. ("I am not going into the general doctrine here: in many such cases we may even say the act was 'void' (or voidable for duress or undue influence) and so forth. Now I suppose that some very general high-level doctrine might embrace both what we have called infelicities *and* these other 'unhappy' features of the doing of actions—in our case actions containing a performative utterance—in a single doctrine: but we are not including this kind of unhappiness—we must just remember, though, that features of this sort can and do *constantly obtrude* into any case we are discussing. Features of this sort would normally come under the heading of 'extenuating circumstances' or of 'factors reducing or abrogating the agent's responsibility,' and so on"; p. 21; my italics). The second gesture of exclusion concerns us more directly here. In question, precisely, is the possibility that every performative utterance (and a priori every other utterance) may be "cited." Now, Austin excludes this eventuality (and the general doctrine which would account for it) with a kind of lateral persistence, all the more significant in its off-sidedness. He insists upon the fact that this possibility remains *abnormal, parasitical*, that it constitutes a kind of extenuation, that is an agony of language that must firmly be kept at a distance, or from which one must resolutely turn away. And the concept of the "ordinary," and therefore of "ordinary language," to which he then has recourse is indeed marked by this exclusion. This makes it all the more problematic, and before demonstrating this, it would be better to read a paragraph from this Second Lecture:

"(ii) Secondly, as *utterances* our performatives are *also* heir to certain other kinds of ill which infect *all* utterances. And these likewise, though again they might be brought into a more general account, we are deliberately at present excluding. I mean, for example, the following: a performative utterance will, for example, be *in a peculiar way* hollow or void if said by an actor on the stage, or if introduced in a poem, or spoken in soliloquy. This applies in a similar manner to any and every utterance—a sea-change in special circumstances. Language in such circumstances is in special ways—intelligibly—used not *seriously* [I am italicizing here, J. D.], but in ways *parasitic* upon its normal use—ways which fall under the doctrine of the *etiolations* of language. All this we are *excluding* from consideration. Our performative utterances, felicitous or not, are to be understood as issued in ordinary circumstances" (pp. 21–22). Austin therefore excludes, along with what he calls the *sea-change*, the "non-serious," the "parasitic," the "etiolations," the "non-ordinary" (and with them the general theory which in accounting for these oppositions no longer would be governed by them), which he nevertheless recognizes as the possibility to which every utterance is open. It is also as a "parasite" that writing has always been treated by the philosophical tradition, and the rapprochement, here, is not at all fortuitous.

Therefore, I ask the following question: is this general possibility necessarily that of a failure or a trap into which language might *fall*, or in which language might lose itself, as if in an abyss situated outside or in front of it? What about *parasitism*? In other words, does the generality of the risk admitted by Austin *surround* language like a kind of *ditch*, a place of external perdition into which locution might never venture, that it might avoid by remaining at home, in itself, sheltered by its essence or *telos*? Or indeed is this risk, on the contrary, its internal and positive condition of possibility? this outside its inside? the very force and law of its emergence? In this last case, what would an "ordinary" language defined by the very law of language signify? Is it that in excluding the general theory of this structural parasitism, Austin, who nevertheless pretends to describe the facts and events of ordinary language, makes us accept as ordinary a teleological and ethical determination (the univocality of the statement—which he recognizes elsewhere remains a philosophical "ideal," pp. 72–73—the self-presence of a total context, the transparency of intentions, the presence of meaning for the absolutely singular oneness of a speech act, etc.)?

For, finally, is not what Austin excludes as anomalous, exceptional, "non-serious,"[11] that is, *citation* (on the stage, in a poem, or in a soliloquy), the determined modification of a general citationality—or rather, a general iterability—without which there would not even be a "successful" performative? Such that—a paradoxical, but inevitable consequence— a successful performative is necessarily an "impure" performative, to use the word that Austin will employ later on when he recognizes that there is no "pure" performative.[12]

Now I will take things from the side of positive possibility, and no longer only from the side of failure: would a performative statement be possible if a citational doubling did not eventually split, dissociate from itself the pure singularity of the event? I am asking the question in this form in order to forestall an objection. In effect, it might be said to me: you cannot allege that you account for the so-called graphematic structure of locution solely on the basis of the occurrence of failures of the performative, however real these failures might be, and however effective or general their possibility. You cannot deny that there are also performatives that succeed, and they must be accounted for: sessions are opened, as Paul Ricoeur did yesterday, one says "I ask a question," one bets, one challenges, boats are launched, and one even marries occasionally. Such events, it appears, have occurred. And were a single one of them to have taken place a single time, it would still have to be accounted for.

I will say "perhaps." Here, we must first agree upon what the "occurring" or the event-hood of an event consists in, when the event supposes in its allegedly present and singular intervention a statement which in itself can be only of a repetitive or citational structure, or rather, since these last words lead to confusion, of an iterable structure. Therefore, I come back to the point which seems fundamental to me, and which now concerns the status of the event in general, of the event of speech or by speech, of the strange logic it supposes, and which often remains unperceived.

Could a performative statement succeed if its formulation did not repeat a "coded" or iterable statement, in other words if the expressions I use to open a meeting, launch a ship or a marriage were not identifiable as *conforming* to an iterable model, and therefore if they were not identifiable in a way as "citation"? Not that citationality here is of the same type as in a play, a philosophical reference, or the recitation of a poem. This is why there is a relative specificity, as Austin says, a "relative purity" of performatives. But this relative purity is not constructed *against* citationality or iterability, but against other kinds of iteration within a general iterability which is the effraction into the allegedly rigorous purity of every event of discourse or every speech act. Thus, one must less oppose citation or iteration to the noniteration of an event, than construct a differential typology of forms of iteration, supposing that this is a tenable project that can give rise to an exhaustive program, a question I am holding off on here. In this typology, the category of intention will not disappear; it will have its place, but from this place it will no longer be able to govern the entire scene and the entire system of utterances. Above all, one then would be concerned with different types of marks or chains of iterable marks, and not with an opposition between citational statements on the one hand, and singular and original statement-events on the other. The first consequence of this would be the following: given this structure of iteration, the intention which animates utterance will never be completely present in itself and its content. The iteration which structures it a priori introduces an essential dehiscence and demarcation. One will no longer be able to exclude, as Austin wishes, the "non-serious," the *oratio obliqua*, from "ordinary" language. And if it is alleged that ordinary language, or the ordinary circumstance of language, excludes citationality or general iterability, does this not signify that the "ordinariness" in question, the thing and the notion, harbors a lure, the teleological lure of consciousness whose motivations, indestructible necessity, and systematic effects remain to be analyzed? Especially since this essential absence of intention for the actuality of the statement, this structural unconsciousness if you will, prohibits every saturation of a context. For a context to be exhaustively determinable, in the sense demanded by Austin, it at least would be necessary for the conscious intention to be totally present and actually transparent for itself and others, since it is a determining focal point of the context. The concept of or quest for the "context" therefore seems to suffer here from the same theoretical and motivated uncertainty as the concept of the "ordinary," from the same metaphysical origins: an ethical and teleological discourse of consciousness. This time, a reading of the connotations of Austin's text would confirm the reading of its descriptions; I have just indicated the principle of this reading.

Différance, the irreducible absence of intention or assistance from the performative statement, from the most "event-like" statement possible, is what authorizes me, taking into account the predicates mentioned just now, to posit the general graphematic structure of every "communication." Above all, I will not conclude from this that there is no relative specificity of the effects of consciousness, of the effects of speech (in opposition to writing in the traditional sense), that there is no effect of the performative, no effect of ordinary language, no effect of presence and of speech acts. It is simply that these effects do not exclude what is generally opposed to them term by term, but on the contrary presuppose it in dyssemtrical fashion, as the general space of their possibility.

Signatures

This general space is first of all spacing as the disruption of presence in the mark, what here I am calling writing. That all the difficulties encountered by Austin intersect at the point at which both presence and writing are in question, is indicated for me by a passage from the Fifth Lecture in which the divided agency of the legal *signature* emerges.

Is it by chance that Austin must note at this point: "I must explain again that we are floundering here. To feel the firm ground of prejudice slipping away is exhilarating, but brings its revenges" (p. 61). Only a little earlier an "impasse" had appeared, the impasse one comes to each time "any *single simple* criterion of grammar or vocabulary" is sought in order to distinguish between performative or constative statements. (I must say that this critique of linguisticism and of the authority of the code, a critique executed on the basis of an analysis of language, is what most interested me and convinced me in Austin's enterprise.) He then attempts to justify, with nonlinguistic reasons, the preference he has shown until now for the forms of the first-person present indicative in the active voice in the analysis of the performative. The justification of last appeal is that in these forms reference is made to what Austin calls the *source* (origin) of the utterance. This notion of the *source*—whose stakes are so evident—often reappears in what follows, and it governs the entire analysis in the phase we are examining. Not only does Austin not doubt that the source of an oral statement in the first person present indicative (active voice) is *present* in the utterance and in the statement (I have attempted to explain why we had reasons not to believe so), but he no more doubts that the equivalent of this link to the source in written utterances is simply evident and ascertained in the *signature*: "Where there is *not*, in the verbal formula of the utterance, a reference to the person doing the uttering, and so the acting, by means of the pronoun 'I' (or by his personal name), then in fact he will be 'referred to' in one of two ways:

"(a) In verbal utterances, *by his being the person who does* the uttering—what we may call the utterance-origin which is used generally in any system of verbal reference-co-ordinates.

"(b) In written utterances (or 'inscriptions'), *by his appending his signature* (this has to be done because, of course, written utterances are not tethered to their origin in the way spoken ones are)" (pp. 60–61). Austin acknowledges an analogous function in the expression "hereby" used in official protocols.

Let us attempt to analyze the signature from this point of view, its relation to the present and to the source. I take it as henceforth implied in this analysis that all the established predicates will hold also for the oral "signature" that is, or allegedly is, the presence of the "author" as the "person who does the uttering," as the "origin," the source, in the production of the statement.

By definition, a written signature implies the actual or empirical nonpresence of the signer. But, it will be said, it also marks and retains his having-been present in a past now, which will remain a future now, and therefore in a now in general, in the transcendental form of nowness (*maintenance*). This general *maintenance* is somehow inscribed, stapled to present punctuality, always evident and always singular, in the form of the signature. This is the enigmatic originality of every paraph. For the attachment to the source to occur, the absolute singularity of an event of the signature and of a form of the signature must be retained: the pure reproducibility of a pure event.

Is there some such thing? Does the absolute singularity of an event of the signature ever occur? Are there signatures?

Yes, of course, every day. The effects of signature are the most ordinary thing in the world. The condition of possibility for these effects is simultaneously, once again, the condition of their impossibility, of the impossibility of their rigorous purity. In order to function, that is, in order to be legible, a signature must have a repeatable, iterable, imitable form; it must be able to detach itself from the present and singular intention of its production. It is its sameness which, in altering its identity and singularity, divides the seal. I have already indicated the principle of the analysis above.

To conclude this very *dry*[13] discourse:

1. As writing, communication, if one insists upon maintaining the word, is not the means of transport of sense, the exchange of intentions and meanings, the discourse and "communication of consciousnesses." We are not witnessing an end of writing which, to follow McLuhan's ideological representation, would restore a transparency or immediacy of social relations; but indeed a more and more powerful historical unfolding of a general writing of which the system of speech; consciousness, meaning, presence, truth, etc., would only be an effect, to be analyzed as such. It is this questioned effect that I have elsewhere called *logocentrism*.

2. The semantic horizon which habitually governs the notion of communication is exceeded or punctured by the intervention of writing, that is of a *dissemination* which cannot be reduced to a *polysemia*. Writing is read, and "in the last analysis" does not give rise to a hermeneutic deciphering, to the decoding of a meaning or truth.

3. Despite the general displacement of the classical, "philosophical," Western, etc., concept of writing, it appears necessary, provisionally and strategically, to conserve the *old name*. This implies an entire logic of *paleonymy* which I do not wish to elaborate here.[14] Very schematically: an opposition of metaphysical concepts (for example, speech/writing, presence/absence, etc.) is never the face-to-face of two terms, but a hierarchy and an order of subordination. Deconstruction cannot limit itself or proceed immediately to a neutralization: it must, by means of a double gesture, a double science, a double writing, practice an *overturning* of the classical opposition *and* a general *displacement* of the system. It is only on this condition that deconstruction will provide itself the means with which to *intervene* in the field of oppositions that it criticizes, which is also a field of nondiscursive forces. Each concept, moreover, belongs to a systematic chain, and itself constitutes a system of predicates. There is no metaphysical concept in and of itself. There is a work—metaphysical or not—on conceptual systems. Deconstruction does not consist in passing from one concept to another, but in overturning and displacing a conceptual order, as well as the nonconceptual order with which the conceptual order is articulated. For example, writing, as a classical concept, carries with it predicates which have been subordinated, excluded, or held in reserve by forces and according to necessities to be analyzed. It is these predicates (I have mentioned some) whose force of generality, generalization, and generativity find themselves liberated, grafted onto a "new" concept of writing which also corresponds to whatever always has *resisted* the former organization of forces, which always has constituted the *remainder* irreducible to the dominant force which organized the—to say it quickly—logocentric hierarchy. To leave to this new concept the old name of writing is to maintain the

structure of the graft, the transition and indispensable adherence to an effective *intervention* in the constituted historic field. And it is also to give their chance and their force, their power of *communication*, to everything played out in the operations of deconstruction.

But what goes without saying will quickly have been understood, especially in a philosophical colloquium: as a disseminating operation *separated* from presence (of Being) according to all its modifications, writing, if there is any, perhaps communicates, but does not exist, surely. Or barely, hereby, in the form of the most improbable signature.

(*Remark*: the—written—text of this—oral—communication was to have been addressed to the *Association of French Speaking Societies of Philosophy* before the meeting. Such a missive therefore had to be signed. Which I did, and counterfeit here. Where? There. J.D.)

J. DERRIDA

Notes

1. TN. *Essai sur l'origine des connaissances humaines*, with an introductory essay by Jacques Derrida (Paris: Galilée, 1973).

2. Rousseau's theory of language and writing is also proposed under the general rubric of *communication*. ("On the Various Means of Communicating Our Thoughts" is the title of the first chapter of the *Essay on the Origin of Languages*.)

3. Language supplements action or perception, articulated language supplements the language of action, writing supplements articulated language, etc.

4. "So far we have considered expressions as used in communication, which last depends essentially on the fact that they operate indicatively. But expressions also play a great part in uncommunicated, interior mental life. This change in function plainly has nothing to do with whatever makes an expression an expression. Expressions continue to have *Bedeutungen* as they had before, and the same *Bedeutungen* as in dialogue." *Logical Investigations*, trans. J. N. Findlay (London: Routledge and Kegan Paul, 1970), p. 278. What I am asserting here implies the interpretation I proposed of Husserlian procedure on this point. Therefore, I permit myself to refer to *Speech and Phenomena*.

5. "In the First Edition I spoke of 'pure grammar,' a name conceived and expressly devised to be analogous to Kant's 'pure science of nature.' Since it cannot, however, be said that pure formal semantic theory comprehends the entire *a priori* of general grammar—there is, e.g., a peculiar *a priori* governing

relations of mutual understanding among minded persons, relations very important for grammar—talk of pure logical grammar is to be preferred." *Logical Investigations*, vol. 2, p. 527. [In the paragraph that follows I have maintained Findlay's translation of the phrase Derrida plays upon, i.e. "green is or," and have given the French necessary to comprehend this passage in parentheses.]

6. TN. J. L. Austin. *How to Do Things with Words* (New York: Oxford University Press, 1962). Throughout this section I have followed the standard procedure of translating *enoncé* as statement, and *énonciation* as utterance.

7. G. Lane, Introduction to the French translation of *How to Do Things with Words*.

8. ". . . two fetishes which I admit to an inclination to play Old Harry with, viz., 1) the true/false fetish, 2) the value/fact fetish" (p. 150).

9. See e.g. pp. 52 and 147.

10. Which sometimes compels Austin to reintroduce the criterion of truth into the description of performatives. See, e.g., pp. 51–52 and 89–90.

11. The very suspect value of the "non-serious" is a frequent reference (see e.g. pp. 104, 121). It has an essential link with what Austin says elsewhere about the *oratio obliqua* (pp. 70–71) and about *mime*.

12. From this point of view one might examine the fact recognized by Austin that "the *same* sentence is used on different occasions of utterance in *both* ways, performative and constative. The thing seems hopeless from the start, if we are to leave utterances *as they stand* and seek for a criterion" (p. 67). It is the graphematic root of citationality (iterability) that provokes this confusion, and makes it "not possible," as Austin says, "to lay down even a list of all possible criteria" (ibid.).

13. TN. Derrida's word here is *sec*, combining the initial letters of three words that form his title, *s*ig-nature, *e*vent, *c*ontext.

14. See *Dissemination* and *Positions*.

Gilles Deleuze

Eighth Series of Structure

Lévi-Strauss has indicated a paradox in the form of an antinomy, which is similar to Lacan's paradox: two series being given, one signifying and the other signified, the first presents an excess and the latter a lack. By means of this excess and this lack, the series refer to each other in eternal disequilibrium and in perpetual displacement. As the hero of *Cosmos* says, there are always too many signifying signs. The primordial signifier is of the order of language. In whatever manner language is acquired, the elements of language must have been given all together, all at once, since they do not exist independently of their possible differential relations. But the signified in general is of the order of the known, though the known is subject to the law of a progressive movement which proceeds from one part to another—*partes extra partes*. And whatever totalizations knowledge may perform, they remain asymptotic to the virtual totality of langue or language. The signifying series organizes a preliminary totality, whereas the signified series arranges the produced totalities. "The Universe signified long before we began to know what it was signifying . . . Man, since his origin, has had at his disposal a completeness of signifier which he is obstructed from allocating to a signified, given as such without being any better known. There is always an inadequacy between the two."[1]

This paradox might be named Robinson's paradox. It is obvious that Robinson, on his desert island, could reconstruct an analogue of society only by giving himself, all at once, all the rules and laws which are reciprocally implicated, even when they still have no objects. The conquest of nature is, on the contrary, progressive, partial, and advances step by step. Any society whatsoever has all its rules at once—juridical, religious, political, economic; laws governing love and labor, kinship and marriage, servitude and freedom, life and death. But the conquest of nature, without which it would no longer be a society, is achieved progressively, from one source of energy to another, from one object to another. This is why *law* weighs with all its might, even before its object is known, and without ever its object becoming exactly known. It is this disequilibrium that makes revolutions possible. It is not at all the case that revolutions are determined by technical progress. Rather, they are made possible by this gap between the two series, which solicits realignments of the economic and political totality in relation to the parts of the technical progress. There are therefore two errors which in truth are one and the same: the error of reformism or technocracy, which aspires to promote or impose partial arrangements of social relations according to the rhythm of technical achievements; and the error of totalitarianism, which aspires to constitute a totalization of the signifiable and the known, according to the rhythm of the social totality existing at a given moment. The technocrat is the natural friend of the dictator—computers and dictatorship; but the revolutionary lives in the gap which separates technical progress from social totality, and inscribes there his dream of permanent revolution. This dream, therefore, is itself action, reality, and an effective menace to all established order; it renders possible what it dreams about.

Let us return to Lévi-Strauss' paradox: two series being given, signifying and signified, there is a natural excess of the signifying series and a natural lack of the signified series. There is, necessarily, a *"floating signifier*, which is the servitude of all finite thought, but also the promise of all art, all poetry, all mythic and aesthetic invention." We would like to add that it is the promise of all revolutions. And then there is on the other side a kind of *floated signified*, given by the signifier "without being thereby known," without being thereby assigned or realized. Lévi-Strauss proposes to interpret in this way the words "gadget" or "whatnot," "something," "*aliquid*," but also the famous "*mana*" (or, yet again, "*it*" [ça]). This is a value "in itself void of sense and thus susceptible of taking on any sense, whose unique function would be to fill the gap between signifier and signified." "It is a symbolic value zero, that is, a sign marking the necessity of a symbolic content supplementary to that which already charges the signified, but able to take any value whatsoever, on the condition that it belong to the available reserve . . ." It is necessary to understand that the two series are marked, one by excess, the other by lack, and that the two determinations are interchanged without ever reaching equilibrium. What is in excess in the signifying series is literally an empty square and an always displaced place without an occupant. What is lacking in the signified series is a supernumerary and non-situated given—an unknown, an occupant without a place, or something always displaced. These are two sides of the same thing—two uneven sides—by means of which the series communicate without losing their difference. It is the adventure in the Sheep's shop or the story that the esoteric word narrates.

We may, perhaps, determine certain minimal conditions for a *structure* in general: 1) There must be at least two heterogeneous series, one of which shall be determined as "signifying" and the other as "signified" (a single series never suffices to form a structure). 2) Each of these series is constituted by terms which exist only through the relations they maintain with one another. To these relations, or rather to the values of these relations, there correspond very particular events, that is, *singularities* which are assignable within the structure. The situation is very similar to that of differential calculus, where the distributions of singular points correspond to the values of differential relations.[2] For example, the differential relations among phonemes assign singularities within language, in the "vicinity" of which the sonorities and significations characteristic of the language are constituted. Moreover, it seems that the singularities attached to a series determine in a complex manner the terms of the other series. In any case, a structure includes two distributions of singular points corresponding to the base series. And for this reason, it is imprecise to oppose structure and event: the structure includes a register of ideal *events*, that is, an entire *history* internal to it (for example, if the series include "characters," it is a history which connects all the singular points corresponding to the positions of the characters relative to one another in the two series). 3) The two heterogeneous series converge toward a paradoxical element, which is their "differentiator." This is the principle of the emission of singularities. This element belongs to no series; or rather, it belongs to both series at once and never ceases to circulate throughout them. It has therefore the property of always being displaced in relation to itself, of "being absent from its own place," its own identity, its own resemblance, and its own equilibrium. It appears in one of the series as an excess, but only on the condition that it would appear at the same time in the other as a lack. But if it is in excess in the one, it is so only as an empty square; and if it is lacking in the other, it is so only as a supernumerary pawn or an occupant without a compartment. It is both word and object at once: esoteric word and exoteric object.

It has the function of articulating the two series to one another, of reflecting them in one another, of making them communicate, coexist, and be ramified. Again, it has the function of joining the singularities which correspond to the two series in a "tangled tale," of assuring the passage from one distribution of singularities to the next. In short, it has the function of bringing about the distribution of singular points; of determining as signifying the series in which it appears in excess, and, as signified, the series in which it appears correlatively as lacking and, above all, of assuring the bestowal of sense in both signifying and signified series. For sense is not to be confused with signification; it is rather what is attributed in such a way that it determines both the signifier and the signified as such. We can conclude from this that there is no structure without series, without relations between the terms of each series, or without singular points corresponding to these relations. But above all, we can conclude that there is no structure without the empty square, which makes everything function.

Twenty-Fourth Series of the Communication of Events

One of the boldest moments of the Stoic thought involves the splitting of the causal relation. Causes are referred in depth to a unity which is proper to them, and effects maintain at the surface specific relations of another sort. Destiny is primarily the unity and the link of physical causes among themselves. Incorporeal effects are obviously subject to destiny, to the extent that they are the effect of these causes. But to the extent that they differ in nature from these causes, they enter, with one another, into relations of quasi-causality. Together, they enter into a relation with a quasi-cause which is itself incorporeal and assures them a very special independence, not exactly with respect to destiny, but rather with respect to necessity, which normally would have had to follow destiny. The Stoic paradox is to affirm destiny and to deny necessity.[3] The wise person is free in two ways which conform to the two poles of ethics: free in the first instance because one's soul can attain to the interiority of perfect physical causes; and again because one's mind may enjoy very special relations established between effects in a situation of pure exteriority. It would then seem that incorporeal causes are inseparable from a form of interiority, but that incorporeal effects are inseparable from a form of exteriority. On one hand, events-effects maintain a relation of causality with their physical causes, without this relation being one of necessity; it is rather a relation of expression. On the other hand, they have between them, or with their ideational quasi-cause, no longer a relation of causality, but rather, once again and this time exclusively, a relation of expression.

The question becomes: what are these expressive relations of events? Between events, there seem to be formed extrinsic relations of silent compatibility or incompatibility, of conjunction or disjunction, which are very difficult to apprehend. What makes an event compatible or incompatible with another? We cannot appeal to causality, since it is a question of a relation of effects among themselves. What brings destiny about at the level of events, what brings an event to repeat another in spite of all its difference, what makes it possible that a life is composed of one and the same Event, despite the variety of what might happen, that it be traversed by a single and same fissure, that it play one and the same air over all possible tunes and all possible words—all these are not due to relations between cause and effect; it is rather an aggregate of noncausal correspondences which form a system of echoes, of resumptions and resonances, a system of signs—in short, an expressive quasi-causality, and not at all a necessitating causality. When Chrysippus insists on the transformation of hypothetical propositions into conjunctives or disjunctives, he shows well the impossibility of events expressing their conjunctions and disjunctions in terms of brute causality.[4]

Is it necessary, then, to invoke identity and contradiction? Would two events be incompatible because they were contradictory? Is this not a case, though, of applying rules to events, which apply only to concepts, predicates, and classes? Even with respect to hypothetical propositions (if it is day, it is light), the Stoics noted that contradiction must be defined on a single level. Rather, contradiction must be defined in the space between the principle itself and the negation of the consequence (if it is day, it is not light). This difference of levels in the contradiction, we have seen, assures that contradiction results always from a process of a different nature. Events are not like concepts; it is their alleged contradiction (manifest in the concept) which results from their incompatibility, and not the converse. It is held, for example, that a species of butterfly cannot be at once gray and vigorous. Either the specimens are gray and weak, or they are vigorous and black.[5] We can always assign a causal physical mechanism to explain this incompatibility, a hormone, for example, on which the predicate gray would depend, and which would soften or weaken the corresponding class. And we can conclude from this causal condition that there is a logical contradiction between gray and vigorous. But if we isolate the pure events, we see that *to turn gray* is no less positive than *to turn black*: it expresses an increase in security (to be hidden, to be taken for the bark of a tree), as much as the becoming black is an increase of vigor (to invigorate). Between these two determinations, each one of which has its advantage, there is initially a relation of primary, "eventmental" incompatibility. Physical causality inscribes the incompatibility only secondarily in the depth of the body, and the logical contradiction translates it only in the content of the concept. In short, the relations of events among themselves, from the point of view of an ideational or noematic quasi-causality, first expresses noncausal correspondence—alogical compatibilities or incompatibilities. The Stoics' strength was in committing themselves to this line of thought: according to what criteria are events *copulata, confatalia* (or *inconfatalia*), *conjuncta*, or *disjuncta*? Astrology was perhaps the first important attempt to establish a theory of alogical incompatibilities and noncausal correspondences.

It seems, however, if we follow the surviving partial and deceiving texts, that the Stoics may not have been able to resist the double temptation of returning to the simple physical causality or to the logical contradiction. The first theoretician of alogical incompatibilities, and for this reason the first important theoretician of the event, was Leibniz. For what Leibniz called "compossible" and "incompossible" cannot be reduced to the identical and the contradictory, which govern only the possible and the impossible. Compossibility does not even presuppose the inherence of predicates in an individual subject or monad. It is rather the inverse; inherent predicates are those which correspond to events from the beginning compossible (the monad of Adam the sinner includes in predicative form only future and past events which are compossible with the sin of Adam). Leibniz was thus extremely conscious of the anteriority and originality of the event in relation to the predicate. Compossibility must be defined in an original manner, at a pre-individual level, by the convergence of series which singularities of events form as they stretch themselves out over lines of ordinary points. Incompossibility must be defined by the divergence of such series: if another Sextus than the one we know is incompossible with our world, it is because he would correspond to a singularity the series of which would diverge from the series of our world, clustered about the Adam, the Judas, the Christ, and the Leibniz that we know. Two events are compossible when the series which are organized around their singularities extend in all directions; they are incompossible when the series diverge in the vicinity of constitutive singularities. Convergence and divergence are entirely original relations which cover the rich domain of alogical compatibilities and incompatibilities, and therefore form an essential component of the theory of sense.

Leibniz though makes use of this rule of incompossibility in order to exclude events from one another. He made a negative use of divergence of disjunction—one of exclusion. This is justified, however, only to the extent that events are already grasped under the hypothesis of a God who calculates and chooses, and from the point of view of their actualization in distinct worlds or individuals. It is no longer justified, however, if we consider the pure events and the ideal play whose principle Leibniz was unable to grasp, hindered as he was by theological exigencies. For, from this other point of view, the divergence of series or the disjunction of members (*membra disjuncta*) cease to be negative rules of exclusion according to which events would be incompossible or incompatible. Divergence and disjunction are, on the contrary, affirmed as such. But what does it mean to make divergence and disjunction the objects of affirmation? As a general rule, two things are simultaneously affirmed only to the extent that their difference is denied, suppressed from within, even if the level of this suppression is supposed to regulate the production of difference as much as its disappearance. To be sure, the identity here is not that of indifference, but it is generally *through identity* that opposites are affirmed at the same time, whether we accentuate one of the opposites in order to find the other, or whether we create a synthesis of the two. We speak, on the contrary, of an operation according to which two things or two determinations are affirmed *through* their difference, that is to say, that they are the objects of simultaneous affirmation only insofar as their difference is itself affirmed and is itself affirmative. We are no longer faced with an identity of contraries, which would still be inseparable as such from a movement of the negative and of exclusion.[6] We are rather faced with a positive distance of different elements: no longer to identify two contraries with the same, but to affirm their distance as that which relates one to the other insofar as they are "different." The idea of a positive distance as distance (and not as an annulled or overcome distance) appears to us essential, since it permits the measuring of contraries through their finite difference instead of equating difference with a measureless contrariety, and contrariety with an identity which is itself infinite. It is not difference which must "go as far as" contradiction, as Hegel thought in his desire to accommodate the negative; it is the contradiction which must reveal the nature of *its* difference as it follows the distance corresponding to it. The idea of positive distance belongs to topology and to the surface. It excludes all depth and all elevation, which would restore the negative and the identity. Nietzsche provides the example for such a procedure, which must not, under any circumstances, be confused with some unknown identity of contraries (as is commonplace in spiritualist and dolorist philosophy). Nietzsche exhorts us to live health and sickness in such a manner that health be a living perspective on sickness and sickness a living perspective on health; to make of sickness an exploration of health, of health an investigation of sickness: "Looking from the perspective of the sick toward *healthier* concepts and values and, conversely, looking again from the fullness and self-assurance of a *rich* life down into the secret work of the instinct of decadence—in this I have had the longest training, my truest experiences; if in anything, I became master in *this*. Now I know how, have the know-how, to *reverse perspectives*. . . ."[7] We cannot identify contraries, nor can we affirm their entire distance, except as that which relates one to the other. Health affirms sickness when it makes its distance from sickness an object of affirmation. Distance is, at arm's length, the affirmation of that which it distances. This procedure which makes of health an evaluation of sickness and sickness an evaluation of health—is this not the Great Health (or the Gay Science)? Is it not this which permits Nietzsche to experience a superior health at the very moment that he is sick? Conversely, Nietzsche does not lose his health when he is sick, but when he can no longer affirm the distance, when he is no longer able, by means of his health, to establish sickness as a point of view on health (then, as the Stoics say, the role is over, the play has ended). "Point of view" does not signify a theoretical judgment; as for "procedure," it is life itself. From Leibniz, we had already learned that there are no points of view on things, but that things, beings, are themselves points of view. Leibniz, however, subjected the points of view to exclusive rules such that each opened itself onto the others only insofar as they converged: the points of view on the same town. With Nietzsche, on the contrary, the point of view is opened onto a divergence which it affirms: another town corresponds to each point of view, each point of view is another town, the towns are linked only by their distance and resonate only through the divergence of their series, their houses and their streets. There is always another town within the town. Each term becomes the means of going all the way to the end of another, by following the entire distance. Nietzsche's perspective—his perspectivism—is a much more profound art than Leibniz's point of view; for divergence is no longer a principle of exclusion, and disjunction no longer a means of separation. Incompossibility is now a means of communication.

It is not that the disjunction has become a simple conjunction. Three sorts of synthesis are distinguished: the connective synthesis (if . . . , then), which bears upon the construction of a single series; the conjunctive series (and), as a method of constructing convergent series; and the disjunctive series (or), which distributes the divergent series: *conexa, conjuncta, disjuncta*. But the whole question, and rightly so, is to know under what conditions the disjunction is a veritable synthesis, instead of being a procedure of analysis which is satisfied with the exclusion of predicates from one thing in virtue of the identity of its concept (the negative, limitative, or exclusive use of disjunction). The answer is given insofar as the divergence or the decentering determined by the disjunction become objects of affirmation as such. The disjunction is not at all reduced to a conjunction; it is left as a disjunction, since it bears, and continues to bear, upon a divergence as such. But this divergence is affirmed in such a way that the *either . . . or* itself becomes a pure affirmation. Instead of a certain number of predicates being excluded from a thing in virtue of the identity of its concept, each "thing" opens itself up to the infinity of predicates through which it passes, as it loses its center, that is, its identity as concept or as self. The communication of events replaces the exclusion of predicates. We have already seen the procedure of this affirmative synthetic disjunction: it consists of the erection of a paradoxical instance, an aleatory point with two uneven faces, which traverses the divergent series as divergent and causes them to resonate through their distance and in their distance. Thus, the ideational center of convergence is by nature perpetually decentered, it serves only to affirm divergence. This is why it seemed that an esoteric, ex-centric path was opened to us, a path altogether different from the ordinary one. For ordinarily the disjunction is not properly speaking a synthesis, but only a regulative analysis at the service of conjunctive syntheses, since it separates the nonconvergent series from one another. As for the conjunctive synthesis, it tends also toward being subordinated to the synthesis of connection, since it organizes the converging series over which it bears as it prolongs them under a condition of continuity. Now, the whole sense of *esoteric words* was to turn this path around: a disjunction which had become a synthesis introduced its *ramifications* everywhere, so that the conjunction was already *coordinating* in a global way divergent, heterogeneous, and disparate series, and that, affecting the details, the connection already *contracted* a multitude of divergent series in the successive appearance of a single one.

This is a new reason for distinguishing the becoming of depths and the Aion of surfaces. For both, at first glance, seemed to dissolve the identity of each thing within infinite identity as the identity of contraries. And from all points of view, whether of quantity, quality, relation, or modality, contraries appeared connected at the surface as much as in depth and to have the same sense no less than the same infra-sense. But, once again, everything changes nature as it climbs to the surface. And it is necessary to distinguish two ways whose personal identity is lost, two ways by means of which the contradiction is developed. In depth, it is through infinite identity that contraries communicate and that the identity of each finds itself broken and divided. This makes each term at once the moment and the whole; the part, the relation, and the whole; the self, the world, and God; the subject, the copula, and the predicate. But the situation is altogether different at the surface where only infinitive events are deployed; each one communicates with the other through the positive characters of its distance and by the affirmative character of the disjunction. The self merges with the very disjunction which it liberates and places outside of itself the divergent series as so many impersonal and pre-individual singularities. Counter-actualization is already infinitive distance instead of infinite identity. Everything happens through the resonance of disparates, point of view on a point of view, displacement of perspective, differentiation of difference, and not through the identity of contraries. It is true that the form of the self ordinarily guarantees the connection of a series; that the form of the world guarantees the convergence of continuous series which can be extended; and that the form of God, as Kant had clearly seen, guarantees disjunction in its exclusive or limitative sense. But when disjunction accedes to the principle which gives to it a synthetic and affirmative value, the self, the world, and God share in a common death, to the advantage of divergent series as such, overflowing now every exclusion, every conjunction, and every connection. It is Klossowski's merit to have shown how the three forms had their fortunes linked, not by a dialectical transformation and the identity of contraries, but by a common dissipation at the surface of things. If the self is the principle of manifestation, in relation to the proposition, the world is the principle of denotation, and God the principle of signification. But sense expressed as an event is of an entirely different nature: it emanates from nonsense as from the always displaced paradoxical instance and from the eternally decentered ex-centric center. It is a pure sign whose coherence excludes merely, and yet supremely, the coherence of the self, world, and God.[8] This quasi-cause, this surface nonsense which traverses the divergent as such, this aleatory point which circulates throughout singularities, and emits them as pre-individual and impersonal, does not allow God to subsist. It does not tolerate the subsistence of God as an original individuality, nor the self as a Person, nor the world as an element of the self and as God's product. The divergence of the affirmed series forms a "chaosmos" and no longer a world; the aleatory point which traverses them forms a counter-self, and no longer a self; the disjunction posed as a synthesis exchanges its theological principle for a diabolic principle. It is the decentered center which traces between the series, and for all disjunctions, the merciless straight line of the Aion, that is, the distance whereupon the castoffs of the self, the world, and God are lined up: the Grand Canyon of the world, the "crack" of the self, and the dismembering of God. Upon this straight line of the Aion, there is also an eternal return, as the most terrible labyrinth of which Borges spoke—one very different from the circular or monocentered return of Chronos: an eternal return which is no longer that of individuals, persons, and worlds, but only of pure events which the instant, displaced over the line, goes on dividing into already past and yet to come. Nothing other than the Event subsists, the Event alone, *Eventum tantum* for all contraries, which communicates with itself through its own distance and resonates across all of its disjuncts.

Twenty-Sixth Series of Language

Events make language possible. But making possible does not mean causing to begin. We always begin in the order of speech, but not in the order of language, in which everything must be given simultaneously and in a single blow. There is always someone who begins to speak. The one who begins to speak is the one who manifests; what one talks about is the denotatum; what one says are the significations. The event is not any of these things: it speaks no more than it is spoken of or said. Nevertheless, the event does belong to language, and haunts it so much that it does not exist outside of the propositions which express it. But the event is not the same as the proposition; what is expressed is not the same as the expression. It does not preexist it, but pre-inheres in it, thus giving it a foundation and a condition. To render language possible thus signifies assuring that sounds are not confused with the sonorous qualities of things, with the sound effects of bodies, or with their actions and passions. What renders language possible is that which separates sounds from bodies and organizes them into propositions, freeing them for the expressive function. It is always a mouth which speaks; but the sound is no longer the noise of a body which eats—a pure orality—in order to become the manifestation of a subject expressing itself. One speaks always of bodies and their mixtures, but sounds have ceased being qualities attached to these bodies in order that they may enter into a new relation with them, that of denotation, and that they may express this power of speaking and of being spoken. Denotation and manifestation do not found language, they are only made possible with it. They presuppose the expression. The expression is founded on the event, as an entity of the expressible or the expressed. What renders language possible is the event insofar as the event is confused neither with the proposition which expresses it, nor with the state of the one who pronounces it, nor with the state of affairs denoted by the proposition. And in truth, without the event all of this would be only noise—and an indistinct noise. For not only does the event make possible and separate that which it renders possible, it also makes distinctions within what it renders possible (see, for example, the triple distinction in the proposition of denotation, manifestation, and signification).

How does the event make language possible? We have seen that its essence is that of the pure surface effect, or the impassible incorporeal entity. The event results from bodies, their mixtures, their actions, and their passions. But it differs in nature from that of which it is the result. It is, for example, attributed to bodies, to states of affairs, but not at all as a physical quality; rather, it is ascribed to them only as a very special *attribute*, dialectical or, rather, noematic and incorporeal. This attribute does not exist outside of the proposition which expresses it. But it differs in nature from its expression. It exists in the proposition, but not at all as a name of bodies or qualities, and not at all as a subject or predicate. It exists rather only as that which is expressible or expressed by the proposition, enveloped in a *verb*. The event occurring in a state of affairs and the sense inhering in the proposition are the same entity. Consequently, to the extent that the incorporeal event is constituted and constitutes the surface, it raises to this surface the terms of its double reference: the bodies to which it refers as a noematic attribute, and the propositions to which it refers as an expressible entity. It organizes these terms as two series which it separates, since it is by and in this separation that it distinguishes itself from the bodies from which it ensues and from the propositions it renders possible. This separation, this line-frontier between things and propositions (to eat/to speak), enters as well into the "made possible," that is, into the propositions themselves, between nouns and verbs, or, rather, between denotations and expressions. Denotations refer always to bodies and, in principle, to consumable objects; expressions refer to expressible meanings. But this line-frontier would not enact the separation of series at the surface it if did not finally articulate that which it separates. It operates on both sides by means of one and the same incorporeal power, which, on one hand, is defined as that which occurs in a state of affairs and, on the other, as that which insists in propositions. (This is why language has only one power, though it may have several dimensions.)

The line-frontier brings about the convergence of divergent series; but it neither abolishes nor corrects their divergence. For it makes them converge not in themselves (which would be impossible) but around a paradoxical element, a point traversing the line and circulating throughout the series. This is an always displaced center which constitutes a circle of convergence only for that which diverges as such (the power of affirming the disjunction). This element or point is the quasi-cause to which the surface effects are attached, precisely insofar as they differ in nature from their corporeal causes. It is this point which is expressed in language by means of esoteric words of different kinds, guaranteeing the separation, the coordination, and the ramifications of series at once. Thus the entire organization of language presents three figures: the metaphysical or transcendental *surface*, the incorporeal abstract *line*, and the decentered *point*. These figures correspond to surface effects or events; at the surface, the line of sense immanent to the event; and on the line, the point of nonsense, surface nonsense, being co-present with sense.

The two great ancient systems, Epicureanism and Stoicism, attempted to locate in things that which renders language possible. But they did so in very different ways. For in order to found not only freedom but also language and its use, the Epicureans created a model based on the *declension* of the atom; the Stoics, on the contrary, created a model based on the *conjugation* of events. It is not surprising therefore that the Epicurean model privileges nouns and adjectives; nouns are like atoms or linguistic bodies which are coordinated through their declension, and adjectives like the qualities of these composites. But the Stoic model comprehends language on the basis of "prouder" terms: verbs and their conjugation, in relation to the links between incorporeal events. The question of knowing whether nouns or verbs are primary in language cannot be resolved according to the general maxim "in the beginning, there is the action," however much one makes of the verb the representative of primary action and of the root the primary state of the verb. For it is not true that the verb represents an action; it expresses an event, which is totally different. Moreover, language is not developed from primary roots; it is organized around formative elements which determine it in its entirety. But if language is not formed progressively following the succession of an external time, we should not believe, for this reason, that its totality is homogeneous. It is true that "phonemes" guarantee every linguistic distinction possible within "morphemes" and "semantemes"; but conversely, the signifying and morphological units determine, in the phonematic distinctions, those which are pertinent in a language under examination. The whole cannot be described by a simple movement, but by a two-way movement of linguistic action and reaction which represents the circle of the proposition.[9] And if phonic action forms an open space for language, semantic reaction forms an internal time without which this space could not be determined in conformity with a specific language. Independently, therefore, of elements and only from the point of view of movement, nouns and their declension incarnate action, whereas verbs and their conjugation incarnate reaction. The verb is not an image of external action, but a process of reaction internal to language. This is why, in its most general notion, it envelops the internal temporality of language. It is the verb which constitutes the ring of the proposition, bringing signification to bear upon denotation and the semanteme upon the phoneme. But it is from the verb as well that we infer what the ring conceals or coils up, or what it reveals once it is split, unrolled, and deployed over a straight line: sense or the event as the expressed of the proposition.

The verb has two poles: the present, which indicates its relation to a denotable state of affairs in view of a physical time characterized by succession; and the infinitive, which indicates its relation to sense or the event in view of the internal time which it envelops.

The entire verb oscillates between the infinitive "mood," which represents the circle once unwound from the entire proposition, and the present "time," which, on the contrary, closes the circle over the denotatum of the proposition. Between the two, the verb curves its conjugation in conformity with the relations of denotation, manifestation, and signification—the aggregate of times, persons, and modes. The pure infinitive is the Aion, the straight line, the empty form, and the distance; it permits no distinction of moments, but goes on being divided formally in the double and simultaneous direction of the past and the future. The infinitive does not implicate a time internal to language without expressing the sense or the event, that is to say, the set of problems raised by language. It connects the interiority of language to the exteriority of being. It inherits therefore the communication of events among themselves. As for univocity, it is transmitted from Being to language, from the exteriority of Being to the interiority of language. Equivocity is always the equivocity of nouns. The Verb is the univocity of language, in the form of an undetermined infinitive, without person, without present, without any diversity of voice. It is poetry itself. As it expresses in language all events in one, the infinitive verb expresses the event of language—language being a unique event which merges now with that which renders it possible.

Notes

1. C. Lévi-Strauss, "Introduction à l'oeuvre de Marcel Mauss," in M. Mauss, *Sociologie et anthropologie* (Paris: P.U.F., 1950), pp. 48–49.

2. The parallel with differential calculus may seem both arbitrary and old-fashioned. But what is old-fashioned is only the infinitist interpretation of calculus. Already at the end of the nineteenth century, Weirstrass gave a finite interpretation, *ordinal and static*, very close to a mathematical structuralism. The theme of singularities remains an essential piece of the theory of differential equations. The best study of the history of the differential calculus and its modern structural interpretation is C. B. Boyer's *The History of the Calculus and Its Conceptual Development* (New York: Dover, 1959).

3. A general theme of Cicero's *De Fato*.

4. *De Fato*, 8.

5. See Georges Canguilhem, *Le Normal et le pathologique* (Paris: P.U.F., 1966), p. 90.

6. On the role of exclusion and expulsion, see the chapter on "contradiction" in Hegel's *Logic*.

7. Nietzsche, *Ecce Homo*, trans. Walter Kaufmann in *On the Genealogy of Morals and Ecce Homo* (New York: Vintage Books, 1969), p. 223.

8. Klossowski speaks of "this thought so perfectly coherent that it excludes me at the very instant I think it," "Oubli et anamnèse dans l'expérience vécue de l'éternel retour du même," *Nietzsche* (Paris: Cahiers de Royaumont, Minuit, 1967), p. 234. See also the postface to *Lois de l'hospitalité*. In these texts,

Klossowski develops a theory of the sign, sense, and nonsense, and a profoundly original interpretation of the Nietzschean eternal return, conceived of as an ex-centric power of affirming divergence and disjunction, and which allows neither the identity of the self, nor of the world, nor of God to subsist.

9. With respect to this process of return or reaction and the internal temporality that it implies, see the work of Gustave Guillaume and the analysis of this work carried out by E. Ortigues in *Le Discours et le symbole* (Paris: Aubier, 1962). Guillaume derives from it an original conception of the infinitive in "Epoques et niveaux temporels dans le système de la conjugaison française" (*Cahiers de linguistique structurale,* no. 4, Université de Laval).

V Difference, Subject, and Other

20   Ethics as First Philosophy

Emmanuel Levinas

I

The correlation between *knowledge*, understood as disinterested contemplation, and *being*, is, according to our philosophical tradition, the very site of intelligibility, the occurrence of meaning (*sens*). The comprehension of being—the semantics of this verb—would thus be the very possibility of or the occasion for wisdom and the wise and, as such, is *first philosophy*. The intellectual, and even spiritual life, of the West, through the priority it gives to knowledge identified with Spirit, demonstrates its fidelity to the first philosophy of Aristotle, whether one interprets the latter according to the ontology of book Γ of the *Metaphysics* or according to the theology or onto-theology of book Λ where, the ultimate explanation of intelligibility in terms of the primary causality of God is a reference to a God defined by being *qua* being.

The correlation between knowledge and being, or the thematics of contemplation, indicates both a difference and a difference that is *overcome* in the *true*. Here the known is understood and so *appropriated* by knowledge, and as it were *freed* of its otherness. In the realm of truth, being, as the *other* of thought becomes the characteristic *property* of thought as knowledge. The ideal of rationality or of sense (*sens*) begins already to appear as the immanence of the real to reason; just as, in being, a privilege is granted to the *present*, which is presence to thought, of which the future and the past are modalities or modifications: re-presentations.

But in knowledge there also appears the notion of an intellectual activity or of a reasoning will—a way of doing something which consists precisely of thinking through knowing, of seizing something and making it one's own, of reducing to presence and representing the difference of being, an activity which *appropriates* and *grasps* the otherness of the known. A certain grasp: as an entity, being becomes the characteristic property of thought, as it is grasped by it and becomes known. Knowledge as perception, concept, comprehension, refers back to an act of grasping. The metaphor should be taken literally: even before any technical application of knowledge, it expresses the principle rather than the result of the future technological and industrial order of which every civilisation bears at least the seed. The immanence of the known to the act of knowing is already the embodiment of seizure. This is not something applied like a form of magic to the "impotent spirituality" of thinking, nor is it the guarantee of certain psycho-physiological conditions, but rather belongs to that unit of knowledge in which *Auffassen* (*understanding*) is also, and always has been, a *Fassen* (*gripping*). The mode of thought known as knowledge involves man's concrete existence in the world he inhabits, in which he moves and works and possesses. The most abstract lessons of science—as Husserl showed in his *The Crisis of European Sciences and Transcendental Phenomenology*—have their beginnings in the "world of life" and refer to things within hand's reach. It is to this hand that the idea of a "given world" concretely refers. Things contain the promise of satisfaction—their concreteness puts them on a scale fit for a knowing form of thought. Thought as knowledge is already the labour of thought. A thought that assesses what is equal and adequate, and can give satisfaction. The rationality of beings stems from their presence and adequation. The operations of knowledge reestablish rationality behind the diachrony of *becoming* in which presence occurs or is foreseen. Knowledge is re-presentation, a return to presence, and nothing may remain *other* to it.

Thought is an activity, where something is appropriated by a knowledge that is independent, of course, of any finality exterior to it, an activity which is disinterested and self-sufficient and whose self-sufficiency, sovereignty, *bonne conscience*[1] and happy solitude are asserted by Aristotle. "The wise man can practise contemplation by himself" says Book Ten of the *Nicomachean Ethics*.[2] This is a regal and as it were unconditioned activity, a sovereignty which is possible only as solitude, an unconditioned activity, even if limited for man by biological needs and by death. But it is a notion that allows a second one to be sustained, the notion of the pure *theoretic*, of its freedom, of the equivalence between wisdom and freedom, of that partial coincidence of the human domain with the divine life of which Aristotle speaks at the end of the seventh section of Book Ten of the *Ethics*. Here already the strange and contradictory concept of a *finite freedom* begins to take shape.

Throughout the whole history of Western philosophy, *contemplation* or *knowledge* and the *freedom of knowledge* are inspiration for the mind (*l'esprit*). Knowing is the psyche or pneumatic force of thought, even in the act of *feeling* or *willing*. It is to be found in the concept of *consciousness* at the dawn of the modern age with the interpretation of the concept of *cogito* given by Descartes in his Second Meditation. Husserl, returning to a medieval tradition, then, describes it as intentionality, which is understood as "consciousness of something," and so is inseparable from its "intentional object." This structure has a noetic-noematic composition in which representation or objectivization is the incontestable model. The whole of human lived experience, in the period up to and above all including the present, has been expressed in terms of experience, that is, has been converted into accepted doctrine, teachings, sciences. Relationships with neighbours, with social groups, with God equally represent collective and religious *experiences*.

Modernity will subsequently be distinguished by the attempt to develop from the identification and appropriation of being *by* knowledge toward the identification of being *and* knowledge. The passage from the *cogito* to the *sum* leads to that point where the free activity of knowledge, an activity alien to any external goal, will also find itself on the side of what is known. This free activity of knowledge will also come to constitute the mystery of being *qua* being, whatever is known by knowledge (*le connu du savoir*). The *Wisdom of first philosophy* is reduced to self-consciousness. Identical and non-identical are identified. The labour of thought wins out over the otherness of things and men. Since Hegel, any goal considered alien to the disinterested acquisition of knowledge has been subordinated to the freedom of knowledge as a science (*savoir*); and within this freedom, *being* itself is from that point understood as *the active affirming of that same being*, as *the strength and strain of being*. Modern man persists in his being as a sovereign who is merely concerned to maintain the *powers of his sovereignty*. Everything that is possible is permitted. In this way the experience of Nature and Society would gradually get the better of any exteriority. A miracle of modern Western freedom unhindered by any memory or remorse, and opening onto a "glittering future" where everything can be rectified. Only by death is this freedom thwarted. The obstacle of death is insurmountable, inexorable and fundamentally incomprehensible. The recognition of finitude will of course character-ize a new test for ontology. But finitude and death will not have called into question the *bonne conscience* with which the freedom of knowledge operates. They will simply have put a check on its powers.

II

In this essay we wish to ask whether thought understood as knowledge, since the ontology of the first philosophy, has exhausted the possible modes of meaning for thought, and whether, beyond knowledge and its hold on being, a more urgent form does not emerge, that of wisdom. We propose to begin with the notion of intentionality, as it figures in Husserlian phenomenology, which is one of the culminating points in Western philosophy. The equivalence of thought and knowledge in relation to being is here formulated by Husserl in the most direct manner. Whilst successfully isolating the idea of an originary, non-theoretical intentionality from the active emotional life of consciousness, he continues to base his theory on *representation*, the objectivizing act, adopting Brentano's thesis at this point, in spite of all the precautions he takes in his new formulation of this thesis. Now, within consciousness—which is consciousness of something—knowledge is, by the same token, a relation to an *other* of consciousness and almost the aim or the will of that other which is an *object*. Husserl, inviting us to question the intentionality of consciousness, wants us also to ask "worauf sie eigentlich hinauswill" (*What are you getting at?*), an intention or wish which, incidentally, would justify calling the units of consciousness acts. At the same time, knowledge, within the intuition of truth, is described as a "filling out" that gratifies a longing for the being as object, given and received in the original, *present* in a representation. It is a hold on being which equals a constitution of that being. This Transcendental

Reduction suspends all independence in the world other than that of consciousness itself, and causes the world to be rediscovered as *noema*. As a result, it leads—or ought to lead—to full self-consciousness affirming itself as absolute being, and confirming itself as an *I* that, through all possible "differences," is identified as master of its own nature as well as of the universe and able to illuminate the darkest recesses of resistance to its powers. As Merleau-Ponty in particular has shown, the I that constitutes the world comes up against a sphere in which it is by its very flesh implicated; it is implicated in what it otherwise would have constituted and so is implicated in the world. But it is present in the world as it is present in its own body, an intimate incarnation which no longer purely and simply displays the exteriority of an object.[3]

But this reduced consciousness—which, in reflecting upon itself, rediscovers and masters its own acts of perception and science as objects in the world, thereby affirming itself as self-consciousness and absolute being—also remains a non-intentional consciousness of itself, as though it were a surplus somehow devoid of any willful aim. A non-intentional consciousness operating, if one may put it like this, unknowingly as knowledge, as a non-objectivizing knowledge. As such it accompanies all the intentional processes of consciousness and of the *ego* (*moi*) which, in that consciousness, "acts" and "wills" and has "intentions." Consciousness of consciousness, indirect, implicit and aimless, without any initiative that might refer back to an ego; passive like time passing and ageing me without my intervening (*sans moi*). A "non-intentional" consciousness to be distinguished from philosophical reflection, or the internal perception to which, indeed, non-intentional consciousness might easily offer itself as an internal object and for which it might substitute itself by making explicit the implicit messages it bears. The intentional consciousness of reflection, in taking as its object the transcendental ego, along with its mental acts and states, may also thematize and grasp supposedly implicit modes of non-intentional lived experience. It is invited to do this by philosophy in its fundamental project which consists in enlightening the inevitable transcendental naivety of a consciousness forgetful of its horizon, of its implicit content and even of the time it lives through.

Consequently one is forced, no doubt too quickly, to consider in philosophy all this immediate consciousness merely as a still confused representation to be duly brought to "light." The obscure context of whatever is thematized is converted by reflection, or intentional consciousness, into clear and distinct data, like those which present the perceived world or a transcendental reduced consciousness.

One may ask, however, whether, beneath the gaze of reflected consciousness taken as self-consciousness, the non-intentional, experienced as the counterpoint to the intentional, does not conserve and free its true meaning. The critique of introspection as traditionally practised has always been suspicious of a modification that a supposedly spontaneous consciousness might undergo beneath the scrutinizing, thematizing, objectivizing and indiscreet gaze of reflection, and has seen this as a violation or distortion of some sort of secret. This is a critique which is always refuted only to be reborn.

The question is what exactly happens, then, in this non-reflective consciousness considered merely to be pre-reflective and the implicit partner of an intentional consciousness which, in reflection, intentionally aims for the thinking self (*soi*), as if the thinking ego (*moi*) appeared in the world and belonged to it? What might this supposed confusion or implication really mean? One cannot simply refer to the formal notion of potentiality. Might there not be grounds for distinguishing between the envelopment of the particular in the conceptual, the implicit understanding of the pre-supposition in a notion, the potentiality of what is considered possible within the horizon, on the one hand, and, on the other hand, the intimacy of the non-intentional within what is known as pre-reflective consciousness and which is duration itself?

III

Does the "knowledge" of pre-reflective self-consciousness really know? As a confused, implicit consciousness preceding all intentions—or as duration freed of all intentions—it is less an act than a pure passivity. This is not only due to its being-without-having-chosen-to-be or its fall into a confused world of possibilities already realised even before any choice might be made, as in Heidegger's *Geworfenheit*. It is a "consciousness" that signifies not so much a knowledge of oneself as something that effaces presence or makes it discreet. Phenomenological analysis, of course, describes such a pure duration of time within reflection, as being intentionally structured by a play of retentions and protentions which, in the very duration of time, at least remain non-explicit and suppose, in that they represent a flow, another sort of time. This duration remains free from the sway of the will, absolutely outside all activity of the ego, and exactly like the ageing process which is probably the perfect model of passive synthesis, a lapse of time no act of remembrance, reconstructing the past, could possibly reverse. Does not the temporality of implicit time, like the implication of the implicit, here signify otherwise than as knowledge taken on the run, otherwise than a way of representing presence or the non-presence of the future and the past? Duration as pure duration, non-intervention as being without insistence, as being that dare not speak its name, being that dare not be; the agency of the instant without the insistence of the ego, which is already a lapse in time, which is "over before it's begun!" This implication of the non-intentional is a form of *mauvaise conscience*: it has no intentions, or aims, and cannot avail itself of the protective mask of a character contemplating in the mirror of the world a reassured and self-positing portrait. It has no name, no situation, no status. It has a presence afraid of presence, afraid of the insistence of the identical ego, stripped of all qualities. In its non-intentionality, not yet at the stage of willing, and prior to any fault, in its non-intentional identification, identity recoils before its affirmation. It dreads the insistence in the return to self that is a necessary part of identification. This is either *mauvaise conscience* or timidity; it is not guilty, but accused; and responsible for its very presence. It has not yet been invested with any attributes or justified in any way. This creates the reserve of the stranger or "sojourner on earth," as it says in the Psalms, the countryless or "home-less" person who dare not enter in. Perhaps the interiority of the mental is originally an insufficient courage to assert oneself in one's being or in body or flesh. One comes not into the world but into question. By way of reference to this, or in "memory" of this, the ego (*moi*) which is already declaring and affirming itself (*s'affirme*)—or making itself firm (*s'affermit*)—itself in being, still remains ambiguous or enigmatic enough to recognise itself as hateful, to use Pascal's term, in this very manifestation of its emphatic identity of its ipseity, in the "saying I". The superb priority of $A = A$, the principle of intelligibility and meaning,[4] this sovereignty, or freedom within the human ego, is also, as it were, the moment when humility occurs. This questions the affirmation and strengthening of being found in the famous and facilely rhetorical quest for the meaning of life, which suggests that the absolute ego, already endowed with meaning by its vital, psychic and social forces, or its transcendental sovereignty, then returned to its *mauvaise conscience*.

Pre-reflective, non-intentional consciousness would never be able to return to a moral realization of this passivity, as if, in that form of consciousness, one could already see a subject postulating itself in the "indeclinable nominative," assured of its right to be and "dominating" the timidity of the non-intentional like a spiritual infancy that is outgrown, or an attack of weakness that becomes an impassive psyche. The non-intentional is from the start passivity, and the accusative in some way its "first case." (Actually, this passivity, which does not correlate to any activity, is not so much something that describes the *mauvaise conscience* of the non-intentional [as] something that is described by it.) This *mauvaise conscience* is not the finitude of existence signaled by anguish. My death, which is always going to be premature, does perhaps put a check on being which, *qua* being, perseveres in being, but in anguish this scandal fails to shake the *bonne conscience* of being, or the moral-ity founded upon the inalienable right of the *conatus* which is also the right and the *bonne conscience* of freedom. However, it is in the passivity of the non-intentional, in the way it is spontaneous and precedes the formulation of any metaphysical ideas on the subject, that the very justice of the position within being is questioned, a position which asserts itself with intentional thought, knowledge and a grasp of the here and now. What one sees in this questioning is being as *mauvaise conscience*; to be open to question, but also to question-ing, to have to respond. Language is born in responsibility. One has to speak, to say *I*, to be in the first person, precisely to be me (*moi*). But, from that point, in affirming this *me* being, one has to respond to one's right to be. It is necessary to think through to this point Pascal's phrase, "the I (*mon*) is hateful."

IV

One has to respond to one's right to be, not by referring to some abstract and anonymous law, or judicial entity, but because of one's fear for the Other. My being-in-the-world or my "place in the sun,"[5] my being at home,[6] have these not also been the usurpation of spaces belonging to the other man whom I have already oppressed or starved, or driven out into a third world; are they not acts of repulsing, excluding, exiling, stripping, killing? Pascal's "my place in the sun" marks the beginning of the image of the usurpation of the whole earth. A fear for all the violence and murder my existing might generate, in spite of its conscious and intentional innocence. A fear which reaches back past my "self-consciousness" in spite of whatever moves are made towards a *bonne conscience* by a pure perseverance in being. It is the fear of occupying someone else's place with the *Da* of my *Dasein*; it is the inability to occupy a place, a profound utopia.

In my philosophical essays, I have spoken a lot about the face of the Other as being the original site of the sensible. May I now briefly take up again the description, as I now see it, of the irruption of the face into the phenomenal order of appearances?

The proximity of the other is the face's meaning, and it means from the very start in a way that goes beyond those plastic forms which forever try to cover the face like a mask of their presence to perception. But always the face shows through these forms. Prior to any particular expression and beneath all particular expressions, which cover over and protect with an immediately adopted face or countenance, there is the nakedness and destitution of the expression as such, that is to say extreme exposure, defencelessness, vulnerability itself. This extreme exposure—prior to any human aim—is like a shot "at point blank range." Whatever has been invested is extradited, but it is a hunt that occurs prior to anything being actually tracked down and beaten out into the open. From the beginning there is a face to face steadfast in its exposure to invisible death, to a mysterious forsakenness. Beyond the visibility of whatever is unveiled, and prior to any knowledge about death, mortality lies in the Other.

Does not expression resemble more closely this extreme exposure than it does some supposed recourse to a code? True *self*-expression stresses the nakedness and defencelessness that encourages and directs the violence of the first crime: the goal of a murderous uprightness is especially well-suited to exposing or expressing the face. The first murderer probably does not realize the result of the blow he is about to deliver, but his violent design helps him to find the line with which death may give an air of unimpeachable rectitude to the face of the neighbour; the line is traced like the trajectory of the blow that is dealt and the arrow that kills.

But, in its expression, in its mortality, the face before me summons me, calls for me, begs for me, as if the invisible death that must be faced by the Other, pure otherness, separated, in some way, from any whole, were my business. It is as if that invisible death, ignored by the Other, whom already it concerns by the nakedness of its face, were already "regarding" me prior to confronting me, and becoming the death that stares me in the face. The other man's death calls me into question, as if, by my possible future indifference, I had become the accomplice of the death to which the other, who cannot see it, is exposed; and as if, even before vowing myself to him, I had to answer for this death of the other, and to accompany the Other in his mortal solitude. The Other becomes my neighbour precisely through the way the face summons me, calls for me, begs for me, and in so doing recalls my responsibility, and calls me into question.

Responsibility for the Other, for the naked face of the first individual to come along. A responsibility that goes beyond what I may or may not have done to the Other or whatever acts I may or may not have committed, as if I were devoted to the other man before being devoted to myself. Or more exactly, as if I had to answer for the other's death even before *being*. A guiltless responsibility, whereby I am none the less open to an accusation of which no alibi, spatial or temporal, could clear me. It is as if the other established a relationship or a relationship were established whose whole intensity consists in not presupposing the idea of community. A responsibility stemming from a time before my freedom—before my (*moi*) beginning, before any present. A fraternity existing in extreme separation. *Before*, but in what past? Not in the time preceding the present, in which I might have contracted any commitments. Responsibility for my neighbour dates from before my freedom in an immemorial past, an unrepresentable past that was never present and is more ancient than consciousness of. . . . A responsibility for my neighbour, for the other man, for the stranger or sojourner, to which nothing in the rigorously ontological order binds me—nothing in the order of the thing, of the something, of number or causality.

It is the responsibility of a hostage which can be carried to the point of being substituted for the other person and demands an infinite subjection of subjectivity. Unless this anarchic responsibility, which summons me from nowhere into a present time, is perhaps, the measure or the manner or the system of an immemorial freedom that is even older than being, or decisions, or deeds.

V

This summons to responsibility destroys the formulas of generality by which my knowledge (*savoir*) or acquaintance (*connaissance*) of the other man re-presents him to me as my fellow man. In the face of the other man I am inescapably responsible and consequently the unique and chosen one. By this freedom, humanity in me (*moi*)—that is, humanity as me—signifies, in spite of its ontological contingence of finitude and mortality, the anteriority and uniqueness of the non-*interchangeable*.

This is the anteriority and chosen nature of an excellence that cannot be reduced to the features distinguishing or constituting individual beings in the order of their world or people, in the role they play on history's social stage, as characters, that is, in the mirror of reflection or in self-consciousness.

Fear for the Other, fear for the other man's death, is *my* fear, but is in no way an *individual's* taking fright. It thus stands out against the admirable phenomenological analysis of *Befindlichkeit*[7] found in *Sein und Zeit*: a reflective structure expressed by a pronominal verb, in which emotion is always emotion for something moving you, but also emotion for oneself. Emotion therefore consists in being moved—being scared by something, overjoyed by something, saddened by something, but also in feeling joy or sadness for oneself. All affectivity therefore has repercussions for my being-for-death. There is a double intentionality in the *by* and the *for* and so there is a turning back on oneself and a return to anguish for oneself, for one's finitude: in the fear inspired *by* the wolf, an anguish *for* my death. Fear for the other man's death does not turn back into anguish for my death. It extends beyond the ontology of the Heideggerian *Dasein* and the *bonne conscience* of being in the sight of that being itself. There is ethical awareness and vigilance in this emotional unease. Certainly, Heidegger's being-for-death marks, for the being (*étant*), the end of his being-in-the-sight-of-that-being as well as the scandal provoked by that ending, but in that ending no scruple of being (*être*) is awakened.

This is the hidden human face behind perseverance in being! Hidden behind the affirmation of being persisting analytically—or animally—in its being, and in which the ideal vigour of identity identifying and affirming and strengthening itself in the life of human individuals and in their struggle for vital existence, whether conscious or unconscious or rational, the miracle of the ego vindicated in the eyes of the neighbour—or the miracle of the ego (*moi*) which has got rid of self (*soi*) and instead fears for the Other—is thus like the suspension, or epochè, of the eternal and irreversible return of the identical to itself and of the intangible nature of its logical and ontological privilege. What is suspended is its ideal priority, which wipes out all otherness by murder or by all-encompassing and totalizing thought; or war and politics which pass themselves off as the relation of the Same to the Other (*l'Autre*). It is in the laying down by the ego of its sovereignty (in its "hateful" modality), that we find ethics and also probably the very spirituality of the soul, but most certainly the question of the meaning of being, that is, its appeal for justification. This first philosophy shows through the ambiguity of the identical, an identical which declares itself to be *I* at the height of its unconditional and even logically indiscernable identity, an autonomy above all criteria, but which precisely at the height of this unconditional identity confesses that it is hateful.

The ego is the very crisis of the being of a being (*de l'être de l'étant*) in the human domain. A crisis of being, not because the sense of this verb might still need to be understood in its semantic secret and might call on the powers of ontology, but because I begin to ask myself if my being is justified, if the *Da* of my *Dasein* is not already the usurpation of somebody else's place.

This question has no need of a theoretical reply in the form of new information. Rather it appeals to responsibility, which is not a practical stopgap measure designed to console knowledge in its failure to match being. This responsibility does not deny knowledge the ability to comprehend and grasp; instead, it is the excellence of ethical proximity in its sociality, in its love without concupiscence. The human is the return to the interiority of non-intentional consciousness, to *mauvaise conscience*, to its capacity to fear injustice more than death, to prefer to suffer than to commit injustice, and to prefer that which justifies being over that which assures it.

VI

To be or not to be—is that the question? Is it the first and final question? Does being human consist in forcing oneself to be and does the understanding of the meaning of being—the semantics of the verb to be—represent the first philosophy required by a consciousness which from the first would be knowledge and representation conserving its assurance in being-for-death, asserting itself as the lucidity of a thought thinking itself right through, even unto death and which, even in its finitude—already or still an unquestioned *mauvaise conscience* as regards its right to be—is either anguished or heroic in the precariousness of its finitude? Or does the first question arise rather in the *mauvaise conscience*, an instability which is different from that threatened by my death and my suffering? It poses the question of my right to be which is already my responsibility for the death of the Other, interrupting the carefree spontaneity of my naive perseverance. The right to be and the legitimacy of this right are not finally referred to the abstraction of the universal rules of the Law—but in the last resort are referred, like that law itself and justice—or for the other of my non-indifference, to death, to which the face of the Other—beyond my ending—in its very rectitude is exposed. Whether he regards me or not, he "regards" me. In this question being and life are awakened to the human dimension. This is the question of the meaning of being: not the ontology of the understanding of that extraordinary verb, but the ethics of its justice. The question *par excellence* or the question of philosophy. Not "Why being rather than nothing?", but how being justifies itself.

Notes

1. We have decided to leave the phrases *bonne conscience* and *mauvaise conscience* in the original French. This is because, in addition to suggesting a good and a bad conscience (which is how they are translated in *Time and the Other*, p. 110, for example) or a clear and a guilty conscience, they also carry the connotation of consciousness and *unhappy consciousness*. For Hegel, unhappy consciousness (*das unglückliches Bewusstsein*) is an inwardly disrupted one, with a dual and essentially contradictory nature. It is therefore "the gazing of one self-consciousness into another, and itself *is* both" (*Phenomenology of Spirit*, p. 126). It is the coexistence of master and slave, eternal and mortal, "the Unchangeable" and the "changeable." Critics are divided, however, over whether or not this duality is a sincerely felt representation of Christianity.

2. Aristotle, *The Nicomachean Ethics* (Harmondsworth: Penguin, 1955, 1981).

3. A reference to Merleau-Ponty's "body intentionality." See the *Phenomenology of Perception*, part 1, pp. 67–199. In addition, see *Totality and Infinity*, p. 181.

4. Hegel characterizes the Absolute as A = A in the Preface to the *Phenomenology of Spirit*, p. 9. The equation is in turn a reference to Leibniz, who calls A = A "the law of identity," arguing ultimately that no distinctions are real, and that identity with itself is the only ultimate equivalence.

5. A reference to Pascal's *Pensées* (Brunzschvicq 295/Lafume 112).

6. Levinas is alluding here to Heidegger's sense of *bei sich*, the real and originary sense in which the existent comes to exist "for itself." The meaning of *"bei"* is close to that of "at" in "at home" or *"chez"* in *"chez moi."* Cf. *Being and Time*, p. 80, H.54: "The expression *'bin'* is connected with *'bei,'* and so *'ich bin'* (I am) mean in its turn 'I reside' or 'dwell alongside' the world, as that which is familiar to me in such and such a way. 'Being' (*Sein*), as the infinitive of *'ich bin'* (that is to say, when it is understood as an *existentiale*), signifies 'to reside alongside . . .,' 'to be familiar with . . .' *'Being-in' is thus the formal existential expression for the Being of Dasein, which has Being-in-the-world as its essential state."*

7. *Befindlichkeit* has always been translated into English as "state-of-mind," an expression also used for *"befinden"* and *"befindlich."* More literally, it means "the state in which one may be found," which is the sense it carries here in Levinas. As such, Heidegger's translators make it clear that 'the "of-mind" belongs to English idiom, has no literal counterpart in the structure of the German word, and fails to bring out the important connotation of finding oneself' (*Being and Time*, footnote to H.134, p. 172).

21 Subjectivity in Language

Emile Benveniste

If language is, as they say, the instrument of communication, to what does it owe this property? The question may cause surprise, as does everything that seems to challenge an obvious fact, but it is sometimes useful to require proof of the obvious. Two answers come to mind. The one would be that language is *in fact* employed as the instrument of communication, probably because men have not found a better or more effective way in which to communicate. This amounts to stating what one wishes to understand. One might also think of replying that language has such qualities as make it suited to serve as an instrument; it lends itself to transmitting what I entrust to it—an order, a question, an announcement—and it elicits from the interlocutor a behavior which is adequate each time. Developing a more technical aspect of this idea, one might add that the behavior of language admits of a behaviorist description, in terms of stimulus and response, from which one might draw conclusions as to the intermediary and instrumental nature of language. But is it really language of which we are speaking here? Are we not confusing it with discourse? If we posit that discourse is language put into action, and necessarily between partners, we show amidst the confusion, that we are begging the question, since the nature of this "instrument" is explained by its situation as an "instrument." As for the role of transmission that language plays, one should not fail to observe, on the one hand, that this role can devolve upon nonlinguistic means—gestures and mimicry—and, on the other hand, that, in speaking here of an "instrument," we are letting ourselves be deceived by certain processes of transmission which in human societies without exception come after language and imitate its functioning. All systems of signals, rudimentary or complex, are in this situation.

In fact, the comparison of language to an instrument—and it should necessarily be a material instrument for the comparison to even be comprehensible—must fill us with mistrust, as should every simplistic notion about language. To speak of an instrument is to put man and nature in opposition. The pick, the arrow, and the wheel are not in nature. They are fabrications. Language is in the nature of man, and he did not fabricate it. We are always inclined to that naïve concept of a primordial period in which a complete man discovered another one, equally complete, and between the two of them language was worked out little by little. This is pure fiction. We can never get back to man separated from language and we shall never see him inventing it. We shall never get back to man reduced to himself and exercising his wits to conceive of the existence of another. It is a speaking man whom we find in the world, a man speaking to another man, and language provides the very definition of man.

All the characteristics of language, its immaterial nature, its symbolic functioning, its articulated arrangement, the fact that it has *content*, are in themselves enough to render suspect this comparison of language to an instrument, which tends to dissociate the property of language from man. Certainly in everyday practice the give and take of speaking suggests an exchange, hence a "thing" which we exchange, and speaking seems thus to assume an instrumental or vehicular function which we are quick to hypostasize as an "object." But, once again, this role belongs to the individual act of speech.

Once this function is seen as belonging to the act of speech, it may be asked what predisposition accounts for the fact that the act of speech should have it. In order for speech to be the vehicle of "communication," it must be so enabled by language, of which it is only the actualization. Indeed, it is in language that we must search for the condition of this aptitude. It seems to us that it resides in a property of language barely visible under the evidence that conceals it, which only sketchily can we yet characterize.

It is in and through language that man constitutes himself as a *subject*, because language alone establishes the concept of "ego" in reality, in *its* reality which is that of the being.

The "subjectivity" we are discussing here is the capacity of the speaker to posit himself as "subject." It is defined not by the feeling which everyone experiences of being himself (this feeling, to the degree that it can be taken note of, is only a reflection) but as the psychic unity that transcends the totality of the actual experiences it assembles and that makes the permanence of the consciousness. Now we hold that that "subjectivity," whether it is placed in phenomenology or in psychology, as one may wish, is only the emergence in the being of a fundamental property of language. "Ego" is he who *says* "ego." That is where we see the foundation of "subjectivity," which is determined by the linguistic status of "person."

Consciousness of self is only possible if it is experienced by contrast. I use *I* only when I am speaking to someone who will be a *you* in my address. It is this condition of dialogue that is constitutive of *person*, for it implies that reciprocally *I* becomes *you* in the address of the one who in his turn designates himself as *I*. Here we see a principle whose consequences are to spread out in all directions. Language is possible only because each speaker sets himself up as a *subject* by referring to himself as *I* in his discourse. Because of this, *I* posits another person, the one who, being, as he is, completely exterior to "me," becomes my echo to whom I say *you* and who says *you* to me. This polarity of persons is the fundamental condition in language, of which the process of communication, in which we share, is only a mere pragmatic consequence. It is a polarity, moreover, very peculiar in itself, as it offers a type of opposition whose equivalent is encountered nowhere else outside of language. This polarity does not mean either equality or symmetry: "ego" always has a position of transcendence with regard to *you*. Nevertheless, neither of the terms can be conceived of without the other; they are complementary, although according to an "interior/exterior" opposition, and, at the same time, they are reversible. If we seek a parallel to this, we will not find it. The condition of man in language is unique.

And so the old antinomies of "I" and "the other," of the individual and society, fall. It is a duality which it is illegitimate and erroneous to reduce to a single primordial term, whether this unique term be the "I," which must be established in the individual's own consciousness in order to become accessible to that of the fellow human being, or whether it be, on the contrary, society, which as a totality would preexist the individual and from which the individual could only be disengaged gradually, in proportion to his acquisition of self-consciousness. It is in a dialectic reality that will incorporate the two terms and define them by mutual relationship that the linguistic basis of subjectivity is discovered.

But must this basis be linguistic? By what right does language establish the basis of subjectivity?

As a matter of fact, language is responsible for it in all its parts. Language is marked so deeply by the expression of subjectivity that one might ask if it could still function and be called language if it were constructed otherwise. We are of course talking of language in general, not simply of particular languages. But the concordant facts of particular languages give evidence for language. We shall give only a few of the most obvious examples.

The very terms we are using here, *I* and *you*, are not to be taken as figures but as linguistic forms indicating "person." It is a remarkable fact—but who would notice it, since it is so familiar?—that the "personal pronouns" are never missing from among the signs of a language, no matter what its type, epoch, or region may be. A language without the expression of person cannot be imagined. It can only happen that in certain languages, under certain circumstances, these "pronouns" are deliberately omitted; this is the case in most of the Far Eastern societies, in which a convention of politeness imposes the use of periphrases or of special forms between certain groups of individuals in order to replace the direct personal references. But these usages only serve to underline the value of the avoided forms; it is the implicit existence of these pronouns that gives social and cultural value to the substitutes imposed by class relationships.

Now these pronouns are distinguished from all other designations a language articulates in that *they do not refer to a concept or to an individual.*

There is no concept "I" that incorporates all the *I*'s that are uttered at every moment in the mouths of all speakers, in the sense that there is a concept "tree" to which all the individual uses of *tree* refer. The "I," then, does not denominate any lexical entity. Could it then be said that *I* refers to a particular individual? If that were the case, a permanent contradiction would be admitted into language, and anarchy into its use. How could the same term refer indifferently to any individual whatsoever and still at the same time identify him in his individuality? We are in the presence of a class of words, the "personal pronouns," that escape the status of all the other signs of language. Then, what does *I* refer to? To something very peculiar which is exclusively linguistic: *I* refers to the act of individual discourse in which it is pronounced, and by this it designates the speaker. It is a term that cannot be identified except in what we have called elsewhere an instance of discourse and that has only a momentary reference. The reality to which it refers is the reality of the discourse. It is in the instance of discourse in which *I* designates the speaker that the speaker proclaims himself as the "subject." And so it is literally true that the basis of subjectivity is in the exercise of language. If one really thinks about it, one will see that there is no other objective testimony to the identity of the subject except that which he himself thus gives about himself.

Language is so organized that it permits each speaker to *appropriate to himself* an entire language by designating himself as *I*.

The personal pronouns provide the first step in this bringing out of subjectivity in language. Other classes of pronouns that share the same status depend in their turn upon these pronouns. These other classes are the indicators of *deixis*, the demonstratives, adverbs, and adjectives, which organize the spatial and temporal relationships around the "subject" taken as referent: "this, here, now," and their numerous correlatives, "that, yesterday, last year, tomorrow," etc. They have in common the feature of being defined only with respect to the instances of discourse in which they occur, that is, in dependence upon the *I* which is proclaimed in the discourse.

It is easy to see that the domain of subjectivity is further expanded and must take over the expression of temporality. No matter what the type of language, there is everywhere to be observed a certain linguistic organization of the notion of time. It matters little whether this notion is marked in the inflection of the verb or by words of other classes (particles, adverbs, lexical variations, etc.); that is a matter of formal structure. In one way or another, a language always makes a distinction of "tenses"; whether it be a past and a future, separated by a "present," as in French [or English], or, as in various Amerindian languages, of a preterite-present opposed to a future, or a present-future distinguished from a past, these distinctions being in their turn capable of depending on variations of aspect, etc. But the line of separation is always a reference to the "present." Now this "present" in its turn has only a linguistic fact as temporal reference: the coincidence of the event described with the instance of discourse that describes it. The temporal referent of the present can only be internal to the discourse. The *Dictionnaire générale* defines the "present" as "le temps du verbe qui exprime le temps où l'on est." But let us beware of this; there is no other criterion and no other expression by which to indicate "the time at which one *is*" except to take it as "the time at which one *is speaking*." This is the eternally "present" moment, although it never relates to the same events of an "objective" chronology because it is determined for each speaker by each of the instances of discourse related to it. Linguistic time is *self-referential*. Ultimately, human temporality with all its linguistic apparatus reveals the subjectivity inherent in the very using of language.

Language is accordingly the possibility of subjectivity because it always contains the linguistic forms appropriate to the expression of subjectivity, and discourse provokes the emergence of subjectivity because it consists of discrete instances. In some way language puts forth "empty" forms which each speaker, in the exercise of discourse, appropriates to himself and which he relates to his "person," at the same time defining himself as *I* and a partner as *you*. The instance of discourse is thus constitutive of all the coordinates that define the subject and of which we have briefly pointed out only the most obvious.

The establishment of "subjectivity" in language creates the category of person—both in language and also, we believe, outside of it as well. Moreover, it has quite varied effects in the very structure of languages, whether it be in the arrangement of the forms or in semantic relationships. Here we must necessarily have particular languages in view in order to illustrate some effects of the change of perspective which "subjectivity" can introduce. We cannot say what the range of the particular phenomena we are pointing out may be in the universe of real languages; for the moment it is less important to delimit them than to reveal them. English provides several convenient examples.

In a general way, when I use the present of a verb with three persons (to use the traditional nomenclature), it seems that the difference in person does not lead to any change of meaning in the conjugated verb form. *I eat, you eat,* and *he eats* have in common and as a constant that the verb form presents a description of an action, attributed respectively and in an identical fashion to "I," "you," and "he." Similarly, *I suffer, you suffer, he suffers* have the description of the same state in common. This gives the impression of being an obvious fact and even the formal alignment in the paradigm of the conjugation implies this.

Now a number of verbs do not have this permanence of meaning in the changing of persons, such as those verbs with which we denote dispositions or mental operations. In saying *I suffer,* I describe my present condition. In saying *I feel* (*that the weather is going to change*), I describe an impression which I feel. But what happens if, instead of *I feel* (*that the weather is going to change*), I say *I believe* (*that the weather is going to change*)? The formal symmetry between *I feel* and *I believe* is complete. Is it so for the meaning? Can I consider *I believe* to be a description of myself of the same sort as *I feel*? Am I describing myself believing when I say *I believe* (*that . . .*)? Surely not. The operation of thought is not at all the object of the utterance; *I believe* (*that . . .*) is equivalent to a mitigated assertion. By saying *I believe* (*that . . .*), I convert into a subjective utterance the fact asserted impersonally, namely, *the weather is going to change*, which is the true proposition.

Let us consider further the following utterances: "You are Mr. X., *I suppose.*" "*I presume* that John received my letter." "He has left the hospital, from which I *conclude* that he is cured." These sentences contain verbs that are verbs of operation: *suppose, presume,* and *conclude* are all logical operations. But *suppose, presume,* and *conclude,* put in the first person, do not behave the way, for example, *reason* and *reflect* do, which seem, however, to be very close. The forms *I reason* and *I reflect* describe me as reasoning and reflecting. Quite different are *I suppose, I presume,* and *I conclude.* In saying *I conclude* (*that . . .*), I do not describe myself as occupied in concluding; what could the activity of "concluding" be? I do not represent

myself as being in the process of supposing and presuming when I say *I suppose, I presume.*
I conclude indicates that, in the situation set forth, I extract a relationship of conclusion
touching on a given fact. It is this logical relationship which is materialized in a personal
verb. Similarly, *I suppose* and *I presume*, are very far from *I pose* and *I resume*. In *I suppose* and
I presume, there is an indication of attitude, not a description of an operation. By including
I suppose and *I presume* in my discourse, I imply that I am taking a certain attitude with
regard to the utterance that follows. It will have been noted that all the verbs cited are followed by *that* and a proposition; this proposition is the real utterance, not the personal verb
form that governs it. But on the other hand, that personal form is, one might say, the
indicator of subjectivity. It gives the assertion that follows the subjective context—doubt,
presumption, inference—suited to characterize the attitude of the speaker with respect to
the statement he is making. This manifestation of subjectivity does not stand out except in
the first person. One can hardly imagine similar verbs in the second person except for taking
up an argument again *verbatim*; thus, *you suppose that he has left* is only a way of repeating
what "you" has just said: "*I suppose* that he has left." But if one removes the expression of
person, leaving only "*he supposes that . . .,*" we no longer have, from the point of view of *I*
who utters it, anything but a simple statement.

We will perceive the nature of this "subjectivity" even more clearly if we consider the
effect on the meaning produced by changing the person of certain verbs of speaking. These
are verbs that by their meaning denote an individual act of social import: *swear, promise,*
guarantee, certify, with locutional variants like *pledge to . . . , commit (oneself) to. . . .* In the
social conditions in which a language is exercised, the acts denoted by these verbs are
regarded as binding. Now here the difference between the "subjective" utterance and the
"nonsubjective" is fully apparent as soon as we notice the nature of the opposition between
the "persons" of the verb. We must bear in mind that the "third person" is the form of the
verbal (or pronominal) paradigm that does *not* refer to a person because it refers to an object
located outside direct address. But it exists and is characterized only by its opposition to
the person *I* of the speaker who, in uttering it, situates it as "non-person." Here is its status.
The form *he . . .* takes its value from the fact that it is necessarily part of a discourse uttered
by "I."

Now *I swear* is a form of peculiar value in that it places the reality of the oath upon the
one who says *I*. This utterance is a *performance*; "to swear" consists exactly of the utterance
I swear, by which Ego is bound. The utterance *I swear* is the very act which pledges me, not
the description of the act that I am performing. In saying *I promise, I guarantee*, I am actually
making a promise or a guarantee. The consequences (social, judicial, etc.) of my swearing,
of my promise, flow from the instance of discourse containing *I swear, I promise*. The utterance is identified with the act itself. But this condition is not given in the meaning of the
verb, it is the "subjectivity" of discourse which makes it possible. The difference will be seen
when *I swear* is replaced by *he swears*. While *I swear* is a pledge, *he swears* is simply a description, on the same plane as *he runs, he smokes*. Here it can be seen that, within the conditions

belonging to these expressions, the same verb, according as it is assumed by a "subject" or is placed outside "person," takes on a different value. This is a consequence of the fact that the instance of discourse that contains the verb establishes the act at the same time that it sets up the subject. Hence the act is performed by the instance of the utterance of its "name" (which is "swear") at the same time that the subject is established by the instance of the utterance of its indicator (which is "I").

Many notions in linguistics, perhaps even in psychology, will appear in a different light if one reestablishes them within the framework of discourse. This is language in so far as it is taken over by the man who is speaking and within the condition of intersubjectivity, which alone makes linguistic communication possible.

22 Formula of Communication

Jacques Lacan

* * *

We always come back, then, to our twofold reference to speech and language. In order to free the subject's speech, we introduce him to the language of his desire, that is, to the *primary language* in which—beyond what he tells us of himself—he is already speaking to us unbeknown to himself, first and foremost, in the symbols of his symptom.

It is certainly a language that is at stake in the symbolism brought to light in analysis. This language, corresponding to the playful wish found in one of Lichtenberg's aphorisms, has the universal character of a tongue that would be understood in all other tongues, but at the same time—since it is the language that grabs hold of desire at the very moment it becomes humanized by gaining recognition—it is absolutely particular to the subject.

It is thus a *primary language*, by which I do not mean a primitive language, since Freud—whose merit for having made this total discovery warrants comparison with Champollion's—deciphered it in its entirety in the dreams of our contemporaries. The essential field of this language was rather authoritatively defined by one of the earliest assistants associated with Freud's work, and one of the few to have brought anything new to it: I mean Ernest Jones, the last survivor of those to whom the seven rings of the master were passed and who attests by his presence in the honorary positions of an international association that they are not reserved solely for relic bearers.

In a fundamental article on symbolism,[1] Jones points out on page 102 that, although there are thousands of symbols in the sense in which the term is understood in analysis, all of them refer to one's own body, blood relatives, birth, life, and death.

This truth, recognized *de facto* by Jones, enables us to understand that although the symbol, psychoanalytically speaking, is repressed in the unconscious, it bears in itself no mark of regression or even of immaturity. For it to have its effects in the subject, it is thus enough that it make itself heard, since these effects operate unbeknown to him—as we admit in our everyday experience, when we explain many reactions by normal and neurotic subjects as their response to the symbolic meaning of an act, a relation, or an object.

It is thus indisputable that the analyst can play on the power of symbols by evoking them in a calculated fashion in the semantic resonances of his remarks.

This is surely the path by which a return to the use of symbolic effects can proceed in a renewed technique of interpretation.

We could adopt as a reference here what the Hindu tradition teaches about *dhvani*,[2] defining it as the property of speech by which it conveys what it does not say. This is illustrated by a little tale whose naïveté, which appears to be required in such examples, proves funny enough to induce us to penetrate to the truth it conceals.

A girl, it is said, is awaiting her lover on the bank of a river when she sees a Brahmin coming along. She approaches him and exclaims in the most amiable tones: "What a lucky day this is for you! The dog whose barking used to frighten you will not be on this river bank again, for it was just devoured by a lion that roams around here . . ."

The absence of the lion may thus have as many effects as his spring—which, were he present, would only come once, according to the proverb relished by Freud.

The *primary* character of symbols in fact makes them similar to those numbers out of which all other numbers are composed; and if they therefore underlie all the semantemes of a language, we shall be able to restore to speech its full evocative value by a discreet search for their interferences, following the course of a metaphor whose symbolic displacement neutralizes the secondary meanings of the terms it associates.

To be taught and to be learned, this technique would require a profound assimilation of the resources of a language [*langue*], especially those that are concretely realized in its poetic texts. It is well known that Freud was steeped in German literature, which, by virtue of an incomparable translation, can be said to include Shakespeare's plays. Every one of his works bears witness to this, and to the continual recourse he had to it, no less in his technique than in his discovery. Not to mention his broad background in the classics, his familiarity with the modern study of folklore, and his keeping abreast of contemporary humanism's conquests in the area of ethnography.

Analytic practitioners should be asked not to consider it futile to follow Freud along this path.

But the tide is against us. It can be gauged by the condescending attention paid to the "wording,"* as if to some novelty; and the English morphology here provides a notion that is still difficult to define with a prop that is sufficiently subtle for people to make a big to-do about it.

What this notion covers, however, is hardly encouraging when we see an author[3] amazed at having achieved an entirely different success in the interpretation of one and the same resistance by the use, "without conscious premeditation," he emphasizes, of the term "need for love"* instead of and in the place of "demand for love,* which he had first put forward, without seeing anything in it (as he himself tells us). While the anecdote is supposed to

---

* Words or phrases followed by an asterisk (*) are given by Lacan in English in the French original.—Trans.

confirm the interpretation's reference to the "ego psychology"* in the title of the article, it refers instead, it seems, to the analyst's ego psychology,* insofar as this interpretation makes do with such a weak use of English that he can extend his practice of analysis right to the very brink of gibberish.[4]

The fact is that need* and demand* have diametrically opposed meanings for the subject, and to maintain that they can be used interchangeably for even an instant amounts to a radical ignorance of the *summoning* characteristic of speech.

For in its symbolizing function, speech tends toward nothing less than a transformation of the subject to whom it is addressed by means of the link it establishes with the speaker— namely, by bringing about a signifying effect.

This is why we must return once more to the structure of communication in language and definitively dispel the mistaken notion of "language as signs," a source in this realm of confusions about discourse and of errors about speech.

If communication based on language is conceived as a signal by which the sender informs the receiver of something by means of a certain code, there is no reason why we should not lend as much credence and even more to every other kind of sign when the "something" in question concerns the individual: indeed, we are quite right to prefer every mode of expression that verges on natural signs.

It is in this way that the technique of speech has been discredited among us and we find ourselves in search of a gesture, a grimace, a posture adopted, a face made, a movement, a shudder—nay, a stopping of usual movement—for we are subtle and nothing will stop us from setting our bloodhounds on the scent.

I shall show the inadequacy of the conception of language as signs by the very manifestation that best illustrates it in the animal kingdom, a manifestation which, had it not recently been the object of an authentic discovery, would have to have been invented for this purpose.

It is now generally recognized that, when a bee returns to its hive after gathering nectar, it transmits an indication of the existence of nectar near or far away from the hive to its companions by two sorts of dances. The second is the most remarkable, for the plane in which the bee traces out a figure eight—a shape that gave it the name "wagging dance"*— and the frequency of the figures executed within a given time, designate, on the one hand, the exact direction to be followed, determined in relation to the sun's inclination (by which bees are able to orient themselves in all kinds of weather, thanks to their sensitivity to polarized light), and, on the other hand, the distance at which the nectar is to be found up to several miles away. The other bees respond to this message by immediately setting off for the place thus designated.

It took some ten years of patient observation for Karl von Frisch to decode this kind of message, for it is certainly a code or signaling system, whose generic character alone forbids us to qualify it as conventional.

But is it a language, for all that? We can say that it is distinguished from language precisely by the fixed correlation between its signs and the reality they signify. For, in a language, signs take on their value from their relations to each other in the lexical distribution of semantemes as much as in the positional, or even flectional, use of morphemes—in sharp contrast to the fixity of the coding used by bees. The diversity of human languages takes on its full value viewed in this light.

Furthermore, while a message of the kind described here determines the action of the "socius," it is never retransmitted by the socius. This means that the message remains frozen in its function as a relay of action, from which no subject detaches it as a symbol of communication itself.[5]

The form in which language expresses itself in and of itself defines subjectivity. Language says: "You will go here, and when you see this, you will turn off there." In other words, it refers to discourse about the other [*discours de l'autre*]. It is enveloped as such in the highest function of speech, inasmuch as speech commits its author by investing its addressee with a new reality, as for example, when a subject seals his fate as a married man by saying "You are my wife."

Indeed, this is the essential form from which all human speech derives more than the form at which it arrives.

Hence the paradox that one of my most acute auditors believed to be an objection to my position when I first began to make my views known on analysis as dialectic; he formulated it as follows: "Human language would then constitute a kind of communication in which the sender receives his own message back from the receiver in an inverted form." I could but adopt this objector's formulation, recognizing in it the stamp of my own thinking; for I maintain that speech always subjectively includes its own reply, that "Thou wouldst not seek Me, if thou hadst not found Me" simply validates the same truth, and that this is why, in the paranoiac refusal of recognition, it is in the form of a negative verbalization that the unavowable feeling eventually emerges in a persecutory "interpretation."

Thus when you congratulate yourself for having met someone who speaks the same language as you, you do not mean that you encounter each other in the discourse of everyman, but that you are united to that person by a particular way of speaking.

The antinomy immanent in the relations between speech and language thus becomes clear. The more functional language becomes, the less suited it is to speech, and when it becomes overly characteristic of me alone, it loses its function as language.

We are aware of the use made in primitive traditions of secret names, with which the subject identifies his own person or his gods so closely that to reveal these names is to lose himself or betray these gods; and what our patients confide in us, as well as our own recollections, teach us that it is not at all rare for children to spontaneously rediscover the virtues of that use.

Finally, the speech value of a language is gauged by the intersubjectivity of the "we" it takes on.

By an inverse antinomy, it can be observed that the more language's role is neutralized as language becomes more like information, the more *redundancies* are attributed to it. This notion of redundancy originated in research that was all the more precise because a vested interest was involved, having been prompted by the economics of long-distance communication and, in particular, by the possibility of transmitting several conversations on a single telephone line simultaneously. It was observed that a substantial portion of the phonetic medium is superfluous for the communication actually sought to be achieved.

This is highly instructive to us,[6] for what is redundant as far as information is concerned is precisely what plays the part of resonance in speech.

For the function of language in speech is not to inform but to evoke.

What I seek in speech is a response from the other. What constitutes me as a subject is my question. In order to be recognized by the other, I proffer what was only in view of what will be. In order to find him, I call him by a name that he must assume or refuse in order to answer me.

I identify myself in language, but only by losing myself in it as an object. What is realized in my history is neither the past definite as what was, since it is no more, nor even the perfect as what has been in what I am, but the future anterior as what I will have been, given what I am in the process of becoming.

If I now face someone to question him, there is no cybernetic device imaginable that can turn his response into a reaction. The definition of "response" as the second term in the "stimulus-response" circuit is simply a metaphor sustained by the subjectivity attributed to animals, only to be elided thereafter in the physical schema to which the metaphor reduces it. This is what I have called putting a rabbit into a hat so as to pull it out again later. But a reaction is not a response.

If I press an electric button and a light goes on, there is a response only to *my* desire. If in order to obtain the same result I must try a whole system of relays whose correct position is unknown to me, there is a question only in relation to my expectation, and there will not be a question any more once I have learned enough about the system to operate it flawlessly.

But if I call the person to whom I am speaking by whatever name I like, I notify him of the subjective function he must take up in order to reply to me, even if it is to repudiate this function.

The decisive function of my own response thus appears, and this function is not, as people maintain, simply to be received by the subject as approval or rejection of what he is saying, but truly to recognize or abolish him as a subject. Such is the nature of the analyst's *responsibility* every time he intervenes by means of speech.

The problem of the therapeutic effects of inexact interpretation, raised by Edward Glover in a remarkable paper,[7] thus led him to conclusions where the question of exactness fades into the background. For not only is every spoken intervention received by the subject as a function of his structure, but the intervention itself takes on a structuring function due to its form. Indeed, nonanalytic psychotherapies, and even utterly ordinary medical "prescriptions," have the precise impact of interventions that could be qualified as obsessive systems of suggestion, as hysterical suggestions of a phobic nature, and even as persecutory supports, each psychotherapy deriving its particular character from the way it sanctions the subject's misrecognition of his own reality.

Speech is in fact a gift of language, and language is not immaterial. It is a subtle body, but body it is. Words are caught up in all the body images that captivate the subject; they may "knock up" the hysteric, be identified with the object of *Penisneid*, represent the urinary flow of urethral ambition, or represent the feces retained in avaricious jouissance.

Furthermore, words themselves can suffer symbolic lesions and accomplish imaginary acts whose victim is the subject. Recall the *Wespe* (wasp), castrated of its initial W to become the S.P. of the Wolf Man's initials, at the moment he carried out the symbolic punishment to which he himself was subjected by Grusha, the wasp.

Recall too the S that constitutes the residue of the hermetic formula into which the Rat Man's conjuratory invocations became condensed after Freud had extracted the anagram of his beloved's name from its cipher, and that, tacked onto the beginning of the final "amen" of his jaculatory prayer, eternally inundated the lady's name with the symbolic ejecta of his impotent desire.

Similarly, an article by Robert Fliess,[8] inspired by Abraham's inaugural remarks, shows us that one's discourse as a whole may become eroticized, following the displacements of erogeneity in the body image, momentarily determined by the analytic relationship.

Discourse then takes on a urethral-phallic, anal-erotic, or even oral-sadistic function. It is noteworthy, moreover, that the author grasps its effect above all in the silences that mark inhibition of the satisfaction the subject derives from it.

In this way speech may become an imaginary or even real object in the subject and, as such, debase in more than one respect the function of language. I shall thus relegate such speech to the parenthesis of the resistance it manifests.

But not in order to exclude it from the analytic relationship, for the latter would then lose everything, including its *raison d'être*.

Analysis can have as its goal only the advent of true speech and the subject's realization of his history in its relation to a future.

Maintaining this dialectic is directly opposed to any objectifying orientation of analysis, and highlighting this necessity is of capital importance if we are to see through the aberrations of the new trends in psychoanalysis.

Notes

Editors' note: This chapter is an excerpt of a longer text.

1. "The Theory of Symbolism," *British Journal of Psychology* IX, 2. Reprinted in his *Papers on Psycho-Analysis* (Boston: Beacon, 1961) [the page number given in the text corresponds to this edition]. See [Lacan's article: "À la mémoire d'Ernest Jones: Sur sa théorie du symbolisme,"*La Psychanalyse* V (1960): 1–20] *Écrits* 1966, 697–717.

2. I am referring here to the teaching of Abhinavagupta in the tenth century. See Dr. Kanti Chandra Pandey, "Indian Aesthetics," *Chowkamba Sanskrit Series*, Studies, II. Benares: 1950).

3. Ernst Kris, "Ego Psychology and Interpretation in Psychoanalytic Therapy," *PQ* XX, 1 (1951): 15–29; see the passage quoted on pages 27–28.

4. (Added in 1966:) Paragraph rewritten.

5. This is for the use of whoever can still understand it after looking in the Littré for justification of a theory that makes speech into an "action beside," by the translation that it gives of the Greek *parabole* (why not "action toward" instead?)—without having noticed at the same time that, if this word nevertheless designated what it means, it is because of sermonizing usage that, since the tenth century, has reserved "Word" [*verbe*] for the Logos incarnate.

6. Each language has its own form of transmission, and since the legitimacy of such research is founded on its success, nothing stops us from drawing a moral from it. Consider, for example, the maxim I chose as an epigraph for the preface to this paper. [*En particulier il ne faudra pas oublier que la séparation en embryologie, anatomie, physiologie, psychologie, sociologie, clinique n'existe pas dans la nature et qu'il n'y a qu'une discipline: la neurobiology à laquelle l'observation nous oblige d'ajouter l'épithète d'humaine en ce qui nous concerne.*] Since it is so laden with redundancies, its style may strike you as a bit lackluster. But lighten it of them and its audacity will arouse the enthusiasm it deserves. Hear ye: "Parfaupe ouclaspa nannanbryle anaphi ologi psysocline ixispad anlana—égnia kune n'rbiol' ô blijouter têtumaine ennouconç . . ." Here the purity of its message is finally laid bare. Its meaning raises its head here, the owning of being [*l'aveu de l'être*] begins, and our victorious intelligence bequeaths to the future its immortal stamp.

7. "The Therapeutic Effect of Inexact Interpretation: A Contribution to the Theory of Suggestion," *IJP* XII, 4 (1931): 397–411.

8. "Silence and Verbalization: A Supplement to the Theory of the 'Analytic Rule,'" *IJP* XXX, 1 (1949): 21–30.

23 The Instance of the Letter in the Unconscious, or Reason since Freud

Jacques Lacan

"Of Children Who Are Wrapped in Swaddling Bands"
O cities of the sea, I behold in you your citizens, women as well as men, tightly bound with stout bonds around their arms and legs by folk who will have no understanding of [y]our speech; and you will only be able to give vent to your griefs and sense of loss of liberty by making tearful complaints, and sighs, and lamentation one to another; for those who bind you will not have understanding of your speech nor will you understand them.[1]
—Leonardo Da Vinci

While the theme of the third volume of *La Psychanalyse*[2] commissioned this contribution by me, I owe this deference to what will be discovered here by introducing it in situating it between writing and speech—it will be halfway between the two.

Writing is in fact distinguished by a prevalence of the *text* in the sense that we will see this factor of discourse take on here—which allows for the kind of tightening up that must, to my taste, leave the reader no other way out than the way in, which I prefer to be difficult. This, then, will not be a writing in my sense of the term.

The fact that I contribute something wholly new at each class of my seminar has heretofore prevented me from providing such a text, except in one class, which has nothing particularly outstanding about it in terms of the series, and is only worth referring to for an idea of its overall level.

For the urgency that I am now taking as a pretext for leaving that aim behind merely covers over the problem that, in maintaining it at the level at which I must present my teachings here, it might stray too far from speech, whose very different measures are essential to the training I seek to effect.

This is why I took the opportunity presented to me at that time by an invitation to meet with the philosophy group of the Fédération des étudiants ès lettres[3] to make an appropriate adjustment to my exposé—its necessary generality matching the extraordinary character of their interest, but its sole object encountering the connivance of their common background, a literary background, to which my title pays homage.

Indeed, how could we forget that Freud constantly, and right until the end, maintained that such a background was the prime requisite in the training of analysts, and that he designated the age-old *universitas litterarum* as the ideal place for its institution?[4]

Thus this reference to the real-life context of my lecture, by showing whom I tailored it for, also marked those to whom it is not addressed.

I mean: none of those who, for whatever reason in psychoanalysis, allow their discipline to take advantage of some false identity.

This is a vice of habit and its effect on the mind is such that its true identity may appear among them as just one more diversion, whose refined redoubling one hopes will not escape the notice of subtler minds.

It is thus that we observe with curiosity the beginnings of a new tack concerning symbolization and language in the *International Journal of Psycho-Analysis*, a great many wetted fingers leafing through works by Sapir and Jespersen. These exercises are still green around the edges, but it is above all the tone that is missing. A certain seriousness always raises a smile when it enters the domain of veracity.

And how could a contemporary psychoanalyst not sense, in coming upon speech, that he had reached this domain, when it is from speech that analytic experience receives its instrument, its frame, its material, and even the background noise of its uncertainties?

I. The Meaning of the Letter

My title conveys the fact that, beyond this speech, it is the whole structure of language that psychoanalytic experience discovers in the unconscious. This is to alert prejudiced minds from the outset that the idea that the unconscious is merely the seat of the instincts may have to be reconsidered.

But how are we to take the letter here? Quite simply, literally [*à la lettre*].

By "letter" I designate the material medium [*support*] that concrete discourse borrows from language.

This simple definition assumes that language is not to be confused with the various psychical and somatic functions that serve it in the speaking subject.

The primary reason for this is that language, with its structure, exists prior to each subject's entry into it at a certain moment in his mental development.

Let us note that, although the deficits of aphasia are caused by purely anatomical lesions in the cerebral systems that provide the mental center for these functions, they prove, on the whole, to be distributed between the two aspects of the signifying effect of what I am calling here "the letter" in the creation of signification.[5] This point will become clearer in what follows.

And the subject, while he may appear to be the slave of language, is still more the slave of a discourse in the universal movement of which his place is already inscribed at his birth, if only in the form of his proper name.

Reference to the experience of the community as the substance of this discourse resolves nothing. For this experience takes on its essential dimension in the tradition established by this discourse. This tradition, long before the drama of history is inscribed in it, grounds the elementary structures of culture. And these very structures display an ordering of exchanges which, even if unconscious, is inconceivable apart from the permutations authorized by language.

With the result that the ethnographic duality of nature and culture is giving way to a ternary conception of the human condition—nature, society, and culture—the last term of which may well be reduced to language, that is, to what essentially distinguishes human society from natural societies.

But I shall neither take sides here nor take this as a point of departure, leaving to their own obscurity the original relations between the signifier and labor. To settle accounts with the general function of *praxis* in the genesis of history by way of a quip, I will confine myself to mentioning that the very society that wished to restore the hierarchy responsible for the relations between production and ideological superstructures to its rightful political place, alongside the privilege of the producers, has nevertheless failed to give birth to an Esperanto whose relations to socialist reality [*réel*] would have ruled out from the start any possibility of literary formalism.[6]

For my part, I will put my faith in only those premises whose value has already been proven, in that they have allowed language to attain the status in experience of a scientific object.

This is what permits linguistics[7] to present itself in the pilot position in this domain, around which a reclassification of the sciences is signaling, as is usually the case, a revolution in knowledge; only the necessities of communication have made me term this domain, in the theme of this volume of *La Psychanalyse*, "the sciences of man"—despite the confusion that may hide behind it.

To pinpoint the emergence of the discipline of linguistics, I will say that, as in the case of every science in the modern sense, it consists in the constitutive moment of an algorithm that grounds it. This algorithm is the following:

$$\frac{S}{s}$$

It is read as follows: signifier over signified, "over" corresponding to the bar separating the two levels.

The sign written in this way should be attributed to Ferdinand de Saussure, although it is not reduced to this exact form in any of the numerous schemas in which it appears in the printed version of the various lectures from the three courses he gave in 1906–7, 1908–9, and 1910–11, which a group of his devoted disciples collected under the title, *Cours de linguistique générale*—a publication of prime importance for the transmission of a teaching worthy of the name, that is, that one can stop only on its own movement.

This is why it is legitimate for us to credit him for the formalization $\frac{S}{s}$, which characterizes the modern stage of linguistics, despite the diversity between schools of linguistics.

The major theme of this science is thus based, in effect, on the primordial position of the signifier and the signified as distinct orders initially separated by a barrier resisting signification.

This is what makes possible an exact study of the connections characteristic of the signifier, and of the magnitude of their function in generating the signified.

For this primordial distinction goes well beyond the debate over the arbitrariness of the sign, such as it has been elaborated since the reflections of Antiquity, and even beyond the impasse, already sensed at that time, which opposed the one-to-one correspondence between word and thing, even in the act of naming—despite the appearances suggested by the role imputed to the index finger pointing to an object as an infant learns its mother tongue, or in the use of so-called concrete academic methods in the study of foreign languages [*langues*].

We can take things no further along this path than to demonstrate that no signification can be sustained except by reference to another signification.[8] This ultimately leads us to the remark that there is no existing language [*langue*] whose ability to cover the field of the signified can be called into question, one of the effects of its existence as a language [*langue*] being that it fulfills all needs there. Were we to try to grasp the constitution of the object in language, we could but note that this constitution is found only at the level of the concept—which is very different from any nominative—and that the *thing* [*chose*], when quite obviously reduced to the noun, splits into the double, divergent ray of the cause in which the thing has taken shelter in French, and of the nothing [*rien*] to which the thing has abandoned its Latin dress (*rem*).

These considerations, as existent as they may be to philosophers, divert us from the locus whence language questions us about its very nature. And we will fail to sustain this question as long as we have not jettisoned the illusion that the signifier serves [*répond à*] the function of representing the signified, or better, that the signifier has to justify [*répondre de*] its existence in terms of any signification whatsoever.

For even if it is reduced to this latter formulation, the heresy is the same—the heresy that leads logical positivism in search of the "meaning of meaning,"* as its objective is called in the language [*langue*] in which its devotees snort. It can be seen here how this sort of analysis can reduce the text the most highly charged with meaning to insignificant trifles. Only mathematical algorithms resist this process; they are considered to be devoid of meaning, as they should be.[9]

The fact remains that if we were able to subtract solely the notion of the parallelism of its upper and lower terms from the algorithm $\frac{S}{s}$, each term only being taken globally, it would remain the enigmatic sign of a total mystery. Which, of course, is not the case.

---

* Words or phrases followed by an asterisk (*) are given by Lacan in English in the French original.—Trans.

In order to grasp its function, I will begin by reproducing the faulty illustration by which its usage is classically introduced:

TREE

We can see here how it lends itself to the kind of direction indicated above as erroneous.

In my lecture, I replaced this illustration with another, which can be considered more correct only because it exaggerates in the incongruous dimension psychoanalysts have not yet altogether given up, because of their justified sense that their conformism derives its value from it alone. Here is the other illustration:

GENTLEMEN   **LADIES**

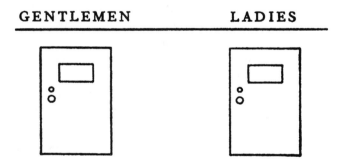

Here we see that, without greatly extending the scope of the signifier involved in the experiment—that is, by simply doubling the nominal type through the mere juxtaposition of two terms whose complementary meanings would seem to have to reinforce each other—surprise is produced by the precipitation of an unexpected meaning: the image of two twin doors that symbolize, with the private stall offered Western man for the satisfaction of his natural needs when away from home, the imperative he seems to share with the vast majority of primitive communities that subjects his public life to the laws of urinary segregation.

The point is not merely to silence the nominalist debate with a low blow, but to show how the signifier in fact enters the signified—namely, in a form which, since it is not immaterial, raises the question of its place in reality. For in having to move closer to the little enamel plaques that bear it, the squinting gaze of a nearsighted person might be justified in wondering whether it is indeed here that we must see the signifier, whose signified would in this case be paid its last respects by the solemn procession in two lines from the upper nave.

But no contrived example can be as telling as what is encountered in the lived experience of truth. Thus I have no reason to be unhappy I invented the above, since it awoke in the person the most worthy of my trust a childhood memory which, having come serendipitously to my attention, is best placed here.

A train arrives at a station. A little boy and a little girl, brother and sister, are seated across from each other in a compartment next to the outside window that provides a view of the station platform buildings going by as the train comes to a stop. "Look," says the brother, "we're at Ladies!" "Imbecile!" replies his sister, "Don't you see we're at Gentlemen."

Aside from the fact that the rails in this story materialize the bar in the Saussurian algorithm in a form designed to suggest that its resistance may be other than dialectical, one would have to be half-blind to be confused as to the respective places of the signifier and the signified here, and not to follow from what radiant center the signifier reflects its light into the darkness of incomplete significations.

For the signifier will raise Dissension—that is merely animal in kind and destined to the natural fog of forgetfulness—to the immeasurable power of ideological warfare, which is merciless to families and a torment to the gods. To these children, Gentlemen and Ladies will henceforth be two homelands toward which each of their souls will take flight on divergent wings, and regarding which it will be all the more impossible for them to reach an agreement since, being in fact the same homeland, neither can give ground regarding the one's unsurpassed excellence without detracting from the other's glory.

Let us stop there. It sounds like the history of France. Which it is more humane to recall here, and rightly so, than that of England, destined to flip from the Large to the Small End of Dean Swift's egg.

It remains to be grasped up what steps and down what corridor the S of the signifier, visible here in the plurals [*hommes* and *dames*] by which it focuses its welcome beyond the train window, must pass to impress its curves upon the ducts by which—like hot air and cold air—indignation and scorn hiss on this side.

One thing is certain: this access must not, in any case, carry any signification with it if the algorithm, $\frac{S}{s}$, with its bar is appropriate to it. For insofar as the algorithm itself is but a pure function of the signifier, it can reveal only a signifying structure in this transfer.

Now the structure of the signifier is, as is commonly said of language, that it is articulated.

This means that its units—no matter where one begins in tracing out their reciprocal encroachments and expanding inclusions—are subject to the twofold condition of being reduced to ultimate differential elements and of combining the latter according to the laws of a closed order.

These elements, the decisive discovery of linguistics, are *phonemes*; we must not look for any *phonetic* constancy in the modulatory variability to which this terra applies, but rather for the synchronic system of differential couplings that are necessary to discern vocables in a given language [*langue*]. This allows us to see that an essential element in speech itself was predestined to flow into moveable type which, in Didots or Garamonds squeezing into lowercases, renders validly present what I call the "letter"—namely, the essentially localized structure of the signifier.

The second property of the signifier, that of combining according to the laws of a closed order, affirms the necessity of the topological substratum, of which the term I ordinarily use, "signifying chain," gives an approximate idea: links by which a necklace firmly hooks onto a link of another necklace made of links.

Such are the structural conditions that define the order of the signifier's constitutive encroachments up to the unit immediately above the sentence as grammar, and the order of the signifier's constitutive inclusions up to the verbal locution as the lexicon.

In the limits within which these two approaches to understanding linguistic usage are confined, it is easy to see that only signifier-to-signifier correlations provide the standard for any and every search for signification; this is indicated by the notion of "usage" of a taxeme or semanteme, which refers to contexts just one degree above that of the units in question.

But it is not because grammatical and lexical approaches are exhausted at a certain point that we must think that signification rules unreservedly beyond it. That would be a mistake.

For the signifier, by its very nature, always anticipates meaning by deploying its dimension in some sense before it. As is seen at the level of the sentence when the latter is interrupted before the significant term: "I'll never . . .," "The fact remains . . .," "Still perhaps . . ." Such sentences nevertheless make sense, and that sense is all the more oppressive in that it is content to make us wait for it.[10]

But the phenomenon is no different, which—making her appear, with the sole postponement of a "but," as comely as the Shulamite, as honest as a virtuous maiden—adorns and readies the Negress for the wedding and the poor woman for the auction block.

Whence we can say that it is in the chain of the signifier that meaning *insists*, but that none of the chain's elements *consists* in the signification it can provide at that very moment.

The notion of an incessant sliding of the signified under the signifier thus comes to the fore—which Ferdinand de Saussure illustrates with an image resembling the wavy lines of the upper and lower Waters in miniatures from manuscripts of Genesis. It is a twofold flood in which the landmarks—fine streaks of rain traced by vertical dotted lines that supposedly delimit corresponding segments—seem insubstantial.

All our experience runs counter to this, which made me speak at one point in my seminar on the psychoses of the "button ties" [*points de capiton*] required by this schema to account for the dominance of the letter in the dramatic transformation that dialogue can effect in the subject.[11]

But while the linearity that Saussure considers to be constitutive of the chain of discourse—in accordance with its emission by a single voice and with the horizontal axis along which it is situated in our writing—is in fact necessary, it is not sufficient. It applies to the chain of discourse only in the direction in which it is oriented in time, even being taken up therein as a signifying factor in all languages [*langues*] in which the time of "Peter hits Paul" is reversed when the terms are inverted.

But it suffices to listen to poetry, which Saussure was certainly in the habit of doing,[12] for a polyphony to be heard and for it to become clear that all discourse is aligned along the several staves of a musical score.

Indeed, there is no signifying chain that does not sustain—as if attached to the punctuation of each of its units—all attested contexts that are, so to speak, "vertically" linked to that point.

Thus, if we take up the word *arbre* (tree) again, this time not in its nominal isolation, but at the endpoint of one of these punctuations, we see that it is not simply because the word *barre* (bar) is its anagram that it crosses the bar of the Saussurian algorithm.

For broken down into the double specter of its vowels and consonants, it calls up—with the robur-oak [*robre*] and the plane tree [*platane*]—the significations of strength and majesty that it takes on in our flora. Tapping all the symbolic contexts in which it is used in the Hebrew of the Bible, it erects on a barren hill the shadow of the cross. Next it reduces to a capital Y, the sign of dichotomy—which, without the illustration that historiates armorials, would owe nothing to the tree, however genealogical it claims to be. Circulatory tree, arbor vitae of the cerebellum, lead tree or silver amalgam [*arbre de Diane*], crystals precipitated into a tree that conducts lightning, is it your countenance that traces our destiny for us in the fire-scorched tortoiseshell, or your flash that brings forth from an infinite night that slow change in being in the Ἐν πάτα of language:

No! says the Tree, it says No! in the scintillating
Of its superb head

verses that I consider to be as legitimately heard in the harmonics of the tree as their reverse:

Which the storm treats universally
As it does a blade of grass.

For this modern verse is organized according to the same law of the parallelism of the signifier, whose concert governs both primitive Slavic epic poetry and the most refined Chinese poetry.

This can be seen in the common mode of beings [*l'étant*] from which the tree and the blade of grass are chosen, so that the signs of contradiction—saying "No!" and "treat as"—can come into being here, and so that, through the categorical contrast between the particularity of "superb" and the "universally" of its reduction, the indiscernible scintillating of the eternal instant may be accomplished in the condensation of *tête* (head) and *tempête* (storm).

But all this signifier can only operate, it may be objected, if it is present in the subject. I answer this objection by assuming that he has shifted to the level of the signified.

For what is important is not whether the subject know more or less about it. (If GENTLEMEN and LADIES were written in a language [*langue*] with which the little boy and girl were unfamiliar, their quarrel would simply be more exclusively a quarrel over words, but it would be no less ready to take on signification for all that.)

What this structure of the signifying chain discloses is the possibility I have—precisely insofar as I share its language [*langue*] with other subjects, that is, insofar as this language [*langue*] exists—to use it to signify *something altogether different* from what it says. This is a function of speech that is more worthy of being pointed out than that of disguising the subject's thought (which is usually indefinable)—namely, the function of indicating the place of this subject in the search for truth.

I need but plant my tree in a locution, *grimper à l'arbre*, or even project onto it the derisive light that a descriptive context gives the word, *arborer*, to not let myself be imprisoned in some sort of *communiqué* of the facts, however official it may be, and if I know the truth, convey it, despite all the censors, *between-the-lines* using nothing but the signifier that can be constituted by my acrobatics through the branches of the tree. These acrobatics may be provocative to the point of burlesque or perceptible only to the trained eye, depending on whether I wish to be understood by the many or the few.

The properly signifying function thus depicted in language has a name. We learned this name in our childhood grammar book on the last page, where the shade of Quintilian, relegated to some phantom chapter to convey final considerations on style, seemed suddenly to hasten its voice due to the threat of being cut off.

It is among the figures of style, or tropes—from which the verb "to find" [*trouver*] comes to us—that this name is, in fact, found. This name is *metonymy*.

I shall refer only to the example of it given there: "thirty sails." For the worry I felt, over the fact that the word "ship" [*bateau*] that was hiding therein seemed to split its presence there in two by having been able to borrow its figurative sense from the very rehashing of this example, veiled [*voilait*] not so much those illustrious sails [*voiles*] as the definition they were supposed to illustrate.

The part taken for the whole—I said to myself, if the thing is supposed to be based on reality [*réel*]—leaves us with hardly any idea what we are to conclude about the size of the fleet these thirty sails are nevertheless supposed to gauge: for a ship to have but one sail is very rare indeed.

This shows that the connection between ship and sail is nowhere other than in the signifier, and that metonymy is based on the *word-to-word* nature of this connection.[13]

I shall designate as metonymy the first aspect of the actual field the signifier constitutes, so that meaning may assume a place there.

The other aspect is *metaphor*. Let me illustrate it immediately; Quillet's dictionary seemed appropriate to me to provide a sample that would not be suspected of being deliberately selected, and I didn't pursue the farce any farther than Victor Hugo's well-known verse, "His sheaf was neither miserly nor hateful . . .," with which I presented metaphor, when the time came for it, in my seminar on the psychoses.

Let us say that modern poetry and the Surrealist school led us to take a major step forward here by showing that any conjunction of two signifiers could just as easily constitute a metaphor, if an additional condition—that of the greatest disparity of the images signified—weren't required for the production of the poetic spark, in other words, for metaphoric creation to occur.

Of course, this radical position is based on the so-called "automatic writing" experiment, which would not have been attempted without the assurance its pioneers drew from Freud's discovery. But it remains marked by confusion because the doctrine behind it is false.

Metaphor's creative spark does not spring forth from the juxtaposition of two images, that is, of two equally actualized signifiers. It flashes between two signifiers, one of which has replaced the other by taking the other's place in the signifying chain, the occulted signifier remaining present by virtue of its (metonymic) connection to the rest of the chain.

One word for another: this is the formula for metaphor, and if you are a poet you will make it into a game and produce a continuous stream, nay, a dazzling weave of metaphors. You will, moreover, obtain the intoxicating effect of Jean Tardieu's dialogue that goes by this title, due solely to the demonstration it provides of the radical superfluousness of all signification to a perfectly convincing representation of bourgeois comedy.

In Hugo's verse, it is obvious that not the slightest light emanates from the assertion that a sheaf is neither miserly nor hateful, because it is clear that the sheaf has no more the merit than the demerit of these attributes, since miserliness and hatred, along with the sheaf, are properties of Booz, who exercises them when he uses the sheaf as he sees fit, without making his feelings known to it.

If "his sheaf" refers back to Booz, as is clearly the case nevertheless, it is because it replaces him in the signifying chain—at the very place that awaited him, because it had been raised up a step by the clearing away of miserliness and hatred. But the sheaf has thus cleared this place of Booz, ejected as he now is into the outer darkness where miserliness and hatred harbor him in the hollow of their negation.

But once *his* sheaf has thus usurped his place, Booz cannot go back to it, the slender thread of the little "his" that attaches him to it being an additional obstacle thereto, because it binds this return with a title of ownership that would detain him in the heart of miserliness and hatred. His asserted generosity is thus reduced to *less than nothing* by the munificence of the sheaf which, being drawn from nature, knows neither our reserve nor our rejections, and even in its accumulation remains prodigal by our standards.

But if, in this profusion, the giver disappears with the gift, it is only to reemerge in what surrounds the figure of speech in which he was annihilated. For it is the radiance of fecundity—which announces the surprise the poem celebrates, namely, the promise of acceding to paternity that the old man receives in a sacred context.

Thus it is between a man's proper name qua signifier and the signifier that metaphorically abolishes it that the poetic spark is produced, and it is all the more effective here in bringing about the signification of paternity in that it reproduces the mythical event through which Freud reconstructed the path along which the mystery of paternity advances in the unconscious of every man.

The structure of modern metaphor is no different. Hence the jaculation, "Love is a pebble laughing in the sun," recreates love in a dimension that I have said strikes me as tenable, as opposed to its ever imminent slippage into the mirage of some narcissistic altruism.

We see that metaphor is situated at the precise point at which meaning is produced in nonmeaning—that is, at the passage which, as Freud discovered, when crossed in the opposite direction, gives rise to the word that is "the word" ["*le mot*"] par excellence in French, the word that has no other patronage there than the signifier *esprit*[14]—and at which it becomes palpable that, in deriding the signifier, man defies his very destiny.

But to return to metonymy now, what does man find in it, if it must be more than the power to skirt the obstacles of social censure? Doesn't this form, which gives oppressed truth its field, manifest a certain servitude that is inherent in its presentation?

It's worth taking the time to read a book in which Leo Strauss, from the land that has traditionally offered asylum to those who have chosen freedom, reflects on the relations between the art of writing and persecution.[15] By honing in on the sort of connaturality that ties this art to this condition, he allows us to glimpse something that imposes its form here, in the effect of truth on desire.

But haven't we been feeling for a while now that, in following the paths of the letter to reach the Freudian truth, we are getting hot, its flames spreading all around us?

Of course, as it is said, the letter kills while the spirit gives life. I don't disagree, having had to pay homage somewhere here to a noble victim of the error of seeking in the letter, but I also ask how the spirit could live without the letter. The spirit's pretensions would nevertheless remain indisputable if the letter hadn't proven that it produces all its truth effects in man without the spirit having to intervene at all.

This revelation came to Freud, and he called his discovery the unconscious.

II. The Letter in the Unconscious

In Freud's complete works, one out of three pages presents us with philological references, one out of two pages with logical inferences, and everywhere we see a dialectical apprehension of experience, linguistic analysis becoming still more prevalent the more directly the unconscious is involved.

Thus what is at stake on every page in *The Interpretation of Dreams* is what I call the letter of discourse, in its texture, uses, and immanence in the matter in question. For this book inaugurates both Freud's work and his royal road to the unconscious. And we are informed of this by Freud, whose confession in letters to Fliess that have since been made public, when he launches this book toward us in the early days of this century,[16] merely confirms what he continued to proclaim to the end: that the whole of his discovery lies in this no-holds-barred expression of his message.

The first clause, articulated already in the introductory chapter because its exposition cannot be postponed, is that the dream is a rebus. And Freud stipulates that it must be understood quite literally [*à la lettre*], as I said earlier. This is related to the instance in the dream of the same "literating" (in other words, phonemic) structure in which the signifier is articulated and analyzed in discourse. Like the unnatural figures of the boat on the roof, or the man with a comma for a head, which are expressly mentioned by Freud, dream images are to be taken up only on the basis of their value as signifiers, that is, only insofar as they allow us to spell out the "proverb" presented by the oneiric rebus. The linguistic structure that enables us to read dreams is at the crux of the "signifierness of dreams," at the crux of the *Traumdeutung*.

Freud shows us in every possible way that the image's value as a signifier has nothing to do with its signification, giving as an example Egyptian hieroglyphics in which it would be ridiculous to deduce from the frequency in a text of a vulture (which is an aleph) or a chick (which is a vau) indicating a form of the verb "to be" and plurals, that the text has anything whatsoever to do with these ornithological specimens. Freud takes his bearings from certain uses of the signifier in this writing that are effaced in ours, such as the use of determinatives, where a categorical figure is added as an exponent to the literal figuration of a verbal term; but this is only to bring us back to the fact that we are dealing with writing where even the supposed "ideogram" is a letter.

But psychoanalysts who have no training in linguistics don't need the current confusion regarding the term "ideogram" to believe in a symbolism deriving from natural analogy, or even from instinct's coaptational image. This is so true that, apart from the French school, which attends to this, it is with a statement like "reading coffee grounds is not the same as reading hieroglyphics" that I must recall to its own principles a technique whose pathways cannot be justified unless they aim at the unconscious.

It must be said that this is admitted only reluctantly, and that the mental vice denounced above enjoys such favor that the contemporary psychoanalyst can be expected to say that he decodes before resolving to take the journey with Freud (turn at the statue of Champollion, says the guide) that is necessary for him to understand that he deciphers—the latter differing in that a cryptogram only takes on its full dimensions when it is in a lost language [*langue*].

Taking this journey simply amounts to going further in the *Traumdeutung*.

Entstellung, translated as "transposition"—which Freud shows to be the general precondition for the functioning of the dream—is what I designated earlier, with Saussure, as the sliding of the signified under the signifier, which is always happening (unconsciously, let us note) in discourse.

But the two aspects of the signifier's impact on the signified are also found here:

Verdichtung, "condensation," is the superimposed structure of signifiers in which metaphor finds its field; its name, condensing in itself the word *Dichtung*, shows the mechanism's connaturality with poetry, to the extent that it envelops poetry's own properly traditional function.

Verschiebung or "displacement"—this transfer of signification that metonymy displays is closer to the German term; it is presented, right from its first appearance in Freud's work, as the unconscious' best means by which to foil censorship.

What distinguishes these two mechanisms, which play a privileged role in the dream-work, *Traumarbeit*, from their homologous function in discourse? Nothing, except a condition imposed upon the signifying material, called *Rücksicht auf Darstellbarkeit*, which must be translated as "consideration of the means of staging" (the translation by "role of the possibility of representation" being overly approximate here). But this condition constitutes a limitation operating within the system of writing, rather than dissolving the system into a figurative semiology in which it would intersect the phenomena of natural expression. This would probably allow us to shed light on problems with certain types of pictography, which we are not justified in regarding as evolutionary stages simply because they were abandoned in writing as imperfect. Let us say, then, that dreams are like the parlor game in which each person, in turn, is supposed to get the spectators to guess some well-known saying or variant of it solely by silent gestures. The fact that dreams have speech at their disposal makes no difference since, for the unconscious, speech is but one staging element among others. It is precisely when games and dreams alike run up against the lack of taxemic material by which to represent logical relationships such as causality, contradiction, hypothesis, and so on that they prove they have to do with writing, not mime. The subtle procedures dreams end up using to represent these logical connections—in a much less artificial way than games usually employ—are taken up specifically in Freud's work, where it is once again confirmed that the dream-work proceeds in accordance with the laws of the signifier.

The rest of the dream revision is termed "secondary" by Freud, taking on its value from what is at stake: they are fantasies or daydreams, *Tagtraum*, to use the term Freud prefers to use to situate them in their wish-fulfilling function (*Wunscherfüllung*). Given that these fantasies may remain unconscious, their distinctive feature is clearly their signification. Now, Freud tells us that their role in dreams is either to serve as signifying elements for the statement of the unconscious thought (*Traumgedanke*), or to be used in the secondary revision that occurs—that is, in a function not to be distinguished, he says, from our waking thought (*von unserem wachen Denken nicht zu unterscheiden*). No better idea of this function's effects can be given than by comparing it to patches of colorwash which, when applied here and there on a stencil, can make stick figures—which are rather unprepossessing in themselves—in a rebus or hieroglyphics look more like a painting of people.

I apologize for seeming to spell out Freud's text myself; it is not merely to show how much is to be gained by not lopping off parts of it. It is to be able to situate what has happened in psychoanalysis in terms of its earliest reference points, which are fundamental and have never been revoked.

Right from the outset, people failed to recognize the constitutive role of the signifier in the status Freud immediately assigned to the unconscious in the most precise and explicit ways.

The reason for this was twofold, the least perceived being, naturally, that this formalization was not sufficient by itself to bring people to recognize the instance of the signifier, because when the *Traumdeutung* was published it was way ahead of the formalizations of linguistics for which one could no doubt show that it paved the way by the sheer weight of its truth.

The second reason is merely the flip side of the first, for if psychoanalysts were fascinated exclusively by the significations highlighted in the unconscious, it was because these significations derived their most secret attraction from the dialectic that seemed to be immanent in them.

I demonstrated to those who attend my seminar that the apparent changes of direction or rather changes in tack along the way—that Freud, in his primary concern to ensure the survival of his discovery along with the basic revisions it imposed upon our knowledge, felt it necessary to apply to his doctrine—were due to the need to counteract the ever-accelerating effects of this partiality.

For, I repeat, given the situation he found himself in, where he had nothing corresponding to the object of his discovery that was at the same level of scientific maturity, he at least never failed to maintain this object at the level of its ontological dignity.

The rest was the work of the gods and took such a course that analysis today finds its bearings in the imaginary forms I have just shown to be sketched out through inverse printing on the text they mutilate. It is to them that the analyst's aim now adapts, confusing them, in the interpretation of dreams, with the visionary liberation of the hieroglyphic aviary, and seeking more generally to verify the exhaustion of the analysis in a sort of "scanning"*[17] of these forms wherever they appear—with the idea that they bear witness both to the exhaustion of the regressions and to the remodeling of "the object-relation" that is supposed to typify the subject.[18]

The technique that is based on such positions can give rise to many varied effects, which are quite difficult to criticize behind their therapeutic aegis. But an internal critique can emerge from the flagrant discordance between the mode of operation by which the technique legitimates itself—namely, the fundamental rule of psychoanalysis, all the instruments of which, starting with "free association," derive their justification from its inventor's conception of the unconscious—and the complete ignorance reigning there of this very conception of the unconscious. The most trenchant supporters of this technique let themselves off the hook here with a mere flourish: the fundamental rule must, they say, be observed all the more religiously since it is only the fruit of a lucky accident. In other words, Freud never really knew what he was doing.

A return to Freud's texts shows, on the contrary, the absolute coherence between his technique and his discovery, and this coherence allows us to situate his procedures at their proper level.

This is why any rectification of psychoanalysis requires a return to the truth of that discovery, which is impossible to obscure in its original moment.

For in the analysis of dreams, Freud intends to give us nothing other than the laws of the unconscious in their broadest extension. One of the reasons why dreams were the most propitious here is, Freud tells us, that they reveal these laws no less in normal subjects than in neurotics.

In neither, however, does the efficacy of the unconscious cease upon awakening. Psychoanalytic experience consists in nothing other than establishing that the unconscious leaves none of our actions outside its field. The presence of the unconscious in the psychological order—in other words, in the individual's relational functions—nevertheless deserves to be more precisely defined. It is not coextensive with that order, for we know that, while unconscious motivation manifests itself just as much in conscious psychical effects as in unconscious ones, conversely it is elementary to note that a large number of psychical effects that are legitimately designated as unconscious, in the sense of excluding the characteristic of consciousness, nevertheless bear no relation whatsoever, by their nature, to the unconscious in the Freudian sense. It is thus only due to an incorrect use of the term that "psychical" and "unconscious" in this sense are confused, and that people thus term psychical what is actually an effect of the unconscious on the soma, for example.

The point is, therefore, to define the topography of this unconscious. I say that it is the very topography defined by the algorithm:

$$\frac{S}{s}$$

What it has permitted me to elaborate concerning the impact of the signifier on the signified allows for its transformation into:

$$f(S)\frac{1}{s}$$

It is on the basis of the copresence in the signified not only of the elements of the horizontal signifying chain but also of its vertical dependencies, that I have demonstrated the effects, distributed in accordance with two fundamental structures, in metonymy and metaphor. We can symbolize them by:

$$f(S\ldots S')S \cong S(-)s$$

that is, metonymic structure, indicating that it is the signifier-to-signifier connection that allows for the elision by which the signifier instates lack of being [*le manque de l'être*] in the object-relation, using signification's referral [*renvoi*] value to invest it with the desire aiming at the lack that it supports. The — sign placed in ( ) manifests here the maintenance of the bar—which, in the first algorithm, denotes the irreducible nature of the resistance of signification as constituted in the relations between signifier and signified.[19]

Now we turn to

$$f\left(\frac{S'}{S}\right)S \cong S(+)s$$

metaphoric structure, indicating that it is in the substitution of signifier for signifier that a signification effect is produced that is poetic or creative, in other words, that brings the signification in question into existence.[20] The + sign in ( ) manifests here the crossing of the bar, —, and the constitutive value of this crossing for the emergence of signification.

This crossing expresses the condition for the passage of the signifier into the signified, whose moment I pointed out above by provisionally conflating it with the place of the subject.

It is the function of the subject, thus introduced, on which we must now dwell since it lies at the crux of our problem.

"I am thinking, therefore I am" (cogito ergo sum) is not simply the formulation in which the link between the transparency of the transcendental subject and his existential affirmation is constituted, at the historical apex of reflection on the conditions of science.

Perhaps I am only object and mechanism (and so nothing more than phenomenon), but assuredly, insofar as I think so, I am—absolutely. Philosophers certainly made important corrections here—namely, that in that which is thinking (cogitans), I am never doing anything but constituting myself as an object (cogitatum). The fact remains that through this extreme purification of the transcendental subject, my existential link to its project seems irrefutable, at least in the form of its actuality, and that "cogito ergo sum" ubi cogito, ibi sum, overcomes this objection.

Of course, this limits me to being there in my being only insofar as I think that I am in my thought; to what extent I really think this concerns me alone and, if I say it, interests no one.[21]

Yet to avoid it on the pretext of its philosophical semblances is simply to demonstrate one's inhibition. For the notion of the subject is indispensable even to the workings of a science such as strategy in the modern sense, whose calculations exclude all "subjectivism."

It is also to deny oneself access to what might be called the Freudian universe—in the sense in which we speak of the Copernican universe. Indeed, Freud himself compared his discovery to the so-called Copernican revolution, emphasizing that what was at stake was once again the place man assigns himself at the center of a universe.

Is the place that I occupy as subject of the signifier concentric or eccentric in relation to the place I occupy as subject of the signified? That is the question.

The point is not to know whether I speak of myself in a way that conforms to what I am, but rather to know whether, when I speak of myself, I am the same as the self of whom I speak. And there is no reason not to bring in the term "thought" here. For

Freud uses the term to designate the elements at stake in the unconscious; that is, in the signifying mechanisms I just pointed to there.

It is nonetheless true that the philosophical *cogito* is at the center of the mirage that renders modern man so sure of being himself in his uncertainties about himself, and even in the distrust he has long since learned to exercise regarding the pitfalls of pride.

Now if, turning the weapon of metonymy against the nostalgia that it serves, I stop myself from seeking any meaning beyond tautology, and if, in the name of "war is war" and "a penny's a penny," I resolve to be only what I am, how can I escape here from the obvious fact that I am in this very act?

And how—in going to the other, metaphoric, pole of the signifying quest, and dedicating myself to becoming what I am, to coming into being—can I doubt that, even if I were to lose myself there, I am there?

Now it is on these very points, where the obvious is subverted by the empirical, that the trick of the Freudian conversion lies.

This signifying game of metonymy and metaphor—up to and including its active tip [*pointe*] that "cotter-pins" my desire to a refusal of the signifier or to a lack of being, and links my fate to the question of my destiny—this game is played, in its inexorable subtlety, until the match is over, where I am not because I cannot situate myself there.

That is, it wasn't going very far to say the words with which I momentarily dumbfounded my audience: I am thinking where I am not, therefore I am where I am not thinking. These words render palpable to an attentive ear with what elusive ambiguity the ring of meaning flees from our grasp along the verbal string.

What we must say is: I am not, where I am the plaything of my thought; I think about what I am where I do not think I am thinking.

This two-sided mystery can be seen to intersect the fact that truth is evoked only in that dimension of ruse whereby all "realism" in creation derives its virtue from metonymy, as well as this other fact that access to meaning is granted only to the double elbow of metaphor, when we hold in our hand their one and only key: namely, the fact that the S and s of the Saussurian algorithm are not in the same plane, and man was deluding himself in believing he was situated in their common axis, which is nowhere.

At least until Freud made this discovery. For if what Freud discovered isn't precisely that, it is nothing.

The contents of the unconscious, in their deceptive ambiguity, supply us no reality in the subject more consistent than the immediate; it is from truth that they derive their virtue in the dimension of being: *Kern unseres Wesen* is Freud's own expression.

Metaphor's two-stage mechanism is the very mechanism by which symptoms, in the analytic sense, are determined. Between the enigmatic signifier of sexual trauma and the term it comes to replace in a current signifying chain, a spark flies that fixes in a symptom—a metaphor in which flesh or function is taken as a signifying element—the signification, that is inaccessible to the conscious subject, by which the symptom may be dissolved.

And the enigmas that desire—with its frenzy mimicking the gulf of the infinite and the secret collusion whereby it envelops the pleasure of knowing and of dominating in jouissance—poses for any sort of "natural philosophy" are based on no other derangement of instinct than the fact that it is caught in the rails of metonymy, eternally extending toward the *desire for something else*. Hence its "perverse" fixation at the very point of suspension of the signifying chain at which the screen-memory is immobilized and the fascinating image of the fetish becomes frozen.

There is no other way to conceive of the indestructibility of unconscious desire—given that there is no need which, when its satiation is prohibited, does not wither, in extreme cases through the very wasting away of the organism itself. It is in a kind of memory, comparable to what goes by that name in our modern thinking-machines (which are based on an electronic realization of signifying composition), that the chain is found which *insists* by reproducing itself in the transference, and which is the chain of a dead desire.

It is the truth of what this desire has been in his history that the subject cries out through his symptom, as Christ said that stones themselves would have cried out, had the children of Israel not lent them their voices.

And this is also why psychoanalysis alone allows us to differentiate in memory the function of remembering. The latter, rooted in the signifier, resolves the Platonic aporias of reminiscence through the ascendancy of history in man.

One need but read *Three Essays on the Theory of Sexuality*—which is covered over for the masses by so many pseudo-biological glosses—to note that Freud has all accession to the object derive from a dialectic of return.

Having thus begun with Hoiderlin's νόστος, Freud arrives less than twenty years later at Kierkegaard's repetition; that is, his thought, in submitting at the outset to the humble but inflexible consequences of the talking cure* alone, was never able to let go of the living servitudes that, starting from the royal principle of the Logos, led him to rethink the deadly Empedoclean antinomies.

And how, if not on the "other scene" Freud speaks of as the locus of the dream, are we to understand his recourse as a man of science to a *Deus ex machina* that is less derisory in that here it is revealed to the spectator that the machine directs the director himself? How can we fathom the fact that a scientist of the nineteenth century valued more highly than all his other works his *Totem and Taboo*—with its obscene, ferocious figure of the primordial father, who is inexhaustibly redeemed in the eternal blinding of Oedipus—before which contemporary ethnologists bow as before the development of an authentic myth, unless we realize that he had to bow to a force of evidence that went beyond his prejudices?

Similarly, the imperious proliferation of particular symbolic creations—such as what are called the sexual theories of children—which account for even the smallest details of the neurotic's compulsions, answer to the same necessities as do myths.

This is why, to bring you to the precise point of the commentary on Freud's work I am developing in my seminar, little Hans, left in the lurch at the age of five by the failings of his symbolic entourage, and faced with the suddenly actualized enigma to him of his sex and his existence, develops—under the direction of Freud and his father, who is Freud's disciple—all the possible permutations of a limited number of signifiers in the form of a myth, around the signifying crystal of his phobia.

We see here that, even at the individual level, man can find a solution to the impossible by exhausting all possible forms of the impossibilities that are encountered when the solution is put into the form of a signifying equation. This is a striking demonstration that illuminates the labyrinth of a case study which thus far has been used only as a scrap heap. It also makes us grasp that the nature of neurosis is revealed in the fact that a symptom's development is coextensive with its elimination in the treatment: whether phobic, hysterical, or obsessive, neurosis is a question that being raises for the subject "from where he was before the subject came into the world" (this subordinate clause is the very expression Freud uses in explaining the Oedipus complex to little Hans).

At stake here is the being that appears in a split second in the emptiness of the verb "to be" and, as I said, this being raises its question for the subject. What does that mean? It does not raise it *before* the subject, since the subject cannot come to the place where being raises it, but being raises it *in* the subject's *place*—in other words, being raises the question in that place *with* the subject, just as one raises a problem *with* a pen and as antiquity's man thought *with* his soul.

Freud brought the ego into his doctrine in this way, defining it by the resistances that are specific to it.[22] I have tried to get people to understand that these resistances are imaginary in nature, like the coaptational lures that ethology shows us in display or combat in animal behavior, these lures being reduced in man to the narcissistic relation introduced by Freud and elaborated by me in "The Mirror Stage." While Freud—by situating in this ego the synthesis of the perceptual functions in which the sensorimotor selections are integrated—seems to agree with the tradition that delegates to the ego the task of answering for reality, this reality is simply all the more included in the suspension of the ego.

For this ego, distinguished first for the imaginary inertias it concentrates against the message of the unconscious, operates only by covering over the displacement the subject is with a resistance that is essential to discourse as such.

This is why an exhaustion of the defense mechanisms, as palpable as Fenichel renders it in his *Problems of Psychoanalytic Technique* because he is a practitioner (whereas his whole theoretical reduction of the neuroses and psychoses to genetic anomalies in libidinal development is pure platitude), turns out to be the other side of unconscious mechanisms, without Fenichel accounting for or even realizing it. Periphrasis, hyperbaton, ellipsis, suspension, anticipation, retraction, negation, digression, and irony, these are the figures of style (Quintilian's *figurae sententiarum*), just as catachresis, litotes, antonomasia, and hypotyposis are the tropes, whose names strike me as the most appropriate ones with which to label these mechanisms. Can one see here mere manners of speaking, when it is the figures themselves that are at work in the rhetoric of the discourse the analysand actually utters?

By obstinately characterizing resistance as having an emotional permanence, thereby making it foreign to discourse, contemporary psychoanalysts simply show that they have succumbed to one of the fundamental truths Freud rediscovered through psychoanalysis. Which is that we cannot confine ourselves to giving a new truth its rightful place, for the point is to take up our place in it. The truth requires us to go out of our way. We cannot do so by simply getting used to it. We get used to reality [*réel*]. The truth we repress.

Now it is especially necessary to the scholar, the sage, and even the quack, to be the only one who knows. The idea that deep within the simplest of souls—and, what's more, in the sickest—there is something ready to blossom is one thing. But that there may be someone who seems to know as much as them about what we ought to make of it . . . come to our rescue yon categories of primitive, pre-logical, and archaic thought—nay, of magical thought, so convenient to attribute to others! It is not fitting that these country bumpkins should keep us breathless by posing enigmas to us that prove overly clever.

To interpret the unconscious as Freud did, one would have to be, as he was, an encyclopedia of the arts and muses, as well as an assiduous reader of the *Fliegende Blätter*. And the task would become no easier were we to put ourselves at the mercy of a thread spun of allusions and quotations, puns and equivocations. Must we make a career out of "antidoted fanfreluches"?

Indeed, we must resolve to do so. The unconscious is neither the primordial nor the instinctual, and what it knows of the elemental is no more than the elements of the signifier.

The three books that one might call canonical with regard to the unconscious—the *Traumdeutung, The Psychopathology of Everyday Life*, and *Jokes (Witz) and Their Relation to the Unconscious*—are but a web of examples whose development is inscribed in formulas for connection and substitution (though multiplied tenfold by their particular complexity, diagrams of them sometimes being provided by Freud outside the main body of the text), which are the formulas I give for the signifier in its *transference* function. For in the *Traumdeutung* it is in terms of such a function that the term *Übertragung*, or transference, which later gave its name to the mainspring of the intersubjective link between analysand and analyst, is introduced.

Such diagrams are not solely constitutive in neurosis of each of the symptoms, but they alone allow us to encompass the thematic of its course and resolution—as the major case histories provided by Freud demonstrate admirably.

To fall back on a more limited fact, but one that is more manageable as it provides a final seal with which to close these remarks, I will cite the 1927 article on fetishism and the case Freud reports there of a patient for whom sexual satisfaction required a certain shine on the nose (*Glanz auf der Nase*).[23] The analysis showed that he owed it to the fact that his early English-speaking years had displaced the burning curiosity that attached him to his mother's phallus—that is, to that eminent want-to-be, whose privileged signifier Freud revealed—into a "glance at the nose,"* rather than a "shine on the nose"* in the forgotten language [*langue*] of his childhood.

It was the abyss, open to the thought that a thought might make itself heard in the abyss, that gave rise to resistance to psychoanalysis from the outset—not the emphasis on man's sexuality, as is commonly said. The latter is the object that has clearly predominated in literature throughout the ages. And the evolution of psychoanalysis has succeeded by a comical stroke of magic in turning it into a moral instance, the cradle and waiting area of oblativity and attraction. The soul's Platonic steed, now blessed and enlightened, goes straight to heaven.

The intolerable scandal when Freudian sexuality was not yet holy was that it was so "intellectual." It was in this respect that it showed itself to be the worthy stooge of all those terrorists whose plots were going to ruin society.

At a time when psychoanalysts are busy refashioning a right-thinking psychoanalysis, whose crowning achievement is the sociological poem of the "autonomous ego," I would like to say, to those who are listening to me, how they can recognize bad psychoanalysts: by the word they use to deprecate all research on technique and theory that furthers the Freudian experience in its authentic direction. That word is "intellectualization"—execrable to all those who, living in fear of putting themselves to the test by drinking the wine of truth, spit on men's bread, even though their spittle can never again have any effect but that of leavening.

III.   The Letter, being, and the other

Is what thinks in my place, then, another ego? Does Freud's discovery represent the confirmation, at the level of psychological experience, of Manichaeism?[24]

There can, in fact, be no confusion on this point: what Freud's research introduced us to was not some more or less curious cases of dual personality. Even at the heroic era I have been describing—when, like animals in the age of fairy tales, sexuality spoke—the diabolical atmosphere that such an orientation might have given rise to never materialized.[25]

The goal Freud's discovery proposes to man was defined by Freud at the height of his thought in these moving terms: *Wo Es war, soll Ich werden.* Where it was, I must come into being.

This goal is one of reintegration and harmony, I might even say of reconciliation (*Versöhnung*).

But if we ignore the self's radical eccentricity with respect to itself that man is faced with—in other words, the very truth Freud discovered—we will renege on both the order and pathways of psychoanalytic mediation; we will make of it the compromise operation that it has, in effect, become—precisely what both the spirit and letter of Freud's work most repudiate. For, since he constantly points out that compromise is behind all the miseries his analysis assuages, we can say that resorting to compromise, whether explicit or implicit, disorients all psychoanalytic action and plunges it into darkness.

But neither does it suffice to rub shoulders with the moralistic tartufferies of our time or to be forever spouting forth about the "total personality" in order to have said anything articulate about the possibility of mediation.

The radical heteronomy that Freud's discovery shows gaping within man can no longer be covered over without whatever tries to hide it being fundamentally dishonest.

Which other is this, then, to whom I am more attached than to myself [*moi*], since, at the most assented to heart of my identity to myself, he pulls the strings?

His presence can only be understood in an alterity raised to the second power, which already situates him in a mediating position in relation to my own splitting from myself, as if from a semblable.

If I have said that the unconscious is the Other's discourse (with a capital O), it is in order to indicate the beyond in which the recognition of desire is tied to the desire for recognition.

In other words, this other is the Other that even my lie invokes as a guarantor of the truth in which my lie subsists.

Here we see that the dimension of truth emerges with the appearance of language.

Prior to this point, we have to admit the existence—in the psychological relation, which can be precisely isolated in the observation of animal behavior—of subjects, not because of some projective mirage, it being the psychologist's vacuous watchword to hack this phantom to pieces, but because of the manifested presence of intersubjectivity. In the animal hidden in his lookout, in the well-laid trap, in the straggler ruse by which a runaway separated from the flock throws a raptor off the scent, something more emerges than in the fascinating erection of display or combat. Yet there is nothing here that transcends the function of a lure in the service of a need, or that affirms a presence in that beyond-the-veil where the whole of Nature can be questioned about its design.

For the question to even arise (and we know that it arose for Freud in *Beyond the Pleasure Principle*), there must be language.

For I can lure my adversary with a movement that runs counter to my battle plan, and yet this movement has its deceptive effect only insofar as I actually make it for my adversary.

But in the proposals by which I initiate peace negotiations with him, what my negotiations propose is situated in a third locus which is neither my speech nor my interlocutor.

This locus is nothing but the locus of signifying convention, as is seen in the comedy of the distressed complaint of the Jew to his pal: "Why are you telling me you are going to Cracow so I'll believe you are going to Lemberg, when you really are going to Cracow?"

Of course the aforementioned flock-movement can be understood in the conventional register of a game's strategy, where it is on the basis of a rule that I deceive my adversary; but here my success is assessed as connoting betrayal—that is, it is assessed in the relationship to the Other who is the guarantor of Good Faith.

Here the problems are of an order whose heteronomy is simply ignored if it is reduced to some "awareness of others," or whatever people choose to call it. For the "existence of the other" having, not long ago, reached the ears of Midas, the psychoanalyst, through the partition that separates him from the phenomenologists' confabs, the news is now being whispered through the reeds: "Midas, King Midas, is the other of his patient. He himself said so."

What sort of breakthrough is that? The other—which other?

Which other was the young André Gide aiming at when he defied the landlady, in whose care his mother had placed him, to treat him as a responsible being by unlocking right in front of her—with a key that was fake only insofar as it opened all locks of the same kind—the lock that she herself considered to be the worthy signifier of her educational intentions? Was it she who would later intervene and to whom the child would laughingly say: "Do you really think a lousy padlock can ensure my obedience?" But by simply remaining out of sight and waiting until that evening before lecturing the kid, after giving him a suitably cold reception upon his return home, it was not simply a female other whose angry face she showed him, but another André Gide, one who was no longer really sure, either then or even later when he thought back on it, what he had wanted to do—who had been changed right down to his very truth by the doubt cast on his good faith.

Perhaps it would be worth dwelling on this realm of confusion—which is simply that in which the whole human *opera buffa* is played out—to understand the pathways by which analysis proceeds, not only to restore order here but also to instate the conditions for the possibility of its restoration.

Kern unseres Wesen, "the core of our being"—it is not so much that Freud commands us to target this, as so many others before him have done with the futile adage "Know thyself," as that he asks us to reconsider the pathways that lead to it.

Or, rather, the "this" which he proposes we attain is not a this which can be the object of knowledge, but a this—doesn't he say as much?—which constitutes my being and to which, as he teaches us, I bear witness as much and more in my whims, aberrations, phobias, and fetishes, than in my more or less civilized personage.

Madness, you are no longer the object of the ambiguous praise with which the sage furnished the impregnable burrow of his fear. And if he is, after all, not so badly ensconced there, it is because the supreme agent at work since time immemorial, digging its tunnels and maze, is reason itself, the same Logos he serves.

Then how do you explain the fact that a scholar like Erasmus, with so little talent for the "commitments" that solicited him in his age, as in any other, could hold such an eminent place in the revolution brought about by a Reformation in which man has as much of a stake in each man as in all men?

It is by touching, however lightly, on man's relation to the signifier—in this case, by changing the procedures of exegesis—that one changes the course of his history by modifying the moorings of his being.

It is precisely in this respect that anyone capable of glimpsing the changes we have lived through in our own lives can see that Freudianism, however misunderstood it has been and however nebulous its consequences have been, constitutes an intangible but radical revolution. There is no need to go seeking witnesses to the fact:[26] everything that concerns not just the human sciences, but the destiny of man, politics, metaphysics, literature, the arts, advertising, propaganda—and thus, no doubt, economics—has been affected by it.

But is this anything more than the dissonant effects of an immense truth where Freud has traced a pure path? It must be said here that a technique that takes advantage of the psychological categorization alone of its object is not following this path, as is the case of contemporary psychoanalysis apart from a return to the Freudian discovery.

Thus the vulgarity of the concepts by which its practice shows its mettle, the embroidery of Freudery [fofreudisme] which is now mere decoration, and what must be called the discredit in which it prospers, together bear witness to the fundamental repudiation of that discovery.

Through his discovery, Freud brought the border between object and being that seemed to mark the limits of science within its ambit.

This is the symptom of and prelude to a reexamination of man's situation in the midst of beings [dans l'étant], as all the postulates of knowledge have heretofore assumed it to be—but please don't be content to classify the fact that I am saying so as a case of Heideggerianism, even prefixed by a "neo-" that adds nothing to the trashy style by which it is common to spare oneself any reflection with the quip, "Separate that out for me from its mental jetsam."

When I speak of Heidegger, or rather when I translate him, I strive to preserve the sovereign signifierness of the speech he proffers.

If I speak of the letter and being, if I distinguish the other from the Other, it is because Freud suggests them to me as the terms to which resistance and transference effects refer—effects against which I have had to wage unequal battle in the twenty years that I have been engaged in the practice that we all, repeating after Freud, call impossible: that of psychoanalysis. It is also because I must help others avoid losing their way there.

It is to prevent the field they have inherited from falling fallow, and to that end to convey that if the symptom is a metaphor, it is not a metaphor to say so, any more than it is to say that man's desire is a metonymy. For the symptom is a metaphor, whether one likes to admit it or not, just as desire is a metonymy, even if man scoffs at the idea.

Thus, if I am to rouse you to indignation over the fact that, after so many centuries of religious hypocrisy and philosophical posturing, no one has yet validly articulated what links metaphor to the question of being and metonymy to its lack, something of the object of this indignation must still be there—something that, as both instigator and victim, corresponds to it: namely, the man of humanism and the irremediably contested debt he has incurred against his intentions.

T.t.y.e.m.u.p.t.

May 14–26, 1957

Notes

1. *Codice Atlantico*, 145. r. a., trans. Louise Services (Paris: Gallimard), vol. II, 400.

2. The theme was "Psychoanalysis and the sciences of man."

3. The talk took place on May 9, 1957, in The Descartes Amphitheater at the Sorbonne, and discussion continued afterward over drinks.

4. "Die Frage der Laienanalyse," *GW* XIV, 281–83.

5. This point—so useful in overturning the concept of "psychological function," which obscures every-thing related to the matter—becomes clear as day in the purely linguistic analysis of the two major forms of aphasia classified by one of the leaders of modern linguistics, Roman Jakobson. See the most accessible of his works (coauthored by Morris Halle), *Fundamentals of Language* (Gravenhage and New York: Mouton, 1956), part II, chapters 1 to 4; see too the collection of translations into French of his works that we owe to Nicolas Ruwet, *Essais de linguistique générale* (Paris: Minuit, 1963).

6. Recall that discussion about the need for a new language in communist society really did take place, and that Stalin, much to the relief of those who lent credence to his philosophy, put an end to it as follows: language is not a superstructure.

7. By "linguistics" I mean the study of existing languages [*langues*] as regards their structure and the laws they reveal; this does not include the theory of abstract codes (incorrectly placed under the heading of communication theory), so-called information theory (originating in physics), or any more or less hypothetically generalized semiology.

8. Cf. St. Augustine's *De Magistro*; I analyzed the chapter "De significatione locutionis" in my seminar on June 23, 1954.

9. Thus I. A. Richards, author of a book about procedures appropriate for reaching this objective, shows us their application in another book. He selects for his purposes a page from Meng Tzu (Mencius, to the Jesuits) and calls the piece *Mencius on the Mind*, given its object. The guarantees provided of the purity of the experiment are nothing compared to the luxury of the approaches employed. And the man of letters, an expert on the traditional Canon that contains the text, is met right on the spot in Peking where our demonstration-model wringer has been transported, regardless of the cost.

But we will be no less transported, though less expensively, upon witnessing the transformation of a bronze, which gives off bell-tones at the slightest contact with thought, into a rag with which to wipe clean the slate of the most depressing British psychologism. And not, alas, without quickly identifying it with the author's own brain—all that remains of his object or of him after he has exhausted the meaning [*sens*] of the one and the common sense of the other.

10. It is in this respect that verbal hallucination, when it takes this form, sometimes opens a door that communicates with the Freudian structure of psychosis—a door which was hitherto missed since it went unnoticed (see my Seminar from 1955–1956).

11. I did so on June 6, 1956, taking as an example the first scene of *Athaliah*, incited, I confess, by an allusion—made in passing by a highbrow* critic in *The New Statesman and Nation*—to the "supreme

bitchery" of Racine's heroines, designed to dissuade us from making reference to Shakespeare's savage tragedies, which has become compulsory in analytic circles where such references serve to whitewash the vulgarity of Philistinism.

12. (Added in 1966:) The publication by Jean Starobinski, in *Le Mercure de France* (February 1964), of the notes left by Saussure on anagrams and their hypogrammatical use, from the Saturnine verses to the writings of Cicero, provide the corroboration I didn't have at the time.

13. I pay homage here to what this formulation owes to Roman Jakobson, that is, to his written work, in which a psychoanalyst can always find something to structure his own experience, and which tenders superfluous the "personal communications" that I could tout as much as anyone else.

Indeed, one can recognize in such oblique forms of allegiance the style of that immortal couple, Rosencrantz and Guildenstern, who are a set that cannot be broken up, not even by the imperfection of their destiny, for it lasts by the same method as Jeannot's knife, and for the very reason for which Goethe praised Shakespeare for presenting the character in their doublet: all by themselves they are the whole *Gesellschaft*, Society in a nutshell (*Wilhelm Meisters Lehrjahre*, Vol. 5, ed. Trunz [Hamburg: Christian Wegner Verlag], 299)—I mean the International Psychoanalytical Association.

(We should extract the whole passage from Goethe: Dieses leise Auftreten, dieses Schmiegen and Biegen, dies Jasagen, Streicheln und Schmeicheln, dieses Behendigkeit, dies Schwäzein, diese Allheit and Leerheit, diese rechtliche Schurkerei, diese Unfähigleit, wie kann sie durch einen Menschen ausgedruckt werden? Es sollten ihrer wenigstens ein Dutzend sein, wenn man sie haben könnte; denn sie bloss in Gesellschaft etwas, sie sind die Gesellschaft.)

Let us be grateful, in this context, to the author of "Some Remarks on the Role of Speech in Psycho-Analytic Technique" (*IJP* XXXVII, 6 [1956]: 467) for taking the trouble to point out that his remarks are "based on" work by him that dates back to 1952. This no doubt explains why he has assimilated nothing of the work published since then, but which he is nevertheless aware of since he cites me as its publisher (*sic*. I know what "editor"* means).

14. *Esprit* is clearly the equivalent of the German *Witz* with which Freud marked the aim of his third fundamental book on the unconscious. The far greater difficulty of finding an equivalent in English is instructive: "wit," weighed down by a discussion running from Davenant and Hobbes to Pope and Addison, left its essential virtues to "humor," which is something else. The only other choice is "pun," but its meaning is too narrow.

15. Leo Strauss, *Persecution and the Art of Writing* (Glencoe, Illinois: The Free Press, 1957).

16. See the correspondence, in particular, letters 107 and 119 selected by its editors.

17. This is the procedure by which a study ensures results through a mechanical exploration of the entire extent of its object's field.

18. (Added in 1966:) By referring only to the development of the organism, the typology neglects the structure in which the subject is caught up in fantasy, the drive, and sublimation, respectively. I am currently developing the theory of this structure.

19. The sign $\cong$ designates congruence.

20. Since S' designates, in this context, the term that produces the signifying effect (or signifierness), one can see that the term is latent in metonymy and patent in metaphor.

21. Things are altogether different if—in raising a question like "Why are there philosophers?"—I become more candid than usual, since I am raising not only a question that philosophers have been asking themselves since time immemorial, but also the one in which they are perhaps the most interested.

22. (Added in December 1968:) This and the next paragraph were rewritten solely to achieve greater clarity of expression.

23. "Fetischismus," *GW* XIV, 311.

24. One of my colleagues went as far as this thought in wondering if the id (*Es*) of Freud's last doctrine wasn't in fact the "bad ego." (Added in 1966:) You see the kind of people I had to work with.

25. Note, nevertheless, the tone with which people spoke in that period of the impish pranks of the unconscious: *Der Zufall und die Koboldstreiche des Unbewussten* ("Chance and the Impish Pranks of the Unconscious"), one of Silberer's titles, which would be absolutely anachronistic in the present context of soul-managers.

26. I'll highlight the most recent in what flowed quite smoothly from François Mauriac's pen, in the *Figaro littéraire* on May 25, by way of an apology for refusing "to tell us his life story." If one can no longer undertake to do this with the old enthusiasm, the reason, he tells us, is that, "for half a century, Freud, whatever we may think of him," has left his mark there. And after briefly yielding to the received idea that it would be to submit to the "history of our body," Mauriac quickly returns to what his writer's sensibility could not help but let slip out: our discourse, in endeavoring to be complete, would publish the deepest confessions of the souls of all our loved ones.

24 Differance

Jacques Derrida

The verb "to differ" [*différer*] seems to differ from itself. On the one hand, it indicates difference as distinction, inequality, or discernibility; on the other, it expresses the interposition of delay, the interval of a *spacing* and *temporalizing* that puts off until "later" what is presently denied, the possible that is presently impossible. Sometimes the *different* and sometimes the *deferred* correspond [in French] to the verb "to differ." This correlation, however, is not simply one between act and object, cause and effect, or primordial and derived.

In the one case "to differ" signifies nonidentity; in the other case it signifies the order of the *same*. Yet there must be a common, although entirely differant[1] [*différante*], root within the sphere that relates the two movements of differing to one another. We provisionally give the name *differance* to this *sameness* which is not *identical*: by the silent writing of its *a*, it has the desired advantage of referring to differing, *both* as spacing/temporalizing and as the movement that structures every dissociation.

As distinct from difference, differance thus points out the irreducibility of temporalizing (which is also temporalization—in transcendental language which is no longer adequate here, this would be called the constitution of primordial temporality—just as the term "spacing" also includes the constitution of primordial spatiality). Differance is not simply active (any more than it is a subjective accomplishment); it rather indicates the middle voice, it precedes and sets up the opposition between passivity and activity. With its *a*, differance more properly refers to what in classical language would be called the origin or production of differences and the differences between differences, the *play* [*jeu*] of differences. Its locus and operation will therefore be seen wherever speech appeals to difference.

Differance is neither a *word* nor a *concept*. In it, however, we shall see the juncture—rather than the summation—of what has been most decisively inscribed in the thought of what is conveniently called our "epoch": the difference of forces in Nietzsche, Saussure's principle of semiological difference, differing as the possibility of [neurone] facilitation,[2] impression and delayed effect in Freud, difference as the irreducibility of the trace of the other in Levinas, and the ontic-ontological difference in Heidegger.

Reflection on this last determination of difference will lead us to consider differance as the *strategic* note or connection—relatively or provisionally *privileged*—which indicates the closure of presence, together with the closure of the conceptual order and denomination, a closure that is effected in the functioning of traces.

I shall speak, then, of a letter—the first one, if we are to believe the alphabet and most of the speculations that have concerned themselves with it.

I shall speak then of the letter *a*, this first letter which it seemed necessary to introduce now and then in writing the word "difference." This seemed necessary in the course of writing about writing, and of writing within a writing whose different strokes all pass, in certain respects, through a gross spelling mistake, through a violation of the rules governing writing, violating the law that governs writing and regulates its conventions of propriety. In fact or theory we can always erase or lessen this spelling mistake, and, in each case, while these are analytically different from one another but for practical purposes the same, find it grave, unseemly, or, indeed, supposing the greatest ingenuousness, amusing. Whether or not we care to quietly overlook this infraction, the attention we give it beforehand will allow us to recognize, as though prescribed by some mute irony, the inaudible but displaced character of this literal permutation. We can always act as though this makes no difference. I must say from the start that my account serves less to justify this silent spelling mistake, or still less to excuse it, than to aggravate its obtrusive character.

On the other hand, I must be excused if I refer, at least implicitly, to one or another of the texts that I have ventured to publish. Precisely what I would like to attempt to some extent (although this is in principle and in its highest degree impossible, due to essential *de jure* reasons) is to bring together an *assemblage* of the different ways I have been able to utilize—or, rather, have allowed to be imposed on me—what I will provisionally call the word or concept of differance in its new spelling. It is literally neither a word nor a concept, as we shall see. I insist on the word "assemblage" here for two reasons: on the one hand, it is not a matter of describing a history, of recounting the steps, text by text, context by context, each time showing which scheme has been able to impose this graphic disorder, although this could have been done as well; rather, we are concerned with the *general system of all these schemata*. On the other hand, the word "assemblage" seems more apt for suggesting that the kind of bringing-together proposed here has the structure of an interlacing, a weaving, or a web, which would allow the different threads and different lines of sense or force to separate again, as well as being ready to bind others together.

In a quite preliminary way, we now recall that this particular graphic intervention was conceived in the writing-up of a question about writing; it was not made simply to shock the reader or grammarian. Now, in point of fact, it happens that this graphic difference (the *a* instead of the *e*), this marked difference between two apparently vocalic notations, between vowels, remains purely graphic: it is written or read, but it is not heard. It cannot be heard, and we shall see in what respects it is also beyond the order of understanding. It is put forward by a silent mark, by a tacit monument, or, one might even say, by a pyramid—keeping in mind not only the capital form of the printed letter but also that passage from Hegel's *Encyclopaedia* where he compares the body of the sign to an Egyptian pyramid. The *a* of differance, therefore, is not heard; it remains silent, secret, and discreet, like a tomb.[3]

It is a tomb that (provided one knows how to decipher its legend) is not far from signaling the death of the king.

It is a tomb that cannot even be made to resonate. For I cannot even let you know, by my talk, now being spoken before the Société Française de Philosophie, which difference I am talking about at the very moment I speak of it. I can only talk about this graphic difference by keeping to a very indirect speech about writing, and on the condition that I specify each time that I am referring to difference with an *e* or differance with an *a*. All of which is not going to simplify matters today, and will give us all a great deal of trouble when we want to understand one another. In any event, when I do specify which difference I mean—when I say "with an *e*" or "with an *a*"—this will refer irreducibly to a *written text*, a text governing my talk, a text that I keep in front of me, that I will read, and toward which I shall have to try to lead your hands and eyes. We cannot refrain here from going by way of a written text, from ordering ourselves by the disorder that is produced therein—and this is what matters to me first of all.

Doubtless this pyramidal silence of the graphic difference between the *e* and the *a* can function only within the system of phonetic writing and within a language or grammar historically tied to phonetic writing and to the whole culture which is inseparable from it. But I will say that it is just this—this silence that functions only within what is called phonetic writing—that points out or reminds us in a very opportune way that, contrary to an enormous prejudice, there is no phonetic writing. There is no purely and strictly phonetic writing. What is called phonetic writing can only function—in principle and *de jure*, and not due to some factual and technical inadequacy—by incorporating nonphonetic "signs" (punctuation, spacing, etc.); but when we examine their structure and necessity, we will quickly see that they are ill described by the concept of signs. Saussure had only to remind us that the play of difference was the functional condition, the condition of possibility, for every sign; and it is itself silent. The difference between two phonemes, which enables them to exist and to operate, is inaudible. The inaudible opens the two present phonemes to hearing, as they present themselves. If, then, there is no purely phonetic writing, it is because there is no purely phonetic phone. The difference that brings out phonemes and lets them be heard and understood [*entendre*] itself remains inaudible.

It will perhaps be objected that, for the same reasons, the graphic difference itself sinks into darkness, that it never constitutes the fullness of a sensible term, but draws out an invisible connection, the mark of an inapparent relation between two spectacles. That is no doubt true. Indeed, since from this point of view the difference between the e and the a marked in "differance" eludes vision and hearing, this happily suggests that we must here let ourselves be referred to an order that no longer refers to sensibility. But we are not referred to intelligibility either, to an ideality not fortuitously associated with the objectivity of theōrein or understanding. We must be referred to an order, then, that resists philosophy's founding opposition between the sensible and the intelligible. The order that resists this opposition, that resists it because it sustains it, is designated in a movement of differance (with an a) between two differences or between two letters. This differance belongs neither to the voice nor to writing in the ordinary sense, and it takes place, like the strange space that will assemble us here for the course of an hour, between speech and writing and beyond the tranquil familiarity that binds us to one and to the other, reassuring us sometimes in the illusion that they are two separate things.

Now, how am I to speak of the *a* of differance? It is clear that it cannot be *exposed*. We can expose only what, at a certain moment, can become *present*, manifest; what can be shown, presented as a present, a being-present in its truth, the truth of a present or the presence of a present. However, if differance $\boxed{is}$ (I also cross out the "is") what makes the presentation of being-present possible, it never presents itself as such. It is never given in the present or to anyone. Holding back and not exposing itself, it goes beyond the order of truth on this specific point and in this determined way, yet is not itself concealed, as if it were something, a mysterious being, in the occult zone of a nonknowing. Any exposition would expose it to disappearing as a disappearance. It would risk appearing, thus disappearing.

Thus, the detours, phrases, and syntax that I shall often have to resort to will resemble—will sometimes be practically indiscernible from—those of negative theology. Already we had to note *that* differance *is not*, does not exist, and is not any sort of being-present (*on*). And we will have to point out everything *that* it *is not*, and, consequently, that it has neither existence nor essence. It belongs to no category of being, present or absent. And yet what is thus denoted as differance is not theological, not even in the most negative order of negative theology. The latter, as we know, is always occupied with letting a supraessential reality go beyond the finite categories of essence and existence, that is, of presence, and always hastens to remind us that, if we deny the predicate of existence to God, it is in order to recognize him as a superior, inconceivable, and ineffable mode of being. Here there is no question of such a move, as will be confirmed as we go along. Not only is differance irreducible to every ontological or theological—onto-theological—reappropriation, but it opens up the very space in which onto-theology—philosophy—produces its system and its history. It thus encompasses and irrevocably surpasses onto-theology or philosophy.

For the same reason, I do not know where *to begin* to mark out this assemblage, this graph, of differance. Precisely what is in question here is the requirement that there be a *de jure* commencement, an absolute point of departure, a responsibility arising from a principle. The problem of writing opens by questioning the *archē*. Thus what I put forth here will not be developed simply as a philosophical discourse that operates on the basis of a principle, of postulates, axioms, and definitions and that moves according to the discursive line of a rational order. In marking out difference, everything is a matter of strategy and risk. It is a question of strategy because no transcendent truth present outside the sphere of writing can theologically command the totality of this field. It is hazardous because this strategy is not simply one in the sense that we say that strategy orients the tactics according to a final aim, a *telos* or the theme of a domination, a mastery or an ultimate reappropriation of movement and field. In the end, it is a strategy without finality. We might call it blind tactics or empirical errance, if the value of empiricism did not itself derive all its meaning from its opposition to philosophical responsibility. If there is a certain errance in the tracing-out of differance, it no longer follows the line of logico-philosophical speech or that of its integral and symmetrical opposite, logico-empirical speech. The concept of *play* [*jeu*] remains beyond this opposition; on the eve and aftermath of philosophy, it designates the unity of chance and necessity in an endless calculus.

By decision and, as it were, by the rules of the game, then, turning this thought around, let us introduce ourselves to the thought of differance by way of the theme of strategy or strategem. By this merely strategic justification, I want to emphasize that the efficacy of this thematics of differance very well may, and even one day must, be sublated, i.e., lend itself, if not to its own replacement, at least to its involvement in a series of events which in fact it never commanded. This also means that it is not a theological thematics.

I will say, first of all, that differance, which is neither a word nor a concept, seemed to me to be strategically the theme most proper to think out, if not master (thought being here, perhaps, held in a certain necessary relation with the structional limits of mastery), in what is most characteristic of our "epoch." I start off, then, strategically, from the place and time in which "we" are, even though my opening is not justifiable in the final account, and though it is always on the basis of differance and its "history" that we can claim to know who and where "we" are and what the limits of an "epoch" can be.

Although "differance" is neither a word nor a concept, let us nonetheless attempt a simple and approximative semantic analysis which will bring us in view of what is at stake [*en vue de l'enjeu*].

We do know that the verb "to differ" [*différer*] (the Latin verb *differre*) has two seemingly quite distinct meanings; in the *Littré* dictionary, for example, they are the subject of two separate articles. In this sense, the Latin *differre* is not the simple translation of the Greek *diapherein*; this fact will not be without consequence for us in tying our discussion to a particular language, one that passes for being less philosophical, less primordially philosophical, than the other. For the distribution of sense in the Greek *diapherein* does not carry one of the two themes of the Latin *differre*, namely, the action of postponing until later, of taking into account, the taking-account of time and forces in an operation that implies an economic reckoning, a detour, a respite, a delay, a reserve, a representation—all the concepts that I will sum up here in a word I have never used but which could be added to this series: *temporalizing*. "To differ" in this sense is to temporalize, to resort, consciously or unconsciously, to the temporal and temporalizing mediation of a detour that suspends the accomplishment or fulfillment of "desire" or "will," or carries desire or will out in a way that annuls or tempers their effect. We shall see, later, in what respects this temporalizing is also a temporalization and spacing, is space's becoming-temporal and time's becoming-spatial, is "primordial constitution" of space and time, as metaphysics or transcendental phenomenology would call it in the language that is here criticized and displaced.

The other sense of "to differ" [*différer*] is the most common and most identifiable, the sense of not being identical, of being other, of being discernible, etc. And in "differents," whether referring to the alterity of dissimilarity or the alterity of allergy or of polemics, it is necessary that interval, distance, *spacing* occur among the different elements and occur actively, dynamically, and with a certain perseverance in repetition.

But the word "difference" (with an *e*) could never refer to differing as temporalizing or to difference as *polemos*. It is this loss of sense that the word differance (with an *a*) will have to schematically compensate for. Differance can refer to the whole complex of its meanings at once, for it is immediately and irreducibly multivalent, something which will be important for the discourse I am trying to develop. It refers to this whole complex of meanings not only when it is supported by a language or interpretive context (like any signification), but it already does so somehow of itself. Or at least it does so more easily by itself than does any other word: here the *a* comes more immediately from the present participle [*différant*] and brings us closer to the action of "differing" that is in progress, even before it has produced the effect that is constituted as different or resulted in difference (with an *e*). Within a conceptual system and in terms of classical requirements, differance could be said to designate the productive and primordial constituting causality, the process of scission and division whose differings and differences would be the constituted products or effects. But while bringing us closer to the infinitive and active core of differing, "differance" with an *a* neutralizes what the infinitive denotes as simply active, in the same way that "parlance" does not signify the simple fact of speaking, of speaking to or being spoken to. Nor is resonance the act of resonating. Here in the usage of our language we must consider that the ending -*ance* is undecided between active and passive. And we shall see why what is designated by "differance" is neither simply active nor simply passive, that it announces or rather recalls something like the middle voice, that it speaks of an operation which is not an operation, which cannot be thought of either as a passion or as an action of a subject upon an object, as starting from an agent or from a patient, or on the basis of, or in view of, any of these *terms*. But philosophy has perhaps commenced by distributing the middle voice, expressing a certain intransitiveness, into the active and the passive voice, and has itself been constituted in this repression.

How are differance as temporalizing and differance as spacing conjoined?

Let us begin with the problem of signs and writing—since we are already in the midst of it. We ordinarily say that a sign is put in place of the thing itself, the present thing— "thing" holding here for the sense as well as the referent. Signs represent the present in its absence; they take the place of the present. When we cannot take hold of or show the thing, let us say the present, the being-present, when the present does not present itself, then we signify, we go through the detour of signs. We take up or give signs; we make signs. The sign would thus be a deferred presence. Whether it is a question of verbal or written signs, monetary signs, electoral delegates, or political representatives, the movement of signs defers the moment of encountering the thing itself, the moment at which we could lay hold of it, consume or expend it, touch it, see it, have a present intuition of it. What I am describing here is the structure of signs as classically determined, in order to define— through a commonplace characterization of its traits—signification as the differance of temporalizing. Now this classical determination presupposes that the sign (which defers presence) is conceivable only *on the basis of* the presence that it defers and *in view of* the deferred presence one intends to reappropriate. Following this classical semiology, the substitution of the sign for the thing itself is both *secondary* and *provisional*: it is second in order after an original and lost presence, a presence from which the sign would be derived. It is provisional with respect to this final and missing presence, in view of which the sign would serve as a movement of mediation.

In attempting to examine these secondary and provisional aspects of the substitute, we shall no doubt catch sight of something like a primordial differance. Yet we could no longer even call it primordial or final, inasmuch as the characteristics of origin, beginning, *telos*, *eschaton*, etc., have always denoted presence—*ousia*, *paronsia*, etc. To question the secondary and provisional character of the sign, to oppose it to a "primordial" differance, would thus have the following consequences:

1. Differance can no longer be understood according to the concept of "sign," which has always been taken to mean the representation of a presence and has been constituted in a system (of thought or language) determined on the basis of and in view of presence.
2. In this way we question the authority of presence or its simple symmetrical contrary, absence or lack. We thus interrogate the limit that has always constrained us, that always constrains us—we who inhabit a language and a system of thought—to form the sense of being in general as presence or absence, in the categories of being or beingness (*ousia*). It already appears that the kind of questioning we are thus led back to is, let us say, the Heideggerian kind, and that differance *seems* to lead us back to the ontic-ontological difference. But permit me to postpone this reference. I shall only note that between differance as temporalizing-temporalization (which we can no longer conceive within the horizon of the present) and what Heidegger says about temporalization in *Sein und Zeit* (namely, that as the transcendental horizon of the question of being it must be freed from the traditional and metaphysical domination by the present or the now)—between these two there is a close, if not exhaustive and irreducibly necessary, interconnection.

But first of all, let us remain with the semiological aspects of the problem to see how differance as temporalizing is conjoined with differance as spacing. Most of the semiological or linguistic research currently dominating the field of thought (whether due to the results of its own investigations or due to its role as a generally recognized regulative model) traces its genealogy, rightly or wrongly, to Saussure as its common founder. It was Saussure who first of all set forth the *arbitrariness of signs* and the *differential character* of signs as principles of general semiology and particularly of linguistics. And, as we know, these two themes—the arbitrary and the differential—are in his view inseparable. Arbitrariness can occur only because the system of signs is constituted by the differences between the terms, and not by their fullness. The elements of signification function not by virtue of the compact force of their cores but by the network of oppositions that distinguish them and relate them to one another. "Arbitrary and differential" says Saussure "are two correlative qualities."

As the condition for signification, this principle of difference affects the *whole sign*, that is, both the signified and the signifying aspects. The signified aspect is the concept, the ideal sense. The signifying aspect is what Saussure calls the material or physical (e.g., acoustical) "image." We do not here have to enter into all the problems these definitions pose. Let us only cite Saussure where it interests us:

> The conceptual side of value is made up solely of relations and differences with respect to the other terms of language, and the same can be said of its material side. . . . Everything that has been said up to this point boils down to this: in language there are only differences. Even more important: a difference generally implies positive terms between which the difference is set up; but in language there are only differences *without positive terms*. Whether we take the signified or the signifier, language has neither ideas nor sounds that existed before the linguistic system, but only conceptual and phonic differences that have issued from the system. The idea or phonic substance that a sign contains is of less importance than the other signs that surround it.[4]

The first consequence to be drawn from this is that the signified concept is never present in itself, in an adequate presence that would refer only to itself. Every concept is necessarily and essentially inscribed in a chain or a system, within which it refers to another and to other concepts, by the systematic play of differences. Such a play, then—differance—is no longer simply a concept, but the possibility of conceptuality, of the conceptual system and process in general. For the same reason, differance, which is not a concept, is not a mere word; that is, it is not what we represent to ourselves as the calm and present self-referential unity of a concept and sound [*phonie*]. We shall later discuss the consequences of this for the notion of a word.

The difference that Saussure speaks about, therefore, is neither itself a concept nor one word among others. We can say this *a fortiori* for differance. Thus we are brought to make the relation between the one and the other explicit.

Within a language, within the *system* of language, there are only differences. A taxonomic operation can accordingly undertake its systematic, statistical, and classificatory inventory. But, on the one hand, these differences *play a role* in language, in speech as well, and in the exchange between language and speech. On the other hand, these differences are themselves *effects*. They have not fallen from the sky ready made; they are no more inscribed in a *topos noētos* than they are prescribed in the wax of the brain. If the word "history" did not carry with it the theme of a final repression of differance, we could say that differences alone could be "historical" through and through and from the start.

What we note as *differance* will thus be the movement of play that "produces" (and not by something that is simply an activity) these differences, these effects of difference. This does not mean that the differance which produces differences is before them in a simple and in itself unmodified and indifferent present. Differance is the nonfull, nonsimple "origin"; it is the structured and differing origin of differences.

Since language (which Saussure says is a classification) has not fallen from the sky, it is clear that the differences have been produced; they are the effects produced, but effects that do not have as their cause a subject or substance, a thing in general, or a being that is somewhere present and itself escapes the play of difference. If such a presence were implied (quite classically) in the general concept of cause, we would therefore have to talk about an effect without a cause, something that would very quickly lead to no longer talking about effects. I have tried to indicate a way out of the closure imposed by this system, namely, by means of the "trace." No more an effect than a cause, the "trace" cannot of itself, taken outside its context, suffice to bring about the required transgression.

As there is no presence before the semiological difference or outside it, we can extend what Saussure writes about language to signs in general: "Language is necessary in order for speech to be intelligible and to produce all of its effects; but the latter is necessary in order for language to be established; historically, the fact of speech always comes first."[5]

Retaining at least the schema, if not the content, of the demand formulated by Saussure, we shall designate by the term *differance* the movement by which language, or any code, any system of reference in general, becomes "historically" constituted as a fabric of differences. Here, the terms "constituted," "produced," "created," "movement," "historically," etc., with all they imply, are not to be understood only in terms of the language of metaphysics, from which they are taken. It would have to be shown why the concepts of production, like those of constitution and history, remain accessories in this respect to what is here being questioned; this, however, would draw us too far away today, toward the theory of the representation of the "circle" in which we seem to be enclosed. I only use these terms here, like many other concepts, out of strategic convenience and in order to prepare the deconstruction of the system they form at the point which is now most decisive. In any event, we will have understood, by virtue of the very circle we appear to be caught up in, that differance, as it is written here, is no more static than genetic, no more structural than historical. Nor is it any less so. And it is completely to miss the point of this orthographical impropriety to want to object to it on the basis of the oldest of metaphysical oppositions—for example, by opposing some generative point of view to a structuralist-taxonomic point of view, or conversely. These oppositions do not pertain in the least to differance; and this, no doubt, is what makes thinking about it difficult and uncomfortable.

If we now consider the chain to which "differance" gets subjected, according to the context, to a certain number of nonsynonymic substitutions, one will ask why we resorted to such concepts as "reserve," "protowriting," "prototrace," "spacing," indeed to "supplement" or "*pharmakon*," and, before long, to "hymen," etc.[6]

Let us begin again. Differance is what makes the movement of signification possible only if each element that is said to be "present," appearing on the stage of presence, is related to something other than itself but retains the mark of a past element and already lets itself be hollowed out by the mark of its relation to a future element. This trace relates no less to what is called the future than to what is called the past, and it constitutes what is called the present by this very relation to what it is not, to what it absolutely is not; that is, not even to a past or future considered as a modified present. In order for it to be, an interval must separate it from what it is not; but the interval that constitutes it in the present must also, and by the same token, divide the present in itself, thus dividing, along with the present, everything that can be conceived on its basis, that is, every being—in particular, for our metaphysical language, the substance or subject. Constituting itself, dynamically dividing itself, this interval is what could be called *spacing*; time's becoming-spatial or space's becoming-temporal (*temporalizing*). And it is this constitution of the present as a "primordial" and irreducibly nonsimple, and, therefore, in the strict sense nonprimordial, synthesis of traces, retentions, and protentions (to reproduce here, analogically and provisionally, a phenomenological and transcendental language that will presently be revealed as inadequate) that I propose to call protowriting, prototrace, or differance. The latter (is) (both) spacing (and) temporalizing.[7]

Given this (active) movement of the (production of) differance without origin, could we not, quite simply and without any neographism, call it *differentiation*? Among other confusions, such a word would suggest some organic unity, some primordial and homogeneous unity, that would eventually come to be divided up and take on difference as an event. Above all, formed on the verb "to differentiate," this word would annul the economic signification of detour, temporalizing delay, "deferring." I owe a remark in passing to a recent reading of one of Koyré's texts entitled "Hegel at Jena."[8] In that text, Koyré cites long passages from the Jena *Logic* in German and gives his own translation. On two occasions in Hegel's text he encounters the expression *"differente Beziehung."* This word (*different*), whose root is Latin, is extremely rare in German and also, I believe, in Hegel, who instead uses *verschieden* or *ungleich*, calling difference *Unterschied* and qualitative variety *Verschiedenheit*. In the Jena *Logic*, he uses the word *different* precisely at the point where he deals with time and the present. Before coming to Koyré's valuable remark, here are some passages from Hegel, as rendered by Koyré:

The infinite, in this simplicity is—as a moment opposed to the self-identical—the negative. In its moments, while the infinite presents the totality to (itself) and in itself, (it is) excluding in general, the point or limit; but in this, its own (action of) negating, it relates itself immediately to the other and negates itself. The limit or moment of the present (*der Gegen-wart*), the absolute "this" of time or the now, is an absolutely negative simplicity, absolutely excluding all multiplicity from itself, and by this very fact is absolutely determined; it is not an extended whole or *quantum* within itself (and) which would in itself also have an undetermined aspect or qualitative variety, which of itself would be related, indifferently (*gleichgültig*) or externally to another, but on the contrary, this is an absolutely different relation of the simple.[9]

And Koyré specifies in a striking note: "Different relation: *differente Beziehung*. We could say: differentiating relation." And on the following page, from another text of Hegel, we can read: "*Diese Beziehung ist Gegenwart, als eine differente Beziehung*" (This relation is [the] present, as a different relation). There is another note by Koyré: "The term '*different*' is taken here in an active sense."

Writing "differing" or "differance" (with an *a*) would have had the utility of making it possible to translate Hegel on precisely this point with no further qualifications—and it is a quite decisive point in his text. The translation would be, as it always should be, the transformation of one language by another. Naturally, I maintain that the word "differance" can be used in other ways, too; first of all, because it denotes not only the activity of primordial difference but also the temporalizing detour of deferring. It has, however, an even more important usage. Despite the very profound affinities that differance thus written has with Hegelian speech (as it should be read), it can, at a certain point, not exactly break with it, but rather work a sort of displacement with regard to it. A definite rupture with Hegelian language would make no sense, nor would it be at all likely; but this displacement is both infinitesimal and radical. I have tried to indicate the extent of this displacement elsewhere; it would be difficult to talk about it with any brevity at this point.

Differences are thus "produced"—differed—by differance. But *what* differs, or *who* differs? In other words, *what is* differance? With this question we attain another stage and another source of the problem.

What differs? Who differs? What is differance?

If we answered these questions even before examining them as questions, even before going back over them and questioning their form (even what seems to be most natural and necessary about them), we would fall below the level we have now reached. For if we accepted the form of the question in its own sense and syntax ("What?," "What is?," "Who is?"), we would have to admit that differance is derived, supervenient, controlled, and ordered from the starting point of a being-present, one capable of being something, a force, a state, or power in the world, to which we could give all kinds of names: a *what*, or being-present as a *subject*, a *who*. In the latter case, notably, we would implicitly admit that the being-present (for example, as a self-present being or consciousness) would eventually result in differing: in delaying or in diverting the fulfillment of a "need" or "desire," or in differing from itself. But in none of these cases would such a being-present be "constituted" by this differance.

Now if we once again refer to the semiological difference, what was it that Saussure in particular reminded us of? That "language [which consists only of differences] is not a function of the speaking subject." This implies that the subject (self-identical or even conscious of self-identity, self-conscious) is inscribed in the language, that he is a "function" of the language. He becomes a *speaking* subject only by conforming his speech—even in the aforesaid "creation," even in the aforesaid "transgression"—to the system of linguistic prescriptions taken as the system of differences, or at least to the general law of differance, by conforming to that law of language which Saussure calls "language without speech." "Language is necessary for the spoken word to be intelligible and so that it can produce all of its effects."[10]

If, by hypothesis, we maintain the strict opposition between speech and language, then differance will be not only the play of differences within the language but the relation of speech to language, the detour by which I must also pass in order to speak, the silent token I must give, which holds just as well for linguistics in the strict sense as it does for general semiology; it dictates all the relations between usage and the formal schema, between the message and the particular code, etc. Elsewhere I have tried to suggest that this differance within language, and in the relation between speech and language, forbids the essential dissociation between speech and writing that Saussure, in keeping with tradition, wanted to draw at another level of his presentation. The use of language or the employment of any code which implies a play of forms—with no determined or invariable substratum—also presupposes a retention and protention of differences, a spacing and temporalizing, a play of traces. This play must be a sort of inscription prior to writing, a protowriting without a present origin, without an *archē*. From this comes the systematic crossing-out of the *archē* and the transformation of general semiology into a grammatology, the latter performing a critical work upon everything within semiology—right down to its matrical concept of signs—that retains any metaphysical presuppositions incompatible with the theme of differance.

We might be tempted by an objection: to be sure, the subject becomes a *speaking* subject only by dealing with the system of linguistic differences; or again, he becomes a *signifying* subject (generally by speech or other signs) only by entering into the system of differences. In this sense, certainly, the speaking or signifying subject would not be self-present, insofar as he speaks or signifies, except for the play of linguistic or semiological differance. But can we not conceive of a presence and self-presence of the subject before speech or its signs, a subject's self-presence in a silent and intuitive consciousness?

Such a question therefore supposes that prior to signs and outside them, and excluding every trace and differance, something such as consciousness is possible. It supposes, more-over, that, even before the distribution of its signs in space and in the world, consciousness can gather itself up in its own presence. What then is consciousness? What does "conscious-ness" mean? Most often in the very form of "meaning" ["*vouloir-dire*"], consciousness in all its modifications is conceivable only as self-presence, a self-perception of presence. And what holds for consciousness also holds here for what is called subjective existence in general. Just as the category of subject is not and never has been conceivable without refer-ence to presence as *hypokeimenon* or *ousia*, etc., so the subject as consciousness has never been able to be evinced otherwise than as self-presence. The privilege accorded to conscious-ness thus means a privilege accorded to the present; and even if the transcendental tempo-rality of consciousness is described in depth, as Husserl described it, the power of synthesis and of the incessant gathering-up of traces is always accorded to the "living present."

This privilege is the ether of metaphysics, the very element of our thought insofar as it is caught up in the language of metaphysics. We can only de-limit such a closure today by evoking this import of presence, which Heidegger has shown to be the onto-theological determination of being. Therefore, in evoking this import of presence, by an examination which would have to be of a quite peculiar nature, we question the absolute privilege of this form or epoch of presence in general, that is, consciousness as meaning [*vouloir-dire*] in self-presence.

We thus come to posit presence—and, in particular, consciousness, the being-next-to-itself of consciousness—no longer as the absolutely matrical form of being but as a "determination" and an "effect." Presence is a determination and effect within a system which is no longer that of presence but that of differance; it no more allows the opposition between activity and passivity than that between cause and effect or in-determination and determination, etc. This system is of such a kind that even to designate consciousness as an effect or determination—for strategic reasons, reasons that can be more or less clearly considered and systematically ascertained—is to continue to operate according to the vocabulary of that very thing to be de-limited.

Before being so radically and expressly Heideggerian, this was also Nietzsche's and Freud's move, both of whom, as we know, and often in a very similar way, questioned the self-assured certitude of consciousness. And is it not remarkable that both of them did this by starting out with the theme of differance?

This theme appears almost literally in their work, at the most crucial places. I shall not expand on this here; I shall only recall that for Nietzsche "the important main activity is unconscious" and that consciousness is the effect of forces whose essence, ways, and modalities are not peculiar to it. Now force itself is never present; it is only a play of differences and quantities. There would be no force in general without the difference between forces; and here the difference in quantity counts more than the content of quantity, more than the absolute magnitude itself.

Quantity itself therefore is not separable from the difference in quantity. The difference in quantity is the essence of force, the relation of force with force. To fancy two equal forces, even if we grant them opposing directions, is an approximate and crude illusion, a statistical dream in which life is immersed, but which chemistry dispels.[11]

Is not the whole thought of Nietzsche a critique of philosophy as active indifference to difference, as a system of reduction or adiaphoristic repression? Following the same logic—logic itself—this does not exclude the fact that philosophy lives *in* and *from* differance, that it thereby blinds itself to the *same*, which is not the identical. The same is precisely differance (with an *a*), as the diverted and equivocal passage from one difference to another, from one term of the opposition to the other. We could thus take up all the coupled oppositions on which philosophy is constructed, and from which our language lives, not in order to see opposition vanish but to see the emergence of a necessity such that one of the terms appears as the differance of the other, the other as "differed" within the systematic ordering of the same (e.g., the intelligible as differing from the sensible, as sensible differed; the concept as differed-differing intuition, life as differing-differed matter; mind as differed-differing life; culture as differed-differing nature; and all the terms designating what is other than *physis*—*technē*, *nomos*, society, freedom, history, spirit, etc.—as *physis* differed or *physis* differing: *physis in differance*). It is out of the unfolding of this "same" as differance that the sameness of difference and of repetition is presented in the eternal return.

In Nietzsche, these are so many themes that can be related with the kind of symptomatology that always serves to diagnose the evasions and ruses of anything disguised in its differance. Or again, these terms can be related with the entire thematics of active interpretation, which substitutes an incessant deciphering for the disclosure of truth as a presentation of the thing itself in its presence, etc. What results is a cipher without truth, or at least a system of ciphers that is not dominated by truth value, which only then becomes a function that is understood, inscribed, and circumscribed.

We shall therefore call differance this "active" (in movement) discord of the different forces and of the differences between forces which Nietzsche opposes to the entire system of metaphysical grammar, wherever that system controls culture, philosophy, and science.

It is historically significant that this diaphoristics, understood as an energetics or an economy of forces, set up to question the primacy of presence qua consciousness, is also the major theme of Freud's thought; in his work we find another diaphoristics, both in the form of a theory of ciphers or traces and an energetics. The questioning of the authority of consciousness is first and always differential.

The two apparently different meanings of differance are tied together in Freudian theory: differing [*le différer*] as discernibility, distinction, deviation, diastem, *spacing*; and deferring [*le différer*] as detour, delay, relay, reserve, *temporalizing*. I shall recall only that:

1. The concept of trace (*Spur*), of facilitation (*Bahnung*), of forces of facilitation are, as early as the composition of the *Entwurf*, inseparable from the concept of difference. The origin of memory and of the psyche as a memory in general (conscious or unconscious) can only be described by taking into account the difference between the facilitation thresholds, as Freud says explicitly. There is no facilitation [*Bahnung*] without difference and no difference without a trace.

2. All the differences involved in the production of unconscious traces and in the process of inscription (*Niederschrift*) can also be interpreted as moments of differance, in the sense of "placing on reserve." Following a schema that continually guides Freud's thinking, the movement of the trace is described as an effort of life to protect itself *by deferring* the dangerous investment, by constituting a reserve (*Vorrat*). And all the conceptual oppositions that furrow Freudian thought relate each concept to the other like movements of a detour, within the economy of differance. The one is only the other deferred, the one differing from the other. The one is the other in differance, the one is the differance from the other. Every apparently rigorous and irreducible opposition (for example, that between the secondary

and primary) is thus said to be, at one time or another, a "theoretical fiction." In this way again, for example (but such an example covers everything or communicates with everything), the difference between the pleasure principle and the reality principle is only differance as detour (*Aufschieben, Aufschub*). In *Beyond the Pleasure Principle*, Freud writes:

> Under the influence of the ego's instincts of self-preservation, the pleasure principle is replaced by the reality principle. This latter principle does not abandon the intention of ultimately obtaining pleasure, but it nevertheless demands and carries into effect the postponement of satisfaction, the abandonment of a number of possibilities of gaining satisfaction and the temporary toleration of unpleasure as a step on the long indirect road (*Aufschub*) to pleasure.[12]

Here we touch on the point of greatest obscurity, on the very enigma of differance, on how the concept we have of it is divided by a strange separation. We must not hasten to make a decision too quickly. How can we conceive of differance as a systematic detour which, within the element of the same, always aims at either finding again the pleasure or the presence that had been deferred by (conscious or unconscious) calculation, and, *at the same time*, how can we, on the other hand, conceive of differance as the relation to an impossible presence, as an expenditure without reserve, as an irreparable loss of presence, an irreversible wearing-down of energy, or indeed as a death instinct and a relation to the absolutely other that apparently breaks up any economy? It is evident—it is evidence itself—that system and nonsystem, the same and the absolutely other, etc., cannot be conceived *together*.

If differance is this inconceivable factor, must we not perhaps hasten to make it evident, to bring it into the philosophical element of evidence, and thus quickly dissipate its mirage character and illogicality, dissipate it with the infallibility of the calculus we know well—since we have recognized its place, necessity, and function within the structure of differance? What would be accounted for philosophically here has already been taken into account in the system of differance as it is here being calculated. I have tried elsewhere, in a reading of Bataille,[13] to indicate what might be the establishment of a rigorous, and in a new sense "scientific," *relating* of a "restricted economy"—one having nothing to do with an unreserved expenditure, with death, with being exposed to nonsense, etc.—to a "general economy" or system that, so to speak, *takes account of* what is unreserved. It is a relation between a differance that is accounted for and a differance that fails to be accounted for, where the establishment of a pure presence, without loss, is one with the occurrence of absolute loss, with death. By establishing this relation between a restricted and a general system, we shift and recommence the very project of philosophy under the privileged heading of Hegelianism.

The economic character of differance in no way implies that the deferred presence can always be recovered, that it simply amounts to an investment that only temporarily and without loss delays the presentation of presence, that is, the perception of gain or the gain of perception. Contrary to the metaphysical, dialectical, and "Hegelian" interpretation of the economic movement of differance, we must admit a game where whoever loses wins and where one wins and loses each time. If the diverted presentation continues to be somehow definitively and irreducibly withheld, this is not because a particular present remains hidden or absent, but because differance holds us in a relation with what exceeds (though we necessarily fail to recognize this) the alternative of presence or absence. A certain alterity—Freud gives it a metaphysical name, the unconscious—is definitively taken away from every process of presentation in which we would demand for it to be shown forth in person. In this context and under this heading, the unconscious is not, as we know, a hidden, virtual, and potential self-presence. It is differed—which no doubt means that it is woven out of differences, but also that it sends out, that it delegates, representatives or proxies; but there is no chance that the mandating subject "exists" somewhere, that it is present or is "itself," and still less chance that it will become conscious. In this sense, contrary to the terms of an old debate, strongly symptomatic of the metaphysical investments it has always assumed, the "unconscious" can no more be classed as a "thing" than as anything else; it is no more of a thing than an implicit or masked consciousness. This radical alterity, removed from every possible mode of presence, is characterized by irreducible aftereffects, by delayed effects. In order to describe them, in order to read the traces of the "unconscious" traces (there are no "conscious" traces), the language of presence or absence, the metaphysical speech of phenomenology, is in principle inadequate.

The structure of delay (*retardement: Nachträglichkeit*) that Freud talks about indeed prohibits our taking temporalization (temporalizing) to be a simple dialectical complication of the present; rather, this is the style of transcendental phenomenology. It describes the living present as a primordial and incessant synthesis that is constantly led back upon itself, back upon its assembled and assembling self, by retentional traces and protentional openings. With the alterity of the "unconscious," we have to deal not with the horizons of modified presents—past or future—but with a "past" that has never been nor will ever be present, whose "future" will never be produced or reproduced in the form of presence. The concept of trace is therefore incommensurate with that of retention, that of the becoming-past of what had been present. The trace cannot be conceived—nor, therefore, can differance—on the basis of either the present or the presence of the present.

A past that has never been present: with this formula Emmanuel Levinas designates (in ways that are, to be sure, not those of psychoanalysis) the trace and the enigma of absolute alterity, that is, the Other [*autrui*]. At least within these limits, and from this point of view, the thought of differance implies the whole critique of classical ontology undertaken by Levinas. And the concept of trace, like that of differance, forms—across these different traces and through these differences between traces, as understood by Nietzsche, Freud, and Levinas (these "authors' names" serve only as indications)—the network that sums up and permeates our "epoch" as the de-limitation of ontology (of presence).

The ontology of presence is the ontology of beings and beingness. Everywhere, the dominance of beings is solicited by differance—in the sense that *sollicitare* means, in old Latin, to shake all over, to make the whole tremble. What is questioned by the thought of differance, therefore, is the determination of being in presence, or in beingness. Such a question could not arise and be understood without the difference between Being and beings opening up somewhere. The first consequence of this is that differance is not. It is not a being-present, however excellent, unique, principal, or transcendent one makes it. It commands nothing, rules over nothing, and nowhere does it exercise any authority. It is not marked by a capital letter. Not only is there no realm of differance, but differance is even the subversion of every realm. This is obviously what makes it threatening and necessarily dreaded by everything in us that desires a realm, the past or future presence of a realm. And it is always in the name of a realm that, believing one sees it ascend to the capital letter, one can reproach it for wanting to rule.

Does this mean, then, that differance finds its place within the spread of the ontic-ontological difference, as it is conceived, as the "epoch" conceives itself within it, and particularly "across" the Heideggerian meditation, which cannot be gotten around?

There is no simple answer to such a question.

In one particular respect, differance is, to be sure, but the historical and epochal *deployment* of Being or of the ontological difference. The *a* of differance marks the *movement* of this deployment.

And yet, is not the thought that conceives the *sense* or *truth* of Being, the determination of differance as ontic-ontological difference—difference conceived within the horizon of the question of *Being*—still an intrametaphysical effect of differance? Perhaps the deployment of differance is not only the truth or the epochality of Being. Perhaps we must try to think this *unheard-of* thought, this silent tracing, namely, that the history of Being (the thought of which is committed to the Greco-Western logos), as it is itself produced across the ontological difference, is only one epoch of the *diapherein*. Then we could no longer even call it an "epoch," for the concept of epochality belongs within history understood as the history of Being. Being has always made "sense," has always been conceived or spoken of as such, only by dissimulating itself in beings; thus, in a particular and very strange way, differance (is) "older" than the ontological difference or the truth of Being. In this age it can be called the play of traces. It is a trace that no longer belongs to the horizon of Being but one whose sense of Being is borne and bound by this play; it is a play of traces or differance that has no sense and is not, a play that does not belong. There is no support to be found and no depth to be had for this bottomless chessboard where being is set in play.

It is perhaps in this way that the Heraclitean play of the *hen diapheron heautōi*, of the one differing from itself, of what is in difference with itself, already becomes lost as a trace in determining the *diapherein* as ontological difference.

To think through the ontological difference doubtless remains a difficult task, a task whose statement has remained nearly inaudible. And to prepare ourselves for venturing beyond our own logos, that is, for a differance so violent that it refuses to be stopped and examined as the epochality of Being and ontological difference, is neither to give up this passage through the truth of Being, nor is it in any way to "criticize," "contest," or fail to recognize the incessant necessity for it. On the contrary, we must stay within the difficulty of this passage; we must repeat this passage in a rigorous reading of metaphysics, wherever metaphysics serves as the norm of Western speech, and not only in the texts of "the history of philosophy." Here we must allow the trace of whatever goes beyond the truth of Being to appear/disappear in its fully rigorous way. It is a trace of something that can never present itself; it is itself a trace that can never be presented, that is, can never appear and manifest itself as such in its phenomenon. It is a trace that lies beyond what profoundly ties fundamental ontology to phenomenology. Like differance, the trace is never presented as such. In presenting itself it becomes effaced; in being sounded it dies away, like the writing of the *a*, inscribing its pyramid in differance.

We can always reveal the precursive and secretive traces of this movement in metaphysical speech, especially in the contemporary talk about the closure of ontology, i.e., through the various attempts we have looked at (Nietzsche, Freud, Levinas)—and particularly in Heidegger's work.

The latter provokes us to question the essence of the present, the presence of the present.

What is the present? What is it to conceive the present in its presence?

Let us consider, for example, the 1946 text entitled "Der Spruch des Anaximander." Heidegger there recalls that the forgetting of Being forgets about the difference between Being and beings:

But the point of Being (*die Sache des Seins*) is to be the Being *of* beings. The linguistic form of this enigmatic and multivalent genitive designates a genesis (*Genesis*), a provenance (*Herkunft*) of the pre*sent* from pre*sence* (*des Anwesenden aus dem Anwesen*). But with the unfolding of these two, the essence (*Wesen*) of this provenance remains hidden (*verborgen*). Not only is the essence of this provenance not thought out, but neither is the simple relation between pre*sence* and pre*sent* (*Anwesen und Anwesendem*). Since the dawn, it seems that pre*sence* and being-pre*sent* are each separately something. Imperceptibly, pre*sence* becomes itself a pre*sent*. . . . The essence of pre*sence* (*Das Wesen des Anwesens*), and thus the difference between pre*sence* and pre*sent*, is forgotten. *The forgetting of Being is the forgetting of the difference between Being and beings.*[14]

In recalling the difference between Being and beings (the ontological difference) as the difference between presence and present, Heidegger puts forward a proposition, indeed, a group of propositions; it is not our intention here to idly or hastily "criticize" them but rather to convey them with all their provocative force.

Let us then proceed slowly. What Heidegger wants to point out is that the difference between Being and beings, forgotten by metaphysics, has disappeared without leaving a trace. The very trace of difference has sunk from sight. If we admit that differance (is) (itself) something other than presence and absence, if it *traces*, then we are dealing with the forgetting of the difference (between Being and beings), and we now have to talk about a disappearance of the trace's trace. This is certainly what this passage from "Der Spruch des Anaximander" seems to imply:

The forgetting of Being is a part of the very essence of Being, and is concealed by it. The forgetting belongs so essentially to the destination of Being that the dawn of this destination begins precisely as an unconcealment of the pre*sent* in its pre*sence*. This means: the history of Being begins by the forgetting of Being, in that Being retains its essence, its difference from beings. Difference is wanting; it remains forgotten. Only what is differentiated—the present and presence (*das Anwesende und das Anwesen*)—becomes uncovered, but not *insofar as* it is differentiated. On the contrary, the matinal trace (*die frühe Spur*) of difference effaces itself from the moment that presence appears as a being-present (*das Anwesen wie ein Anwesendes erscheint*) and finds its provenance in a supreme (being)-present (*in einem höchsten Anwesenden*).[15]

The trace is not a presence but is rather the simulacrum of a presence that dislocates, displaces, and refers beyond itself. The trace has, properly speaking, no place, for effacement belongs to the very structure of the trace. Effacement must always be able to overtake the trace; otherwise it would not be a trace but an indestructible and monumental substance. In addition, and from the start, effacement constitutes it as a trace—effacement establishes the trace in a change of place and makes it disappear in its appearing, makes it issue forth from itself in its very position. The effacing of this early trace (*die frühe Spur*) of difference is therefore "the same" as its tracing within the text of metaphysics. This metaphysical text must have retained a mark of what it lost or put in reserve, set aside. In the language of metaphysics the paradox of such a structure is the inversion of the metaphysical concept which produces the following effect: the present becomes the sign of signs, the trace of traces. It is no longer what every reference refers to in the last instance; it becomes a function in a generalized referential structure. It is a trace, and a trace of the effacement of a trace.

In this way the metaphysical text is *understood*; it is still readable, and remains to be read. It proposes *both* the monument and the mirage of the trace, the trace as simultaneously traced and effaced, simultaneously alive and dead, alive as always to simulate even life in its preserved inscription; it is a pyramid.

Thus we think through, without contradiction, or at least without granting any pertinence to such contradiction, what is perceptible and imperceptible about the trace. The "matinal trace" of difference is lost in an irretrievable invisibility, and yet even its loss is covered, preserved, regarded, and retarded. This happens in a text, in the form of presence.

Having spoken about the effacement of the matinal trace, Heidegger can thus, in this contradiction without contradiction, consign or countersign the sealing of the trace. We read on a little further:

The difference between Being and beings, however, can in turn be experienced as something forgotten only if it is already discovered with the presence of the present (*mit dem Anwesen des Anwesenden*) and if it is thus sealed in a trace (*so eine Spur geprägt hat*) that remains preserved (*gewahrt bleibt*) in the language which Being appropriates.[16]

Further on still, while meditating upon Anaximander's τὸ χρεών, translated as *Brauch* (sustaining use), Heidegger writes the following:

Dispensing accord and deference (*Fug und Ruch verfügend*), our sustaining use frees the pre*sent* (*das Anwesende*) in its sojourn and sets it free every time for its sojourn. But by the same token the present is equally seen to be exposed to the constant danger of hardening in the insistence (*in das blosse Beharren verhärtet*) out of its sojourning duration. In this way sustaining use (*Brauch*) remains itself and at the same time an abandonment (*Aushändigung*: handing-over) of presence (*des Anwesens*) *in den Un-fug*, to discord (disjointedness). Sustaining use joins together the dis- (*Der Brauch fügt dress Un-*).[17]

And it is at the point where Heidegger determines *sustaining use* as *trace* that the question must be asked: can we, and how far can we, think of this trace and the *dis-* of differance as *Wesen des Seins*? Doesn't the *dis* of differance refer us beyond the history of Being, beyond our language as well, and beyond everything that can be named by it? Doesn't it call for—in the language of being—the necessarily violent transformation of this language by an entirely different language?

Let us be more precise here. In order to dislodge the "trace" from its cover (and whoever believes that one tracks down some *thing*?—one tracks down tracks), let us continue reading this passage:

The translation of τò χρεών by "sustaining use" (*Brauch*) does not derive from cogitations of an etymo-logico-lexical nature. The choice of the word "sustaining use" derives from an antecedent *trans*lation (*Über*setzen) of the thought that attempts to conceive difference in the deployment of Being (*im Wesen des Seins*) toward the historical beginning of the forgetting of Being. The word "sustaining use" is dictated to thought in the apprehension (*Erfahrung*) of the forgetting of Being. Tò χρεών properly names a trace (*Spur*) of what remains to be conceived in the word "sustaining use," a trace that quickly disappears (*alsbald verschwindet*) into the history of Being, in its world-historical unfolding as Western metaphysics.[18]

How do we conceive of the outside of a text? How, for example, do we conceive of what stands opposed to the text of Western metaphysics? To be sure, the "trace that quickly disappears into the history of Being, . . . as Western metaphysics," escapes all the determinations, all the names it might receive in the metaphysical text. The trace is sheltered and thus dissimulated in these names; it does not appear in the text as the trace "itself." But this is because the trace itself could never itself appear as such. Heidegger also says that difference can never appear *as such*: "Lichtung des Unterschiedes kann deshalb auch nicht bedeuten, dass der Unterschied als der Unterschied erscheint." There is no essence of differance; not only can it not allow itself to be taken up into the *as such* of its name or its appearing, but it threatens the authority of the *as such* in general, the thing's presence in its essence. That there is no essence of differance at this point also implies that there is neither Being nor truth to the play of writing, *insofar* as it involves differance.

For us, differance remains a metaphysical name; and all the names that it receives from our language are still, so far as they are names, metaphysical. This is particularly so when they speak of determining difference as the difference between presence and present (*Anwesen/Anwesend*), but already and especially so when, in the most general way, they speak of determining differance as the difference between Being and beings.

"Older" than Being itself, our language has no name for such a differance. But we "already know" that if it is unnamable, this is not simply provisional; it is not because our language has still not found or received this *name*, or because we would have to look for it in another language, outside the finite system of our language. It is because there is no *name* for this, not even essence or Being—not even the name "differance," which is not a name, which is not a pure nominal unity, and continually breaks up in a chain of different substitutions.

"There is no name for this": we read this as a truism. What is unnamable here is not some ineffable being that cannot be approached by a name; like God, for example. What is unnamable is the play that brings about the nominal effects, the relatively unitary or atomic structures we call names, or chains of substitutions for names. In these, for example, the nominal effect of "differance" is itself involved, carried off, and reinscribed, just as the false beginning or end of a game is still part of the game, a function of the system.

What we do know, what we could know if it were simply a question of knowing, is that there never has been and never will be a unique word, a master name. This is why thinking about the letter *a* of differance is not the primary prescription, nor is it the prophetic announcement of some imminent and still unheard-of designation. There is nothing kerygmatic about this "word" so long as we can perceive its reduction to a lowercase letter.

There will be no unique name, not even the name of Being. It must be conceived without *nostalgia*; that is, it must be conceived outside the myth of the purely maternal or paternal language belonging to the lost fatherland of thought. On the contrary, we must *affirm* it—in the sense that Nietzsche brings affirmation into play—with a certain laughter and with a certain dance.

After this laughter and dance, after this affirmation that is foreign to any dialectic, the question arises as to the other side of nostalgia, which I will call Heideggerian *hope*. I am not unaware that this term may be somewhat shocking. I venture it all the same, without excluding any of its implications, and shall relate it to what seems to me to be retained of metaphysics in "Der Spruch des Anaximander," namely, the quest for the proper word and the unique name. In talking about the "first word of Being" (*das frühe Wort des Seins: τὸ χρεών*), Heidegger writes,

The relation to the pre*sent*, unfolding its order in the very essence of pre*sence*, is unique (*ist eine einzige*). It is pre-eminently incomparable to any other relation; it belongs to the uniqueness of Being itself (*Sie gehört zur Einzigkeit des Seins selbst*). Thus, in order to name what is deployed in Being (*das Wesende des Seins*), language will have to find a single word, the unique word (*ein einziges, das einzige Wort*). There we see how hazardous is every word of thought (every thoughtful word: *denkende Wort*) that addresses itself to Being (*das dem Sein zugesprochen wird*). What is hazarded here, however, is not something impossible, because Being speaks through every language; everywhere and always.[19]

Such is the question: the marriage between speech and Being in the unique word, in the finally proper name. Such is the question that enters into the affirmation put into play by differance. The question bears (upon) each of the words in this sentence: "Being / speaks / through every language; / everywhere and always /."

Notes

1. [The reader should bear in mind that "differance," or difference with an *a*, incorporates two significations: "to differ" and "to defer."—Translator.]

2. [For the term "facilitation" (*frayage*) in Freud, cf. "Project for a Scientific Psychology I" in *The Complete Psychological Works of Sigmund Freud*, 24 vols. (New York and London: Macmillan, 1964), I, 300, note 4 by the translator, James Strachey: "The word 'facilitation' as a rendering of the German '*Bahnung*' seems to have been introduced by Sherrington a few years after the *Project* was written. The German word, however, was already in use." The sense that Derrida draws upon here is stronger in the French or German; that is, the opening-up or clearing-out of a pathway. In the context of the "Project for a Scientific Psychology I," facilitation denotes the conduction capability that results from a difference in resistance levels in the memory and perception circuits of the nervous system. Thus, lowering the resistance threshold of a contact barrier serves to "open up" a nerve pathway and "facilitates" the excitatory process for the circuit. Cf. also J. Derrida, *L'Ecriture et la différence*, Chap. VII, "Freud et la scène de l'écriture" (Paris: Seuil, 1967), esp. pp. 297–305.—Translator.]

3. [On "pyramid" and "tomb" see J. Derrida, "Le Puits et la pyramide" in *Hegel et la pensée moderne* (Paris: Presses Universitaires de France, 1970), esp. pp. 44–45.—Translator.]

4. Ferdinand de Saussure, *Cours de linguistique générale*, ed. C. Bally and A. Sechehaye (Paris: Payot, 1916); English translation by Wade Baskin, *Course in General Linguistics* (New York: Philosophical Library, 1959), pp. 117–18, 120.

5. *Course in General Linguistics*, p. 18.

6. [On "supplement" see above, *Speech and Phenomena*, Chap. 7, pp. 88–104. Cf. also Derrida, *De la grammatologie* (Paris: Editions de Minuit, 1967). On "*pharmakon*" see Derrida, "La Pharmacie de Platon," *Tel Quel*, No. 32 (Winter, 1967), pp. 17–59; No. 33 (Spring, 1968), pp. 4–48. On "hymen" see Derrida, "La Double séance," *Tel Quel*, No. 41 (Spring, 1970), pp. 3–43; No. 42 (Summer, 1970), pp. 3–45. "La Pharmacie de Platon" and "La Double séance" have been reprinted in a recent text of Derrida, *La Dissémination* (Paris: Editions du Seuil, 1972).—Translator.]

7. [Derrida often brackets or "crosses out" certain key terms taken from metaphysics and logic, and in doing this, he follows Heidegger's usage in *Zur Seinsfrage*. The terms in question no longer have their full meaning, they no longer have the status of a purely signified content of expression—no longer, that is, after the deconstruction of metaphysics. Generated out of the play of differance, they still retain a vestigial trace of sense, however, a trace that cannot simply be gotten around (*incontourable*). An extensive discussion of all this is to be found in *De la grammatologie*, pp. 31–40.—Translator.]

8. Alexandre Koyré, "Hegel à Jéna," *Revue d'histoire et de philosophie religieuse*, XIV (1934), 420–58; reprinted in Koyré, *Etudes d'histoire de la pensée philosophique* (Paris: Armand Colin, 1961), pp. 135–73.

9. Koyré, *Etudes d'histoire*, pp. 153–54. [The quotation from Hegel (my translation) comes from "Jenenser Logik, Metaphysik, und Naturphilosophie," *Sämtliche Werke* (Leipzig: F. Meiner, 1925), XVIII, 202. Koyré reproduces the original German text on pp. 153–54, note 2.—Translator.]

10. De Saussure, *Course in General Linguistics*, p. 37.

11. G. Deleuze, *Nietzsche et la philosophie* (Paris: Presses Universitaires de France, 1970), p. 49.

12. Freud, *Complete Psychological Works*, XVIII, 10.

13. Derrida, *L'Ecriture et la difference*, pp. 369–407.

14. Martin Heidegger, *Holzwege* (Frankfurt: V. Klostermann, 1957), pp. 335–36. [All translations of quotations from *Holzwege* are mine.—Translator.]

15. *Ibid.*, p. 336.

16. *Ibid.*

17. *Ibid.*, pp. 339–40.

18. *Ibid.*, p. 340.

19. *Ibid.*, pp. 337–38.

VI Exchange, Gift, Communication

25   The Fetishism of the Commodity and Its Secret | The Process of Exchange

Karl Marx

The Fetishism of the Commodity and Its Secret

A commodity appears at first sight an extremely obvious, trivial thing. But its analysis brings out that it is a very strange thing, abounding in metaphysical subtleties and theological niceties. So far as it is a use-value, there is nothing mysterious about it, whether we consider it from the point of view that by its properties it satisfies human needs, or that it first takes on these properties as the product of human labour. It is absolutely clear that, by his activity, man changes the forms of the materials of nature in such a way as to make them useful to him. The form of wood, for instance, is altered if a table is made out of it. Nevertheless the table continues to be wood, an ordinary, sensuous thing. But as soon as it emerges as a commodity, it changes into a thing which transcends sensuousness. It not only stands with its feet on the ground; but, in relation to all other commodities, it stands on its head, and evolves out of its wooden brain grotesque ideas, far more wonderful than if it were to begin dancing of its own free will.[1]

The mystical character of the commodity does not therefore arise from its use-value. Just as little does it proceed from the nature of the determinants of value. For in the first place, however varied the useful kinds of labour, or productive activities, it is a physiological fact that they are functions of the human organism, and that each such function, whatever may be its nature or its form, is essentially the expenditure of human brain, nerves, muscles and sense organs. Secondly, with regard to the foundation of the quantitative determination of value, namely the duration of that expenditure or the quantity of labour, this is quite palpably different from its quality: In all situations, the labour-time it costs to produce the means of subsistence must necessarily concern mankind, although not to the same degree at different stages of development.[2] And finally, as soon as men start to work for each other in any way, their labour also assumes a social form.

Whence, then, arises the enigmatic character of the product of labour, as soon as it assumes the form of a commodity? Clearly, it arises from this form itself. The equality of the kinds of human labour takes on a physical form in the equal objectivity of the products of labour as values; the measure of the expenditure of human labour-power by its duration takes on the form of the magnitude of the value of the products of labour; and finally the relationships between the producers, within which the social characteristics of their labours are manifested, take on the form of a social relation between the products of labour.

The mysterious character of the commodity-form consists therefore simply in the fact that the commodity reflects the social characteristics of men's own labour as objective characteristics of the products of labour themselves, as the socio-natural properties of these things. Hence it also reflects the social relation of the producers to the sum total of labour as a social relation between objects, a relation which exists apart from and outside the producers. Through this substitution, the products of labour become commodities, sensuous things which are at the same time supra-sensible or social. In the same way, the impression made by a thing on the optic nerve is perceived not as a subjective excitation of that nerve but as the objective form of a thing outside the eye. In the act of seeing, of course, light is really transmitted from one thing, the external object, to another thing, the eye. It is a physical relation between physical things. As against this, the commodity-form, and the value-relation of the products of labour within which it appears, have absolutely no connection with the physical nature of the commodity and the material [*dinglich*] relations arising out of this. It is nothing but the definite social relation between men themselves which assumes here, for them, the fantastic form of a relation between things. In order, therefore, to find an analogy we must take flight into the misty realm of religion. There the products of the human brain appear as autonomous figures endowed with a life of their own, which enter into relations both with each other and with the human race. So it is in the world of commodities with the products of men's hands. I call this the fetishism which attaches itself to the products of labour as soon as they are produced as commodities, and is therefore inseparable from the production of commodities.

As the foregoing analysis has already demonstrated, this fetishism of the world of commodities arises from the peculiar social character of the labour which produces them.

Objects of utility become commodities only because they are the products of the labour of private individuals who work independently of each other. The sum total of the labour of all these private individuals forms the aggregate labour of society. Since the producers do not come into social contact until they exchange the products of their labour, the specific social characteristics of their private labours appear only within this exchange. In other words, the labour of the private individual manifests itself as an element of the total labour of society only through the relations which the act of exchange establishes between the products, and, through their mediation, between the producers. To the producers, therefore, the social relations between their private labours appear as what they are, i.e., they do not appear as direct social relations between persons in their work, but rather as material [*dinglich*] relations between persons and social relations between things.

It is only by being exchanged that the products of labour acquire a socially uniform objectivity as values, which is distinct from their sensuously varied objectivity as articles of utility. This division of the product of labour into a useful thing and a thing possessing value appears in practice only when exchange has already acquired a sufficient extension and importance to allow useful things to be produced for the purpose of being exchanged, so that their character as values has already to be taken into consideration during production. From this moment on, the labour of the individual producer acquires a twofold social character. On the one hand, it must, as a definite useful kind of labour, satisfy a definite social need, and thus maintain its position as an element of the total labour, as a branch of the social division of labour, which originally sprang up spontaneously. On the other hand, it can satisfy the manifold needs of the individual producer himself only in so far as every particular kind of useful private labour can be exchanged with, i.e., counts as the equal of, every other kind of useful private labour. Equality in the full sense between different kinds of labour can be arrived at only if we abstract from their real inequality, if we reduce them to the characteristic they have in common, that of being the expenditure of human labour-power, of human labour in the abstract. The private producer's brain reflects this twofold social character of his labour only in the forms which appear in practical intercourse, in the exchange of products. Hence the socially useful character of his private labour is reflected in the form that the product of labour has to be useful to others, and the social character of the equality of the various kinds of labour is reflected in the form of the common character, as values, possessed by these materially different things, the products of labour.

Men do not therefore bring the products of their labour into relation with each other as values because they see these objects merely as the material integuments of homogeneous human labour. The reverse is true: by equating their different products to each other in exchange as values, they equate their different kinds of labour as human labour. They do this without being aware of it.[3] Value, therefore, does not have its description branded on its forehead; it rather transforms every product of labour into a social hieroglyphic. Later on, men try to decipher the hieroglyphic, to get behind the secret of their own social product: for the characteristic which objects of utility have of being values is as much men's social product as is their language. The belated scientific discovery that the products of labour, in so far as they are values, are merely the material expressions of the human labour expended to produce them, marks an epoch in the history of mankind's development, but by no means banishes the semblance of objectivity possessed by the social characteristics of labour. Something which is only valid for this particular form of production, the production of commodities, namely the fact that the specific social character of private labours carried on independently of each other consists in their equality as human labour, and, in the product, assumes the form of the existence of value, appears to those caught up in the relations of commodity production (and this is true both before and after the above-mentioned scientific discovery) to be just as ultimately valid as the fact that the scientific dissection of the air into its component parts left the atmosphere itself unaltered in its physical configuration.

What initially concerns producers in practice when they make an exchange is how much of some other product they get for their own; in what proportions can the products be exchanged? As soon as these proportions have attained a certain customary stability, they appear to result from the nature of the products, so that, for instance, one ton of iron and two ounces of gold appear to be equal in value, in the same way as a pound of gold and a pound of iron are equal in weight, despite their different physical and chemical properties. The value character of the products of labour becomes firmly established only when they act as magnitudes of value. These magnitudes vary continually, independently of the will, foreknowledge and actions of the exchangers. Their own movement within society has for them the form of a movement made by things, and these things, far from being under their control, in fact control them. The production of commodities must be fully developed before the scientific conviction emerges, from experience itself, that all the different kinds of private labour (which, are carried on independently of each other, and yet, as spontaneously developed branches of the social division of labour, are in a situation of all-round dependence on each other) are continually being reduced to the quantitative proportions in which society requires them. The reason for this reduction is that in the midst of the accidental and ever-fluctuating exchange relations between the products, the labour-time socially necessary to produce them asserts itself as a regulative law of nature. In the same way, the law of gravity asserts itself when a person's house collapses on top of him.[4] The determination of the magnitude of value by labour-time is therefore a secret hidden under the apparent movements in the relative values of commodities. Its discovery destroys the semblance of the merely accidental determination of the magnitude of the value of the products of labour, but by no means abolishes that determination's material form.

Reflection on the forms of human life, hence also scientific analysis of those forms, takes a course directly opposite to their real development. Reflection begins *post festum,** and therefore with the results of the process of development ready to hand. The forms which stamp products as commodities and which are therefore the preliminary requirements for the circulation of commodities, already possess the fixed quality of natural forms of social life before man seeks to give an account, not of their historical character, for in his eyes they are immutable, but of their content and meaning. Consequently, it was solely the analysis of the prices of commodities which led to the determination of the magnitude of value, and solely the common expression of all commodities in money which led to the establishment of their character as values. It is however precisely this finished form of the world of commodities—the money form—which conceals the social character of private labour and the social relations between the individual workers, by making those relations appear as relations between material objects, instead of revealing them plainly. If I state that coats or boots stand in a relation to linen because the latter is the universal incarnation of abstract human labour, the absurdity of the statement is self-evident. Nevertheless, when the producers of coats and boots bring these commodities into a relation with linen, or with gold or silver (and this makes no difference here), as the universal equivalent, the relation

* "After the feast," i.e. after the events reflected on have taken place.

between their own private labour and the collective labour of society appears to them in exactly this absurd form.

The categories of bourgeois economics consist precisely of forms of this kind. They are forms of thought which are socially valid, and therefore objective, for the relations of production belonging to this historically determined mode of social production, i.e. commodity production. The whole mystery of commodities, all the magic and necromancy that surrounds the products of labour on the basis of commodity production, vanishes therefore as soon as we come to other forms of production.

As political economists are fond of Robinson Crusoe stories,[5] let us first look at Robinson on his island. Undemanding though he is by nature, he still has needs to satisfy, and must therefore perform useful labours of various kinds: he must make tools, knock together furniture, tame llamas, fish, hunt and so on. Of his prayers and the like, we take no account here, since our friend takes pleasure in them and sees them as recreation. Despite the diversity of his productive functions, he knows that they are only different forms of activity of one and the same Robinson, hence only different modes of human labour. Necessity itself compels him to divide his time with precision between his different functions. Whether one function occupies a greater space in his total activity than another depends on the magnitude of the difficulties to be overcome in attaining the useful effect aimed at. Our friend Robinson Crusoe learns this by experience, and having saved a watch, ledger, ink and pen from the shipwreck, he soon begins, like a good Englishman, to keep a set of books. His stock-book contains a catalogue of the useful objects he possesses, of the various operations necessary for their production, and finally of the labour-time that specific quantities of these products have on average cost him. All the relations between Robinson and these objects that form his self-created wealth are here so simple and transparent that even Mr Sedley Taylor* could understand them. And yet those relations contain all the essential determinants of value.

Let us now transport ourselves from Robinson's island, bathed in light, to medieval Europe, shrouded in darkness. Here, instead of the independent man, we find everyone dependent—serfs and lords, vassals and suzerains, laymen and clerics. Personal dependence characterizes the social relations of material production as much as it does the other spheres of life based on that production. But precisely because relations of personal dependence form the given social foundation, there is no need for labour and its products to assume a fantastic form different from their reality. They take the shape, in the transactions of society, of services in kind and payments in kind. The natural form of labour, its

---

* The original German has here "Herr M. Wirth," chosen by Marx as a run-of-the-mill vulgar economist and propagandist familiar to German readers. Engels introduced "Mr Sedley Taylor," a Cambridge don against whom he polemicized in his preface to the fourth German edition (see above, p. 117).

particularity—and not, as in a society based on commodity production, its universality—is here its immediate social form. The *corvée* can be measured by time just as well as the labour which produces commodities, but every serf knows that what he expends in the service of his lord is a specific quantity of his own personal labour-power. The tithe owed to the priest is more clearly apparent than his blessing. Whatever we may think, then, of the different roles in which men confront each other in such a society, the social relations between individuals in the performance of their labour appear at all events as their own personal relations, and are not disguised as social relations between things, between the products of labour.

For an example of labour in common, i.e. directly associated labour, we do not need to go back to the spontaneously developed form which we find at the threshold of the history of all civilized peoples.[6] We have one nearer to hand in the patriarchal rural industry of a peasant family which produces corn, cattle, yarn, linen and clothing for its own use. These things confront the family as so many products of its collective labour, but they do not confront each other as commodities. The different kinds of labour which create these products—such as tilling the fields, tending the cattle, spinning, weaving and making clothes—are already in their natural form social functions; for they are functions of the family, which, just as much as a society based on commodity production, possesses its own spontaneously developed division of labour. The distribution of labour within the family and the labour-time expended by the individual members of the family, are regulated by differences of sex and age as well as by seasonal variations in the natural conditions of labour. The fact that the expenditure of the individual labour-powers is measured by duration appears here, by its very nature, as a social characteristic of labour itself, because the individual labour-powers, by their very nature, act only as instruments of the joint labour-power of the family.

Let us finally imagine, for a change, an association of free men, working with the means of production held in common, and expending their many different forms of labour-power in full self-awareness as one single social labour force. All the characteristics of Robinson's labour are repeated here, but with the difference that they are social instead of individual. All Robinson's products were exclusively the result of his own personal labour and they were therefore directly objects of utility for him personally. The total product of our imagined association is a social product. One part of this product serves as fresh means of production and remains social. But another part is consumed by the members of the association as means of subsistence. This part must therefore be divided amongst them. The way this division is made will vary with the particular kind of social organization of production and the corresponding level of social development attained by the producers. We shall assume, but only for the sake of a parallel with the production of commodities, that the share of each individual producer in the means of subsistence is determined by his labour-time. Labour-time would in that case play a double part. Its apportionment in accordance with a definite social plan maintains the correct proportion between the different functions of labour and the various needs of the associations. On the other hand, labour-time also serves as a measure of the part taken by each individual in the common labour, and of his share in the part of the total product destined for individual consumption. The social relations of the individual producers, both towards their labour and the products of their labour, are here transparent in their simplicity, in production as well as in distribution.

For a society of commodity producers, whose general social relation of production consists in the fact that they treat their products as commodities, hence as values, and in this material [*sachlich*] form bring their individual, private labours into relation with each other as homogeneous human labour, Christianity with its religious cult of man in the abstract, more particularly in its bourgeois development, i.e., in Protestantism, Deism, etc., is the most fitting form of religion. In the ancient Asiatic, Classical-antique, and other such modes of production, the transformation of the product into a commodity, and therefore men's existence as producers of commodities, plays a subordinate role, which however increases in importance as these communities approach nearer and nearer to the stage of their dissolution. Trading nations, properly so called, exist only in the interstices of the ancient world, like the gods of Epicurus in the *intermundia*,* or Jews in the pores of Polish society. Those ancient social organisms of production are much more simple and transparent than those of bourgeois society. But they are founded either on the immaturity of man as an individual, when he has not yet torn himself loose from the umbilical cord of his natural species-connection with other men, or on direct relations of dominance and servitude. They are conditioned by a low stage of development of the productive powers of labour and correspondingly limited relations between men within the process of creating and reproducing their material life, hence also limited relations between man and nature. These real limitations are reflected in the ancient worship of nature, and in other elements of tribal religions. The religious reflections of the real world can, in any case, vanish only when the practical relations of everyday life between man and man, and man and nature, generally present themselves to him in a transparent and rational form. The veil is not removed from the countenance of the social life-process, i.e. the process of material production, until it becomes production by freely associated men, and stands under their conscious and planned control. This, however, requires that society possess a material foundation, or a series of material conditions of existence, which in their turn are the natural and spontaneous product of a long and tormented historical development.

Political economy has indeed analysed value and its magnitude, however incompletely,[7] and has uncovered the content concealed within these forms. But it has never once asked

* According to the Greek philosopher Epicurus (*c.* 341–*c.* 270 B.C.), the gods existed only in the *intermundia*, or spaces between different worlds, and had no influence on the course of human affairs. Very few of the writings of Epicurus have been preserved in the original Greek, and this particular idea survived only by being included in Cicero, *De natura deorum*, Book I, Section 18.

the question why this content has assumed that particular form, that is to say, why labour is expressed in value, and why the measurement of labour by its duration is expressed in the magnitude of the value of the product.[8] These formulas, which bear the unmistakable stamp of belonging to a social formation in which the process of production has mastery over man, instead of the opposite, appear to the political economists' bourgeois consciousness to be as much a self-evident and nature-imposed necessity as productive labour itself. Hence the pre-bourgeois forms of the social organization of production are treated by political economy in much the same way as the Fathers of the Church treated pre-Christian religions.[9]

The degree to which some economists are misled by the fetishism attached to the world of commodities, or by the objective appearance of the social characteristics of labour, is shown, among other things, by the dull and tedious dispute over the part played by nature in the formation of exchange-value. Since exchange-value is a definite social manner of expressing the labour bestowed on a thing, it can have no more natural content than has, for example, the rate of exchange.

As the commodity-form is the most general and the most undeveloped form of bourgeois production, it makes its appearance at an early date, though not in the same predominant and therefore characteristic manner as nowadays. Hence its fetish character is still relatively easy to penetrate. But when we come to more concrete forms, even this appearance of simplicity vanishes. Where did the illusions of the Monetary System come from? The adherents of the Monetary System did not see gold and silver as representing money as a social relation of production, but in the form of natural objects with peculiar social properties. And what of modern political economy, which looks down so disdainfully on the Monetary System? Does not its fetishism become quite palpable when it deals with capital? How long is it since the disappearance of the Physiocratic illusion that ground rent grows out of the soil, not out of society?

But, to avoid anticipating, we will content ourselves here with one more example relating to the commodity-form itself. If commodities could speak, they would say this: our use-value may interest men, but it does not belong to us as objects. What does belong to us as objects, however, is our value. Our own intercourse as commodities proves it. We relate to each other merely as exchange-values. Now listen how those commodities speak through the mouth of the economist:

"Value (i.e. exchange-value) is a property of things, riches (i.e. use-value) of man. Value, in this sense, necessarily implies exchanges, riches do not."[10]

"Riches (use-value) are the attribute of man, value is the attribute of commodities. A man or a community is rich, a pearl or a diamond is valuable . . . A pearl or a diamond is valuable as a pearl or diamond."[11]

So far no chemist has ever discovered exchange-value either in a pearl or a diamond. The economists who have discovered this chemical substance, and who lay special claim to critical acumen, nevertheless find that the use-value of material objects belongs to them independently of their material properties, while their value, on the other hand, forms a part of them as objects. What confirms them in this view is the peculiar circumstance that the use-value of a thing is realized without exchange, i.e. in the direct relation between the thing and man, while, inversely, its value is realized only in exchange, i.e. in a social process. Who would not call to mind at this point the advice given by the good Dogberry to the night-watchman Seacoal?*

"To be a well-favoured man is the gift of fortune; but reading and writing comes by nature."[12]

The Process of Exchange

Commodities cannot themselves go to market and perform exchanges in their own right. We must, therefore, have recourse to their guardians, who are the possessors of commodities. Commodities are things, and therefore lack the power to resist man. If they are unwilling, he can use force; in other words, he can take possession of them.[13] In order that these objects may enter into relation with each other as commodities, their guardians must place themselves in relation to one another as persons whose will resides in those objects, and must behave in such a way that each does not appropriate the commodity of the other, and alienate his own, except through an act to which both parties consent. The guardians must therefore recognize each other as owners of private property. This juridical relation, whose form is the contract, whether as part of a developed legal system or not, is a relation between two wills which mirrors the economic relation. The content of this juridical relation (or relation of two wills) is itself determined by the economic relation.[14] Here the persons exist for one another merely as representatives and hence owners, of commodities. As we proceed to develop our investigation, we shall find, in general, that the characters who appear on the economic stage are merely personifications of economic relations; it is as the bearers[†] of these economic relations that they come into contact with each other.

What chiefly distinguishes a commodity from its owner is the fact that every other commodity counts for it only as the form of appearance of its own value. A born leveller and cynic, it is always ready to exchange not only soul, but body, with each and every other commodity, be it more repulsive than Maritornes herself.[††] The owner makes up for this lack in the commodity of a sense of the concrete, physical body of the other commodity, by his own five and more senses. For the owner, his commodity possesses no direct use-value. Otherwise, he would not bring it to market. It has use-value for others; but for himself its only direct use-value is as a bearer of exchange-value, and consequently, a means of

* In Shakespeare's comedy *Much Ado About Nothing*, Act 3, Scene 3.

† The concept of an object (or person) as the receptacle, repository, bearer [*Träger*] of some thing or tendency quite different from it appears repeatedly in *Capital*, and I have tried to translate it uniformly as "bearer."

†† Maritornes: a character from Cervantes' novel *Don Quixote*.

exchange.[15] He therefore makes up his mind to sell it in return for commodities whose use-value is of service to him. All commodities are non-use-values for their owners, and use-values for their non-owners. Consequently, they must all change hands. But this changing of hands constitutes their exchange, and their exchange puts them in relation with each other as values and realizes them as values. Hence commodities must be realized as values before they can be realized as use-values.

On the other hand, they must stand the test as use-values before they can be realized as values. For the labour expended on them only counts in so far as it is expended in a form which is useful for others. However, only the act of exchange can prove whether that labour is useful for others, and its product consequently capable of satisfying the needs of others.

The owner of a commodity is prepared to part with it only in return for other commodities whose use-value satisfies his own need. So far, exchange is merely an individual process for him. On the other hand, he desires to realize his commodity, as a value, in any other suitable commodity of the same value. It does not matter to him whether his own commodity has any use-value for the owner of the other commodity or not. From this point of view, exchange is for him a general social process. But the same process cannot be simultaneously for all owners of commodities both exclusively individual and exclusively social and general.

Let us look at the matter a little more closely. To the owner of a commodity, every other commodity counts as the particular equivalent of his own commodity. Hence his own commodity is the universal equivalent for all the others. But since this applies to every owner, there is in fact no commodity acting as universal equivalent, and the commodities possess no general relative form of value under which they can be equated as values and have the magnitude of their values compared. Therefore they definitely do not confront each other as commodities, but as products or use-values only.

In their difficulties our commodity-owners think like Faust: "In the beginning was the deed."* They have therefore already acted before thinking. The natural laws of the commodity have manifested themselves in the natural instinct of the owners of commodities. They can only bring their commodities into relation as values, and therefore as commodities, by bringing them into an opposing relation with some one other commodity, which serves as the universal equivalent. We have already reached that result by our analysis of the commodity. But only the action of society can turn a particular commodity into the universal equivalent. The social action of all other commodities, therefore, sets apart the particular commodity in which they all represent their values. The natural form of this commodity thereby becomes the socially recognized equivalent form. Through the agency of the social process it becomes the specific social function of the commodity which has been set apart to be the universal equivalent. It thus becomes—money.

* "Im Anfang war die Tat" (Goethe, Faust, Part I, Scene 3, Faust's Study, line 1237).

"Illi unum consilium habent et virtutem et potestatem suam bestiae tradunt . . . Et ne quis possit emere aut vendere, nisi qui habet characterem aut nomen bestiae, aut numerum nominis eius" (Apocalypse).*

Money necessarily crystallizes out of the process of exchange, in which different products of labour are in fact equated with each other, and thus converted into commodities. The historical broadening and deepening of the phenomenon of exchange develops the opposition between use-value and value which is latent in the nature of the commodity. The need to give an external expression to this opposition for the purposes of commercial intercourse produces the drive towards an independent form of value, which finds neither rest nor peace until an independent form has been achieved by the differentiation of commodities into commodities and money. At the same rate, then, as the transformation of the products of labour into commodities is accomplished, one particular commodity is transformed into money.[16]

The direct exchange of products has the form of the simple expression of value in one respect, but not as yet in another. That form was x commodity A = y commodity B. The form of the direct exchange of products is x use-value A = y use value B.[17] The articles A and B in this case are not as yet commodities, but become so only through the act of exchange. The first way in which an object of utility attains the possibility of becoming an exchange-value is to exist as a non-use-value, as a quantum of use-value superfluous to the immediate needs of its owner. Things are in themselves external to man, and therefore alienable. In order that this alienation [*Veräusserung*] may be reciprocal, it is only necessary for men to agree tacitly to treat each other as the private owners of those alienable things, and, precisely for that reason, as persons who are independent of each other. But this relationship of reciprocal isolation and foreignness does not exist for the members of a primitive community of natural origin, whether it takes the form of a patriarchal family, an ancient Indian commune or an Inca state. The exchange of commodities begins where communities have their boundaries, at their points of contact with other communities, or with members of the latter. However, as soon as products have become commodities in the external relations of a community, they also, by reaction, become commodities in the internal life of the community. Their quantitative exchange-relation is at first determined purely by chance. They become exchangeable through the mutual desire of their owners to alienate them. In the meantime, the need for others' objects of utility gradually establishes itself. The constant repetition of exchange makes it a normal social process. In the course of time, therefore, at least some part of the products must be produced intentionally for the purpose of exchange. From that moment the distinction between the usefulness of things for direct consumption and their usefulness in exchange becomes firmly established. Their use-value becomes distinguished from their exchange-value. On the other hand, the quantitative proportion in

---

* "These have one mind, and shall give their power and strength unto the beast" (Revelation 17: 13). "And that no man might buy or sell, save that he had the mark, or the name of the beast, or the number of his name" (Revelation 13: 17).

which the things are exchangeable becomes dependent on their production itself. Custom fixes their values at definite magnitudes.

In the direct exchange of products, each commodity is a direct means of exchange to its owner, and an equivalent to those who do not possess it, although only in so far as it has use-value for them. At this stage, therefore, the articles exchanged do not acquire a value-form independent of their own use-value, or of the individual needs of the exchangers. The need for this form first develops with the increase in the number and variety of the commodities entering into the process of exchange. The problem and the means for its solution arise simultaneously. Commercial intercourse, in which the owners of commodities exchange and compare their own articles with various other articles, never takes place unless different kinds of commodities belonging to different owners are exchanged for, and equated as values with, one single further kind of commodity. This further commodity, by becoming the equivalent of various other commodities, directly acquires the form of a universal or social equivalent, if only within narrow limits. The universal equivalent form comes and goes with the momentary social contacts which call it into existence. It is transiently attached to this or that commodity in alternation. But with the development of exchange it fixes itself firmly and exclusively onto particular kinds of commodity, i.e., it crystallizes out into the money-form. The particular kind of commodity to which it sticks is at first a matter of accident. Nevertheless there are two circumstances which are by and large decisive. The money-form comes to be attached either to the most important articles of exchange from outside, which are in fact the primitive and spontaneous forms of manifestation of the exchange-value of local products, or to the object of utility which forms the chief element of indigenous alienable wealth, for example cattle. Nomadic peoples are the first to develop the money-form, because all their worldly possessions are in a movable and therefore directly alienable form, and because their mode of life, by continually bringing them into contact with foreign communities, encourages the exchange of products. Men have often made man himself into the primitive material of money, in the shape of the slave, but they have never done this with the land and soil. Such an idea could only arise in a bourgeois society, and one which was already well developed. It dates from the last third of the seventeenth century, and the first attempt to implement the idea on a national scale was made a century later, during the French bourgeois revolution.*

In the same proportion as exchange bursts its local bonds, and the value of commodities accordingly expands more and more into the material embodiment of human labour as such, in that proportion does the money-form become transferred to commodities which are by nature fitted to perform the social function of a universal equivalent. Those commodities are the precious metals.

The truth of the statement that "although gold and silver are not by nature money, money is by nature gold and silver,"[18] is shown by the appropriateness of their natural

---

* The issue of the *assignats* in 1789, backed by confiscated Church lands.

properties for the functions of money.[19] So far, however, we are acquainted with only one function of money, namely to serve as the form of appearance of the value of commodities, that is as the material in which the magnitudes of their values are socially expressed. Only a material whose every sample possesses the same uniform quality can be an adequate form of appearance of value, that is a material embodiment of abstract and therefore equal human labour. On the other hand, since the difference between the magnitudes of value is purely quantitative, the money commodity must be capable of purely quantitative differentiation, it must therefore be divisible at will, and it must also be possible to assemble it again from its component parts. Gold and silver possess these properties by nature.

The money commodity acquires a dual use-value. Alongside its special use-value as a commodity (gold, for instance, serves to fill hollow teeth, it forms the raw material for luxury articles, etc.) it acquires a formal use-value, arising out of its specific social function.

Since all other commodities are merely particular equivalents for money, the latter being their universal equivalent, they relate to money as particular commodities relate to the universal commodity.[20]

We have seen that the money-form is merely the reflection thrown upon a single commodity by the relations between all other commodities. That money is a commodity[21] is therefore only a discovery for those who proceed from its finished shape in order to analyse it afterwards. The process of exchange gives to the commodity which it has converted into money not its value but its specific value-form. Confusion between these two attributes has misled some writers into maintaining that the value of gold and silver is imaginary.[22] The fact that money can, in certain functions, be replaced by mere symbols of itself, gave rise to another mistaken notion, that it is itself a mere symbol. Nevertheless, this error did contain the suspicion that the money-form of the thing is external to the thing itself, being simply the form of appearance of human relations hidden behind it. In this sense every commodity is a symbol, since, as value, it is only the material shell of the human labour expended on it.[23] But if it is declared that the social characteristics assumed by material objects, or the material characteristics assumed by the social determinations of labour on the basis of a definite mode of production, are mere symbols, then it is also declared, at the same time, that these characteristics are the arbitrary product of human reflection. This was the kind of explanation favoured by the eighteenth century: in this way the Enlightenment endeavoured, at least temporarily, to remove the appearance of strangeness from the mysterious shapes assumed by human relations whose origins they were unable to decipher.

It has already been remarked above that the equivalent form of a commodity does not imply that the magnitude of its value can be determined. Therefore, even if we know that gold is money, and consequently directly exchangeable with all other commodities, this still does not tell us how much 10lb. of gold is worth, for instance. Money, like every other commodity, cannot express the magnitude of its value except relatively in other commodities. This value is determined by the labour-time required for its production, and is expressed in the quantity of any other commodity in which the same amount of labour-time is congealed.[24] This establishing of its relative value occurs at the source of its production by means of barter. As soon as it enters into circulation as money, its value is already given. In the last decades of the seventeenth century the first step in the analysis of money, the discovery that money is a commodity, had already been taken; but this was merely the first step, and nothing more. The difficulty lies not in comprehending that money is a commodity, but in discovering how, why and by what means a commodity becomes money.[25]

We have already seen, from the simplest expression of value, x commodity A = y commodity B, that the thing in which the magnitude of the value of another thing is represented appears to have the equivalent form independently of this relation, as a social property inherent in its nature. We followed the process by which this false semblance became firmly established, a process which was completed when the universal equivalent form became identified with the natural form of a particular commodity, and thus crystallized into the money-form. What appears to happen is not that a particular commodity becomes money because all other commodities express their values in it, but, on the contrary, that all other commodities universally express their values in a particular commodity because it is money. The movement through which this process has been mediated vanishes in its own result, leaving no trace behind. Without any initiative on their part, the commodities find their own value-configuration ready to hand, in the form of a physical commodity existing outside but also alongside them. This physical object, gold or silver in its crude state, becomes, immediately on its emergence from the bowels of the earth, the direct incarnation of all human labour. Hence the magic of money. Men are henceforth related to each other in their social process of production in a purely atomistic way. Their own relations of production therefore assume a material shape which is independent of their control and their conscious individual action. This situation is manifested first by the fact that the products of men's labour universally take on the form of commodities. The riddle of the money fetish is therefore the riddle of the commodity fetish, now become visible and dazzling to our eyes.

Notes

1. One may recall that China and the tables began to dance when the rest of the world appeared to be standing still—*pour encourager les autres.**

* "To encourage the others." A reference to the simultaneous emergence in the 1850s of the Taiping revolt in China and the craze for spiritualism which swept over upper-class German society. The rest of the world was "standing still" in the period of reaction immediately after the defeat of the 1848 Revolutions.

2. Among the ancient Germans the size of a piece of land was measured according to the labour of a day; hence the acre was called *Tagwerk, Tagwanne* (*jurnale*, or *terra jurnalis*, or *diornalis*), *Mannwerk, Mannskraft, Mannsmaad, Mannshauet*, etc. See Georg Ludwig von Maurer, *Einleitung zur Geschichte der Mark-, Hof-, usw. Verfassung*, Munich, 1854, p. 129 ff.

3. Therefore, when Galiani said: Value is a relation between persons (*"La Ricchezza è una ragione tra due persone"*) he ought to have added: a relation concealed beneath a material shell. (Galiani, *Della Moneta*, p. 221, Vol. 3 of Custodi's collection entitled *Scrittori classics italiani di economia politica, Parte moderna*, Milan, 1803.)

4. "What are we to think of a law which can only assert itself through periodic crises? It is just a natural law which depends on the lack of awareness of the people who undergo it" (Friedrich Engels, *Umrisse zu einer Kritik der Nationalökonomie*, in the *Deutsch-Französische Jahrbücher*, edited by Arnold Ruge and Karl Marx, Paris, 1844) [English translation in Marx/Engels' *Collected Works*, Vol. 3, London, 1975, p. 433].

5. Even Ricardo has his Robinson Crusoe stories. "Ricardo makes his primitive fisherman and primitive hunter into owners of commodities who immediately exchange their fish and game in proportion to the labour-time which is materialized in these exchange-values. On this occasion he slips into the anachronism of allowing the primitive fisherman and hunter to calculate the value of their implements in accordance with the annuity tables used on the London Stock Exchange in 1817. Apart from bourgeois society, the 'parallelograms of Mr Owen' seem to have been the only form of society Ricardo was acquainted with"* (Karl Marx, *Zur Kritik etc.*, pp. 38–9) [English translation, p. 60].

* The "parallelograms" were the utopian socialist Robert Owen's suggestion for the most appropriate layout for a workers' settlement, made in *A New View of Society* (1813) and immediately seized on by his critics. Ricardo's reference to them is from his *On Protection of Agriculture*, London, 1822, p. 21.

6. "A ridiculous notion has spread abroad recently that communal property in its natural, spontaneous form is specifically Slav, indeed exclusively Russian. In fact, it is the primitive form that we can prove to have existed among Romans, Teutons and Celts, and which indeed still exists to this day in India, in a whole range of diverse patterns, albeit sometimes only as remnants. A more exact study of the Asiatic, and specifically of the Indian form of communal property would indicate the way in which different forms of spontaneous, primitive communal property give rise to different forms of its dissolution. Thus the different original types of Roman and Germanic private property can be deduced from the different forms of Indian communal property" (Karl Marx, *Zur Kritik, etc.*, p. 10) [English translation, p. 33].

7. The insufficiency of Ricardo's analysis of the magnitude of value—and his analysis is by far the best—will appear from the third and fourth books of this work.* As regards value in general, classical political economy in fact nowhere distinguishes explicitly and with a clear awareness between labour as it appears in the value of a product, and the same labour as it appears in the product's use-value. Of course the distinction is made in practice, since labour is treated sometimes from its quantitative aspect, and at other times qualitatively. But it does not occur to the economists that a purely quantitative distinction between the kinds of labour presupposes their qualitative unity or equality, and therefore their reduction to abstract human labour. For instance, Ricardo declares that he agrees with Destutt de Tracy when the latter says: "As it is certain that our physical and moral faculties are alone our original riches, the employment of those faculties, labour of some kind, is our original treasure, and it is always from this employment that all those things are created which we call riches . . . it is certain too, that all those things only represent the labour which has created them, and if they have a value, or even two distinct values, they can only derive them from that" (the value) "of the labour from which they emanate" (Ricardo, *The Principles of Political Economy*, 3rd edn, London, 1821, p. 334).† We would here

only point out that Ricardo imposes his own more profound interpretation on the words of Destutt. Admittedly Destutt does say that all things which constitute wealth "represent the labour which has created them," but, on the other hand, he also says that they acquire their "two different values" (use value and exchange-value) from "the value of labour." He thus falls into the commonplace error of the vulgar economists, who assume the value of one commodity (here labour) in order in turn to use it to determine the values of other commodities. But Ricardo reads him as if he had said that labour (not the value of labour) is represented both in use-value and in exchange-value. Nevertheless, Ricardo himself makes so little of the dual character of the labour represented in this twofold way that he is forced to spend the whole of his chapter "Value and Riches, their Distinctive Properties" on a laborious examination of the trivialities of a J. B. Say. And at the end he is therefore quite astonished to find that while Destutt agrees with him that labour is the source of value, he nevertheless also agrees with Say about the concept of value.[††]

* These are the books that appeared, respectively, as Volume 3 of *Capital*, and *Theories of Surplus-Value* (3 volumes).
[†] Destutt de Tracy, *Élémens d'idéologie*, Parts 4 and 5, Paris, 1826, pp. 35–6.
[††] "I am sorry to be obliged to add that M. de Tracy supports, by his authority, the definitions which M. Say has given of the words 'value,' 'riches,' and 'utility'" (Ricardo, op. cit., p. 334).

8. It is one of the chief failings of classical political economy that it has never succeeded, by means of its analysis of commodities, and in particular of their value, in discovering the form of value which in fact turns value into exchange-value. Even its best representatives, Adam Smith and Ricardo, treat the form of value as something of indifference, something external to the nature of the commodity itself. The explanation for this is not simply that their attention is entirely absorbed by the analysis of the magnitude of value. It lies deeper. The value-form of the product of labour is the most abstract, but also the most universal form of the bourgeois mode of production; by that fact it stamps the bourgeois mode of production as a particular kind of social production of a historical and transitory character. If then we make the mistake of treating it as the eternal natural form of social production, we necessarily overlook the specificity of the value-form, and consequently of the commodity-form together with its further developments, the money form, the capital form, etc. We therefore find that economists who are entirely agreed that labour-time is the measure of the magnitude of value, have the strangest and most contradictory ideas about money, that is, about the universal equivalent in its finished form. This emerges sharply when they deal with banking, where the commonplace definitions of money will no longer hold water. Hence there has arisen in opposition to the classical economists a restored Mercantilist System (Ganilh, etc.), which sees in value only the social form, or rather its insubstantial semblance. Let me point out once and for all that by classical political economy I mean all the economists who, since the time of W. Petty, have investigated the real internal framework [*Zusammenhang*] of bourgeois relations of production, as opposed to the vulgar economists who only flounder around within the apparent framework of those relations, ceaselessly ruminate on the materials long since provided by scientific political economy, and seek there plausible explanations of the crudest phenomena for the domestic purposes of the bourgeoisie. Apart from this, the vulgar economists confine themselves to systematizing in a pedantic way, and proclaiming for everlasting truths, the banal and complacent notions held by the bourgeois agents of production about their own world, which is to them the best possible one.

9. "The economists have a singular way of proceeding. For them, there are only two kinds of institutions, artificial and natural. The institutions of feudalism are artificial institutions, those of the bour-

geoisie are natural institutions. In this they resemble the theologians, who likewise establish two kinds of religion. Every religion which is not heirs is an invention of men, while their own is an emanation of God . . . Thus there has been history, but there is no longer any" (Karl Marx, *Misère de la philosophie. Réponse à la philosophie de la misère de M. Proudhon*, 1847, p. 113).* Truly comical is M. Bastiat, who imagines that the ancient Greeks and Romans lived by plunder alone. For if people live by plunder for centuries there must, after all, always be something there to plunder; in other words, the objects of plunder must be continually reproduced. It seems, therefore, that even the Greeks and the Romans had a process of production, hence an economy, which constituted the material basis of their world as much as the bourgeois economy constitutes that of the present-day world. Or perhaps Bastiat means that a mode of production based on the labour of slaves is based on a system of plunder? In that case he is on dangerous ground. If a giant thinker like Aristotle could err in his evaluation of slave-labour, why should a dwarf economist like Bastiat be right in his evaluation of wage-labour? I seize this opportunity of briefly refuting an objection made by a German-American publication to my work *Zur Kritik der Politischen Ökonomie*, 1859. My view is that each particular mode of production, and the relations of production corresponding to it at each given moment, in short "the economic structure of society," is "the real foundation, on which arises a legal and political superstructure and to which correspond definite forms of social consciousness," and that "the mode of production of material life conditions the general process of social, political and intellectual, life."† In the opinion of the German–American publication this is all very true for our own times, in which material interests are preponderant, but not for the Middle Ages, dominated by Catholicism, nor for Athens and Rome, dominated by politics. In the first place, it strikes us as odd that anyone should suppose that these well-worn phrases about the Middle Ages and the ancient world were unknown to anyone else. One thing is clear: the Middle Ages could not live on Catholicism, nor could the ancient world on politics. On the contrary, it is the manner in which they gained their livelihood which explains why in one case politics, in the other case Catholicism, played the chief part. For the rest, one needs no more than a slight acquaintance with, for example, the history of the Roman Republic, to be aware that its secret history is the history of landed property. And then there is Don Quixote, who long ago paid the penalty for wrongly imagining that knight errantry was compatible with all economic forms of society.

* English translation: Karl Marx, *The Poverty of Philosophy*, London, 1966, p. 105.

† These passages are taken from the Preface to *A Contribution to the Critique of Political Economy*, written in January 1859 (English translation, pp. 20–21).

10. *Observations on Some Verbal Disputes in Pol. Econ., Particularly Relating to Value, and to Supply and Demand*, London, 1821, p. 16.

11. S. Bailey, op. cit., p. 165.

12. Both the author of *Observations etc.*, and S. Bailey accuse Ricardo of converting exchange-value from something relative into something absolute. The reverse is true. He has reduced the apparent relativity which these things (diamonds, pearls, etc.) possess to the true relation hidden behind the appearance, namely their relativity as mere expressions of human labour. If the followers of Ricardo answer Bailey somewhat rudely, but by no means convincingly, this is because they are unable to find in Ricardo's own works any elucidation of the inner connection between value and the form of value, or exchange-value.

13. In the twelfth century, so renowned for its piety, very delicate things often appear among these commodities. Thus a French poet of the period enumerates among the commodities to be found in the fair of Lendit, alongside clothing, shoes, leather, implements of cultivation, skins, etc., also *"femmes folles de leur corps."**

* "Wanton women." This passage comes from the *Dit du Lendit*, a satirical poem by the medieval French poet Guillot de Paris.

14. Proudhon creates his ideal of justice, of *"justice éternelle,"* from the juridical relations that correspond to the production of commodities: he thereby proves, to the consolation of all good petty bourgeois, that the production of commodities is a form as eternal as justice. Then he turns round and seeks to reform the actual production of commodities, and the corresponding legal system, in accordance with this ideal. What would one think of a chemist who, instead of studying the actual laws governing molecular interactions, and on that basis solving definite problems, claimed to regulate those interactions by means of the "eternal ideas" of *"naturalité"* and *"affinité"*? Do we really know any more about "usury," when we say it contradicts *"justice éternelle,"* *"équité éternelle,"* *"mutualité éternelle,"* and other *"vérités éternelles"* than the fathers of the church did when they said it was incompatible with *"grâce éternelle,"* *"foi éternelle,"* and *"la volonté éternelle de Dieu"*?

15. "For twofold is the use of every object . . . The one is peculiar to the object as such, the other is not, as a sandal which may be worn and is also exchangeable. Both are uses of the sandal, for even he who exchanges the sandal for the money or food he is in need of, makes use of the sandal as a sandal. But not in its natural way. For it has not been made for the sake of being exchanged" (Aristotle, *Republic*, I, i, c. 9).

16. From this we may form an estimate of the craftiness of petty-bourgeois socialism, which wants to perpetuate the production of commodities while simultaneously abolishing the "antagonism between money and commodities," i.e., abolishing money itself, since money only exists in and through this antagonism.* One might just as well abolish the Pope while leaving Catholicism in existence. For more on this point see my work *Zur Kritik der Politischen Ökononzie*, p. 61 ff. [English translation, pp. 83–6].

* This is directed at the proposal of John Gray, in *The Social System* (1831), for the introduction of labour-money, later taken up by Proudhon.

17. So long as a chaotic mass of articles is offered as the equivalent for a single article (as is often the case among savages), instead of two distinct objects of utility being exchanged, we are only at the threshold of even the direct exchange of products.

18. Karl Marx, op. cit., p. 135. [English translation, p. 155]. "The metals . . . are by their nature money" (Galiani, *Delia Moneta*, in Custodi's collection, *Parte moderna*, Vol. 3, p. 137).

19. For further details on this subject see the chapter on "The Precious Metals" in my work cited above [English translation, pp. 153–7].

20. "Money is the universal commodity" (Verri, op. cit., p. 16).

21. "Silver and gold themselves, which we may call by the general name of Bullion, are . . . commodities . . . rising and falling in . . . value . . . Bullion then may be reckoned to be of higher value, where the smaller weight will purchase the greater quantity of the product or manufacture of the country

etc." (S. Clement, *A Discourse of the General Notions of Money, Trade, and Exchange, as They Stand in Relations to Each Other. By a Merchant*, London, 1695, p. 7). "Silver and gold, coined or uncoined, tho' they are used for a measure of all other things, are no less a commodity than wine, oyl, tobacco, cloth or stuffs" (J. Child, *A Discourse Concerning Trade, and That in Particular of the East-Indies etc.*, London, 1689, p. 2). "The stock and riches of the kingdom cannot properly be confined to money, nor ought gold and silver to be excluded from being merchandize" (T. Papillon, *The East-India Trade a Most Profitable Trade*, London, 1677, p. 4).

22. "Gold and silver have value as metals before they are money" (Galiani, op. cit., p. 72). Locke says, "The universal consent of mankind gave to silver, on account of its qualities which made it suitable for money, an imaginary value" (John Locke, *Some Considerations etc.*, 1691, in *Works*, ed. 1777, Vol. 2, p. 15). Law, on the other hand, says "How could different nations give an imaginary value to any single thing . . . or how could this imaginary value have maintained itself?" But he himself understood very little of the matter, for example "Silver was exchanged in proportion to the use-value it possessed, consequently in proportion to its real value. By its adoption as money it received an additional value (*une valeur additionnelle*)" (Jean Law, *Considérations sur le numéraire et le commerce*, in E. Daire's edition of *Économistes financiers du XVIII siècle*, pp. 469–70).

23. "Money is their (the commodities') symbol" (V. de Forbonnais, *Élémens du commerce*, new edn, Leyden, 1776, Vol. 2, P. 143). "As a symbol it is attracted by the commodities" (ibid. p. 155). "Money is a symbol of a thing and represents it" (Montesquieu, *Esprit des lois, Œuvres*, London, 1767, Vol. 2, p. 3). "Money is not a mere symbol, for it is itself wealth; it does not represent the values, it is their equivalent" (Le Trosne, op. cit., p. 910). "If we consider the concept of value, we must look on the thing itself only as a symbol; it counts not as itself, but as what it is worth" (Hegel, op. cit., p. 100).* Long before the economists, lawyers made fashionable the idea that money is a mere symbol, and that the value of the precious metals is purely imaginary. This they did in the sycophantic service of the royal power, supporting the right of the latter to debase the coinage, during the whole of the Middle Ages, by the traditions of the Roman Empire and the conceptions of money to be found in the Digest. "Let no one call into question," says their apt pupil, Philip of Valois, in a decree of 1346, "that the trade, the composition, the supply, and the power of issuing ordinances on the currency . . . belongs exclusively to us and to our royal majesty, to fix such a rate and at such a price as it shall please us and seem good to us." It was a maxim of Roman Law that the value of money was fixed by Imperial decree. It was expressly forbidden to treat money as a commodity. "*Pecunias vero nulli emere fas erit, nam in usu publico constitutas oportet non esse mercem.*"† There is a good discussion of this by G. F. Pagnini, in *Saggio sopra il giusto pregio delle cose*, 1751, printed in Custodi's collection, *Parte moderna*, Vol. 2. In the second part of his work Pagnini directs his polemic especially against the legal gentlemen.

* This is a reference to the *Philosophy of Right*, para. 63, Addition (English translation, p. 240).
† "However, it shall not be lawful for anyone to buy money, for, as it was created for public use, it is not permissible for it to be a commodity" (*Codex Theodosianus*, lib. 9, tit. 23).

24. "If a man can bring to London an ounce of silver out of the Earth of Peru, in the same time that he can produce a bushel of corn, then the one is the natural price of the other: now, if by reason of new or more easie mines a man can procure two ounces of silver as easily as he formerly did one, the corn will be as cheap at ten shillings the bushel as it was before at five shillings, *caeteris paribus*" (William Petty, *A Treatise of Taxes and Contributions*, London, 1667, p. 32).

25. The learned Professor Roscher, after first informing us that "the false definitions of money may be divided into two main groups: those which make it more, and those which make it less, than a commodity," gives us a motley catalogue of works on the nature of money, which does not provide even the glimmer of an insight into the real history of the theory. He then draws this moral: "For the rest, it is not to be denied that most of the later economists do not bear sufficiently in mind the peculiarities that distinguish money from other commodities" (it is then, after all, either more or less than a commodity!) . . . "So far, the semi-mercantilist reaction of Ganilh is not altogether without foundation" (Wilhelm Roscher, *Die Grundlagen der Nationalökonomie*, 3rd edn, 1858, pp. 207–10). More! Less! Not sufficiently! So far! Not altogether! What a way of determining one's concepts! And this eclectic professorial twaddle is modestly baptized by Herr Roscher "the anatomico-physiological method" of political economy! However, he does deserve credit for one discovery, namely, that money is "a pleasant commodity."

26   The Reason of the Gift

Jean-Luc Marion

A Contradiction in Terms

We give without account. We give without accounting, in every sense of the word. First, because we give *without ceasing*. We give in the same way we breathe, every moment, in every circumstance, from morning until evening. Not a single day passes without our having given, in one form or another, something to someone, even if we rarely, if ever, "give everything."[1] Also, we give without keeping account, *without measure*, because giving implies that one gives at a loss, or at least without taking into account either one's time or one's efforts: one simply does not keep account of what one gives. Finally, we give without account because, for lack of time and attention, most of the time we give *without* a clear *consciousness* of our giving, such that we give almost mechanically, automatically, and without knowing it.

So, at first glance, the attitude of giving appears obvious enough, since its exercise is imperceptible; it happens without reflection and without concern. It could be that the gift's very evidence renders any consciousness of the gift and its giving almost superfluous. Thus, there would be nothing more to discuss about the gift, and no essence to interrogate; the gift would simply need to be made. The gift would not give something to reflect on, something of which one would need to become conscious. Instead, it would directly determine an ethical demand and a social obligation. If it still presented a difficulty, it would not be the difficulty of its definition, but of its exercise. For there would be nothing to say about the gift; instead, as with love, it would only be a question of making it.

Yet as soon as it seems to give us certitude, this evidence takes it back again. For these three ways of giving cannot be brought together without contradiction. Indeed, the third way of giving without account—to give without being conscious of it—manifestly cancels the preceding two ways. For if we truly give without ceasing and without measure, how could we not be conscious of it in the end? Reciprocally, if we give without being conscious of it, how could we know that we are giving without ceasing and without measure? More exactly, how can we be assured that this "without ceasing and without measure" makes our gift a true gift, if we are not conscious of it? In short, how can we give without account if we give without rendering an account of it?

But, beyond this formal contradiction, another contradiction takes shape that is incomparably more profound and that puts the gift as a whole in question. Indeed, the gift that claims to give without account in fact always accounts and even accounts too much. The gift gives in such a way that it loses nothing, and is never lost, but always finds its account and is recovered as at least equal to that which it would have remained had it never given anything. In fact and in principle, the gift does not give without account, because at the end of the account, it is always accounted for in one way or another. The gift gives cheaply (*à bon compte*) because it remains intact after having given—it recovers itself as it is. In short, it always finds its account and recovers itself. At the very least, we can always interpret a gift in such a way that it seems to collapse inescapably, not because of an obstacle that comes from elsewhere, but because of the simple fact that it occurs spontaneously and is brought about perfectly. It suffices to analyze its three dimensions—the giver (*le donateur*), the givee[2] (*le donataire*), and the given gift (*le don donné*)—to see how the gift is abolished in favor of its contrary: *the exchange*.

Let us first consider the giver. In fact, he never gives without receiving as much as he gave in return. If he gives and is acknowledged as the giver, he at least receives the givee's recognition, even if his gift is never rendered to him; and, even in the absence of any recognition from the givee, the giver still receives the esteem of those who witness his gift. If by chance he gives without anybody acknowledging him as the giver, perhaps because the gift remains a strictly private affair (without a witness), or perhaps because the beneficiary is unaware of the gift, or rejects it (ingratitude), the giver will still receive esteem from himself (for having been generous and having given freely). This esteem, which is in fact perfectly well deserved, will provide the giver with a sense of self-satisfaction, and thus with the sovereign independence of a wise man. He will feel—justly—that he is morally superior to the miser that he was able to avoid resembling. This gain will compensate in large part for his loss. But, suddenly, the giver has abolished his gift in favor of an exchange—and disappeared as a giver, to become the purchaser of his own esteem. To be sure, this happens at the price of an asset that is lost but then recovered. "A good deed is never wasted" (*Un bienfait n'est jamais perdu*), according to a French proverb.

Let us next consider the givee. In receiving, he receives not only an asset but, especially, a debt. He becomes indebted to his benefactor and therefore is obliged to him. If he immediately gives something back for the good received, he will be even—but precisely because he has canceled his debt by substituting an exchange in place of the gift, and thus canceled the gift, which disappears. If he cannot give something back immediately, he will remain obligated in the future, either provisionally or definitively. Throughout the course of his debt, he will have to express his gratitude and acknowledge his dependence. In this instance, he will bring about his release by repaying his debt with his indebted submission, even to the point of taking on the status of a servant before his master. If, perhaps, he denies having received a gift, at the price of a lie and a denial of justice, he will have to argue that it was only a matter of something that was due to him, or that he received nothing. In each of these cases, the givee erases the gift and establishes an exchange in its place—whether real or fictitious is of little importance, since it always ends up abolishing his status as a givee.

Finally, let us examine the given gift, which inexorably tends to erase in itself all trace and all memory of the gesture by which it was given. Indeed, as soon as it is given, that which is given, whatever it may be, imposes its presence, and this evidence obfuscates the act by which it is delivered. The given gift occupies the whole stage of the giving givenness, and relegates this givenness to the nonactuality of its past. If we must always remind ourselves to thank a benefactor before taking possession of the gift (as we constantly remind small children), this is less because of bad manners than because of phenomenological necessity. The gift captivates all our attention and thus annuls its provenance. As soon as it is possessed, as soon as its receipt is confirmed, the given gift is detached from its giver; in one blow, it loses its status of being given in givenness, appearing instead in its pure and naked market value. The gift is judged in terms of its price, cleansed of the giver's intention, becoming again an autonomous object endowed with its own exchange value: it is ready to return to the commercial circuit (to be resold, exchanged, "cashed in"). As soon as it is given, the gift disappears as a given gift, to be solidified in its value as an object for possible—and hence almost inevitable—exchange.

How can one not conclude that the gift, as soon as it becomes actual and appears in the cold light of day, is inescapably transformed into its contrary, according to a threefold assimilation to exchange and commerce? How can one not conclude that this self-suppression implies a radical phenomenal instability that gives the gift the appearance of a phenomenon but leaves it incapable of being constituted as an objective phenomenon? The gift contradicts itself by a contradiction in terms—a contradiction in terms of exchange.

Either the gift appears as actual but disappears as a gift, or it remains a pure gift but becomes unapparent, nonactual, excluded from the instance of things, a pure idea of reason, a simple noumenon incompatible with the conditions of experience. That which appears according to the real conditions of actual experience must, from the gift that it was, be cashed in as an exchange. Either the gift remains true to givenness but never appears or it does appear, but in the economy of an exchange, where it is transformed into its contrary—to be precise, into an exchange, a given that is returned (*do ut, des* [I give so that you will give]), something given for a return and returned for a given, part of the trade and management of goods. Exchange is imposed as the truth of the gift, and cancels it. By submitting itself to an economy, the gift exchanges its essence as gift for an actuality that denies it—precisely in exchange. For an economy economizes the gift.[3]

The Economy

Does this critique of the gift—perhaps so effective because so abstract—in turn escape criticism? Obviously, it is open to a counterattack, since it rests on at least one unexamined presupposition: namely, that the gift implies a perfect and pure gratuity, in which it is necessary to give for nothing, without there ever being a return.

However, the postulate of gratuity is debatable. First, because for both the giver and for the givee, to receive or to grant a reward that is moral (esteem or recognition), symbolic (obligation), and therefore unreal (not a thing, nothing to do with value or a price) is not purely and simply equivalent to a real reimbursement (an amount, a thing, an asset). Indeed, to confuse the two kinds of gains—received or given—implies annulling all difference between the real and the unreal, and between the thing and the symbol. Suspended between cynicism (which realizes the unreal) and idealism (which dismisses the thing), such a description simplifies the specificity of the phenomena that are at stake here to the point where it annihilates them.

Moreover, it is not evident that the gift disappears as soon as the least satisfaction accompanies it. One may very well be satisfied as a result of a gift, without that satisfaction having been foreseen and preceding the gift as its motivation, or anticipating it as its prior intention. It is entirely possible to discover that we are happy to have given or received, without that giving or receiving having been done solely with the aim of being happy. It could even be that we receive this satisfaction only because we have *not* looked for it, nor forecast it, nor foreseen it—in short, it could be that satisfaction engulfs us precisely because it happens to us unexpectedly, as a bonus *(par surcroît)*. The joy of a gift does not motivate the gift any more than it precedes it; rather, it is added to it each time, as a grace that is unexpected, unforeseeable, and in a sense undeserved.

Finally, how is one to avoid suspecting that to require such a strict purity of the gift would imply its absolute independence from every possible other *(autrui)*? This purity would finally lead to a total independence in which not only exchanges and gifts are prohibited, but also alterity in general. Also, how can one not have the feeling that such gratuity would put in question, along the alterity of the gift's other *(l'altérité de l'autre du don)*, the very selfhood of the ego, which I put at stake as giver or givee? In the end, to give with full gratuity, without desire, would we not have to annul our selfhood—or, on the contrary, claim to be a god? At the least, wouldn't this so-called gratuity be reduced to a pure and simple indifference that, with eyes closed, gave nothing to anyone and received nothing from anyone?[4]

The aporias of gratuity seem so obvious that we should never have been ignorant of them: if the gift contradicts itself when we impose gratuity on it, why have we made that imposition? Of course, there is an excellent reason to do so: because gratuity seems to be—and, in a sense yet to be determined, actually is—the best defense against the economic process of exchange, its absolute contrary. But in what way is gratuity exempted from the economy? To this first question, a second must be added: Why must the gift disappear as soon as it satisfies the conditions of gratuity, as if being exempted from the economy were the equivalent of being excluded also from experience in general? What could the requirements of exchange and of the economy have in common with the conditions of possibility of experience? In fact, they end up coinciding, provided that we reconstitute several stages of their convergence.

First of all, an economic process presupposes and produces an equality of exchange:

> In exchanging, it is necessary that each party should agree to the quantity and quality of each of the things exchanged. In this agreement it is natural that each should desire to receive as much, and to give as little, as he can.[5]

It remains to be understood where the power of this equality comes from and how it almost inevitably extends its empire. It is, of course, not only an issue that concerns formal rigor, nor even the requirements of honesty. Rather, it is an issue of a theoretical possibility. According to Cournot:

> Whatever man can measure, calculate, and systematise, ultimately becomes the object of measurement, calculation, and system. Wherever fixed relations can replace indeterminate, the substitution finally takes place. It is thus the sciences and all human institutions are organized.

Thus, he continues, "as the abstract idea of wealth . . . constitutes a perfectly determinate relation, like all precise conceptions it can become the object of theoretical deductions."[6] Measure (mathematical quantification) makes equality possible, and therefore also makes exchange possible. In these conditions, the gift becomes an object by the exchange that "equalizes" it—an object of exchange, and therefore an object of commerce, according to "the abstract idea of *value in exchange,* which supposes that the objects to which such value is attributed *are in commercial circulation.*"[7] Commerce allows the exchange of goods only by fixing a measure of equality between objects of value. However, it fixes these measures of equality in terms of value only because it has already determined the gift in terms of exchange. Now, these terms of exchange are in turn constituted as objects by a measure that arranges them according to equalities and equivalents, and thus puts them in an order. Consequently, the gift enters into exchange and commerce because it is transcribed in terms of an economic exchange and thereby transposed in terms of an object.

We thus understand how the economy can fix the conditions of possibility of experience for objects of exchange: it deploys and puts directly into play the requirements of the *mathesis universalis,* according to its strictest Cartesian definition. Order imposes exchange, and measure guarantees equality in the field of the gift, which thereby becomes problematic as such, even aporetic, insofar as it is converted into an exchange. Either the gift arrives at its concept—exchange—and satisfies its proper conditions of possibility, or it remains gratuitous—that is, without order or measure—and thus contradicts the conditions of its possibility. The gift can be thought only by being transposed into an exchange—in accordance with the properly metaphysical requirements of rationality.[8]

The abolition of the gift, such that it passes into the (measured) equality of exchange, also defines the conditions of possibility of its appearance in experience. For the equality of exchange matters only to the extent that it renders a reason (*rend raison*)[9] for its possibility and its actuality in experience. The economy thus claims to measure exchange on the level of reason, and to render reason to it. Every exchange will have its reason, for no longer will anything be exchanged in vain. In fact, the "economy strives not to consume anything in vain," since what is at issue in "political economics," as in every other science (even human sciences), is a "way of connecting effects to causes"—in this case by means of exchange, which alone defines value.[10] In an economy, just as elsewhere, to render reason allows one to render account, because reason calculates, restores equality, and provides self-identity—which in this instance is value. Reason renders reason because it identifies the conditions of exchange, and therefore assigns conditions to possibility and justifies wealth (as with so many other phenomena) as an effect, by attributing adequate causes to it.

That the equality of exchange renders reason to the economy was in fact confirmed by Marx *a contrario*. Marx objects to the "jurist's consciousness [that] recognises in this [comparison between exchanges involving labour and all other exchanges], at most, a material difference, expressed in the juridically equivalent formulae: *Do ut des, do ut facias, facio ut des, facio ut facias* [I give so that you will give, I give so that you will act, I act so that you will give, I act so that you will act]" and insists on a contrary view:

Capital, therefore, is not only, as Adam Smith says, the command over labour. It is essentially the command over *unpaid labour* . . . a definite quantity of other people's unpaid labour.

In so doing, Marx not only unveils the mechanism of "the secret of profit making" but also, by denying the supposed equality in the exchange between salary and labor, destroys the whole "political economy."[11] Thus, the economy as such consists in restoring equality between the terms of exchange in order to provide this phenomenon—the exchange—with the means of satisfying the conditions of its possibility and thereby actually appearing.[12]

Thus, exchange suffices for rendering reason—rendering its due to the gift (in the economy) and rendering its cause to the effect (in experience). Reason always suffices, and its sufficiency restores equality, intelligibility, and justice. In principle, nothing has the right to exempt itself from the demand of reason. Every pronouncement, every action, every event, every fact, every object, and every being[13] must furnish a response to the question that asks it why? διότι? *cur*? Even the very simplest of ideas must do this, even God[14]; therefore, even—especially—the gift. On the contrary, if the gift rests on gratuity, sufficient reason cannot but economize it, precisely in the name of the economy in which reason carries on. Consequently, sufficient reason owes it to itself to exclude the gift from experience, and therefore from phenomenally: one must render invisible everything for which one cannot render reason—and first of all the gift.

In this way, one can understand the annulment of gratuity by the economy. Rendering reason to the gift means demonstrating that no one gives without rendering account, nor without rendering an account for it—thus, without being reimbursed, in either real or symbolic terms. In short, it means demonstrating that one gives only with an account, and for the sake of satisfaction. Sufficient reason can indeed always seize the gift by assigning a reason of exchange to each of its moments. The gift's self-contradiction, which I have formally indicated above, can then be repeated more concretely, in the form of a threefold response to the demand of sufficient reason. To arrive at this interpretation, it suffices to distinguish between external reasons (or causes) and internal reasons (or motives).

The giver does not give gratuitously because, as we have seen, he is always reimbursed, either in real or in symbolic terms. But most of all, one can cancel the giver's merit by arguing that he has given only what he was able to give, and thus that he has given from his surplus. By definition, he was able to dispose of this surplus, and therefore it did not really belong to him. By giving it, he has merely redistributed an excess of property that he had unjustly confiscated. In principle, the duty of justice obliged the giver to distribute that which—in all justice—did not belong to him. In claiming to give, he has done nothing more than fulfill his duty of justice. Justice, which is the motive (internal reason) for the apparent gift, explains it and commands it as a simple duty. Consequently, the giver's claim to gratuity, and even the gift's entitlement to be called such, collapse in the face of a simple duty of justice—the duty to render to each his account, his due.

Reciprocally, the givee can put forward sound motives for receiving an asset as part of a simple exchange and denying that he is the beneficiary of a gift. It suffices for him to maintain that this supposed gift has come about simply as his due. Consider the case where I find that I am impoverished and in real need—I am destitute. This means not only that I am in need, but that I need that which I lack because my condition as a human being requires it—necessarily and by right. On the basis of human rights, I have the right (and not simply the need) to nourishment, to clothing, to housing, and even to earn a salary. Therefore, that which public or private assistance might give me is delivered as my due, and no longer as a gift. Not only would there not be a question of gratuity, but gratuity would do me injury and an injustice. I claim my due in virtue of a right, and those who give me my due owe it to me by virtue of a duty that is imposed on them in accordance with an objective right. In fact, if they abandon me to my misery, they would put at risk not only my life but also my humanity, which they would debase to animality.

By the same token, they would lose their own humanity by abolishing mine. They must render reason to the humanity that is in me, but also in themselves. If they do not come to my rescue (by simple solidarity among fellow human beings), they put at risk their own status as human beings and their ethical dignity as subjects with rights. Thus, by giving me what I need in order to remain a human being, others only fulfill their duty. They do not give me a gift, but render to me what is due, which in return guarantees their own human dignity. It is a question of an exchange—symbolic, to be sure—between my humanity and theirs. However, the symbol is here infused with the highest possible reality, for it reunites us in the same equality, the same humanity. The gift is abolished in that which is due, and gratuity is abolished in solidarity. All that is operative is the symbolic exchange of sociality— the ultimate economy.

If we now consider, beyond motives (internal reasons), the causes (external reasons), we can in the same way draw the given gift (the object itself, the thing) back into the economy.

Let us take a banal example: when a "humanitarian" organization (to avoid calling it: "charitable") or a local community association "gives" (let us accept this problematic term for the moment) food, clothing, housing, or employment ("social" or reserved jobs), that organization certainly distributes these goods gratuitously, without payment or an economic transaction. However, this does not mean that these goods have no value for exchange, no market price. On the contrary, to dispense these goods gratuitously, they must be produced and distributed; that is, procured. How? Obviously, by means of gifts: the surplus of individuals, the unsold stock of businesses, or subsidies from community funds. In each case, it is a matter of consumable goods and equipment, with a market value that is calculable with precision and already inscribed in the economic sphere.

These goods and values are removed from the economic sphere by those who, having acquired or produced them within the economy, part with them at an economic loss (pure gratuity, or gratuity mixed with realism—these goods having become useless, unsalable, depreciated in value, etc.). During the period of time in which they are under the control of "humanitarian" associations—that is, until their redistribution—these goods remain outside the economy, with their exchange value neutralized. However, as soon as they are given, they recover this value; and it is precisely for this reason that they are a real assistance to those in need, in that these people are provided with goods for which they do not have to pay a price, but which nevertheless have an exchange value, a value in the economy. The advantage of the "humanitarian" stage of this process obviously does not lie in a definitive suspension of the exchange cycle, nor in an illusory escape from the economy. On the contrary, the advantage lies in the goods finally being reinscribed in the economy, almost gratuitously, in what is close to a neutralization of the exchange. The short moment in which the exchange is suspended (the gift in a strict sense) is directed solely toward finally reinscribing the gift in the economy, and thus making it *disappear* as a gift.

Moreover, the moment of the gift—which is now to be regarded as provisional—is not the first to suspend the economy. On the contrary, the first to do this is the poverty of the one who is poor, which excludes him from entering into exchange, thus canceling the economy, because it does not operate here (*annulait par défaut l'économie*). Therefore, the gift suspends (in a second and positive way) only the initial suspension (the poverty of the first instance); then, by paying on behalf of the one who is insolvent, it reinstates him in the cycle of exchange. The gift is therefore not a gift, in two senses: first, because in the end it restores the economy; second; because it "buys back" (so to speak) poverty and need by providing them with the means for paying, buying, and exchanging anew. Hence, the gift labors for the economy's reinstatement, and not at all for its suppression. The gift restores the poor person's former unbalanced accounts in order to allow him to render accounts anew—in short, to render reason for future exchanges. Thus we often speak of these "humanitarian" associations not only as an associative *economy* but also as vehicles for integration. Integration into what, if not into the economy? The moment of the gift not only is provisional, but appears in the end as a wayward economic agent—a cause or reason, and so powerful that it restores the economy at the very point where it was blocked.

The gift, in its three figures, can and even must (by virtue of a simple care for social functioning) either allow itself to be drawn back into an exchange (justice between giver and givee) or work toward reinstating exchange (insertion by the gift). Hence, it must be abolished in the economy that it restores, rather than being exempted from it. There is therefore always a motive or cause for submitting the gift to an economic interpretation and rendering it reason according to exchange. Either the gift remains provisional and a simple appearance, or it appears, but as an object and according to an exchange, by satisfying sufficient reason, which assimilates it into the economy. The economy economizes the gift because it renders it reason sufficiently.

Reducing the Gift to Givenness

After all this, is it possible to understand the gift as it is given and spoken—that is, as a gift— without in the end rendering it to economic reason or dissipating it in the phantom of an empty gratuity? Such an understanding would demand, at the very least, preserving the gift from the logic that demands not that it give what it claims to give, but instead that it give *reasons* for giving (or, rather, for *not* giving). In other words: How is it possible to avoid compelling the gift to render itself to a reason that authorizes it only by canceling it? The gift is unthinkable in the economy because it is interpreted there as necessarily being a relationship of giving–giving, like an exchange of gifts, where the first gift is recovered in the gift that is returned for it, and where the returned gift is registered as the return on the initial gift (*do ut des*). Paradoxically, the gift is lost here because it does not manage really to give at a loss—in short, it is lost because it has lost the freedom to be lost. Consequently, how is one to conceive of a gift as such: a lost gift that has lost its head, a loss without return—and nevertheless not without a thinkable meaning, even a certain reason adapted to it?

Evidently, we will not arrive at an answer to this question as long as we investigate the gift in terms of exchange and describe it on the economic horizon. We will succeed only if we stop approaching the gift as a concealed exchange that is yet to be interpreted according to economic reason—either as an unconscious exchange or as a supposedly gratuitous exchange (presuming that this is not a contradiction in terms). In short, we will succeed only if we think the gift as such, irreducible to exchange and economy. However, if the gift is not related to exchange, even as an exception to it, we would have to be able to think it starting from precisely that which exchange abolishes—that is, excess and loss, which are in fact the same thing. But we can do justice to excess and loss, and therefore to the gift as such, only by leaving the horizon of exchange and economy.

But is there any other horizon than this, and how is one to identify it? This other horizon could be discovered—if that is to be done without illusion or arbitrariness—only starting from the gift itself, or rather from the point where its phenomenon wells up just before it is dissolved into exchange, during the fragile moment where its three moments are not yet rendered to the economy's sufficient reason. We can discover this other horizon only by restraining the phenomenon of the gift from sliding down into an exchange, and by maintaining it in itself; that is, by reducing the gift to itself, hence to givenness, which is the gift's own proper horizon.

Givenness is opened as a horizon only to the extent that we reduce the gift to it, in the double sense of drawing the gift back to givenness and of submitting the gift to a phenomenological reduction by establishing it in givenness. Yet, givenness is not self-evident and, because it always precedes the gift, it seems to us that it is even less accessible than is the gift. Nevertheless, we can presume that if givenness opens a horizon for the gift, it will testify to itself at least by not immediately assigning the gift to a social process or an ethical behavior (even if it eventually does this), but rather by allowing the gift to appear without requiring that it be dissolved into exchange. In order to appear, the gift reduced to givenness would only have to be given—no more and no less—without having to render reason for itself by coming back to a revenue and making the least return on investment. That would mean describing the gift without reconstituting the terms of exchange; that is, without the two terms that are the minimum basis for any exchange. For, if the giver were to give without a givee to acknowledge this, or if the givee were to receive without any giver to honor, or even if both the giver and the givee were to exchange no given thing, then in each case one of the conditions of possibility of an exchange would be missing, and the gift would be brought about absolutely and as such. Let us attempt such a threefold description of a gift that is liberated from the terms of exchange.

First, a gift can be brought about as a gift without any giver being rewarded (in either real or symbolic terms), because it can be brought about without any giver at all. To see this, it suffices to analyze the hypothesis of a gift that is received from an anonymous or even nonexistent giver. These two conditions in fact coincide in the case of an inheritance, where death steals the giver, forbidding that anything at all be rendered to him. By definition, I am so much unable to render anything to him that this very impossibility constitutes the condition of the gift that is made to me. Indeed, it needs the testator's death for the will to come into effect; thus, it is necessary that I have no one to thank if I am to be able to receive the gift he gives me. The testator will not receive recognition from me (nor recognition of a debt), since he will no longer be here to enjoy it; and, if I declare my recognition, this will be before precisely that social group that knew him, yet of which he is no longer part. It could even happen that I receive the gift of this inheritance without the testator having wanted that, and even against his intentions, because either he was completely unknown to me up until that point, or I to him, with only a genealogical inquiry having led his executor to me. In each of these cases, the giver is lacking, thus excluding recognition and reimbursement. Nevertheless, the gift is brought about perfectly. Therefore, it appears fully, even though it is unexpected, undeserved, unpaid, without recognition or return. On the contrary, it takes on its full meaning in the very absence of motive and sufficient reason.

Second, the gift can be brought about as a gift without a givee of any sort. To establish this, would it not suffice to take the argument from anonymity again, this time applying it to the givee? Indeed, in the vast majority of cases, when we contribute to a "humanitarian" organization, we do not know the individual person who is going to benefit from our help. The organization mediates our gift, such that we remain anonymous to the givee, who in turn is anonymous to us. The gift is carried out even though no givee is made known, such that, by definition, he or she can never render anything to me. However, this argument from anonymity could be contested by arguing that here, in the final instance, it is not a question of a gift, because the intermediary (the association)—even if it does its work scrupulously (distributing contributions, helping efficiently)—precisely refuses to make a gift by rendering the recipients anonymous and merging them into the crowd of those who are helped. As we have seen in the preceding section, here it is more a question of solidarity and what is due by right than it is a question of a gift.

There is still another case where a gift is brought about perfectly, with a clearly identified givee, without, however, any risk that he will be able to make a reimbursement and thus transform the gift into an exchange: the case where I give to an enemy. Whether an enemy is private or public matters little, since in either case the hate he bears toward me will make him return my gift with an insult, and every claim to generosity with additional humiliation. Not only will he not render a gift in return for mine; not only will he deny that there is even a gift at issue; but he will also foster a still greater hate for me. He will return the favor I give him (*il me rendra la monnaie de ma pièce*), inverting the debt a hundredfold. I will deserve to be even more hated by him, because I have wanted to make him benefit from my wealth, to render him slave to my protection, to overpower him by my generosity, and so on.[15] He will therefore take vengeance on me in order to free himself from the least obligation of recognition. He will kill me rather than acknowledge that he owes me the least recognition. Even so, is my gift compromised by this? Not at all, for a gift that is scorned and denied, even transformed into an affront, nonetheless remains perfectly and definitively given; this desolation even makes it appear with a more sovereign force. It is only to an enemy that I can make a gift without risk of finding it taken up in an exchange or trapped in reciprocity. Paradoxically, only my enemy takes care of the gift by protecting it from a relationship of giving–giving. Whoever gives to his enemy does so without return, without anything coming back, and without sufficient reason—incontestably.

Third, the gift can be brought about without giving any object that can be brought back to an exchange value. Indeed, what can I give that is more precious than such a gift? Without doubt, there is nothing more precious than my attention, my care, my time, my faith, or even my life. And, in the end, the other person expects nothing less and can hope for nothing more. Nor I from him. For in giving these nonobjective gifts, which elude being either understood or possessed, which supply no gain or assignable return, and which really provide *nothing* (*nothing real; ne rem*), I in fact give myself in my most complete selfhood. In giving this *nothing*, I give all that I have, because I am not giving something that I possess apart from myself, but rather that which I am. Hence, the paradox that I give (myself) more, the more I give nothing: the given gift does not consist in a substrate or a real predicate. Therefore, from here on, I am giving outside the horizon of possession (and dispossession) of anything whatever, and therefore outside both objectness (*objectité*) and the reason that could render an account for the gift.

It should not be objected that by giving no object, I would give less, or would even dispense with actually giving at all. On the contrary (and here the argument repeats itself), I am excused from really giving—that is, from giving *myself*, me in person—when I settle for giving an object in place of myself. Thus, I give money in order to be excused from giving my time and attention. I pay into an annuity in order to be excused from having to love, and so regain my liberty. What happens, for example, when I give a woman a magnificent piece of jewelry? Two hypotheses: Either I give her this object alone, but in order to admit to her that I am leaving her or that I do not really love her (i.e., to settle accounts); or I give it to her as an indication that I love her irrevocably, thus simply as a sign of the true gift, which remains nonobjectifiable and invaluable—the gift of my time, my attention, my faith, my life—in short, the gift of myself. This is a gift that I can give only symbolically now, since it will require the entire duration of my lifetime to carry it out in reality.[16] In summary, either the object that is given remains alone and signifies the denial of the full gift (the gift of self), or it is presented as a simple indication and marks the promise of the full gift (this same gift of self), which is always still unaccomplished. Every gift that is given—insofar as it implies more than actuality—must become unreal, nonobjectifiable, and invaluable.

Thus, the gift, in its three moments, can be reduced to the givenness in it and can dispense with itself—and it can do this all the better when it lacks one of the terms of reciprocity and is freed from that to which the economy attempts to debase it in each instance: the giving–giving relation of exchange. The gift is given more perfectly the more it is ignorant either of the giver who is compensated by his (good) conscience, or of the givee who is freed from all consciousness (of debt), or of the given that is recoverable as an exchange value by a (commercial) consciousness. The gift is reduced to givenness by being brought about without any consciousness of giving (*conscience*[17] *de don*)—without the self-consciousness that would make it render reason of its accounts and multiply reciprocity. The gift reduced to givenness has no consciousness of what it does; it has hands to do it with, but it does it only on condition that the right hand does not know what the left hand is doing.

The Case of the Gift: Fatherhood

However, this result may still raise a concern. Does it not prove too much, and too quickly, for it to offer a rational argument—is it not simply a question of a polemical response? Does not bracketing each term of the exchange, aside from avoiding reciprocal exchange, come at the price of the disappearance of all of the gift's real process? Does not suspending the exchange's sufficient reason also entail the abolition of all rationality of the gift itself? For we have arrived at an outright contradiction: instead of being defined in relation to the givee, the giver would give all the better by disappearing (as unknown or deceased) from the givee's view; the givee, far from appearing by dealing with his debt, would appear all the better by denying it (as anonymous or an enemy); and that which is given, far from being concretized in a manifest object, would appear all the better by evaporating into the unreal or the symbolic (as an indication). Under the pretext of clarifying the gift in light of its givenness alone, have we not, rather, dissolved phenomenality? In short, does not the would-be phenomenological reduction of the gift to its givenness in the end prohibit it from even having the dignity of a phenomenon?

This difficulty cannot be dodged, but neither should it be overestimated, for it is the consequence, essentially, of beginning the examination at the wrong point. We began our inquiry into the gift by starting with its contrary—exchange—and we recovered proper access to it only by disqualifying that which prevented it—reciprocity. Having left the economic point of view, and making our way through the debris of exchange, we continue to be entangled there at the very moment when we are doing our best to free ourselves from it. Thus, we may need to attempt a direct description, starting from itself, of a phenomenon of the same kind as the gift, but this time inscribed from the outset on the horizon of givenness: a phenomenon that could never allow itself to be recaptured by the economic horizon, a gift that is always already reduced and drawn back to givenness, free of any degradation into economy, born free of sufficient reason. In short, a gift that is naturally reduced to givenness, an exceptional case where the difficulty would not consist in overcoming the natural attitude so as to carry out the reduction but, rather, in face of a phenomenon that is already (naturally) reduced, in reconstituting it (so to speak), starting from that to which it is reduced. Which phenomenon would be able to satisfy this inverted description of appearing *only as always already reduced?* Let me suggest one: *fatherhood.*

Fatherhood is undeniably a phenomenon, since it appears wherever people live; it is a phenomenon that is regularly observable, since it stretches over the duration of each lifetime; finally, it is unchallengeable, since no human being can claim not to have experienced it. No one can deny it, least of all those who themselves are either fatherless or childless, since the phenomenon is even more apparent in such absences, as we shall see. Fatherhood (provided that we do not bring it down to exchange straightaway) never puts itself forward as a simple biological product of procreation, nor as a primary interest group, nor as an elementary political category. Doubtless, fatherhood is connected to all of these things, but only after the fact, once it is subjected to an economic interpretation in terms of exchange, according to which it is a first stage in a series of increasingly complex communities that lead, in principle, up to the state. However, no matter how powerful and widely accepted this interpretation might be, it still belongs to metaphysics and, above all, it conceals the determinations of the gift, in the form in which it appears on the horizon of givenness.

First of all, as with every phenomenon, fatherhood appears insofar as it gives itself. But it gives *itself*, unlike most other phenomena, *insofar as it gives.*[18] Fatherhood manifests all the given phenomenon's characteristics, though they are exhibited not only in the mode of a given but also in the mode of a giving. For if fatherhood did not give, neither would it give itself as a phenomenon that shows itself. Thus, it gives, but with a style that is absolutely remarkable and proper to it.

Fatherhood does indeed give, but *without being able to be foreseen*; for the intention to procreate is never enough for procreation to happen, any more than the intention not to procreate is a guarantee against its happening. Again, fatherhood gives, but *without cause* and without any univocally assignable reason. This is proved by the inability of demographic science to calculate the evolution of the fertility rate or to anticipate long-term population growth or decline. This inability is so pronounced that demographic science resorts to the unquantifiable consideration of psychological, cultural, and even religious factors that at best allow a simple intelligibility a posteriori but never a serious forecast. Thus, fatherhood produces—or, rather; produces itself—as an *event* and not as a simple fact: welling up from pure possibility, it does not produce a finished result, determined and concluded once it is delivered, but rather brings about a possibility (the child), whose future, in turn, cannot be foreseen, nor deduced from causes, nor anticipated, but must be waited for.

All these determinations also characterize the phenomenon in general, considered as given,[19] except for one decisive difference. Here, the phenomenon that is given also gives, and thus lays claim to an exemplary role among all given phenomena: that of the given that itself gives (*donné donnant*). That the given gives not only itself, but also a given other than itself, implies the opening of an uncontrollable excess, growth, and negative entropy, which misery, death, and fear are not enough to extinguish (on the contrary, in fact). Simply put, here the given always and necessarily gives something other than itself, and thus more than itself; it proves to be uncontrollable and inexhaustible, irrepressible and impossible (in other words, it makes possible the impossible), having neither master nor god. But there is more, for the given gives insofar as it phenomenalizes both itself and that which it gives. This means that the visible itself—in fact, nothing less than the sum of all the phenomena visible up until this point—will also grow, with an irrepressible, incalculable, and inexhaustible excess that nothing will conquer. By giving itself and showing itself, fatherhood in principle gives and manifests more than itself; the event of its arrival in the visible thus provokes a phenomenal event that is endless by right. Nowhere else does the given's character (*Gegebenheit*)—in other words, the character of appearing in the mode of the given (which would almost deserve the neologism "givenence" [*donnéité*][20])—announce itself as clearly as here, thus conferring on fatherhood an exceptional phenomenological privilege.

However, this exceptional privilege (the highest form of givenness) is echoed or balanced by another characteristic, which can only be conceived negatively, at least upon first glance. This very phenomenon that gives itself in giving cannot, for its part, give itself without first having been given to itself—that is, received from elsewhere; namely, from a(nother) father. But the father's gift brings about anew the threefold paradox of the gift reduced to givenness.

First, the giver remains essentially absent and bracketed here. For *the father is missing.* To start with, the father is missing because he procreates in only a moment and, having become useless, withdraws immediately—in contrast to the mother, who remains, and in whom the child remains. The mother's immanence to the child stigmatizes the father's unfortunate transcendence. The father is also missing later because he leaves (must leave), and attracts the child's attention by—in principle—being lacking to him. Not that he always leaves like a paradoxical thief, forcibly abandoning mother and child. Rather, he is lacking because he can never merge with the given child (in contrast to the mother, who can, and even must, do this for a time), since he can remain united with the child only by taking leave—precisely so as then to pass on his help: as extroverted provider, hunter, warrior, or traveler; in short, as one who constantly returns, coming back to the hearth from which he must distance himself if he wants to maintain it. In order to live there, the father must be missing, and thus shine by his absence. He appears insofar as he disappears.[21] Finally, and most of all, the father is missing because (in consequence of the previous two absences) his fatherhood can never rely on an immediate empirical confirmation. Even a genetic identification is mediated (since it requires time, instruments, and study), and still results in a juridical process of recognition (or denial) of paternity: inevitably, the father remains putative. This does not mean that he conceals or disavows himself as father, but rather that he can declare himself only by recognizing—necessarily after the fact—the child whom he could, by definition, never know from the outset. He can claim the child as his (therefore also deny him) only with a delay, through a mediate word and a juridical declaration. He can really give a father to his child only by giving to him again—after the gift of biological life that is always somewhat random—this time, a status and a name: in short, an identity. This symbolic identity must be constantly given again, endlessly, in every moment, and can be made secure only by repeating it until the end. The father must spend his whole lifetime giving and regiving identity to his child; this identity is his child's status as gift without return, but also without certainty. Fatherhood, or the redundancy of the gift that lacks. For these three reasons—withdrawal, departure, and redundancy—the father appears as the giver who is perfectly reduced to givenness: the bracketed giver.

Second, the gift reduced to givenness is further confirmed in the phenomenon of fatherhood in that the child, however much he appears to be a givee (par excellence, since he receives not only a gift but also himself as the gift of a possibility), by definition cannot make good on the least consciousness of a debt. Indeed, no matter how deeply he is moved by the feeling of indebtedness, nor how earnestly filial piety is sometimes at work in him, nor how seriously he strives to correspond to the father's gift, an obstacle always stands in the way. It is not a question here of subjective ingratitude or of empirical hate, though these are always possible and at least looming. It is a more radical question of an in principle impossibility. Whether he wants to or not, whether he feels bound to it or not, the child can never "render," and will remain ungrateful, inadequate, and inconsiderate, because it will never be given to him to render to his father what he has received from him—life. The child can render him time, care, and attention (watching over his advanced years, ensuring that he is lacking nothing, surrounding him with affection, etc.), possibly until the very end; but the child will never be able to give him life in return at the hour of his death. At best, the child will render a peaceful death to his father, but he will never give back (or render) him life.

It should not be objected that the child will be able to give life in turn. True, the child may be able to do this, but whomever he may give it to, it will not be to his father. For he, too, will give it to those who, by the same principle, will be able to give it only to their own children, and never to their father. These children will, in turn, be exposed as givees who are absent and, in turn, installed as givers who are missing. This is how the arrow of time is pointed, with a genuinely original differance (from which even the differance of the delay of intuition also derives). The child responds adequately, even justly, to the father—the giver who is missing—only by avowing himself to be a givee who defaults. Genealogy extends onward by virtue of these ineluctable impossibilities of rendering the gift, of closing the gift that is reduced to givenness back into the loop of exchange.

As for the gift that is given in fatherhood, at this point it goes without saying that it can in no way be converted into an object or a being (whether a subsistent being or a utensil being does not matter). The father gives nothing to the child other than life (and a name that sanctions this). The given gift is reduced here precisely to life, which, exactly because it renders possible—and potentially actual—every being and every object, itself belongs neither to beingness (*l'étantité*) nor to objectness (*l'objectité*). Life is not, since nothing is without it; it is not seen, or defined, or grasped as something real—as one thing among others. A corpse lacks nothing real that would allow it to be distinguished from the living— "he almost looks like he could talk" (*il ne lui manque que la parole*), as one says of someone who has just died. But speech is not one real thing among others; it triggers things by naming them and, making them appear, it never itself appears as a thing. Life that is given does not appear, is not, and is not possessed. It gives us our appearing, our being, and our possessing of ourselves. In it, the gift is perfectly reduced to givenness—that nothing which tears everything away from nothingness.

Fatherhood thus lays out, in fact and by right, the whole phenomenality of a gift reduced to pure givenness. With fatherhood, the giver is manifested even insofar as he is absent, the givee insofar as he defaults, and the gift in direct proportion to its unreality. Not only do the phenomenological requirements of a reduction of the given to givenness not contradict the description of the gift as a phenomenon in its own right (*de plein droit*); not only are these demands fulfilled, here at least, almost perfectly; but above all, father-hood appears as a phenomenon in its own right (given) and even privileged (the given that itself gives [*donné donnant*]) only if the phenomenological view interprets (*déchiffre*) it as always already naturally reduced, by reconstituting (so to speak) that on the basis of which it is discovered as reduced, and in the face of which the models of exchange, pro-creation, and production definitively show themselves to be impotent (*impuissants*) and inadequate. The contemporary difficulty with conceiving fatherhood follows directly from an incapacity (*impuissance*) to reduce the gift to the givenness in it.

The Gift Without the Principle of Identity

Thus reduced without remainder to givenness, the given and giving phenomenon of fatherhood opens new domains to the phenomenality of givenness (or givenence [*donnéité*]) in general, which we cannot explore here. But we can at least emphasize a characteristic of the gift's phenomenality in the strict sense, which is brought into clear light here.

Fatherhood is clearly distinguished in that it is unfolded without reciprocity and with excess. What importance is to be accorded to these two particularities? It is without reciprocity because the father can give (life) as father only on the express condition of never being able to receive it in return from the one to whom he has given it. The father cannot give in order to receive in return—and is singled out precisely by this privilege. The privilege becomes paradoxical only if one persists in envisaging it on the economic horizon, where it seems to arise from a lost exchange and a disappointed reciprocity; but this privilege is easily demonstrated, on the contrary, as soon as analysis takes the chance to transgress the economic horizon for good and enter onto the horizon of givenness. The father appears without contest as he for whom I, as the child, can do nothing, as he to whom I can render nothing, as he whom I will allow to die alone. However, the neglect in which I must finally abandon him, regardless of what may happen and what my filial sentiments may be, has nothing to do with a bitter impotence or a harsh injustice. For, before all else, it marks the sole indisputable transcendence that all human life can and must recognize in its own immanence; with the result that if we ever have to name God with a name, it is very appropriate to call Him "Father"—and Him alone: "Call no one on earth your father, for you have only one Father, and He is in heaven" (Matthew 23:9).

The father—as him to whom we can render nothing, precisely because we owe him our inscription in the given—makes evident the son, he who could not give to himself that which he has nonetheless received as most his own—and vice versa. For we do not experience ourselves solely as given, like every other phenomenon, but as gifted (*adonné*)—as those who receive themselves in the reception of the given, far from waiting for this given in the position of a receiver who is already available and secure in itself. To what extent does the experience of oneself as a gifted also imply the recognition of filiation in myself? The response to this question perhaps (and no more than perhaps) exceeds the scope of philosophy and possibly touches on a domain that is already theological; but the phenomenology of the reduced gift leads one inevitably at least to pose it as a question.[22]

Beyond the transcendence that it unveils in the gifted's intimate immanence, fatherhood also and especially imposes a strictly phenomenal determination: the invalidation of reciprocity. For if the reduced gift attests to itself as irreducible to exchange, that depends, as has just been seen, on the fact that it has no need to rest on the two (or three) terms of the exchange in order to be brought about; it can give its all, as money thrown away, to receive without being able to render, and to be realized without transferring any reality susceptible of being possessed. Consequently, not only can fatherhood, like every other reduced gift, be dispensed of reciprocity, but it cannot even tolerate it nor give it the least right. The reduced gift gives (and receives) without return or revenue, even on condition of having nothing in common with these.

What does this abandonment of reciprocity signify? This question does not concern ethics, whose operations (altruism, justice, generosity, disinterestedness, etc.) themselves become intelligible and determinant only once reciprocity is overcome, and on the basis of this overcoming. Therefore, this overcoming, coming before ethics, goes back to the fundamental determination of metaphysics, of which it puts a radical principle in question: the principle of identity. This principle supposes that nothing can be, at the same moment and in the same respect, other than itself; in other words, possibility is founded on logical noncontradiction: "We judge to be false that which contains contradiction, and to be true that which is opposed or contradictory to the false."[23] Logical noncontradiction, which founds the formal possibility of each thing on its thinkability, hence on its essence, rests on self-equality. In consequence, reciprocity in exchange reproduces between two beings and their two (or more) essences the single requirement of noncontradiction. The economy extends and applies this requirement to the relations of production, possession, and consumption of objects, which are woven by societies and which support their cohesion. Inversely, not to respect this requirement provokes contradiction, and therefore in the end prevents exchanges and societies. The political ideals of equality and solidarity take up the same requirement at a higher level of complexity. Under all its figures, reciprocity generalizes the same principle of identity and the same requirement of noncontradiction.

Henceforth, if the reduced gift attests to itself only in subverting reciprocity—and thus the self-equality of things—not only does it contradict the economy and its conditions of possibility for experience, but it also and especially contradicts the principle of noncontradiction itself. As the case of fatherhood proves, the reduced gift allows for a thing not being left equal to itself, but becoming (or, rather, giving) more than itself, or as much as it loses in the exchange of being accomplished as gift. The reduced gift always gives (or receives) more (or less) than itself, for if the balance stayed equal, the gift would not actually take place—but, in its place, an exchange. For exchange respects the principle of identity, and so it offers only an elementary variant on the case of a relation between two terms. The father, for example, loses himself in giving a life, which will never be rendered to him; and he contradicts himself in renouncing an equal exchange, precisely to fulfill the office of father; but, moreover, he gives much more than he possesses, in giving a life that in one sense he does not have (in and of) himself, because it is not identified with him, who himself remains the son of another father. Fatherhood manifests the nonidentity of each self with itself, this contradiction of self to self then being unfolded in all the figures of inequality. In general, the gift is produced only by provoking this nonidentity with itself, then in releasing an inequality without end: that of the giver with the gift, of the givee with the gift, and of the gift with itself. These nonidentical inequalities can be described successively and even alternatively as a loss, as an excess, or as an equivocation—but they can never be understood on the model of self-identity.

This essential and polysemous nonidentity, which liberates the gift everywhere it operates, in the end imposes nothing less than a new definition of possibility. Henceforth, it must no longer be conceived as bare noncontradiction—namely, the self-identity of an essence, which attests to its rationality in posing no contradiction for the understanding— but as the excess (or, just as well, the deficit) of the self over the self, which, in giving without return, gives more than itself and provokes an other different from the first self (and hence itself also different from itself). Possibility does not consist in self-identity with the self, but in the self's excess over itself. Following the paradoxical logic of the gift, which excludes exchange and reciprocity, everything always ends up as much more (or less) than itself, without any impossibility being opposed to this. For the impossibility that would have to be opposed to this would remain a simple nonpossibility, in the sense of non–self-identity and the principle of identity, the contradiction of which defines *precisely* the new acceptance of possibility that is set to work by the gift—which, far from perishing from its nonidentity and its inequality with itself, wells up only if these latter are unfolded to their end. This means that no impossibility can prevent the new possibility of the gift, since it is fed on impossibility and on the very contradiction of self-identity, self-equality, and the reciprocity of exchange. To that which gains itself only in losing itself—namely, the gift, which gives itself in abandoning itself—nothing is impossible any longer. Not only does that which does not give itself lose itself, but nothing can ruin (*perdre,* lose) the gift, since it consists in the contradiction even of its possibility.

The Horizon Proper to the Gift: Unconditioned Possibility

Such as we have just reestablished it on its own terms under the figure of fatherhood, the phenomenon of the gift unfolds only by eliminating in itself the terms of exchange, to the point of contradicting the principle of (non)contradiction. This result, supposing that it is admitted, far from solidly establishing the phenomenality of the gift and illuminating its logic, could lead to a reinforced difficulty. First, because the exception made to the principle of identity seems to reinforce the tendency to marginalize the gift, with this extreme case of phenomenality being a contrast that makes clear the common regularity of exchange, which is left conforming to identity and noncontradiction. After all, if the gift in general is exemplified principally by the case of fatherhood, would it not be necessary to confine to this indisputable phenomenal exception (a gift naturally reduced to givenness, a gift responding to the gifted) the possibility of contradicting (non)contradiction, indeed the possibility of impossibility? Only the exemplary gift—fatherhood (hence also the gifted)— could be an exception to the principle of identity, which, for remaining phenomena and even for other gifts, would continue to be the rule. But as reasonable as this evasion may seem, it fixes nothing.

First, because *all* gifts without exception are brought about by contradicting the identity in themselves, because they contradict the equality between their terms. Fatherhood offers an example only because it manifests precisely this contradiction of identity not only in itself but in all possible gifts. Next, because the gift as such (in other words, all gifts) exempts itself not only from the first principle of metaphysics—the principle of identity and non-contradiction—but also from the second: "that of Sufficient Reason, in virtue of which we consider that no fact can be real or actual, and no proposition true, without there being a sufficient reason for its being so and not otherwise."[24] For this principle posits that everything—facts, propositions, and hence (especially) phenomena—must have a reason that justifies its actuality. In other words, for a phenomenon to be brought about, it is not sufficient that the possibility of its essence (noncontradiction) be shown; it is also necessary to justify the actuality of its existence, and that can happen only if a term other than it comes, as cause or reason, to render intelligible this transition. But can we always assign a reason or a cause to the phenomenon that gives itself?

I have shown elsewhere the phenomenological fragility of this claim: the phenomenon, in the strict sense, has the essential property of showing itself in itself and on the basis of itself—hence of not becoming manifest in the way an effect becomes actual, namely, by means of another cause or reason than itself. A phenomenon shows *itself* all the more as itself, in that it gives *itself* on the basis of itself.[25] Is the particular case where the given phenomenon takes the figure of the gift, one in which we could more readily assign to its phenomenalization another *self* than itself? Merely formulating the question is sufficient to see that the gift, even less than any other phenomenon, permits another instance to preside at its phenomenalization. The gift shows itself on the basis of itself because, like every other phenomenon, it gives *itself* on the basis of itself, but also because, more radically than every other phenomenon, it gives its *self* on the basis of *itself*. The gift that gives (itself) gives only on the basis of itself, hence without owing anything to another reason (or cause) than itself. One need only return to the precise description of the gift to verify that this phenomenon manifests itself and gives itself as it gives—*of itself*, on the basis of itself alone, without any other reason than itself.

Let us suppose the simple illustrative case where a gift appears to its giver before he gives it (the givee remaining bracketed here). How does the reduced gift come (*advient*) to this giver so that it becomes an actual gift? Let us consider first the uncritical answer: the gift passes to actuality when this same giver decides to give it and lays claim to establishing himself as its efficient cause and last reason. But this response is not valid, for the decision itself remains an appearance. More essentially, we must understand how the giver himself comes to the decision of actually giving this gift, hence how (the decision of) taking the decision happens (*advient*) to him. And the response to this question is not as easily established as one might expect.

For, evidently, the giver does not decide to give some gift because of the object that he is giving. First, because an object as such can decide nothing, in particular it cannot decide between itself and all the other objects susceptible of being considered as what one might give. Next, because the reasons for preferring to give one object rather than another could not result from calculations, which in any case the object would suffer, without producing them or justifying them. Neither does the giver decide on some gift because of some potential beneficiary, who could have begged for it more than the others—the number of needy discourages, and the impudence of the claims disgusts, without allowing one to decide. It must therefore be that the giver alone decides to give, by himself. But he must still decide to *give* and not only to part with an available object following rules that include a benefit for him, nor only to share it out by calculation (even by justice, which is itself an equality), nor to distribute it following economic laws (an exchange). It must be, here again, that a gift gives itself, reduced purely to the givenness in it. And that can happen only if the gift wells up from itself and imposes itself as such on its giver. It can do this only by coming (*advenant*) to this giver as something to give, as that which demands that one give it (*donandum est*)—by appearing among many other objects or beings like itself, in the midst of which the gift imposes itself of itself: as so useful for a distress close to its actual (and provisional) proprietor, that henceforth he or she must become the leaseholder whose time has expired, and finally the giver; or as so beautiful that it is only fitting for a beauty greater than that of its possessor, who is obliged to pay homage with it; or finally as so rare that its finder feels constrained to convey it to a jewel box more exceptional than himself. The examples of this silent constraint—political (devolutions: Lear to his daughters), moral (renunciations: the Princess of Cleves), religious (consecrations: the stripping of Francis of Assisi), or others—abound to the point of dispensing us from describing them further.

Here, before being given, the gift comes (*advient*) to this point on the basis of itself, on the basis of a *self* that imposes itself doubly. First, it imposes itself as that which must be given—a phenomenon distinguished among other phenomena by a prominence such that no one can legitimately proclaim himself its possessor, as a phenomenon that burns the fingers, and of which the very excellence demands that one be rid of it. Next, the gift imposes itself in imposing on its initial possessor that it be let go to a recipient who is always other; for the gift makes the possessor's decision about to whom it is to be given, hence also demands of this possessor that he make himself the giver and dispossess himself of it (in this order, and not the inverse). Thus the gift reduced to givenness is brought about in virtue of nothing other than its own *givability*: in appearing as givable, it transforms its reality as a being or an object and thus convinces its possessor to be rid of it, so as to allow it to appear precisely according to a perfect givability. The gift decides its givenness by itself and decides its giver by itself, in appearing indisputably as givable and making itself be given. And this phenomenality comes to it from nothing other than itself. It has no recourse to any cause, nor to any reason, other than the pure demand of givenness that it show itself as it gives itself—namely, in itself and of itself. It comes (*advient*) on the basis of its own possibility, such that it gives this possibility originarily to itself.

Inversely, let us suppose the illustrative case where a gift appears to its givee, who receives it (the giver remaining bracketed here). How does the reduced gift come (*advient*) to this givee as an actual gift? Because this same givee decides to receive it and lays claim to establishing himself as its final cause and initial reason. But it still remains to be understood how the givee comes to accept this gift as gift, hence first to decide by himself to accept it. Now the difficulties mount up. First, it is necessary that the final beneficiary accepts the receiving of a gift; but this acceptance implies a prior renunciation—and a considerable renunciation—since it is a matter of abandoning the posture of self-sufficiency and calm possession of oneself and one's world; in short, renunciation of that most powerful of fantasies, which is the foundation of the whole economy and every calculation of interest in an exchange, that fantasy of the self-identity of the "I" (contradicting the principle of identity). Before accepting a gift—which would nevertheless seem easy, since it appears to be a matter of gain, pure and simple—it is necessary first to accept to accept, which implies recognizing that one no longer increases oneself by oneself, but rather by a dependence on that which one is not, more exactly on that which the "I" in one is not.

And this consent supposes that one abandons self-equality; hence, not only that which morality would label egoism, but above all that which the reduction to givenness has stigmatized as exchange and economy. It is a matter of nothing less than abandoning one logic to let oneself take up another, which no sufficient reason governs and no cause controls. Next, it is necessary to distinguish between that which it is appropriate to accept and that which one cannot or should not accept; for not every good is offered as a gift that is to be received—whether it remains the possession of an absent or unknown proprietor (desire for a lost object, abandoned and then found, that belongs by right to another), or whether it can in no way become an appropriable good for the enjoyment of whomsoever (such as environmental goods, which belong to nobody), or whether what appears as a gift ends up proving to be an evil in reality (the horse abandoned to the Trojans by the Greeks), and so on. Whence this conclusion: to discern if and when it is a matter of a gift, it is first of all necessary that the gift itself appear given as such; namely, as given to be received.

The beneficiary cannot, as such, satisfy these two requirements—accepting to accept and knowing what to accept—since he himself becomes a givee only at the moment when they are satisfied in his eyes, and hence before him. Therefore, there remains only a sole hypothesis: the gift itself must make itself accepted by the one who accepts it, and that it must declare itself from itself as a gift to be received. And the gift succeeds in this precisely when, from the innumerable crowd of beings and objects that are available, but undistinguished or ruled by possession, one detaches itself and imposes itself by appearing as the one that I must accept (*accipiendum est*). It appears then as a phenomenon that has welled up under the aspect of *acceptability*. It appears in designating itself as to be received, and in making itself accepted by the one who, at first and most of the time, neither sees it as a gift nor conceives of himself as the givee. Such an acceptability is exerted on the one who, without it, would not recognize himself as a givee; and it is not exerted solely, nor at first, in the manner of a moral pressure or a sensual seduction, but in virtue of a privileged aspect of phenomenality—the phenomenality of that which in itself and by itself gives itself to be received. The gift phenomenalizes itself of itself insofar as it shows itself as it gives itself—as that which none can begin to see without first receiving it. The gift thus received refers back to no cause, nor to any reason, other than its pure logic of givenness, appearing in its own right (*deplein droit*). Presupposing neither its givee nor its giver, it comes (*advient*) on the basis of its own possibility, such that it gives this possibility originarily to itself: it shows itself in itself because it gives itself in itself.[26]

At the end of this inchoate description, we arrive at the outline of a result: if one seriously undertakes to reduce the gift to givenness, the gift gives itself on the basis of itself alone; not only can it be described by bracketing its givee, its giver, or its objectness, but above all it gives rise to them all under the two aspects of its own phenomenality—givability and acceptability. Therefore, the reduced gift comes to pass (*advient*) with no cause or reason that would suffice for rendering account of it, other than itself—not that it renders an account to itself, but because it renders itself (reason) inasmuch as it gives itself in and by itself. Actually, it renders itself in multiple senses. It renders itself in that it abandons itself to its givee, to allow him the act of acceptance. It also renders itself to its giver, in that it puts itself at his disposal to allow the act of giving. Finally, it renders itself to itself in that it is perfectly accomplished in dissipating itself without return, as a pure abandoned gift, possible in all impossibility.

Thus, the reduced gift—which is illustrated with the phenomenon of the gift giving itself and making itself received—accomplishes the *self* of the full phenomenon (*phénomène plénier*). That which appears, appears as that which shows itself (Heidegger); but that which shows itself, shows itself and can show itself only in itself, hence on the basis of itself. But once again, it can do this showing of itself on the basis of itself only if, in showing itself, it puts its self in play (which, in short, can happen only if it gives itself in itself). A phenomenon shows itself in itself only if it gives its *self*.[27] And giving itself here signifies giving itself in the visible, without reserve or retreat, hence without condition or measure, hence without cause or reason. Unless it is said that the real reason for appearing, like that for givenness, consists in not having a reason. The gift gives itself of itself without borrowing anything from a possibility that comes from elsewhere, such as the parsimonious calculation of sufficient reason—in short, without any other possibility than its own. The gift reduced to givenness requires no (privileged) rights ([*passe-*]*droit*) in order to give itself or to show itself as it gives itself. It requires no possibility from anything, but gives possibility to all on the basis of that which it opens in and by itself.

The Gift Without Principle of Sufficient Reason

Whence it follows that, in exceeding the requirement for a cause and a reason, not only does the gift not lack rationality but, completely to the contrary, it could also be able to constitute itself as a "greater reason" than the tight *ratio reddenda* of metaphysics. Or again: Could it not be that the gift provides the nonmetaphysical figure of possibility par excellence, and that the possibility that is "higher than actuality" opens itself first of all as gift? In other words, if the phenomenon in the strict sense opens itself in itself and on the basis of itself, welling up from a possibility that is absolutely its own, unforeseeable, and new, then could not the gift offer itself as the privileged phenomenon—more exactly, as the figure of all phenomenality?[28]

That the gift reduced to givenness, and—on its basis—the phenomenon as pure given arise from no other cause or reason, but only from themselves, in no way implies that they lack rationality or that they have a conceptual deficiency. For nothing proves that the highest rationality of a phenomenon is defined by the requirement to render reason for its phenomenality to an instance other than itself. It could be that such a figure of reason—a metaphysical figure of heteronomous reason—suffers from an immeasurable deficiency, and that it compromises and even censures the phenomenality of all phenomena, to the point that, in these nihilistic times, it could be that the only phenomena that can still burst forth into broad daylight are those whose intuitive saturation frees them from the grasp of the principle of reason. And to contest the primacy of the principle of reason over the phenomenon—or, what here amounts to the same, of the economy over the gift—is in no way a misguided undertaking, since one and the other, in their respective formulations, spell out a fundamental contradiction precisely from the point of view of givenness.

For the economy, which is founded on exchange, requires equality and its justice, since it is itself defined thus: "Proprius actus justitiae nihil aliud est quam reddere unicuique quod suum est (The proper act of justice is none other than to *render* to each his own)."[29] But what does *reddere* signify here, if not "render" (that is, "regive," hence first of all "give")? Justice would therefore consist in giving to each, possibly (but not necessarily) in return and by reaction, what is due to him. But then justice is no longer based on exchange, since exchange itself is understood here as a particular (moreover, devalued) mode of the gift! Hence, on the contrary, like exchange itself, justice would presume an original intervention, however dissimulated, of the gift itself. Could the reason of exchange and justice lie hidden in the gift, and not at all the inverse? To be sure, the economy could neither reduce the gift nor be reduced to it, but it could arise from it by simplification and neutralization; in short, it could in the end require it and attest to it as its real reason.

Is it the same for the principle of reason? Actually, Leibniz constantly bases it—the "great metaphysical principle" that he proclaims it to be—on the same surrender to *reddere*: "Axioma magnum./Nihil est sine ratione./Sive, quod idem est, nihil existit quin aliqua ratio reddi possit (saltem ab omniscio) cur sit potius quam non sit et cur sic sit potius quam aliter" (The great axiom/Nothing is without reason./Or, what amounts to the same: Nothing exists without it being possible [(at least for (one who has) omniscience] to *render* some reason why it is rather than is not and why it is so rather than otherwise).[30] One can render a reason for everything—but how is one to render a reason for it being necessary to *render* this very reason? Though the solidity of the principle of reason has nothing to fear from attempts to submit it to, for example, the principles of contradiction or identity, and though it can resist the quietist pretensions of gratuity or indeterminism, it nevertheless wavers before the immanence of *reddere* in it. For to provide a sufficient reason, it is necessary that a mind (an omniscient mind, as it turns out, for contingent statements) renders it. But rendering it (*re-dare*) implies that one regives it, that one gives it in return, hence essentially that one gives it. For the French *rendre* (render) derives from the colloquial Latin *rendere*, formed from *reddere* in relation to *prendre* (take).[31]

In the end, it may also be possible to translate "render reason" by "re-presentation" (Heidegger); but this re-presentation neither exhausts nor replaces givenness, from which it arises, and which allows it as one of its derived operations. That even (sufficient) reason—which is so foreign to the gift—needs to be given is plainly no longer justified by the principle of rendering reason, which in this instance is capable of nothing and understands nothing. Since it is even necessary to render reason, it, too, rests on the gift, and not at all on itself. Therefore reason, which does not know how to give, never suffices for *giving* this other "reason" for rendering reason—hence the gift alone can give it. Reason becomes truly sufficient only if the gift (reduced to givenness) gives it (and renders it) to itself. Reason suffices no more for thinking itself than for thinking the gift. In short, if it is necessary to regive reason, this implies that the *ratio* remains, in itself, secondary and derivative from a more originary instance—the givenness that puts it in the position of operating as a complete reason and a final argument. Givenness governs the *ratio reddenda* more intimately than exchange rules the gift, because no reason can be dispensed from being rendered (that is, from a gift putting it on the stage and preceding it). The gift alone renders reason to itself, for it alone suffices for giving it. This time the gift no longer waits for its good standing by right (*bon droit*) of reason, but on the contrary justifies reason, because it precedes reason, as a "greater reason" than reason.

The gift alone gives reason and renders reason to itself. It thus challenges the second principle of metaphysics, just as it contradicted the first. How, precisely, is this privilege of the gift's metaphysical extraterritoriality to be understood, and how is it to be extended to phenomenality in general?

The gift gives reason, and gives it to reason itself; in other words, it renders to reason its full validity, because it gives itself reason, without any condition or exception. In fact, the characteristic of a gift consists in its never being wrong and always being right (literally, having reason): it depends on no due or duty, hence it never appears owing or in debt. Having no presupposition (not even the justice of equality or the equality of exchange), no prior condition, no requisite, the gift gives (itself) absolutely freely. For it always comes (*advient*) unhoped-for and unexpectedly, in excess and without being weighed on a balance. It can never be refused or declined; or, if it is refused (and we have clearly seen that this can often be done), it can never be refused with legitimate reason nor, above all, can it be refused the right to give itself, since it gives itself without price, without salary, without requirement or condition. Always coming in excess, it demands nothing, removes nothing, and takes nothing from anybody. The gift is never wrong, because it never does wrong. Never being wrong, it is always right (literally, has reason). Therefore, it delivers its reason at the same time as itself—reason that it gives in giving itself and without asking any other authority than its own advent. The gift coincides with its reason, because its mere givenness suffices as reason for it. Reason sufficing for itself, the gift gives itself reason in giving itself.

But isn't it the same for the phenomenon in general, at least provided that it truly shows itself in and on the basis of itself, because it gives itself of itself in an accomplished givenness (according to the anamorphosis, the unpredictable landing [*arrivage*], the fait accompli, the incident and eventness [*événementalité*])?[32] Isn't it clearer still if first of all one considers saturated phenomena (the event, the idol, the flesh, and the icon or the face)?[33] When it shows itself on the basis of itself and in itself, the phenomenon comes to pass (*parvient*) only in giving itself, hence in coming (*advenant*), without any other condition than its sovereign possibility. It shows itself in that it imposes itself in visibility, without cause or principle that would precede it (for if they are found, they will come only after its coming, reconstituted a posteriori). Moreover, it does not simply show itself in the visible, such that its horizon defines it *ne varietur* (without anything changing); it adds itself there at the same time as each new instant; and it adds itself there because it adds a new visible that until then had remained unseen and that would have remained so without this unexpected event. Hence, it redefines the horizon to the measure of its own new dimensions, pushing back its limits. Every painter knows perfectly well that in bringing about a painting, he reproduces nothing in the world, but produces a new visible, introduces a new phenomenon, and makes it an irrevocable gift. The phenomenon is never wrong, but always right (literally, has reason), a reason that appears with its gift—its sole and intrinsic reason.

Notes

1. "To give everything" [*tout donner*] is perhaps an odd expression because on the occasions when I say that I give "everything," most of the time I in fact give nothing (nothing real, no thing—first paradox), and this very fact allows me to give all that I can, namely, to give myself (almost) without reserve of restraint (second paradox). But what is the significance of this gift where I give nothing in order to give myself—precisely not as a thing, but as an "unreal" gift, completely given and yet repeatable? From the very outset, we find ourselves in an aporia.

2. The normal English translation of *donataire* is "recipient." However, in *Being Given*, Kosky introduces "givee," which preserves the common root of *donateur, donataire, don,* and *donner*. Because of the parallels between *Being Given* and this chapter, we have followed Kosky's choice. (Trans.)

3. On the question of the gift, its possible contradiction, and the critique of my treatment of it in *RG*, see, in succession: Jacques Derrida's remarks in *Given Time. I: Counterfeit Money,* trans. Peggy Kamuf (Chicago: University of Chicago Press, 1992), esp. pp. 12ff. and 50ff.; translation of *Given Time, Donner le temps. 1: La fausse monnaie,* in the series La Philosophie en Effet (Paris: Éditions Galilée, 1991), pp. 24ff. and 72ff.; my response in *BG,* 74ff./*ED,* 108ff; and our debate, *OTG.*

4. It is appropriate here to acknowledge the analyses of Camille Tarot, *De Durkheim à Mauss, l'invention du symbolique: Sociologie des sciences de la religion* (Paris: La Découverte, 1999); and Alain Caillé, *Anthropologie du don: Le tiers paradigme* (Paris: Desclée de Brouwer, 2000).

5. Anne Robert Jacques Turgot, *Reflections on the Formation and Distribution of Wealth* (written in 1766, published in 1768–70), in *The Economics of A .R. J. Turgot,* ed. and trans. P. D. Groenewegen (The Hague: Martinus Nijhoff, 1977), §31, p. 57.

6. Antoine-Augustin Cournot, *Researches into the Mathematical Principles of the Theory of Wealth,* trans. Nathaniel T. Bacon, in the series Reprints of Economic Classics (New York: Macmillan, 1927; repr. New York: Kelley, 1971), §2, p. 10, and §6, pp. 16–17.

7. Ibid., §2, p. 8; Cournot's emphasis.

8. Though one could easily refer to Descartes (e.g., *Discourse on Method, AT,* VI, 61-62), Cournot refers more to Leibniz: "We have already sketched elsewhere [*Traité de l'enchaînement des ideés fondamentales,* II, chap. 7] the principles of this *superior dynamic* for which Leibniz had the idea, and which shows us, in the laws that govern the work of machines, a proper example for conceiving the much more general laws under whose empire the perpetual conversion of natural forces into one another is brought about; in the same way one can establish a comparison between the phenomenon of economic production and the work of machines, so as to adjust [*render sensible*] the analogies they present" (*Principes de la théorie de richesses* [1860], ed. Gerard Jorland, in Cournot's *Oeuvres complètes,* vol. 9 [Paris: Vrin, 1981], p. 39; Cournot's emphasis). In his own way, Diderot fully recognized and stated that the "economy" is inscribed in the deployment of a *mathesis universalis* in its strictly Cartesian meaning, on which it depends from beginning to end for the radicality of objectification: "One holds forth, one investigates, one feels little and reasons much; one *measures everything to the scrupulous level of method,* of logic and even of truth. . . . Economic science is a fine thing, but it stupefies us." *Salon de 1769,* in Diderot's *Oeuvres complètes,* vol. 16, *Beaux-arts III,* ed. Herbert Dieckmann and Jean Varloot (Paris: Hermann, 1990), 657; emphasis added.

9. *Rendre raison* means to give a rational explanation or reason, thereby making something appear reasonable. However, because both "render" and "reason" are important terms in this chapter, *render raison* is translated throughout by the somewhat clumsy "render reason." (Trans.)

10. Jean-Baptiste Say, *A Treatise on Political Economy or The Production, Distribution and Consumption of Wealth* (New York: Claxton, Remsen & Haffelinger, 1880), translation of *Traité d'économie politique ou Simple exposition de la manière dont se forment, se distribuent et se consomment les richesses,* 6th ed., ed. Horace Say (Paris: Guillaumin, 1841; 1st ed., 1803), vol. 1, p. 455, and vol. 1, p. 117.

11. Karl Marx, *Capital: A Critique of Political Economy. Book One: The Process of Production of Capital,* trans. From the 3rd German ed. by Samuel Moore and Edward Aveling, ed. Frederick Engels (London: Lawrence

and Wishart, 1954), chap. 19, p. 506; chap. 18, p. 500; chap. 6, p. 172; chap.1, sec. 4, pp. 84f. (emphasis added). The excess of surplus value, which does not appear in the exchange's formulation, destroys its equality. This fact contradicts not only social justice, and Ricardo's or Smith's theory of value, but also invalidates the very notion of a political economy (henceforth dubbed "bourgeois"). Excess—even the invisible excess of surplus value—destroys the terms of exchange, and thus the economy. Certainly, Bataille envisages an economy based on excess: "The solar radiance . . . finally finds nature and the meaning of the sun: it is necessary for it to give, *to lose itself without calculation*. A living system grows, or lavishes itself *without reason*," such that "in practical terms, from the perspective of riches, the radiance of the sun is distinguished by its unilateral character: it loses itself *without counting, without consideration. The solar economy* is founded on this principle" ("The Economy to the Proportion of the Universe," trans. Michael Richardson, in *Georges Bataille: Essential Writings*, ed. Michael Richardson [London: Sage, 1998], pp. 75 and 74; translation of "L'économie à la mesure de l'univers," first published in *La France libre* no. 65 [July 1946], repr. In Bataille's *Oeuvres complètes* [Paris: Gallimard, 1976], vol. 7, p. 10; Bataille's emphasis). But one can question the legitimacy of thinking (and naming) this excess (without reason or measure) of expenditure starting from an economy, unless one assumes an economy deprived of exchange, price, and calculation; that is, the contrary of what economists understand by this term.

12. Marx relies here on Aristotle's arguments. On the one hand, equality defines justice, and therefore exchange: "Since the unjust man is unequal and the unjust act unequal, it is clear that there is also an intermediate for the unequal. And this is the equal." On the other hand, injustice consists in upsetting equality by appropriating "more" (value): "The man who acts unjustly has too much, and the man who is unjustly treated too little, of what is good." *Nicomachean Ethics*, trans. W. D. Ross, rev. J. O. Urmson, in *The Complete Works of Aristotle: The Revised Oxford Translation*, ed. Jonathan Barnes, Bollingen Series 71:2, vol. 2 (Princeton, N.J.: Princeton University Press, 1984), V.3.1131a10–11; V.3.1131b19–20.

13. Leibniz strongly emphasizes that this universality of the principle of sufficient reason extends to the contingency of the event. *"No fact* can be real or actual, and no proposition true, without there being a sufficient reason for its being so and not otherwise" (*G. W. Leibniz's Monadology: An Edition for Students*, trans. Nicholas Rescher [Pittsburgh, Pa.: University of Pittsburgh Press, 1991], §32, p.116; emphasis added); or "The principle in question is the principle of the want of a sufficient reason *for a thing to exist, for an event to happen*" ("Fifth Letter to Clarke," in *G. W. Leibniz: Philosophical Essays*, ed. and trans. Roger Ariew and Daniel Garber [Indianapolis, Ind.: Hackett, 1989], §125, p. 346; emphasis added). Or again: "Constat ergo omnes veritates *etiam maxime contingentes* probationem a priori seu rationem aliquam cur sint potius quam non sint habere. Atque hoc ipsum est quod volgo dicunt, nihil fieri sine causa, seu nihil esse sine ratione (It is therefore established that all truths, *even the most contingent*, have an a priori proof or some reason why they are rather than are not. And this is what the vulgar say: Nothing comes to be without cause; or: Nothing is without reason)"; untitled text described on the contents page by the editor [Gerhardt] as "Ohne Überschrift, in Betreff [Untitled, in] der Mittel der philosophischen Beweisführung [Reference to the Means of Philosophical Demonstration]," in *Die philosophischen Schriften von Gottfried Wilhelm Leibnix*, ed. C. I. Gerhardt, 7 vols. (Berlin: Weidmann, 1875–90), vol. 7, p. 301; emphasis added.

14. Without repeating the Cartesian *causa sui*, which submits even God to causality (*de ipso Deo quaeri potest* [which can be asked even about God himself], *IIae Responsiones*, AT VII, 164, 1. 29)—or, in His case alone, to reason—Leibniz nevertheless thinks God as being a reason (His own sufficient reason)

for Himself: "Vides quid ex illo theoremate sequatur, *nihil est sine ratione* . . . omnia, quae sibi ipsi ratio cur sint, no sunt . . . ea tamdiu in rationem, et rationem rationis, reducenda esse, donec reducantur in id quod sibi ipsi ratio est, id est Ens a se, seu Deum (You see what follows from the thesis: *nothing is without reason* . . . everything that is not a reason for its own existence . . . is to be reduced to its reason, and its reason's reason, until it is reduced to what is its own reason, namely, the Being of itself, that is, God)"; *Confessio philosophi,* in Leibniz's *Sämtliche Schriften und Briefe,* ser. 6, vol. 3, *Philosophische Schriften: 1672–1676,* ed. Leibniz-Forschungsstelle der Universität Münster (Berlin: Akademie-Verlag, 1980), p. 120; Leibniz's italics.

15. Pierre Corneille: "Cinna, let us be friends! An end to strife!/You were my enemy; I spared your life;/Despite your base designs—that plot insane—/I'll spare my would-be killer's life again!/ Let's now compete and time its view deliver/On who fares best—recipient or giver./My bounties you've betrayed; I'll shower more:/You shall be overwhelmed, as ne'er before!" (*Cinna or The Clemency of Augustus,* in *Le Cid; Cinna; Polyeuct: Three Plays,* trans. Noel Clark [Bath: Absolute Classics, 1993], V, 3, vv. 1701–8). Admittedly, Cinna receives the gift as it is given—but we are here in Corneille's world and not in ours.

16. See my analysis in *IEIDS,* chap. 5.

17. The French *conscience* can mean either "conscience" or "consciousness." (Trans.)

18. Fatherhood gives *itself* only to the extent that it gives. Thus it inverts and bears out the definition of "the gifted [*l'adonné*]," who receives *himself* from what he receives. See *BG,* §26, esp. pp. 266ff./*ED,* 366ff.

19. On the phenomenon's determinations as given, see *BG,* bk. 3, pp. 119ff./*ED,* 169ff. I mention only some of them here, but fatherhood also validates the others (anamorphosis, facticity, fait accompli, incident, etc.).

20. "Givenness" is the obvious English translation for both *donnéité* and the German *Gegebenheit.* "Givenness" is, however, already well established as the English translation for Marion's *donation.* To avoid any confusion, "givenence" has been introduced as an alternative. (Trans.)

21. See Roland Barthes: "Historically, the discourse of absence is carried on by the woman: Woman is sedentary, Man hunts, journeys; Woman is faithful (she waits), man is fickle (he sails away, he cruises). . . . It follows that, in every man who speaks of the absence of the other, *the feminine* declares itself: this man who waits and who suffers from it, is miraculously feminised." Roland Barthes, *A Lover's Discourse: Fragments,* trans. Richard Howard (London: Jonathan Cape, 1979), pp. 13–14; translation of *Fragments d'un discours amoureux* (Paris: Seuil, 1977), p. 20; Barthes' emphasis.

22. Michel Henry does this with an exemplary rigor, by opposing reciprocity—"The phenomenon that is at the economy's origin is exchange, the concept of which cannot be formed independently of that of reciprocity"—to that which goes beyond it—"the nonreciprocity of the interior relation that connects us to God signifies the intervention of another relation than that which is established among men," that [relation] precisely where "each person is son of God and of him alone . . . no living being having the power to bring itself into life." *Paroles du Christ* (Paris: Seuil, 2002), pp. 37, 46, 47.

23. Leibniz, *Monadology,* §31, p. 21.

24. Leibniz, *Monadology,* §32, p. 21

25. See *BG*, §§17–18 (and bk. 3, passim).

26. This gift, which imposes itself to be given and received of itself, could be described, with Barthes, as *adorable*, for "*Adorable* means: this is my desire, insofar as it is unique: 'That's it! That's it exactly (which I love)!' Yet the more I experience the specialty of my desire, the less I can give it a name; to the precision of the target corresponds a wavering [*tremblement*] of the name; what is characteristic of desire, proper to desire, can produce only an impropriety of the utterance. Of this failure of language, there remains only one trace: the word 'adorable' (the right translation of 'adorable' would be the Latin *ipse*: it is the self, himself, herself, in person)" (Barthes, *A Lover's Discourse*, p. 20/*Fragments d'un discours amoureux*, p. 27). In fact, the ipseity and the pure self of this phenomenon—that which it is a question of loving, hence of receiving, hence of giving—come to it perhaps from precisely what they liberate from my desire and from its language, which, in this adorable, see only fire, only a manifest object of an obscure desire.

27. On the transition from "show itself" to "give itself," see *BG*, §6, pp. 58ff.

28. Thus this remark, which Barthes makes in passing, would take on all its weight: "The gift then reveals the test of strength of which it is the instrument" (*A Lover's Discourse,* p. 76/*Fragments d'un discours amoureux*, p. 91).

29. Thomas Aquinas, *Summa theologiae*, IIa IIae, q. 58, a. 11 (emphasis added), referring to Aristotle (*Nicomachean Ethics*, V), who does not, however, use this exact formula.

30. Leibniz, *Elementa verae pietatis* (1677–78), in Gaston Grua, *Textes inédits*, 2 vols. (Paris: Presses Universitaires de France, 1948), vol. 1, p. 13; emphasis added. See also vol. 1, p. 25; and "Specimen inventorum de admirandis naturae generalis arcanis," in Leibniz's *Die philosophischen Schriften*, vol. 7, p. 309.

31. See Oscar Bloch and Walther von Wartburg, *Dictionnaire étymologique de la langue française*, 8th ed. (Paris: Presses Universitaires de France, 1989; 1st ed., 1932), p. 546; Alfred Ernout, Morphologie historique du latin, 3rd ed., Nouvelle Collection à l'Usage des Classes, no. 32 (Paris: Klincksieck, 1953; 1st ed., 1914), §207, p. 136; and Antonio Maria Martin Rodriguez, *Los verbos de "dar" en latín arcaico y clásico* (Grand Canary: Universidad de Las Palmas, 1999), *ad loc*. This is confirmed by Vincent Carraud, who emphasizes this "fundamental meaning" (*donner la raison* [to give reason], *ratio redenda/ratio reddita*, etc.) even in the formulas of the history of metaphysics (*Causa sive ratio: La raison de la cause, de Suarez à Leibniz* [Paris: Presses Universitaires de France, 2002], pp. 27ff., 436, 462 and n. 1, 492, etc.).

32. On the determinations of the phenomenon as pure given, see *BG*, bk. 3.

33. On the analysis of saturated phenomena, see *BG*, bk. 4, §§21–35, and *IE*, passim.

27 The Madness of Economic Reason: A Gift without Present

Jacques Derrida

At the same time we are thinking the impossible, and it is at the same time.

What does "at the same time" mean to say? Where could one ever place oneself in order to say "at the same time"? And to say what is meant, for example in some language or another, by "at the same time"?

It is as if we were looking for complications, for *midi à quatorze heures* as we say in French, literally, for noon at two o'clock, and as if we wanted to show that we were given to, and even gifted at, tracking the impossible. That is what the narrator of "Counterfeit Money" says when speaking of the "exhausting faculty" that "nature" has given him as a "gift." To look for noon at two o'clock is to torment one's mind trying to find that which, by defini-tion, cannot be found where one is looking for it and especially not at the moment one is looking for it. At no *given moment*, at no *desired moment* [moment voulu] can one reasonably hope to find, outside any relativity, noon at two o'clock. This contradiction is the logical and chronological form of the *impossible* simultaneity of two times, of two events separated in time and which therefore cannot be given *at the same time*. To look for the impossible is that form of madness in which we seem to have enclosed ourselves up to now. It is true that looking for "noon" is not just any madness and it is not looking for just any moment; perhaps it is to dream, at whatever time and always too late (at two o'clock it's already too late), of an origin without shadow, without dialectical negativity, in the solar course on the basis of which we calculate time; it is to dream while strolling along, like the two friends in "Counterfeit Money"; it is to sleepwalk in the vicinity of the impossible.

Perhaps what was said or told the last time sounded a little mad. How is one to speak reasonably, in a sensible fashion, that is, accessible to common sense, of a gift that could not be what it was except on the condition of not being what it was? On the condition of not being or appearing to be the gift of anything, of anything that is or that is present, come from someone and given to someone? On the condition of "being" a gift without given and without giving, without presentable thing and act? A gift that would neither give *itself*, nor give itself *as such*, and that could not take place except on the condition of not taking place—and of remaining impossible, without dialectical sublation of the contradiction? To desire, to desire to think the impossible, to desire, to desire to give the impossible—this is obviously madness. The discourse that orders itself on this madness cannot not let itself be contaminated by it. This discourse on madness appears to go mad in its turn, *alogos* and *atopos*. *Alogos* as well because it claims to render an account (the demand to *render account* that we mentioned at the conclusion), to render account and reason (*reddere rationem*) of that very thing, the gift, that demands an unheard-of-accounting since it must not conclude in either a balancing of income and expenses, in an economic circle, or in the regulated rationality of a calculation, a metrics, a symmetry, or any kind of relation, which is to say in a *logos*, to stay with this injunction of the Greek term, which means at once reason, discourse, relation, and account. It is *logos* and *normos* that, as we saw, are sent into crisis by the madness of the gift—but perhaps as well *topos*. *Atopos*, as we know, means that which is not in its place (noon at two o'clock) and thus it means the extraordinary, the unusual, the strange, the extravagant, the absurd, the mad. Only an *atopic* and *utopic* madness, *perhaps* (a certain *perhaps* or *maybe* will be both the modality and the modality to be modified or our meditation), could thus give rise to the gift that can give only on the condition of not taking place, taking up residence or domicile: *the gift may be, if there is any.*

This madness, let us recall, would also be that of a forgetting, of a given and desired forgetting, not as a negative experience therefore, like an amnesia and a loss of memory, but as the affirmative condition of the gift. How, without madness, can one desire the forgetting of that which will have been, like the gift, a gift without ambivalence, a gift that would not be a *pharmakon* or a poisoned present (*Gift/gift*)[1] but a good, a good that would not be an object (a good given as a thing) but the good of the gift, of giving or donation itself? How does one desire forgetting? How does one desire not to keep? How does one desire mourning (assuming that to mourn, to work at mourning does not amount to keeping—and here we touch on what remains no doubt the unavoidable problem of mourning, of the relation between gift and grief, between what should be non-work, the non-work of the gift, and the work of mourning)? How does one desire forgetting or the non-keeping of the gift if, implicitly, the gift is evaluated as good, indeed as the very origin of what is good, of the good, and of value?

Linked to the double bind (double ligature, double stricture,[2] double obligation to link and unlink absolutely, thus to absolve and to forgive by giving), this madness is all the more maddened and maddening that it besieges reason at its two borders, so to speak, from the inside and the outside. It is at once reason and unreason because it also manifests that madness of the rational *logos* itself, that madness of the economic circle the calculation of which is constantly reconstituted, logically, rationally, annulling the excess that itself, as we underscored at the conclusion of the preceding chapter, entails the circle, makes it turn without end, gives it its movement, a movement that the circle and the ring can never comprehend or annul. Whence the difficulty in knowing whom and what one is talking about. Is madness the economic circulation annulling the gift in equivalence? Or is it the excess, the expenditure, or the destruction?

To make another indicative and preliminary appeal to *The Gift*, we will lift an exemplary fragment from it in which madness is named. Evoking it in passing and in the form of an adverb ("madly"), Mauss seems to be quite unaware of what he is naming and whether one can still call one thing by the name of gift and another thing by the name of exchange.

Mauss is describing the potlatch.[3] He speaks of it blithely as "gifts exchanged." But he never asks the question as to whether gifts can remain gifts once they are exchanged. A long *nota bene* has just specified that "there are potlatches everywhere. . . . As in Melanesia it is a constant give-and-take." This latter expression, also in English in the original, is translated "donner et recevoir." So, translating "take" by "recevoir," Mauss continues: "The potlatch *itself*, so typical a phenomenon, and at the same time so characteristic of these tribes, *is none other than* the system of gifts exchanged" (p. 35). (We underscore "itself," this word that marks the assurance and the certainty that one has touched the essential property of an identifiable thing corresponding to a proper name: potlatch; we also underscore the locution "is none other than": It confirms once again the identificatory tranquility of this assurance.)

Mauss does not worry enough about this incompatibility between gift and exchange or about the fact that an exchanged gift is only a tit for tat, that is, an annulment of the gift. By underscoring this, we do not mean to say that *there is no* exchanged gift. One cannot deny the *phenomenon*, nor that which presents this precisely phenomenal aspect of exchanged gifts. But the apparent, visible contradiction of these two values—gift and exchange—must be problematized. What must be interrogated, it seems, is precisely this being-together, the at-the-same-time, the synthesis, the symmetry, the syntax, or the system, the *syn* that joins together two processes that are by rights as incompatible as that of the gift and that of exchange. Can one speak without any second thoughts of something that would be "none other," in "*itself*," "than the system of gifts exchanged"?

The *syn* of this system, as we shall see in a moment, has an essential relation to *time*, to a certain delay, to a certain *deferral/differing* [différer] in time. The "it is none other than" takes on all its relief when, right after this, Mauss marks a difference: "the only differences are . . . ," he is going to note. This difference is precisely that of the *excessive*. An essential exaggeration marks this process. Exaggeration cannot be here a feature among others, still less a secondary feature. The problem of the gift has to do with its nature that is *excessive in advance, a priori exaggerated*. A donating experience that would not be delivered over, *a priori*, to some immoderation, in other words, a moderate, measured gift would not be a gift. To give and thus do something other than calculate its return in exchange, the most modest gift must pass beyond measure. Mauss continues:

The potlatch . . . is none other than the system of gifts exchanged. The only differences are in the violence, exaggeration, and antagonisms it arouses, on the one hand and, on the other, by a certain lack of juridical concepts, and in a simpler, more brutal structure than in Melanesia, especially with the two northern nations, the Tlingit and the Haida . . . (Ibid.)

And before describing this exaggeration of the Indians in a passage where precisely "madness" will be named and where, at least twice, the question of the lexicon will appear inevitable, Mauss stays a moment longer with the Melanesians or the Polynesians so as to describe both the circle, the regular circulation of what he insists on calling *gifts*, and the role played by *time* in this circulation. The decisive concepts here are those of "credit" and "term" (in the sense of the term of a loan or a debt) in the potlatch:

Gifts *circulate* [emphasis added; how can gifts circulate?], as we have seen, in Melanesia and Polynesia, with the certainty that they will be reciprocated. Their "guarantee" [*sûreté*: also security deposit] is in the virtue of the thing given [we will come back to this] which is itself that "guarantee." But in every possible form of society, it is in the nature of a gift to impose an obligatory *time limit or term* [emphasis added]. By definition, even a meal shared in common, a distribution of *kava*, or a talisman that one takes away, cannot be reciprocated immediately. "Time" [an expression that Mauss puts in quotation marks, no doubt aware of the obscure character of this notion and the fact that, beneath the word time, it is no doubt a matter, in the homogeneous element of chronology, of a more complex and qualitatively more heterogeneous structure of delay, of interval, of maturation, or of differance] is needed to perform any counter-service. The notion of a *time limit or term* [emphasis added again] is thus logically implied when it is a question of paying or returning visits [*rendre des visites*: an interesting expression in the French idiom: a visit is always repaid or returned even when it is the first], contracting marriages and alliances, establishing peace, attending games or regulated contests, celebrating alternative festivals, rendering ritual and honorific services [*rendre les services*: an equally interesting expression: This language of restitution is necessary even for services that one "gives" for the first time], "showing reciprocal respect" [a Tlingit expression]—all the things that are exchanged at the same time as other things that become increasingly numerous and valuable, as these societies become richer. (P. 36)

The term "term" marks a mark: It is the limit of a due date, the cadence of a falling due [*échéance*]. It thus implies time, the interval that separates reception from restitution, In Mauss's view, the *term* forms the original and essential feature of the *gift*. The interval of this delay to deadline allows Mauss to pass unnoticed over that contradiction between gift and exchange on which I have insisted so much and which leads to madness in the case both where the gift must remain foreign to circular exchange as well as where it is pulled into that exchange, unless it is the gift itself that does the pulling. The differance marked by the term "term" is comparable here to a guardrail, *un garde-fou*, against the madness of the gift. Mauss is not at all bothered about speaking of exchanged gifts; he even thinks there is gift only in exchange. However the *syn-*, the *syn*thesis, the *sys*tem, or the *syn*tax that joins together gift and exchange is temporal—or more precisely temporizing—differance, the delay of the term or the term of delay that dislocates any "at the same time." The identity between gift and exchange would not be immediate and analytical. It would have in effect the form of an *a priori* synthesis: a synthesis because it requires temporization and *a priori*—in other words necessary—because it is required at the outset by *the thing itself*, namely by the very object of the gift, by the force or the virtue that would be inherent to it. Here is, it seems, the most interesting idea, the great guiding thread of *The Gift*: For those who participate in the experience of gift and countergift, the requirement of restitution "at term," at the delayed "due date," the requirement of the circulatory differance *is inscribed in the thing itself* that is given or exchanged. Before it is a contract, an intentional gesture of individual or collective subjects, the movement of gift/countergift is a *force* (a "virtue of the thing given," says Mauss), a property immanent to the thing or in any case apprehended as such by the donors and donees. Moved by a mysterious force, the thing itself demands gift *and* restitution, it requires therefore "time," "term," "delay," "interval" of temporization, the becoming-temporization of temporalization, the animation of a neutral and homogeneous time by the desire of the gift and the restitution. Differance, which (is) nothing, is (in) the thing itself. It is (given) in the thing itself. It (is) the thing itself. It, differance, the thing (itself). It, without anything other. Itself, nothing.

The transformation of temporalization into temporization would be the movement of this desire for the gift/countergift. It would be inscribed in, *upon* [à même] the given-exchanged thing. This demand of the thing, this demand for term and temporization, would be the very structure of the thing. The thing would demand limit and time, at once the mark or the margin—that is, the measure that sets a boundary—and temporality. And the thing would be a thing, that is, it would have its "virtue" or its essence of thing, only in this demand. The demand dawns in what is called the gift-counter-gift.

What is a thing that one can talk about it in this fashion? Later we will have to encounter this question in or beyond its Heideggerian modality, but it seems to be posed in a certain way at the very opening of *The Gift*, right after the definition of a program and the quotation of a poetic text in epigraph. (Why must one begin with a poem when one speaks of the gift? And why does the gift always appear to be the *gift of the poem*, the *don du poème* as Mallarmé says?) Here are the first words in italics: "*What rule of legality and self-interest, in societies of a backward or archaic type, compels the present that has been received to be obligatorily reciprocated? What force is there in the given thing that causes its recipient to pay it back?*" (p. 3).

One can translate as follows: The gift is not a gift, the gift only gives to the extent it *gives time*. The difference between a gift and every other operation of pure and simple exchange is that the gift gives time. *There where there is gift, there is time.* What it gives, the gift, is time, but this gift of time is also a demand of time. The thing must not be restituted *immediately and right away*. There must be time, it must last, there must be waiting—without forgetting [*l'attente—sans oubli*]. It demands time, the thing, but it demands a delimited time, neither an instant nor an infinite time, but a time determined by a term, in other words, a rhythm, a cadence. The thing is not *in* time; it is or it has time, or rather it demands to have, to give, or to take time—and time as rhythm, a rhythm that does not befall a homogeneous time but that structures it originarily.

The gift gives, demands, and takes time. The thing gives, demands, or takes time. That is one of the reasons this thing of the gift will be linked to the—internal—necessity of a certain narrative [*récit*] or of a certain poetics of narrative. That is why we will take account of "Counterfeit Money" and of the impossible account [*compte-rendu*] that is Baudelaire's tale. The thing as given thing, the given of the gift arrives, if it arrives, only in narrative. And in a poematic simulacrum of narrative. The opening of *The Gift* inscribes, then, in epigraph an "old poem from the Scandinavian *Edda*" of which one stanza (45) is made to stand out:

It is better not to beg [ask for something]
Than to sacrifice too much [to the gods]:
A present given always expects one in return.
It is better not to bring any offering
Than to spend too much on it. (P. 2)

Mauss maneuvers laboriously with this notion of time or term. He is seeking in it the distinctive trait of the gift, that which distinguishes the latter from credit, debt, or payment as these are determined by modern Western law or economy. In criticizing the vocabulary of certain authors, Mauss tries to restitute, so to speak, the value of gift, of "present made" and of "present repaid" where others wanted to describe the same operation of exchange with interest as a purely economic, commercial, or fiduciary operation, without needing in the least to have recourse to the category of the gift. For it might seem tempting to get rid of the mysterious and elusive character of this value of gift. And since we are saying with such insistence that it is impossible, why not denounce it as an illusion, even a sophism or paralogism, as well as a pseudo-problem that reason would require us, in good logic, to evacuate? Does it not suffice in fact to describe scientifically the objective exchange of values with usurious supplement, in short, the logic of credit, of interest rates, and of repayment due dates? By reintroducing the word and the category of gift where other authors attempt or are tempted to get by without it, Mauss would like to bring off several operations (and this is one of the admirable things about his essay: it seeks to match the stubbornness of this impossible non-thing that would be the gift with a certain stubbornness of its own): (1) to succeed in maintaining an originary specificity of the process of gift in relation to cold economic rationality, to capitalism, and mercantilism—and in that way to recognize in the gift that which sets the circle of economic exchange going; (2) to succeed in describing the symbolicity that runs throughout cold economic reason, to render an account of religious, cultural, ideological, discursive, esthetic, literary, poetic phenomena that are inseparable from the process of the gift and that organize it from within this *total social fact* which Mauss makes the very object of sociology (here it would be necessary to evoke his critique of a certain economism in Marx and the whole context of the *Cahiers de Sociologie*, and so forth); (3) to succeed in understanding the at least relative homogeneity of all human cultures, whatever may be the type or the level of economic and juridical functioning; (4) to succeed in making credit, time, "term"—or the supplementary differance (the "return-more-later")—into a demand, an *interest of the thing itself*, thus an interest that cannot be derived from anything other than the thing, an interest of the given thing, of the thing that calls for the gift, of the given "it" or *ça* (*ça* is not in Mauss's vocabulary): not the *ça* of *ça donne* (*es gibt, il y a*, there is) but of the *ça donné*, of the given it, although the thing's requirement that it be given-returned allows one to dispense with the distinction between the *it* of *it gives* and the *it* of the *given*. The given *it* will have required that *it* gives. The *it* is giving-given, giving-giving.[4] Finally, with the sole difference of a distancing in time and of the interest of usury, the *it* is at once, "at the same time," given-given and giving-giving.

To substantiate these remarks, let us consider a certain lexical maneuver by Mauss. We will give or take two examples of it.

First example. This example can interest us as well for the relation between the *date* and the *gift*, a relation that Mauss does not thematize.[5] On the question of the credit demanded by the thing in the potlatch among tribes of northwestern Canada, a note quotes Boas:

"In all his undertakings, the Indian trusts to the aid of his friends. He promises to pay them for this assistance at a later date. If the aid provided consists of valuable things, which are measured by the Indians in blankets, just as we measure them in money, he promises to pay back the value of the loan with interest. The Indian has no system of writing and consequently, to guarantee the transaction, the promise is made in public. To contract debts on the one hand, and to pay those debts on the other, constitutes the potlatch. This economic system is developed to such an extent that the capital possessed by all the individuals associated with the tribe far exceeds the quantity of available valuables that exists; in other words, the conditions are entirely analogous to those prevailing in our own society: if we desired to pay off all our debts, we would find that there was not nearly enough money, in fact, to settle them. The result of an attempt by all creditors to seek reimbursement of their loans [that is, together and immediately] is a disastrous panic that the community takes a long time to recover from." (P. 11, n. 131)

Let us notice first of all, in passing, this allusion to writing. To repeat the, in our view, very problematic expression of Boas, "the Indian has no system of writing." We thus see a certain relation shaping up between writing or its substitute (but what is a substitute for writing if not a writing?) and the process of the gift. The latter is perhaps not determined only as the content or the theme of a piece of writing—accounting, archive, memoirs, narrative, or poem—but already, in itself, as the marking of a trace. The gift would always be the gift of a writing, a memory, a poem, or a narrative, in any case, the legacy of a text; and writing would not be the formal auxiliary, the external archive of the gift, as Boas suggests here, but "something" that is tied to the very act of the gift, *act* in the sense both of the archive and the performative operation.

Boas concludes that, in the potlatch, the Indian wants *both* to pay his debts in public and to invest the fruits of his labor for the future, to prepare an inheritance for his children. Now, what does Mauss do after having quoted this long passage? He raises no essential objection, he judges the description to be exact, but he proposes a correction to the vocabulary. Here it is: "By correcting the terms 'debt,' 'payment,' 'reimbursement,' 'loan' and replacing them with such terms as 'presents made' and 'presents repaid,' terms that Boas moreover ends up by using himself, we have a fairly exact idea of how the notion of credit functions in the potlatch."

This correction inverts, therefore, the direction of the definitional circle. It appears tautological, but what is at stake in this correction is important for Mauss. For him, it is a matter of thinking the economic rationality of credit on the basis of the gift and not the reverse. The gift would be originary. It would be the true producer of value, being in itself the value of values. As Valéry says of spirit, the gift would be at once a value and the—priceless—origin of all value.[6] For Mauss's discourse is oriented by an ethics and a politics that tend to valorize the generosity of the giving-being. They oppose a liberal socialism to the inhuman coldness of economism, of those two economisms that would be capitalist mercantilism *and* Marxist communism.

Second example. Right after this, another apparently lexical maneuver objects to a sort of evolutionism. In failing to understand debt in its relation to the originary gift, in failing to understand "term" and deferred interest as gift effects, evolutionism ends up believing credit to be a late invention of very evolved societies.

Current economic and juridical history is largely mistaken in this matter. Imbued with modern ideas, it forms *a priori* ideas of development,* and follows a so-called necessary logic. All in all, it remains within old traditions. There is nothing more dangerous than this "unconscious sociology," as Simiand has termed it. For example, Cuq still states: "In primitive societies, only the barter regime is conceived of; in those more advanced, sales for cash are the practice. Sale on credit is characteristic of a higher phase in civilization. It first appears in an oblique form as a combination of cash sale and loans." In fact, the point of departure lies elsewhere. It is provided in a category of rights neglected by jurists and economists as uninteresting. This is the gift, a complex phenomenon, particularly in its most ancient form, that of *the total prestation which we are not studying in this essay. Now, the gift necessarily entails the notion of credit* [emphasis added]. The evolution in economic law has not been from barter to sale, and from cash sale to credit sale. It is on the foundation of a system of gifts given and returned over time [*à terme*] that have been established both barter, through simplification, by drawing together moments of time earlier dissociated, and purchase and sale, both credit and cash sale, as well as loans. For we have no evidence that any of the legal systems that have evolved beyond the phase we are describing (in particular, Babylonian law) remained ignorant of the credit process that is known in every archaic society that still survives today. This is another simple, realistic way of resolving the problem of the two "moments of time" brought together in the contract, which Davy has already studied. (P. 36)

*Note: We have failed to notice that the notion of "term" was not only as ancient, but also as simple, or, if you wish, as complex, as the notion of cash. (P. 111, n. 133)

These propositions belong to a subchapter titled "Honor and Credit," that is, two motifs that would be proper to this American potlatch. The subject of credit has just been addressed. It is on the subject of honor that madness irrupts into the scene that, in truth, it secretly organizes. We have made ourselves take this detour in order to arrive at this madness. The madness that insinuates itself even into Mauss's text is a certain excess of the gift. It goes so far perhaps as to burn up the very meaning of the gift; at the very least it threatens the presumed semantic unity that authorizes one to continue speaking of gift. Whereas, in the preceding paragraphs, he has shown himself to be so scrupulous, so demanding with regard to the *name* gift and the necessity of calling a gift a gift, Mauss will begin to proliferate signs—to give signs, as one says—of a lexical uncertainty, as if his language were about to go a little mad one page after it had insisted so strenuously on keeping the meaning of gift for the gift. His language goes mad at the point where, in the potlatch, the process of the gift *gets carried away with itself* [s'emporte lui-même] and where, as Mauss comes to say, "it is not even a question of giving and returning, but of destroying, so as not to want even to appear to desire repayment. . . ." The trembling of this uncertainty affects the word "gift" but also the word "exchange" with which Mauss regularly associates it. Here is the passage of madness:

No less important in these transactions of the Indians is the role played by honor. Nowhere is the individual prestige of a chief and that of his clan so closely linked to what is spent and to the meticulous repayment with interest of gifts that have been accepted, so as to transform those who have obligated you into the obligated ones. Consumption and destruction are here really without limits. In certain kinds of potlatch, one must expend all that one has, keeping nothing back. It is a competition to see who is the richest and also *the most madly* extravagant [le plus follement *dépensier*; emphasis added]. Everything is based upon the principles of antagonism and of rivalry. The political status of individuals in the brotherhoods and clans, and ranks of all kinds are gained in a "war of property," just as they are in real war, or through chance, inheritance, alliance, and marriage. Yet everything is conceived of as if it were a "struggle of wealth."* Marriages for one's children and places in the brotherhoods are only won during the potlatch exchanged and returned. They are lost at the potlatch as they are lost in war, by gambling or in running and wrestling. In a certain number of cases, *it is not even a question of giving and returning, but of destroying, so as not to want even to appear to desire repayment* [emphasis added]. Whole boxes of olachen (candlefish) oil or whale oil are burnt, as are houses and thousands of blankets. The most valuable copper objects are broken and thrown into the water, in order to crush and to "flatten" one's rival. In this way one not only promotes oneself, but also one's family, up the social scale. It is therefore a system of law and economics in which considerable wealth is constantly being expended and transferred. *One may, if one so desires, call these transfers by the name of exchange or even trade and sale; but* [emphasis added] such trade is noble, replete with etiquette and generosity. At least, when it is carried on in another spirit, with a view to immediate gain, it is the object of very marked scorn. (P. 37)

*Note: See especially the myth of Haiyas . . . who has lost face while gambling and dies. His sisters and his nephews go into mourning, give a "revenge" potlatch, and he comes to life again. On this subject it would be necessary to study gambling, which even in French society, is not considered to be a contract, but a situation in which honor is committed and where goods are handed over that, after all, one could refuse to hand over. Gambling is a form of potlatch and the gift system. Its spread even as far as the American Northwest is remarkable. (P. 112, n. 138 and 139)

This madness has a somewhat monstrous face, but its face or its defacement is regular up to a certain point. One can recognize in it a few interlaced traits. Linked to the redoubled double bind, between the bind and the non-bind or the letting loose [*débandade*], this madness is surely double since it threatens *a priori* the closed circle of exchangist rationality as well as frantic expenditure, without return, of a gift that forgets itself: madness of keeping or of hypermnesic capitalization *and* madness of the forgetful expenditure. But because it wreaks havoc on the two sides of the circle, this madness manages to eat away at language itself. It ruins the semantic reference that would allow one reasonably to say, to state, to describe this madness, in short, it ruins everything that claims to know what gift and non-gift *mean to say*. There is always a moment when this madness begins to burn up the word or the meaning "gift" itself and to disseminate without return its ashes as well as its terms or germs. We could interrogate this essential passage between the gift and this dissemination—what I in the past defined as that which does not return to the father, or that which does not *return* in general.[7] Let us, then, try to find the unifying principle of all the idiomatic locutions in which one finds the noun "gift," the verb "to give," the adjective "given." Such a semantic *center* [foyer] around which an organized economy or polysemia would gather seems indeed to be lacking. If this lack were to be confirmed, one would have to give up a concept of language regulated by deep semantic anchoring points that would authorize, for example, questions of the type: What is the guiding sense or *etymon* of the gift on the basis of which all semantic diversities, all idioms, and all usages are diffracted? What is the con-sensus on the basis of which an implicit linguistic contract would permit us to understand one another, to pre-understand one another, right here, to extend credit to each other when we speak of gift, giving, or given? What would happen if the lack of a guiding sense or of a regulated polysemia were to force us to renounce this style of question in favor of a certain concept of dissemination? This concept, which would not be the only one possible, would lead us to consider only usage, play, and the contextual functionings of idioms, if indeed it were still possible to speak of idioms in this sense, without postulating a semantic regula-tion, a system of prescriptions inscribed in language or in the continuum of a linguistic tradition. This alternative, let us note in is passing, would in both cases concern a sort of given of the language: what is given by the language or the language as given, as a given language [*une sorte de donné ou de donnée de la langue*], in other words, two ways of determin-ing the gift of the language said to be maternal or natural.

This hypothesis of a dissemination without return would prevent the locution from circling back to its meaning. It thus also concerns—whence this paradoxical fold—the without-return of the gift. One must say that we are constantly encouraged in this direction by the experience of language each time that the words "gift," "to give," "given," "dona-tion," "donee," or "donor" occur there. Not only because of great frontiers, great lines of demarcation that seem to set up a secure barrier between different meanings or different functionings. For example, one might wonder if the same semantic order governs the logic of the gift whether it is under the regime of *to have* or *to be*. In general, it is thought that one can give only what one has, what one possesses as one's own, and give it to the other who, in his or her turn, can thus have it, come into possession. The very paradox of "giving what one does not have," which we have already talked about, has the value of paradox only because of what links, in common sense, giving with having. One might wonder if the same semantic order governs locutions that, on the contrary, imply the transfer of what one *is* to the other who takes—or becomes—what is thereby given to him or her. Think of the expression "to give oneself," of the metonymies or synecdoches concerning partial "objects," the fragments or signs of what one is and which one can give as something one has, abandons, or lets be taken. All the figures of this tropic are difficult to contain within the limits of a rhetoric the margins or "terms" of which can no longer, in principle and in all rigor, be fixed.

Likewise, one might wonder if the same order governs locutions which imply that one gives something (a determined object, either material or symbolic, to make provisional use of this distinction) and those in which the given of the donation is not an object, a material thing, but a symbol, a person, or a discourse. In other words, does not the direct "object" of the act of "giving," does not the given of the giving alter radically the meaning of the act each time? What do the following have in common: on the one hand, to give a ring, a bracelet, to give something to drink and to eat and, on the other hand, to give an impression, to give a feeling, to give a show or a play? The latter are all expressions that appeal irreducibly to the idiom and in principle therefore they have only a limited translatability. What is common to and what is the connection between "to give the time" and "to give a price" (in the sense of the auction bid: "I will give you so much for it"), between "donner une facilité" [to facilitate, as in a facilitated payment plan] and "give an order," between "give information," "give a course, a class, and a seminar," "give a lesson" (which is something completely different) and "give chase,"[8] "give signs," and so forth? Each time a structural difference of the given presents itself: It can be an apparently natural or material thing (water), a symbolic thing (a ring), a person (to give one's daughter or son in marriage, to give a child, to give a king to one's country),[9] a discourse (still another order of the gift: to give a lecture, to give an order; once again the nature of the discourse alters each time the structure of the gift). Each time, then, the structural difference of the giv*en* seems, and we do say *seems*, to transmit to the operation of the giv*ing* an irremediable heterogeneity.

In this very short list of examples, we have all the same tried to put things in order. We distinguished, for the convenience of the presentation, between the orders of *given* (to be *vs.* to have; sensible, natural thing, if such exists in the pure state, *vs.* symbol, person, discourse, and so forth—all of which are problematic categories since all of them determine being-given and since, thereby, the gift may perhaps efface their boundaries). We have indeed tried to establish an order, a principled taxonomy, a classification (given as either to be or to have, either thing or person, either natural, sensible thing or signifying, symbolic thing, either thing or word, and so forth), but if you consult the *Littré* or what is called an analogic dictionary, you would be at great pains to find a unifying or classifying principle for all the idiomatic locutions. We could take as guide *four types of questions:*

1. In the style of analytic philosophy or of ordinary language analysis, one could ask oneself: What are the conditions (conventional, contextual, intentional, and so forth) for the functioning of, for example, an expression or a speech act that consists in, let us say it in French, *donner sa parole*, giving one's word (to promise or to swear) or *donner un ordre*,

giving an order (jussive act) and what is going on with giving in each of these cases? Such an analysis can go back before speech acts, in the phenomenological style of an intentional analysis, toward the intentional act of giving in general. On what conditions does it take place? What is a "donating consciousness"? and so on. This latter expression, moreover, is immediately and massively complicated by reason of a figure of donation that is constantly used by phenomenologists, beginning with Husserl, to designate the ultimate recourse, phenomenology's principle of principles, namely the originary *donating* intuition (*gebende Anschauung*),[10] the one that delivers up the thing or the sense themselves, in person or in flesh and blood, as people still say, in their immediate presence.

2. One may wonder whether this multiplicity of meanings that transmits the multiplicity of *givens* and refracts it in the multiplicity of the *to give* has a sort of general equivalent which would permit translation, metaphorization, metonymization, exchange within an ultimately homogeneous semantic circle. This general equivalent would be a transcendental signified or signifier. Playing the role of a transcendental given, it would orient the multiplicity and furnish the transcendental category of which all the other categories of given (to be/to have; thing/person; sensible, natural/symbolic; and so forth) would be particular determinations, metaphorico-metonymic substitutes. We know that the adjective "transcendental" modifies first of all the category that surpasses every genus (*transcendit omne genus*), thereby making possible every other categorial determination. This great transcendentalist tradition can inscribe the transcendental given in the present in general (the present appearing of that which appears in the light, or else created being, the originary given of a gift which comes down to and comes back to [*revient à*] Nature, Being, God, the Father—or the Mother) as well as in the phallus in general (transcendental signifier sealing, according to Lacan, a "symbolic order" that guards the gift against its dissemination, which is perhaps to say, against itself). For this tradition, which is the most powerful and the most irrefutable, there must be a general equivalent of the given if one is to understand what happens with the gift in general and how gifts and exchanges in general (total or partial) are ordered—and, finally, what the Thing given is. For in the end, it must always be the Thing, the same thing that gives itself, even if it does so by dividing itself or by partitioning itself into partial objects. But the Thing is not a partial object, which is why Lacan, for example, insists on the fact that the phallus, the signifier of all signifiers, condition of every gift and every exchange, cannot be a partial object.[11] Difficult problematic of the partial object and the whole chain of supposed gifts (*cadeaux*, feces, penis, child, weapons of war). It is this problematic that we are talking about here, directly or indirectly.

3. How is one to explain these breaks, within certain idioms (French for example), between the syntax of giving (verb), and the syntax of the gift (noun)? From the meaning of "to give" to the meaning of "gift," is the idiom logically consistent? For example, I would say in French that a window "*donne* sur la rue," it gives onto the street (understanding by that, I suppose, that it gives visual access, just as a stairway gives onto, gives access to, and so forth). But it would never occur to me (and why?) that what we have here is a gift. In

any case, I would not say literally the gift of the window or of the staircase. What is the significance of these breaks? Why does "giving someone up to the police" not amount to offering a gift, a generous gift, of someone to the police (although the latter may indeed receive it as such), whereas parents who give one of their children in marriage or to the fatherland could more easily speak of a gift, since they could think that they are depriving themselves of what they give? Let us not accumulate these examples; they would be numerous but also different from one language to another. Let us merely draw from them a *conclusion* (which is that the essential link that passes from the thinking of the gift to language, or in any case to the trace, will never be able to avoid idioms) and a *doubt* (is it not impossible to isolate a concept of the essence of the gift that transcends idiomatic difference?).

4. The transcendental question or rather the question *on* the transcendental gets complicated, it even goes a little mad if, among all the *givens*, all the "things" given that we have so far enumerated, one attempts to draw a line dividing two major structures of the gift, such at least as these are to be located in the idiom. There would be, *on the one hand*, the gift that gives something determinate (a given, a present in whatever form it may be, personal or im-personal thing, "natural" or symbolic thing, thing or sign, nondiscursive or discursive sign, and so forth) and, *on the other hand*, the gift that gives not a given but the *condition* of a present given in general, that gives therefore the element of the given in general. It is thus, for example, that "to give time" is not to give a given present but the condition of presence of any present in general; "donner le jour" (literally to give the day, but used in the sense of the English expression "to give birth") gives nothing (not even the life that it is supposed to give "metaphorically," let us say for convenience) but the *condition* of any given in general. To give time, the day, or life is to give nothing, nothing determinate, even if it is to give the giving of any possible giving, even if it gives the condition of giving. What distinguishes in principle this division from the transcendental division it resembles? One perceives there no longer the sharp line that separates the transcendental from the conditioned, the conditioning from the conditioned, but rather the fold of undecidability that allows all the values to be inverted: The gift of life amounts to the gift of death, the gift of day to the gift of night, and so on. And we will say nothing further—it would take us into another dimension—about the strange crossings of idioms such as those that translate "se donner la mort" by "to take one's life." This inversion follows from the great law of the *Gift-gift*.[12] It was the locution "donner le jour" that elsewhere led us to explore this logic, which is a logic of madness but also of narration, the condition of possibility and impossibility of narration, in the margins of a text by Blanchot titled *La folie du jour, The Madness of the Day*.[13]

All these questions concern a certain madness of the gift, which is first of all the madness of the dissemination of the meaning "gift." To look for a unity of this meaning would be, to quote the narrator of "Counterfeit Money," to "look for noon at two o'clock." Mauss is not unaware of this madness. His essay *The Gift* begins more and more to look like an essay not on the gift but on the word "gift." It would basically be an attempt to see if one can speak of the gift, an assaying of the "gift" (in quotation marks because it is mentioned rather than used), an assaying, in a word, of the word "gift" to see if and how it can be used. At the end of this essay, of these assays, a few pages before the final word, he writes the following, which leaves one wondering or perplexed since it comes from someone who has taken an incessant pleasure in giving self-satisfied terminology lessons to the authors he has been citing:

> However, we can go even farther than we have gone up to now. We can dissolve, mix up, color, and redefine the principal notions that we have used. The terms that we have used—present, gift, *cadeau*—are not themselves entirely exact. It's just that we can find no others. These concepts of law and economics that we like to oppose: freedom and obligation; liberality, generosity, and luxury, as against savings, interest, and utility—it would be good to put them into the melting pot once more. (P. 73)

In place of this impossible concept and of this missing term, Mauss then proposes only brief indications and an example, an "example," an example of, precisely, a "hybrid," which defies the oppositions permitting one to construct concepts. Is this significant? Here is how Mauss in fact continues:

> We can only give the merest indications on this subject. Let us choose, for example,* the Trobriand Islands. There they still have a complex notion that inspires all the economic acts we have described. Yet this notion is neither that of the free, purely gratuitous prestation, nor that of production and exchange purely interested in what is useful. It is a sort of hybrid that has flourished there.
>
> *Note: We could just as well have chosen the Arab *sadaqa:* alms, price of the betrothed, justice, tax.

The madness of this essay: It ends where it should have begun, and the result is that, just as in Blanchot's *Madness of the Day*, one no longer knows according to what impossible figure an interminable end is included in an interminable beginning.[14] It is a narrative, but an interdicted narrative in this sense. As if Mauss were saying to us: Forget everything that has been said in all the preceding pages; we will have to begin all over again.

This madness still hesitates between the "I am talking madness" and the "don't go off thinking that I am talking madness even when I speak of madness." And it is inscribed in the command to forget that is uttered with every gift. But the command to forget, the command given to forget is a strange command, whose very structure remains as maddened as it is maddening. One sees it appear in "Aumône" (Alms) by Mallarmé:

Ne t'imagine pas que je dis des folies
La terre s'ouvre vieille à qui crève la faim
Je hais une autre aumône et veux que tu m'oublies.
Et surtout ne va pas, frère, acheter du pain.

Do not suppose that I am talking madness
The earth opens up old to one dying of hunger
I hate another alms and want you to forget me.
And most of all, brother, do not go buy bread

We will not interpret this poem, not even this last line. It gives the command, it requires, it asks that the gift not be converted into its equivalent merchandise, into some useful goods (in the first two versions, it was "Je hais l'aumône utile," "I hate the useful alms") and especially into edible food, into an incorporable thing. Let us merely underscore the structure of an impossible command: "I want you to forget me." Like every negative command, like every interdiction that folds back in a contradictory manner toward the subject who utters it (for example, "do not listen to me," "do not read me"), it engenders that schism in the response or the responsibility in which some have sought to recognize the schizo-pathogenic power of the double bind.

Here the addressee must keep the command not to keep, without forgetting the request to forget: Grieve for me, therefore keep me enough to lose me as you must.

We will encounter later, in all its dimensions (religious, anthropological, cultural, socioeconomic), the question of alms—and of whether alms is a gift. For the moment, let us not forget the fold of a supplementary question: Is that which is given, whether or not it is alms, the content, which is to say the "real" thing one offers or of which one speaks? Is it not rather the act of address to the other, for example the work as textual or poetic performance? Along with all the internal perversion or madness we are talking about, is not the gift first of all the essay titled *The Gift*, precisely to the extent to which it would be incapable of speaking adequately of the gift that is its theme? Or the poem titled "Aumône"? Or very close to it, that song of mourning which is "Don du poème" (The Gift of the Poem)? "Aumône" also names "tabac," "opium," the "pharmacie," and the act of "supputer" (calculation), all of which are motifs that will stay with us. This poem went through at least four versions and several earlier titles: "Haine du pauvre" (Hatred of the Poor Man), "A un mendiant" (To a Beggar), and "A un pauvre" (To a Poor Man).[15]

Aumône

Prends ce sac, Mendiant! tu ne le cajolas
Sénile nourrisson d'une tétine avare
Afin de pièce à pièce égoutter ton glas.
Take this bag, Beggar! you cajoled it
Senile nurseling of a miser teat
Only to drain from it coin by coin your *glas.*

A un mendiant

Pauvre, voici cent sous . . . Longtemps tu cajolas,
—Ce vice te manquait,—le songe d'être avare?
Ne les enfouis pas pour qu'on te sonne un glas.
Poor man, here is twenty cents . . . Long you cajoled,
—You lacked this vice—the dream of being miserly?
Don't bury them to have a *glas* sounded for you.

A un pauvre

Prends le sac, Mendiant. Longtemps tu cajolas
—Ce vice te manquait—le songe d'être avare?
N'enfouis pas ton or pour qu'il te sonne un glas.
Take the bag, Beggar. Long you cajoled
—You lacked this vice—the dream of being miserly?
Don't bury your gold so it will sound a *glas* for you.[16]

The sadistic aggressivity with regard to the donee, the perversity which threatens a beggar suspected of speculating, all this already belongs to a certain tradition. We will attempt to recognize that tradition and we cite Mallarmé here only in order to sketch in this descent. It is for example the tradition of Baudelaire's "Counterfeit Money" and "Assommons les pauvres," (Beat Up the Poor). This tradition will have left traces in *The Madness of the Day* where one may read, for instance: "At forty, somewhat poor, I was becoming destitute. . . . What is irritating about poverty is that it is visible, and anyone who sees it thinks: You see, I'm being accused; who is attacking me? But I did not in the least wish to carry justice around on my clothes."[17] Is not the gift precisely the madness of the day?[18] Like "Aumône," Mallarmé's "Don du poème" went through several versions. One of them was titled precisely "Le jour" (The Day), and the other "Le poème nocturne" (The Nocturnal Poem) and the "Dédicace du poème nocturne" (Dedication of the Nocturnal Poem). Like the narrative of "Counterfeit Money" that we will take up soon, like its dedication, which gives itself by giving nothing other than the gift in question with no possible oversight [*surplomb*] of that performance, this "Gift of the Poem" would be given as the gift itself, enacted; it begins "Je t'apporte l'enfant d'une nuit d'Idumée!" [I bring you the child of an Idumean night!]. Idumea, the land of the Edom, would be the pre-Adamic kingdom: Before Esau was replaced by Jacob, who received his blind father's blessing, the kings of Idumea were supposed to reproduce themselves without sex and without woman. They were not hermaphrodites but men without sex and without women. The poem is compared to a work that would have been born from the poet alone, without couple or without woman. "Horrible naissance" (Horrible birth), says "Don du poème," a birth in which the child, that is, the poem, finds itself thus *given*, confided, offered—to the reader to whom it is dedicated, to its addressee or its donee, to be sure, but by the same token to the nurse who *in her turn, in exchange, will give* it the breast (". . . *accueille une horrible naissance: / Et ta voix rappelant viole et clavecin, / Avec le doigt fané presseras-tu le sein / Par qui coule en blancheur sibylline la femme / Pour les lèvres que l'air du vierge azur affame?*" [. . . receive a horrible birth: / And your voice recalling viola and harpsichord, / With faded finger will you press the breast / From which flows the woman in sibylline whiteness / For the lips famished by the virgin azure air?])[19]

From the hand of the donor to that of the beggar, we have just seen the passage of gifts in the form of cash money. We can no longer avoid the question of what money is: true money or counterfeit money, which can only be what it is, false or counterfeit, to the extent to which no one knows it is false, that is, to the extent to which it circulates, appears, functions *as good and true money*. The enigma of this simulacrum should begin to orient us toward the triple and indissociable question of the *gift*, of *forgiveness*, and of the *excuse*. And to the question of whether a gift can or *ought* to *secure itself* against counterfeit money.

At the end of a long note on the notion of money (pp. 93–94), Mauss deems it necessary to excuse himself. He does so in the grammar of the magisterial "we": "We excuse ourselves for having been obliged to take sides on these very vast questions, but they touch too closely upon our subject and it was necessary to be clear." He does not ask to be excused; he *excuses himself*. In the code of French etiquette, it is not the most refined formula of politeness. What is he excusing himself for? Well, for having been obliged to take sides. When one is obligated, in principle, one does not have to excuse oneself; one has every excuse as when one does something "beyond one's control." In this formulation, which must not be pushed too far, he excuses himself for having been obligated. This may seem strange. But since he has a good excuse, he does not have to ask forgiveness. Without waiting for the reader's reply, he takes the liberty of excusing himself. What is the fault he was obligated to commit and for which he has such a good excuse? Having "taken sides" ["*pris parti*"] and having taken sides on "very vast questions." He would thus have the right to excuse himself because these questions "touch too closely" upon the subject and it was necessary to be rather "clear." In this unique sentence, which is all of a piece, one cannot tell what the real fault is. In "taking sides" or in taking sides on "very vast questions"? One first has the feeling that, in his view, a sociologist, a theoretician, a scholar guided by a principle of objectivity and neutrality should not take sides, should not be *involved* or *committed* [engagé]. He should not give any *token* [gage] in the debate or in the problem. In this scene, he should not occupy a position (*take* a position, as one says) in order to try to win, to win his case, as if the normative ideal for whoever would speak scientifically—for instance of the *gift*—were to neither give nor take, nor to make of one's scientific discourse a *piece* of the analyzed structure, a piece in the play [*pièce*] or in the scene, an act in the play or a scene in the play (the word *pièce* in French, which means piece, play, but also coin as in "pièce de monnaie," could give the title to any possible discourse on the gift, indeed of any possible gift, if one did not immediately have to say the same thing of the word "title").[20]

Unless Mauss is excusing himself not for having broken with a sort of metalinguistic neutrality or uninvolved distant reserve but for having taken sides where he should not have done so: on "very vast questions." He would have gone too quickly and too superficially over questions that deserve a wider treatment, an analysis that would be fitting to their—very vast—scale. Mauss would be excusing himself for having concluded too quickly, for having given insufficient *guarantees* of his statements, for having insufficiently demonstrated his justificatory reasons. Which implies that by good ethical standards—and here the good ethical standards of scientific discourse—one must not take sides unless one is able to do so neither in the dark, nor at random, nor by making allowance for chance, that is, for what cannot be thoroughly anticipated or controlled. One should only take sides rationally, one should not get involved beyond what analysis can *justify* and beyond what can accredit or legitimate the taking of sides; one should accredit, guarantee, and legitimate the discourse in which the taking of sides, the *parti pris* or bias is stated. Otherwise, one pays with words or *on se paie de mots*, as we say in French, [one gets paid in words, i.e., one talks a lot of hot air], by which one understands that words in this case are simulacra, money without value—devalued or counterfeit—that is, without gold reserves or without the correspondent accrediting value. By excusing himself for having been obliged to take sides on very vast questions, Mauss excuses himself for not having given to his taking of sides, that is, to the discourse that explains his taking of sides, a kind of fiduciary guarantee. He has not been able to accredit sufficiently the signs he has given of his taking of sides. He excuses himself, therefore, for seeming to take the risk of giving us a kind of counterfeit money without corresponding gold reserves.

He does not say, of course, that in taking sides he is unjustified or that the money he gives us is counterfeit, that he is paying us with words (which implies without proven value [*titre*]). No, he says that perhaps it looks as if—but this is only an appearance—he is giving us counterfeit money, or more exactly and what is even worse (since giving someone money that the other knows to be counterfeit is not a deception), money that we cannot know to be sufficiently credited, true or counterfeit, guaranteed or not, since the relation is not established, visible, or verifiable between the terms of his taking sides and the extent of these "very vast questions." He may be deceiving us, he may have the appearance of being able to deceive us by deceiving himself, paying us with words while talking a lot of hot air. This is in sum what he excuses himself for in this long note on money ("A *Note* of principle concerning the use of the notion of money").

For Mauss is not opposed to all taking of sides. Even if it does not look that way, we can verify that *The Gift*, from beginning to end, is one long taking of sides, a continuous involvement [*engagement*]. And it cannot be otherwise. A discourse on the gift, a treatise on the gift *must* and can only be *part* or *party* [partie prenante *ou* parti pris] in the field it describes, analyzes, defines. That is why, that is the way in which, *that is the very thing he must, he owes, he ought to* [il doit]: He is first of all and from the first *indebted*. The theoretical and supposedly constative dimension of an essay on the gift is *a priori* a piece, only a part, a part and a party, a *moment* of a performative, prescriptive, and normative operation that gives or takes, indebts itself, gives and takes, refuses to give or accepts to give—or does both at the same time according to a necessity that we will come back to. But in every case, this discursive gesture is from the outset an example of that about which it claims to be speaking. It is part of the whole, it belongs [*appartient*] to the whole process, it is part of it even as it claims to designate only an object of that process or a part of a set that would be dominated by its discourse. Thus the mass of prescriptive (ethical, moral, juridical, political) "il faut" (it is necessary, one must, one should, one ought to and so forth) that are unleashed in the last chapter titled "Conclusion" and especially in its first subchapter ("Moral Conclusions"). These "il faut" accumulate according to a regular law. Not that the "il faut" are lacking before this moral conclusion. But here they are assumed in a declared fashion and are regulated by a law that may appear strange but that alone can account for the little sentence I began by quoting. No doubt, as with every "il faut," this law of the "il faut" is that one must—*il faut*—go beyond constatation and prescribe. One must—*il faut*—opt *for* the gift, for generosity, for noble expenditure, for a practice and a morality of the gift ("il faut donner," one must give). One cannot be content to speak of the gift and to describe the gift without giving and without saying *one must* give, without giving by saying one must give, without giving to think that one must give but a thinking that would not consist merely in thinking but in doing what is called giving, a thinking that would call upon one to give in the proper sense, that is, to do more than call upon one to give in the proper sense of the word, but to give beyond the call, beyond the mere word.

But—because with the gift there is always a "but"—the contrary is also necessary: It is necessary [*il faut*] to limit the excess of the gift and of generosity, to limit them by economy, profitability, work, exchange. And first of all by reason or by the principle of reason: It is *also* necessary to render an account, it is also necessary to give consciously and conscientiously. It is necessary *to answer for* [répondre] the gift, the given, and the call to giving. It is necessary to answer to it and answer for it. One must be *responsible* for what one gives and what one receives.

Whence a series of "il faut" worked over, as you will hear, by this contradiction, sometimes going so far as to take the most ingenuous and naïvely hypocritical form, which is also the most inconsistent and incoherent, betraying thereby Mauss's predicament when he tries to define the right rule, the right economy: *between* economy and non-economy, in the "not too much," "neither too much this nor too much that," "a good but moderate blend of reality and the ideal." In this long litany of "il faut," we will also underscore, among other things, the words "to state," "revolution," and "return."

But it is not enough *to state* the fact. *One must* [il faut] deduce practice from it, and a moral precept. It is not sufficient to say that law is in the process of ridding itself of a few abstractions such as the distinction between real law and personal law; or that it is intent on adding other rights to the cold-hearted law of sale and payment for services. One *must* [Il faut] *also say* that this is a salutary *revolution.*

First of all, we *return*, as *return we must* [il faut], to customs of "noble expenditure." *It is essential* [Il faut] that, as in Anglo-Saxon countries and so many other contemporary societies, both primitive and highly civilized ones, that the rich *return*, freely or by obligation, to considering themselves as the financial guardians, as it were, of their fellow citizens. Among ancient civilizations, from which ours has sprung, some had a (debtors') jubilee, others liturgies (of duty) such as choregies and trierarchies, and *syussitia* (meals in common), and the obligatory expenditure by the aedile and the consular dignitaries. *We should* [On devra] go back to laws of this kind. Then *there must be* [il faut] more care for the individual, his life, his health, his education (which is, moreover, a profitable investment), his family, and their future. *There must be* [Il faut] more good faith, more sensitivity, more generosity in contracts dealing with hiring of services, the renting of houses, the sale of vital foodstuffs. And *it will indeed be necessary* [il faudra bien] to find a way to limit the rewards of speculation and interest.

However, the individual *must* work [il faut *que l'individu travaille*]. He *must* [il faut] be made to rely upon himself rather than upon others. On the other hand, *he must* [il faut] defend his interests, both personally and as a member of a group. Over-generosity and communism would be as harmful to himself and to society as the egoism of our contemporaries and the individualism of our laws. In the *Mahabharata* a malevolent genie of the woods explains to a Brahmin who gave away too much, and too injudiciously: "That is why you are thin and pale." The life of the monk and the life of a Shylock *must be* [doivent] equally shunned. This new morality will surely consist of a *good but moderate blend of reality and the ideal*. (Pp. 68–69)

A few remarks, since perhaps not everything goes without saying upon first encountering these declarations:

1. First of all, it would be wrong to consider these "Moral Conclusions" (in a final chapter that is itself titled "Conclusion") as a moral epilogue external to the work, as a taking sides that could be harmlessly dissociated from the work that goes before. These axiomatics were at work in *all* the preceding analyses. They provided the conceptual material, the instruments of analysis, the theoretical organization of the discourse.

2. It would be rather thoughtless to laugh at the often indecent mediocrity of the mediating desire, at this median, measured, measuring morality, this rule of the compromise and of the "good but moderate blend of reality and the ideal." The moderation of this *mediocritas* signals perhaps the most difficult task. Better—or worse—it announces perhaps a sort of paradoxical *hubris*, the *hubris* of the right measure (who ever dares to fix the right measure?) and even that vocation of the impossible to which all responsibility and every effective decision has to answer. What is recommended is not just any compromise; it is the good one, the right one. Now, from his reflection and his inquiry into the gift, Mauss has learned that the *pure* gift or the gift that is *too good*, the excess of generosity of the gift—in which the pure and good gift would consist—turns into the bad; it is even the worst. The best becomes the worst. It is because he has understood this turnabout to be the law of the gift that the anthropologist tends toward this wisdom, this policy, this morality of the *mediocritas* and of the happy medium. And as we have just suggested, but it should be said in Mauss's favor perhaps, this "happy medium" is, moreover, as impossible, as untenable, and as inaccessible as the two extremes, just as the role of Sancho Panza is as unlivable as that of Don Quixote.

3. Mauss repeatedly says that one must *return to*—. Return to what? This "returning" is not a regression but a revolution. Analogous to the natural revolution of the Earth around the Sun, of the absolute sun at its high noon (and this is why we began by making the question of the gift turn around a Sun-King), it would bring about a return to man's nature, to that "eternal morality" ("This morality is eternal," Mauss will write further on), to that "bedrock" which has remained closest to the surface in those societies said to be "the least advanced that we can imagine"—those societies that have been the object of *The Gift*, its particular but also obviously *exemplary* object in Mauss's eyes. They offer the example of a natural—and thus universal—structure of this *socius* set in motion by the gift. That description ought to hold true beyond those societies. To be sure, Mauss does not *directly* extend his analysis to "evolved" societies, but by way of the axis of a certain historicity and a certain

exemplarity, with the ethicopolitical movement of the "one must return . . . ," he assures a revolutionary circulation to his discourse. We must return to the *example* given us by those "least advanced societies" that are closer to "bedrock." We must return to the example they give us concerning the gift. "Thus we can and we ought to return to the archaic and to the elemental," says Mauss.

We will rediscover motives for living and acting that are still prevalent in many societies and classes: the joy of public giving; the delight in generous expenditure on the arts; the pleasure in hospitality and in private and public festival. Social security, the solicitude of the mutuality, of the cooperative, of the professional group, of all those legal entities upon which English law bestows the name of "Friendly Societies"—all are of greater value than the mere personal security that the lord guaranteed to his tenant, better than the mean life afforded by the daily wage set by management, and even better than capitalist saving—which is only based on a changing form of credit. (Ibid.)

We will find a surer guide back to this archaic originarity, which we have left behind or allowed to become perverted, in a non-Marxist socialism, a liberal anti-capitalism or anti-mercantilism. That is the morality or the politics that organizes the structure, even the theoretical *telos*, of this essay. As for the formal characteristic of this profound identity between the theoretical and the ethical, we could invoke a Platonic or Aristotelian tradition. However, as for its content, one glimpses rather a Rousseauist schema. This is not only the model that will soon be reclaimed by the very one who introduces, not without formulating a few admiring criticisms, Mauss's essay, namely Lévi-Strauss; it is already Mauss's model, even if he does not refer to it as explicitly as Lévi-Strauss does.

This question of the natural or exemplary universality of the "bedrock" and the (inductive or reflexive) extension of Mauss's analyses is formulated or resolved in his very language. A question of *restitution*: The anthropologist proposes to *give back* and to *come back* in a circular manner to the good example, to return to the good inheritance that archaic societies have given or rather bequeathed us. The inheritance that is thus passed down is nothing other, finally, than nature. It is nature that gives, and one must show oneself worthy of this gift. One must take and learn [*prendre et apprendre*] the gift of nature. From giving nature, one must learn to give, in a manner that is both generous and ordered; and by giving as nature says one must give, one will give it back its due, one will show oneself to be worthy, one will mark the right equivalence. This equivalence (whose naturalist law we will find staged once again in "Counterfeit Money") is nothing other that that of the giving-returning or of the giving-taking. It is the logic of exchange or the symbolics of *restitution*—or one could also say of the *re-institution*—of nature, beyond the opposition nature/culture, *phusis/nomos*, or *phusis/thesis*, and so forth.

Archaic society, the archaic, or the originary in general can be replaced by *anything whatsoever* (by X or by Chi), by nature, the mother, father, creator, supreme being, prime mover, *logos*, masculine or feminine possessor of the *phallus*: One will always find again the same schema, one will find (oneself) back there all the time—in a circular manner. And it is by setting out from the question of the "giving-taking" or the "giving-returning" that one accedes to all the instances we have just enumerated or piled up. Now, this equivalence of giving-taking is precisely stated in the form of a "beautiful Maori proverb" that, once again as epiloguing epigraph, comes to close the "Moral Conclusions":

"Ko Maru kai atu
Ko Maru kai mai
Ka ngohe ngohe"

"Give as much as you take, all shall be very well." (P. 69)

In a note to the translation, Mauss clarifies as follows: "Rev. Taylor, *Te Ika a Maui, Old New Zealand* (p. 130, proverb 42), translates very briefly as 'give as well as take and all will be right,' but the literal translation is probably as follows: 'As much as Maru gives, so much Maru takes, and this is good, good' (Maru is the god of war and justice)."

The equivalence of the taken and the given is *posed*, it is a thesis and a theme. It happens to be posed as the moral, ethical, and political rule: the rule of what there is but also of *what is necessary* [*de ce qu'il* faut], of what *there must be* [*de ce qu'il* doit y avoir]. The law of what happens implies an imperative: "give as much as you take." The original text has a descriptive form and not, precisely, an imperative one; yet the statement is followed by a positive evaluation that transforms natural necessity into a good thing: "As much as Maru [god of war and justice] gives, so much Maru takes, *and this is good*." The logic of the utterance remains complex. By posing the equivalence between what the god gives and what he takes, by posing this equivalence as "good," one affirms the excess of the gift; one lets the gift overflow. The equivalence given by Maru or that he gives by his example is good and this *goodness* of the given equivalence is in *excess* over the equivalence itself. It will thus be necessary to restore, reconstitute, give back, *restitute* the equilibrium by following the *example*, by reflecting it in imitation. We are not through with this "logic," and what is more one is never through with it.

The schema of exemplarity is all the more significant in this precise place in that it poses the equivalence of the giving and taking, of the given and the taken, but on the basis of their opposition or at least their distinction. To say that *one must* reach equivalence and that equivalence is good is to recall that it is not simply given and that giving is not taking. There is at the outset neither real equivalence nor semantic equivalence: To give does not mean to take—on the contrary!

But like the *il faut*, the *on doit* [one must, one ought, one owes]—which, along with debt and duty, supposes an inequality—regulates itself according to an "it is thus," *there is* [il y a] equivalence; this is a natural law of nature, a necessity. One must therefore think this equivalence of equivalence and non-equivalence. Any discourse on this problematic must then presuppose a clarity, if possible and even before taking sides, concerning the values of "giving" and "taking," concerning their possible opposition or their equivalence, whether real or semantic. Now, Mauss makes a brief allusion to the fact that, in certain languages, notably in Papuan and Melanesian, there is "one single term to designate buying and selling, lending and borrowing," in the words of Holmes who has studied these tribes and according to whom operations that are "opposites are expressed by the same word" (p. 32). This concerns only the opposition of selling and buying (and not in general that of giving and taking). Mauss notes that the uncertainty of this verbal opposition "selling/buying" is not specific to the societies of the Pacific; it is present in Chinese where only a tonal difference distinguishes the two monosyllables that designate the purchase as well as the sale; and in our ordinary language, the word "sale" ["*vente*"] covers the sale as well as the purchase. This seems rather careless on Mauss's part: Although the word *vente* can cover a chain of operations of which purchase is one link, there is no ambiguity in ordinary language regarding the opposition between selling and buying, but that little matters here. What matters more is this possibility of an effacement, inside and outside of language, of the opposition in general, and singularly of the opposition between giving and taking. There would be, there should be an equivalence between what one gives and what one takes, between the given and the taken, but also between the meaning of giving and the meaning of taking. This is the logical lever of two, almost contemporary texts that each have a very different relation to the essay *The Gift*. I mean first *The Introduction to the Work of Marcel Mauss*, by Lévi-Strauss. It opens the 1950 volume of *Sociologie et Anthropologie* in which Mauss's essay was reprinted. One should remember that Mauss died during the printing of this volume.[21] The other text is that of Benveniste, "Gift and Exchange in Indo-European Vocabulary."[22] This pair of texts will lead us back to the excuses presented by Mauss and then to the forgiveness refused by one of the two friends in Baudelaire's "Counterfeit Money."

The same unrest will never quiet down, that of the gift as well as that of forgiveness. *Ought* they not—but beyond duty and debt[23]—*deprive themselves of any security* against the counterfeit, of any mistrust regarding counterfeit money, so as to preserve the chance of being what they *ought to be*, but ought to be beyond duty and debt? A gift that would claim to control money and preserve itself from any simulacrum, will that still be a gift or already a calculation clinging or recalling one—naïvely, sometimes with authority—to the reassuring distinction between the natural and the artificial, the authentic and the inauthentic, the originary and the derived or borrowed?

Notes

1. In a note to "Plato's Pharmacy" (*Dissemination*, pp. 150–51/131–32), the subject of which is therefore being continued here, I had already cited this note of Mauss's:

Mélanges Ch. Andler, Strasbourg, 1924. We are asked why we do not examine the etymology of *gift*, translation of the Latin *dosis*, itself a transcription of the Greek *dosis*, dose, dose of poison. This etymology supposes that High and Low German dialects had retained a scientific word for a commonly used thing, which is contrary to the usual semantic rule. Moreover, one would still have to explain the choice of the word *gift* for this translation and the inverse linguistic taboo that has weighed on the sense of "gift" for this word in certain Germanic languages. Finally, the Latin and especially Greek use of *dosis* to mean poison shows that with the Ancients as well there was association of ideas and moral rules of the kind we are describing.

We compare the uncertainty of the meaning of *gift* with that of the Latin *venenum* and the Greek *philtron* and *pharmakon*; one should also add (cf. Bréal, *Mélanges de la société linguistique*, Vol. 3, p 140) *venia, vernus, venenum*, from *vanati* (Sanskrit, to give pleasure) and *gewinnen, win*.

Cf. as well Gloria Goodwin Raheja, *The Poison in the Gift: Ritual, Prestation, and the Dominant Caste in a North Indian Village* (Chicago: University of Chicago Press, 1988). There, one may follow an interesting discussion of Mauss on the subject of the gift and the (non-reciprocal) reception of the *dan* (pp. 249ff.).

2. Cf. on this subject *Glas* and *The Post Card*.

3. In Chapter 2, section 3, "The American Northwest: Honor and Credit," pp. 33ff.

4. That is, *donnant donnant*. This is also a colloquial expression in French that might be translated: fair's fair, i.e., you give me this and I'll give you that. (Trans.)

5. I take the liberty of referring here to *Schibboleth, pour Paul Celan* (Paris: Galilée, 1986), in particular pp. 72–77, 93–108.

6. Paul Valéry, *Oeuvres complètes* (Paris: Bibliothèque de la Pléiade, 1960), vol. 2, pp. 1077–85. Cf. on this subject, *L'Autre cap*, pp. 94ff.

7. Cf. *Dissemination*, passim, especially "Outwork."

8. Derrida's example here is "donner le change," which is a hunting expression that means to decoy or to put off the scent. (Trans.)

9. Or to give a slave: When this lecture was read in Chicago, W. J. T. Mitchell elaborated the question of the slave in a very interesting manner and linked it to that of narrative (in an unpublished text to which I hope to return one day). In a word, what happens when "the Given is a person," the slave who "has nothing to give"? Slavery is that which gives back or gives ("What gives?" in American slang) but also deprives of "narrative."

10. Following here the problematic outline I tried to put in place during the 1977–78 seminar, I will not for the moment enter into the long developments, the patient reading and discussion that would be required concerning the important work since published by Jean-Luc Marion (*Réduction et donation, Recherches sur Husserl, Heidegger et la phénoménologie* [Paris: Presses Universitaires de France, 1989]). In order to indicate a few preliminary points of reference in the space of this future exchange and in order to situate the stakes of the semantics of donation in phenomenology, I will quote the conclusion of the first chapter, where Marion discusses in particular certain aspects of my reading of Husserl's *Logical Investigations in Speech and Phenomena:*

Categorial intuition allows one only to take the measure—which is from now on measureless—of donation. It marks the open abyss of donation without covering it over—at least in Heidegger's view, if not in Husserl's. For here, the most sober of the two in the face of the fascination with superabundant and unconditional presence is no doubt not the one you expected. Husserl, in fact, completely dazzled by limitless donation, does not seem to realize the strangeness of such a beyond-measure [*démesure*], and does nothing more than *manage* its excess, without interrogating it. Unless the bedazzlement betrays—by covering it over—a fright in face of the broadening of presence by donation.

This is no doubt where the question arises that Husserl could not answer, perhaps because he never understood it as an authentic question: What then is given? Not only "What is it that is given?" but more essentially: "What does giving mean, what is then being played out by the fact that everything is given, how is one to think the fact that everything that is only is insofar as it is given?" It seems legitimate to suppose that Husserl, as if he were submerged by the imperative—at once threatening and jubilatory—to *manage* the superabundance of givens in presence, at no point (at least in the *Logical Investigations*) inquires into the status, the scope, and even the identity of this donation. This silence amounts to admitting (following Jacques Derrida's thesis) that Husserl, leaving donation uninterrogated even though he had accomplished its broadening, does not free it from the prison of presence; rather he maintains it in metaphysical detention. Heidegger, on the contrary . . ." (p. 62; cf. as well especially pp. 68ff., 87ff., and naturally all the pages called up by the whole course of the book [unless it is the book that is called up by them] on the basis of a thinking of the *call* as thinking of the gift: ("After thetranscendental reduction and the existential reduction, the reduction of and to the call intervenes. What is given is given only to whoever gives himself over to the call and only in the pure form of a confirmation of the appeal, repeated because received. . . . The call thus appears as the originary schema of the two former reductions, precisely because it alone permits one to go back to . . . in that it demands that one give oneself over to the call as such—to answer the call, in the double sense of abandoning oneself to it and of going toward it. . . . It would already suffice to specify that which, before or without *Dasein*, receives or challenges the call, in short hears it. Neither the constituting *I* nor *Dasein* which is—if precisely it can still be—the one that gives itself over to the call that gives?" [Pp. 296–97])

What I have attempted to articulate on the subject of the call, as well as of the "come," the "yes," especially their irreducible iterability, of the "destinerrance" of a sending determined by the response, and of the "gift" in general would lead me no doubt to subscribe to the "logic" and the necessity of this analysis.

To limit ourselves here to the most basic schema, let us say that the question, if not the discussion, would remain open at the point of the determination of the call or of the demand, there where the circle seems to turn between the call of Being (*Anspruch des Seins*), the call of the father (*Anspruch des Vaters*), the primacy of which Heidegger contests, and a "call which is brother to the one Heidegger dismisses," namely, the one that "Levinas will not fail to take up." Nor, I will add, does Marion, who seems to me also to make *"the* call as such," "the pure form of the call," conform to the call of the father, to the call that returns to the father and that, in truth, would speak the truth of the father, even the name of the father, and finally of the father inasmuch as he gives the name.

Marion indeed writes: "In fact, the speech that demands 'Listen!' does not so much pronounce *a* call among other possible ones to the advantage of some authority or other as it performs *the* call as such— the call to answer the call itself, in the sole intention of holding oneself to it by exposing oneself to it. The call even intervenes as such, without or before any other 'message' except to *overtake* with surprise [surprendre] whoever hears it, to *take* up [prendre] even whoever does not expect it. The model of the call is in practice before the simple claim of Being and more fully." And then this in a note: "In fact the claim is no longer exerted here in the name of Being (but of the Father), neither at destination nor from a being. Thus the pure form of the call arises" (p. 295; I have italicized the words "prendre" and "surprendre" in order to situate, in advance, some stakes that will appear later on, notably in the reading of "Counterfeit Money"). Having *declared* that it excludes any determinable content, why does Marion determine "the pure form of the call" (and therefore of the gift) as call "in the name of the Father"? As unique call, despite "the gap between the two calls (the one Christian, the other Jewish)" that it is "important to maintain"? Is it possible to hear a "pure form of the call" (and first of all must one presume such a purity? And if one does, on what basis?) that would still not be from Being, nor from the father, nor in the fraternal difference of the "there," if one can put it that way, between the Jew and the Christian, nor therefore in the language of the "Hear, O Israel: The Lord our God is one Lord" (*Deuteronomy* 6:4) in which, Marion tells us, they "both have their source" (p. 295)? Cf. also Marion, "Réponses à quelques questions," *Revue de Métaphysique et de Morale*, no. 1 (1991), in particular p. 69.

11. Cf. "Le Facteur de la vérité," in *The Post Card*, pp. 500ff./pp. 470ff.

12. See above, note 1, p. 561.

13. Cf. *Parages*, pp. 240ff. and pp. 280ff.

14. Ibid., pp. 232ff. and pp. 266ff.

15. On this poem and on the "glas" that comes to resonate there, cf. *Glas*, pp. 171ff./150ff.

16. Stéphane Mallarmé, *Oeuvres complètes*, ed. Henri Mondor et G. Jean-Aubry (Paris: Bibliothèque de la Pléiade, 1961), pp. 39, 1434–36.

17. "A quarante, un peu pauvre, je devenais misérable . . . la misère a ceci d'ennuyeux qu'on la voit et ceux qui la voient pensent: Voilà qu'on m'accuse; qui m'attaque là? Or je ne souhaitais pas du tout porter la justice sur mes vêtements" (Paris: Fata Morgana, 1973), pp. 23–24; *The Madness of the Day*, trans. Lydia Davis (Barrytown, N.Y.: Station Hill Press, 1981), p. 13.

18. Cf. *Parages*, pp. 234ff. and 278ff.

19. *Oeuvres complètes*, pp. 40, 1438–39.

20. We have attempted to analyze this word "pièce" and put it in play in a reading of *Droit de regards* by M.-F. Plissart (Paris: Minuit, 1985), pp. XVII, XX ("Right of Inspection," trans. David Wills, in *Art & Text*, no. 32, Autumn 1989 pp. 60, 62).

21. This fact is recalled in the Postscriptum (at once extraordinary and flatly conventional) that Georges Gurvitch, who was then director of the collection and professor at the Sorbonne, adds on 12 April 1950 to the Foreword dated 20 September 1949. The several lines of this Postscriptum deserve to be quoted. In their fashion, perhaps inadvertently, they say something about the *Gift-gift*, the poisoned gift of which legacies are made, particularly those exemplary legacies that are intellectual legacies: gifts, in sum, whose poison almost never fails to call forth the counter-poison which is presented in the guise of the counter-gift (restitution, tribute, celebration, commentary, critical reading, "personal interpretation"). And when a third party says of an "interpretation," which an inheritor offers to the one from whom he inherits, that it is a "very personal interpretation," one may suspect that there is more here than a disagreement or reservation: some venom is surely being distilled, like a counter-poison in its turn, in the body of this tribute to a tribute, to this already venomous tribute that was the interpretation in question. Not that death *really* results, or always, but here is that which sometimes—impressive *imprimatur*, murderous perfidy of academic politeness, mask over mortuary mask—literally follows death: "Postscriptum—During the printing of this volume, Marcel Mauss died. The reader will find in M. Claude Lévi-Strauss's introduction an impressive image of the inexhaustible wealth of the intellectual legacy bequeathed by this great scholar, as well as a very personal interpretation of his work. Georges Gurvitch, *Paris, 12 April 1950*."

22. *L'Année sociologque*, vol. 2, 1950; reprinted in *Problèmes de linguistique générale* (Paris: Gallimard, 1966); *Problems in General Linguistics*, trans. Mary Elizabeth Meek (Coral Gables, Fla.: University of Miami Press, 1971).

23. Another form of the same aporia, this *ought-to without owing, duty without duty* [devoir sans devoir] prescribes that the gift not only *owes* nothing, remains foreign to the circle of the debt, but must not

answer to its own essence, must not even be what it has to be, namely, a gift. On the immense question (at once etymological, semantic, philosophical, and so forth) of what does or does not link duty to debt, we will refer not only to the well-known texts of Nietzsche, Heidegger, and so forth, but, closer to home, to the analyses of Emile Benveniste (*Le vocabulaire des institutions européennes* [Paris: Minuit, 1969], vol. 1, chap. 16, "Prêt, emprunt et dette," and chap. 17, "Gratuité et reconnaissance," pp. 181ff.). Cf. as well Charles Malamoud's admirable "Présentation" of the very rich contributions, including his own ("Dette et devoir dans le vocabulaire sanscrit et dans la pensée brahmanique"), collected in *Lien de vie, noeud mortel, Les représentations de la dette en Chine, an Japon et dans to monde indien* (Paris: EHESS, 1988). The question of the "false money of a true sacrifice" is evoked there in relation to "Les Monnaies de la Trésorerie et la notion de Destin fondamental," by Hou Chinlang (p. 14). Cf. aussi Charles Malamoud, "La théologie de la dette dans le brâhmanisme," in *Purusartha* 4: "La Dette" (Paris: EHESS, 1980).

These questions have also been approached in *The Post Card*, notably at the beginning of "To Speculate—on 'Freud'" (pp. 278ff./260ff.). On the indissociable question of the fetish, in Marx or Freud, on its link to the "rest of time" to be given, cf. *Glas*, pp. 231ff./206ff.

28   Something Like: "Communication . . . without Communication"

Jean-Francois Lyotard

With a view to dramatizing the question laid down, "Art and Communication," I would just like to recall the regime of representation which is proper, or which has been thought proper, at least since Kant, to aesthetic reception; and, in order to pick out this regime, I will just quote two sentences, aphorisms, which appear to contradict one another perfectly:

No work of art should be described or explained through the categories of communication.

One could even define taste as the faculty of judging what renders our feeling, proceeding from a given representation, universally *communicable* without the mediation of a concept.

The first is from Theodore Adorno (*Aesthetic Theory*), the second from Immanuel Kant (*Critique of Judgement*, § 40).

These two aphorisms appear to be contradictory, one saying that art has nothing to do with communication, and the other that the reception of art presupposes and demands a universal communicability without concept. The philosopher is used to contrary theses. The Adorno passage is one of the objections he makes to the Hegelian reduction of the work to the dialectic of the concept. Adorno, not without premonition, discerns in Hegelian thought the beginnings of something like *a communicationalist* ideology, and probably—here we come back to Kant's formulation—for the very reason that in Hegel's speculative philosophy there is an absolute hegemony of the concept. Now in what Adorno calls *communication*, the idea is also implicitly required that if there is a communication in art and through art, it must be without concept. So much so, that in spite of the apparent contradiction, Adorno is at this point inserting himself into a tradition of thinking about art which we get from Kant. There is a thinking about art which is not a thinking of non-communication but of non-conceptual communication.

The question I want to dramatize is this: what about communication without concept at a time when, precisely, the "products" of technologies applied to art cannot occur without the massive and hegemonic intervention of the concept? In the conflict surrounding the word *communication*, it is understood that the work, or at any rate anything which is received as art, induces a feeling—before inducing an understanding—which, constitutively and therefore immediately, is universally communicable, by definition. Such a feeling is thereby distinguishable from a merely subjective preference. This communicability, as a demand and not as a fact, precisely because it is assumed to be originary, *ontological*, eludes communicational activity, which is not a receptiveness but something which is managed, which is done. This, in my view, is what governs our problematic of "new technologies and art," or, put differently, "art and postmodernity." This communicability, as it is developed in the Kantian analysis of the beautiful, is well and truly "anterior" to communication in the sense of "theories of communication," which include communicative pragmatics (*pragma* is the same thing as *Handeln*). This assumed communicability, which takes place immediately in the feeling of the beautiful, is always presupposed in any conceptual communication.

By showing that the feeling of beauty differs from the other affects or affections with which it is tempting to confuse it, including the feeling of sublimity, Kant signifies that it *must* be *made transitive* immediately, without which there is no feeling of beauty. The requirement that there be such an assenting, universal in principle, is constitutive of aesthetic judgement. So if we keep to a psychological or social or pragmatic or generally anthropological kind of description, we give up on according to art a specific status as to its reception, and basically, we grant that there is no art. If we abandon this transitivity—potential, immediate, capable of being demanded in the judgement of taste and, simultaneously, demanded in order for there to be art—by the same token we abandon the idea of a community deriving from what Kant calls *sensus communis*, which is to say from an immediately communicable *sentimentality*.

And it cannot be said of a feeling that it must gather everyone's agreement without mediation, im-mediately, without presupposing a sort of *community of feeling* such that every one of the individuals, placed before the same situation, the same work, can at least dispose of an identical judgement without elaborating it conceptually. In the analysis of aesthetic feeling, there is thus also an issue of the analysis of what goes on with a community in general. In the reception of works of art, what is involved is the status of a sentimental, aesthetic community, one certainly "anterior" to all communication and all pragmatics. The cutting out of intersubjective relations has not yet happened and there would be an assenting, a unanimity possible and capable of being demanded, within an order which cannot "yet" be that of argumentation between rational and speaking subjects.

The hypothesis of another type of community thus emerges, irreducible to theories of communication. If we accept that assumed communicability is included in the singular aesthetic feeling, and if we accept that this singular aesthetic feeling is the im-mediate mode, which is no doubt to say the poorest and the purest, of a possibility to space and time, necessary forms of *aesthesis*, then can this communicability persist when the forms which should be its occasion are conceptually determined, whether in their generation or in their transmission? What happens to aesthetic feeling when *calculated* situations are put forward as aesthetic?

The opposition between linear system and figurative system indicated in the conference's rubric, not to mention the hopes invested in the calculated production of figures, seems to me irrelevant in relation to the one I am trying to state between *passibility* and activity. Passibility as the possibility of experiencing (*pathos*) presupposes a donation. If we are in a state of passibility, it's that something is happening to us, and when this passibility has a fundamental status, the donation itself is something fundamental, originary. What happens to us is not at all something we have first controlled, programmed, grasped by a concept [*Begriff*]. Or else, if what we are passible to has first been plotted conceptually, how can it *seize us*? How can it test us if we already know, or if we can know—of what, with what, for what, it is done? Or else, if such a feeling, in the very radical sense that Kant tries to give this term, takes place, it must be admitted that what happens to us disconcerts us. When Kant speaks of the *matter* of sensation, which he opposes to its form, its formation, it is precisely to do with what we cannot calculate. We have nothing to say about what it is that administers this matter to us, gives it to us. We cannot conceptualize this sort of *Other* with a capital O which Kant calls a big X. It must certainly be granted that the donation proceeds from an X, which Heidegger called *Being*. This donation which is experienced before (or better, *in*) any capture or conceptualization *gives matter* for reflection, for the conception, and it is *on it*, for it, that we are going to construct our aesthetic philosophy and our theories of communication. There does have to be something which is given first. The feeling is the immediate *welcoming* of what is given. Works produced by the new *techne* necessarily, and to quite diverse degrees, and in diverse parts of themselves, bear the traces of having been determined to be one or more *calculations*, whether in their constitution and/or their restitution, or only in their distribution. And by "calculation" I don't only mean the kind that occupies the time of computer engineers, but also taking in the inevitable measurability of spaces and times, of all the times, including those dubbed "working" times, expended in the production of these works and their distribution.

Any industrial reproduction pays homage to this profound and fundamental problematic of *re*-presentation, and aesthetic feeling presupposes something which necessarily is implied, and forgotten, in representation: *presentation*, the fact that something is *there now*. All representations presuppose space and time as that by and in which something happens to us and which is always here and now: the place and the moment. It has to do not with concepts but simply with modes of presentation. As soon as we are within the arts of representation, the question of the here-and-now is hidden. How can there be an *aesthetic* feeling issuing from calculated *re*-presentation alone? How could the traces of the conceptual determination of the forms proposed by the new *techne* leave free the play of reflexive judgement which constitutes aesthetic pleasure? How could the communicability constitutive of this pleasure, which remains potential, promised and not affected, not be excluded by the conceptual, argumentative and techno-scientific—"realistic"—determination of what is communicated in the product of these new technologies?

In urging this strange problematic of aesthetic feeling in Kant, in its im-mediacy *and* its demand for universal communicability, without which it's not art we're dealing with, I only mean to suggest the following hypothesis: what is hit first of all, and complains, in our modernity, or our postmodernity, is perhaps space and time. What is attacked would be space and time as forms of the donation of what happens. The real "crisis of foundations" was doubtless not that of the foundations of reason but of any scientific enterprise bearing on so-called real objects, in other words given in sensory space and time.

There are already two aesthetics in Kant, two senses of the word *aesthetic*. In the first Aesthetic (*Critique of Pure Reason*), the question posed is restricted to the elaboration of the sensible (its "synthesis") through which it is knowable by concept. How is it that concepts can find application in reality? It must be that there are already, in the sensible as it is given to us, types of syntheses of elements, sensible unities which prepare it for its being taken into intelligibility under concepts. There is an affinity between what is given in the sensible and what the concept is going to do with it. For example in the temporal series of sounds, there is what permits the application of the numerical series. It is this first synthesis which Kant calls *schema* and which, in the sensible prepares for the conceptual application. We can know the sensible because it has an affinity with the intelligence. In the third Critique, the Aesthetic elaborates the question of the forms. The object at this point is not to understand how science is possible but to understand how it is that in the here-and-now of donation a feeling is produced such that it is only the affective transcription of the forms which float freely in space and time. Kant attributes this feeling to the inscription on the subject of the forms attributable to the productive imagination. The syntheses which take place in the sensible are no longer conceived here by Kant a preparing for science but as permitting *feeling* which is itself preparatory to all knowledge. It is the way that the forms are received by a subject which interests him; he also calls them *monograms*.

There is thus first of all this schema/form problem, but there is further the division of the apprehension of the forms into two aesthetic feelings: the feeling of the beautiful and the feeling of the sublime. This last, whose Analytic Kant introduces without any sort of justification, contrary to rule, has the interesting property of including no im-mediate communicability. The feeling of the sublime is manifested when the presentation of free forms is lacking. It is compatible with the form-less. It is even when the imagination which presents forms finds itself lacking that such a feeling appears. And this latter must go via the *mediation* of an Idea of reason which is the Idea of freedom. We find sublime those spectacles which exceed any real presentation of a form, in other words where what is signified is the superiority of our power of freedom *vis-à-vis* the one manifested in the spectacle itself. In singling out the sublime, Kant places the accent on something directly related to the problem of the failing of space and time. The free-floating forms which aroused the feeling of the beautiful come to be lacking. In a certain way the question of the sublime is closely linked to what Heidegger calls the retreat of Being, retreat of donation. For Heidegger, the welcome accorded something sensory, in other words some meaning embodied in the here-and-now before any concept, no longer has place and moment. This retreat signifies our current fate.

In *The Principle of Reason* and *The Age of the World-Picture*, the opposition is at its greatest between the poetic, receptivity in the sense of this Kantian sentimentality, and the *Gestell* [untranslatable: enframing?], which is to be credited to techno-science. For Heidegger, techno-science at its height was nuclear science; we have done much better in *Gestell* nowadays. It is clear that the in-stallation [same "root" as *stellen*] of the concept as far as space-time is infinitely more fine in the new technologies than it was in what Heidegger was familiar with. Opposition between two forms of reception: on one side the poetic form which he imputes to the Greeks, and on the other techno-scientific reception (it is still an ontological reception) which occurs under the general regime of the principle of reason and whose explicit birth he sees in Leibniz's thought. It is clear that the idea of the combinatory, and thus of all that governs computer science and communication, is one of the things whose birth is in this, including the infinitesimal.

This problematic should be taken up again, revised and corrected: it seems to me central in the question of "art and communication." In Hölderlin's *Remarks* on Oedipus, which it would be necessary for us to ponder, the poet notes that the true tragedy of Oedipus is that the god has categorically turned away from man. The real tragedy is not *Oedipus Tyrannos* (the plot, the murder, the misunderstanding) but *Oedipus at Colonus*, in other words when fate is accomplished and nothing more happens to the hero, nothing is destined for him any more. The loss of all destiny is the essential feature of the drama and in this "nothing happens" also lies the essential feature of our problematic. It is clear that what is called communication is always, in every case, that nothing happens, that we are not destined. And in this connection Hölderlin adds this quite remarkable sentence: "At the extreme limit of distress, there is in fact nothing left but the conditions of time and space."

At the horizon of what is called the "end of art," which Hegelian thought discovers at the start of the nineteenth century, we find the melancholy of "there is nothing left but the conditions of time and space," which tends and bandages itself in that immense work of mourning, that immense remission which is Hegelian dialectical thought. Not only is it going to be necessary to absorb the fact that "there is nothing left but time and space" as pure conditions (which is done from the start of the first great work, the *Phenomenology of Spirit*, where it is demonstrated that space and time have their truth not in themselves but in the concept, that there is no here-and-now, that the sensible is always already mediated by the understanding), but the theme of the end of art reveals on another level the persistence of the theme of the retreat of the donation and the crisis of the aesthetic. If there is no time, if time is the concept, there is no art except by mistake, or rather the moment of the end of art coincides with that of the hegemony of the concept. We should connect this problematic back with the one we are immersed in nowadays, generalized logocentrism, and show that the art-industry belongs indirectly to this way of finishing art off. The art-industry would be a completion of speculative metaphysics, a way in which Hegel is present, has succeeded, in Hollywood. To be elucidated through Paul Virilio's remarks on the problem of space and time which he calls *critical*, in a strategic sense: that of the Pentagon. The position of Husserl in the face of the crisis of the sciences in Europe should also be elaborated.

A study of the advant-gardes is imperative. Their movement is not only due to the end of art. If they are in a problematic analogous to the one through which Hegel thematizes the end of art, they have "exploited" this "there remains only" in an exemplary way. If there remain only the conditions of space and time, in other words, basically, if representation, the staging of plots, are not interesting and what is interesting is Oedipus without a fate, then let's elaborate a painting of the fate-less. The avant-gardes get to work on the conditions of space and time. Attempts which have been going on for a century without having finished yet. This problematic makes it possible to resituate the real issue of the avant-gardes by putting them back in their domain. They have been inflexible witnesses to the crisis of these foundations of which theories of communication and the new technologies are other aspects, much less lucid ones than the avant-gardes. They at least had the sense of drama, and in this they are completely analogous in their own field to what has happened in the sciences.

From the end of the nineteenth century, there has been an immense amount of discussion under the heading of "crisis of the sciences"—bearing on arithmetic, in other words the science of number which is the science of time; on geometry, the science of space; and on mechanics, the science of movement, which is to say the science of space and time. It is very hard to believe that what has been being discussed between scientists and philosophers for a century must be of no interest to the little ideology of communication. The problems out of which emerged non-Euclidean geometry axiomatic forms of arithmetic and non-Newtonian physics are also those which gave rise to the theories of communication and information.

Is it the case that in this crisis, which bears on the conditions of space and time (with its two expressions: modern—there no longer remains anything but space and time; and postmodern—we no longer *even* have space and time left)—is it the case that in this work, which we take up under the aspect of communication, there is simply the loss of something (donation or presentation) without there being some gain? We are losing the earth (Husserl), which is to say the here-and-now, but are we gaining something and how are we gaining it? Can the uprooting which is linked to the new technology promise us an emancipation?

As is indicated in the conference's programme, the question of the body comes up here; but we must not put too much trust in this word, for if space and time are hit and attacked by the new technologies, then the body is too and has to be. Perhaps we should also set ourselves to the work of mourning the body.

About the confusion between passible and passive. These two problems are distinct: passivity is opposed to activity, but not passibility. Even further, this active/passive opposition presupposes passibility and at any rate is not what matters in the reception of works of art. The demand for an activity or "interactivity" instead proves that there should be more intervention, and that we are thus through with aesthetic feeling. When you painted, you did not ask for "interventions" from the one who looked, you claimed there was a community. The aim nowadays is not that sentimentality you still find in the slightest sketch by a Cézanne or a Degas, it is rather that the one who receives should not receive, it is that s/he does not let him/herself be put out, it is his/her self-constitution as active subject in relation to what is addressed to him/her: let him/her reconstitute himself immediately and identify himself or herself as someone who intervenes. What we live by and judge by is exactly this will to action. If a computer invites us to play or *lets* us play, the interest valorized is that the one receiving should manifest his or her capacity for initiative, activity, etc. We are thus still derivatives from the Cartesian model of "making oneself master and possessor. . . ." It implies the retreat of the passibility by which alone we are fit to receive and, as a result, to modify and do, and perhaps even to enjoy. This passibility as *jouissance* and obligatory belonging to an immediate community is repressed nowadays in the general problematic of communication, and is even taken as shameful. But to take action in the direction of this activity which is so sought-after is only to *react*, to repeat, at best to conform feverishly to a game that is already given or installed [*gestellt?*]. Possibility, in contrast, has to do with an immediate community of feeling demanded across the singular aesthetic feeling, and what is lost is more than simple capacity, it is propriety. Interactional ideology is certainly opposed to a passivity but it remains confined in a completely secondary opposition.

The true issue is to know whether or not are maintained the actuality and immediacy of a feeling which appeals to the co-belonging to a "ground" presupposed by concept and calculation in their eluding of it. The work is only first *received* in the name of this immediate community, even if afterwards it can be presented in a gallery, at a distance. We are dealing with a problem of the modality of presence and not a problem of content or simple form. The question of unanimity of feeling bears not on what is presented or on the forms of presentation, but on the modality of reception, as demand for unanimity. It is not a matter of situating passibility as a moment, even a brief one, in a process of appropriation, of the work, it is a matter of saying (and this is what is meant by *transcendental critique* in Kant) that without this dimension, we are incapable of so much as recognizing a work *of art*. It is an a priori condition even if it is never marked in a perceptible way in the psycho-social process.

What is absolutely specific in art? What do space and time have to do with it? What is the gain from techno-science? What will become of our body? It is not in the discourse of techno-science, which *de facto* and *de jure* takes place outside this situation, but in the quite different field of the will to identification, that we will be able so much as to broach these questions.

Passibility: the opposite of "impassibility"? Something is not destined for you, there is no way to feel it. You are touched you will only *know* this afterwards. (And in thinking you know it, you will be mistaken about this "touch.") We imagine that minds are made anxious by not intervening in the production of the product. It is because we think of presence according to the exclusive modality of masterful intervention. Not to be contemplative is a sort of implicit commandment, contemplation is perceived as a devalorized passivity.

In Kant, passibility does not disappear with the sublime but becomes a passibility *to lack*. It is precisely the beautiful forms with their destination, our own destiny, which are missing, and the sublime includes this sort of pain due to the finitude of "flesh," this ontological melancholy.

The question raised by the new technologies in connection with their relation to art is that of the here-and-now. What does "here" mean on the phone, on television, at the receiver of an electronic telescope? And the "now"? Does not the "tele-"element necessarily destroy presence, the "here-and-now" of the forms and their "carnal" reception? What is a place, a moment, not anchored in the immediate "passion" of what happens? Is a computer in any way here and now? Can anything *happen* with it? Can anything happen *to* it?

VII Community and Incommunicability

29 Of Being Singular Plural

Jean-Luc Nancy

* * *

We say "people are strange."[1] This phrase is one of our most constant and rudimentary ontological attestations. In fact, it says a great deal. "People" indicates everyone else, designated as the indeterminate ensemble of populations, lineages, or races [*gentes*] from which the speaker removes himself. (Nevertheless, he removes himself in a very particular sort of way, because the designation is so general—and this is exactly the point—that it inevitably turns back around on the speaker. Since I say that "people are strange," I include myself in a certain way in this strangeness.)

The word "people" does not say exactly the same thing as the Heideggerian[2] "one,"[3] even if it is partly a mode of it. With the word "one," it is not always certain whether or not the speaker includes himself in the anonymity of the "one." For example, I can say "someone said to me" ["on m'a dit"] or else "it is said that" ["on dit que"] or else "that is how it is done" ["c'est comme ça qu'on fait"] or else "one is born; one dies" ["on naît, on meurt"]. These uses are not equivalent and, moreover, it is not certain that it is always the case that the "one" speaks of himself (from and about himself). Heidegger understood that "one" would only be said as a response to the question "who?" put to the subject of *Dasein*, but he does not pose the other inevitable question that must be asked in order to discover *who* gives this response and who, in responding like this, removes himself or has a tendency to remove himself. As a result, he risks neglecting the fact that there is no pure and simple "one," no "one" in which "properly existing" existence [*l'existant* "proprement existant"] is, from the start, purely and simply immersed. "People" clearly designates the mode of "one" by which "I" remove myself, to the point of appearing to forget or neglect the fact that I myself am part of "people." In any case, this setting apart [*mise à l'ecart*] does not occur without the recognition of identity. "People" clearly states that we are all precisely *people*, that is, indistinctly persons, humans, all of a common "kind," but of a kind that has its existence only as numerous, dispersed, and indeterminate in its generality. This existence can only be grasped in the paradoxical simultaneity of togetherness (anonymous, confused, and indeed massive) and disseminated singularity (these or those people(s)," or "a guy," "a girl," "a kid").

"People" are silhouettes that are both imprecise and singularized, faint outlines of voices, patterns of comportment, sketches of affects, not the anonymous chatter of the "public domain." But what is an affect, if not each time a sketch? A comportment, if not each time a pattern? A voice, if not each time a faint outline? What is a singularity, if not each time its "own" clearing, its "own" imminence, the imminence of a "propriety" or propriety itself as imminence, always touched upon, always lightly touched: revealing itself *beside*, always beside. ("Beside himself" ["a côté de ses pompes"[4]], as the saying goes. The comedy of this expression is no accident, and, whether it masks an anxiety or liberates the laughter of the ignorant, it is always a matter of an escape, an evasion, and an emptying out of what is closest, an oddity presented as the rule itself.)

"I" take refuge in an exception or distinction when I say "people," but I also confer this distinction on each and every person, although in just as obscure a way. This is undoubtedly why people so often make the judgment "people are strange" or "people are incredible." It is not only, or even primarily, a question of the tendency (however evident) to set up our own *habitus* as the norm. It is necessary to uncover a more primitive level of this particular judgment, one where what is apprehended is nothing other than singularity as such. From faces to voices, gestures, attitudes, dress, and conduct, whatever the "typical" traits are, everyone distinguishes himself by a sort of sudden and headlong precipitation where the strangeness of a singularity is concentrated. Without this precipitation there would be, quite simply, no "someone." And there would be no more interest or hospitality, desire or disgust, no matter who or what it might be for.

"Someone" here is understood in the way a person might say "it's him all right" about a photo, expressing by this "all right" the covering over of a gap, making adequate what is inadequate, capable of relating only to the "instantaneous" grasping of an instant that is precisely its own gap. The photo—I have in mind an everyday, banal photo—simultaneously reveals singularity, banality, and our curiosity about one another. The principle of indiscernability here becomes decisive. Not only are all people different but they are also all different from one another. They do not differ from an archetype or a generality. The typical traits (ethnic, cultural, social, generational, and so forth), whose particular patterns constitute another level of singularity, do not abolish singular differences; instead, they bring them into relief. As for singular differences, they are not only "individual," but infraindividual. It is never the case that I have met Pierre or Marie per se, but I have met him or her in such and such a "form," in such and such a "state," in such and such a "mood," and so on.

This very humble layer of our everyday experience contains another rudimentary ontological attestation: what we receive (rather than what we perceive) with singularities is the discreet passage of *other origins of the world*. What occurs there, what bends, leans, twists, addresses, denies—from the newborn to the corpse—is neither primarily "someone close," nor an "other," nor a "stranger," nor "someone similar." It is an origin; it is an affirmation of the world, and we know that the world has no other origin than this singular multiplicity of origins. The world always appears [*surgit*][5] each time according to a decidedly local turn [of events]. Its unity, its uniqueness, and its totality consist in a combination of this reticulated multiplicity, which produces no result.

Without this attestation, there would be no first attestation of *existence* as such, that is, of the nonessence and non-subsistence-by-itself that is the basis of being-oneself. This is why the Heideggerian "one" is insufficient as the initial understanding of *existentielle* "everydayness." Heidegger confuses the everyday with the undifferentiated, the anonymous, and the statistical. These are no less important, but they can only constitute themselves in relation to the differentiated singularity that the *everyday* already is by itself: each day, each time, day to day. One cannot affirm that the meaning of Being must express itself starting from everydayness and then begin by neglecting the general differentiation of the everyday, its constantly renewed rupture, its intimate discord, its polymorphy and its polyphony, its relief and its variety. A "day" is not simply a unit for counting; it is the turning of the world—each time singular. And days, indeed every day, could not be similar if they were not first different, difference itself. Likewise "people," or rather "peoples," given the irreducible strangeness that constitutes them as such, are themselves primarily the exposing of the singularity according to which existence exists, irreducibly and primarily—and an exposition of singularity that experience claims to communicate with, in the sense of "to" and "along with," the totality of beings. "Nature" is also "strange," and we exist there; we exist *in* it in the mode of a constantly renewed singularity, whether the singularity of the diversity and disparity of our senses or that of the disconcerting profusion of nature's species or its various metamorphoses into "technology." Then again, we say "strange," "odd," "curious," "disconcerting" *about* all of being.

Themes of "wonder" and the "marvel of Being" are suspect if they refer to an ecstatic mysticism that pretends to escape the world. The theme of scientific curiosity is no less suspect if it boils down to a collector's preoccupation with rarities. In both cases, desire for the exception presupposes disdain for the ordinary. Hegel was undoubtedly the first to have this properly modern consciousness of the violent paradox of a thinking whose own value is as yet unheard of, and whose domain is the grayness of the world. This ordinary grayness, the insignificance of the everyday—which the Heideggerian "one" still bears the mark of—assumes an absent, lost, or far away "grandeur." Yet, truth can be nothing if not the truth of being in totality, that is, the totality of its "ordinariness," just as meaning can only be right at [*à même*] existence and nowhere else. The modern world asks that this truth be thought: that meaning is right at. It is in the indefinite plurality of origins and their coexistence. The "ordinary" is always exceptional, however little we understand its character as origin. What we receive most communally as "strange" is that the ordinary itself is originary. With existence laid open in this way and the meaning of the world being what it is, the exception is the rule. (Is this not the testimony of the arts and literature? Is not the first and only purpose of their strange existence the presentation of this strangeness? After all, in the etymology of the word *bizarre*,[6] whether the word comes from Basque or Arabic, there is a sense of valor, commanding presence, and elegance.)

Gaining Access to the Origin

As a consequence, gaining access to the origin,[7] entering into meaning, comes down to exposing oneself to this truth.

What this means is that we do not gain access to the origin: access is refused by the origin's concealing itself in its multiplicity. We do not gain access; that is, we do not penetrate the origin; we do not identify with it. More precisely, we do not identify ourselves in it or as it, but *with* it, in a sense that must be elucidated here and is nothing other than the meaning of originary coexistence.

The alterity of the other is its being-origin. Conversely, the originarity of the origin is its being-other, but it is a being-other *than* every being *for* and *in crossing through* [à travers] all being. Thus, the originarity of the origin is not a property that would distinguish a being from all others, because this being would then have to be something other than itself in order to have its origin in its own turn. This is the most classic of God's aporias, and the proof of his nonexistence. In fact, this is the most immediate importance of Kant's destruction of the ontological argument, which can be deciphered in a quasi-literal manner; the necessity of existence is given right at the existing of all existences [*l'exister de tout l'existant*], in its very diversity and contingency. In no way does this constitute a supplementary Being. The world has no supplement. It is supplemented in itself and, as such, is indefinitely supplemented by the origin.

This follows as an essential consequence: the being other of the origin is not the alterity of an "other-than-the-world." It is not a question of an Other (the inevitably "capitalized Other.")[8] *than* the world; it is a question of the alterity or alteration *of* the world. In other words, it is not a question of an *aliud* or an *alius*, or an *alienus*, or an other in general as the essential stranger who is opposed to what is proper, but of an *alter*, that is, "one of the two." This "other," this "lowercase other," is "one" among many insofar as they are many; it *is each one*, and it is *each time* one, one *among* them, one among all and one *among* us all. In the same way, and reciprocally; "we" is always inevitably "us all," where no one of us can be "all" and each one of us is, in turn (where all our turns are simultaneous as well as successive, in every sense), the other origin of the same world.

The "outside" of the origin is "inside"—in an inside more interior than the extreme interior, that is, more interior than the *intimacy* of the world and the intimacy that belongs to each "me." If intimacy must be defined as the extremity of coincidence with oneself, then what exceeds intimacy in interiority is the distancing of coincidence itself. It is a coexistence of the origin "in" itself, a coexistence of origins; it is no accident that we use the word "intimacy" to designate a relation between several people more often than a relation to oneself. Our being-with, as a being-many, is not at all accidental, and it is in no way the secondary and random dispersion of a primordial essence. It forms the proper and necessary status and consistency of originary alterity as such. *The plurality of beings is at the foundation* [fondment] *of Being.*

A single being is a contradiction in terms. Such a being, which would be its own foundation, origin, and intimacy, would be incapable of *Being*, in every sense that this expression can have here. "Being" is neither a state nor a quality, but rather the action according to which what Kant calls "the [mere] positing of a thing"[9] takes place ("is"). The very simplicity of "position" implies no more, although no less, than its being discrete, in the mathematical sense, or its distinction *from*, in the sense of *with*, other (at least possible) positions, or its distinction *among*, in the sense of *between*, other positions. In other words, every position is also dis-position, and, considering the appearing that takes the place of and takes place in the position, all appearance is co-appearance [*com-parution*]. This is why the meaning of Being is given as existence, being-in-oneself-outside-oneself, which *we* make explicit, we "humans," but which we make explicit, as I have said, *for* the totality of beings.

If the origin is irreducibly plural, if it is the indefinitely unfolding and variously multiplied intimacy of the world, then not gaining access to the origin takes on another meaning. Its negativity is neither that of the abyss, nor of the forbidden, nor of the veiled or the concealed, nor of the secret, nor that of the unpresentable. It need not operate, then, in the dialectical mode where the subject must retain in itself its own negation (since it is the negation of its own origin). Nor does it have to operate in a mystical mode, which is the reverse of the dialectical mode, where the subject must rejoice in its negation. In both of these, negativity is given as the *aliud*, where alienation is the process that must be reversed in terms of a reappropriation. All forms of the "capitalized Other" presume this alienation from the proper as their own; this is exactly what constitutes the "capitalization" of the "Other," its unified and broken transcendence. But, in this way, all forms of the capitalized "Other" represent precisely the exalted and overexalted mode of the propriety of what is proper, which persists and consists in the "somewhere" of a "nowhere" and in the "sometime" of a "no time," that is, in the *punctum aeternum* outside the world.

The outside is inside; it is the spacing of the dis-position of the world; it is our disposition and our co-appearance. Its "negativity" changes meaning; it is not converted into positivity, but instead corresponds to the mode of Being which is that of disposition/co-appearance and which, strictly speaking, is neither negative nor positive, but instead the mode of being-together or being-*with*. The origin is together with other origins, originally divided. As a matter of fact, we do have access to it. We have access exactly in the mode of having access; we get there; we are on the brink, closest, at the threshold; we *touch* the origin. "(Truly) we have access (to the truth). . . ."[10] ["À la verité, nous accédons . . ."] is Bataille's phrase,[11] the ambiguity of which I repeat even though I use it in another way (in Bataille, it precedes the affirmation of an immediate loss of access). Perhaps everything happens between loss and appropriation: neither one nor the other, nor one and the other, nor one in the other, but much more strangely than that, much more simply.

"To reach[12] [*toucher*] the end" is again to risk missing it, because the origin is not an end. End, like Principle, is a form of the Other. To reach the origin is not to miss it; it is to be properly exposed to it. Since it is not another thing (an *aliud*), the origin is neither "missable" nor appropriable (penetrable, absorbable). It does not obey this logic. It is the plural singularity of the Being of being. We reach it to the extent that we are in touch with *ourselves* and in touch with the rest of beings. We are in touch with ourselves insofar as we exist. Being in touch with ourselves is what makes us "us," and there is no other secret to discover buried behind this very touching, behind the "with" of coexistence.

We have access to the truth of the origin as many times as we are in one another's presence and in the presence of the rest of beings. Access is "coming to presence," but presence itself is dis-position, the spacing of singularities. Presence is nowhere other than in "coming to presence." We do not have access to a thing or a state, but only to a coming. We have access to an access.

"Strangeness" refers to the fact that each singularity is another access to the world. At the point where we would expect "something," a substance or a procedure, a principle or an end, a signification, there is nothing but the manner, the turn of the other access, which conceals itself in the very gesture wherein it offers itself to us—and whose concealing *is* the turning itself. In the singularity that he exposes, each child that is born has already concealed the access that he is "for himself" and in which he will conceal himself "within himself," just as he will one day hide under the final expression of a dead face. This is why we scrutinize these faces with such curiosity, in search of identification, looking to see whom the child looks like, and to see if death looks like itself. What we are looking for there, like in the photographs, is not an image; it is an access.

Is this not what interests us or touches us in "literature" and in "the arts"? What else interests us about the disjunction of the arts *among* themselves, by which they are what they are as arts: plural singulars? What else are they but the exposition of an access concealed in its own opening, an access that is, then, "inimitable," untransportable, untranslatable *because* it forms, each time, an absolute point of translation, transmission, or transition of the origin *into origin*. What counts in art, what makes art art (and what makes humans the artists of the world, that is, those who expose the world for the world), is neither the "beautiful" nor the "sublime"; it is neither "purposiveness without a purpose" nor the "judgment of taste"; it is neither "sensible manifestation" nor the "putting into work of truth." Undoubtedly, it is all that, but in another way: it is access to the scattered origin in its very scattering; it is the plural touching of the singular origin. This is what "the imitation of nature" has always meant. Art always has to do with cosmogony, but it exposes cosmogony for what it is: necessarily plural, diffracted, discreet, a touch of color or tone, an agile turn of phrase or folded mass, a radiance, a scent, a song, or a suspended movement, exactly because it is the birth of a *world* (and not the construction of a system). A world is always as many worlds as it takes to make a world.

We only have access to ourselves—and to the world. It is only ever a question of the following: full access is there, access to the whole of the origin. This is called "finitude" in Heideggerian terminology. But it has become clear since then that "finitude" signifies the infinite singularity of meaning, the infinite singularity of access to truth. Finitude *is* the origin; that is, it is an infinity of origins. "Origin" does not signify that from which the world comes, but rather the coming of each presence of the world, each time singular.

✳ ✳ ✳

Being Singular Plural

Being singular plural: these three apposite words, which do not have any determined syntax ("being" is a verb or noun; "singular" and "plural" are nouns or adjectives; all can be rearranged in different combinations), mark an absolute equivalence, both in an indistinct *and* distinct way. Being is singularly plural and plurally singular. Yet, this in itself does not constitute a particular predication of Being, as if Being is or has a certain number of attributes, one of which is that of being singular-plural—however double, contradictory, or chiasmatic this may be. On the contrary, the singular-plural constitutes the essence of Being, a constitution that undoes or dislocates every single, substantial essence of Being itself. This is not just a way of speaking, because there is no prior substance that would be dissolved. Being does not preexist its singular plural. To be more precise, Being absolutely does not *preexist*; nothing preexists; only what exists exists. Ever since Parmenides, one of philosophy's peculiarities has been that it has been unfolding this unique proposition, in all of its senses. This proposition proposes nothing but the placement [*la position*] and dis-position of existence. It is its plural singularity. Unfolding this proposition, then, is the only thing philosophy has to do.[13]

That which exists, whatever this might be, coexists because it exists. The co-implication of existing [*l'exister*] is the sharing of the world. A world is not something external to existence; it is not an extrinsic addition to other existences; the world is the coexistence that puts these existences together. But one could object that there exists something [which does not first coexist]. Kant established that there exists something, exactly because I can think of a possible existence: but the possible comes second in relation to the real, because there already exists something real.[14]

It would also be worth adding that the above inference actually leads to a conclusion about an element of existence's plurality [*un pluriel d'existence*]: there exists something ("me") *and* another thing (this other "me" that represents the possible) to which I relate myself in order for me to ask myself if there exists something of the sort that I think of as possible. This something coexists at least as much as "me." But this needs to be drawn out in the following way: there does not exist just these "me's," understood as subjects-of-representation, because along with the real difference between two "me's" is given the difference between things in general, the difference between my body and many bodies.

This variation on an older style of philosophizing is only meant to point out that there has never been, nor will there ever be, any [real] philosophical solipsism. In a certain way, there never has been, and never will be, a philosophy "of the subject" in the sense of the final [*infinie*] closure in itself of a for-itself.

However, there is for the whole of philosophy what is exemplified in Hegel's statement "the I is in essence and act the universal: and such partnership (*Gemeinschaftlichkeit*) is a form, though an external form, of universality."[15] It is well known that dialectical logic requires the passage through exteriority as essential to interiority itself. Nevertheless, within this logic, it is the "interior" and subjective form of the "Me" that is needed in order to finish the project of finding itself and posing itself as the *truth* of the universal and its community. As a consequence, what is left for us to hold onto is the moment of "exteriority" as being of almost essential value, so essential that it would no longer be a matter of relating this exteriority to any individual or collective "me" without also unfailingly attaining [*maintenir*] to *exteriority itself and as such*.

Being singular plural means the essence of Being is only as coessence. In turn, coessence, or *being-with* (being-with-many), designates the essence of the *co-*, or even more so, the *co-* (the *cum*) itself in the position or guise of an essence. In fact, coessentiality cannot consist in an assemblage of essences, where the essence of this assemblage as such remains to be determined. In relation to such an assemblage, the assembled essences would become [mere] accidents. Coessentiality signifies the essential sharing of essentiality, sharing in the guise of assembling, as it were. This could also be put in the following way: if Being is being-with, then it is, in its being-with, the "with" that constitutes Being; the with is not simply an addition. This operates in the same way as a collective [*collégial*] power: power is neither exterior to the members of the collective [*collège*] nor interior to each one of them, but rather consists in the collectivity [*collégialité*] as such.

Therefore, it is not the case that the "with" is an addition to some prior Being; instead, the "with" is at the heart of Being. In this respect, it is absolutely necessary to reverse the order of philosophical exposition, for which it has been a matter of course that the "with"— and the other that goes along with it—always comes second, even though this succession is contradicted by the underlying [*profonde*] logic in question here. Even Heidegger preserves this order of succession in a remarkable way, in that he does not introduce the co-originarity of *Mitsein* until after having established the originary character of *Dasein*. The same remark could be made about the Husserlian constitution of the *alter ego*, even though this too is in its own way contemporaneous (once again, the *cum*) with the *ego* in the "single universal community."[16]

To the contrary; it can also be shown that when Hegel begins the *Phenomenology of Spirit* with the moment of "sense certainty," where it appears that consciousness has not yet entered into relation with another consciousness, this moment is nonetheless characterized by the language with which consciousness appropriates for itself the truth of what is immediately sensible (the famous "now it is night"). In doing so, the relation to another consciousness remains surreptitiously presupposed. It would be easy to produce many observations of this kind. For example, the evidence for the *ego sum* comes down to, constitutively and co-originarily, its possibility in each one of Descartes's readers. The evidence as evidence owes its force, and its claim to truth, precisely to this possibility in each one of us—one could say, the copossibility. *Ego sum = ego cum*.[17]

In this way, it can be shown that, for the whole of philosophy, the necessary successivity [*la successivité*] of any exposition does not prevent the deeply set [*profond*] order of reasons from being regulated by a co-originarity [*soit réglé sur une co-orginarité*]. In fact, in proposing to reverse the order of ontological exposition, I am only proposing to bring to light a resource that is more or less obscurely presented throughout the entire history of philosophy—and presented as an answer to the situation described above: philosophy begins with and in "civil" ["concitoyenne"] coexistence as such (which, in its very difference from the "imperial" form, forces power to emerge as a problem). Or rather, the "city" is not primarily a form of political institution; it is primarily being-with *as such*. Philosophy is, in sum, the thinking of being-with; because of this, it is also thinking-with as such.

This is not simply a matter of clarifying a still, faulty exposition. . . . It is just as much a question of doing justice to the essential reasons for why, across the whole history of philosophy, being-with is subordinated to Being *and*, at the same time and according to this very subordination, is always asserting [*de faire valoir*] its problem as the very problem of Being. In sum, *being-with is Being's own most problem*. The task is to know why and how this is so.[18]

Let us take up the matter again, then, not beginning from the Being of being and proceeding to being itself being with-one-another [*étant l'un-avec-l'autre*], but starting from being—and all of being—determined in its Being as being with-one-another. [This is the] singular plural in such a way that the singularity of each is indissociable from its being-with-many and *because*, in general, a singularity is indissociable from a plurality. Here again, it is not a question of any supplementary property of Being. The concept of the singular implies its singularization and, therefore, its distinction from other singularities (which is different from any concept of the individual, since an immanent totality, without an other, would be a perfect individual, and is also different from any concept of the particular, since this assumes the togetherness of which the particular is a part, so that such a particular can only present its difference from other particulars as numerical difference). In Latin, the term *singuli* already says the plural, because it designates the "one" as belonging to "one by one." The singular is primarily *each* one and, therefore, also *with* and *among* all the others. The singular is a plural. It also undoubtedly offers the property of indivisibility, but it is not indivisible the way substance is indivisible. It is, instead, indivisible in each instant [*au coup par coup*], within the event of its singularization. It is indivisible like any instant is indivisible, which is to say that it is infinitely divisible, or *punctually* indivisible. Moreover, it is not indivisible like any particular is indivisible, but on the condition of *pars pro toto*: the singular is each time *for* the whole, in its place and in light of it. (If humanity is *for* being in totality in the way I have tried to present it, then it is the exposing of the singular as such and in general.) A singularity does not stand out against the background of Being; it is, when it is, Being itself or its origin.

Once again, it is fairly easy to see to what extent these features answer to those of the Cartesian *ego sum*. The singular is an *ego* that is not a "subject" in the sense of the relation of a self to itself. It is an "ipseity" that is not the relation of a "me" to "itself."[19] It is neither "me" nor "you"; it is what is distinguished in the distinction, what is discreet in the discretion. It is being-a-part of Being itself and in Being itself, Being in each instant [*au coup par coup*], which attests to the fact that Being only takes place in each instant.

The essence of Being is the shock of the instant [*le coup*]. Each time, "Being" is always an instance [*un coup*] of Being (a lash, blow, beating, shock, knock, an encounter, an access). As a result, it is also always an instance of "with": singulars singularly together, where the togetherness is neither the sum, nor the incorporation [*englobant*], nor the "society," nor the "community" (where these words only give rise to problems). The togetherness of singulars is singularity "itself." It "assembles" them insofar as it spaces them; they are "linked" insofar as they are not unified.

According to these conditions, Being as being-with might no longer be able to say itself in the third person, as in "it is" or "there is." Because there would no longer be a point of view that is exterior to being-together from which it could be announced that "there is" being and a being-with of beings, one with the other. There would be no "it is" and, therefore, no longer the "I am" that is subjacent to the announcement of the "it is." Rather, it would be necessary to think the third-person singular in the first person. As such, then, it becomes the first-person plural. Being could not speak of itself except in this unique manner: "we are." The truth of the *ego sum* is the *nos sumus*; this "we" announces itself through humanity for all the beings "we" are with, for existence in the sense of being-essentially-with, as a Being whose essence is the with.

("One will speak . . .": Which one? We will speak: Who is this "we"? How can I say "us" for those of you who are reading this? How can I say "us" for me? Although this is what we are in the process of doing, how do we think together, whether we are "in accord" or not? How are we with one another? All of this is to ask: What is at play in our communication, in this book, in its sentences, and in the whole situation that more or less gives them some meaning? [This is the] question of philosophy as "literature," which is about asking how far it is possible to take the third-person discourse of philosophy. At what point must ontology become . . . what? Become conversation? Become lyricism? . . .The strict conceptual rigor of being-with exasperates the discourse of its concept. . . .)

What is known as "society," therefore, in the broadest and most diffuse sense of the word, is the figure [*chiffre*] of an ontology yet to be put into play. Rousseau presented [a glimpse of] it by making the poorly named "contract" the very event that "made a creature of intelligence and a man . . . from a stupid, limited animal,"[20] and not simply an arrangement

between individuals. (Nietzsche confirms this presentation in a paradoxical way when Zarathustra says, "human society: that is an experiment . . . a long search . . . and *not* a 'contract'."[21]) Marx saw it when he qualified humanity as social in its very origin, production,
and destination, and when the entire movement and posture of his thinking assigned Being
itself to this social being. Heidegger designated it in positing being-with as constitutive of
being-there. No one, however, has radically thematized the "with" as the essential trait of
Being and as its proper plural singular coessence. But they have brought us, together and
individually, to the point where we can no longer avoid thinking about this in favor of that
to which all of contemporary experience testifies. In other words, what is at stake is no
longer thinking:

—beginning from the one, or from the other,
—beginning from their togetherness, understood now as the One, now as the Other,
—but thinking, absolutely and without reserve, beginning from the "with," *as the proper
essence of one whose Being is nothing other than with-one-another* [l'un-avec-l'autre].

The one/the other is neither "by," nor "for," nor "in," nor "despite," but rather "with."
This "with" is at once both more and less than "relation" or "bond," especially if such relation or bond presupposes the preexistence of the terms upon which it relies; the "with" is
the exact contemporary of its terms; it is, in fact, their contemporaneity. "With" is the
sharing of time-space; it is the at-the-same-time-in-the-same-place as itself, in itself, shat-
tered. It is the instant scaling back of the principle of identity: Being is at the same time in
the same place only on the condition of the spacing of an indefinite plurality of singularities. Being is with Being; it does not ever recover itself, but it is near to itself, beside itself,
in touch with itself, its very self, in the paradox of that proximity where distancing [*éloigne-
ment*] and strangeness are revealed. We are each time an other, each time with others. "With"
does not indicate the sharing of a common situation any more than the juxtaposition of
pure exteriorities does (for example, a bench with a tree with a dog with a passer-by).

The question of Being and the meaning of Being has become the question of being-with
and of being-together (in the sense of the world). This is what is signified by [our] modern
sense of anxiety, which does not so much reveal a "crisis of society" but, instead, reveals
that the "sociality" or "association" of humans is an injunction that humanity places on
itself, or that it receives from the world: to have to be only what it is and to have to, itself,
be Being as such. This sort of formula is primarily a desperate tautological abstraction—and
this is why we are all worried. Our task is to break the hard shell of this tautology. What is
the being-with of Being?

In one sense, this is the original situation of the West that is always repeating itself; it is
always the problem of the city, the repetition of which, for better or worse, has already
punctuated our history. Today, this repetition produces itself as a situation in which the
two major elements [*données*] compose a sort of antinomy: on the one hand, there is the
exposure of the world and, on the other, the end of representations of the world. This means

nothing short of a transformation in the relation [that we name] "politico-philosophy": it can no longer be a matter of a single community, of its essence, closure, and sovereignty; by contrast, it can no longer be a matter of organizing community according to the decrees of a sovereign. Other, or according to the *telos* [fins] of a history. It can no longer be a matter of treating sociability as a regrettable and inevitable accident, as a constraint that has to be managed in some way or another. Community is bare, but it is imperative.

On the one side, the concept of community or the city is, in every sense, diffracted. It is that which signifies the chaotic and multiform appearance of the infranational, supranational, para-national and, moreover, the dis-location of the "national" in general. On the other side, the concept of community appears to have its own prefix as its only content: the *cum*, the *with* deprived of substance and connection, stripped of interiority, subjectivity, and personality. Either way, sovereignty is nothing.[22] Sovereignty is nothing but the *com-*; as such, it is always and indefinitely "to be completed," as in com-munism or com-passion.

This is not a matter of thinking the annihilation of sovereignty. It is a matter of thinking through the following question: If sovereignty is the grand, political term for defining community (its leader or its essence) that has nothing beyond itself, with no foundation or end but itself, what becomes of sovereignty when it is revealed that it is nothing but a singularly plural spacing? How is one to think sovereignty as the "nothing" of the "with" that is laid bare? At the same time, if political sovereignty has always signified the refusal of domination (of a state by another or by a church, of a people by something other than itself), how is one to think the bare sovereignty of the "with" and against domination, whether this is the domination of being-together by some other means or the domination of togetherness by itself (by the regulation of its "automatic" control)? In fact, one could begin to describe the present transformation of "political space"[23] as a transition toward "empire," where empire signifies two things: (1) domination without sovereignty (without the elaboration of such a concept); and (2) the distancing, spacing, and plurality opposed to the concentration of interiority required by political sovereignty. The question then becomes: How is one to think the spacing of empire against its domination?

In one way or another, bare sovereignty (which is, in a way, to transcribe Bataille's notion of sovereignty) presupposes that one take a certain distance from the politico-philosophical order and from the realm of "political philosophy." This distance is not taken in order to engage in a depoliticized thinking, but in order to engage in a thinking, the site of which is the very constitution, imagination, and signification of the political, which allows this thinking to retrace its path in its retreat and beginning from this retreat. The retreat of the political does not signify the disappearance of the political. It only signifies the disappearance of the philosophical presupposition of the whole politico-philosophical order, which is always an ontological presupposition. This presupposition has various forms, it can consist in thinking Being as community and community as destination, or, on the contrary, thinking Being as anterior and outside the order of society and, as such, thinking Being as the accidental exteriority of commerce and power. But, in this way, being-together is never properly [brought to the fore as an explicit] theme and as the ontological problem. The retreat of the political[24] is the uncovering, the ontological laying bare of being-with.

Being singular plural: in a single stroke, without punctuation, without a mark of equivalence, implication, or sequence. A single, continuous-discontinuous mark tracing out the entirety of the ontological domain, being-with-itself designated as the "with" of Being, of the singular and plural, and dealing a blow to ontology—not only another signification but also another syntax. The "meaning of Being": not only as the "meaning of with," but also, and above all, as the "with" of meaning. Because none of these three terms precedes or grounds the other, each designates the coessence of the others. This coessence puts essence itself in the hyphenation—"being-singular-plural"—which is a mark of union and also a mark of division, a mark of sharing that effaces itself, leaving each term to its isolation *and* its being-with-the-others.

From this point forward, then, the unity of an ontology must be sought in this traction, in this drawing out, in this distancing and spacing which is that of Being and, at the same time, that of the singular and the plural, both in the sense that they are distinct from one another and indistinct. In such an ontology, which is not an "ontology of society" in the sense of a "regional ontology," but ontology itself as a "sociality" or an "association" more originary than all "society," more originary than "individuality" and every "essence of Being." Being is *with*; it is *as the with* of Being itself (the cobeing of Being), so that Being does not identify itself *as such*[25] (*as Being of the being*), but *shows itself* [se pose], *gives itself, occurs, dis-poses itself* (made event, history, and world) as its own singular plural *with*. In other words, *Being is not without Being*, which is not another miserable tautology as long as one understands it in the co-originary mode of being-with-being-itself.

According to this mode, Being is simultaneous. Just as, in order to say Being, one must repeat it and say that "Being is," so Being is only simultaneous with itself. The time of Being (the time that it is) is this simultaneity, this coincidence that presupposes "incidence" in general. It assumes movement, displacement, and deployment; it assumes the originary temporal derivative of Being, its spacing.

In one sense, this is all a matter of repeating the Aristotelian axiom *pollakôs legomenon*; Being is said in many ways. But to say it once more, according to the "with," the "also," the "again" of a history that repeats this excavation and drawing out [*traction*] of Being, the singularity of Being is its plural. But this plurality is no longer said in multiple ways that all begin from a presumed, single core of meaning. The multiplicity of the said (that is, of the sayings) belongs to Being as its constitution. This occurs with each said, which is always singular; it occurs in each said, beyond each said, and as the multiplicity of the totality of being [*l'étant en totalité*].

Being, then, does not coincide *with* itself unless this coincidence immediately and essentially marks itself out [*se remarque*] according to the *co*structure of its occurrence [*l'événement*] (its incidence, encounter, angle of declination, shock, or discordant accord). Being coincides with Being: it *is* the spacing and the unexpected arrival [*survenue*], the unexpected spacing, of the singular plural *co-*.

It might be asked why it is still necessary to call this "Being," since the essence of it is reduced to a prefix of Being, reduced to a *co-* outside of which there would be nothing, nothing but beings or existences [*les existants*], and where this *co-* has none of the substance or consistency proper to "Being" as such. This is, in fact, the matter in question. Being consists in nothing other than the existence of all existences [*tous les existants*]. However, this consistency itself does not vanish in a cloud of juxtaposed beings. What I am trying to indicate by speaking of "dis-position" is neither a simple position nor a juxtaposition. Instead, the *co-* defines the unity and uniqueness of what is, in general. What is to be understood is precisely the constitution of this unique unity as *co-*: the *singular plural*.

(Incidentally, one could show without much trouble that this is a question that has been taken up and repeated throughout a long tradition: in Leibniz's monadology, in all the various considerations of the "originary division," and, most of all, in all the various forms of the difference between the in-itself and the for-itself. But exactly what is important is this repetition, the concentration on and repeated excavation of the question—which does not necessarily signify some sort of progress or degeneration, but rather a displacement, a fit of, or drift toward something else, toward another philosophical posture.)

At the very least, and provisionally, one could try to say it in the following way: it is no more a matter of an originary multiplicity and its correlation (in the sense of the One dividing itself in an arch-dialectical manner, or in the sense of the atoms' relationship to the clinamen) than it is a matter of an originary unity and its division. In either case, one must think an anteriority of the origin according to some event that happens to it unexpectedly (even if that event originates within it). It is necessary then, to think plural unity originarily. This is indeed the place to think the plural as such.

In Latin, *plus* is comparable to *multus*. It is not "numerous"; it is "more." It is an increase or excess of origin in the origin. To put it in terms of the models just alluded to above: the One is more than one; it is not that "it divides itself," rather it is that one equals more than one, because "one" cannot be counted without counting more than one. Or, in the atomist model, there are atoms *plus* the clinamen. But the clinamen is not something else, another element outside of the atoms; it is not in addition to them; it is the "more" of their exposition. Being many, they cannot but incline or decline; they are ones in relation to others. Immobility or the parallel fall [*la chute parallèl*] would do away with this exposition, would return to the pure position and not distinguish itself from the One-purely-one (or, in other words, from the Other). The One as purely one is less than one; it cannot be, be put in place, or counted. One as properly one is always more than one. It is an excess of unity; it is one-with-one, where its Being in itself is copresent.

The *co-* itself and as such, the copresence of Being, is not presentable as that Being which "is," since it is only in the distancing. It is unpresentable, not because it occupies the most withdrawn and mysterious region of Being, the region of nothingness, but quite simply because it is not subject to a logic of presentation. Neither present nor to be presented (nor, as a result, "unpresentable" in the strict sense), the "with" is the (singular plural) condition of presence in general [understood] as copresence. This co-presence is neither a presence withdrawn into absence nor a presence *in* itself or *for* itself.

It is also not pure *presence to*, to *itself*, to *others*, or to the *world*. In fact, none of these modes of presence can take place, insofar as presence takes place, unless copresence first takes place. As such, no single subject could even designate *itself* and *relate itself* to itself as subject. In the most classical sense of the term, a subject not only assumes its own distinction from the object of its representation or mastery, it also assumes its own distinction from other subjects. It is possible, then, to distinguish the ipseity of these other subjects (which is to say, the aesity) *from* [d'avec] its own source of representation or mastery. Therefore, the with is the supposition of the "self" in general. But this supposition is no longer subjacent to the self, in the sense of an infinite self-presupposition of sub-jective substance. As its syntactic function indicates, "with" is the pre-position of the position in general; thus, it constitutes its dis-position.

The "self," of the "self" in general, takes place with before taking place as itself and/or as the other. This "aseity" of the self is anterior to the same and to the other and, therefore, anterior to the distinction between a consciousness and its world. Before phenomenological intentionality and the constitution of the ego, but also before thinglike consistency as such, there is co-originarity according to the with. Properly speaking, then, there is no anteriority: co-originarity is the most general structure of all con-sistency, all con-stitution, and all con-sciousness.

[This is] presence-with: *with* as the exclusive mode of being-present, such that being present and the present of Being does not coincide in itself, or with itself, inasmuch as it coincides or "falls with" ["tombe avec"] the other presence, which itself obeys the same law. Being-many-together is the originary situation; it is even what defines a "situation" in general. Therefore, an originary or transcendental "with" demands, with a palpable urgency, to be disentangled and articulated for itself. But one of the greatest difficulties of the concept of the with is that there is no "getting back to" or "up to" [*remonter*] this "originary" or "transcendental" position; the with is strictly contemporaneous with all existence, as it is with all thinking.

❋   ❋   ❋

Co-appearing

It might be, then, that the current situation of "social Being" has to be understood in some other way than by starting from the schema of an immense, spectacular self-consumption, a schema where the truth of community is dissolved and engulfed—whether community [is understood] as subject or as occurring between subjects. If only we made the effort to decipher it in a new way, it might be that the phenomenon of the generalized "spectacle," along with what we call the "tele-global dimension," which accompanies it and is cosubstantial with it, would reveal something else altogether. What is of primary importance in this is to avoid presupposing that the subject of "social Being" or the subject of Being *tout court* is already established.

But this cannot simply be a matter of the classic gesture of wanting to begin without presuppositions (which always assumes that this desire [*volonté*] itself is not already the whole presupposition). It is a matter of rigorously thinking what Being-without-presuppositions-about-itself means, which is, once again, the "creation of the world." In a general way, indeed in an absolutely general way, the primordial requirement of ontology or first philosophy must now be that Being not be presupposed in any way or in any respect, and, more precisely, that *every presupposition of Being must consist in its nonpresupposition.*

Being cannot be pre-sup-posed [*pré-sup-posé*] if it is only the Being of what exists, and is not itself some other existence that is previous or subjacent to existence by which existence exists. For existence exists in the plural, singularly plural. As a result, the most formal and fundamental requirement [of ontology] is that "Being" cannot even be assumed to be the simple singular that the name seems to indicate. Its being singular is plural in its very Being. It follows, then, that *not only must being-with-one-another not be understood starting from the presupposition of being-one, but on the contrary, being-one* (Being as such, complete Being or *ens realissimum*) *can only be understood by starting from being-with-one-another.* That question which we still call a "question of social Being" must, in fact, constitute *the* ontological question.

If one really understands the necessity of this groundless presupposition, one would also have to try to say the following: if the situation of being-social is not that of a spectacular self-alienation that presupposes a lost or dissimulated "real presence," neither is it that of a general communicational arrangement, which presupposes a "rational subject" of communication. This does not mean that there is nothing to the illusions of spectacular self-alienation or to the rationality of a general communicational arrangement, but it does mean that "real presence" and "rationality" can only be thought or evaluated by beginning from something else; and they cannot themselves constitute the groundless presupposition. If left to itself, as a sort of grand, hermeneutical antinomy of the modern world (and one that is clearly at work everywhere), this contrary double form of the "[illusory] spectacle" and "[rational] communication" could even switch their predicates around, such that the "spectacle" would be nothing other than "communication" and vice versa. This chiasma or circle worries us in our confused and anxiety-ridden awareness that society just "turns round and around," without substance, without foundation, without end.

In fact, it might be that what is happening to us is just another sort of "Copernican revolution," not of the cosmological system, or of the relation of subject and object, but rather of "social Being" revolving [*tournant*] around itself or turning on itself, and no longer revolving around something else (Subject, Other, or Same).

What happens to us, then, is the stripping bare [*mis à nu*] of social reality, the very *reality* of being-social in, by, and as the symbolicity that constitutes it, where "spectacle," "communication," "commodity," and "technology" would be different figures of this symbolicity. These are, however, perverse figures that still have to be thought.

It is still necessary to understand what this word "symbolic" means. The proper value of symbolism is in making a *symbol*, that is, in making a connection or a joining,[26] and in giving a face [*figure*] to this liaison by making an *image*. Insofar as the relation is imagined [*se représente*], and because the relation as such is nothing other than its own representation, the symbolic is what is real in such a relation. By no means, however, is such a relation the representation of something that is real (in the secondary, mimetic sense of representation), but the relation is, and is nothing other than, what is real in the representation—its effectiveness and its efficacy. (The paradigm for this is "I love you" or, perhaps more originally, "I am addressing myself to you.")

In this respect, it is important to emphasize that the symbolic and the imaginary are far from opposites. But the way in which they are not opposites is even contrary to how the common way of speaking [*vulgate*] conflates the image (understood as manifestation and recognition) with the simulacrum (understood as a captivating and mystifying hypostasis). The simple, or simplistic, critique of "the image" (and of the "civilization of images"), which has become a sort of ideological trope in theories of the "spectacle" and in theories of "communication," is nothing but the mythic and mystifying effect of the frantic desire for a "pure" symbolization (and a symptomatic manifestation of the weakness of "critique" in general). The sole criterion of symbolization is not the exclusion or debasement of the image, but instead the capacity for allowing a certain play, in and by the image-symbol, with the joining, the distancing, the opened interval that articulates it as *sym-bol*: this word simply means "put with" (the Greek *sun* equals the Latin *cum*), so that the dimension, space, and nature of the "with" are in play here. Therefore, the "symbolic" is not simply an aspect of being-social: on the one hand, it is this Being itself; on the other hand, the symbolic does not take place without (re)presentation, the (re)presentation of one another [*des uns aux autres*] according to which they are with one another [*les-uns-avec-les-autres*].

If I speak of "social" reality's being stripped bare as its symbolicity, then I am talking about "society" uncovered, society no longer being the appearance of only itself, society no longer reduced to a sort of background "symbolizing" (in the ordinary sense) nothing (no community, no mystical body). I am talking about society making a symbol of itself, society making its appearance by facing [*face à*] itself in order to be all that it is and all that it has to be. In this way, being-social is not reduced to any assumption of an interior or superior unity. Its unity is wholly symbolic; it is wholly of the with. Being-social is Being that is by appearing in the face of itself, faced with itself: it is *co-appearing* [com-parution].

Co-appearing does not simply signify that subjects appear together. In that case (which is the "social contract"), it would still need to be asked from where it is that they "appear," from which remote depth do they come into being-social as such, from what origin. We must also wonder why they appear "together" ["ensemble"] and for what other depth they are destined, destined "all together" or "further-on [outre] together." Either the predicate "together" is only a qualification that is extrinsic to subjects, which does not belong to the appearance of each one as such, but designates a pure, indifferent juxtaposition, or it adds a particular quality, one granted a meaning of its own that must be worked out for all subjects "together" and as "together." These two questions lead straight to the dead ends of a metaphysics—and its politics—in which (1) social co-appearance is only ever thought of as a transitory epiphenomenon, and (2) society itself is thought of as a step in a process that always leads either to the hypostasis of togetherness or the common (community, communion), or to the hypostasis of the individual.

In either case, one comes to a dead end because being-social as such—or again, what might be called the *association* [sociation] *of Being*—is instrumentalized, related to something other than itself. On this account, the essence of the "social" is not itself "social." As a result, it is never presentable under the heading of the "social," but only under the heading of either a simple, extrinsic, and transitory "association," or of a transsocial presupposition, the unitary entelechy of common Being—which are both ways to repress and foreclose the problem of "association."

The very meaning of the word "together," just like the meaning of the word "with," seems to oscillate indefinitely between two meanings, without ever coming to a point of equilibrium: it is either the "together" of juxtaposition *partes extra partes*, isolated and unrelated parts, or the "together" of gathering *totum intra totum*, a unified totality [*unitotalité*] where the relation surpasses itself in being pure. But it is clear from this that the resources found in the term are situated precisely on the point of equilibrium between the two meanings: "together" is neither *extra* nor *intra*. In fact, the pure outside, like the pure inside, renders all sorts of togetherness impossible. They both suppose a unique and isolated pure substance, but pure in such a way that one cannot even say "isolated," exactly: because one would be deprived of all relation with it. As such, then, God is not together with anything or anyone, but is—at least in Spinoza and Leibniz, although in different, but equally exemplary, ways—the togetherness or being-together of all that is: God is not "God."[27]

Togetherness and being-together are not equivalent. (On the contrary; the equivocation between the two makes the status of the gods of onto-theology uncertain. [Whether it is a matter of] pantheism, panentheism, polytheism, monotheism, atheism, deism, and so on, [are such gods] representable or unrepresentable? [Do they] ground representation or remove it? Or [might they] even be representation itself?) Togetherness, in the sense of being a substantive entity, is a collection (as in the theory of togethernesses [*ensembles*]). Collection assumes a regrouping that is exterior and indifferent to the being-together ("in common") of the objects of the collection. In a general way, the themes and practices of the "collective" or of "collectivism" move in this register. It could be said, then, that the ontological *togetherness* which we must think through is never substantive; it is always the adverb of a *being-together*. But, this adverb is not a predicate of "Being"; it brings to it no particular and supplementary qualification. Like all adverbs, it modifies or modifies the verb, but here modalization is of the essence and of the origin. Being is together, and it is not a togetherness.

"Together" means simultaneity (*in*, *simul*), "at the same time." Being together is being at the same time (and in the same place, which is itself the determination of "time" as "contemporary time"). "Same time / same place" assumes that "subjects," to call them that, share this space-time, but not in the extrinsic sense of "sharing"; they must share it between *themselves*; they must themselves "symbolize" it as the "same space-time" without which there would not be time or space. The space-time itself is first of all the possibility of the "with." Very long analyses are called for here. Cutting them far too short, let me say that time cannot be the pure moment [*instant*], or pure succession, without being simultaneity "at the same time." Time itself implies "at the same time." Simultaneity immediately opens space as the spacing of time itself. Starting from the simultaneity of "subjects," time is possible, but above all, it is necessary. For in order to be together and to communicate, a correlation of places *and* a transition of passages from one place to another is necessary. Sharing [*partage*] and passage control each other reciprocally. Husserl writes, "It is essentially necessary that the *togetherness* of monads, their mere *co*-existence, be a *temporal* co-existence . . ."[28] In fact, simultaneity is not a matter of indistinction; on the contrary, it is the distinctness of places taken together. The passage from one place to another *needs time* [*D'un lieu à l'autre*, il faut le temps]. And moving in place [*du lieu à lui-même*] as such also needs time: the time for the place to open itself as place, the time to space itself. Reciprocally, originary time, appearing as such, *needs space* [il lui faut l'espace], the space of its own dis-tension, the space of the passage that divides [*partage*] it. Nothing and nobody can be born without being born to and with others who come into this encounter, who are born in their own turn. The "together," therefore, is an absolutely originary structure. What is not together is in the no-time-no-place of non-Being.

Co-appearance, then, must signify—because this is what is now at stake—that "appearing" (coming into the world and being in the world, or existence as such) is strictly inseparable, indiscernable from the *cum* or the *with*, which is not only its place and its taking place, but also—and this is the same thing—its fundamental ontological structure.

That Being is being-with, absolutely, this is what we must think."[29] The *with* is the most basic feature of Being, the mark [*trait*] of the singular plurality of the origin or origins in it.

Undoubtedly, the *with* as such is not presentable. I have already said so, but I have to insist upon it. The *with* is not "unpresentable" like some remote or withdrawn presence, or like an Other. If there is a subject only with other subjects, the "with" itself is not a subject. The "with" is or constitutes the mark of unity/disunity, which in itself does not designate unity or disunity as that fixed substance which would undergird it; the "with" is not the sign of a reality, or even of an "intersubjective dimension." It really is, "in truth," a mark drawn out over the void, which crosses over it and underlines it at the same time, thereby constituting the drawing apart [*traction*] and drawing together [*tension*] of the void. As such, it also constitutes the traction and tension, repulsion/attraction, of the "between"-us. The "with" stays between us, and we stay between us: just us, but only [as] the interval between us.

In fact, one should not say the "with"; one should only say "with," which would be a preposition that has no position of its own and is available for every position. But if the unpresentability of "with" is not that of a hidden presence, then it is because "with" is the unpresentability of this pre-position, that is, the unpresentability of presentation itself. "With" does not add itself to Being, but rather creates the immanent and intrinsic condition of presentation in general.

Presence is impossible except as copresence. If I say that the Unique is present, I have already given it presence as a companion (even if such presence constitutes the Unique, and I have split it in two). The *co-* of copresence is the unpresentable par excellence, but it is nothing other than—and not the Other of—presentation, the existence which co-appears.

If we now have to think about social Being in some other way than according to its spectacular-market self-mockery or its communicational self-assurance, both of which take place on the basis of an unlikely and nostalgic inauthenticity, it is quite likely that there would be nothing else for us to meditate on, nothing to ruminate about or mull over between us. What is proper to community is neither a creativity nor a rationality laid down like some fundamental internal resource, readily available to be put into practice through critique. In this respect, we are definitely no longer in the age of Enlightenment or Romanticism. We are elsewhere, which does not mean we are opposed to them or beyond them, as if we had dialectically surpassed them. We are in a sort of simultaneous drawing together [*tension*] of these two epochs; they are contemporaries of ours and we see them wearing thin. One is worn thin to the point of being an extremely dull platitude; the other is stretched out toward the night of extermination. We are thus in a suspension of history where an enigma is gathering anew; we are contemporaries of ourselves, contemporaries of the stripping bare of being-in-common.

What is proper to community, then, is given to us in the following way: it has no other resource to appropriate except the "with" that constitutes it, the *cum* of "community," its interiority without an interior, and maybe even its *interior intimo sui*. As a result, this *cum* is the *cum* of a co-appearance, wherein we do nothing but appear together with one another, co-appearing before no other authority [*l'instance*][30] than this "with" itself, the meaning of which seems to us to instantly dissolve into insignificance, into exteriority, into the inorganic, empirical, and randomly contingent [*aléatoire*] inconsistency of the pure and simple "with."

So it appears to us that what is proper to community is nothing more than the generalized impropriety of banality, of anonymity, of the lonely crowd and gregarious isolation. The simplest solidarities, the most elementary proximities seem to be dislocated. As such, then, "communication" is only the laborious negotiation of a reasonable and disinterested image of community devoted to its own maintenance, which constantly reveals itself as nothing but the maintenance of the spectacular-market machine.

It must be said, however, that co-appearance might only be another name for capital. At the same time, it might be a name that runs the risk of once again masking what is at-issue, providing a consoling way of thinking that is secretly resigned. But this danger is not a sufficient reason to be satisfied, with a critique of capital that is still held prisoner to the presupposition of an "other subject" of history, economics, and the appropriation of the proper in general. In pointing to "capital," Marx designated a general depropriation [*dépropriation*] that does not allow for the presupposition or preservation of the other, or the Other, which would be the subject of the general reappropriation.

Or more precisely, the presupposition cannot take the form of presupposing a "subject"; rather, it must take the form of being-with-one-another, and must do so in a way that is much more problematic, but far more radical, than Marx could have suspected. It must also be said, then, that the classic critique of capital, even in its latest post-Marxist forms, is not sufficient for taking hold of what capital exposes. At the very least, a thinking of co-appearance must awaken this anxiety.

The intuition buried in Marx's work is undoubtedly located in the following ambivalence: at one and the same time, capital exposes the general alienation of the proper—which is the generalized disappropriation, or the appropriation of misery in every sense of the word— *and* it exposes the stripping bare of the *with* as a mark of Being, or as a mark of meaning. Our thinking is not yet adequate to this ambivalence. This is why, since Marx and up through Heidegger, such ambivalence constantly revives a great, undefined hesitation on the subject of "technology," the limit-object—and perhaps the screen [*l'objet-écran*]—of a thinking which projects onto it either the promise of a self-overcoming of capital or the assurance of the implacable character of its machinery carrying on uncontrolled—and, thereby, controlling everything thanks to this absence of control.

This is also why the truth of our time can only be expressed in Marxist or post-Marxist terms. This why it is a question of the market, of misery, of social-democratic ideology, or the substantial reappropriations that give a reply to it (nationalism, fundamentalism, and fascism in all their various forms). But this truth itself demands that it be thought starting from the *with* of co-appearance, so long as bringing it to life and stripping it bare signifies at least this—to put it in a formulaic way: what is at stake is not a reappropriation of the *with* (of the essence of a common Being), but rather a *with* of reappropriation (where the proper does not return, or returns only *with*).

(This is why we do not make an economy out of an ontology, but it is also why this ontology must be both an *ethos* and a *praxis*, identically. This will have to be developed later.[31] Let us hold the following in reserve: an ontology of being-with can only be located within the distinction of these terms: to be, to act, event, meaning, end, conduct, just as much as, and because, it must be located within the distinction of the "singular" and the "plural," the "in oneself" ["à soi"] and the "in several" ["à plusieurs"].)

Notes

1. "Les gens sont bizarres." The word *bizarre* is translated as "strange" throughout the text in order to preserve the idiom. This presents a particular difficulty only in the final sentence of the first paragraph of p. 10 where Nancy draws attention to the etymology of the French (and also the English) word *bizarre*.—Trans.

2. Heidegger's *das Man* is generally translated into French as *le "on"* but has generally appeared in English as the "they." We have avoided that habit here because a plural pronoun is unwarranted and would only serve to confuse what is, after all, an analysis of singularity and plurality. Translating it as the "one" has the added advantage of preserving echoes of both the author's French and Heidegger's German.—Trans.

3. Although the exercise might be instructive, I will not stop here to examine what "people" and "one" designate in various languages, or the history of the word "people" ["les gens"] (*gentes*, "Gentiles," nations, and so on).

4. This *argot* expression means "his head in the clouds" or "not down-to-earth," or even "out of his mind," but we have used the literal translation as the only way to preserve the author's play on "beside" [*à côté*].—Trans.

5. Although reasonably accurate, "appears" is a somewhat pale translation of *surgit*, so some additional connotations should be born in mind: appears suddenly, abruptly, even violently, emerges, wells up, surges forth. The emphasis, however, here and elsewhere, is on the moment of appearing.—Trans.

6. *Bizarre* is the French word we have translated as "strange" throughout this passage.—Trans.

7. Having, gaining, and being access is what is at issue here, but it should be remembered that *accéder* also means "to accede to" or "to accommodate."—Trans.

8. Let me be quite clear that the allusion to Lacan is deliberate.

9. Immanuel Kant, *Critique of Pure Reason*, trans. Norman Kemp Smith (New York: St. Martin's Press, 1965), 504. Also presupposed here is Martin Heidegger's *Kants These Über das Sein* (Frankfurt am Main: Vittorio Klosterman, 1963).

10. The complex ambiguity Nancy emphasizes here is not easily captured in English. It operates along two axes, one having to do with the expression *à la verité*, the other with the verb *accéder*. The phrase could be rendered as "We have access to the truth," or as "Truly, we have access," but either "We accede to the truth" or "Truly, we accede" would also be warranted. In Bataille's text, the latter axis is dissolved (indeed, does not arise) but, as the note below makes clear, Nancy will not allow the connotations of accession or accommodation to disappear.—Trans.

11. Georges Bataille, *Histoire des rats. Oeuvres complètes, III* (Paris: Gallimard, 1971), 114. As a matter of fact [*à la verité*], my memory fails me and Bataille writes "we attain" ["nous atteignons"]: to attain, to gain access [to accede]: as the splitting of the "almost there" ["l'a-peu-pres"] character of reaching the origin. But I must cite the whole passage from Bataille: "We do not have the means of attaining at our disposal: we attain to truth; we suddenly attain to the necessary point and we spend the rest of our

days looking for a lost moment: but we miss it only at times, precisely because looking for it diverts us from it, to unite us is undoubtedly) a means of . . . forever missing the moment of return. Suddenly, in my night, in my solitude, anxiety gives way to conviction: it is sly, no longer even disturbing (by dint of its being disturbing, it no longer disturbs), *suddenly the heart of B. is in my heart.*"

12. In Section 2, we translated *toucher à* as "to touch" since the context specified surfaces that touch one another. Here, the primary sense is of reaching or attaining an end, but it is also important to bear in mind the tactile sense, as well as the more common sense of "being in touch with."—Trans.

13. Jean-François Marquet's *Singularité et événement* (Grenoble: Jérome Millon, 1995) gives a full account of the tradition of thinking about the one, in the sense of each one and the singular, and what differences there are among our various perspectives. But even before going there, one should look at those texts where this preoccupation comes to us in the first place: the texts of Gilles Deleuze along with those of Jacques Derrida (and this *with* will demand its own commentary some day). Basically, this preoccupation travels in the same direction as that undertaken by Giorgio Agamben, on one side, and Alain Badiou, on the other (even if Badiou wants to put the question in the form of an opposition by playing multiplicity against the One). All of this is to make the point that we are only thinking about the ones *with* the other [*les uns* avec *les autres*] (by, against, in spite of, close to, far from, in touch with, in avoiding it, in digging through it).

14. See Part 1, §3 of Immanuel Kant's *Der einzig mögliche Beweisgrund: The One Basis for a Demonstration of the Existence of God*, trans. Gordon Treash (New York: Abaris Books, 1979).

15. G. W. F. Hegel, *Hegel's Logic*, trans. William Wallace (Oxford: Oxford University Press, 1975), 31.

16. Edmund Husserl, *Cartesian Meditations: An Introduction to Phenomenology*, trans. Dorion Cairns (The Hague: Martinus Nijhoff, 1977), 140.

17. Descartes himself attests to this, that we all participate in the process and discourse of the *ego sum*: ". . . by that internal awareness which always precedes reflective knowledge. This inner awareness of one's thoughts and existence is so innate in all men that, although we may pretend that we do not have it . . . we cannot in fact fail to have it" ("Author's Replies to the Sixth Set of Objections," *The Philosophical Writings of Descartes, Volume II*, trans. John Cottingham, Robert Stoothoof, and Dugald Murdoch [Cambridge: Cambridge University; Press, 1984], 285).

18. In a sense, Levinas testifies to this problematic in an exemplary manner. But what he understands as "otherwise than Being" is a matter of understanding "the ownmost of Being," exactly because it is a matter of thinking being-with rather than the opposition between the other and Being.

19. Martin Heidegger, *Beiträge zur Philosophie* (Frankfurt am Main: Vittorio Klostermann, 1989), 319.

20. Jean-Jacques Rousseau, *The Social Contract*, trans. Maurice Cranston. (New York: Penguin Books, 1968), 65.

21. Friedrich Nietzsche, *Thus Spake Zarathustra*, trans. R. J. Hollingdale (New York: Penguin Books, 1969), 229.

22. This is, of course, an expression that is dear to Bataille. One could even say that this constituted his expression, absolutely.

23. See Antonio Negri's "La crise de l'espace politique," and the rest of the articles gathered in number 27, "En attendant l'empire," of *Futur Antérieur* (Paris: l'Harmattan, January 1995).

24. See the work gathered together not long ago in *Recreating the Political*; ed. Simon Sparks (London: Routledge, 1997), and in *Rejouer le politique* (Paris: Galilée, 1983).

25. For a deconstructive reading of the "as such" of Being in fundamental ontology see the work of Yves Dupeux (thesis, Université de Strasbourg, 1994).

26. Of course, the Greek *sumbolon* was a piece of pottery broken in two pieces when friends, or a host and his guest, parted. Its joining would later be a sign of recognition.

27. A trinitarian God represents a Being-together as its very divinity: and it is clear, therefore, that he is no longer "God," but Being-with of the onto-theological species. Here, another motif of the "deconstruction of Christianity," which I invoked in relation to the Creation, is touched upon. It is also possible to discern here the intimate connection of all the great motifs of Christian dogma, none of which deconstruction can leave intact.

28. Husserl, *Cartesian Meditations*, 139. It is undoubtedly here, more than anywhere else, that Husserl shows how phenomenology itself reaches its limit, and exceeds it: it is no longer the egoistic kernel, but the world "as a constituted sense" that shows itself to be constitutive (137). The constitution is itself constituted: in these terms, this is undoubtedly the ultimate structure of "language" and of the "with," of language *as* "with." The immediate context of the passage shows how Husserl means to give his most direct reply to Heidegger and to a thinking of *Mitsein* still insufficiently founded in the "essential necessity" of the "given Objective world" and its "sociality of various levels" (137). A highly remarkable chiasma is produced, here, between two thoughts that provoke and cross through one another according to what can only be called *two styles of the essentiality of the with*. Broadly speaking, they might be described as the style of cobelonging (in *Being as truth*, Heidegger) and the style of correlation (in *ego as meaning*, Husserl). But these somewhat schematic characteristics could just as easily be reversed. This is not what is most important. What is important is in the *common* testimony of the era (with Freud, with Bataille, with . . .), according to which ontology must, from that point on, be the ontology of the "with," or of nothing.

29. As Francis Fisher, a longtime companion in the recognition of this demand, said, "The 'with' is a strict determination of the inessence of existence. Being-at is immediately 'with' because *Dasein* has no essence" ("Heidegger et la question de l'homme" [thesis, Université de Strasbourg, 1995]).

30. One should keep in mind that "coappear" translates *com-parution*, the exact English equivalent of which is "compearing." This itself is a legal term that is used to designate appearing before a judge together with another person.—Trans.

31. See the forthcoming volume *Léthique originaire* (which starts with Heidegger).

Giorgio Agamben

§1 The Paradox of Sovereignty

1.1. The paradox of sovereignty consists in the fact the sovereign is, at the same time, outside and inside the juridical order. If the sovereign is truly the one to whom the juridical order grants the power of proclaiming a state of exception and, therefore, of suspending the order's own validity, then "the sovereign stands outside the juridical order and, nevertheless, belongs to it, since it is up to him to decide if the constitution is to be suspended *in toto*" (Schmitt, *Politische Theologie*, p. 13). The specification that the sovereign is "*at the same time* outside and inside the juridical order" (emphasis added) is not insignificant: the sovereign, having the legal power to suspend the validity of the law, legally places himself outside the law. This means that the paradox can also be formulated this way: "the law is outside itself," or: "I, the sovereign, who am outside the law, declare that there is nothing outside the law [*che non c'è un fuori legge*]."

The topology implicit in the paradox is worth reflecting upon, since the degree to which sovereignty marks the limit (in the double sense of end and principle) of the juridical order will become clear only once the structure of the paradox is grasped. Schmitt presents this structure as the structure of the exception (*Ausnahme*):

The exception is that which cannot be subsumed; it defies general codification, but it simultaneously reveals a specifically juridical formal element: the decision in absolute purity. The exception appears in its absolute form when it is a question of creating a situation in which juridical rules can be valid. Every general rule demands a regular, everyday frame of life to which it can be factually applied and which is submitted to its regulations. The rule requires a homogeneous medium. This factual regularity is not merely an "external presupposition" that the jurist can ignore; it belongs, rather, to the rule's immanent validity. There is no rule that is applicable to chaos. Order must be established for juridical order to make sense. A regular situation must be created, and sovereign is he who definitely decides if this situation is actually effective. All law is "situational law." The sovereign creates and guarantees the situation as a whole in its totality. He has the monopoly over the final decision. Therein consists the essence of State sovereignty, which must therefore be properly juridically defined not as the monopoly to sanction or to rule but as the monopoly to decide, where the word "monopoly" is used in a general sense that is still to be developed. The decision reveals the essence of State authority most clearly. Here the decision must be distinguished from the juridical regulation, and (to formulate it paradoxically) authority proves itself not to need law to create law. . . . The exception is more interesting than the regular case. The latter proves nothing; the exception proves everything. The exception does not only confirm the rule; the rule as such lives off the exception alone. A Protestant theologian who demonstrated the vital intensity of which theological reflection was still capable in the nineteenth century said: "The exception explains the general and itself. And when one really wants to study the general, one need only look around for a real exception. It brings everything to light more clearly than the general itself. After a while, one becomes disgusted with the endless talk about the general—there are exceptions. If they cannot be explained, then neither can the general be explained. Usually the difficulty is not noticed, since the general is thought about not with passion but only with comfortable superficiality. The exception, on the other hand, thinks the general with intense passion." (*Polisische Theologie*, pp. 19–22)

It is not by chance that in defining the exception Schmitt refers to the work of a theologian (who is none other than Søren Kierkegaard). Giambattista Vico had, to be sure, affirmed the superiority of the exception, which he called "the ultimate configuration of facts," over positive law in a way which was not so dissimilar: "An esteemed jurist is, therefore, not someone who, with the help of a good memory, masters positive law [or the general complex of laws], but rather someone who, with sharp judgment, knows how to look into cases and see the ultimate circumstances of facts that merit equitable consideration and exceptions from general rules" (*De antiquissima*, chap. 2). Yet nowhere in the realm of the juridical sciences can one find a theory that grants such a high position to the exception. For what is at issue in the sovereign exception is, according to Schmitt, the very condition of possibility of juridical rule and, along with it, the very meaning of State authority. Through the state of exception, the sovereign "creates and guarantees the situation" that the law needs for its own validity. But what is this "situation," what is its structure, such that it consists in nothing other than the suspension of the rule?

ℵ The Vichian opposition between positive law (*ius theticum*) and exception well expresses the particular status of the exception. The exception is an element in law that transcends positive law in the form of its suspension. The exception is to positive law what negative theology is to positive theology. While the latter affirms and predicates determinate qualities of God, negative (or mystical) theology, with its "neither . . . nor . . . ," negates and suspends the attribution to God of any predicate whatsoever. Yet negative theology is not outside theology and can actually be shown to function as the principle grounding the possibility in general of anything like a theology. Only because it has been negatively presupposed as what subsists outside any possible predicate can divinity become the subject of a predication. Analogously, only because its validity is suspended in the state of exception can positive law define the normal case as the realm of its own validity.

1.2. The exception is a kind of exclusion. What is excluded from the general rule is an individual case. But the most proper characteristic of the exception is that what is excluded in it is not, on account of being excluded, absolutely without relation to the rule. On the contrary, what is excluded in the exception maintains itself in relation to the rule in the form of the rule's suspension. *The rule applies to the exception in no longer applying, in withdrawing from it.* The state of exception is thus not the chaos that precedes order but rather the situation that results from its suspension. In this sense, the exception is truly, according to its etymological root, *taken outside* (*ex-capere*), and not simply excluded.

It has often been observed that the juridico-political order has the structure of an inclusion of what is simultaneously pushed outside. Gilles Deleuze and Félix Guattari were thus able to write, "Sovereignty only rules over what it is capable of interiorizing" (Deleuze and Guattari, *Mille plateaux*, p. 445); and, concerning the "great confinement" described by Foucault in his *Madness and Civilization*, Maurice Blanchot spoke of society's attempt to "confine the outside" (*enfermer le dehors*), that is, to constitute it in an "interiority of expectation or of exception." Confronted with an excess, the system interiorizes what exceeds it through an interdiction and in this way "designates itself as exterior to itself" (*L'entretien infini*, p. 292). The exception that defines the structure of sovereignty is, however, even more complex. Here what is outside is included not simply by means of an interdiction or an internment, but rather by means of the suspension of the juridical order's validity—by letting the juridical order, that is, withdraw from the exception and abandon it. The exception does not subtract itself from the rule; rather, the rule, suspending itself, gives rise to the exception and, maintaining itself in relation to the exception, first constitutes itself as a rule. The particular "force" of law consists in this capacity of law to maintain itself in relation to an exteriority. We shall give the name *relation of exception* to the extreme form of relation by which something is included solely through its exclusion.

The situation created in the exception has the peculiar characteristic that it cannot be defined either as a situation of fact or as a situation of right, but instead institutes a paradoxical threshold of indistinction between the two. It is not a fact, since it is only created through the suspension of the rule. But for the same reason, it is not even a juridical case in point, even if it opens the possibility of the force of law. This is the ultimate meaning of the paradox that Schmitt formulates when he writes that the sovereign decision "proves itself not to need law to create law." What is at issue in the sovereign exception is not so much the control or neutralization of an excess as the creation and definition of the very space in which the juridico-political order can have validity. In this sense, the sovereign exception is the fundamental localization (*Ortung*), which does not limit itself to distinguishing what is inside from what is outside but instead traces a threshold (the state of exception) between the two, on the basis of which outside and inside, the normal situation and chaos, enter into those complex topological relations that make the validity of the juridical order possible.

The "ordering of space" that is, according to Schmitt, constitutive of the sovereign nomos is therefore not only a "taking of land" (Landesnahme)—the determination of a juridical and a territorial ordering (of an Ordnung and an Ortung)—but above all a "taking of the outside," an exception (Ausnahme).

א Since "there is no rule that is applicable to chaos," chaos must first be included in the juridical order through the creation of a zone of indistinction between outside and inside, chaos and the normal situation—the state of exception. To refer to something, a rule must both presuppose and yet still establish a relation with what is outside relation (the nonrelational). The relation of exception thus simply expresses the originary formal structure of the juridical relation. In this sense, the sovereign decision on the exception is the originary juridico-political structure on the basis of which what is included in the juridical order and what is excluded from it acquire their meaning. In its archetypal form, the state of exception is therefore the principle of every juridical localization, since only the state of exception opens the space in which the determination of a certain juridical order and a particular territory first becomes possible. As such, the state of exception itself is thus essentially unlocalizable (even if definite spatiotemporal limits can be assigned to it from time to time).

The link between localization (*Ortung*) and ordering (*Ordnung*) constitutive of the "*nomos* of the earth" (Schmitt, *Das Nomos*, p. 48) is therefore even more complex than Schmitt maintains and, at its center, contains a fundamental ambiguity, an unlocalizable zone of indistinction or exception that, in the last analysis, necessarily acts against it as a principle of its infinite dislocation. One of the theses of the present inquiry is that in our age, the state of exception comes more and more to the foreground as the fundamental political structure and ultimately begins to become the rule. When our age tried to grant the unlocalizable a permanent and visible localization, the result was the concentration camp. The camp—and not the prison—is the space that corresponds to this originary structure of the *nomos*. This is shown, among other things, by the fact that while prison law only constitutes a particular sphere of penal law and is not outside the normal order, the juridical constellation that guides the camp is (as we shall see) martial law and the state of siege. This is why it is not possible to inscribe the analysis of the camp in the trail opened by the works of Foucault, from *Madness and Civilization* to *Discipline and Punish*. As the absolute space of exception, the camp is topologically different from a simple space of confinement. And it is this space of exception, in which the link between localization and ordering is definitively broken, that has determined the crisis of the old "*nomos* of the earth."

1.3. The validity of a juridical rule does not coincide with its application to the individual case in, for example, a trial or an executive act. On the contrary, the rule must, precisely insofar as it is general, be valid independent of the individual case. Here the sphere of law shows its essential proximity to that of language. Just as in an occurrence of actual speech, a word acquires its ability to denote a segment of reality only insofar as it is also meaningful in its own not-denoting (that is, as *langue* as opposed to *parole*, as a term in its mere lexical consistency, independent of its concrete use in discourse), so the rule can refer to the individual case only because it is in force, in the sovereign exception, as pure potentiality in the suspension of every actual reference. And just as language presupposes the nonlinguistic as that with which it must maintain itself in a virtual relation (in the form of a *langue* or, more precisely, a grammatical game, that is, in the form of a discourse whose actual denotation is maintained in infinite suspension) so that it may later denote it in actual speech, so the law presupposes the nonjuridical (for example, mere violence in the form of the state of nature) as that with which it maintains itself in a potential relation in the state of exception. *The sovereign exception (as zone of indistinction between nature and right) is the presupposition of the juridical reference in the form of its suspension.* Inscribed as a presupposed exception in every rule that orders or forbids something (for example, in the rule that forbids homicide) is the pure and unsanctionable figure of the offense that, in the normal case, brings about the rule's own transgression (in the same example, the killing of a man not as natural violence but as sovereign violence in the state of exception).

א Hegel was the first to truly understand the presuppositional structure thanks to which language is at once outside and inside itself and the immediate (the nonlinguistic) reveals itself to be nothing but a presupposition of language. "Language," he wrote in the *Phenomenology of Spirit*, "is the perfect element in which interiority is as external as exteriority is internal" (see *Phänomenologie des Geistes*, pp. 527–29). We have seen that only the sovereign decision on the state of exception opens the space in which it is possible to trace borders between inside and outside and in which determinate rules can be assigned to determinate territories. In exactly the same way, only language as the pure potentiality to signify, withdrawing itself from every concrete instance of speech, divides the linguistic from the nonlinguistic and allows for the opening of areas of meaningful speech in which certain terms correspond to certain denotations. Language is the sovereign who, in a permanent state of exception, declares that there is nothing outside language and that language is always beyond itself. The particular structure of law has its foundation in this presuppositional structure of human language. It expresses the bond of inclusive exclusion to which a thing is subject because of the fact of being in language, of being named. To speak [*dire*] is, in this sense, always to "speak the law," *ius dicere*.

1.4. From this perspective, the exception is situated in a symmetrical position with respect to the example, with which it forms a system. Exception and example constitute the two modes by which a set tries to found and maintain its own coherence. But while the exception is, as we saw, an *inclusive exclusion* (which thus serves to include what is excluded), the example instead functions as an *exclusive inclusion*. Take the case of the grammatical example (Milner, "L'exemple", p. 176): the paradox here is that a single utterance in no way distinguished from others of its kind is isolated from them precisely insofar as it belongs to them. If the syntagm "I love you" is uttered as an example of a performative speech act, then this syntagm both cannot be understood as in a normal context and yet still must be treated as a real utterance in order for it to be taken as an example. What the example shows is its belonging to a class, but for this very reason the example steps out of its class in the very moment in which it exhibits and delimits it (in the case of a linguistic syntagm, the example thus *shows* its own signifying and, in this way, suspends its own meaning). If one now asks if the rule applies to the example, the answer is not easy, since the rule applies to the example only as to a normal case and obviously not as to an example. The example is thus excluded from the normal case not because it does not belong to it but, on the contrary, because it exhibits its own belonging to it. The example is truly a *paradigm* in the etymological sense: it is what is "shown beside," and a class can contain everything except its own paradigm.

The mechanism of the exception is different. While the example is excluded from the set insofar as it belongs to it, the exception is included in the normal case precisely because it does not belong to it. And just as belonging to a class can be shown only by an example—that is, outside of the class itself—so non-belonging can be shown only at the center of the class, by an exception. In every case (as is shown by the dispute between anomalists and analogists among the ancient grammarians), exception and example are correlative concepts that are ultimately indistinguishable and that come into play every time the very sense of the belonging and commonality of individuals is to be defined. In every logical system, just as in every social system, the relation between outside and inside, strangeness and intimacy, is this complicated.

א The *exceptio* of Roman court law well shows this particular structure of the exception. The *exceptio* is an instrument of the defendant's defense that, in the case of a judgment, functions to neutralize the conclusiveness of the grounds proffered by the plaintiff and thus to render the normal application of the *ius civile* impossible. The Romans saw it as a form of exclusion directed at the application of the *ius civile* (*Digesta*, 44 r. 2; Ulpianus, 74: *Exceptio dicta est quasi quaedam exclusio, quae opponi actioni solet ad excludendum id, quod in intentionem condemnationemve deductum est*, "It is said to be an exception because it is almost a kind of exclusion, a kind of exclusion that is usually opposed to the trial in order to exclude what was argued in the *intentio* and the *condemnatio*"). In this sense, the *exceptio* is not absolutely outside the law, but rather shows a contrast between two juridical demands, a contrast that in Roman law refers back to the opposition between *ius civile* and *ius honorarium*, that is, to the law introduced by the magistrate to temper the excessive generality of the norms of civil law.

In its technical expression in the law of the Roman court, the *exceptio* thus takes the form of a conditional negative clause inserted between the *intentio* and the *condemnasio*, by means of which the condemnation of the defendant is subordinated to the nonexistence of the fact excepted by both *intentio* and *condemnatio* (for example: *si in ea re nihil malo A. Agerii factum sit neque fiat*, "if there has not been malice"). The case of the exception is thus excluded from the application of the *ius civile* without, however, thereby calling into question the belonging of the case in point to the regulative provision. The sovereign exception represents a further dimension: it displaces a contrast between two juridical demands into a limit relation between what is inside and what is outside the law.

It may seem incongruous to define the structure of sovereign power, with its cruel factual implications, by means of two innocuous grammatical categories. Yet there is a case in which the linguistic example's decisive character and ultimate indistinguishability from the exception show an unmistakable involvement with the power of life and death. We refer to the episode in *Judges* 12: 6 in which the Galatians recognize the fleeing Ephraimites, who are trying to save themselves beyond the Jordan, by asking them to pronounce the word "Shibboleth," which the Ephraimites pronounce "Sibboleth" ("The men of Gilead said unto him, 'Art thou an Ephraimite?' If he said, 'Nay'; then they said unto him, 'Say now Shibboleth': and he said Sibboleth: for he could not frame to pronounce it right. Then they took him, and slew him at the passages of Jordan"). In the Shibboleth, example and exception become indistinguishable: "Shibboleth" is an exemplary exception or an example that functions as an exception. (In this sense, it is not surprising that there is a predilection to resort to exemplary punishment in the state of exception.)

1.5. Set theory distinguishes between membership and inclusion. A term is included when it is part of a set in the sense that all of its elements are elements of that set (one then says that b is a subset of a, and one writes it $b \subset a$). But a term may be a member of a set without being included in it (membership is, after all, the primitive notion of set theory, which one writes $b \in a$), or, conversely, a term may be included in a set without being one of its members. In a recent book, Alain Badiou has developed this distinction in order to translate it into political terms. Badiou has membership correspond to presentation, and inclusion correspond to representation (re-presentation). One then says that a term *is a member of* a situation (in political terms, these are single individuals insofar as they belong to a society). And one says that a term is *included* in a situation if it is represented in the metastructure (the State) in which the structure of the situation is counted as one term (individuals insofar as they are recodified by the State into classes, for example, or into "electorates"). Badiou defines a term as *normal* when it is both presented and represented (that is, when it both is a member and is included), as *excrescent* when it is represented but not presented (that is, when it is included in a situation without being a member of that situation), and as *singular* when it is presented but not represented (a term that is a member without being included) (*L'être*, pp. 95–115).

What becomes of the exception in this scheme? At first glance, one might think that it falls into the third case, that the exception, in other words, embodies a kind of membership without inclusion. And this is certainly Badiou's position. But what defines the character of the sovereign claim is precisely that it applies to the exception in no longer applying to it, that it includes what is outside itself. The sovereign exception is thus the figure in which singularity is represented as such, which is to say, insofar as it is unrepresentable. What cannot be included in any way is included in the form of the exception. In Badiou's scheme, the exception introduces a fourth figure, a threshold of indistinction between excrescence (representation without presentation) and singularity (presentation without representation), something like a paradoxical inclusion of membership itself. *The exception is what cannot be included in the whole of which it is a member and cannot be a member of the whole in which it is always already included.* What emerges in this limit figure is the radical crisis of every possibility of clearly distinguishing between membership and inclusion, between what is outside and what is inside, between exception and rule.

א Badiou's thought is, from this perspective, a rigorous thought of the exception. His central category of the event corresponds to the structure of the exception. Badiou defines the event as an element of a situation such that its membership in the situation is undecidable from the perspective of the situation. To the State, the event thus necessarily appears as an excrescence. According to Badiou, the relation between membership and inclusion is also marked by a fundamental lack of correspondence, such that inclusion always exceeds membership (theorem of the point of excess). The exception expresses precisely this impossibility of a system's making inclusion coincide with membership, its reducing all its parts to unity.

From the point of view of language, it is possible to assimilate inclusion to sense and membership to denotation. In this way, the fact that a word always has more sense than it can actually denote corresponds to the theorem of the point of excess. Precisely this disjunction is at issue both in Claude Lévi-Strauss's theory of the constitutive excess of the signifier over the signified ("there is always a lack of equivalence between the two, which is resolvable for a divine intellect alone, and which results in the existence of a superabundance of the signifier over the signifieds on which it rests" [Introduction à Mauss, p, xlix]) and in Émile Benveniste's doctrine of the irreducible opposition between the semiotic and the semantic. The thought of our time finds itself confronted with the structure of the exception in every area. Language's sovereign claim thus consists in the attempt to make sense coincide with denotation, to stabilize a zone of indistinction between the two in which language can maintain itself in relation to its *denotata* by abandoning them and withdrawing from them into a pure *langue* (the linguistic "state of exception"). This is what deconstruction does, positing undecidables that are infinitely in excess of every possibility of signification.

1.6. This is why sovereignty presents itself in Schmitt in the form of a decision on the exception. Here the decision is not the expression of the will of a subject hierarchically superior to all others, but rather represents the inscription within the body of the *nomos* of the exteriority that animates it and gives it meaning. The sovereign decides not the licit and illicit but the originary inclusion of the living in the sphere of law or, in the words of Schmitt, "the normal structuring of life relations," which the law needs. The decision concerns neither a *quaestio iuris* nor a *quaestio facti*, but rather the very relation between law and fact. Here it is a question not only, as Schmitt seems to suggest, of the irruption of the "effective life" that, in the exception, "breaks the crust of a mechanism grown rigid through repetition" but of something that concerns the most inner nature of the law. The law has a regulative character and is a "rule" not because it commands and proscribes, but because it must first of all create the sphere of its own reference in real life and *make that reference regular*. Since the rule both stabilizes and presupposes the conditions of this reference, the originary structure of the rule is always of this kind: "If (a real case in point, e.g.: *si membrum rupsit*), then (juridical consequence, e.g.: *talio esto*)," in which a fact is included in the juridical order through its exclusion, and transgression seems to precede and determine the lawful case. That the law initially has the form of a *lex talionis* (*talio*, perhaps from *talis*, amounts to "the thing itself") means that the juridical order does not originally present itself simply as sanctioning a transgressive fact but instead constitutes itself through the repetition of the same act without any sanction, that is, as an exceptional case. This is not a punishment of this first act, but rather represents its inclusion in the juridical order, violence as a primordial juridical fact (*permittit enim lex parem vindictam*, "for the law allows equitable vengeance" [Pompeius Festus, *De verborum significatione*, 496. 15]). In this sense, the exception is the originary form of law.

The cipher of this capture of life in law is not sanction (which is not at all an exclusive characteristic of the juridical rule) but guilt (not in the technical sense that this concept has in penal law but in the originary sense that indicates a being-in-debt: *in culpa esse*), which is to say, precisely the condition of being included through an exclusion, of being in relation to something from which one is excluded or which one cannot fully assume. *Guilt refers not to transgression, that is, to the determination of the licit and the illicit, but to the pure force of the law, to the law's simple reference to something.* This is the ultimate ground of the juridical maxim, which is foreign to all morality, according to which ignorance of the rule does not eliminate guilt. In this impossibility of deciding if it is guilt that grounds the rule or the rule that posits guilt, what comes clearly to light is the indistinction between outside and inside and between life and law that characterizes the sovereign decision on the exception. The "sovereign" structure of the law, its peculiar and original "force," has the form of a state of exception in which fact and law are indistinguishable (yet must, nevertheless, be decided on). Life, which is thus obliged, can in the last instance be implicated in the sphere of law only through the presupposition of its inclusive exclusion, only in an *exceptio*. There is a limit-figure of life, a threshold in which life is both inside and outside the juridical order, and this threshold is the place of sovereignty.

The statement "The rule lives off the exception alone" must therefore be taken to the letter. Law is made of nothing but what it manages to capture inside itself through the inclusive exclusion of the *exceptio*: it nourishes itself on this exception and is a dead letter without it. In this sense, the law truly "has no existence in itself, but rather has its being in the very life of men." The sovereign decision traces and from time to time renews this threshold of indistinction between outside and inside, exclusion and inclusion, *nomos* and *physis*, in which life is originarily excepted in law. Its decision is the position of an undecidable.

ℵ Not by chance is Schmitt's first work wholly devoted to the definition of the juridical concept of guilt. What is immediately striking in this study is the decision with which the author refutes every technico-formal definition of the concept of guilt in favor of terms that, at first glance, seem more moral than juridical. Here, in fact, guilt is (against the ancient juridical proverb "There is no guilt without rule") first of all a "process of inner life," which is to say, something essentially "intrasubjective," which can be qualified as a real "ill will" that consists in "knowingly positing ends contrary to those of the juridical order" (*Über Schuld*, pp. 18–24, 92).

It is not possible to say whether Benjamin was familiar with this text while he was writing "Fate and Character" and "Critique of Violence." But it remains the case that his definition of guilt as an originary juridical concept unduly transferred to the ethico-religious sphere is in perfect agreement with Schmitt's thesis—even if Benjamin's definition goes in a decisively opposed direction. For Benjamin, the state of demonic existence of which law is a residue is to be overcome and man is to be liberated from guilt (which is nothing other than the inscription of natural life in the order of law and destiny). At the heart of the Schmittian assertion of the juridical character and centrality of the notion of guilt is, however, not the freedom of the ethical man but only the controlling force of a sovereign power (*katechon*), which can, in the best of cases, merely slow the dominion of the Antichrist.

There is an analogous convergence with respect to the concept of character. Like Benjamin, Schmitt clearly distinguishes between character and guilt ("the concept of guilt," he writes, "has to do with an *operari*, and not with an *esse*" [*Über Schuld*, p. 46]). Yet in Benjamin, it is precisely this element (character insofar as it escapes all conscious willing) that presents itself as the principle capable of releasing man from guilt and of affirming natural innocence.

1.7. If the exception is the structure of sovereignty, then sovereignty is not an exclusively political concept, an exclusively juridical category, a power external to law (Schmitt), or the supreme rule of the juridical order (Hans Kelsen): it is the originary structure in which law refers to life and includes it in itself by suspending it. Taking up Jean-Luc Nancy's suggestion, we shall give the name *ban* (from the old Germanic term that designates both exclusion from the community and the command and insignia of the sovereign) to this potentiality (in the proper sense of the Aristotelian *dynamis*, which is always also *dynamis mē energein*, the potentiality not to pass into actuality) of the law to maintain itself in its own privation, to apply in no longer applying. The relation of exception is a relation of ban. He who has been banned is not, in fact, simply set outside the law and made indifferent to it but rather *abandoned* by it, that is, exposed and threatened on the threshold in which life and law, outside and inside, become indistinguishable. It is literally not possible to say whether the one who has been banned is outside or inside the juridical order. (This is why in Romance languages, to be "banned" originally means both to be "at the mercy of" and "at one's own will, freely," to be "excluded" and also "open to all, free.") It is in this sense that the paradox of sovereignty can take the form "There is nothing outside the law." *The originary relation of law to life is not application but Abandonment.* The matchless potentiality of the *nomos, its originary "force of law,"* is that it holds life in its ban by abandoning it. This is the structure of the ban that we shall try to understand here, so that we can eventually call it into question.

א The ban is a form of relation. But precisely what kind of relation is at issue here, when the ban has no positive content and the terms of the relation seem to exclude (and, at the same time, to include) each other? What is the form of law that expresses itself in the ban? The ban is the pure form of reference to something in general, which is to say, the simple positing of relation with the nonrelational. In this sense, the ban is identical with the limit form of relation. A critique of the ban will therefore necessarily have to put the very form of relation into question, and to ask if the political fact is not perhaps thinkable beyond relation and, thus, no longer in the form of a connection.

※　※　※

§4   Form of Law

4.1. In the legend "Before the Law," Kafka represented the structure of the sovereign ban in an exemplary abbreviation.

Nothing—and certainly not the refusal of the doorkeeper—prevents the man from the country from passing through the door of the Law if not the fact that this door is already open and that the Law prescribes nothing. The two most recent interpreters of the legend, Jacques Derrida and Massimo Cacciari, have both insisted on this point, if in different ways. "The Law," Derrida writes, "keeps itself [se garde] without keeping itself, kept [gardée] by a doorkeeper who keeps nothing, the door remaining open and open onto nothing" ("Préjugés," p. 356). And Cacciari, even more decisively, underlines the fact that the power of the Law lies precisely in the impossibility of entering into what is already open, of reaching the place where one already is: "How can we hope to 'open' if the door is already open? How can we hope to enter-the-open [entrare-l'aperto]? In the open, there is, things are there, one does not enter there. . . . We can enter only there where we can open. The already-open [il già-aperto] immobilizes. The man from the country cannot enter, because entering into what is already open is ontologically impossible" (Icone, p. 69).

Seen from this perspective, Kafka's legend presents the pure form in which law affirms itself with the greatest force precisely at the point in which it no longer prescribes anything—which is to say, as pure ban. The man from the country is delivered over to the potentiality of law because law demands nothing of him and commands nothing other than its own openness. According to the schema of the sovereign exception, law applies to him in no longer applying, and holds him in its ban in abandoning him outside itself. The open door destined only for him includes him in excluding him and excludes him in including him. And this is precisely the summit and the root of every law. When the priest in The Trial summarizes the essence of the court in the formula "The court wants nothing from you. It receives you when you come, it lets you go when you go," it is the originary structure of the nomos that he states.

א In an analogous fashion, language also holds man in its ban insofar as man, as a speaking being, has always already entered into language without noticing it. Everything that is presupposed for there to be language (in the forms of something nonlinguistic, something ineffable, etc.) is nothing other than a presupposition of language that is maintained as such in relation to language precisely insofar as it is excluded from language. Stéphane Mallarmé expressed this self-presuppositional nature of language when he wrote, with a Hegelian formula, "The logos is a principle that operates through the negation of every principle." As the pure form of relation, language (like the sovereign ban) always already presupposes itself in the figure of something nonrelational, and it is not possible either to enter into relation or to move out of relation with what belongs to the form of relation itself. This means not that the nonlinguistic is inaccessible to man but simply that man can never reach it in the form of a nonrelational and ineffable presupposition, since the nonlinguistic is only ever to be found in language itself. (In the words of Benjamin, only the "crystal-pure elimination of the unsayable in language" can lead to "what withholds itself from speech" [*Briefe*, p. 127].)

4.2. But does this interpretation of the structure of law truly exhaust Kafka's intention? In a letter to Benjamin dated September 20, 1934, Gerschom Scholem defines the relation to law described in Kafka's *Trial* as "the Nothing of Revelation" (*Nichts der Offenbarung*), intending this expression to name "a stage in which revelation does not signify [*bedeutet*], yet still affirms itself by the fact that it is in force. Where the wealth of significance is gone and what appears, reduced, so to speak, to the zero point of its own content, still does not disappear (and Revelation is something that appears), there the Nothing appears" (Benjamin and Scholem, *Briefwechsel*, p. 163). According to Scholem, a law that finds itself in such a condition is not absent but rather appears in the form of its unrealizability. "The students of whom you speak," he objects to his friend, "are not students who have lost the Scripture . . . but students who cannot decipher it" (ibid., p. 147).

Being in force without significance (Geltung ohne Bedeutung): nothing better describes the ban that our age cannot master than Scholem's formula for the status of law in Kafka's novel. What, after all, is the structure of the sovereign ban if not that of a law that *is in force* but does not *signify*? Everywhere on earth men live today in the ban of a law and a tradition that are maintained solely as the "zero point" of their own content, and that include men within them in the form of a pure relation of abandonment. All societies and all cultures today (it does not matter whether they are democratic or totalitarian, conservative or progressive) have entered into a legitimation crisis in which law (we mean by this term the entire text of tradition in its regulative form, whether the Jewish Torah or the Islamic Shariah, Christian dogma or the profane *nomos*) is in force as the pure "Nothing of Revelation." But this is precisely the structure of the sovereign relation, and the nihilism in which we are living is, from this perspective, nothing other than the coming to light of this relation as such.

4.3. In Kant the pure form of law as "being in force without significance" appears for the first time in modernity. What Kant calls "the simple form of law" (*die bloß Form des Gesetzes*) in the *Critique of Practical Reason* is in fact a law reduced to the zero point of its significance, which is, nevertheless, in force as such (*Kritik der praktischen Vernunft*, p. 28). "Now if we abstract every content, that is, every object of the will (as determining motive) from a law," he writes, "there is nothing left but the simple form of a universal legislation" (ibid., p. 27).

A pure will, thus determined only through such a form of law, is "neither free nor unfree," exactly like Kafka's man from the country.

The limit and also the strength of the Kantian ethics lie precisely in having left the form of law in force as an empty principle. This being in force without significance in the sphere of ethics corresponds, in the sphere of knowledge, to the transcendental object. The transcendental object is, after all, not a real object but "merely the idea of relation" (*bloß eine Idee des Verhältnisses*) that simply expresses the fact of thinking's being in relation with an absolutely indeterminate thought (*Kants opus postuum*, p. 671).

But what is such a "form of law"? And how, first of all, is one to conduct oneself before such a "form of law," once the will is not determined by any particular content? What is the *form of life*, that is, that corresponds to the *form of law*? Does the moral law not become something like an "inscrutable faculty"? Kant gives the name "respect" (*Achtung*, reverential attention) to the condition of one who finds himself living under a law that is in force without signifying, and that thus neither prescribes nor forbids any determinate end: "The motivation that a man can have, before a certain end is proposed to him, clearly can be nothing other than the law itself through the respect that it inspires (without determining what goals it is possible to have or reach by obeying it). For once the content of free will is eliminated, the law is the only thing left in relation to the formal element of the free will" ("Über den Gemeinspruch," p. 282).

It is truly astounding how Kant, almost two centuries ago and under the heading of a sublime "moral feeling," was able to describe the very condition that was to become familiar to the mass societies and great totalitarian states of our time. For life under a law that is in force without signifying resembles life in the state of exception, in which the most innocent gesture or the smallest forgetfulness can have most extreme consequences. And it is exactly this kind of life that Kafka describes, in which law is all the more pervasive for its total lack of content, and in which a distracted knock on the door can mark the start of uncontrollable trials. Just as for Kant the purely formal character of the moral law founds its claim of universal practical applicability in every circumstance, so in Kafka's village the empty potentiality of law is so much in force as to become indistinguishable from life. The existence and the very body of Joseph K. ultimately coincide with the Trial; they *become* the Trial. Benjamin sees this clearly when he writes, objecting to Scholem's notion of a being in force without significance, that a law that has lost its content ceases to exist and becomes indistinguishable from life: "Whether the students have lost the Scripture or cannot decipher it in the end amounts to the same thing, since a Scripture without its keys is not Scripture but life, the life that is lived in the village at the foot of the hill on which the castle stands" (Benjamin and Scholem, *Briefwechsel*, p. 155). And this provokes Scholem (who does not notice that his friend has grasped the difference perfectly well) to insist that he cannot agree that "it is the same thing whether the students have lost their Scripture or cannot decipher it, and it even seems to me that this is the greatest mistake that can be made. I refer to precisely the difference between these two stages when I speak of a 'Nothing of Revelation'" (ibid., p. 163).

If, following our analyses, we see in the impossibility of distinguishing law from life—that is, in the life lived in the village at the foot of the castle—the essential character of the state of exception, then two different interpretations confront each other here: on the one hand, that of Scholem, which sees in this life the maintenance of the pure form of law beyond its own content—a being in force without significance—and, on the other hand, that of Benjamin, for which the state of exception turned into rule signals law's fulfillment and its becoming indistinguishable from the life over which it ought to rule. Confronted with the imperfect nihilism that would let the Nothing subsist indefinitely in the form of a being in force without significance, Benjamin proposes a messianic nihilism that nullifies even the Nothing and lets no form of law remain in force beyond its own content.

Whatever their exact meaning and whatever their pertinence to the interpretation of Kafka's text, it is certain that every inquiry into the relation between life and law today must confront these two positions.

א The experience of being in force without significance lies at the basis of a current of contemporary thought that is not irrelevant here. The prestige of deconstruction in our time lies precisely in its having conceived of the entire text of tradition as being in force without significance, a being in force whose strength lies essentially in its undecidability and in having shown that such a being in force is, like the door of the Law in Kafka's parable, absolutely impassable. But it is precisely concerning the sense of this being in force (and of the state of exception that it inaugurates) that our position distinguishes itself from that of deconstruction. Our age does indeed stand in front of language just as the man from the country in the parable stands in front of the door of the Law. What threatens thinking here is the possibility that thinking might find itself condemned to infinite negotiations with the doorkeeper or, even worse, that it might end by itself assuming the role of the doorkeeper who, without really blocking the entry, shelters the Nothing onto which the door opens. As the evangelical warning cited by Origen concerning the interpretation of Scripture has it: "Woe to you, men of the Law, for you have taken away the key to knowledge: you yourselves have not entered, and you have not let the others who approached enter either" (which ought to be reformulated as follows: "Woe to you, who have not wanted to enter into the door of the Law but have not permitted it to be closed either").

4.4. This is the context in which one must read both the singular "inversion" that Benjamin, in his essay on Kafka, opposes to law's being in force without significance, and the enigmatic allusion, in his eighth "Theses on the Philosophy of History," to a "real" state of exception. A life that resolves itself completely into writing corresponds, for Benjamin, to a Torah whose key has been lost: "I consider the sense of the inversion toward which many of Kafka's allegories tend to lie in an attempt to transform life into Scripture" (Benjamin and Scholem, *Briefwechsel*, p. 155). Analogously, the eighth thesis opposes a "real" (*wirklich*) state of exception, which it is our task to bring about, to the state of exception in which we live, which has become the rule: "The tradition of the oppressed teaches us that the 'state of exception' in which we live is the rule. We must arrive at a concept of history that corresponds to this fact. Then we will have the production of the real state of exception before us as a task" (Benjamin, "Über den Begriff," p. 697).

We have seen the sense in which law begins to coincide with life once it has become the pure form of law, law's mere being in force without significance. But insofar as law is maintained as pure form in a state of virtual exception, it lets bare life (K.'s life, or the life lived in the village at the foot of the castle) subsist before it. Law that becomes indistinguishable from life in a real state of exception is confronted by life that, in a symmetrical but inverse gesture, is entirely transformed into law. The absolute intelligibility of a life wholly resolved into writing corresponds to the impenetrability of a writing that, having become indecipherable, now appears as life. Only at this point do the two terms distinguished and kept united by the relation of ban (bare life and the form of law) abolish each other and enter into a new dimension.

4.5. Significantly, in the last analysis all the interpreters read the legend as the tale of the irremediable failure or defeat of the man from the country before the impossible task imposed upon him by the Law. Yet it is worth asking whether Kafka's text does not consent to a different reading. The interpreters seem to forget, in fact, precisely the words with which the story ends: "No one else could enter here, since this door was destined for you alone. Now I will go and shut it." If it is true the door's very openness constituted, as we saw, the invisible power and specific "force" of the Law, then we can imagine that all the behavior of the man from the country is nothing other than a complicated and patient strategy to have the door closed in order to interrupt the Law's being in force. And in the end, the man succeeds in his endeavor, since he succeeds in having the door of the Law closed forever (it was, after all, open "only for him"), even if he may have risked his life in the process (the story does not say that he is actually dead but only that he is "close to the end"). In his interpretation of the legend, Kurt Weinberg has suggested that one must see the figure of a "thwarted Christian Messiah" in the shy but obstinate man from the country (*Kafkas Dichtungen*, pp. 130–31). The suggestion can be taken only if it is not forgotten that the Messiah is the figure in which the great monotheistic religions sought to master the problem of law, and that in Judaism, as in Christianity or Shiite Islam, the Messiah's arrival signifies the fulfillment and the complete consummation of the Law. In monotheism, messianism thus constitutes not simply one category of religious experience among others but rather the limit concept of religious experience in general, the point in which religious experience passes beyond itself and calls itself into question insofar as it is law (hence the messianic aporias concerning the Law that are expressed in both Paul's Epistle to the Romans and the Sabbatian doctrine according to which the fulfillment of the Torah is its transgression). But if this is true, then what must a messiah do if he finds himself, like the man from the country, before a law that is in force without signifying? He will certainly not be able to fulfill a law that is already in a state of suspension, not simply substitute another law for it (the fulfillment of law is not a new law).

A miniature painting in a fifteenth-century Jewish manuscript containing Haggadoth on "He who comes" shows the arrival of the Messiah in Jerusalem. The Messiah appears on horseback (in other illustrations, the mount is a donkey) at the sacred city's wide-open gates, behind which a window shows a figure who could be a doorkeeper. A youth in front of the Messiah is standing one step from the open door and pointing toward it. Whoever this figure is (it might be the prophet Elijah), he can be likened to the man from the country in Kafka's parable. His task seems to be to prepare and facilitate the entry of the Messiah—a paradoxical task, since the door is wide open. If one gives the name "provocation" to the strategy that compels the potentiality of Law to translate itself into actuality, then his is a paradoxical form of provocation, the only form adequate to a law that is in force without signifying and a door that allows no one to enter on account of being too open. The messianic task of the man from the country (and of the youth who stands before the door in the miniature) might then be precisely that of making the virtual state of exception real, of compelling the doorkeeper to close the door of the Law (the door of Jerusalem). For the Messiah will be able to enter only after the door is closed, which is to say, after the Law's being in force without significance is at an end. This is the meaning of the enigmatic passage in Kafka's notebooks where he writes, "The Messiah will only come when he is no longer necessary, he will only come after his arrival, he will come not on the last day, but on the very last day." The final sense of the legend is thus not, as Derrida writes, that of an "event that succeeds in not happening" (or that happens in not happening: "an event that happens not to happen," *un événement qui arrive à ne pas arriver* ["Préjugés," p. 359]), but rather precisely the opposite: the story tells how something has really happened in seeming not to happen, and the messianic aporias of the man from the country express exactly the difficulties that our age must confront in attempting to master the sovereign ban.

א One of the paradoxes of the state of exception lies in the fact that in the state of exception, it is impossible to distinguish transgression of the law from execution of the law, such that what violates a rule and what conforms to it coincide without any remainder (a person who goes for a walk during the curfew is not transgressing the law any more than the soldier who kills him is executing it). This is precisely the situation that, in the Jewish tradition (and, actually, in every genuine messianic tradition), comes to pass when the Messiah arrives. The first consequence of this arrival is that the Law (according to the Kabbalists, this is the law of the Torah of Beriah, that is, the law in force from the creation of man until the messianic days) is fulfilled and consummated. But this fulfillment does not signify that the old law is simply replaced by a new law that is homologous to the old but has different prescriptions and different prohibitions (the Torah of Aziluth, the originary law that the Messiah, according to the Kabbalists, would restore, contains neither prescriptions nor prohibitions and is only a jumble of unordered letters). What is implied instead is that the fulfillment of the Torah now coincides with its transgression. This much is clearly affirmed by the most radical messianic movements, like that of Sabbatai Zevi (whose motto was "the fulfillment of the Torah is its transgression").

From the juridico-political perspective, messianism is therefore a theory of the state of exception—except for the fact that in messianism there is no authority in force to proclaim the state of exception; instead, there is the Messiah to subvert its power.

א One of the peculiar characteristics of Kafka's allegories is that at their very end they offer the possibility of an about-face that completely upsets their meaning. The obstinacy of the man from the country thus suggests a certain analogy with the cleverness that allows Ulysses to survive the song of the Sirens. Just as the Law in "Before the Law" is insuperable because it prescribes nothing, so the most terrible weapon in Kafka's "The Sirens" is not song but silence ("it has never happened, but it might not be altogether unimaginable that someone could save himself from their song, but certainly never from their silence.") Ulysses' almost superhuman intelligence consists precisely in his having noticed that the Sirens were silent and in having opposed them with his trick "only as a shield," exactly as the man from the country does with respect to the doorkeeper of the Law. Like the "doors of India" in "The New Lawyer," the door of the Law can also be seen as a symbol of those mythic forces that man, like Bucephalus, the horse, must master at all costs.

4.6. Jean-Luc Nancy is the philosopher who has most rigorously reflected upon the experience of law that is implicit in this being in force without significance. In an extremely dense text, he identifies its ontological structure as that of abandonment and, consequently, attempts to conceive not only our time but the entire history of the West as the "time of abandonment." The structure he describes nevertheless remains inside the form of law, and abandonment is conceived as abandonment to the sovereign ban, without any way out of the ban being envisaged:

To *abandon* is to remit, entrust, or turn over to . . . a sovereign power, and to remit, entrust, or turn over to its *ban,* that is, to its proclaiming, to its convening, and to its sentencing.

One always abandons to a law. The destitution of abandoned Being is measured by the limitless severity of the law to which it finds itself exposed. Abandonment does not constitute a subpoena to present oneself before this or that court of law. It is a compulsion to appear absolutely under the law, under the law as such and in its totality. In the same way—it is the same thing—to be *banished* amounts not to coming under a provision of the law but rather to coming under the entirety of the law. Turned over to the absolute of the law, the abandoned one is thereby abandoned completely outside its jurisdiction. . . . Abandonment respects the law; it cannot do otherwise. (*L'impératif catégorique*, pp. 149–50)

The task that our time imposes on thinking cannot simply consist in recognizing the extreme and insuperable form of law as being in force without significance. Every thought that limits itself to this does nothing other than repeat the ontological structure that we have defined as the paradox of sovereignty (or sovereign ban). Sovereignty is, after all, precisely this "law beyond the law to which we are abandoned," that is, the self-presuppositional power of *nomos*. Only if it is possible to think the Being of abandonment beyond every idea of law (even that of the empty form of law's being in force without significance) will we have moved out of the paradox of sovereignty toward a politics freed from every ban. A pure form of law is only the empty form of relation. Yet the empty form of relation is no longer a law but a zone of indistinguishability between law and life, which is to say, a state of exception.

Here the problem is the same one that Heidegger confronts in his *Beiträge zur Philosophie* under the heading of "Seinsverlassenheit," the abandonment of the entity by Being, which, in fact, constitutes nothing less than the problem of the unity and difference between Being and being in the age of the culmination of metaphysics. What is at issue in this abandonment is not something (Being) that dismisses and discharges something else (the being). On the contrary: *here Being is nothing other than the being's being abandoned and remitted to itself*; here Being is nothing other than the ban of the being:

> What is abandoned by whom? The being by Being, which does and does not belong to it. The being then appears *thus*, it appears as object and as available Being, as if Being were not. . . . Then this is shown: that Being abandons the being means: Being dissimulates itself in the being-manifest of the being. And Being itself becomes essentially determined as this withdrawing self-dissimulation. . . . Abandoned by Being: that Being abandons the being, that Being is consigned to itself and becomes the object of calculation. This is not simply a "fall" but the first history of Being itself. (*Beiträge zur Philosophie*, p. 115)

If Being in this sense is nothing other than Being *in the ban* of the being [*l'essere* a bandono *dell'ente*], then the ontological structure of sovereignty here fully reveals its paradox. The relation of abandonment is now to be thought in a new way. To read this relation as a being in force without significance—that is, as Being's abandonment *to* and *by* a law that prescribes nothing, and not even itself—is to remain inside nihilism and not to push the experience of abandonment to the extreme. Only where the experience of abandonment is freed from every idea of law and destiny (including the Kantian form of law and law's being in force without significance) is abandonment truly experienced as such. This is why it is necessary to remain open to the idea that the relation of abandonment is not a relation, and that *the being together of the being and Being does not have the form of relation*. This does not mean that Being and the being now part ways; instead, they remain without relation. But this implies nothing less than an attempt to think the politico-social *factum* no longer in the form of a relation.

א Alexandre Kojève's idea of the end of history and the subsequent institution of a new homogenous state presents many analogies with the epochal situation we have described as law's being in force without significance (this explains the contemporary attempts to bring Kojève to life in a liberal-capitalist key). What, after all, is a State that survives history, a State sovereignty that maintains itself beyond the accomplishment of its *telos*, if not a law that is in force without signifying? To conceive of a fulfillment of history in which the empty form of sovereignty still persists is just as impossible as to conceive of an extinction of the State without the fulfillment of its historical forms, since the empty form of the State tends to generate epochal contents that, in turn, seek out a State form that has become impossible (this is what is happening in the ex–Soviet Union and in ex-Yugoslavia).

The only thought adequate to the task would be one capable of both thinking the end of the State and the end of history together and mobilizing the one against the other.

This is the direction in which the late Heidegger seems to move, if still insufficiently, with the idea of a final event or appropriation (*Ereignis*) in which what is appropriated is Being itself, that is, the principle that had until then determined beings in different epochs and historical figures. This means that with the *Ereignis* (as with the Hegelian Absolute in Kojève's reading), the "history of Being comes to an end" (Heidegger, *Zur Sache des Denkens*, p. 44), and the relation between Being and being consequently finds its "absolution." This is why Heidegger can write that with the *Ereignis* he is trying to think "Being without regard to the being," which amounts to nothing less than attempting to think the ontological difference no longer as a relation, and Being and being beyond every form of a connection.

This is the perspective from which we must situate the debate between Kojève and Georges Bataille. What is at play here is precisely the figure of sovereignty in the age of the fulfillment of human history. Various scenarios are possible. In the note added to the second edition of his *Introduction to the Reading of Hegel*, Kojève distances himself from the first edition's claim that the end of history simply coincides with man's becoming an animal again and the disappearance of man in the proper sense (that is, as the subject of negating action). During a trip to Japan in 1959, Kojève had maintained the possibility of a posthistorical culture in which men, while abandoning their negating action in the strict sense, continue to separate forms from their contents not in order to actively transform these contents but to practice a kind of "pure snobbism" (tea ceremonies, etc.). On the other hand, in the review of Raymond Queneau's novels he sees in the characters of *Dimanche de vie*, and particularly in the "lazy rascal" (*voyou desœuvré*), the figure of the satisfied wise man at the end of history (Kojève, "Les romans," p. 391). In opposition to the *voyou desœuvré* (who is contemptuously defined as *homo quenellenesis*) and the satisfied and self-conscious Hegelian wise man, Bataille proposes the figure of a sovereignty entirely consumed in the instant (*la seule innocence possible: celle de l'instant*) that coincides with "the forms in which man gives himself to himself: . . . laughter, eroticism, struggle, luxury."

The theme of *desœuvrement*—inoperativeness as the figure of the fullness of man at the end of history—which first appears in Kojève's review of Queneau, has been taken up by Blanchot and by Nancy, who places it at the very center of his work *The Inoperative Community*. Everything depends on what is meant by "inoperativeness." It can be neither the simple absence of work nor (as in Bataille) a sovereign and useless form of negativity. The only coherent way to understand inoperativeness is to think of it as a generic mode of potentiality that is not exhausted (like individual action or collective action understood as the sum of individual actions) in a *transitus de potentia ad actum*.

✳ ✳ ✳

§6   The Ban and the Wolf

6.1. "The entire character of *homo sacer* shows that it was not born on the soil of a constituted juridical order, but goes all the way back to the period of pre-social life. It is a fragment
of the primitive life of Indo-European peoples. . . . In the bandit and the outlaw (*wargus,
vargr,* the wolf and, in the religious sense, the sacred wolf, *vargr y veum*), Germanic and
Scandinavian antiquity give us a brother of *homo sacer* beyond the shadow of any doubt.
. . . That which is considered to be an impossibility for Roman antiquity—the killing of the
proscribed outside a judge and law—was an incontestable reality in Germanic antiquity"
(Jhering, *L'esprit du droit romain*, p. 282).

   Rodolphe Jhering was, with these words, the first to approximate the figure of *homo
sacer* to that of the *wargus,* the wolf-man, and of the *Friedlos*, the "man without peace"
of ancient Germanic law. He thus placed *sacratio* in the context of the doctrine of
Friedlosigkeit that Wilhelm Eduard Wilda had elaborated toward the middle of the nineteenth century, according to which ancient Germanic law was founded on the concept
of peace (*Fried*) and the corresponding exclusion from the community of the wrongdoer,
who therefore became *friedlos,* without peace, and whom anyone was permitted to kill
without committing homicide. The medieval ban also presents analogous traits: the
bandit could be killed (*bannire idem est quod dicere quilibet possit eum offendere*, "'To ban'
someone is to say that anyone may harm him." [Cavalca, *Il bando*, p. 42]) or was even
considered to be already dead (*exbannitus ad mortem de sua civitate debet haberi pro mortuo*,
"Whoever is banned from his city on pain of death must be considered as dead" [ibid.,
p. 50]). Germanic and Anglo-Saxon sources underline the bandit's liminal status by
defining him as a wolf-man (*wargus, werwolf,* the Latin *garulphus,* from which the French
loup garou, "werewolf," is derived): thus Salic law and Ripuarian law use the formula
wargus sit, hoc est expulsus in a sense that recalls the *sacer esto* that sanctioned the sacred
man's capacity to be killed, and the laws of Edward the Confessor (1030–35) define the
bandit as a *wulfesheud* (a wolf's head) and assimilate him to the werewolf (*lupinum enim
gerit caput a die utlagationis suae, quod ab anglis wulfesheud vocatur*, "He bears a wolf's
head from the day of his expulsion, and the English call this *wulfesheud*"). What had
to remain in the collective unconscious as a monstrous hybrid of human and animal,
divided between the forest and the city—the werewolf—is, therefore, in its origin the
figure of the man who has been banned from the city. That such a man is defined as
a wolf-man and not simply as a wolf (the expression *caput lupinum* has the form of a
juridical statute) is decisive here. The life of the bandit, like that of the sacred man, is
not a piece of animal nature without any relation to law and the city. It is, rather, a
threshold of indistinction and of passage between animal and man, *physis* and *nomos*,
exclusion and inclusion: the life of the bandit is the life of the *loup garou*, the werewolf,
who is precisely *neither man nor beast*, and who dwells paradoxically within both while
belonging to neither.

6.2. Only in this light does the Hobbesian mythologeme of the state of nature acquire its true sense. We have seen that the state of nature is not a real epoch chronologically prior to the foundation of the City but a principle internal to the City, which appears at the moment the City is considered *tanquam dissoluta*, "as if it were dissolved" (in this sense, therefore, the state of nature is something like a state of exception). Accordingly, when Hobbes founds sovereignty by means of a reference to the state in which "man is a wolf to men," *homo hominis lupus,* in the word "wolf" (*lupus*) we ought to hear an echo of the *wargus* and the *caput lupinem* of the laws of Edward the Confessor: at issue is not simply *fera bestia* and natural life but rather a zone of indistinction between the human and the animal, a werewolf, a man who is transformed into a wolf and a wolf who is transformed into a man—in other words, a bandit, a *homo sacer.* Far from being a prejuridical condition that is indifferent to the law of the city, the Hobbesian state of nature is the exception and the threshold that constitutes and dwells within it. It is not so much a war of all against all as, more precisely, a condition in which everyone is bare life and a *homo sacer* for everyone else, and in which everyone is thus *wargus, gerit caput lupinum.* And this lupization of man and humanization of the wolf is at every moment possible in the *dissolutio civitatis* inaugurated by the state of exception. This threshold alone, which is neither simple natural life nor social life but rather bare life or sacred life, is the always present and always operative presupposition of sovereignty.

Contrary to our modern habit of representing the political realm in terms of citizens' rights, free will, and social contracts, from the point of view of sovereignty *only bare life is authentically political.* This is why in Hobbes, the foundation of sovereign power is to be sought not in the subjects' free renunciation of their natural right but in the sovereign's preservation of his natural right to do anything to anyone, which now appears as the right to punish. "This is the foundation," Hobbes states, "of that right of Punishing, which is exercised in every Common-wealth. For the Subjects did not give the Soveraign that right; but onely in laying down theirs, strengthned him to use his own, as he should think fit, for the preservation of them all: so that it was not *given,* but *left* to him, and to him onely; and (excepting the limits set him by naturall Law) as entire, as in the condition of meer Nature, and of warre of every one against his neighbour" (*Leviathan*, p. 214, emphasis added).

Corresponding to this particular status of the "right of Punishing," which takes the form of a survival of the state of nature at the very heart of the state, is the subjects' capacity not to disobey but to resist violence exercised on their own person, "for . . . no man is supposed bound by Covenant, not to resist violence; and consequently it cannot be intended, that he gave any right to another to lay violent hands upon his person" (ibid.). Sovereign violence is in truth founded not on a pact but on the exclusive inclusion of bare life in the state. And just as sovereign power's first and immediate referent is, in this sense, the life that may be killed but not sacrificed, and that has its paradigm in *homo sacer,* so in the person of the sovereign, the werewolf, the wolf-man of man, dwells permanently in the city.

א In *Bisclavret,* one of Marie de France's most beautiful lays, both the werewolf's particular nature as the threshold of passage between nature and politics, animal world and human world, and the werewolf's close tie to sovereign power are presented with extraordinary vividness. The lay tells of a baron who is particularly close to his king (*de sun seinur esteit privez* [v. 19]), but who, every week, after hiding his clothes under a stone, is transformed into a werewolf (*bisclavret*) for three days, during which time he lives in the woods stealing and preying on other creatures (*al plus espés de la gaudine / s'i vif de preie e de ravine*). His wife, who suspects something, induces him to confess his secret life and convinces him to reveal where he hides his clothes, even though he knows that he would remain a wolf forever if he lost them or were caught putting them on (*kar si jes eusse perduz / e de ceo feusse aparceuz / bisclavret serei a tuz jours*). With the help of an accomplice who will become her lover, the woman takes the clothes from their hiding place, and the baron remains a wolf forever.

What is essential here is the detail, to which Pliny's legend of Antus also bears witness (*Natural History*, bk. 8), of the temporary character of the metamorphosis, which is tied to the possibility of setting aside and secretly putting on human clothes again. The transformation into a werewolf corresponds perfectly to the state of exception, during which (necessarily limited) time the city is dissolved, and men enter into a zone in which they are no longer distinct from beasts. The story also shows the necessity of particular formalities marking the entry into—or the exit from—the zone of indistinction between the animal and the human (which corresponds to the clear proclamation of the state of exception as formally distinct from the rule). Contemporary folklore also bears witness to this necessity, in the three knocks on the door that the werewolf who is becoming human again must make in order to be let into the house:

When they knock on the door the first time, the wife must not answer. If she did, she would see her husband still entirely as a wolf, and he would eat her and then run away into the forest forever. When they knock on the door the second time, the woman must still not answer: she would see him with a man's body and a wolf's head. Only when they knock on the door the third time can the door be opened: for only then are they completely transformed, only then has the wolf completely disappeared and has the man of before reappeared. (Levi, *Cristo si è fermato a Eboli*, pp. 104–5)

The special proximity of werewolf and sovereign too is ultimately shown in the story. One day (so the lay tells), the king goes hunting in the forest in which Bisclavret lives, and the dogs find the wolf-man as soon as they are let loose. But as soon as Bisclavret sees the sovereign, he runs toward him and grabs hold of his stirrup, licking his legs and his feet as if he were imploring the King's mercy. Amazed at the beast's humanity ("this animal has wits and intelligence / . . . I will give my peace to the beast / and for today I will hunt no more"), the king brings him to live with him, and they become inseparable. The inevitable encounter with the ex-wife and the punishment of the woman follow. What is important, however, is that Bisclavret's final transformation back into a human takes place on the very bed of the sovereign.

The proximity of tyrant and wolf-man is also shown in Plato's *Republic,* in which the transformation of the guardian into a tyrant is approximated to the Arcadian myth of Lycean Zeus:

What, then, is the cause of the transformation of a protector into a tyrant? Is it not obviously when the protector's acts begin to reproduce the myth that is told of the shrine of Lycean Zeus in Arcadia? . . . The story goes that whoever tastes of one bit of human entrails minced up with those of other victims is inevitably transformed into a wolf. . . . Thus, when a leader of the mob [*dēmos*], seeing the multitude devoted to his orders, does not know how to abstain from the blood of his tribe . . . will it not then be necessary that he either be killed by his enemies or become a tyrant and be transformed from a man into a wolf? (*Republic,* 565d–565e)

6.3. The time has come, therefore, to reread from the beginning the myth of the foundation of the modern city from Hobbes to Rousseau. The state of nature is, in truth, a state of exception, in which the city appears for an instant (which is at the same time a chronological interval and a nontemporal moment) *tanquam dissoluta.* The foundation is thus not an event achieved once and for all but is continually operative in the civil state in the form of the sovereign decision. What is more, the latter refers *immediately* to the life (and not the free will) of the citizens, which thus appears as the originary political element, the *Urphänomen* of politics. Yet this life is not simply natural reproductive life, the *zoē* of the Greeks, nor *bios,* a qualified form of life. It is, rather, the bare life of *homo sacer* and the *wargus,* a zone of indistinction and continuous transition between man and beast, nature and culture.

This is why the thesis stated at the logico-formal level at the end of the first part above, according to which the originary juridico-political relation is the ban, not only is a thesis concerning the formal structure of sovereignty but also has a substantial character, since what the ban holds together is precisely bare life and sovereign power. All representations of the originary political act as a contract or convention marking the passage from nature to the State in a discrete and definite way must be left wholly behind. Here there is, instead, a much more complicated zone of indiscernability between *nomos* and *physis,* in which the State tie, having the form of a ban, is always already also non-State and pseudo-nature, and in which nature always already appears as *nomos* and the state of exception. The understanding of the Hobbesian mythologeme in terms of *contract* instead of *ban* condemned democracy to impotence every time it had to confront the problem of sovereign power and has also rendered modern democracy constitutionally incapable of truly thinking a politics freed from the form of the State.

The relation of abandonment is so ambiguous that nothing could be harder than breaking from it. The ban is essentially the power of delivering something over to itself, which is to say, the power of maintaining itself in relation to something presupposed as nonrelational. What has been banned is delivered over to its own separateness and, at the same rime, consigned to the mercy of the one who abandons it—at once excluded and included, removed and at the same time captured. The age-old discussion in juridical historiography between those who conceive exile to be a punishment and those who instead understand it to be a right and a refuge (already at the end of the republic, Cicero thought exile in opposition to punishment: *Exilium enim non supplcium est, sed perfugium portusque supplicii,*

"Exile is not a penalty, but a haven and a refuge from penalty" [*Pro Caec.*, 34]) has its root in this ambiguity of the sovereign ban. Both for Greece and for Rome, the oldest sources show that more ancient than the opposition between law and punishment is the status—which "cannot be qualified either as the exercise of a law or as a penal situation" (Crifò, *L'esclusione dall città*, p. 11)—of the person who goes into exile as a consequence of committing homicide, or who loses his citizenship as a result of becoming a citizen of a *civitas foederata* that benefits from an *ius exilii*.

The originary political relation is marked by this zone of indistinction in which the life of the exile or the *aqua et igni interdictus* borders on the life of *homo sacer*, who may be killed but not sacrificed. This relation is more original than the Schmittian opposition between friend and enemy, fellow citizen and foreigner. The "estrarity" of the person held in the sovereign ban is more intimate and primary than the extraneousness of the foreigner (if it is possible to develop in this way the opposition established by Festus between *extrarius*, which is to say, *qui extra focum sacramentum iusque sit* ["whoever is outside the hearth, the sacrament, and the law"], and *extraneus*, which is to say, *ex altera terra, quasi exterraneus* ["whoever is from another land and almost extraneous"]).

Now it is possible to understand the semantic ambiguity that we have already noted, in which "banned" in Romance languages originally meant both "at the mercy of" and "out of free will, freely," both "excluded, banned" and "open to all, free." The ban is the force of simultaneous attraction and repulsion that ties together the two poles of the sovereign exception: bare life and power, *homo sacer* and the sovereign. Because of this alone can the ban signify both the insignia of sovereignty (*Bandum, quod postea appellatus fuit Standardum, Guntfanonum, italice Confalone* [Muratori, *Antiquitates*, p. 442]) and expulsion from the community.

We must learn to recognize this structure of the ban in the political relations and public spaces in which we still live. *In the city, the banishment of sacred life is more internal than every interiority and more external than every extraneousness.* The banishment of sacred life is the sovereign *nomos* that conditions every rule, the originary spatialization that governs and makes possible every localization and every territorialization. And if in modernity life is more and more clearly placed at the center of State politics (which now becomes, in Foucault's terms, biopolitics), if in our age all citizens can be said, in a specific but extremely real sense, to appear virtually as *homines sacri,* this is possible only because the relation of ban has constituted the essential structure of sovereign power from the beginning.

References

Badiou, Alain. *L'être et le l'événement*. Paris: Seuil, 1988.

Benjamin, Walter. *Briefe*. Vol. 1. Edited by Gerschom Scholem and Theodor W. Adorno. Frankfurt am Main: Suhrkamp, 1966 (*The Correspondence of Walter Benjamin, 1919—1940*. Edited by Gerschom Scholem and Theodor W. Adorno. Translated by Manfred R. Jacobsen and Evelyn M. Jacobsen. Chicago: University of Chicago Press, 1994).

Benjamin, Walter. "Über den Begriff der Geschichte." In Walter Benjamin, *Gesammelte Schriften*, 2 volumes. ("Thesis on the Philosophy of History." Translated by Harry Zohn. In Walter Benjamin, *Illuminations*. Edited by Hannah Arendt. New York: Schoken Books, 1968.)

Benjamin, Walter, and Gerschom Scholem. *Briefwechsel 1933—1940*. Edited by Gerschom Scholem. Frankfurt am Main: Suhrkamp, 1988. (*The Correspondence of Walter Benjamin and Gerschom Scholem, 1932—1940*. Edited by Gerschom Scholem. Translated by Gary Smith and Andre Lefevere. Cambridge, MA.: Harvard University Press, 1992).

Blanchot, Maurice. *L'entretien infini*. Paris: Gallimard, 1969. (*The Infinite Conversation*. Translated by Susan Hanson. Minneapolis: University of Minnesota Press, 1993).

Cacciari, Massimo. *Icone della legge*. Milan: Adelphi, 1985.

Crifò, Giuliano. *L'esclusione dall città: Altri studi sull'exilium romano*. Perugia: Università di Perugia, 1985.

Deleuze, Gilles, and Félix Guattari. *Mille plateaux*. Paris: Minuit, 1980. (*A Thousand Plateaus: Capitalism and Schizophrenia*. Trans. Brian Massumi. Minneapolis: University of Minnesota Press, 1987.)

Derrida, Jacques. "Préjugés." In *Spiegel und Gleichnis*. Edited by N. W. Bolz and W. Hübener. Würzburg: Königshausen und Neuman, 1983. ("Before the Law." Translated by Avital Ronnell and Christine Roulston. In Jacques Derrida, *Acts of Literature*. Edited by Derek Attridge. London: Routledge, 1992.)

Hegel, Georg Wilhelm Friedrich. *Phänomenologie des Geistes*. In G. W. F. Hegel, *Werke in zwanzig Bänden*, Vol. 3. Frankfurt: Suhrkamp, 1971. (*Phenomenology of Spirit*. Translated by A. V. Miller. Oxford: Oxford University Press, 1977).

Heidegger, Martin. *Beiträge zur Philosophie*. In Martin Heidegger, *Gesamtausgabe*, Vol. 65. Frankfurt am Main: Vittorio Klostermann, 1989.

Heidegger, Martin. *Zur Sache des Denkens*. Tubingen: Max Niemeyer, 1976. (*On Time and Being*. Translated by Joan Stambaugh. New York: Harper and Row, 1972).

Hobbes, Thomas. *Leviathan*. Edited by R. Tuck. Cambridge: Cambridge University Press, 1991.

Jhering, Rodolphe. *L'esprit du droit romain dans les diverses phases de son développement*. Translated by O. de Meulenaere. Vol. I. Paris: Marescq, 1886.

Kojève, Alexandre. "Les romans de la sagesse," *Critique*, 60 (1952).

Kant, Immanuel. *Kants opus postuum*. Edited by Adickes. Berlin: Reuther & Reichard, 1920. (*Opus Postuum. Cambridge Edition of the Works of Immanuel Kant*. Translated by Eckhard Förster. Cambridge: Cambridge University Press, 1993).

Kant, Immanuel. *Kritik der praktischen Vernunft*. In *Kants Gesammelte Schriften*, Akademieausgabe, Vol. 5. Berlin: G. Reimer, 1913. (*Critique of Practical Reason*. Translated by Lewis White Beck. New York: Macmillan, 1993).

Kant, Immanuel. "Über den Gemeinspruch: Das mag in der Theorie richtig sein, taugt aber nicht für die Praxis." In *Kants Gesammelte Schriften*, Akademieausgabe, Vol. 8. Berlin: G. Reimer, 1914. ("On the Common Saying: 'This May Be True in Theory but It Does Not Apply in Practice." In *Kant, Political*

Writings. Edited by Hans Riess, translated by N. B. Nisbet. Cambridge: Cambridge University Press, 1991).

Levi, Carlo. *Cristo si é fermato a Eboli*. Turin: Einaudi, 1946. (*Christ Stopped at Eboli: The Story of a Year*. Translated by Frances Frenaye. New York: Terpino, 1982).

Lévi-Strauss, Claude. "Introduction à l'oeuvre de Marcel Mauss." In Marcel Mauss, *Sociologie et anthropologie*. Paris: Presses Universitaire de France, 1950.

Milner, J.-C. "L'exemple et la fiction." In *Transparence et opacité: Littérature et sciences cognitives*. Edited by Tibor Papp and Pierre Pira. Paris: Cerf, 1988.

Muratori, Lodovico Antonio. *Antiquitates italicae Medii Aevi*. Vol. 2. Milan: Mediolani, 1739.

Nancy, Jean-Luc. *L'impératif catégorique*. Paris: Flammarion, 1983. ("Abandoned Being." In Jean-Luc Nancy, *The Birth to Presence*. Translated by Brian Holmes. Stanford: Stanford University Press, 1993).

Schmitt, Carl. *Das Nomos von der Erde*. Berlin: Duncker & Humbolt, 1974.

Schmitt, Carl. *Politische Theologie, Vier Kapitel zur Lehre von der Souveränität*. Munich-Leipzig: Duncker & Humbolt, 1922. (*Political Theology: Four Chapters on the Concept of Sovereignty*. Translated by George Schwab. Cambridge, MA.: MIT Press, 1985).

Schmitt, Carl. *Über Schuld und Schuldarten, Eine terminologische Untersuchung*. Breslau: Schletter, 1910.

Weinberg, Kurt. *Kafkas Dichtungen. Die Travestien des Mythos*. Bern: Francks, 1963.

31 Becoming-Media: Galileo's Telescope

Joseph Vogl

Medium means middle and in the middle, mediation and mediator; it calls for a closer questioning of the role, workings, and materials of this "in-between." Media studies' field of inquiry is quite rightly a broad one, stretching from prehistoric registers of the tides and stars to the ubiquitous contemporary mass media, encompassing physical transmitters (such as air and light), as well as schemes of notation, whether hieroglyphic, phonetic, or alphanumeric. It includes technologies and artifacts like electrification, the telescope, or the gramophone alongside symbolic forms and spatial representations such as perspective, theater, or literature as a whole. However, the very size of the field only highlights the relative inability of media studies to provide reliable information on how media work, on what they actually do, and even on what they are. In this wide area, we see a mixing and clashing of methods and disciplinary traditions: approaches from literary study, history, art history, information engineering, journalism, economics, communications, and the history of science all muddle together without any particular guiding principle. Furthermore, the unclear relationship between media studies and other disciplines highlights its lack of a defined, common disciplinary space and its problematic (to say the least) definition of an object of study. Across many disciplines, questions about the functioning, effects, and history of media continue to be posed, but in answering them we still have no single, stable, well-demarcated canon of knowledge to rely on, in spite of the widespread institutional and disciplinary establishment of media studies.

Media theory might thus axiomatically claim that no such thing as a medium exists, at least not in a stable generic, disciplinary, substantial, or historical sense. Media cannot be reduced to means of representation, like film and theater; or to technologies, like printing or telecommunications; or to machines, like the telegraph or the computer; or to symbolic systems, like writing, images, or numbers. Nonetheless, all these things are emphatically "medial." The concept of media cannot be adequately explained by reference to the material bases or the forms of communication, to symbolic systems or to distribution techniques. Recent theoretical positions may give us a common horizon and a better understanding of media as something more than a set of procedures for information storage, processing, and distribution, for the spatial and temporal transmission of data. Rather, media are specific, systematizable objects of study for the following reason: everything they store and mediate is stored and mediated under conditions that are created by the media themselves and that ultimately comprise those media.

This is what is meant by the well-known dictum that the medium is the message; or that media determine our situation; or that everything we learn and know, we learn and know through media. What media are and what they do, how they work and the effects they create, their places in cultural and social practices, their specific roles as cultural technologies, not to mention the concept of medium itself—none of this can be reduced to a simple definition, template, or set of facts. In this respect, media analysis is not simply about communications, devices, and codes but also about media-events. These are events in a particular, double sense: the events are communicated through media, but the very act of communication simultaneously communicates the specific event-character of media *themselves*. Media make things readable, audible, visible, perceptible, but in doing so they also have a tendency to erase themselves and their constitutive sensory function, making themselves imperceptible and "anesthetic." This double *becoming-media* cannot be predetermined with any certainty because it is in each case differently constituted as an assemblage, a "dispositive" (in Foucault's sense) of heterogeneous conditions and elements. Becoming-media opens up perspectives on the cultural effects of media and a culture constituted by media and takes the analysis of media away from the monopolies of literary studies, the history of technology, and the history of communications.

Above all, the history and theory of media must address the singular scenes or situations where media (more strictly: the functions and functioning of media) come into existence in a coming together of heterogeneous elements—apparatuses, codes, symbolic systems, forms of knowledge, specific practices, and aesthetic experiences. The following analysis examines a prominent and exemplary case. In 1610 Galileo Galilei, in *Sidereus nuncius* (News from the Stars), speaks of incredible messages transmitted from the stars to the telescope, from telescope to eye, eye to hand, and then, in black and white, to paper, book, and reader. But this event contains more than just a demonstration of Copernicanism, more than the arrival of a new cosmology, more than the birth of a startling new view of the heavens scribbled down in just a few nights. In addition, this event marks a change in how the meaning of seeing and visibility is determined, as well as the meaning of the relationship between the eye, the gaze, and the viewed object. Furthermore, this event also involves a technological transformation—in Galileo's hands and before his eyes, the telescope fundamentally changes its nature from the simple device supposedly brought to Italy by Dutch lens grinders, displayed at fairgrounds, and eventually plagiarized by Galileo. The device now gives data of a unique kind: having been an instrument, it becomes a medium. How can we describe these historical steps, this transformation, as the telescope's "becoming-media"?

Denaturing the Senses

The significance of Galileo's telescope is not limited to his turning of the telescope from Earth to sky—"having dismissed [the use of the telescope to observe] earthly things, I applied myself to the exploration of the heavens";[1] it goes further than the far-reaching theoretical shift noted by Hans Blumenberg, who discerned in Galileo's action the first technologization of natural science. Before any investigation of the firmament, Galileo begins with an investigation of the device itself. The investigation brings his astronomical studies back to "the complete theory of this instrument" and turns a two-lens lead-and-paper pipe into an object almost as unfathomable as the stars.[2] Thus Galileo begins by experimenting on and with the device, testing its performance, its magnification and measurement of angles. The view through the telescope is supplemented by a view of the laws that govern that view. Everything the view makes visible also allows seeing itself to be seen. The telescope here appears as constructed, materialized *theoria* (in the Greek sense of the word), as vision. The device is no longer simply for enlarging, for bringing things closer or reproducing them. The telescope is not just an extension of the senses nor an auxiliary device to improve or correct the senses, one whose usefulness would ultimately lie in the "advantages of the instrument . . . on land and at sea."[3] Rather, the telescope creates the senses anew: it defines the meaning of vision and sensory perception, turning any and all visible facts into constructed and calculated data. Ultimately, all the phenomena and "messages" it produces bear the mark of theory. The sensory evidence transmitted by these messages is conveyed alongside the procedure by which that evidence was established.

This experimentalization of seeing relates to the fact that the eye and its natural vision are now merely parts of a single optical case among many others. The telescope does not enlarge any more than the eye makes smaller, and the telescopic view is no less natural than the eye's vision is artificial. Galileo's telescope thus erases the coordinates of natural vision, the natural view, and the natural eye. Johannes Kepler, enthusiastically following up on Galileo's work, grasped this immediately in his *Dioptrik*, subtitled "A sketch of the results of the recent invention of the telescope for vision and visible things." The telescope should not, he suggested, be "considered to be an ordinary instrument." Furthermore, a "theory of the instrument" touches directly on the theory of the eye, and vice versa. One cannot be developed without the other. Because their reciprocal determination is so close, the telescope, its optics and laws, now defines the sensory capacities of the eye. Like the telescope, the eye is an example of applied geometry, by virtue of which the retina is "painted, with the colored rays of visible things."[4] In 1604, Kepler had already established that the eye is an optical device—made up of a lens, lightproof chamber, and retina/screen—and so showed how vision is itself an optical distortion and that sensory perception is based on sensory deception.[5] The example of the telescope allowed him to bring this more clearly into focus: eye and telescope are both optical systems, and any natural difference between the two is erased. In both cases, the view implies its own construction. In both cases, any object seen implies the technical operation that makes it visible. Since Galileo, changes in vision cannot be understood in terms of given, natural vision: what the eye sees is now itself understood to be a construction. The eye is no longer the reliable organ of Aristotelian world-disclosure. What the eye sees is deception as much as it is truth. Vision has lost its status as natural evidence. The telescope is more than an auxiliary instrument. To the extent that it becomes a theoretical object, to the extent that it presents itself as constructed theory, it cracks open the world of natural vision. From now on, vision is denatured.

Producing a Fundamental Self-referentiality

The telescope's "self-referentiality" means three things. First, the telescopic view pinpoints the observer as much as the object observed. Second, any relation to the object in Galileo's observations is also a relation of observation to itself. Finally, the telescope's medial character is also revealed in its self-referential structure. The surprising turn taken by Galileo's viewing of the sky through the telescope is that when Galileo looks through his telescope at the planets, and in particular at the moon, what he sees above all is the Earth. When Galileo examines the moon's surface, he establishes that it does not have the crystalline smoothness and roundness suggested by Aristotle's *quinta essentia* but instead is raw and cratered, an absolutely earthly landscape. The surface of the moon is, he writes, "not smooth . . . but, on the contrary, [is] uneven, rough and crowded with depressions and bulges. And it is like the face of the Earth itself, which is marked here and there with chains of mountains and depths of valleys."[6] He discovers dark patches and bright zones and notes that

we have an almost entirely similar sight on Earth, around sunrise, when the valleys are not yet bathed in light but the surrounding mountains facing the Sun are already seen shining with light. And just as the Sun climbs higher, so those lunar spots lose their darkness as the luminous part grows.[7]

These examples continue in his reflections as to whether the Earth lights the moon like the moon lights the Earth and whether the Earth rises and sets on the moon as the moon does on the Earth. When Galileo looks through the telescope at the moon, he not only sees another Earth, that is, a world, his concept of "world" changes with this view: the difference between Earth and other heavenly bodies is erased, and the Earth itself appears as a star among stars. The Earth is no longer the "dump heap of the filth and dregs of the universe" but becomes one in a multitude of worlds.[8]

Among the effects of this combined observation and self-observation is that observation itself is made conditional. This effect is deeply embedded in the textual structure of *Sidereus nuncius*. Time and again, we find formulations claiming that a particular heavenly object is "thicker," not in itself but in relation to our view; that, were one to look at the Earth from the moon, this or that would be seen; or that "seen from a certain point," a particular condition would be fulfilled or a conclusion made possible.[9] Even at the level of formulations and syntax a "telescope-effect" is apparent—things are made relative or hypothetical, and the standpoint of the speaking subject is made conditional. Correct observation can only be expressed in the conditional. Just as every observer in a Copernican system must factor in the mobility and thus the relativity of his standpoint, so every description and every observation is made conditional and incorporated into a self-referential system. In this respect the telescope pointed at the heavens is in fact a Copernican instrument, an organ or medium for the creation of a Copernican world, with a relativized observer who observes him- or herself as an observer. The new sky is not simply a constellation (an assemblage) of planets and stars distributed into a new universe (or a pluriverse). The new sky is above all a constellation of *views*, a system of intersecting observations. This means that whoever, along with Galileo, looks at the sky through a telescope is at the same time looking back at him- or herself—seeing is self-seeing, observation is self-observation, locating is self-locating. By setting up these constitutive relations of self-reference, the telescope—and this is another aspect of its becoming-media—produces a world.

Generating an Anesthetic Field

In this way perception becomes a complex process that affects in turn the status of the visibilities seen through the telescope. The field of the visible is inextricably linked, with a constitutive invisibility, revealing a further insight into media-transformation: The critical point of the historical analysis of media is not to be found in what a medium makes visible, tangible, audible, readable or perceptible; it is not so much located in the aesthetic of the data and in-formation provided by a medium but rather in the anesthetic side of a media process. Again, what does Galileo Galilei see when he turns his telescope toward the sky? What exactly are the visibilities that Galileo observes, then captures in his texts and drawings—the lunar surface, unknown fixed stars, the Milky Way, the moons of Jupiter? *Sidereus nuncius* leaves no doubt: Galileo sees, newly perceptible in his telescope, not just sun, moon, and stars but the difference between the visible and the invisible. Telescopic vision becomes a second order of vision.

Consider Galileo's comments on his diagrams, based on telescope observations, of Orion and the Pleiades:

[I]n order that you may see one or two illustrations of the almost inconceivable crowd of them, and from their example form a judgment about the rest of them, I decided to reproduce two star groups. In the first I had decided to depict the entire constellation of Orion, but overwhelmed by the enormous multitude of stars and a lack of time, I put off this assault until another occasion. For there are more than five hundred new stars around the old ones, spread over a space of 1 or 2 degrees. For this reason, to the three in Orion's belt and the six in his sword that were observed long ago, I have added eighty others seen recently, and I have retained their separations as accurately as possible. For the sake of distinction, we have depicted the known or ancient ones larger and outlined by double lines, and the other inconspicuous ones smaller and outlined by single lines.[10]

Galileo explicitly states that both the visible and the invisible are represented here. More precisely, he documents the *relation* of the visible to the invisible. We have here a double image, a reproduction of Galileo's view through the telescope and a schematic record of the difference between the visible and the invisible.

As Blumenberg pointed out, this clearly marks the end of "the visibility postulate"—the belief, held from antiquity to the middle ages, that human beings' organic equipment was adequate to comprehend nature and the cosmos. In Galileo's telescope-view, a new, variable visibility appears, an alterable horizon of the visible. A dark background of invisibility now appears, reaching far into the representation of visible things. This change is intimately bound up with the telescope and the new ways of using it, as well as with other factors, like perspectival construction. Sight is now turned toward that which withdraws from sight; it is incorporated into a process that calls up immensities of invisible and hidden things along with the visible data. Galileo, in his "Letter to the Grand Duchess," writes,

> If we want to grasp the deeper concepts which stand written in the map of the heavens, we do not believe that it is enough to take in the shine of the sun and stars and to observe their rising and setting. This can be seen even by the eyes of animals and of the uneducated mob. But behind this are hidden secrets so deep and thoughts so sublime that the efforts and vigils of hundreds of the keenest minds, in their millennia of work and learning, have not yet fully fathomed them. What is given to us by the mere sense of our sight is as nothing compared to the wonders discovered by the reason of reasonable men.[11]

What the telescope thus brings into view is the difference between the visible and the invisible, and what it produces above all is invisibility, visible invisibility. The naked eye and unaided appearance are found wanting, and any apparent optical gain is counterbalanced by that which now lies, irretrievably, just beyond our view. Blumenberg declared this to be an antinomy in Galileo's epistemology, but it is also one of the effects of the telescope's becoming-media. On the one hand, the telescope increases visibility, produces an increase in empirical knowledge and gives certain evidence for the Copernican system. On the other hand, this very evidence is called into question by the telescope-effect: every visibility now bears a stigma of provisionality; every visibility is surrounded by an ocean of invisibility. Everything visible remains contingent, forever encompassed by the imperceptible and the unknown. Hence the antinomy: the telescopic view gives proof of certain hypotheses (e.g., the Copernican system)—in fact, the whole question of proof is given over to the empirical facts of vision as the final instance of truth—but visibility itself is rendered extremely problematic, a questionable, endangered, risky option riddled with uncertainty, dependent on coincidence, threatened by illusion (including optical illusion), and relativized by its segmentarity.[12] A trace of provisionality always remains: every truth that appears through the telescope is bordered by as-yet-undiscovered truths, by the "countless truths remaining to be discovered," as Galileo put it. We might understand this as the birth of a certain idea of science, positioned in the awkward space between sensory evidence and abstraction. Exactly here, however, the media-historical argument applies: along with the visible, the becoming-media of Galileo's telescope creates something invisible, nonperceptible, and anesthetic.

With every deepening of clarity comes a new depth of the unclarifiable. With Galileo's telescope, the heavens' star-spangled vault becomes an immeasurable black void.

In laying out these points, I have tried to describe a limited, local historical situation in which we can observe the becoming-media of the telescope; that is, its transformation from a mere optical instrument into a medium. A number of quite heterogeneous conditions were needed for this becoming-media: the technology of Dutch lens grinders; the invention (initially anonymous) of a device whereby two lenses mounted in a tube create an enlargement effect; a new knowledge, the Copernican hypotheses that define a new field of application for the telescope; certain experimental practices, which for Galileo meant the testing of vision itself against the telescope; a physical knowledge expressed in the formulation of optical problems; finally, a particular manner of drawing and representation, to be found in Galileo's drawings but also in the relationship of these images to his text. Further factors could be added: the laws of perspective, for example, which condition Galileo's way of seeing and representing things, which encode the flux of light and dark into geometric forms;"[13] more broadly, printing, which immediately turned the telescope-effect, into one of the first great Europe-wide scientific events.[14] All these factors meet in Galileo's telescope, which is no longer a simple object but a complex formation comprising material, discursive, practical, and theoretical elements.

Although the transformation of these disparate elements, devices, and arrangements into a medium is at issue, the specific case does not imply a generally valid concept of media. Rather, in each case, it is a question of a specific, local, and limited becoming-media, in which the confluence of various factors decides on the emergence of a medial function. Any general history of media will be the task of a historiography whose representation of events takes into account the way in which events become representable and in which events are always presented with a certain ambiguity. A history of media will always be tainted by histories that are themselves enabled and created by media: the history of writing, which first produced the distinction between myth and history; or the history of the printing press, whose "typographical persistence" made possible a history of progressive knowledge.[15] A history of media must be a history of media-events in a double sense: a history of events that determine the production, the representation, and the formation of events. Perhaps we might identify a kind of general determination, usable for our (historical) observation of media but resistant to a more general, transhistorical definition or determination. Ambiguous becoming-media such as these cannot be predetermined. In each case of becoming-media—as when series of letters become writing or polished lenses become an optical instrument—the transformation of apparatuses, symbolic orders, or institutions comes about through a specific assemblage of diverse conditions, factors and elements. For the future of media studies, I would like to suggest that we should set aside any general concept of media in favor of examining historically singular constellations in which we can identify the metamorphosis into media of things, symbolic systems, or technologies. No such thing as a medium exists in any permanent sense. That media denaturalize the senses and allow their historicization; that media can be understood as self-referential, world-creating organs; that media are defined by the anesthetic space they produce—these might form the outline of a framework in which the history of media is constituted in nothing more and nothing less than the mere events of a discontinuous becoming-media.

Notes

1. Galileo Galilei, *Sidereus nuncius, or, The Sidereal Messenger,* trans. Albert van Helden (Chicago: University of Chicago Press, 1989), 38. The following considerations draw in particular on the groundbreaking analyses of Hans Blumenberg. See Hans Blumenberg, "Das Fernrohr und die Ohnmacht der Wahrheit," in Galileo Galilei, *Sidereus nuncius,* ed. Hans Blumenberg (Frankfurt: Insel, 1965); Hans Blumenberg, *The Genesis of the Copernican World* (Cambridge: MIT Press, 1987); and Hans Blumenberg, *The Legitimacy of the Modern Age* (Cambridge: MIT Press, 1983).

2. Galileo, *Sidereus nuncius,* 39.

3. Galileo, *Sidereus nuncius,* 38.

4. Johannes Kepler, *Dioptrik* (1611; Leipzig: Engelmann, 1904), 3–4, 28,

5. Svetlana Alpers, *The Art of Describing* (Chicago: University of Chicago Press, 1983), 34. Alpers cites Kepler's *Ad vitellionem porolipomena, quibus astronomioe pars optica traditur* (1604).

6. Galileo, *Sidereus nuncius,* 40.

7. Galileo, *Sidereus nuncius,* 41.

8. Galileo, *Sidereus nuncius,* 57.

9. Galileo, *Sidereus nuncius,* 53–57.

10. Galileo, *Sidereus nuncius,* 59–61.

11. Galileo Galilei, "Letter to the Grand Duchess," in *The Galileo Affair: A Documentary History,* ed. Maurice A. Finocchiaro (Berkeley and Los Angeles: University of California Press, 1989), 103–104; translation modified. See also Blumenberg, "Das Fernrohr und die Ohnmacht der Wahrheit," 21, 38.

12. Or, the media-function is documented in the constitutive distortion of that which is mediated. See Michel Serres, *The Parasite,* trans. Lawrence R. Schehr (Baltimore: Johns Hopkins University Press, 1982).

13. See Joseph Vogl, "Kraterlandschaft," in *Umwege des Lesens: Aus dem Labor philologischer Neugierde,* ed. Caroline Welsh and Christoph Hoffmann (Berlin: Parerga, 2006), 303–316.

14. See Elizabeth L. Eisenstein, *The Printing Revolution in Early Modern Europe* (Cambridge, UK: Cambridge University Press, 1993), 83.

15. See Jack Goody and Ian Watt, "The Consequences of Literacy," *Literacy in Traditional Societies,* ed. Jack Goody (Cambridge, UK: Cambridge University Press, 1968), 27–68; Eisenstein, 226–237.

32 *Actio in Distans*: On Forms of Telerational World-Making

Peter Sloterdijk

The crisis of the philosophical *epoché* is the defining characteristic of the present age. Orientation in complex realities has become extremely difficult; in the turbulence of contemporary life, it is hard to perform Husserl's basic philosophical operation—stepping back from the image of reality while bracketing one's own existential intentions—with any degree of conviction. This experience is not entirely new: in *One-Way Street*, written between the two world wars, Walter Benjamin already bade farewell to illusions of adequate distance:

Fools lament the decay of criticism. For its day is long past. Criticism is a matter of correct distancing. It was at home in a world where perspectives and prospects counted and where it was still possible to take a standpoint. Now things press too closely on human society.[1]

Benjamin's leave-taking from critique was done in relatively good spirits: his encounter with Marxism had convinced him that he had an Ariadne's thread for the labyrinth of late-capitalism's Minos—a thread woven from dialectical materialism and messianic hermeneutics. Even if we no longer share this standpoint, Benjamin's observation nonetheless remains useful. It helps us to understand that the crisis of the *epoché* is also a crisis of contemplative rationality and in some sense a crisis of all logical escapism and all seigneurial theorizing. Benjamin's aphorism can even be taken to foresee a mode of world-making [*Welterzeugung*] primarily characterized by the shift to globally-scaled neighborhoods and telecausal interactions.

Bearing this in mind, the following analysis must forego the advantages of a distancing theoretical gaze. Stepping back can still sometimes be a productive gesture, as when standing in front of a painting or a landscape. However, it makes no sense inside a labyrinth or in any other situation characterized by the subject's loss of distance to the world. In these circumstances, we can best defend the interests of totalizing theory by adopting an alternative method. In our case, this alternative entails a systematic estrangement of the "close pressing" phenomena of the contemporary world, its technical labyrinths and its chaotic data flows. Two procedures in particular can be useful. The first estrangement consists of viewing contemporary occurrences through the eyes of classical metaphysics. These newly estranged phenomena are then defamiliarized a second time, now through the lens of archaic logic and historical anthropology, or more precisely paleoanthropology.

To sum up the procedure in a phrase: "Technology contains nothing that was not already present in metaphysics. Metaphysics contains nothing that was not already present in archaic logic." In this respect, the progression from magic to metaphysics and from metaphysics to technology can be seen as a process of *explication* (see the third volume of *Sphären* for a discussion of this term). These movements of explication are a technical realization of pre-technical fantasies, but they also instantiate a tendency inherent to modernization: the transformation of vague, symbolic immune structures into operational techniques of immunization.

These premises lead to a somewhat subversive culture-theoretical thesis: by mapping modern technology, above all, advanced media technology, onto paleoanthropological concepts and the workings of archaic intelligence, we gain particular insights into its nature and historical development [*Wesen und Tendenz der neuzeitlichen Technologie*]. Applied more directly to contemporary concerns, this means that a genuine, unironic attempt to grasp early Stone Age logic can help us understand what drives media technology and design. This is supplemented by a second approach, dealing with the transformation of archaic thought by classical metaphysics.

Unless I am mistaken, discourses on new media have two focal points, which structure the vast majority of mediological and media-sociological arguments. The first focus is on the impact that new media have on human beings under their sway—here the talk is of "cultural revolutions" and the teletechnological reconfiguration of the field of human experience. In hotbeds of the theoretical avant-garde, new disciplines have—literally and metaphorically—sprung up out of the ground: telematics, artificial intelligence, Internet anthropology, and so on. A creative theoretical milieu continually exploits these innovations in ideological terms, a sign that intellectuals continue to gravitate to events marking out a radical break with a previous epoch. The same mindset that up until the 1960s and 70s was powerfully drawn to History—more precisely to a Revolution always about to happen and always already here—is now attracted by the Internet and the turbulences of the virtual. The personal and intellectual biographies of Régis Debray and Jean Baudrillard are exemplary in this respect. Another set of questions cluster at the *second* pole of media discourse: these ask how individual media deal with the broader medial plurality of which they form a part. Here, the standard answer is that they *converge*. Media—in this view—are coming ever closer to one another, they are joining forces and combining, ever more successfully enmeshing and interconnecting. Previously there were two main branches of media technology, each with their own mode of evolution: on the one hand, classical, one-way transmission media (radio and TV), on the other, the classical two-way media of the telephone paradigm. Increasingly, however, digitalization means the two branches are merging, a phenomenon leading to the coinage of the term "mediamatics" by trend-theoreticians. (These theoreticians, formerly known as "critics," now aspire to go beyond theory and to themselves become the makers and breakers of trends.) In this process, one trend clearly emerges—the growing primacy of mobile and individualized tele-technologies at the expense of traditional one-way media.

In the following, I will confine myself to a few observations on the *second* focus of media-theoretical debate. I want to put together a number of observations about what media do to other media and about the forms of cooperation that result from this, on both an inter-apparative and inter-programmatic level. This will give us a sense of the connection between interapparativity and intersubjectivity; here the decisive factor is how new "tele-functions" can modify the form of subjectivity. As mentioned, I do not propose a direct approach to these phenomena. Rather, the discussion will detour through two successive estrangements, first metaphysically, then archaeologically and paleontologically.

Let's begin with a media-theoretical thesis which is broad enough to encompass both Stone Age and modern conditions, and which is equally valid for animistic, personalistic and mechanistically-influenced mentality structures. To forestall any doubts as to the pos-sibility of such an overarching thesis, I will say straight away what I think it might be: *all media history is the history of the transmission of thought.* The term "thought transmission" is of course mostly associated with parapsychology, but I want to show that the concept is vital to any rational inquiry into interpersonal relations, either proximate or distant. Without it, the whole field resists our approach.

From the early Stone Age up to the present day, the whole history of communication and information can be best understood as a series of answers—biological, semiotic and technical—to one persistently pressing question: how to achieve contact with other relevant beings. The common factor in all the answers to this question is media convergence, although this takes quite different forms at different evolutionary moments. It should be clear that the concept of medium only makes sense if we understand "medium" in terms of supplementing other media, or in terms of an accommodation with them, as *co*-media. McLuhan's famous aphorism comes to mind—the content of one medium is always another medium (thus text reproduces spoken language and television reproduces photography or film). In this context, however, we need to expand the concept of a medium, taking it beyond the border between humans and technologies, entering a region of thought beyond all narrowly technocentric conceptions of media. The further we go back in time, away from modernity's densely mediated world into a pre-history far more sparsely equipped with tools and signs, the more the concept of a medium changes, moving away from one based on things and apparatuses to one centred on the mediumistic properties of humans and their predecessors. Nowadays, this is understood only by those who believe in clairvoyance [*Hellsehen*] and clairaudience [*Hellhören*] as well as in television [*Fernsehen*].[2] While the "medium" of television is a technical device, in the context of occult vision or the hearing of spirit voices, the medium is a person—the telepathic individual or the prophet.

The further back we go, to the oldest forms of human world-making [*Welterzeugungsfor-men*], the more do personal media overshadow the mediality of things, apparatuses and devices. Going back far enough, we find *homo sapiens* at his most naked and least equipped, the purest representative of a regime of personified mediality. Indeed, the "sapiential" character *of homo sapiens* lay above all in his intermediary capacity, his potential to be a mediating element between two or more of his kind.

To put it in less mysterious and more physiological terms: prehistoric humans had the capacity to address each other's minds because the brains they used came from the same biological series. The irony of the term "use" is worth emphasizing—ancient man was very much a *user* of a non-transparent technical system, the operator of his intelligence equipment. By definition, a *user* is restricted to a system's front end, even if he retains a vague notion of a Beyond on the other side of the interface. For humans as brain-users this means they navigate across the psychic surface (we might perhaps say the inner surface) of brain states. They may move amongst thoughts, perceptions, feelings, sensations and moods [*Atmosphären*], but they are incapable of going beyond these surface phenomena to reach the underlying technical substructure. Of course they do develop intuitions of something beyond these thoughts, perceptions, feelings, sensations and atmospheres, but these intuitions tend to move in the wrong directions, transcending off towards the world of gods and spirits rather than honing in on the brain itself. Thus for a long time, the brain remained occult, as a hidden basis for mental contents and states. Only much later was the brain incorporated into the explication process and dramatically revealed as the physical carrier and generator of all psychic phenomena. In fact, only today's neurocybernetics allows us to articulate the idea that the gods are not absolute, transcendental values, but simply grammatical and emotional phenomena in the user interface of the brain. Even if God did represent a supreme reality, the highest ranking ontological entity, our conception of Him would be made using brains—and a symbolic toolkit—ultimately formed by evolution.

With this in mind, we can begin to get a better grip on the main argument, moving from the proposition that "all media history is the history of the transfer of thought" to more specific theses: first, that brains were themselves the primordial media, and second that they were, above all, media for the reproduction and transmission of brain states and conception. This appears trivial if it is simply a question of local communications among small groups. However, as soon as local brain communications give way to communications at a distance, the medial functioning of the brain becomes mysterious and takes on a sublime aspect: developed human culture as traditionally understood only begins with the emergence of symbolic telecommunications and of *actiones in distans*. The reciprocal, neurologically-conditioned "opening" of co-existent brains is the starting point for all media co-operation and convergence. (This opening is unthinkable, of course, without the prior systemic closing of the cerebral system itself.) A communicative biological demand for the networking of several cerebral agents gave rise to an evolved human audiovisuality, which could be combined with a highly intensified sensitivity to interpersonal atmospheres [*interpersonale Atmosphären*].

At this point, we should focus on a ubiquitous fallacy. It is widely believed that one person's thoughts are invisible to another, that the skull is a kind of safe, filled with ideas and dreams kept under lock and key, that mental reflection produces a book unreadable outside the mind, that personal ideas and knowledge solely belong exclusively to the self, and that they are transparent to the subject and impenetrable to others. All this is true—so goes the belief—to the point where the self can even withstand torture, in a willed refusal to share what it knows. It is impossible to overestimate the significance achieved by this syndrome of ideas during the short epoch of the privacy illusion. So it may seem provocative to suggest that the very idea of subjective privacy was based on an image of the concealment of thoughts in the closed interior of the self. In our culture, these notions are barely more than two and a half thousand years old. For the macrohistorian, ideas of psychic individualism are no more than a light moss on the ancient rock formations of psychological-anthropological reality; were it not for their contemporary dominance, they would be almost nothing against the sheer weight of hominization's long history. For the vast majority of human evolution, nearly everything a human thought and felt was transparent, open to others to the point where his experience might as well also be theirs. There is no indication that private conception, shared through explicit linguistic formulations, had any impact whatever on prehistoric experience or on patterns of social space. There were as yet no cells or apartments for the individual, either in the physical architecture of lived space or in the "social" imaginary. For small groups living under the law of reciprocity, the action of one is the action of the other. As a rule, the thoughts of one are the thoughts of others. In this kind of permeable world, accessing the minds of others is unproblematic, particularly in known and repeatable situations. Telecommunicators and mediamatics specialists would quite literally have nothing to do: in and of themselves, these early human groups were already pure mediamatic formations. This was the case even in archaic "shame cultures," where the individual suffered from the exposure of his affect and wanted to conceal his interiority. It seems likely that the affect of shame is itself an evolutionary sedimentation, produced by the impossibility of hiding one's interiority from the penetrating empathetic gaze of others. From a paleopsychological point of view, the notion of private thought is an absurdity. The idea of a protected inner sphere into which the subject can retreat, shutting the door behind him for introspection and self-expression, simply did not exist before antiquity's proto-individualistic turn. When the idea did appear, the men who were propagandists first went by the name *wise men,* then *philosophers,* they themselves being the forerunners of modern intellectuals and of postmodern singles.[3] These men, the inventors of individualism's psychological apartheid, were the first to formulate the revolutionary idea that true thought was only possible as the self's own thought, distinct and different from the thoughts of the stupid masses. These early impulses would eventually lead to the influential model of "mind as conclave" [*Klausur im Kopf*], with its well-known political motto: *thoughts are free, others cannot guess them.* [*Die Gedanken sind frei, keiner kann sie erraten.*] However, this nineteenth-century German liberal slogan implies that only *new* and unexpected thoughts can lend thinking subjects opacity against the custodians of conventional thought. In a world of new thoughts, the axiom that "the thoughts of one are the thoughts of all" increasingly loses its validity: I cannot conjecture a thought in the mind of another if I myself do not think it or have never thought it. In internally differentiated societies, different people do in fact have different thoughts. For this reason, these social systems suffer from telecommunications inflation, reflecting the fact that thought-transmission among strangers can no longer take the form of participatory empathy. Instead, it functions through explicit communication-at-a-distance, using very expensive symbolic systems. The expense of these systems—consider the enormous costs associated with the introduction of alphabetic writing—has been completely forgotten, because it has been one hundred percent socialized. (If the alphabet cost as much as a telephone network, people would be more sparing with the written word.) In differentiated societies with a division of labor and a division of thoughts it is the job of psychotherapists, entertainers and telecommunications networks to keep the individual from drifting too deeply into the pathological privacy of his own thoughts and feelings. Consider how, from about the turn of the twentieth century on, pathological privacy was discussed in terms of the "unconscious." This discursive turn was plausible to the degree that the Unconscious could be explained as a transmission system which directed thoughts into an unknowing subject with the individual unaware of the transmissions he received. In this sense the concept of the unconscious corresponded to a modern version of possession, with psychotherapy as modern exorcism.

By contrast, in the earlier sociosphere thoughts were general, public and non-occult. A basic media-physiological fact underlies this: human brains, like genitals, are essentially built for coupling, as elements within a social system. Their basic condition is promiscuity; their normal state implies long-term relationships with supplementary or parallel brains. While the ominous phrase "my belly belongs to me"[4] at least has specific polemical meaning (only a woman should decide on an abortion), the equivalent sentence "any brain belongs to me" is both morally unacceptable and factually incorrect. The statement is simply untrue, whether taken to mean that an individual is the sole author of his thoughts or that the individual can be exempted from sharing them with others. Even to claim that *I can think what I want* is inherently untenable. This kind of cerebral individualism fails to recognize that the brain only achieves functionality when linked with a second and a third similarly-structured brain, and ultimately with a much larger ensemble. Brains are media for what other brains do and have done; one intelligence serves as the release-stimulus for another, triggering its autonomous functioning. As with language and emotion, intelligence is not a subject but a milieu, a system of resonances.

Unlike later forms of distance-capable, alphabetic human intelligence, pre-alphabetic intelligence is predicated on a dense climate of participation. Entirely embedded in close-range communication, this kind of intelligence only develops amidst the rich experiential stimulation of a co-present milieu. Thus from the very beginning, brains exist in a convergent relation to other brains. This convergence is medial in a precise sense: cerebrality, as we have here understood it, emerges in a structurally multiple form. To put it another way, the brain is always already dyadically associated with another brain in a resonant relationship. It is always already triadically—or even more—constituted, located as a mediating element between two other brains, informing one, informed by the other. (This means that beyond the mediality of beings and persons, there is always a deeper level of intercerebral processes.) Any realistic discussion of brains' experience [*Um von realen Gehirnwelten zu sprechen*] must thus presume, at a minimum, that they exist in groups of three, in brain-trinities, so to speak. Unfortunately, this aspect has been neglected by both popular debate and scientific research, which conceive of the brain only as a *singular* phenomenon. In this way, in the name of neurological Enlightenment, both popular and scientific discourse aid the disinformation of a merciless individualism.

This discussion leads us to modify our initial theorem at a key point. From now on, we must also attend to the economics of thought transmissions. All media history is the history of thought transmission, but the earliest moments of this history are characterized by a principle of communicational thrift. The sheer expense of explicit symbolization had to be kept to a minimum in the communal syncing of primordial brains. In other words, it was less a question of reciprocal information exchange than a kind of collective tonization. Homeostatic brain communes—often colloquially called "peoples"—can be understood as an ensemble, resonating in synchronous redundancy. (We can observe this even today in the famous phenomenon of Munich's "beer tent socialism.") What is sometimes referred to as "a sense of being at home" [*Heimatlichkeit*] is essentially a participation in this kind of communication, one marked with high reduncancy and almost without informational content. Once this sense of home has been lost—in the forced, overwhelming exposure to an excess of non-redundant, individualizing information—it can nonetheless persist, now experienced as a promise of happiness. Even today, among the last remaining anti-rhetorical and anti-telecommunicative subcultures—residual agrarian milieus, a few remote spiritual communities—a resonant, wordless understanding is known and prized as the only true communication between human beings. For ancient man, to speak a word too many was to lose a word forever.

As I will discuss later, modernity's long-term trend is from a thrifty use of words to their squandering, a tendency to compulsive word-wasting incited and commercially exploited by the media industry, above all the telephone companies. Understood in terms of paleolithic modes of communication, the goal of all communicative intention is to supply a number of individual cerebra with the same ideation and, in as much as possible, with concordant situational perception. This can only succeed under two conditions. First—as in hunting or ritual behavior—the members of a technically or symbolically cooperating group are so tightly coupled together that there is immediate common awareness of the actions and thoughts of all. Or, second, convergence happens by a simultaneous turn towards an acute perceptual presence. The sudden appearance of a leopard at the edge of a camp, for example, would be an equally pressing event for all, an acute visual impression guaranteeing the simultaneous conception of leopards across the whole brain community. (The mechanism persists into our own differentiated media societies, available for use by the advertising industry. Just before the evening news an entire population may perceive the sudden virtual presence of an elk[5]—a windfall of simultaneous mass thought-transfer in modern mediated space.)

From an economic point of view, the Stone Age paradigm aimed to a greater or lesser degree at the radical reduction of information to communication. Or to put it another way, it sought the reduction of new thoughts into old ones. It would never occur to an average Stone Age human to ask what someone else was thinking. There was simply nothing to be gained from an experience of others' different thoughts; in this respect, there was as yet no useful otherness. Prehistoric interest in the contents of someone else's head was not about ideas but about edible delicacies. A few years ago, a skull fragment of the oldest known European was discovered at Atapuerca, a Spanish palaeontological gravesite. Its age was a sensation—at 780,000 years old, it was ten times older than the standard estimates for *Homines sapientes*. Along with its age, there was another surprise. The scratches and scrapings on the child's skull showed it to be a relic of a cannibalistic feast—an early sign of hominids' concern for the brain-contents of their fellow (or rather, their not-yet-fellow[6]) pre-humans.

This oldest paradigm of media convergence—brain convergence—is therefore regulated by a double principle. First, thoughts are transmitted from one brain to another with the least possible expenditure of manifest signs. This goes along with a second aspect, the suppression of any potentially new, individualizing thoughts and their reduction to already existing, communitized ones. This tendency to reduction is characteristic of the *mythic* stage of all ages and peoples: myth has always been the sponge which wipes away individualizing difference.

At this point let us make a further paradigmatic leap, from archaicism to metaphysics. One reason for the emergence of philosophy was that a key struggle of early antiquity was gradually revealed to be a paradoxical undertaking: the struggle waged by modes of redundant communication and communion against information and the new experiences disseminated by it. While early tribes and peoples had communicated resonantly through a vast number of myths and legendary tales, these proved to be an ineffective means of information reduction for a new age of population movements and mixing. The great trading port of Athens, where goods and opinions arrived from all corners of the Earth, served as a kind of political and media-technical laboratory, testing how humans would cope in polymythic situations. As we know, it was here that Plato came to the conclusion that myths, poetry, and tales of the gods were no longer adequate guides for post-Socratean humans. In this polymythic city, those in search of communicational resonance could no longer use stories to achieve something like pre-linguistic thought-communion. There was no syntony, no resonance, no *con-cordia*. They were, rather, sucked ever more strongly into the proliferation of speech and *eo ipso* into the permanent escalation of differences of opinion. Plato could rightly uphold that humans do not communicate too little, but too much. Thus, he suggested, they also lie too much; in speaking, they distance themselves further and further from the truth. For Plato, this also carried a political danger: the proliferation of nonsense called the existing urban synthesis into question. What he had in mind was nothing less than a logical-semantic modernization of the archaic principle of communicative thrift; hence the epistemic filter he used to reduce the metastatizing communications of quarrelling, lying, fabricating human beings. He aimed to contain the proliferating, dissensus-building chatter of poets, wet nurses, sophists and—not least—democratic warmongers. To do so, his ingenious method placed the entirety of local communications under the control of a divine telecommunications monopoly. Here we see the invention of a philosophical version of universal top-down communications.

For over two millenia, generations of thinkers have found Plato's world-projection [*Weltentwurf*] powerfully suggestive, largely because it excludes the possibility of relevant new thoughts, an exclusion even more effective than that of myth, working on a deeper level. Philosophy presents itself as the definitive salvation from information; not coincidentally, philosophy's role model was the wise man who is no longer amazed by anything. For this reason, *nil adminari* served as the motto for philosophy's method of transforming information into recollection. Philosophical reflection may—supposedly at least—have its origin in a sense of wonder, but its ultimate aim is in fact the destruction of wonder, executed by the deployment of final proofs. A priori ousts a posteriori, separating the wheat of knowledge from the chaff of opinion. And true knowledge—so it would be claimed—comes not from the exchange of information, but from memories of the soul's ancient time, filled with the perception of essential Forms.

To return to the main thesis, we can thus see how Plato's intervention introduces a new element into our account of media history as the history of thought-transmission. From now on, it is no longer simply a question of "horizontal" transmission of brain-states across a local neurological exchange. Plato cuts away at the communicative link between immediately co-present human beings, leaving only a thin thread, the minimum needed to run a school and seek truth by academic conversation. Truth, however, is no longer something transmitted through *face-to-face* or *ear-to-ear* communications. Instead, any individual intelligence gains access to truth only through a radicalized philosophical recollection of a world of Forms before his birth. In a Platonic universe, players of the collective language game can no longer be immersively socialized, as everywhere till then, in the back-and-forth of group chatter [*durch das Mitschwingen im Gruppengeschwätz*]. What takes place instead is a kind of depth socialization, based on the free and lonely relation between the individual and a universal firmament of Ideas common to all. In going beyond polymythic babble— suggested as not only informationally sterile but "polemogenic" (war-creating)—Plato put all thinking souls into direct relation with the noetic God, the ultimate transmitter of all valid knowledge. In the school's preferred terminology, the name of this god was no longer Zeus or Apollo, but Agathon, the Good.

Philosophy is the informatics of the Good, or rather an anti-informatics, since it refuses to collate the empirical bric-a-brac of information. Instead, it is concerned exclusively with the labor of recollection and therapeutic anamnesis. The decisive thought-transfer now takes place between the individual human brain and a divine central one, as with the transmission between Plato and the Good in the medium of logical evidence. Only this kind of thought-transfer—from a single, common God to the individual—can serve as the basis of a communicative regime in which all human minds can participate (at least virtually, if not actually) and in which distinctions can be made between true statements and mere gossip.

The subsequent fate of the philosophical media revolution is well-known. Over the course of European history, the Platonic system collapsed, largely due to two unintended side-effects, or perhaps structural flaws. First, Platonism brought with it an uncontrollable problem with elites, because no practical distinction was ever worked out between those who clearly recollected ante-natal Ideas, and those whose memories were too clouded to give coherent evidence. This meant that the Enlightenment ultimately dispensed with the ideal of the wise man. Instead, it turned to *common sense*, now given an opportunity to exact heavy revenge for two thousand years of philosophical disparagement. (If I'm not mistaken, this revenge orgy reached its peak some time in the late twentieth century. After the overkilling of philosophy in vitalism and in postmodern entertainment ideologies, there are signs of a new division of labor between philosophical thought and other modes of intelligent behavior.) Second, Platonic measures towards logos-conservation were condemned to failure, not least since they did not quantitatively reduce the circulation of speech in the world. On the contrary, philosophical discourse—with its own kind of infinitude—was simply added to existing varieties of quotidian babble. The attempt to reduce information to communication failed across the board. Of course, this failure had its productive side: although early philosophy was unable to stabilize absolute knowledge, one of its by-products—the sciences of old Europe—took on an important life of its own. The rise of scholarly disciplines led to an accumulation of authentic information, but also a boundless proliferation of informative and pseudo-informative discourses. In view of this development, it is unsurprising that the mainstream of philosophy branched into two. One branch led into mysticism, where the understanding of God and the soul remained wordless, as in archaic communion and direct thought-transmission. The other, discursive-scientific branch formed an overflowing river of speech, an information stream bursting its banks; here, any idea of using communication to control information has long since been forgotten.

In the long term, the structural faults of classical metaphysics led it to unintentionally give rise to two characteristic elements of modernity. First, there is the cognitive egalitarianism of modern discursive culture, a knowledge system which awards no participant privileged access to first or last causes. Second there is the emancipation of information and the positive valence given to new knowledge, now favorably evaluated for the first time in the history of the cognitive system. Modernity is the strange time when the Good dissolves its alliance—once thought eternal—with the Old and the Long-Established, in favor of a new pact with the New and the Latest. The newly positive valence of information brought together brains, media and institutions of knowledge in a historically unprecedented configuration, the one in which we must find our way today.

Let us make another historical leap, moving forward into the space of contemporary problems and concerns. As I have indicated, modernity became aggressively self-conscious at the moment when the failure of the metaphysical project (which made all worldly affairs subject to a vertical thought-transmission between a monotheistic God and the thinking individual) became clear. Depending on which of modernity's philosophical provinces they inhabited, intelligent Europeans sensed this final failure of metaphysics some time between the seventeenth and the twentieth centuries. This epoch saw the realization that the key mode of thought transmission in our world structure would not be the archaic communion of brains in local co-present telepathy. Nor would it be the subtle anamneses communicated long-distance between the individual soul-intelligence and the philosophers' God. What now became significant was a deregulated, mixed transmission of thoughts, conducted both horizontally and vertically, conducted in media which were both communicational *and* informational. Among these media, the book was initially the most prominent, but since the late nineteenth century it has faced strong competition from electric and electronic systems. This process increasingly drove out verticality in favor of horizontality, until a point where participants in society's communicative-informational games realize nothing more can be expected from Above, that they are alone on this disenchanted Earth with their brains, their media, their errors and their illusions. They are condemned to an electronic world-citizenship, whose categories are determined by the fact of an ever more concentrated world and of the ever more ubiquitous proximity of all. What we blithely call "telecommunications" in fact brings with it a teleoperative world-form [*Weltform*] determined by *actiones in distans* of all kinds. This world-form accords with a consciousness coming to increasing awareness of its own telemoral responsibilities.

It is time to add some nuance to the proposition that all media history is the history of thought transfer, focusing on its most sensitive point, i.e., the concept of thought itself. In our discussion of the prehistoric world, the term "thought" was so broadly defined as to include almost any mental state experienceable by brains in communication. However, in discussing classical metaphysics, we used a notion of thought which, at a stretch, could be taken to mean "a priori knowledge" or "archetypal intuition." For the deregulated information market of the modern world yet another understanding of "thought" is required, broadly corresponding to what traditional epistemology would call empirical propositions, or in Kantian terms, synthetic a posteriori judgments. Here we beg to approach modern system-theoretical definitions of information, in which information is a unit of measurement for the changes brought into an information storage system by a new message. Once innovation is *per se* given a positive valence, information can also be viewed in positive terms. In this way, we come to the typically modern equation of New, Better and More, an equation essential for the business of thought-transfer to flourish. The new concept of information brings with it an ontological advantage: it enables descriptions of thought transfer which do not subordinate all transferrable thoughts to a Someone who "has" them. We can allow thoughts—now transformed into units of information—to subsist below the threshold of persons and subjects; this means that technical systems can converse with each other without the intervention of an experiencing self. Seen from the point of view of relieved human brains, this technological takeover of communicative work holds considerable emancipatory potential.

With information now seen in positive terms, participants in the marketplace of innovation faced a new ecological problem—the disposal of informational waste. In the age of the book, the problem could be kept under control; as vehicles for information, books are low capacity, infrequent and slow. In the age of electronic information transmission, however, the problem exploded dramatically. Bear in mind that conventionally constituted brains are configured for low idea-consumption. Or to put it another way, as organisms, brains are set up to defend themselves against unwelcome new experience. Self-reflection confirms that this is clearly still the case. A moment's introspection makes clear that brains tend to seek out the nearest homeostatic level. In other words, they tend toward a condition which maximizes comfort and preserves existing structures—an experience of self-satisfaction reinforcing our sense of rightness in the world and granting us extended license to play the game of identity. We all know how creatively humans can avoid revising their Judgment of Self. Modernity's decisive mutation comes with the demand that human brains switch from fending off information to welcoming it. Even in the print era, this led to an anthropological revolution, giving rise to typically modern figures like the magician-scholar, the artist, the engineer, the intellectual and the literate citydweller. Time is almost up for all of these figures, as the historic marriage between brains and flows of printed information draws to a close, or more precisely, as the humanist constellation is de-optimized. In its aftermath come new social types. These exhibit a high degree of flexibility, along with an exceptional ability to play along with ubiquitous programs of "lifelong learning." Since information has been given a positive valence, participants in modern information and communication systems face inevitable information inflation, too powerful for processing by biologically-evolved brains. Therefore brains are increasingly being withdrawn from the front line of information reception; in their place, media—that is, media apparatuses—increasingly maintain direct contact with each other. This is prompted by the realization that the laws of technical evolution apply to heavy communicational labor as much as they do to physical labor; here too, machines can alleviate or even entirely replace the burden of work.

This brings the account of the telecommunicative relation to the world [*des telekommunikativen Weltverhältnisses*] to the threshold of the present day. With the shift from semiotic conservation to an extravagant expenditure of signs, the contemporary world-form retains almost nothing of a morality of thrift or the ideal of neurological communion. Only the realization is left that human brains are insufficiently robust for what information providers in the open communications market want to push down their throats. The only adequate reaction seems to be the formation of a kind of spam ontology. *Eo ipso,* thought-transmission in the information age cannot be directed towards natural brains for very long since most information is useless for them. As in the Stone Age, brains still tend to seek the reduction of information to communication. This underlies the modern interest in extra-cerebral processing of the flood of information; this is why we need the convergence of information and communication technologies. Not coincidentally, evidence is now emerging of the benefits of direct communications between technologies. These machines were designed for informatic heavy labor, unlike nerve-creatures, who—in theory at least—have better things to do than the stressful processing of superfluous information. This can be put in terms less favorable to the nervous system, as in Friedrich Kittler's observation that protein-based processors ultimately cannot compete with silicon-based ones.

I will conclude these very abstract remarks with some even more abstract ones, returning to the Platonic caesura and the world of archaic communion. If, in structural terms, all media history really is the history of the transmission of thought, then the immanent tele-ology of all telecommunicative acts is made concrete in the dream of a return to brain communications, in a future where others' brains could be directly accessed without passing through external media. If the technical really does tend to repeat the archaic, then we may be heading towards a return to an older local form of communications, based on mutually attuned neuro-sympathy systems, but now reproduced within the horizon of mass long-distance communications. This can be seen in the immense success of the mobile telephone, which has done much to reproduce archaic orality on the level of the global village. But speculative mediology must push far beyond even this level. In the last days of media time [*Am Ende aller Medientage*], communicators will be able to transmit their own thoughts directly into the minds of absent partners: all that will be needed is a neurotelepathy system with advanced addressing technology. The sender-subject will simply set his logical inten-tionality to a particular group of neurological addresses—known in the medial dark ages as "persons"—immediately triggering the addressees' internal receivers. Nothing would be required of recipients except to have their systems set for external reception. In the days of the media end-time, eyes and ears—today so heavily overloaded—will be bypassed neuro-telepathically. Gentle skull-rupture technologies will allow us to steer remotely into neuro-social environments [*Nervenmitwelten*] at any distance. (References to the self-referential closure of neural systems—so fashionable at the end of the twentieth century—will no longer seem convincing.) In that time, perhaps only one century of R & D into the future, technologies and mass media may achieve something which today is only claimed by psycho-psychics and a few religious telecommunicators: without any physical encounter, by thought alone, we will discreetly telecommunicate each other into possessed states, marvellous or horrific.

Immersed in each others' psyches along ultra-long-distance intercerebral radio relays, we will not only—as in Platonism—send and receive archetypes and eternal Ideas, but will exchange individualized ideation, messages with a specific time, place and addressee. Today's "new media" will be remembered as antiquated technology—heavy, clunking and external. People will look back in bemusement at the superfluous, pernicious middlemen who once attempted to monopolize and exploit human thought-transmission. The last problem remaining to be solved will be the protection of the cerebral private sphere. To prevent reception, humans may have to wear ANT-helmets—anti-neurotelepathy caps which remove the wearer from the omnipresent symphonies of transmitted information. The intellectual buzzword of the day will be "neuroglobalization." In those last days of thought-transmission, today's most widespread form of information-defence—*incomprehension*—will no longer function. Every refusal of comprehension will have to be performed explicitly and consciously, realized like a work of art, subject to aesthetic rules. Given these future perspectives, we should enjoy our natural reserves of non-comprehension while there is still time.

Translated by Brian Hanrahan

Notes

1. Walter Benjamin, *One-Way Street and Other Writings*, translated by Edmund Jephcott & Kingsley Shorter (London: NLB, 1979), 45.

2. Sloterdijk here plays on the close relation in German between technical and occult vocabularies of "medium": *Fernsehen* (literally: to see far) is the term for television in all its standard meanings, but it also historically referred to a kind of clairvoyant vision. *Hellsehen* (literally: to see clearly) and *Hellhören* (to hear clearly) are related terms for, respectively, clairvoyance and clairaudience (hearing spirit voices). On this relation, see Stefan Andriopoulos, "Psychic Television," *Critical Inquiry 31,* no. 3 (Spring): 618–637.—Trans.

3. *Singles* is in English in the original, i.e., unattached urban dwellers of the contemporary era, whose spatial habitat and psychological disposition Sloterdijk sees as the culmination of metaphysical individualism.—Trans.

4. *Mein Bauch gehört mir!* was a slogan of the German women's movement in the early 1970s.—Trans.

5. A reference to the long-running use of an elk in early Ikea television advertising campaigns.—Trans.

6. Sloterdijk here plays with compounds of "pre-human" and "fellow human": . . . *die Anteilnahme von Vormenschen an den Kopfinhalten ihrer Mitvormenschen—oder Vormitmenschen.*—Trans.

Index